WE THE PEOPLE

2

TRANSFORMATIONS

WE THE PEOPLE

2

TRANSFORMATIONS

Bruce Ackerman

THE BELKNAP PRESS OF
HARVARD UNIVERSITY PRESS
CAMBRIDGE, MASSACHUSETTS
LONDON, ENGLAND

Copyright © 1998 by the President and Fellows of Harvard College
All rights reserved
Printed in the United States of America

Library of Congress cataloging information is on page 516.

For Susan

Contents

PART THREE
Modernity

Acknowledgments

I generally write books in the way they are read—beginning with the beginning, and slogging on to the end. But this one is an exception. After struggling with the first chapter of *We the People* for months with little to show other than increasing gloom, I took my wife's advice and began in the middle. I threw myself into the history of Reconstruction, and then the New Deal. Four years later, I emerged with a long manuscript that explored many forgotten questions but had lost sight of the big picture. With something resembling despair, I put my draft away and tried to write in my accustomed manner—from the beginning.

The result was *Foundations,* the first volume in this series. The years spent with the sources had not been wasted. I could now describe the forest as well as the trees, and develop my main themes without too many distractions.

But the day of reckoning could not be indefinitely postponed: *Foundations* made many controversial historical claims, and I was obliged to substantiate them if I hoped to be taken seriously. I returned to my historical manuscripts with trepidation. Rereading them, I was impressed with the number of relevant investigations that I had not even attempted. Was I cut out for this job?

The last five years have been intellectually demanding, and I am very conscious of the crucial role played by my conversation-partners. Neal Katyal and David Golove were wonderfully resourceful collaborators. The full extent of their contribution is revealed in two publications: Ackerman and Katyal, "Our Unconventional Founding,"

62 *University of Chicago Law Review* 475 (1995), and Ackerman and Golove, *Is NAFTA Constitutional?* (1995). Other students made outstanding contributions as research assistants, including Michael Aprahamian, Lynda Dodd, Rachel Harmon, Stephen Keogh, Mahmood Mabood, Cynthia Powell, Jon Shepard, Greg Silverman, Michael Splete, and Jan Trafimow. As always, Gene Coakley provided priceless assistance in unlocking the resources of the Yale libraries. Over the years, my friends among historians provided guidance. Bob Cover and Bill Nelson gave much-needed assistance in the early years. Richard Friedman reviewed an early draft of chapters on the New Deal; as did Michael Les Benedict and Eric Foner on Reconstruction; and Jack Rakove and Henry Monaghan on the Founding. I find it impossible to enumerate my debt to all the other friends who have suffered through a project that has bulked so large for fifteen years. They know how much they have helped.

Turning to institutions, the law schools at Columbia and Yale gave me a tremendous amount of freedom to teach courses that allowed for in-depth exploration of the themes explored here. Deans Benno Schmidt and Barbara Black at Columbia, and Guido Calabresi and Tony Kronman at Yale, were unstinting in their support. In addition to research leaves provided by my universities, I gained extra assistance from two research institutes: the Wissenschaftskolleg in Berlin and the Woodrow Wilson Center in Washington. My year in Berlin was almost too seductive, encouraging me to write a book, *The Future of Liberal Revolution,* that delayed publication of the present volume. Nonetheless, I spent a lot of time in Germany rethinking *Transformations,* and this helped in the long run. My academic year at the Wilson Center in 1995–96 gave me the chance to reduce my sprawling historical manuscripts into readable size and shape. Last but not least, my secretaries Joan Pacquette-Sass and Jill Tobey helped with countless tasks that otherwise would have made sustained writing impossible.

As these paragraphs suggest, I am a lucky man. I hope this book partially repays my enormous debt to the institutions, and the country, that made it possible.

I have included revised versions of some materials published previously. Parts of Chapter 1 appeared as "Higher Lawmaking?" in

Responding to Imperfection (Princeton: Princeton University Press, 1995), edited by Sanford Levinson; parts of Chapters 2 and 3 in Bruce Ackerman and Neal Katyal, "Our Unconventional Founding," 62 *University of Chicago Law Review* 475 (1995); and parts of Chapter 13 appeared as "Transformative Appointments," 101 *Harvard Law Review* 1164 (1988). These sections are reprinted with the kind permission of the original publishers.

PART ONE

In the Beginning

CHAPTER ONE

Higher Lawmaking

THE PROPHETIC VOICE

MY FELLOW AMERICANS, we are in a bad way. We are drifting. Our leaders are compromising, compromised. They have lost sight of government's basic purposes.

It is past time for us to take the future into our hands. Each of us has gained so much from life in America. Can we remain idle while this great nation drifts downward?

No: We must join together in a movement for national renewal, even if this means self sacrifice. We will not stop until the government has heard our voice.

The People must retake control of their government. We must act decisively to bring the law in line with the promise of American life.

Since the first Englishmen colonized America, this voice has never been silent. We have never lived for long without hearing its diagnoses of decline, its calls for renewal. For good and for ill, there can be no thought of silence—no way to proclaim that our generation has reached the promised land. Americans have become too diverse, too free, to suppose that their struggle over national identity will end before the death of the Republic. If the future is like the past, the substance of our collective commitments will change, and for the better?

Yet the voice will remain—calling upon Americans to rethink and revitalize their fundamental commitments, to recapture government in the name of the People. It is this voice that will concern us here, as well as the distinctive attitude Americans have cultivated in its exercise. While we have long since learned to live with prophets in our midst, we have not learned to love them.

Talk is cheap. It is one thing for self-proclaimed saviors to call for national renewal; quite another to convince millions of ordinary Americans to work together to redefine the national purpose. Many are called, but few are chosen to speak with the authority of We the People of the United States.

The normal American's reaction to some politico's claim of a popular "mandate" is incredulity, not commitment. Authority to speak for the People cannot be lightly presumed. It must be earned through years of work in the political wilderness—arguing, mobilizing, recruiting a broadening commitment to a revitalized understanding of the public good. Even relatively successful movements have met with different fates. Sometimes Americans have responded to impassioned calls for renewal by reaffirming the status quo; sometimes, by adopting important, but interstitial, constitutional amendments; sometimes, by endorsing sweeping moral transformations in the meaning of the Union.

The twists and turns of centuries have done more than reshape the substance of political identity. They have redefined the constitutional processes through which Americans have engaged the prophetic voice. The earliest calls for spiritual renewal expressed themselves in the explicit accents of Protestant Christianity.[1] But since the Revolution and Founding, national debate has been conducted primarily in secular terms. The constitutional system has not allowed transformative movements to excommunicate nay-sayers in the name of a jealous God. It has required would-be spokesmen for the People to confront the skeptical doubts of their opponents; to give them a fair chance to mobilize their own supporters. Only after the reformers carry their initiative repeatedly in deliberative assemblies and popular elections has our Constitution finally awarded them the solemn authority to revise the foundations of our polity in the name of We the People.

I shall be asking two questions about this extraordinary process of democratic definition, debate, and decision. How has it worked in the past? How should it work in the future?

FOUNDATIONS

These questions are especially significant in America. This country's Constitution focuses with special intensity on the rare moments when transformative movements earn broad and deep support for their initiatives. Once a reform movement survives its period of trial, the Constitution tries to assure that its initiatives have an enduring place in future political life. Elected politicians will not be readily allowed to undermine the People's solemn commitments through everyday legislation. If they wish to revise preexisting principles, they must return to the People and gain the deep, broad, and decisive popular support that earlier movements won during their own periods of institutional testing.

This focus upon successful moments of mobilized popular renewal distinguishes the American Constitution from most others in the modern world. It motivates a distinctive system of government involving the construction of two lawmaking tracks. The normal lawmaking track is designed for countless decisions made in the absence of mobilized and politically self-conscious majority sentiment. The higher lawmaking system imposes specially rigorous tests upon political movements that hope to earn the heightened sense of democratic legitimacy awarded to spokesmen for We the People. When this two-track system is operating well, it encourages Americans to distinguish between ordinary decisions made by government and considered judgments made by the People. I have this distinctive aspiration in mind in describing America as a dualist democracy.

Foundations, the first volume in this series, located the historical origin of dualism in the Founding generation's revolutionary experience. Washington, Madison, and the rest could have played the normal political game according to the rules laid down by Imperial Britain. They refused, but were not rewarded by the life of frustration, exile, death that usually accompanies revolutionary rejection. After years of arduous effort, they lived to see most of their countrymen support their vision of a federal union—but only after a complex and demanding process of constitutional ratification. Little wonder, then, that they thought they had achieved something special. Nor were they content to allow their great achievements to be eroded by politicians who had failed to gain the mobilized and deliberate assent of the People that marked (in their eyes at least) their revolutionary triumph. As children of the Enlightenment, they used the best political science of their time to write a two-track Constitution—and thereby set the terms for the future development of dualistic democracy.

Moving from history to philosophy, *Foundations* argued that dualism still makes sense, perhaps even more sense than it did two centuries ago. A dualistic process responds to a characteristic complexity in the modern American's approach to politics. On the one hand, most of us recognize a responsibility to do our part as citizens—talking about the issues of the day at home and at work, paying our taxes, coming out to vote. On the other hand, we usually spend most of our time and effort in more private spheres of life. Normal politics is a sideline, one that competes with national sports, the latest movies, and the like.

But at other times, politics can take center stage with compelling force. The events catalyzing a rise in political consciousness have been as various as the country's history—war, economic catastrophe, or urgent appeals to the national conscience. For whatever reason, political talk and action begin to take on an urgency and breadth lacking most of the time. Normally passive citizens become more active— arguing, mobilizing, and sacrificing their other interests to a degree that seems to them extraordinary.

This ebb and flow has been noted by social scientists and historians.[2] *Foundations* made it the basis of a normative argument. Dualistic government is especially appropriate for a citizenry whose engagement with politics varies substantially from decade to decade, generation to generation. During periods of constitutional politics, the higher lawmaking system encourages an engaged citizenry to focus on fundamental issues and determine whether any proposed solution deserves its considered support. During periods of normal politics, the system prevents the political elite from undermining the hard-won achievements of the People "behind the citizenry's back"— requiring leaders to return to the People and mobilize their considered support before foundational principles may be revised in a democratic way.

This conclusion returns us to the special concerns of the present volume. We shall be exploring how American institutions have in fact operated to organize popular debate and decision during our most creative periods of constitutional politics. The aim is to learn what history can teach about the ways Americans have translated the heady rhetoric of constitutional politics into enduring judgments of higher law. Only after canvasing our past two centuries of practice can we turn toward the future: Is our existing system of higher lawmaking in good repair? If not, how should it be reformed?

THE PROFESSIONAL NARRATIVE

Our task will require a critical reexamination of the tools we use to interpret the past. Modern Americans know their Constitution has changed fundamentally over two centuries. Only they have been taught to conceptualize these changes in ways that trivialize them.

Lawyers are most to blame for this. Day after day, the courts try to control our most powerful elected officials by discerning the meaning of decisions made in the name of the People a century or two ago. The things they allow themselves to see in the past determine, sometimes dramatically, what all of us can do in the here and now. It is their professional narrative, as I shall call it, that blocks insight into the distinctive character of our historical experience.

The problem does not involve the outright denial of change. No serious judge, lawyer, or scholar has trouble recognizing that today's Constitution is very different from the eighteenth-century version. Nor do they experience difficulty in identifying the crucial transformative periods. While particular doctrines are due to the work of different generations, two periods stand out. The first is the Republican reconstruction of the Union after the Civil War. The second is the Democrats' legitimation of activist national government during and after the Great Depression.

As with the original Founding, neither of these sweeping changes came about overnight. Each was preceded by a generation and more of political agitation that prepared the way for a decade of decisive change. In 1860, constitutionalists argued endlessly about secession of the states and slavery in the territories; by 1870, such questions were no longer open to fair dispute. The agonies of the Civil War had been translated into new constitutional meanings that shaped legal discourse for generations.

The same pattern—lengthy critique capped by a transformational decade—marks the constitutional legitimation of the activist welfare state. As late as 1935, the national government's power to regulate the economy was constrained by a complex set of constitutional limitations—whose precise character served as the centerpiece of ceaseless doctrinal debate. By 1941, this intricate web had disintegrated and the Constitution allowed ongoing governmental intervention in economic and social life. The agonies of the Great Depression had provoked a fundamental reworking of constitutional identity.

After these two transformations, American government was very different from anything the Founders had experienced or envisioned. No longer had "We the People" established a decentralized federal system enabling white men to pursue their self-interest within a market economy. Americans had constituted a powerful national government with unquestioned authority to secure the legal equality and economic welfare of all its citizens.

So much, I take it, is common ground for all students of the American constitution—citizens no less than scholars, politicians no less than judges. Whenever some new current of opinion gains political prominence, the popular mind—as if by reflex—recurs to these great achievements to measure the new movement's significance. The constitutional importance of Ronald Reagan's Presidency can be reduced to a single question: To what extent did it succeed in leading the American People to repudiate the welfare state legitimated during the New Deal? The same is true of the modern civil rights movement: Is it not past time for the American People to redeem the promise of equality made after the Civil War?

My problem arises when we turn from constitutional substance to higher lawmaking process: How did Americans of the nineteenth and twentieth centuries define, debate, and finally endorse the transformative proposals championed by their respective parties of constitutional reform?

The Existing Story Line

Today's Americans come to this question at a great disadvantage. The great struggles of Reconstruction are now beyond the recall of our grandparents. Darkness is now settling over the New Deal. The Americans who lived through the Roosevelt years are now vanishing with accelerating speed. The enduring meaning of their achievements is now in the hands of their children and their children's children.

Here is where lawyers have let their fellow citizens down. To measure their collective act of trivialization, consider the standard story lawyers tell themselves about the 1780's. If anything, modern constitutionalists are increasingly prepared to recognize, and reflect upon, the truly revolutionary character of the Founding. The Philadelphia Convention met not in a Lockean state of nature but in a dense legal environment established by the constitutions of thirteen states joined in "perpetual Union" through the Articles of Confederation. If the Federalists had played the game defined by these authoritative documents, their constitution would have been decisively rejected.

The Federalists responded by asserting their right to redefine the rules in the name of the People. Even more remarkably, most of their opponents accepted the legitimacy of this revolutionary breach. As the next chapter shows, the Federalists won their opponents' grudging consent by using old institutions in new ways to enhance their claim to speak for the People. This fascinating process of *unconventional adaptation* will be the central object of our study. Americans owe their remarkable constitutional continuity to their repeated success in negotiating these unconventional adaptations during their gravest crises as a People.

This point is lost in standard professional discussions of Reconstruction and the New Deal. When modern lawyers turn to the Thirteenth Amendment's abolition of slavery and the Fourteenth's commitment to equal protection and due process, they do not pause to consider how these great texts became part of the Constitution. They simply assume that the Reconstruction Republicans enacted them into law in strict conformity with the provisions for constitutional amendment laid down by Article Five of the 1787 Constitution.

The New Deal is treated even more dismissively. At least lawyers are willing to admit that the Civil War amendments changed the substantive law in fundamental ways. But when it comes to the New Deal, the story they tell denies that anything creative was going on. They treat the constitutional struggles of the 1930's as if they were the product of an intellectual mistake made by a handful of judicial conservatives on the Supreme Court. On the regnant view, the epic battles between the Old Court and the New Deal should never have happened. The Court should have immediately dressed the Roosevelt regime up in the clothes of the Founding Fathers. The anti-Roosevelt majority on the Supreme Court were fools or knaves to use the Constitution as a weapon against the New Deal.

Once we combine these stories about the Founding, Reconstruction, and New Deal, the overarching message is a continuing decline in constitutional creativity. Apparently, the most sweeping transformation of the twentieth century is best understood through a myth of rediscovery—it was not Franklin Roosevelt, but James Madison, who laid the constitutional foundations for the New Deal. Even the changes that followed Civil War and Reconstruction are not understood as a second American Revolution. When viewed from the legal angle, the Fourteenth Amendment is no different from the most trivial amendment to our sacred text. The last time the American People engaged in unconventional forms of popular sovereignty was at the Founding.

Revision: A Third Way?

Every time a lawyer rises in court to tell these familiar stories about the Founding, Reconstruction, and New Deal, he is casting modern Americans as tired epigones who lack any experience of successful constitutional politics. Such an insult would be acceptable if it were based on the hard truth. But if it isn't true, why should serious lawyers continue to tell a story of decline?

Throughout this series, I point to many professional advantages that may follow from a revision of the reigning professional narrative. A new approach will clarify many modern problems of constitutional interpretation; it will give us added insights into the interpretive dilemmas of the past; it will open new frontiers of interdisciplinary collaboration with historians, political scientists, and philosophers. But all these specialist advantages pale next to the simple question of integrity:[3] Can lawyers allow themselves to abuse their special knowledge and power by systematically demeaning the constitutional creativity of their fellow citizens?

It would be naive to rely on this single question to carry the day. The received narrative has one priceless advantage. It exists as a pervasive cultural reality in the life of the law, and you can't beat something with nothing. If we hope to do better, constitutionalists must return to the sources and discover that they tell a very different story. They reveal both Reconstruction Republicans and New Deal Democrats refusing to follow the path for constitutional amendment set out by their predecessors. Like the Federalists before them, these reformers self-consciously validated their initiatives through a series of unconventional institutional appeals to the People. It is we, not they, who have forgotten the truth about the revolutionary character of their higher lawmaking effort.

Our story will challenge two familiar views of constitutional change. On the first view, the distinctive feature of American democracy is the remarkable staying power of the "rules of the game." The American Constitution is the oldest in the world because we have remained remarkably faithful to established principles of democratic lawmaking for a longer period than fickle foreigners.

There is only one problem with this vision of procedural consensus: it is false. Neither Founding Federalists nor Reconstruction Republicans nor New Deal Democrats showed deep respect for established modes of constitutional revision. They changed them in the very process of changing the substance of fundamental values: from loose confederation to federal union, from slavery to freedom, from laissez-faire to the activist regulatory state.

But their revisionary activities do not comfortably fall within a second familiar framework. This position emphasizes the arbitrary character of acts of constituent power. Here is where the law ends, and pure politics (or war) begins: if revolutionaries succeed in establishing a new constitution, their rule-breaking activities are irrelevant; and if they fail, they fail.[4]

This simple account fails to capture the distinctive character of American history. The Founding, Reconstruction, and the New Deal were all acts of constituent authority. But they were not sheer acts of will. While Federalists, Republicans, and Democrats failed to follow well-established rules and principles, they experienced powerful institutional constraints on their revisionary authority. Much of this book describes the character of these constraints. Begin by considering a threshold question: if the participants weren't respectful of established legal norms, why did they feel any legal constraints at all?

My answer distinguishes between a challenge to well-established norms and a challenge to an entire constitutional tradition. As an example of this second assault, consider the Bolshevik Revolution of 1917. Before the Communists seized power in October, the previous provisional government had scheduled elections for a constituent assembly whose task was to frame a new constitution. The Bolsheviks allowed these elections to proceed, only to find themselves in the minority. At this point they confronted the question of total revolution: Would they disband the constituent assembly and thereby break their last institutional links to the past?[5]

This question provoked much anxious indecision before Lenin convinced his comrades to disband the assembly and break decisively with the old legal order.[6] Rather than adapting preexisting constitutional ideas and institutions to broaden support and gain consent, the Leninists embraced total revolution. They would ground their new regime on institutions—most notably the Red Army and Communist Party—that had *no* constitutional relationship, however remote, to the preexisting system.

But this is not what happened in America in the 1780's or the 1860's or the 1930's. In each case, the protagonists were not yearning for root-and-branch repudiation but for the revolutionary reform of the old regime. This distinctive aspiration motivated a distinctive form of revisionary practice. Though the rising constitutional movement did not respect established norms for revision, it did not seek to destroy the entire matrix of preexisting institutions. Instead, it constructed new higher lawmaking processes out of older institutions, using them as platforms for an unconventional argument:

> Granted, we did not play by the old rules and principles. But we did something just as good. We have beaten our opponents time after time in an arduous series of electoral struggles within a large number of familiar lawmaking institutions. True, our repeated victories don't add up to a formal constitutional amendment under the existing procedures. But we would never have emerged victorious in election after election without the considered support of a mobilized majority of the American People. We therefore claim that our repeated institutional and electoral victories have provided us with *a mandate from the People* adequate to authorize new constitutional law. Forcing us to play by the old procedures would only allow a minority to stifle the living voice of the People by manipulating legalisms that have lost their underlying functions.

This is a difficult and dangerous argument—but one that we will hear Madison and Bingham and Roosevelt advance at decisive turning points of American history. Before we examine its operation at particular times and places, consider the special conditions under which revolutionary reformers will be driven to embrace its logic.

America is a legalistic country. As soon as reformers attempt an end run around established principles and procedures, they will hand their opponents a potent political weapon. Previously, conservatives could only complain about the substantive merit of the reform. Now they can present themselves as guardians of legality—portraying their opponents as dangerous demagogues who are assaulting basic constitutional understandings in their lust for uncontrolled power.

Men like Patrick Henry and Andrew Johnson and Burton Wheeler sounded this alarm as they confronted the hubristic efforts of the Federalists, Republicans, and Democrats to make higher law in the name of the People. But normally such clarion calls will be unnecessary, since their prospect suffices to keep reformers in check. Rather than handing their opponents such a powerful weapon, transformative movements will try to fulfill their objectives within the existing constitutional order. They will make a break only when continued obedience threatens their reform agenda with defeat.

The reformers' reluctance will be reinforced by the distinctive character of their strategy. They are not proposing to destroy all the institutions of the old regime, but are embarking on a remarkable form of institutional jujitsu. They hope to win repeated support from a large number of existing institutions despite the incompatibility of their higher lawmaking initiative with the existing system of revision. Many of these institutions will initially be dominated by conservatives profoundly committed to the old legality. To put it mildly, they will not be thrilled at the prospect of helping their opponents dig their own graves.

All this means that our revolutionary reformers must be prepared for a long hard struggle—and one they may well lose in the end. Nonetheless, history reveals common themes emerging from the more successful struggles. The most persistent leitmotiv has been nationalism: Federalists, Republicans, and Democrats all complain that the preexisting system of revision gives too much power to the states, and that unconventional institutional moves are needed to express the constitutional will of the nation.

Successful appeals to popular sovereignty have also become increasingly inclusionary over time. Most of the Federalists were notoriously comfortable with the exclusion of slaves and women from any role in constitutional decisionmaking. But as we shall see, their appeal to the People to ratify the Constitution was remarkably inclusionary for its time and place. An inclusionary thrust is even more evident during Reconstruction and the New Deal—where appeals to blacks and workers played crucial roles in consolidating revolutionary reforms.

Given their inclusionary nationalism, reformers had a powerful response to conservative opponents who insisted upon strict fidelity to established procedures for constitutional amendment. These procedures, after all, had been devised by representatives of an earlier age, who had defined We the People in ways that later generations considered objectionably narrow. Now that the next wave of reformers were prepared to revise the earlier definition to embrace more of their fellow citizens, why should they be bound by the revisionary processes handed down by a much narrower group of Americans from a distant past? Was it not right and proper to revise these procedures if they threatened to stifle the voice of a more expansively conceived People?

To which conservatives replied that the reformers' unconventional actions would provoke a destructive cycle of incivility. As the constitutional fabric disintegrated, rival factions would simply give up the entire enterprise of talking to one another in a common language; they would simply seek dominion through unmediated violence. The end would come only with the establishment of tyranny, in which a bunch of power-drunk politicians confused their own arbitrary will with the will of the People.

Here is where reformers drew upon a remarkable aspect of American tradition. For Americans, law-breaking does not necessarily imply lawlessness. It is sometimes seen as a civic gesture indicating high seriousness. Consider the phenomenon of civil disobedience. The disobedient break the law, but they deny they are outlaws. They accept punishment to symbolize the depth of their commitment to the community. By putting their bodies on the line, they call on their fellow citizens to confront the true nature of justice and build a new legal order on firmer foundations.

By breaking the law we will find higher law. This paradoxical thought has obvious roots in Christianity, but modern Americans have appropriated it for more secular purposes, including the remarkable events reported in these pages. Like civil disobedience, unconventional activity heightens the seriousness of collective dialogue. But it occurs under much more dangerous conditions, at times when constitutional order is unraveling. And yet, for all the risks, the revolutionary activities of Federalists, Republicans, Democrats led not to chaos but to a renewed sense that the People really do rule in America. Part of this success is due to sheer luck, part to individual statesmanship, and much to other social conditions. But part is also due to the character of American constitutional law, which has always contained much more than formal rules and principles. Our task is to understand these deeper structures—both how they operated in the past and how they may discipline the future.

BEYOND ARTICLE FIVE

Wherever our story ends, it is clear where it should begin: the fifth article of the original Constitution provides future generations with a special set of procedures for constitutional amendment. The Founding system is dimly familiar to all Americans who have survived the terrors of high school civics. Future movements in constitutional politics are invited either to gain the support of two-thirds of both houses of Congress for their initiative, or to invoke an onerous procedure that will lead to the convocation of a new constitutional convention. Even if reformers persuade Congress or a convention to endorse their proposals, they confront a second obstacle course. They must gain the assent of three-fourths of the states, acting through legislatures or conventions. Only then does Article Five explicitly authorize them to reform higher law in the name of the People.

As one might expect, these rules are not as clear as high school civics suggests. But I mean to raise a more fundamental question: Should modern Americans read Article Five as if it described the only mechanisms they may appropriately use for constitutional revision at the dawn of the twenty-first century?

The text does not provide an answer. None of its 143 words say anything like "this Constitution may only be amended through the following procedures, and in no other way." The article makes its procedures sufficient, but not necessary, for the enactment of a valid amendment. It is up to us, not the text, to decide whether to convert a sufficient condition into a necessary one and give the Founding procedure a monopoly over future development.

Given the importance of this decision, we should not make it arbitrarily. Much of the lawyer's craft involves the thoughtful resolution of indeterminacy. We will be ranging over the full range of interpretive disciplines—from the intention of the Framers to the decisions of the modern Supreme Court. For this introductory sketch, it will be enough to confront the monopolistic reading with the challenge posed by Reconstruction.

Some simple mathematics serves to introduce the problem. During the 1860's, there were never more than 37 states in the Union. Under the terms of Article Five, this gave an absolute veto over constitutional initiatives to any ten states—one-fourth plus one. Despite the Union's victory in the Civil War, it was all too easy for such a veto bloc to assemble. There were no less than eleven states returning to the Union from the former Confederacy—as well as a number of Northern states that were not reliably in the Republican column. The reformers' opponents—and there were millions in the North as well as the South—were confident of victory so long as constitutional amendments were processed in the way envisioned by Article Five. They insisted that the Republicans play the game in strict accordance with traditional principles, confident that the Founders had dealt them a losing hand.

The Republican leadership responded with anxiety—and grim determination. As the constitutional crisis reached its climax in the struggle over the Fourteenth Amendment, they refused to allow their opponents' legalistic interpretation of Article Five block Reconstruction. In the face of dramatic challenges by conservatives, they gained popular support to press the established system beyond its breaking point. Only in this way did they finally win the constitutional authority to validate the Fourteenth Amendment in the name of the People.

Part Two of this book will be largely dedicated to establishing this single conclusion. But if you find it persuasive, I think I have earned the right to dismiss the monopolistic interpretation of the Founding text. After all, the original Constitution does *not* explicitly monopolize the procedures used by future generations; indeed, as the next chapter argues, such a monopoly is inconsistent with both the Founding practice and its theory of popular sovereignty. Why, then, read such a demand into the text at the cost of delegitimizing the Fourteenth Amendment?

I shall argue for a pluralistic reading of the Founding text, one that permits its harmonious coexistence with the Reconstruction experience. Pluralists understand the amendment system established in

1787 as a facilitative device, always available when the American people choose to use it. But they refuse to allow this system to monopolize our legal vision. If we aim for a *comprehensive* statement of the modern law, we must move beyond the Founding and consider Reconstruction as a fundamental precedent in the evolving law of higher lawmaking.

This means, first, that we should state the relevant facts as dispassionately as we can: What fundamental legal problems did Republicans confront in using Article Five? Second, how did presidents, congressmen, courts, and ordinary voters deal with these problems? Third, how did individual responses to particular problems develop into larger patterns of constitutional decision? By answering these questions, we shall reach a fourth stage—in which we may reflect upon the larger patterns of practical decisionmaking that have come into view.

This four fold task requires a lot of work, but it should seem familiar to any competent lawyer. In principle, it is no different from the job she might do in examining the basic precedents defining the law of free speech (or the common law of accidents). If there is anything distinctive, it has less to do with legal method and more with the actors whose words and deeds are at the center of the analysis. While decisions of the Supreme Court play a role, a larger part will be played by Presidents and Congresses—and their efforts to gain the support of the American people at general elections. We will be studying Congressional committee reports, Presidential proclamations, and party campaign platforms with the same care that lawyers usually reserve for Supreme Court opinions.

This shift in focus is only natural, given the nature of our question. Our subject is the law of constitutional lawmaking, not the way courts and others have interpreted the law once it has been enacted. How, then, did nineteenth-century Americans define, debate, and decide which proposals for Reconstruction deserved to gain the authority of We the People of the United States?

PATTERNS OF RECONSTRUCTION

First and foremost, the Republicans challenged the Federalists' view that the states should be an equal partner in the amendment process, with the right to veto any innovation that did not meet with their overwhelming approval. During the debate over slavery, the Presidency served as the principal vehicle for the Republicans' assault on this Federalist premise. Not only did Abraham Lincoln's Emancipation Proclamation shift the constitutional status quo before the Thirteenth Amendment was formally proposed, but Andrew Johnson's role was no less remarkable. President Johnson did not allow the Southern states to suppose that the original Federalist idea of an equal nation-state partnership applied to their consideration of the Emancipation Amendment.

The President fundamentally restructured the conditions under which Southern states would consider the Thirteenth Amendment. These actions violated original Federalist principles, but they fell far short of coercion. They did not, for example, deter Mississippi from formally rejecting the Thirteenth Amendment, but they did suffice to induce other Southern states to give their reluctant consent to this great nationalizing initiative on behalf of universal freedom. Overall, the ratification process is best described as a Presidentially led effort that diminished, but did not eliminate, the role of the states—an artful weave of old Federalist and new Presidential patterns that culminated in Secretary of State Seward's proclamation of December 1865, declaring the Thirteenth Amendment part of our higher law.

This precedent will prove especially important when we encounter the New Deal—which represents yet another quantum leap in the development of the *model of Presidential leadership*. As we turn to the Fourteenth Amendment, our analysis takes a different turn. Johnson refused to throw the Presidency's support behind this amendment's broad-ranging commitment to equal protection for American citizens of all races. Opposing further unconventional actions on the higher lawmaking front, he inaugurated a dramatic struggle with the Reconstruction Congress for the mantle of national leadership. The result was the elaboration of a *model of Congressional leadership* in which the Republicans on Capitol Hill finally gained the acceptance of the President (and the Supreme Court) of their claim that the Fourteenth Amendment was a valid expression of We the People.

The unconventional process evolved in five stages. During most of 1866, Congress and the President struggled to an impasse from their citadels on either end of Pennsylvania Avenue: each challenging the very authority of its antagonist to speak on fundamental matters in the name of We the People.

This first period of point-counterpoint induced both the President and Congress to transform the next regular election into one of the greatest higher lawmaking events of American history. The Congressional leadership proposed the Fourteenth Amendment as the platform on which they called upon the American people to renew their mandate. Andrew Johnson used the Presidency to mobilize the people against the Republicans by electing solid conservatives to Congress who would repudiate the Fourteenth Amendment.

The result was a decisive electoral victory for the party of revolutionary reform. This inaugurated the second stage of the process. The returning Republicans claimed a mandate from the People for the Fourteenth Amendment; the conservatives, led by Johnson, denied that the People had spoken decisively. The President encouraged ten Southern states to exercise the veto seemingly offered them by the Federalist's Article Five. This put Congress in an awkward position, since these Southern governments had been instrumental in giving the Thirteenth Amendment its three-fourths majority. Nonetheless, the Republicans refused to allow Federalist norms to monopolize their lawmaking options. Rather than accept an Article Five veto of the Fourteenth Amendment, they took unconventional action to redeem their mandate from the People.

This tactic inaugurated a third phase, involving an unconventional assault upon dissenting institutions. It began with the enactment of the Reconstruction Act of March 2, 1867, and continued through the impeachment of Andrew Johnson one year later. During this period, Congress claimed a popular mandate to destroy the autonomy of any institution—the Southern governments, the Presidency, and the Supreme Court—that opposed the legitimation of the Fourteenth Amendment. At the same time, the dissenters were under no compulsion to bend their knee before Congressional demands. They were free to resist until the next round of elections in 1868 in the hope that conservatives might gain a decisive victory at the polls.

The dissenters chose the path of resistance until they confronted their moment of truth in March of 1868—when the voters in the South, the conservatives on the Supreme Court, and Andrew Johnson in the White House made some of the pivotal decisions in our history. The central event was the President's impeachment trial, precipitated by Johnson's effort to slow down ratification of the Fourteenth Amendment so that its validity could remain a campaign issue in the upcoming 1868 elections. Would the President continue to resist the Republicans' vision of the Union—and thereby suffer conviction at the hands of the Senate? Or would he try to save his Presidency by negotiating a "switch in time," in which he would accept Congress's authority to override the South's Article Five veto?

The President chose the latter course, inaugurating a fourth stage— the "switch in time." Virtually simultaneous "switches" by the other dissenting institutions also allowed them to preserve their institutional autonomy. As a consequence, a new institutional situation emerged in the months after the impeachment trial. After years of intense struggle, all three branches in Washington, together with the reconstructed governments of the South, were converging on the legitimacy of the Fourteenth Amendment.

With the outlines of the Republican solution emerging from Washington D.C., the elections of 1868 provided leading Democrats with another opportunity to denounce the constitutional legitimacy of the Fourteenth Amendment. But the Democratic challenge had the very opposite effect from its intended aim. Rather than provoking a further debate over first principles, 1868 served as a consolidating election, making it plain that most Americans wanted to bring the period of turbulent constitutional politics to an end. With Grant replacing Johnson in the White House, and the Republicans in firm control of Congress and the Court, nobody remained in authority to continue agitating public opinion about the constitutional irregularities involved in the enactment of the Civil War amendments. After the consoliding election of 1868, there was no longer a serious question whether the Civil War amendments were legal; the question, instead, was what they meant, and whether Americans would live up to their promise.

To summarize this five-stage process in terms of a simple schema:

Constitutional Impasse → Electoral Mandate →
Challenge to Dissenting Institutions → Switch in Time →
Consolidating Election

Consider how this schema challenges basic premises of the Federalist model of constitutional change. As we have seen, the Federalists used the division of powers between state and nation as their basic building block in constructing the Founding system: new amendments would be forged through a joint decisionmaking process dominated by popularly elected assemblies on both levels of government. As this system threatened to doom the Fourteenth Amendment, the Republicans adapted a second building block—the separation of powers—to a new constitutional use. For the Federalists, the separation between Congress, President, and Court played no significant role in higher lawmaking; it was simply a mechanism for passing normal legislation within higher-law constraints. But now it became the means by which contending protagonists tested each others' claims to a decisive "mandate" from the People on behalf of rival visions of the Union. The Fourteenth Amendment became higher law only because the Republican Congress emerged victorious from this test. It was the separation of powers, not the division of power, that became the nineteenth century's great engine of higher lawmaking.

One adaptation led to another. The protagonists in the White House and on Capitol Hill were given powerful incentives to impress new plebiscitarian meanings on national elections. The election of 1866 is paradigmatic, with both sides trying to break the impasse by gaining a decisive electoral victory. But the consolidating election of 1868 was hardly less important. In both cases, the election decisively changed the balance of perceived legitimacy, endowing the victors with a new credibility for their claim that the People had given broad and emphatic support for their constitutional solutions.

Putting these two interlocking innovations together, the successful struggle for the Fourteenth Amendment introduces a new nationalistic pattern into our higher lawmaking repertoire—one which supplements, but does not displace, the classical Federalist model. In contrast to its predecessor, the Republican model contemplates a constitutional dynamic dominated by a debate between rival branches of the national government—which, if successful, is culminated by a series of decisive electoral victories by the transformative movement after a sustained period in which its vision is subjected to withering criticism by the more conservative branches.

Having recovered this model, we come to the next question: how are lawyers going to use it? Those heavily invested in the reigning professional narrative may be tempted by a strategy of trivialization: "Granted, there is something fishy about the Fourteenth Amendment. But surely Reconstruction was an exceptional time, full of the passions of Civil War. It was the blood and sacrifice at battles like Gettysburg, not the nationalistic model of constitutional change, that legitimated the *Civil War* amendments. Whatever anomalies may have accompanied these amendments, they are of no relevance to the larger enterprise of constitutional understanding."[7]

This easy answer allows lawyers to make their peace with Reconstruction, but only at a great cost in historical understanding. All that the victory of the Union army established was the failure of secession. It did not establish the terms for reunion, and certainly did not establish that most Americans supported a move beyond the Thirteenth Amendment. As the Republicans well understood, President Johnson was speaking for a large portion of the public when he rejected the Fourteenth Amendment's promise of equal protection to black Americans. The challenge was to organize a constitutional process that came to a decisive conclusion only after both sides were given a fair chance to bring their case to the country and mobilize their supporters for a series of focused electoral struggles.

Here is where the enduring status of the Federalist model became central. Quite simply, if the Republicans had respected the initial Article Five veto of the Fourteenth Amendment, Johnson would have won the struggle over the constitutional meaning of the Civil War. It was only through unconventional innovation that the Republicans finally won legitimacy for their more egalitarian understanding of the Union. Battlefield victories were necessary but not sufficient conditions for the Reconstruction amendments. Change in the higher law-making system was also crucial.

Putting the point more broadly, the Republicans' relationship to the Civil War is no different from the Federalists' relation to the Revolutionary War. George Washington, after all, gained his place at the Constitutional Convention by virtue of his wartime triumphs. But the war against England, like the war between the states, only established the military conditions for American independence. The enduring constitutional terms would be determined by the People during the peace that followed.

The parallel with the Federalists goes further. As we shall see, the 1787 Constitution would never have been ratified if the Federalists had played by the established rules. In 1787 as in 1868, unconventional adaptation was a necessary, if not a sufficient, condition for constitutional victory in the name of the People. Why, then, should the professional narrative give pride of place to the Federalist model while ignoring the Republican model?

We ignore these questions only by blinding ourselves to some deep truths about American identity expressed by the Republican model. After the searing experience of Civil War, Americans did become more of a nation. This is made plain by the very first sentence of the Fourteenth Amendment, which expressly affirms that national citizenship is primary and makes state citizenship derivative. The nation-centered character of the Republican model of constitutional change meshes perfectly with this substantive change. A professional narrative that ignores the Republican model would have us pretend that we still lived in the Federalist era, when Americans were still uncertain whether We the People of the *United* States were anything more than a confederation of sovereign states.

I do not deny the continuing importance of the Federalist system. Article Five provides an enduring resource for the American people when they wish to exercise their constituent power through the states. Rather than choosing between Federalism and Republicanism, I want to affirm both aspects of our higher lawmaking legacy.

Finally, the trivializing response goes wrong in suggesting that the Republican achievement is an anomaly in American history. As we shall see, it is the Republican model, more than the Federalist, which permits deeper insights into the dynamics of twentieth-century development.

FROM RECONSTRUCTION TO NEW DEAL

I shall be inviting you to reflect upon a series of remarkable parallels between the 1860's and the 1930's. The effort will reveal that the New Deal Democrats' struggle for activist government went through a five-stage process that was broadly similar to the one encountered by the Republicans in their struggle for freedom and equality.

The New Deal Pattern

As in Reconstruction, the separation of powers served as the central engine for constitutional debate and decision during the New Deal.

The big difference between the two periods concerns the identity of the leading reformist and conservative branches. After Lincoln was shot, the Presidency turned conservative, and Congress was left alone as the champion of revolutionary reform. In contrast, Roosevelt remained at the helm throughout the New Deal, leaving it up to the Court to defend the conservative view of the Constitution. With this variation, however, the five-phase pattern repeats itself.

Roosevelt's first term marks the first phase of institutional impasse, as the Supreme Court struck down a series of revolutionary reforms. As in 1866, the New Dealers responded by using the next regularly scheduled election as a device to break the constitutional impasse. When they gained a crushing victory in the Presidential and Congressional elections of 1936, they claimed a mandate from the People for their activist vision of American government.

A third phase followed, characterized by an unconventional assault on dissenting institutions. Since the leading conservative branch during Reconstruction was the Presidency, the Republicans threatened Johnson with impeachment unless he accepted their constitutional reforms. Since the leading conservative branch in the 1930's was the Court, the President threatened the Justices with court-packing if they continued to defend the principles of laissez-faire constitutionalism. While impeachment and court-packing differ in legal form, their constitutional function was identical: to confront the leading conservative institution with a distinctive, and fundamental, question. Should it continue supporting the older constitutional tradition at the risk of permanent damage to its institutional autonomy?

Just as President Johnson made his "switch in time" in the late 1860's, so did the Court in the 1930's. Both retreats, in turn, allowed the dissenting institution to escape grievous long-term damage. Once the switch was made, conservatives managed to convince the Senate to reject court-packing in the 1930's, just as it had rejected impeachment in the 1860's. This not only enabled the separation of powers to survive. It encouraged the endangered branch to rehabilitate itself over time by playing a constructive role in the emerging constitutional order. As in 1868, so in 1937, all three branches were beginning to converge upon a new constitutional solution.

But this new solution had not yet been woven into the fabric of higher law. While the Supreme Court had supported some key New

Deal programs by narrow margins in 1937, a Republican Presidential victory in 1940 could have led to a reappraisal of these transitional decisions. As in the case of Reconstruction, the party of constitutional reform required a "consolidating election" before it could definitively set constitutional law on a new course.

Roosevelt's election to an unprecedented third term marked the point of no return. By 1941, the President and the Senate had replaced the last holdover Justices from the Republican era with convinced believers in activist national government. The 5-to-4 decisions of 1937 were now transformed into unanimous judgments that self-consciously swept away the fundamental doctrines of an earlier age.

What Was New about the New Deal?

The New Deal pattern is, then, best viewed as a variation on historic precedents established during Reconstruction. It was the Reconstruction Republicans, not the New Deal Democrats, who first combined the separation of powers with decisive electoral victories to gain the constitutional authority to speak in the voice of We the People of the *United* States—a voice distinct from, but no less authentic than, the voice of We the People of the United *States* expressed through the Federalist rules of Article Five. But, of course, it is crucially important to clarify the variations introduced in the 1930's—since they mark the parameters of modern constitutional development. I shall be emphasizing three themes.

The first, and most important, involves the Presidency. While Lincoln and Johnson played unprecedented roles in the constitutional emancipation of the slaves, Presidential leadership came to an end with Andrew Johnson's defection. In contrast, New Deal Democrats could rely on the Presidency to provide ongoing constitutional leadership.

The Democrats' good fortune gave them more lawmaking options. They did not need to follow the example of the Reconstruction Congress as it destroyed state governments when they vetoed the Fourteenth Amendment. Nor did they need to threaten a hostile President with impeachment. Roosevelt could target the Supreme Court, and codify the New Deal vision, by flooding the bench with new Justices prepared to endorse a revolutionary transformation of traditional doctrine.

This led to a second fundamental change—the self-conscious use of *transformative judicial appointments* as a central tool for constitutional change. Roosevelt introduced this device in his famous court-packing proposal of 1937—which would have given him the right to make six new nominations immediately. When the Old Court switch took the political wind out of this radical proposal, President and Congress elaborated a more gradual, but similar, approach. As traditionalist Justices resigned or died, they were systematically replaced by appointees prepared to support and elaborate a transformative vision of constitutional law.

By the early 1940's the stage had been set for the third change: the use of *transformative judicial opinions* to establish the basic contours of constitutional doctrine. These New Deal cases not only rejected leading decisions of the old regime, like *Lochner v. New York,* which struck down maximum-hours legislation in the name of "freedom of contract." They transformed *Lochner* into a symbol of an entire constitutional order that had been thoroughly repudiated by the American people. These New Deal opinions have operated as the functional equivalent of formal constitutional amendments, providing a solid foundation for activist intervention in national social and economic life for the past sixty years.

I do not claim that this New Deal jurisprudence is an unchangeable element of our Constitution—but then again, neither is most of the formal text. I do claim that any future transformation of New Deal principles should require a higher lawmaking process comparable to the one led by President Roosevelt in the 1930's.

FROM ROOSEVELT TO REAGAN—AND BEYOND

The enduring significance of New Deal precedents has been paradoxically confirmed during the last generation. As in the 1930's, so in the 1980's, Ronald Reagan refused to put the Presidency's principal energies behind formal amendments—in his case, amendments to balance the budget and overrule *Roe v. Wade.* Like Roosevelt, he claimed a mandate from the People for a new breed of Supreme Court Justice—and sought to fulfill this mandate through a series of transformative judicial appointments. The aim, as in the Roosevelt years, was to gain a commanding judicial majority for transformative opinions that would demonize the leading cases of the prior era: if Mr. Justice Scalia had his way, *Roe* would be treated with the same contempt that the New Deal Court reserved for Old Court decisions like *Lochner* that had protected the free market from activist regulation.

The parallel ends at this point. Reagan's effort did not culminate in transformative opinions proclaiming a decisive break with the past. Rather than demonizing *Roe* as the New Dealers demonized *Lochner*, the reconstituted Court of the 1990's pledged continued fidelity to the past. The crucial decision was *Planned Parenthood v. Casey*—in which Reagan-Bush Justices cast the decisive votes to preserve *Roe* against the angry dissent of Mr. Justice Scalia.

While the outcome of the 1980's was different from the 1930's, the process by which the American people debated their constitutional future was similar. In both cases, the Presidency served as the institutional engine of constitutional transformation; in both cases, the operational question was whether the President could convince Congress and the Court to accept his demand for fundamental change in the name of the People; in both cases, the fate of the President's higher lawmaking pretensions was climaxed by a struggle in the Senate over his effort to make transformative appointments to the Supreme Court.

The substantive views of Robert Bork were different from Felix Frankfurter's. But the two nominations played uncannily similar functions in the evolving practice of Presidential leadership. Both men were nominated by transformative Presidents in the seventh year of their tenures; both were archetypal transformative appointments—immensely capable scholars who had provided intellectual leadership to the political movements ascendant in the White House, they were transparently eager to write transformative opinions that repudiated key elements of existing doctrine. The fact that Roosevelt succeeded with Frankfurter and Reagan failed with Bork should not blind us to the striking similarity in the processes through which the Presidency sought to revolutionize higher law in the name of the People.

Having isolated a recurring model of Presidential leadership, I conclude by considering its reform. Should the precedents inherited from the Roosevelt and Reagan years be radically repudiated, interstitially modified, or wholeheartedly accepted?

BEYOND FORMALISM

There is lots of history in this book, some political science, a little philosophy—but these interdisciplinary excursions are in the service of a fundamentally legal enterprise. Except for the last chapter, I am focusing on a single question: If Americans of the 1990's wish to revise their Constitution, what are the *legal* alternatives they may legitimately pursue?

Now it would be nice if I could answer in a page or two or ten. Such a clear statement would not only satisfy lawyers, whose desire for conceptual neatness sometimes verges on the pathological. It would also yield very real advantages for all Americans if higher lawmaking could be conducted under some crisply stated rules.

The first advantage is fair notice. From the very beginning, each side would know precisely what it must do in order to emerge victorious from the struggle. As a consequence, partisans would be given a fair opportunity to marshal their political forces at the critical moments. A rulebook would also make it harder for the losing side to explain away defeat by saying that it wasn't aware that a critical decision was about to be made.

A formalist process also has the substantial merit of signaling the point at which a particular exercise in constitutional lawmaking comes to an end—at a predetermined point the new amendment will turn out a clear winner or a clear loser. While committed activists would retain the right to begin again from the beginning, normal Americans could choose to relax their political attention and turn to other things. In a dualist democracy, this is no mean achievement. The Constitution does not, and should not, try to force citizens to remain in a constant state of constitutional agitation.[8] Normal Americans have a right to assert their constitutional will in politics without making this project their life's work; bringing constitutional exertions to an unambiguous end is as great a service to democratic government as helping a new movement to signal a new set of constitutional intentions to the public at large.

And yet formalism cannot escape the vices of its virtues. It achieves clarity and structure only at the cost of *presuming* the existence of a mobilized and considered popular judgment by pointing to some readily observable institutional criteria—say, the affirmative vote of two-thirds of Congress and three-fourths of the state legislatures. Underlying this presumption is something I call the theory of institutional resistance. The idea is that an elaborate institutional obstacle course will exhaust all political groups who fail to mobilize and sustain the massive public-regarding support required for constitutional legitimacy. Institutional resistance, in short, will frustrate the cynical manipulation of the idea of a higher law by coalitions of narrow pressure groups. While there is something to this idea, the design of the perfect obstacle course is a tricky business. For the obstacle course cannot be so exhausting that it resists even a massive public-regarding majority on those rare occasions when the People-with-a-capital-P *do* have something new to say.

To put the point broadly, any formalist system of rules suffers two dangers. The first danger is the *false positive:* here the formal system signals that the People have spoken even though the supporters of the initiative have not in fact mobilized the sustained and considered support that dualist principles require of a new constitutional solution. This is a bad thing, and any formal rule system should be designed to make it unlikely.

As this risk is diminished, it inevitably increases the risk of *false negatives.* By making it hard for a momentary special interest coalition to impersonate the People, the formalist's obstacle course may stifle the expression of constitutional movements that have won the continuing support of a decisive and sustained majority after years of mobilized debate penetrating deeply into the consciousness of ordinary citizens.[9] This is also a bad thing—indeed, if lawyerly elites were allowed to use the rules to stifle the considered judgments of constitutional politics, most Americans would eventually despair at the very idea that We the People can meaningfully give our representatives their marching orders.

Formalists might dismiss this second danger if, after two centuries of history, it has proved merely hypothetical. But the truth is different. At two of the greatest crises in their history, Americans faced the very grave risk of a false negative. If they chose to play punctiliously by the rules of Article Five, Reconstruction Republicans and New Deal Democrats confronted the clear and present danger that their long and successful struggle to mobilize the People for fundamental change would be stifled by legalistic nit-picking. In response, they sought to win the support of the People for a change in the rules of revision.

Given the success of both Republicans and Democrats, we cannot responsibly pretend that the rules for amendment propounded by the Federalists remain the sole source of law for the twenty-first century. Granted, the study of the unconventional precedents left by Americans of the 1860's and 1930's requires some hard work. But we will find it quite possible to elaborate principles that will help identify the conditions under which future movements might *legitimately* claim that the People have given them a mandate for fundamental constitutional change.

This claim supposes that there is more to law than rules. But this is a very uncontroversial notion in jurisprudence.[10] Every thoughtful lawyer, I would hope, recognizes that law includes the study of principles and precedents no less than rules—and that he or she must try to state the law in a way that takes all three into account. Sometimes, it may prove possible to set the principles, precedents, and rules into a neatly ordered sequence—with the leading precedents falling under crisp rules, which are in turn illuminated by fundamental principles. While such neo-classical reasoning structures aren't fashionable right now, they are often persuasive.

But sometimes they aren't. After two centuries of unruly but creative constitutional politics, neo-classical order is simply unattainable. While the great historical precedents do not fall under crisp rules, they do display important family resemblances. So long as we do not expect to reduce these precedents to simple-seeming rules, it is possible to elaborate fundamental constitutional criteria that future political movements must satisfy before gaining higher lawmaking authority.

This is the purpose of the model of Presidential leadership—to provide historically rooted criteria for appraising future efforts by political movements to use the White House as a springboard for a new beginning in constitutional law. The next time that a President comes forward aggressively to claim some sweeping mandate from the People, constitutionalists should be better prepared to use the experience of the past to test these claims. Despite the rise of Presidential leadership in the modern republic, the Chief Executive has not (yet) won the authority to jolt the Constitution into a new direction on the basis of a victory or two at the polls. The precedents continue to constrain the occasions upon which the separation of powers may be used to legitimate a new constitutional beginning in the name of We the People. The challenge for the legal community is to begin a serious conversation that will allow us to play a disciplined role in the next crisis of Presidential leadership.

CHAPTER TWO

Reframing the Founding

CONVENTIONAL WISDOM

O SCILLATING between idolizing the Founders and demonizing them, Americans have a hard time defining their relationship to their constitutional beginnings. The dark side was powerfully sketched by Charles Beard early in the century.[1] His image of the Founding as the American Thermidor still haunts. Beard's Founders did not come to fulfill the Revolution, but to lead an antipopular putsch for property rights. This Beardian image has been darkened further by increasing reflection upon the Founders' racist and sexist presuppositions—to the point where Justice Thurgood Marshall could publicly deny that the Founding provided an adequate moral basis for modern American government.[2] These moral doubts fuel the powerful antioriginalism of much modern constitutional law: surely the prejudiced opinions of white men, many of them slaveholders, cannot be allowed to serve as the fixed points of our community's search for a more perfect Union?

Such questions have darkened, but never obliterated, the older heroic image. The Founders may have had feet of clay, but don't they stand as the most remarkable statesmen in American history? The miracle in Philadelphia remains just that—there can be no denying that the Framers divined the future course of American history and came down with governing formulae that deserve our continuing respect. If anything, this mythic image has reemerged with renewed force in recent years—to the point where Justice Clarence Thomas could embrace the words and wisdom of the Framers with an enthusiasm unprecedented in modern constitutional law.

I reject both images. I aim to push the Fathers off the pedestal

without dropping them into the dustbin of history. There is no denying Thurgood Marshall's point. The Founders shared the prejudices
of their age. If we are to grasp their enduring importance, we cannot
look upon them as demigods with final answers. Later generations
have reversed many Founding judgments about the place of equality,
liberty, and federalism in our higher law—without these latter-day
contributions, the Constitution of 1787 would have long since proved
inadequate. If we are to grasp 1787's enduring importance, we must
approach it with different expectations. We must search for the
deeper ways that the Founding language, institutions, and ideals have
shaped the very process through which later generations have revised
the substantive commitments of the eighteenth century. Even at this
level of higher lawmaking process, Founding models have not survived untouched by time. Nevertheless, we will never grasp the genius
of modern American government without assessing their continuing
importance.

Unfortunately, this interpretive effort has also been distorted by the
demonization/glorification cycle. Either the Founding contribution to
the law of higher lawmaking is ignored in free-form (if often perceptive) discussions of the "living constitution."[3] Or the Federalists are
treated as superheroes whose timeless commands have rigorously controlled all constitutional transformations of the next two centuries. To
break this cycle, we must take the Founders off their pedestal and
learn to look upon them as mere mortals facing a serious problem—
and one that would recur at later points in American history. Quite
simply, the Federalists confronted a preexisting system for higher
lawmaking that made demands upon them that they could never
realistically hope to fulfill. But Madison & Co. refused to accept
defeat for their constitutional enterprise. They also refused to launch
an all-out assault against the system.

They carved out a third way. They created a new higher lawmaking
system by using preexisting institutions as key building blocks. By
gaining these institutions' assent to their own reorganization, the Federalists vastly enhanced their claim to speak for the People.

They were not the first to take this path. As we shall see, they were
elaborating a great precedent from English constitutional history, established by the Convention of 1688 in consolidating the principles of
the Glorious Revolution.

Nor were they the last. Reconstruction and the New Deal are best viewed as similar "convention-like" adaptations. But before this thesis can be rigorously formulated, let alone tested, we should follow the Federalists, step by step, as they pursued their third path to constitutional legitimacy.

THE PROBLEM

Only six years before Philadelphia, all thirteen states had finally agreed upon Articles of Confederation, whose final provision reads:

> 13. And the Articles of this confederation shall be inviolably observed by every state, and the Union shall be perpetual; nor shall any alteration at any time hereafter be made in any of them; unless such alteration be agreed to in a congress of the United States, and be afterwards confirmed by the legislatures of every state.

Article XIII's emphasis on unanimity is hardly accidental, since it took a lot of work to get all of the states to agree to the terms of Confederation in the first place.[4]

And yet the Federalists were now refusing to play by the rules. After a summer of secret meetings, they went public with a bombshell. Article Seven blandly asserted that "[t]he Ratification of the Conventions of nine States shall be sufficient for the Establishment of this Constitution between the States so ratifying the Same." This declaration of independence created three sorts of legal problems.

Problems under the Articles

Article Seven assaults the established revisionary process on four fronts. First, it invited secession, rejecting the Articles' assertion that "the Union shall be perpetual" and authorizing a walkout of nine states. As we shall see, this threat of secession was crucial in pushing states like New York and Virginia to give the Constitution their reluctant endorsement. The first Congress after ratification began as a secessionist body, meeting without North Carolina or Rhode Island— and the latter state's consent was only procured after the secessionist Congress began threatening it with economic sanctions.

Second, the Founding text ignored the power over amendments

granted by the Articles to the Continental Congress. This omission was especially remarkable since a number of states refused to send delegates to Philadelphia until the Constitutional Convention received express Congressional approval.

The Federalists were no less contemptuous of existing state authorities. In the teeth of the Articles' express command, their proposed Constitution cut the legislatures out of the ratifying process, leaving it up to special conventions meeting in each state.

Finally, all this was done in the face of the Articles' express claim to specify the exclusive means for its revision.

Problems with the Convention

Consider the assembly that was taking the law into its own hands. The Convention was itself a secessionist body. Rhode Island was the obvious holdout, refusing to send any delegates. New York and Delaware posed problems as well.

New York sent three delegates to the Convention, but two walked out as the centralizing bias of the Federalist majority became clear. Since New York required a majority of its delegates to bind the state, the vote of the only remaining representative, Alexander Hamilton, was legally insufficient. The Convention did not pretend otherwise. Its journal treated New York like Rhode Island on the final question of whether to approve the Constitution. Neither state is recorded as casting a ballot.[5]

Delaware's legislature expressly barred its delegation from agreeing to any proposal that deprived it of the equal voting power it enjoyed under the Articles. Its delegates signed the Constitution in contempt of their commission.[6]

We are presented, then, with the spectacle of ten delegations urging nine states to bolt a solemn agreement ratified by all thirteen members of the Confederation. Even this understates the difficulty. In calling for the Convention, the Continental Congress had charged the delegates to meet "for the *sole and express* purpose of revising the Articles."[7] Did this limited grant authorize the delegates to rip up the Articles and propose an entirely new text?

This question was raised repeatedly. In the two key states of New York and Massachusetts, it was reinforced by delegate commissions that expressly incorporated Congress' restrictive language.[8] Delegates from other states came with a broader mandate, allowing them to make any constitutional proposal they thought appropriate.[9] While key delegates may well have acted beyond their commission, this was not true of all.

But no delegation had any similar warrant for an end run around the amendment rules found in the Articles of Confederation. The precise language varied from state to state, but Virginia's commissions were typical: its delegation could engage in "*devising* and *discussing* all such alterations and further provisions, as may be necessary to render the Federal Constitution adequate . . . *reporting* such an Act for that purpose, *to the United States in Congress, as, when agreed to by them, and duly confirmed by the several states, will effectually provide for the same.*"[10]

Such language expressly subordinated the Convention to existing institutions and procedures. So did the Continental Congress in stipulating that the Philadelphians' proposals could become law only if "agreed to in Congress and confirmed by the states."[11] The delegates had absolutely no authority to set up a new higher lawmaking mechanism for the exercise of popular sovereignty. Indeed, some delegates to the Continental Congress refused appointments to Philadelphia because, as Richard Henry Lee explained, "Being a Member of Congress where the plan of Convention must be approved," he would be required to "pass judgment at New York upon their opinion at Philadelphia."[12]

Problems with State Constitutions

The Federalists ran into more legal trouble in calling for ratifying conventions in the thirteen states. By virtue of its Supremacy Clause, their proposed Constitution amounted to a vast revision of each state's constitution, and yet they were proceeding in willful contempt of each state's existing revisionary mechanism.

The legal status of each ratifying convention depended upon its particular state constitution, but it will pay to distinguish between two broad types—those that contemplated the use of conventions; and those that did not.

Those that did included Massachusetts, New Hampshire, and

Pennsylvania. In the first two, a special convention had initially proposed the state constitution, which was then approved by popular votes in town meeting. Pennsylvania's 1776 constitution was enacted by its legislature, but it was widely recognized as the most radically democratic document of its time.[13] It is therefore revealing how these three states dealt with the convention mechanism. In each case, the constitutional text refused to give the legislature, or anybody else, the unfettered right to call a convention. Such an extraordinary assembly could only meet after a specified number of years had passed—seven years in New Hampshire and Pennsylvania; fifteen in Massachusetts. New Hampshire was the sole state to make the summoning of a convention automatic; Massachusetts required two-thirds of the towns to agree; Pennsylvania required two-thirds of a specially elected body of Censors.[14]

These cumbersome processes reflected a deep concern with stability characteristic of early republican thought.[15] Americans were painfully aware of the Tory claim that their infant republics would disintegrate amidst constant factional strife. The careful structuring of conventions expressed a commitment to stability coupled with an ultimate faith in popular sovereignty.

Unhappily for the Federalists, their 1787 call came at the wrong time in these three states. Pennsylvania's Censors had rejected a convention in 1784 and their next meeting was set for 1791; New Hampshire, for 1791; Massachusetts, for 1795. Worse yet, the Federalists were calling for the wrong kind of convention. In all three states, it was the convention's task to make constitutional proposals, not rubber-stamp those made by others. In the two New England states, these proposals were put up to the voters in town meeting. If the legislatures of these three heeded Philadelphia's call for ratifying conventions, they would be acting in contempt of their own constitutions.

The legal situation in other states was more propitious in one sense, less in another. Most of these constitutions had been proposed by the legislature, and often enacted into law without any special form of consultation with the electorate. Rhode Island and Connecticut continued to operate under Royal Charters which had always given them great political autonomy—the legislatures simply striking the clauses from the text that offered fealty to the English Crown.[16]

These texts gave greater legal warrant to legislatures that chose to go along with the Philadelphia call. Since the legislatures were the source of the existing state constitutions, weren't they legally free to propose a new method for revision? Yes, but the Federalists' end run around the legislature, and their demand for popular ratifying conventions, seemed more of a frontal assault on existing constitutional processes. Especially when the Philadelphians altogether lacked the legal authority from these legislatures to make such an end run; especially when they were calling on popular conventions to rubber-stamp proposals that they, without any direct authorization by the voters, saw fit to make.

To sum up, here is the young John Quincy Adams's shocked reaction to the news from Philadelphia:

> But to crown the whole the 7th article, is an open and bare-faced violation of the most sacred engagements which can be formed by human beings. It violates the *Confederation,* the 13th article of which I wish you would turn to, for a complete demonstration of what I affirm; and it violates the Constitution of this State, which was the only crime of our Berkshire & Hampshire insurgents [in Shays' Rebellion].
>
> As a justification for this, it is said, that in times of great distress and imminent danger, the Constitution of any country whatever must give way; and that no agreements can be put in competition, with the existence, of a nation; but here, in order to apply this proposition, which is undoubtedly true, two points are to be established: the first, that we are now in this tremendous situation, where our very national existence, is at stake; the second that no better remedy can be found than that of a revolution.—The first it appears to me, no man in his Senses, can pretend to assert: our situation it is true is disagreeable; but it is confessedly growing better every day, and might very probably be prosperous in a few years without any alteration at all. but even if some alteration be *necessary,* where is the necessity of introducing a *despotism;* yes, a *despotism;* for if there shall be any limits to the power of the federal Congress, they will only be such as they themselves shall be pleased to establish.[17]

These remarks suggest the opening of a generation gap. For Washington and Madison, the Founding was the consolidation of a lifetime of revolutionary activity. For the young fogie Adams, it was a shocking outbreak of lawlessness. In the aftermath of Shays' rebellion, many of Adams's elders shared his anxieties. How, then, did the Federalists respond?

By preparing the ground for their break with legality through a fascinating set of exchanges with established institutions that began in 1785 and ended in 1791.

THE BANDWAGON EFFECT

Call it the "bandwagon effect." At each stage, the Federalists suffered grave legal difficulties in advancing their enterprise. At each stage, some important institutions refused to cooperate on legalistic grounds. Nonetheless, the Federalists gained enough acceptance by enough standing institutions to sustain their momentum. Winning these *official confirmations* made it plausible for them to embark on another illegal initiative, which—confirmed once again by more standing institutions—made it plausible for them to proceed to another illegal initiative. And so forth, until they had earned a deep sense of constitutional authority even though they had not played by the rules.

There is much that is puzzling about this unconventional process. Before speculating further, we need a firmer grounding in the facts. There were five phases to the Founders' unconventional activities. During the first, the Federalists sought to establish that an anomalous body like the Convention was an appropriate response to the country's problems. The construction of a credible constitutional signal was fundamental to the overall success of the enterprise: How did the Federalists manage the obvious dangers involved in their frontal challenge to established authority?

A successful answer only served to open up other questions. After constructing a credible signal, they faced the problem of legitimating their proposal. It was one thing to suggest a few amendments to the Articles, quite another to write an entirely new Constitution. How did they deal with the shocked response of existing institutions to this sweeping reorganization?

But the Convention did more than propose; it triggered a change in the rules for ratification. How did the Founders win support for this revolutionary step? Call this the triggering problem.

As the Federalists were trying to solve it, they proceeded to a fourth stage and embarked on the struggle for ratification on a state-by-state basis. This struggle only confirmed the importance of their triggering solution. Ratification would never have occurred without general acceptance of the new ratification rules.

Fifth and finally, the Federalists confronted dissenting states like Rhode Island and North Carolina, which continued to affirm the prior constitutional solution. How to induce them to renounce their legalistic opposition and confirm the legitimacy of the new regime? Call this the problem of constitutional consolidation.

THE SIGNALING PROBLEM

The effort to amend the Articles began as soon as they were ratified. For a long time, however, the stage was dominated by actors who played by the rules.

The first legalistic campaign aimed at granting Congress the power to levy a five percent impost on foreign commerce. Proposed by Congress in 1781, the impost gained the consent of all states but Rhode Island two years later. Before Rhode Island could be induced to join, Virginia backed out, and Congress returned to the drawing boards.[18] After some pulling and hauling, it proposed new initiatives. The most successful was another impost, which passed Congress in April of 1783.[19] By 1786, only New York remained a holdout, and even it had formally accepted the initiative—though with so many conditions that Congress found it unacceptable.[20] Trying to sustain the momentum, Congress proposed a new package of seven amendments in August of 1786.[21]

This meant that the Federalists were constantly encountering objections from supporters of a strengthened Union who denied the need to break the rules: Wouldn't the Federalist bandwagon only derail the legally unproblematic initiatives then underway?[22] Granted that New York was holding up the impost, why suppose that it would accept a lawless break into the unknown?[23] Wasn't it wiser to continue pressing for the impost, and use a success as a springboard for more sweeping reforms, like those Congress had sent to the states in 1786?[24]

Along with these questions of efficacy came deeper problems of legitimacy. Given the ongoing efforts by existing institutions to solve their problems, how did Madison & Co. earn sufficient authority to challenge the status quo?

The Mount Vernon Conference

The first step toward a convention had such humble origins that it did not immediately provoke widespread legalistic opposition. Only as the Federalists gained experience with the bandwagon effect did they begin to confront the deep philosophical problems involved in its legitimation.

Our story begins with the 1785 Mount Vernon Conference, where commissioners from Maryland and Virginia met at George Washington's mansion. Though their commissions were limited to the regulation of the Potomac and Pocomoke rivers, they agreed to "sweeping, if sensible recommendations . . . [that] went considerably beyond the instructions that the respective legislatures had given to them."[25] Nonetheless, both legislatures approved the proposed interstate compact.

Madison, who had been behind the initiative,[26] moved that the Virginia legislature submit the agreement to the Continental Congress in compliance with Article VI of the Articles, which required this whenever "two or more states" entered into "any treaty, confederation, or alliance."[27] I don't know why, but the Virginia Assembly rejected his proposal. As to Maryland, its legislature cited the Articles' grant of authority to "enter into a firm league of friendship with the other states respectively, for their mutual and general welfare," but also failed to explain why it did not submit the compact to Congress for approval.[28]

The result may have provided Madison with a learning experience on three fronts. It suggested, first, that delegates to *ad hoc* assemblies might move beyond their commissions and get away with it; second, that this could happen even though the "whole proceeding was distinctly unconstitutional";[29] and, third, that unconventional activity might prove especially rewarding in a context, like Mount Vernon, that promised plain economic benefits to the states involved.

The Virginia Federalists made their next move on January 21, 1786, convincing the legislature to authorize seven commissioners (including Madison) to invite deputies from other states to attend a meeting at Annapolis "to consider and recommend a federal plan for regulating commerce."[30] Even at this early stage, there is evidence that Madison was aware of the bandwagon dynamic. He wrote to Monroe:

> Will it not be best on the whole to suspend measures for a more thorough cure of our federal system, till the partial experiment shall have been made [to regulate commerce at Annapolis]. If the spirit of the Conventioners should be friendly to the Union, and their proceedings well conducted, their return into the Councils of their respective States will greatly facilitate any subsequent measures which may be set on foot by Congress, or by any of the States.[31]

Madison was already mastering a key insight into unconventional legitimation. Rather than aiming for a single grand victory, he was setting up a stepwise process—in which one partial initiative built on the next in a series of sequential ratifications:

> The efforts of bringing about a correction thro' the medium of Congress have miscarried. Let a Convention then be tried. If it succeeds in the first instance, it can be repeated as other defects force themselves on the public attention, and as the public mind becomes prepared for further remedies. The Assembly here [in Virginia] would refer nothing to Congress. They would have revolted equally against a plenipotentiary commission to their deputies for the Convention. The option therefore lay between doing what was done and doing nothing. Whether a right choice was made time only can prove. I am not in general an advocate for temporizing or partial remedies. But a rigor in this respect, if pushed too far may hazard everything.[32]

The bandwagon process had begun in earnest.

Annapolis

Despite its questionable legality,[33] Virginia's call proved surprisingly successful, leading nine states to appoint delegates to a convention at Annapolis in September 1786. At the same time, it provoked expressions of dissent from three states. South Carolina refused, on the ground that it had "an appearance of either revoking or infringing on those powers" the legislature granted to Congress when it approved the five percent impost.[34] The Annapolis proposal led to an impasse in Connecticut, as legislators feared that it would undermine Congress and set a precedent for other illegal movements.[35] Maryland's rejection was more elaborate:

> [T]he meeting proposed may be misunderstood or misrepresented in Europe, give umbrage to Congress, and disquiet the citizens of the United States, who may be thereby led erroneously to suspect, that the great council of this country wants either the will or wisdom to digest a proper uniform plan for the regulation of their commerce. The power must be given to Congress to effectuate any system which might be adopted by the proposed meeting of commissioners.[36]

Worse yet, the meeting "may produce other meetings, which may have consequences which cannot be foreseen. Innovations in Government, when not absolutely necessary, are dangerous, particularly to republics, generally too fond of novelties, and subject to change."[37]

The Annapolis commissioners would convene in a state that had formally denounced them as dangerous revolutionaries. The early turnout of delegates was less impressive than expected.[38] When only twelve delegates from five states arrived, the Federalists desperately sought to sustain institutional momentum. Before disbanding, they endorsed Hamilton's call for another convention—this time in Philadelphia. According to the Commissioners' Report, the new convention should not be limited to "commercial regulation," but would have power to consider a broader range of "defects [which], upon a closer examination, may be found greater and more numerous." This call raised an obvious question—who, after all, had given these commercial emissaries such expansive authority? The Report answered: "If in expressing this wish or in intimating any other sentiment, Your Commissioners should seem to exceed the strict bounds of their appointment, they entertain a full confidence, that a conduct, dictated by an anxiety for the welfare, of the United States, will not fail to receive an indulgent construction."[39]

The upshot was a striking combination of hubris and humility. The commissioners had asserted the immense authority of calling for a convention, unknown to the established system, to propose amendments to the Articles. Having taken a revolutionary step, they covered their tracks to gain the cooperation of existing institutions.[40] First, they specified that any constitutional proposals emerging from Philadelphia should be approved by Congress and all thirteen legislatures. This was precisely what didn't happen—moreover, given their willingness to go beyond their mandate, how seriously could one take their assurance about the future convention? Nonetheless, the stipulation softened the challenge to existing authorities implicit in the call for a convention that, once in existence, might serve as a formidable rival.

Second, the commissioners did not take decisive action unilaterally. They called upon Congress and the thirteen states to issue calls to Philadelphia. Surely there was little harm in that? If existing authorities ignored the invitation, it would be quickly forgotten.

But if it struck a responsive chord, the Report's hubristic aspect would reemerge. In particular, did its initiative require the assent of all thirteen states and Congress before the convention could appropriately assemble? If not, how much support would be enough? The commissioners were silent on these crucial operational questions. It was enough to precipitate the bandwagon effect: as more and more existing institutions recognized the need for a convention, would the dynamic of consent create its own kind of legitimation?

Shays' Rebellion

Some have attributed Hamilton's call at Annapolis to the news of the Massachusetts uprising we know as Shays' Rebellion.[41] A comprehensive study of original sources gives no support to this claim. However, news of the Rebellion did rapidly overtake reports about Annapolis and profoundly affected its public reception.

But in a complicated way. Some accounts, relying on Beardian understandings, stress the class anxieties generated by Shays' Rebellion amongst the revolutionary elite—fears that led them to embrace strong measures like a constitutional convention.[42] This is only part of the story. Shays and the other rebels of rural New England were not only closing down courts and refusing to pay debts. They were engaging in more constructive forms of politics—meeting in illegal county conventions and making extraordinary demands for fundamental change.

These acts predictably led opponents to assault the farmers' use of conventions. Pamphleteers, like An Other Citizen, distinguished sharply between the illegal conventions of the American Revolution and the current rebellious assemblies. When the colonists were fighting the British, they had no alternative but to break the law and meet in convention. But the situation had changed radically in 1780, when the people of Massachusetts solemnly approved a constitution. Since that time, no group of men could properly meet in convention and "dare, with impunity, to lay the foundations of a CIVIL WAR in the state, or to molest that Government in the execution of its Constitutional powers."[43] An address to Governor James Bowdoin of Massachusetts elaborated this argument:

> In the same compact, the people solemnly agreed to support the Constitution for the space of fifteen years, and made ample provision for the revision of it at the end of that period, if it should then be thought necessary.—There is no officer, either high or low, within the commonwealth, who does not derive his whole authority from the people, and who is not amenable to a proper and adequate tribunal for his conduct.
>
> . . . If the citizens of the State labour under grievances which can be redressed by the acts of the legislature, we conceive that their privileges in this case can never be enlarged, for the General Court are chosen annually by the people; and though in one year our complaints are not attended to, yet we can in the next election place men in power who will answer our reasonable expectations; and, we are constrained to say, that we are ignorant of the time when the representatives of the people in this state have not duly attended to the Instructions of their constituents. . . . Fellow citizens, we now entreat you, by the *sacred* compact which holds us in one society—by the *blood* of our brethren *shed to obtain our freedom*—by the tender regard we feel for our *rising offspring,* claiming freedom from our hands, as *their* inheritance by the *grant* of heaven—to use your endeavours that redress of grievances be fought for in *a Constitutional and orderly way only.*[44]

Given these emphatic principles, it was going to be tough for Shaysite opponents to embrace the Annapolis initiative. Why wasn't the call for a convention in Philadelphia as illegitimate as the ones organized by the rebel farmers?[45]

The question soon reverberated in the Massachusetts legislature. Both Rufus King and Nathan Dane opposed the Annapolis proposal as unconstitutional. As King explained: "The Confederation was the act of the people. No part could be altered but by consent of Congress and confirmation of the several Legislatures. Congress therefore ought to make the examination first, because, if it was done by a convention, no Legislature could have a right to confirm it . . . Besides, if Congress should not agree upon a report of a convention, the most fatal consequences might follow."[46]

King and Dane are important figures. A few months later, they will write the Congressional resolution calling upon the states to send delegates to Philadelphia. But during the fall of 1786, they were more impressed with the county conventions of the Shaysites. Rather than serving as a prod to the upper classes, Shays' Rebellion served as an example of the ease with which illegality could spiral out of control.

Given these anxieties, it should be no surprise that New York and New England were slow to respond to Annapolis' call to Philadelphia.[47] But Federalists further south were successful in winning a number of favorable responses,[48] maintaining momentum through the winter of 1786, until the bandwagon effect could be renewed by another round of official confirmation.

The Continental Congress Gets on the Bandwagon

Congress received the Annapolis proceedings on September 20 and referred them to a special committee, which took no action for months. By early February, Madison and Hamilton had come to Congress to campaign for endorsement, but others continued to be impressed by the illegality of it all. Richard Henry Lee, a member of the special Congressional committee, surveyed the scene:

> With difficulty the friends to the system adopted by the convention [at Annapolis] induced Congress to commit your report, altho' all were . . . zealous to accomplish the objects proposed by the authors of the commercial convention. Indeed their conviction of the inadequacy of the present federal government render them particularly zealous to amend, and strengthen it. But different opinions prevail as to the mode; some think with the Annapolis meeting, others consider Congress not only the Constitutional but the most eligible body to originate and propose necessary amendments to the confederation, and others prefer State conventions for the express purpose, and a Congress of deputys, appointed by these conventions with plenipotentiary powers.[49]

Despite these hesitations, Congressional endorsement was imperative if Philadelphia were to become credible. Many states, especially in the

North, were unprepared to send delegates to an unconstitutional convention unless Congress expressly endorsed it.

Within this context, the partisans of the convention were reinforced from a surprising direction: the same King and Dane who had opposed Philadelphia in Massachusetts now came to its defense as Congressional delegates. After some preliminary sparring in mid-February, the two Massachusetts delegates wrote the resolution that gained Congressional approval on February 21, calling the states to send delegates to Philadelphia "for the *sole and express* purpose of revising the Articles."[50] What accounted for the shift?

King answers in a letter to Elbridge Gerry: "For a number of reasons, although my sentiments are the same as to the legality of this measure, I think we ought not to oppose, but to coincide with this project. . . . Events are hurrying to a crisis; prudent and sagacious men should be ready to seize the most favourable circumstances to establish a more permanent and vigorous government."[51] Close observers had little difficulty explaining King's conversion. By this point, Massachusetts was effectively crushing Shays' Rebellion.[52] Stephen Higginson, who had been appointed a Massachusetts delegate to the Annapolis Convention, drolly observed that King and Dane "will not now think there is so great a resemblance between our County Conventions . . . and that proposed to be held in Philadelphia in May, as they thought, nor will they now imagine that the same danger can result to the Union from the latter, as our experience has proved was justly apprehended from the former to this Commonwealth."[53]

Despite the explicit acknowledgment of formal illegality by its draftsmen, the resolution sufficed to propel the institutional bandwagon forward. With Shays' Rebellion under control, Northern states joined Southern laggards in responding affirmatively to the Congressional invitation to Philadelphia.

With one exception.

Rhode Island

"Permit the legislature of this state to address you," Governor John Collins of Rhode Island wrote to the President of the Continental Congress, in explanation of his state's refusal to send delegates to Philadelphia:

[A]s a legislative body, we could not appoint delegates to do that which only the people at large are entitled to do. By a law of our state, the delegates in Congress are chosen by the suffrages of all the freemen therein, and are appointed to represent them in Congress; and for the legislative body to have appointed delegates to represent them in convention, when they cannot appoint delegates in Congress (unless upon their death or other incidental matter,) must be absurd; as that delegation in convention is for the express purpose of altering a constitution, which the people at large are only capable of appointing the members.[54]

Collins's objection was by no means unique. Others, including John Jay, were deeply troubled by the fact that the Philadelphia Convention was a creature of state legislatures, and so could not claim a sufficiently direct connection to "the People."[55] After challenging the legitimacy of the Convention, Collins quoted the final Article of Confederation verbatim, emphasizing Rhode Island's "diffiden[ce] of power, and apprehension of dissolving a compact which was framed by the wisdom of men who gloried in being instrumental in preserving the religious and civil rights of a multitude of people . . . ; and fearing, when the compact should once be broken, we must all be lost in a common ruin."[56]

And yet, for all its rhetorical force, this letter is a token of the Federalists' success in solving their signaling problem. The first tip-off is its date: September 15, a time when the Convention's proceedings are almost at end. With both Congress and twelve states on record in support of the Convention, Rhode Island has been reduced to mere letter writing. Indeed, the governor is writing an apology for something that generally requires no defense—the state's refusal to cooperate in a transparently unconstitutional effort to disrupt the status quo.

I do not wish to exaggerate the Federalist accomplishment. While their bandwagon effect had made the Philadelphia Convention into a credible constitutional signal, they had many more obstacles to confront before their Constitution could gain recognition as the collective endeavor of We the People.

Nonetheless, it is not easy to create a plausible alternative to the existing higher lawmaking system, and it is important to reflect upon the Federalists' distinctive methods. Consider the number of times they had gained official confirmation of their extraconstitutional activities. In the following summary, I have *italicized* the roles of legal bodies in the ongoing sequence and used SMALL CAPITALS for extra-legal assemblies:

From the dispatch of commercial delegates by *Virginia and Maryland* to the MOUNT VERNON CONFERENCE to its confirmation by the *two states* and *Virginia's call for* ANNAPOLIS.

To the confirmation by *nine states* of the ANNAPOLIS MEETING over the legalistic dissent of *four others;* to the CALL AT ANNAPOLIS FOR A CONVENTION AT PHILADELPHIA and its confirmation by some of the *Southern states* while the *Northern ones* remained in legalistic indecision.

To the *Congressional recommendation* of PHILADELPHIA and its confirmation by *New York and New England* over the legalistic dissent of *Rhode Island.*

To the PHILADELPHIA CONVENTION.

THE PROPOSAL AND TRIGGERING FUNCTIONS

By the time the Convention met, there was a general expectation that it would make a constitutional proposal. But it was hardly obvious that it would propose the creation of an entirely new regime. No less shocking was the Founding effort to trigger an entirely new procedure for ratification. These two initiatives—proposing a new regime, triggering a new ratification procedure—are analytically distinct. But the Federalists often combined them in their effort to overcome resistance, and so I will consider them together.

Illegality at Philadelphia

Illegality was a leitmotif at the Convention from first to last. The theme was provoked during the first six weeks by a bitter debate between nationalists and decentralizers over the scope of the Convention's proposal. The nationalists seized the agenda with their fifteen-point Virginia Plan, which contemplated a powerful national government with legislative, executive, and judicial institutions operating independently of the states.[57] The decentralizers responded with the New Jersey Plan, which enhanced the powers of the existing Congress without challenging basic premises—especially the principle that gave each state equal voting power in the Continental Congress.

The decentralizers repeatedly wrapped themselves in the cloak of legality. Here is William Paterson introducing the New Jersey Plan:

> The Convention he said was formed in pursuance of an Act of Congs. that this act was recited in several of the Commissions, particularly that of Massts. which he required to be read: That the amendment of the confederacy was the object of all the laws and commissions on the subject; that the articles of the confederation were therefore the proper basis of all the proceedings of the Convention. We ought to keep within its limits, or we should be charged by our constituents with usurpation. that the people of America were sharpsighted and not to be deceived. But the Commissions under which we acted were not only the measure of our power. they denoted also the sentiments of the States on the subject of our deliberation. The idea of a national Govt. as contradistinguished from a federal one, never entered into the mind of any of them, and to the public mind we must accommodate ourselves. . . . We must follow the people; the people will not follow us.[58]

On Paterson's widely shared view,[59] it was only a moderate plan, like New Jersey's, that qualified as a revision. Nationalist proposals championed by Madison, Wilson, and Hamilton were simply beyond the Convention's authority: "If the confederacy was radically wrong, let us return to our States, and obtain larger powers, not assume them of ourselves."[60]

Especially problematic was the nationalists' desire to deprive the small states of equal voting power: "He reads the 5th art: of Confederation giving each State a vote—& the 13th declaring that no alteration shall be made without unanimous consent. This is the nature of all treaties. What is unanimously done, must be unanimously undone."[61] Throughout these bitter weeks, Paterson's legalistic concerns were reinforced by his allies.[62]

With the exception of Madison,[63] the nationalists were strikingly unconcerned with legal technicalities. Edmund Randolph, who had presented the Virginia Plan, responded to recurring legalisms by explaining that he "was not scrupulous on the point of power. When the salvation of the Republic was at stake, it would be treason to our trust, not to propose what we found necessary."[64] Such sentiments were sometimes buttressed by appeals to popular sovereignty, as with James

Wilson's: "We have powers to conclude nothing—we have power to propose anything—we expect the Approbation of Cong. we hope for that of the Legis. of the several States perhaps it will not be inconsistent with Revolution principles, to promise ourselves the Assent of the People provided a more regular establishment cannot be obtained &c &c."[65]

This debate ended in July with the Great Compromise—in which the Convention (by a narrow margin) accepted much of the centralizing thrust of the Virginia Plan and mollified the decentralizers by giving an equal vote to all states in the Senate. Shortly thereafter, New Yorkers Robert Yates and John Lansing walked out, loudly denouncing the illegalities contemplated by the runaway Convention.[66]

But those who remained had not yet finished with the problem. Although they were moving in the direction of a revolutionary proposal, they had not squarely confronted Article XIII of the Confederation: Were they prepared, in the end, to accept a humble role and submit their recommendations to Congress and all thirteen state legislatures?

After some inconclusive sparring, the question came to the floor in late August: "Mr. Sherman doubted the propriety of authorizing less than all the States to execute the Constitution, considering the nature of the existing Confederation. Perhaps all the States may concur, and on that supposition it is needless to hold out a breach of faith."[67] Gouverneur Morris then moved to "leav[e] the states to pursue their own modes of ratification." This immediately led Daniel Carroll of Maryland to open another hornet's nest: "Mr. Carrol [*sic*] mentioned the mode of altering the Constitution of Maryland pointed out therein, and that no other mode could be pursued in that State."[68] Madison tried to reassure the delegates:

> The difficulty in Maryland was no greater than in other States, where no mode of change was pointed out by the Constitution, and all officers were under oath to support it. The people were in fact, the fountain of all power, and by resorting to them, all difficulties were got over. They could alter constitutions as they pleased. It was a principle in the Bills of rights, that first principles might be resorted to.[69]

The Marylanders were not impressed, James McHenry noting "that the officers of Govt. in Maryland were under oath to support the mode of alteration prescribed by the Constitution."[70] King recalled that the constitution of Massachusetts, which did have an explicit procedure for calling conventions, "was made unalterable till the year 1790."[71]

He reassured his fellows, however, that "this was no difficulty with him. The State must have contemplated a recurrence to first principles before they sent deputies to this Convention"[72]—a remarkable statement from a man who had repeatedly confessed the illegality of the entire enterprise. Previously, however, he had already made clear the grounds for his insistence on overriding state constitutions: "Mr. King thought that striking out 'Conventions' as the requisite mode was equivalent to giving up the business altogether. Conventions alone, which will avoid all the obstacles from the complicated formation of the Legislatures, will succeed, and if not positively required by the plan, its enemies will oppose that mode."[73]

King's predictions would be fulfilled during the struggle for ratification. There is no way that the Constitution would have succeeded without the Convention's revolutionary breach with Article XIII. This was probably why the debate was so brief, with nobody other than Madison trying to answer the dissenters' legalistic doubts. The Federalists had the votes, and that was that. The Convention majority then made it plain that it would not formally ask Congress for its approval, leaving unanswered Elbridge Gerry when he "dwelt on the impropriety of destroying the existing Confederation, without the unanimous Consent of the parties to it."[74]

The die had been cast; but then there was a moment of hesitation. At one of the Convention's final working meetings, Alexander Hamilton urged caution. Not otherwise noted for timidity, he drew the line at a frontal assault on the higher lawmaking system. He moved "that the foregoing plan of a Constitution be transmitted to the U.S. in Congress assembled, in order that if the same shall be agreed to by them, it may be communicated to the Legislatures of the several States." After strictly complying with the Articles, his motion went on to "recommend" that each state consider whether it might voluntarily change its ratification practices. Hamilton suggested that legislatures refrain from considering the Constitution itself and call a special constitutional convention. He was even more tentative in confronting the Articles' insistence on unanimous approval by all thirteen states. This time, his motion merely contained a doubly conditional "recommendation" to the legislatures. It did not urge them to break with the unanimity rule but simply to authorize its state convention to make the break "if" the convention "should be of the opinion" that nine states were enough to bring the Constitution into life.[75]

Hamilton's caution was undoubtedly based on the legalistic denunciations that Yates and Lansing were already publishing in New York; even at this late moment, his pleas were joined by dissenting legalists like Elbridge Gerry, who then refused to sign: "If nine out of thirteen can dissolve the compact, Six out of nine will be just as able to dissolve the new one hereafter."[76]

As was typical, this last legalistic plea was countered not with a legalistic defense but with some cold truths from James Wilson:

> He expressed in strong terms his disapprobation, particularly the suspending the plan of the Convention on the approbation of Congress. He declared it to be worse than folly to rely on the concurrence of the Rhode Island members of Congs. in the plan. Maryland had voted on this floor for requiring the unanimous assent of the 13 States to the proposed change in the federal System. N—York has not been represented for a long time past in the Convention. Many individual deputies from other States have spoken much against the plan. Under these circumstances Can it be safe to make the assent of Congress necessary. After spending four or five months in the laborious & arduous task of forming a Government for our Country, we are ourselves at the close throwing insuperable obstacles in the way of its success.[77]

Hamilton's legalistic hesitations were swept aside by a vote of ten states to one.[78] But Wilson's vivid description of the prospective opposition made it clear how vulnerable the Convention's proposals would be in the months ahead. Out of fifty-five delegates, only thirty-eight signed the final proposal. Luther Martin and John Francis Mercer of Maryland had recently followed Yates and Lansing of New York in a loud and public walkout. Would the reputation of George Washington and a few other famous names be enough to sustain the institutional bandwagon?

Confirmation in New York

On the same day it approved the Constitution, the Convention also "RESOLVED that the preceding Constitution be laid before the

United States in Congress assembled," without conceding the right to veto or revise its final product.[79]

This unconventional move should now begin to seem familiar. But it was also very dangerous: once Congress seized hold of the Constitution, would it try to change the rules of the game once more? Once the Convention dissolved in Philadelphia, how could it respond to a Congressional counterassertion of authority?

Not idle questions, as events showed. When Congress took up the Constitution nine days later, Richard Henry Lee of Virginia led the critics. Lee had refused to serve at Philadelphia since it was improper for him to participate in a decision that he was going to review as a Congressman. Now he was confronted with a fait accompli:

> Strangest doctrine he ever heard, that [in] referring a matter of report, that no alterations should be made. . . . The states and Congress, he thinks, had the idea that Congress was to amend if they thought proper. He wishes to give it a candid inquiry, and proposes such alterations as are necessary . . . To insist that it should go as it is without amendments is like presenting a hungry man 50 dishes and insisting he should eat all or none.[80]

Hastily returning to his seat in Congress,[81] Madison conceded that Congress had the legal right to revise the Convention's text.[82] He sought to ward off intervention with one of the most remarkable arguments in constitutional history: "that as the Act of the Convention, when altered would instantly become the mere act of Congress, and must be proposed by them, and of course be addressed to the Legislatures, not conventions of the States, and require the ratification of thirteen instead of nine States, and as the unaltered act would go forth to the States directly from the Convention under the auspices of that body."[83] In other words, if Congress wanted to get anything done, it could not touch the Convention's proposal—since only that proposal could be processed by the extraconstitutional triggering rule of nine out of thirteen! If Congress did not want to run into the stone wall of Article XIII, it could not convert the revolutionary proposal into a "mere" act of law!

It was all or nothing—the Convention's revolutionary triggering decision was being invoked to ward off efforts to whittle down its revolutionary proposal. And yet, these anxieties about "mere" legality did not deter Madison from seeking a Congressional message to the states unambiguously approving the merits of the Constitution. Rather than *substituting* its legal warrant for the Convention's revolutionary assertion, Madison wanted it to *complement* the Convention's authority with its own, giving new momentum to the institutional bandwagon.

Contrast this with Lee's resolution:

> Resolved, That Congress after due attention to the Constitution under which this body exists and acts find that the said Constitution in the thirteenth article thereof limits the power of Congress to the amendment of the present Confederacy of thirteen states, but does not extend it to the creation of a new confederacy of nine states; and the late Convention having been constituted under the authority of twelve states in this Union it is deemed respectful to transmit, and it is accordingly ordered, that the plan of a new Federal Constitution laid before Congress by the said Convention be sent to the executive of every state in the Union to be laid before their respective legislatures.[84]

Madison's response: "Can't accede to it. . . . If this House can't approve [the Constitution], it says the crisis is not yet arrived and implies disapp[robation]."[85] At the end of the debate, Madison had to settle for something less than explicit approval, but something more than Lee's emphasis on the Convention's illegality. On September 28, Congress resolved that "said report . . . be transmitted to the several legislatures in order to be submitted to a convention of delegates chosen in each state by the people thereof in conformity to the resolves of the Convention."[86] While Congress refrained from passing on the merits of the Constitution, this explicit confirmation of the Convention's triggering decision was crucial, as events soon proved.[87]

Violence in Philadelphia

Even before they received word of Congress's resolution, the Federalists sought to maintain momentum by pressing ahead in the Pennsylvania Assembly, demanding an immediate call for a state ratifying convention.[88]

A substantial minority were unimpressed. They pointed out that Pennsylvania's constitution required a six-month pause between proposal of amendments and the election of delegates to a convention.[89]

Since the Federal Constitution amounted to a massive amendment of Pennsylvania's, should not the Assembly wait six months? Surely the people should be given a chance to digest the proposal before electing delegates?

The Federalist majority ignored these very reasonable complaints and proposed to hold an election within nine days. The dissenters described their response in a joint letter to their constituents:

> In these circumstances we had no alternative; we were under a necessity of either returning to the House, and by our presence, enabling them to call a convention before our constituents could have the means of information or time to deliberate on the subject, or by absenting ourselves from the House, prevent the measure taking place. Our regard for you induced us to prefer the latter and we determined not to attend in the afternoon. . . .
> [W]e determined the next morning again to absent ourselves from the House, when James M'Calmont, Esquire, a member from Franklin, and Jacob Miley, Esquire, a member from Dauphin, were seized by a number of citizens of Philadelphia, who had collected together for that purpose; their lodgings were violently broken open, their clothes torn, and after much abuse and insult, they were forcibly dragged through the streets of Philadelphia to the State House, and there detained by force, and in the presence of the majority . . . treated with the most insulting language; while the House so formed proceeded to finish their resolutions, which they mean to offer to you as the doings of the legislature of Pennsylvania.[90]

Note the menace of the final line. Had the House lost its status as "the legislature of Pennsylvania" by procuring its quorum through blatant coercion? Should the dissenters urge their constituents to boycott the elections for the Convention?

News of the Federalist mob, and its coercive actions, swept the nation.[91] The threads of political legitimacy were visibly beginning to unravel—a process more easily started than stopped.

Would the unraveling have spun out of control had not Congress confirmed the Convention's triggering decision? Without unconventional reinforcement, would Philadelphia's call for ratifying conventions have precipitated a series of mob scenes, and legislative manipulations, discrediting the entire initiative?

The Stabilizing Role of the Continental Congress

Throughout the coming months, the Continental Congress continued to play an active role,[92] and the Federalists made repeated and self-conscious[93] use of their unconventional strategy to prop up the Convention's revolutionary triggering decision.

A crucial moment came on July 2, 1788, when Congress learned that New Hampshire was the ninth state to ratify. It quickly took the lead in organizing the new government. Within a week, a special committee proposed that Presidential Electors be appointed in the states that had ratified the Constitution by the first Wednesday in December, who would then "Assemble in their respective States and Vote for a President, and that the first Wednesday in February next be the time, and —— the place for Commencing proceedings under the said Constitution."[94] Throughout the summer, there was a fierce struggle to fill in the blank with the name of the nation's next capital—which was finally resolved in favor of New York on September 13. For much of this time, all thirteen states voted—including states which had not ratified.[95]

To glimpse the importance of this ongoing official confirmation of the Convention's nine-state rule, indulge a thought-experiment. As you read onward, imagine that Congress had responded to New Hampshire's ninth yea by solemnly declaring that its governing charter, the Articles of Confederation, required the unanimous consent of all thirteen states before it would cede its constitutional authority to the new President, House, and Senate. How would this have changed the outcome of the ratification struggle?

RATIFICATION: THE BANDWAGON IN THE STATES

Although the proposed Constitution completely cut state legislatures out of the ratification process, the text did not accurately describe institutional realities. Success depended heavily on the Federalists' unconventional use of existing institutional authority. In each state, the revolutionaries sought to persuade the legislature to ignore the legalistic quibblings of their opponents and get on the institutional bandwagon by calling for a ratifying convention. They then used these legislative anchors to respond to charges of illegality down the road.[96]

This strategy did not get off to an auspicious start in Pennsylvania. But the violent violation of the Pennsylvania constitution allowed the Federalists to catch their opponents by surprise in a six-week election campaign and win a two-to-one margin in the Pennsylvania convention. At about the same time, Federalists were winning in four small states that depended on a strong central government for their economic survival.[97] By January 9, 1788, the revolutionaries had once again established institutional momentum.

But nobody could be optimistic about the future. On February 13, 1788, the New Hampshire Federalists found themselves outnumbered at their convention by more than a two-to-one margin. Foreseeing disaster if they pushed forward, they postponed their meetings for three months in the hope that the closely divided Massachusetts convention would ratify in the interim.[98]

Things were going no better in North Carolina. There is evidence of "heated debates" in the legislature prior to the call for a ratifying convention.[99] When elections were held on March 28, the Anti-Federalists won a landslide victory of 184–84, despite the fact that Federalists had twice precipitated riots at polling places and run off with some ballot boxes.[100] The convention would meet in July, but nobody was optimistic.

The news was even worse in New York. On January 31, Cornelius Schoonmaker generated a bitter debate in the General Assembly when he proposed to amend the call for a ratifying convention by declaring that the Philadelphia Convention had exceeded its powers and that ratification would "materially alter" New York's constitution "and greatly affect the rights and privileges" of New York residents.[101] This was voted down 27 to 25 after the parchment containing the proposal was discovered to contain scratched-out writing hostile to the Constitution. In the Senate, Robert Yates, who had walked out of Philadelphia, proposed a resolution denouncing the Convention for going "beyond their powers" and asserting that "they have not amended, but made a new system."[102] This motion was rejected by 12–7, and the Senate voted 11 to 8 to accept the Assembly's call for a June 17 convention, with balloting for delegates on April 29. This election returned forty-six Anti-Federalists and only nineteen Federalists.[103] The June convention threatened disaster.

And then there was Rhode Island. In its February session, the legislature refused to call a convention, putting the Constitution to the people in a special referendum: "[We] cannot make any innovation in a Constitution which has been agreed upon and the compact settled between the governors and governed, without the express consent of the freemen at large by their own voices individually taken in town meetings assembled."[104] The vote was 2,708 against the Constitution and 237 in favor, with an indeterminate number of Federalists boycotting the election. In a letter of April 5 to the Continental Congress, Governor Collins reported the result and defended the procedure:

> Although this state has been singular from her sister states in the mode of collecting the sentiments of the people upon the Constitution, it was not done with the least design to give any offence to the respectable body who composed the convention, or a disregard to the recommendation of Congress, but upon pure republican principles, founded upon that basis of all governments originally deriving from the body of the people at large.[105]

We can now glimpse the supreme importance of the Philadelphia Convention's triggering decision. With four states pointing decisively in a negative direction by spring, the Constitution was a dead letter under the Articles' requirement of unanimity.

Especially when opponents could cloak their opposition with attractive rhetoric. Rather than opposing the Constitution outright, they often proposed a middle road: Why not condition ratification upon the acceptance of perfecting amendments like the Bill of Rights?

In rebuttal, Federalists extended the revolutionary arguments Madison had made before the Continental Congress. They opposed preratification amendments on the ground that these would be governed by the unanimity rule laid down by Article XIII of the Confederation. If opponents were interested in amendments that might actually pass, they should ratify first and then take advantage of Article Five's more relaxed approach![106]

But it would take more than clever rhetoric to gain success. Even with the nine-state rule, the Federalists barely squeaked through. A crucial turning point came in Massachusetts. Federalists found themselves outnumbered by opponents at the convention.[107] In desperation, they focused on John Hancock, who "had it in his power to throw the convention's vote either way."[108] The vain Hancock was assured of the Vice Presidency or even the Presidency if Virginia did not ratify the Constitution in time to put forth Washington. As Forrest McDonald says, "[n]othing could have appealed to Hancock more, and he gave his support to ratification."[109] After five hard weeks, the Federalists gained a narrow majority by supporting a "conciliatory proposition" insisting on a series of amendments as soon as the new government was established.[110] The vote was 187 to 168, with nine abstentions.

Then two more states came through. Maryland was won rather easily, despite the powerful, and often legalistic, denunciations of Luther Martin and others.[111] Victory in South Carolina was owed entirely to a gerrymander that converted the Federalists' 40 percent of the popular vote into 60 percent of the convention seats.[112]

That made eight, which permitted the Federalists to squeeze the two major outstanding states, Virginia and New York. In Virginia, the Anti-Federalists proved better at clever tactics. Though the polls returned 85 Federalists and only 66 Anti-Federalists, the Antis managed to convert a substantial number at the convention. Twelve delegates from the district of Kentucky yielded especially good pickings, making the outcome uncertain.[113]

The convention opened with Patrick Henry demanding that the relevant legal papers—from the Annapolis Report onward—be read on the floor to establish the illegality of the entire initiative. The Federalist Edmund Pendleton responded, characteristically, by urging his fellow delegates "not to consider whether the federal Convention exceeded their powers. It strikes my mind that this ought not to influence our deliberations."[114]

Although Henry withdrew his motion, his speeches were full of legalistic attacks upon "a proposal that goes to the utter annihilation of the most solemn engagements of the states—a proposal of establishing nine states into a confederacy, to the eventual exclusion of four states. . . . The people gave them no power to use their name. That they exceeded their power is perfectly clear."[115] Governor Randolph, who had been a delegate at Philadelphia, presented a characteristic response:

[Henry] objects because nine states are sufficient to put the government in motion. What number of states ought we to have said? Ought we to have required the concurrence of all the thirteen? Rhode Island—in rebellion against integrity—Rhode Island plundered all the world by her paper money; and, notorious for her uniform opposition to every federal duty, would then have it in her power to defeat the Union . . . Therefore, to have required the ratification of all the thirteen states would have been tantamount to returning without having done any thing. What other number would have been proper? Twelve? The same spirit that has actuated me in the whole progress of the business, would have prevented me from leaving it in the power of any one state to dissolve the Union; for would it not be lamentable that nothing could be done, for the defection of one state? A majority of the whole would have been too few. Nine states therefore seem to be a most proper number.[116]

Hear the voice of the confident revolutionary, defending the Convention's decision by an unmediated appeal to necessity and the public good. Rather than apologizing for their revolutionary nine-state rule, the Federalists constantly threatened the delegates with the secessionist consequences that would follow if Virginia rejected the Constitution and another state supplied the missing vote.[117]

This forced the Anti-Federalists onto the defensive. William Grayson found himself responding to fears that Pennsylvania and Maryland would invade Virginia if it did not ratify: "Have they not agreed, by the old Confederation, that the Union shall be perpetual, and that no alteration should take place without the consent of Congress, and the confirmation of the legislatures of every state? I cannot think that there is such depravity in mankind as that, after violating public faith so flagrantly, they should make war upon us, also, for not following their example."[118] And Patrick Henry, responding to such Federalist charges, predicted that the Constitution could not survive if Virginia rejected it:

They would intimidate you into an inconsiderate adoption, and frighten you with ideal evils, and that the Union shall be dissolved. 'Tis a bugbear, sir: the fact is, sir, that the eight adopting states can hardly stand on their own legs. Public fame tells us that the adopting states have already heart-burnings and animosity, and repent their precipitate hurry: this, sir, may occasion exceeding great mischief. When I reflect on these and many other circumstances, I must think those states will be found to be in confederacy with us. If we pay our quota of money annually, and furnish our ratable number of men, when necessary, I can see no danger from a rejection.[119]

"Bugbear" or no, the final words voiced in the Convention suggest how large the nine-state rule played in the outcome. As we have seen, Randolph had defended the Convention's revolutionary break with Article XIII, but his general position was more complex. As a delegate in Philadelphia, he ultimately refused to sign the proposal, and as the sitting governor of Virginia, his opinion was influential with many fence-sitters.[120] Here is how he justified his affirmative vote:

> Mr. Chairman, one parting word I humbly supplicate. The suffrage which I shall give in favor of the Constitution will be ascribed, by malice, to motives unknown to my breast. But, although for every other act of my life I shall seek refuge in the mercy of God, for this I request his *justice* only. Lest, however, some future annalist should, in the spirit of party vengeance, deign to mention my name, let him recite these truths—*that I went to the federal Convention* with the strongest affection for the Union; that I acted there in full conformity with this affection; *that I refused to subscribe, because I had, as I still have, objections to the Constitution,* and wished a free inquiry into its merits; and that the accession of eight states reduced our *deliberations* to the single question of *Union or no Union.*[121]

The final vote was 89–79.[122]

The nine-state rule was yet more decisive in New York.[123] Facing a hostile 46-to-19 majority, the Federalists played a waiting game when the convention began on June 17.[124] With both New Hampshire and Virginia deliberating, they moved that the convention debate the Constitution clause by clause—stalling for time until one of these states contributed the ninth vote for secession from the Confederation.[125]

The gambit worked. News of New Hampshire's ratification reached the convention on June 24, and the event is mentioned the next day:

> Mr. Chancellor LIVINGSTON observed, that it would not, perhaps, be altogether impertinent to remind the committee, that, since the intelligence of yesterday, it had become evident that the circumstances of the country were greatly altered, and the ground of the present debate changed. The Confederation, he said, was now *dissolved.*
>
> The question before the committee was now a question of policy and expediency. He presumed the convention would consider the situation of their country. He supposed, however, that some might contemplate disun-

ion without pain. They might flatter themselves that some of the Southern States would form a league with us; but he could not look without horror at the dangers to which any such confederacy would expose the state of New York. He said, it might be political cowardice in him, but he had felt since yesterday an alteration of circumstances, which had made a most solemn impression on his mind.[126]

But Governor George Clinton, the leading opponent of the Constitution, was no "political coward." He remained steadfast, though his troops were uncertain as to their next step.[127]

Hamilton, still desperate, wrote to Madison on June 25 that "[o]ur chance of success here is infinitely slender, and none at all if you go wrong."[128] After news of Virginia's ratification arrived, he was still writing that "[o]ur arguments confound, but do not convince—some of the leaders however appear to me to be convinced *by circumstances.*"[129] Only on July 26 did the New York convention approve by a vote of 30–27, with eight abstentions. To make their unhappiness abundantly clear, the delegates sent a circular letter to all state governors:

> We, the members of the Convention of this state, have deliberately and maturely considered the Constitution proposed for the United States. Several articles in it appear so exceptionable to a majority of us, that nothing but the fullest confidence of obtaining a revision of them by a general convention, and an invincible reluctance to separating from our sister states, could have prevailed upon a sufficient number to ratify it, without stipulating for previous amendments. We all unite in opinion, that such a revision will be necessary to recommend it to the approbation and support of a numerous body of our constituents.[130]

This theme dominates the entire letter, which urges the governors to ask their legislatures to call a second convention.

I hope you have been keeping in mind the contrarian scenario which introduced this analysis: Suppose that the Continental Congress had repudiated the Convention's nine-state rule and had repeatedly declared itself duty-bound to defend the Articles' proud assertion that "the Union shall be perpetual" unless and until all thirteen states agreed to its revision. Would Governor Randolph have led the fence-sitters to endorse the Constitution in Virginia? And what of Governor Clinton and the overwhelming Anti-Federalist majority in New York?

Under the contrarian scenario, the First Congress after ratification would have begun with a bare quorum of nine states in attendance— with New York and Virginia joining North Carolina and Rhode Island in a chorus of legalistic condemnation of their secession from the "perpetual" Union. Under these conditions, would the new Constitution have survived?[131]

CONSOLIDATION

And yet, for all of the Federalists' unconventional success, the First Congress began as a secessionist body. Rhode Island's legislature remained defiant after the referendum, refusing to call a ratifying convention. North Carolina's convention refused to crumple upon the news of Federalist success in Virginia and New York. After eleven days of debate that rehearsed familiar charges of illegality,[132] Anti-Federalist leader Willie Jones carried a resolution, 184–84, neither rejecting nor ratifying the Constitution but taking up New York's call for a second federal convention. Urging this convention to consider a twenty-item Bill of Rights and twenty-six other amendments prior to ratification, the Anti-Federalists triumphantly adjourned on August 2.[133]

The ball was now in the Federalists' court. Unless and until the dissenters got on the bandwagon, the problematic legality of the new regime would be a matter of open and endless contestation. There was an ever-present possibility that the Federalist success would unravel— as one or another key state reconsidered its secessionist impulses or demanded a second constitutional convention as a price for remaining within the Union. How then did the Federalists solve their problem of constitutional consolidation?

By a mix of democratic countermobilization and coercive threat. The democratic strategy was on display in North Carolina, where Federalists waged an energetic campaign for a new convention, which was granted by a newly elected legislature in November of 1788. With elections scheduled for August 1789, the Federalists had plenty of time to organize a successful grass-roots campaign: North Carolina's second convention ratified in November by 195–77.

Rhode Island posed a more difficult problem. Despite the disastrous referendum, Federalists continued to campaign for a convention and persuaded the legislature to reconsider in January 1790. When the departure of a legislator for church deadlocked the General Assembly, Governor Collins cast the tie-breaking vote, citing "the extreme distress we were reduced to by being disconnected with the other States."[134] But Rhode Islanders were unimpressed. The Anti-Federalists won a slim majority at the convention. After four days of desultory debate, the meeting adjourned.[135]

Congress then began to play tough. In May 1790, the Senate approved the Rhode Island Trade Bill, which embargoed all trade with the state and demanded immediate payment in hard currency of all its debts to the United States.[136] The Senate's debates were not then published, but the notes of Senator William Maclay of Pennsylvania reveal that he called the action "premature" and distinguished between imposing sanctions as "a punishment for rejection" of the Constitution and doing so on the basis of a "supposition that they would ruin our revenue." The latter course might be legitimate if the facts could be established, and this may be why he called the statute "premature." But at the present time, "the bill could not be justified on the Principles of freedom law the Constitution or any other Mode Whatever."[137]

According to Maclay, Pierce Butler of South Carolina rose to defend the bill: "It is no infringement of Her Sovereignty to withdraw your trade . . . Granted—Mr Izard says their little State is brought into Compact with the other States."[138] Despite the legal compunctions of Ralph Izard and Maclay, the Senate passed the bill by a vote of 13 to 8 and sent it to the House.

Meanwhile the Rhode Island convention reassembled, and once again the Anti-Federalist majority moved for adjournment, but this time they were defeated. The trading centers of Providence and Newport threatened secession if the Constitution were to fail again.[139] Finally, on May 29, two Anti-Federalist delegates defied their instructions, and the Constitution was ratified by a vote of 34–32.

Just in time: the House of Representatives had already considered the Rhode Island bill briefly, but dropped it upon learning of ratification on June 3, 1790.[140]

The bandwagon had finally lurched to its ultimate destination.

From Practice to Theory

I have been trying to redeem the promise of Anglo-American legal method. Rather than indulging heady abstractions about constitutional change, we have been approaching the Founding in the way lawyers address any important precedent—beginning with a "statement of the facts" that describes the Federalists' legal problems, and how they went about solving them step by step.

My approach has been functional, as was the Federalists'. It turns out that transforming a nation's constitutional order is not one problem, but many. There is a Sisyphean aspect to the Federalist enterprise—just as Madison and his friends managed to push one big boulder to the top of the hill, another came hurtling down.

But it is a mistake to think of the Federalists' problems as if they were random bolts from the blue. There was a pragmatic logic to the sequence—the Federalists' problems did not merely follow one another; the solution of one generated a pragmatic imperative to confront the next. Begin with the relationship between the signaling and proposal stages. As the Federalists were well aware, the country would not take their proposal seriously unless painstaking efforts were made to get a strong majority of the states to send delegates to their Convention. Only when they had solved this signaling problem did they have to get serious about their proposal. As they did so, the pragmatic linkage between proposing and triggering became unavoidable: if the Federalists were determined to propose a revolutionary reform of ideals and institutions, they simply could not accept the old ratification rule. A different pragmatic link connected triggering to ratifying: the Federalists could not win their political campaign for ratification without sustaining the credibility of their triggering decision. And finally, problems of constitutional consolidation burst on the scene only after success at each of the four prior stages.

I hope these points seem obvious, because they explain a puzzle raised repeatedly in this book. As we move beyond the Founding to explore other great turning points of the American past, we will find Reconstruction Republicans and New Deal Democrats engaging in the same five Founding activities pioneered by their Federalist predecessors—signaling, proposing, triggering, ratifying, and consolidating their constitutional authority in roughly the same order. At first glance, the recurrence of this pattern seems mysterious—or worse yet, a tell-tale sign of a grim determination to impose my fivefold schema on constitutional history without serious attention to the particularities of particular cases.

But this skeptical treatment of my organizing schema ignores its pragmatic basis. The five-phase pattern recurs because the problems recur. It is, of course, possible to imagine a group trying to compress constitutional transformation into a single moment of time: Not only do they emerge from the blue to announce the coming of the new regime, but all existing institutions rejoice upon hearing the Good News and meekly accept whatever role has been assigned them in the new dispensation.

But this is a version of the Second Coming; when mere mortals seek to reenact it, the predictable result is an attempted putsch ending in civil war or military despotism (or both). The Founding example demonstrates, however, that a democratic effort at revolutionary reform *can* occur through a temporally extended process that enables reformers *to build up* their constitutional credibility by solving a series of discrete, but interrelated, problems.

This point is enough to establish an analytic agenda. If, as I will show, both Reconstruction Republicans and New Deal Democrats understood themselves as confronting the Federalists' problems, we can compare and contrast the ways in which these three groups of revolutionary reformers tried to solve them. As in this chapter's study of the Federalists, we will follow both Republicans and Democrats as they confronted the challenges of signaling, proposing, triggering, ratifying, and consolidating. Unsurprisingly, each generation of revolutionary reformers used different institutional tools to solve their common problems—and it will take a good deal of time and effort to compare and contrast them.

In the end, however, the effort will be rewarded by fresh insights into the enduring dynamics of the American constitutional system. Despite the very important differences in institutional technique elaborated over the generations, there are fundamental similarities in the way Federalists, Republicans, and Democrats confronted the system's challenge to their claim to speak for the People. I have already suggested one recurring pattern: the unconventional methods through which constitutional reformers repeatedly sought and won official confirmation of their popular mandate. But we will uncover many more. By exploring the deeper regularities that organize the different efforts of Federalists, Republicans, and Democrats to speak for the People, we will lay bare the deepest structures of America's dualistic Constitution.

CHAPTER THREE

The Founding Precedent

ON METHOD

W E H A V E B E E N looking at the Federalists as practical statesmen who faced a series of sharp constitutional challenges to their initiative. Without their ongoing display of unconventional statecraft, the Founding would have been a miserable failure. Even with it, the Federalists barely staggered across the finish line they had drawn for themselves.

In crossing the line, they managed to distinguish themselves from many other clever and ambitious men who have yearned to impose their ideals upon the larger public. From the days of Jefferson to the days of Gingrich, movements for constitutional reform have repeatedly tried to repeat the Federalists' success in speaking for the People—with a wide variety of outcomes. Many never got beyond the signaling stage. A few were so successful that they reshaped the criteria the Federalists developed for successful signals, proposals, triggers, ratifications, and consolidations. In principle, each serious movement is entitled to sustained study.

I will be settling for a lot less. I will be focusing on Reconstruction and the New Deal for two reasons. First, they are like the Federalist period in demonstrating sustained popular support for revolutionary reforms. Other successful movements have settled for less sweeping changes. Second, they arose in the remote past, beyond the vivid recollection of modern Americans. Once the active participants are dead and gone, legal scholars have a special role to play in exposing the relevant materials for more general discussion. If they don't present the constitutional problems raised by our past, who will?

The simple passage of time may also free us from knee-jerk partisanship and allow us to see the great constitutional struggles of the past as something that binds us together as Americans—yielding precious resources for assessing our own political efforts. As we move into our third century as a People, one thing is clear—the effort at revolutionary reform has not come to an end, nor has the skepticism it engenders. In the future as in the past, would-be reformers will have to earn huge quantities of institutional credibility before they gain higher lawmaking recognition for their achievements. But how much institutional resistance must they transcend, and of what kinds?

If dualism is to remain a viable constitutional project, constitutionalists must be in a position to provide credible answers to these questions. And I know of no better way than the reflective and critical assessment of the paradigm cases of popular sovereignty given to us by American history. When constitutionalists confront the claim of a rising group of politicians to speak for the People, we should be asking ourselves: Have the newcomers earned their claim to popular sovereignty through a process that measures up to those through which Federalists, Republicans, and Democrats gained their credibility at earlier times?

There is no shortcut to an answer. We must work our way through each of our paradigm cases with the classic tools of reflective legal analysis—searching for analogies between the cases that seem grounded in fundamental legal principles. If we are successful, the result will have the texture of good common law judgments—providing historically rooted criteria that are sufficiently incisive to produce meaningful legal assessment of the unknowable future. What more can Americans reasonably expect from law than this?

This is not a rhetorical question. I have no doubt that many—most?—lawyers will be tempted by a different answer, which is no less grounded in the Founding. On this formalist approach, the Federalists have solved our problem for us in Article Five of their Constitution, which lays down some clear rules for constitutional amendment. Given this set of instructions, lawyers can happily avoid a tedious study of the messy lessons of history before propounding the law of higher lawmaking that should guide Americans into their third century. If future reformers want to change the Constitution, let them play by the rules laid down in Article Five. What could be simpler?

THE MEANING OF ARTICLE FIVE

But what does Article Five really say?

> The Congress, whenever two-thirds of both Houses shall deem it neces-
> sary, shall propose Amendments to this Constitution, or, on the Applica-
> tion of Legislatures of two-thirds of the several States, shall call a Conven-
> tion for proposing Amendments, which, in either Case, shall be valid to all
> Intents and Purposes, as part of this Constitution, when ratified by the
> Legislatures of three-fourths of the several States, or by Conventions in
> three-fourths thereof, as the one or the other Mode of Ratification may be
> proposed by the Congress . . .*

The words describe a complex system. They place four different com-
binations before us: federal convention–state conventions; convention–legislatures; Congress–conventions; Congress–legislatures. Why
the plurality? Why can't the People learn how to speak in a single
way?

Worse yet, the article lacks the clear set of rules presupposed by the
formalist's question. True, if the People choose to express themselves
through the Congress-legislatures combination, it is clear that an
amendment must gain the support of two-thirds of the House and
Senate, and three-fourths of the legislatures. But it is unclear whether
the state legislatures must approve the amendment by two-thirds (like
the Congress) or by some other majority. Things get murkier with the
other modes of revision. What is this beast, the "convention"? How is
it composed? How is it different from those more familiar creatures:
the legislatures sitting on the national and state levels? For example,
could Congress simply call itself a convention (upon receiving appropriate applications from two-thirds of the state legislatures)? If not,
why not? If the convention must meet as a separate body, as it did in
Philadelphia, should it also follow Philadelphia in awarding a single
vote to each state, regardless of population? This proliferating list of

---

*Article Five concludes with two provisos: "Provided that no Amendment which may
be made prior to the Year One thousand eight hundred and eight shall in any Manner
affect the first and fourth Clauses in the Ninth Section of the First Article [dealing with the
slave trade and direct taxation]; and that no State, without its Consent, shall be deprived of
its equal Suffrage in the Senate."

questions[1] should caution against overenthusiastic descriptions of Article Five as containing a "plain meaning."[2] An appeal to the text can provide no escape from the thoughtful exercise of lawyerly judgment.

More generally, I want to embrace a pluralist view of the sources of law. Rather than choosing between the lessons of the text and the lessons of our great historical precedents, we should try to learn from both, coordinating them into a larger understanding of the law of higher lawmaking. My real antagonist, then, is not the thoughtful textualist but someone who treats the Founding text as the exclusive source of law. Hypertextualists, as I will call them, insist that *all* the modern lawyer needs to know about constitutional revision can be found within "the four corners" of Article Five. While this position is not represented too forcefully in the literature,[3] my real-world encounters with ordinary lawyers have led me to take it seriously. As we move into the nineteenth and twentieth centuries, I will return to consider how the twists and turns of history undermine the claims of hypertextualism. Right now, I will be trying to exclude hypertextualism from the starting gate—for the simple reason that it fails to do justice to the complexities of the original understanding. From the very first, our Constitution was based on the pluralist claim that both text and practice deserve weight in the evolving law of higher lawmaking.

The Convention

If the Framers wanted to vindicate hypertextualism decisively, there was an easy way to do it. They could have written an explicit proviso that "This Constitution can *only* be amended when. . . ." In writing such a clause, the Federalists would have self-consciously warned future Americans against treating their own unconventional activities as a precedent: "While we claimed the authority to revise the Articles in the name of the People, we deny future generations an equal right to change the amendment procedures we now lay down in Article Five."

But the Convention made no such claim, despite warnings from the delegates that they were creating a decisive precedent: "Mr. Gerry urged the indecency and pernicious tendency of dissolving in so slight a manner, the solemn obligations of the articles of confederation. If nine out of thirteen can dissolve the compact, Six out of nine will be just as able to dissolve the new one hereafter."[4] Whatever else Article Five may say, it does *not* claim exclusivity.

But, replies the hypertextualist, the Convention didn't need to say so. It could rely on an established legal maxim: "Expressio unius exclusio alterius"—which means "To enumerate one thing is to exclude others." But there is no evidence that the Convention relied on this bit of Latin to resolve the textual indeterminacy. Indeed, the records show that the Convention gave Five remarkably little thought of any kind

This may seem surprising, until we consider that Article Five was not the only constitutional provision devoted to the problem of higher lawmaking. For the Federalists, the other provision, found in Article Seven, was more important. It was here where they decided, after anxious and recurring debate, to break their links with the Articles of Confederation by declaring that nine state ratifications would suffice to validate their new Constitution. In contrast, Five spoke to the day after tomorrow, addressing a problem then triply hypothetical: *If* the Convention gained general acceptance for the nine-state rule announced in Seven, and *if* the Federalists managed to carry nine state conventions, and *if* the People later wished to change the Constitution, how might they go about it?

Little wonder that the Convention delegates had better things to do with their time. While the Federalists produced drafts that briefly noted the need for an amendment article, there was very little discussion until the last working week of the Convention. At that point, the working draft contained a provision that reflected the rudimentary character of the debate: "On the application of the Legislatures of two-thirds of the States in the Union, for an amendment of this Constitution, the Legislature of the United States shall call a Convention for that purpose"[5]—in other words, the process for revision should (more or less) track the process by which the Federalists got to Philadelphia in the first place.

But in their initial encounter with the problem on the floor, the delegates were convinced by Madison (after a very brief discussion) to eliminate the possibility of a second constitutional convention and place control over higher lawmaking firmly in the hands of the new Congress:

The legislature of the U– S– whenever two thirds of both Houses shall deem necessary, or on the application of two thirds of the Legislatures of the several States, shall propose amendments to this Constitution, which shall be valid to all intents and purposes as part thereof, when the same shall have been ratified by three fourths at least of the Legislatures of the several States, or by Conventions in three fourths thereof, as one or the other mode of ratification may be proposed by the Legislature of the U.S.[6]

Then, on their last working day, the delegates returned to Madison's handiwork in a critical spirit:

Col: Mason thought the plan . . . exceptionable & dangerous. As the proposing of amendments is in both the modes to depend, in the first immediately and in the second, ultimately, on Congress, no amendments of the proper kind would ever be obtained by the people, if the Government should become oppressive, as he verily believed would be the case.

Mr. Govr. Morris & Mr. Gerry moved to amend the article so as to require a Convention on application of 2/3 of the Sts.

Mr. Madison did not see why Congress would not be as much bound to propose amendments applied for by two thirds of the States as to call a Convention on the like application. He saw no objection however against providing a Convention for the purpose of amendments, except only that difficulties might arise as to the form, the quorum &c. Which in Constitutional regulations ought to be as much as possible avoided.[7]

The last lines come as close as you get to a hypertextualist assertion at the Convention. Madison was perfectly right to complain that the Morris-Gerry amendment would destroy Article Five's promise of a neat rule system. By explicitly allowing another federal convention, Mason, Morris, and Gerry were opening up vast new areas of ambiguity "as to the form, the quorum &c." which the second Convention might exploit in surprising ways—ambiguities especially threatening given the iconoclastic precedent established at Philadelphia. If the delegates had been genuinely concerned to redeem hypertextualism's promise of clarity, they either would have rejected Morris-Gerry or specified further rules to fill its most troublesome gaps.

They did neither. When the Convention was faced with the stark choice between rule-like clarity and allowing the People to break the Congressional monopoly over higher lawmaking, it was eleven states to none against rule-like clarity. With any pretense at formal perfection shattered, Roger Sherman moved to muddy the waters further, taking

aim at the provision that authorized ratification by three-fourths of
state legislatures or state conventions. He moved to strike the words
"three-fourths . . ., leaving future Conventions to act in this matter,
like the present Conventions according to circumstances."[8] This motion might have set the stage for an extended debate on hypertextualism. On a better day, we might have heard a pluralist assert that
Sherman's amendment was unnecessary since a second convention
could appropriately follow the precedent of the first in moving beyond preexisting ratification rules. But the delegates were in no mood
for extended argument as they rushed toward the finish line. Without
any discussion, they voted Sherman's proposal down by seven states to
three.

This is not, to put it mildly, a picture that puts hypertextualism in its
best light. It is one thing to focus narrowly on some Founding words
when they represent the culmination of deep and wide-ranging
thought; quite another, when they are the by-product of a last-minute
rush—especially when the Federalists, in their all-too-human desire to
go home, did take the time to uphold Mason's appeals to popular
sovereignty over Madison's concerns about the formal perfection of
Article Five's system of rules.

The Founders' nonchalant treatment of Article Five contrasts
sharply with the very deliberate way they proceeded to break with the
Confederation in the name of We the People. Why, then, should
constitutionalists ignore the lessons of their well-considered practice
and concentrate exclusively on the rule fragments so negligently left
behind in Article Five?

Public Understandings and Ordinary Language

I do not want to put too much weight on the secret deliberations—or
lack of them—that went on at the Philadelphia Convention. How
would ordinary Americans have understood the article? Would they
have used *expressio unius* as a key to determining whether it provided
the exclusive modes for amendment? What is the foundation of this
Latin maxim anyway?

I take it to be based on a point about ordinary English usage.
Suppose, for example, your boss said to you, "You can use a hammer
to fix the machine." In certain contexts, you would be right to use

expressio unius to interpret this remark to mean "You can *only* use a hammer *and nothing else* to fix the machine."

But only sometimes. It may be more sensible to understand it as "You can use a hammer *or any like implement* to fix the machine." The right inference depends on context, which makes history important. But before we go down that road, a few thought-experiments may permit some insight into the contextual issues.

Reflect, first, on the fact that Article Five does not merely create a single implement to fix the constitutional machine; it creates four. In ordinary life, this single fact subtly—though not decisively—shifts the balance in favor of pluralism. Suppose the boss says "You can use hammers or screwdrivers, or both together, to fix the machine," and you discover that a wrench is more functional than either of these tools. Doesn't the fact that the boss initially authorized several different instruments, and not only one, make the pluralist reading a bit more plausible?

Consider the same case as before, with one additional fact. Before giving you his instruction about hammers and screwdrivers, the boss had fixed the machine with a wrench. You are now considering whether to use a wrench as well, when a partisan of *expressio unius* intervenes:

> E (for Expressio): The boss said that you could use hammers or screwdrivers, but he said nothing about wrenches! Why are you disobeying?

> P (for Pluralist): But he used a wrench himself. If he didn't want me to use a wrench in an appropriate case, he would have said so.

In many contexts, P's reply would be entirely sensible. Unless E points to a special feature that supports his inference, the contextual balance seems to be tipping in the pluralist direction: "You can use a hammer or a screwdriver *or any like instrument (and especially a wrench)* to fix the machine."

Now a final bit of context: When the boss used a wrench earlier to fix the machine, he himself had a boss, who had *explicitly* told him not to use the wrench. The boss disobeyed, and nevertheless was successful. Now that he has become the highest authority, he fails to follow the example of his previous employer. Rather than explicitly prohibiting the use of a wrench, he simply fails to mention the wrench and merely says that his underlings "can use hammers or screwdrivers." As you are about to use your wrench, E intervenes:

E: The boss said that you could use hammers or screwdrivers, but he said nothing about wrenches! Why are you disobeying?

P: But he used a wrench himself when he was in my position.

E: So what? Unless he explicitly mentions wrenches, you should understand him as implicitly forbidding their use.

P: Nonsense. You just don't understand the boss. He was trying to be helpful in mentioning hammers and screwdrivers. He wasn't trying to stop me from using other tools if they would get the job done.

E: Why didn't he say so?

P: He didn't need to, given the way he dealt with instructions when he was in my position. After all, he ignored his old boss when the guy expressly warned him off wrenches. If he wanted me to take his warnings seriously, he would have gone out of his way to say so, and not leave it to implication.

Of course, a constitution is no ordinary machine. Nevertheless, these dialogues deflate hypertextualist rhetoric that presents *expressio unius* as the only "natural" way to read texts. In a setting like the last one, the linguistic intuitions of native English speakers incline strongly against the maxim, and in favor of pluralism. This is important since this scenario approximates the historical realities.

Recall that the thirteenth Article of Confederation had *explicitly* made its amendment provision exclusive. As in my last hypothetical, the Convention not only ignored these instructions from its nominal boss but refused to claim exclusivity for new amendment procedures. Within this context, isn't it odd to suppose that *expressio unius* should be an appropriate guide?

Public Understandings: History

After all, Americans had been proclaiming the "right of the People to alter and abolish" their government since 1776—both in the Declaration of Independence and in many of the state constitutions of the revolutionary era.[9] Since the Federalists were operating within this

revolutionary tradition, why should the average American have interpreted Article Five as cutting off all future appeals to the People
which did not comply with its requirements?

This is certainly not the impression left by James Wilson, who took
to the floor of Pennsylvania's ratifying convention to insist that "the
people may change the constitutions whenever and however they
please."[10] Wilson's words were widely noted, coming from a man who
rivaled Madison in his leadership at the Convention. Indeed, the
Anti-Federalist leader John Smilie soon tried to turn Wilson's words in
an unexpected direction: "even after this Convention shall have
agreed to ratify the proposed plan, if the people on better information
or maturer deliberation should think it a bad and improper form of
government, they will still have a right to assemble another body to
consult upon other measures and either in the whole, or in part, to
abrogate this federal work so ratified."[11]

Later on in the ratifying campaign, the Federalists sought to use
Smilie's point to their own advantage. Their opponents had focused
on the Philadelphians' failure to include a Bill of Rights as the central
deficiency of the Constitution. Given this major flaw, was it not more
prudent to condition ratification on its successful solution? The Anti-
Federalists urged the conventions to refuse ratification and insist that
a second federal convention meet to frame an appropriate set of
amendments; only then would final ratification by a second set of state
conventions be appropriate. What was the rush anyway?[12]

The Federalists responded to this reasonable question by assuring
their opponents that the First Congress would quickly respond with a
Bill of Rights. But what if these promises were unredeemed? Here is
Edmund Pendleton, president of the Virginia ratifying convention,
responding to these anxieties in his initial address:

> We, the people, possessing all power, form a government, such as we think
> will secure happiness; and suppose, in adopting this plan, we should be
> mistaken in the end; where is the cause of alarm on that quarter? In the
> same plan we point out an easy and quiet method of reforming what may
> be found amiss. No, but, say gentlemen, we have put the introduction of
> that method in the hands of our servants, who will interrupt it from
> motives of self-interest. What then? We will resist, did my friend say?
> conveying an idea of force? Who shall dare to resist the people? No, we

will assemble in Convention; wholly recall our delegated powers, or reform them so as to prevent such abuse. . . .[13]

Pendleton could not have held out this option if Article Five had explicitly claimed exclusivity.

Nor did the Federalists consign Pendleton's sentiments to oblivion once they had fulfilled their purpose during the ratification campaign. In his influential Law Lectures of 1790, James Wilson repeated the same claims he had made on the stump, emphasizing the "one great principle . . . animat[ing] all the others . . . that the supreme or sovereign power of the society resides in the citizens at large; and that, therefore, they always retain the right of abolishing, altering, or amending their constitution, at whatever time, and in whatever manner, they shall deem it expedient."[14] But now Wilson was a Justice of the Supreme Court and his audience included the leaders of the new government.

The same pluralist theme recurs as the First Congress redeemed the Federalists' promise of a Bill of Rights.[15] James Madison's initial draft interweaved the new amendments into the original text, starting with a new beginning to the preambulatory "We the People," which included: "[t]hat the people have an indubitable, *inalienable, and indefeasible* right to reform or change their Government."[16] Nobody denied the merit of this sentiment, but it was rejected on grounds of redundancy. Roger Sherman's remarks are revealing:

> The people of the United States have given their reasons for doing a certain act. Here we propose . . . to let them know that they had a right to exercise a natural and inherent privilege, which they have asserted in the solemn ordination and establishment of the constitution. Now, if this right is indefeasible, and the people have recognized it in practice, the truth is better asserted than it can be by any words whatever. The words "We the people" in the original constitution, are as copious and expressive as possible . . .[17]

This is precisely the pluralist's point. If the principle of popular sovereignty is "better asserted [in practice] than it can be by any words whatever," lawyers should treat the lessons of practice no less seriously than the words of Article Five.

This conclusion is reinforced by the practical construction early Americans gave amendment clauses of the Federalist type. Time and again, legislatures confronted state constitutions that, like the Federalist text of 1787, neither expressly barred nor explicitly authorized nontextual revisionary procedures. On sixteen occasions before the Civil War, state legislatures refused to read this silence to imply exclusivity.[18] They repeatedly called constitutional conventions on occasions not explicitly authorized by their governing texts. Looking back, the leading treatise writer of the nineteenth century—the very conservative Judge Jameson—had no trouble concluding: "upon authority [of the precedents] certainly, and I think also upon principle, it is competent for the people, at the instance and through the ministry of the existing government, to amend their Constitution either in the mode presented [in the text] or in such other mode as custom may have sanctioned, and as sound statesmanship may, under all the circumstances, approve."[19] The few twentieth-century scholars who have seriously studied these sources tend to be equally emphatic.[20]

I do not deny that exclusivism begins to gain serious advocates as the early Republic proceeds. The most notable assertion is in George Washington's Farewell Address:

> If in the opinion of the people the distribution or modification of the constitutional powers be in any particular wrong, let it be corrected by an amendment in the way which the Constitution designates. But let there be no change by usurpation; for though this in one instance may be the instrument of good, it is the customary weapon by which free governments are destroyed. The precedent must always greatly overbalance in permanent evil any partial or transient benefit which the use can at any time yield.[21]

Like many valedictories, this one contrasts sharply with the speaker's deeds when he was an active leader. If Washington had practiced what he preached, he would have walked out of the Constitutional Convention. Nonetheless, his Farewell does inaugurate a school of thought that looks upon the Founding as the end, and not merely the beginning, of the American experiment with popular sovereignty.[22]

The best way to confront this tradition is to move beyond the Founding and see what Americans have actually done with their Constitution in the name of the People. But for now, it is enough to caution that Washington's Farewell does not do justice to the revolutionary thrust of early American thought and practice. As I read the sources, they generally point in the pluralist direction, and caution us against reading the silence of Article Five as if it contained an express effort by the Founding generation to put itself on a pedestal and prevent future generations from following Washington's example, rather than his valedictory.

The Meaning of the Convention

So let us leave the text and return to the Founders' practice, this time searching for deeper legal meanings. The place to begin is with the curious institution that the Federalists brought to center stage. In English constitutional law, a "convention" was a legally defective Parliament, most notably the one presiding over the Glorious Revolution of 1688. Before slipping out of London, King James II cancelled the writs of election he had issued and dropped the Great Seal in the Thames, explaining: "A meeting of a parliament cannot be authorized without writs under the great seal."[23]

His enemies responded with an ersatz process. Members of earlier Commonses met in Westminster as an *ad hoc* body and issued a "circular letter" as a substitute for legal writs of election. Acting under these letters, officials conducted something that looked very much like a traditional ballot for the Commons. Members of this unconventional House joined (some of) the Lords to meet as a "Convention." Even this ersatz Commons + Lords was not enough for a Parliament under English law—since the presence of the King was required, and James was all too absent.[24] But despite the evident break with formal rules, the Whigs had designed a procedure that created as much institutional continuity with the old regime as was plausible under the circumstances.

In the eyes of the victors of the American Revolution, the Convention of 1688 was responsible for some of the greatest achievements in English constitutional history—notably the promulgation of a Bill of Rights and the replacement of a tyrant king with a constitutional monarch. This great precedent provided the Federalists with a language that permitted them to present their rule-breaking initiative in a way that fell short of total revolution. As in 1688, the Federalist conventions of 1787–88 had broken some basic rules but had created credible institutional linkages to the preexisting constitution. Thanks to the English precedents, the Federalists were not required to make up an alien language to explain what they were doing. In calling for "conventions," they could adapt an older vocabulary already rooted in the living political culture.[25]

Modern English has evolved to the point where the Federalists' use of "convention" is anything but conventional. To provide a link with the past, I have been using "unconventional" to describe the same sort of institutional practice. This is a sharp verbal change, but the Federalists were also linguistic reformers. Their conventions were different beasts from their great English predecessor. For one thing, they claimed greater authority. The Convention of 1688 was profoundly embarrassed by its defective legality. As soon as William and Mary were comfortably on the throne, the Convention declared itself a proper Parliament and passed a statute retroactively legalizing the anomalous acts of its legally defective predecessor.[26] In contrast, the Federalist conventions claimed to speak for the People *better* than the established Congress and state legislatures. In a remarkable inversion, the legally problematic character of the conventions was taken as a sign of their superior capacity to speak for the People.

In making this move, the Federalists were not acting entirely without precedent. A few years earlier, the town meetings of both New Hampshire and Massachusetts had refused to approve constitutions proposed by their state legislatures, insisting that special conventions be called instead.[27] The Federalists, then, were nationalizing a precedent that had already gained a foothold on the local level.

But they gave these precedents a different spin. While the town meetings of New Hampshire and Massachusetts had insisted on state conventions to propose constitutions, they saw no need to demand special ratifying conventions but approved the proposals themselves.[28] The Federalists used the convention device twice: after proposing their Constitution at Philadelphia, they demanded special ratifying conventions.

This second round was essential in legitimating their rule-breaking exercise. Otherwise, they would have been obliged to defend themselves before the very bodies that had defined their legal mandates: the state legislatures. By appealing for ratifying conventions, they could redefine the relevant question. Instead of acting defensively when their opponents accused them of breaking the rules, they could go on the offensive and deny that legalistic objections could appropriately prevent a convention of the People from deliberating on its constitutional destiny. After all, if the citizenry found rule-breaking really troubling, they would simply elect so many Anti-Federalists to the ratifying conventions that the Constitution would be doomed.

The Federalists' referendum-like appeal placed their opponents at a distinct ideological disadvantage. The Anti-Federalists were also children of the Revolution. They too had broken countless British laws in the name of the People. They too knew that the Convention of 1688 had played a proud role in the Glorious Revolution. Once the Federalists had adapted convention-imagery on behalf of their revolutionary reforms, the Anti-Federalists were left looking like legalistic nitpickers—and they knew it. Since the calling of ratifying conventions was a bitterly fought question in some of the state legislatures, the Federalists' success in taking the high ideological ground could well have made the difference.

Once again, there doesn't seem to be a standard word to describe the distinctive character of their innovation. So please forgive me when I call the Federalist ratifying conventions an exercise in *quasi-direct* democracy. To grasp this distinctive mixture, begin with the sense in which the Federalist initiative approached the notion of "direct" democracy, as exemplified by a popular referendum. As in a referendum, the elections for convention delegates in 1787 and 1788 were focused on a concrete proposal—the Federalist Constitution of 1787. At the same time, the process was only quasi-direct—the voters did not cast ballots on the merits of the Federalist Constitution but for delegates who would deliberate further. This allowed for a more complex process of decision than the simple Yes-No of a modern plebiscite: delegates could be elected who were publicly uncommitted on the merits; others might choose to pay the political price of changing their public positions from No to Yes. For all this flexibility, delegates had a much clearer sense of a "mandate" from the People to move in a particular direction than normally exists in standard electoral contests.

The convention mode, then, represented a distinctive mix of popular will and elite deliberation—combining the popular involvement of "direct democracy" with the enhanced deliberation of "representative democracy." The aim was for a *deliberative plebiscite*.[29] But by aiming so high, the Federalists risked missing both targets: their conventions might lack the democratic credibility of a referendum while lacking the deliberative quality of the best representative bodies. In fact, the historical record is mixed, and we will soon turn to consider the darker side of Federalist practice.

But for now, consider its affirmative contribution. The Federalist experiment in quasi-direct democracy was way ahead of its time. In the half-century after 1787, thirty-four state constitutions would be enacted into law, but only six would be ratified through a special procedure involving a focused vote by the People—and only two of these ballots occurred outside New England. Popular ratification became a national norm only after the Jacksonian Revolution of the 1830's.[30] When set within its time and place, the Federalist call for ratifying conventions was a radical experiment in democracy.[31]

Their success is impossible to understand without reference to this radically democratic ideal. After all, their opponents could have reacted to Federalist lawlessness by boycotting the elections, thereby depriving them of their legitimacy. Instead, they responded to the Convention's appeal to the People by competing for popular support in a relatively fair and open contest. Their engaged electoral competition vastly enhanced the quality of the Federalists' ultimate victory. Once the Anti-Federalists had jumped on the bandwagon started at Annapolis, it would be hard for them to jump off and condemn the outcome simply because they had lost.

After four years of engaged institutional struggle, the Federalists had reached a point where even their bitter opponents had a hard time denying that the Constitution represented a considered judgment of We the People of the United States. To summarize this bandwagon dynamic, it may be clarifying to distinguish between its negative and positive aspects. Negatively, unconventional action served to constrain the destabilizing consequences of a breach of the basic rules for constitutional revision—providing the political participants with an institutional context for decision that was sufficiently familiar to engage in constructive debate and decision. Positively, the elaboration of new forms of quasi-direct democracy allowed the public to intervene in a specially focused way—without reducing the notion of a mandate to a mechanical yes-no vote. Rather than supposing that the People speak directly at the ballot box, the Federalist precedent promises *legitimation through a deepening institutional dialogue between political elites and ordinary citizens.* The idea is that a form of complex, and temporally extended, institutional practice will ultimately permit a group of revolutionary reformers a kind of popular authority that is qualitatively different from normal electoral victories. The challenge is to understand more precisely the distinctive character of this unconventional practice.

REREADING THE TEXT: THE DYNAMIC OF LEGITIMATION

This was, of course, the aim of the last chapter. Rather than considering Federalist practice as an undifferentiated whole, we followed the Founders through a five-stage process of constitutional legitimation—moving from the problems of signaling through the difficulties of constitutional consolidation. But perhaps we can now deepen this case study by integrating it into this chapter's larger themes. I have been defending a pluralistic legal method, which refuses to choose between the lessons of text and those of precedent but seeks to synthesize them into a mutually enlightening whole. On this integrative line of thinking, lawyers should always be on the lookout for ways in which the text of Article Five confirms, rejects, or refines the conclusions suggested by their study of constitutional practice. We can now begin to cash this promissory note.

As we saw, it is hard for the hypertextualist to read Article Five without embarrassment—as rule systems go, this one is almost criminally negligent in its failure to regulate the most obvious problems. But for the pluralist, the text consolidates and refines the lessons of practice. Consider, first, how it elaborates legitimating patterns of differential complexity as it contemplates different institutions at the center of the stage. Begin with the simplest pattern, involving the standard organs of everyday government—Congress and the state legislatures. When these institutions occupy the foreground, the text describes a truncated pattern: two-thirds of Congress proposes an amendment and sends it on to the state legislatures for ratification. Even here, it is worth noting two minor stages. Between proposal and ratification there is a half-stage during which Congress exercises a triggering function—deciding that its proposal should be ratified by legislatures rather than conventions. At the end of the process, the text gestures to another minor stage. It announces that the amendment "shall be valid to all Intents and Purposes" upon ratification by three-fourths of the states—without, however, explaining how this act of constitutional consolidation should take place. Thus, the Constitution seems to envision a four-phase process when Congress and state legislatures are involved—containing two main stages, proposal and ratification, and two minor ones, triggering and consolidation.

The legitimating dynamic gets more complex when the "convention" gets into the picture. The full-blown treatment extends to four major phases, which alternate between standard and unconventional bodies. First, two-thirds of state legislatures signal the need for a constitutional "convention," a word whose complex resonances we have just explored. In response to this signal, Congress is given no choice: it "shall" issue the call, and allow the convention to take the lead at the proposal stage. But the initiative then returns to a standard institution—Congress—whose triggering decision takes on a larger significance. When faced with the convention's demand for constitutional revision in the name of the People, Congress can either send the proposal down the standard track or call for another round of unconventional activities. By calling for ratification by "conventions," Congress ousts the standard legislative bodies in the states from their accustomed position of authority. Finally, we encounter the weakly articulated consolidation phase, where somebody or other recognizes that three-fourths of state conventions have ratified, and the new revisions come into effect.

In short, the text envisions the very five-stage process through which the Federalists themselves won their own legitimacy. This strikes me as important—most obviously, because it confirms the categories we have used to describe the Founding process. Not only are our five stages rooted in Founding realities, but the Founders themselves made comparable functional distinctions. Even more important, the Founders are commending this model to the future. As we have seen, they self-consciously rejected a draft that gave Congress a monopoly over the process of constitutional amendment. Rather than eliminating all mention of the creative days when "conventions" ruled in the name of the People, their text holds this option out as an essential aspect of American constitutional development.

Not that the text disparages the role of normal institutions of American government. Instead, it seeks to replicate one of the most distinctive features of Founding practice—the unconventional way in which the Federalists repeatedly sought to gain official confirmation of the decisions made in their legally anomalous conventions. Thus the text does not envision the next convention coming out of nowhere. Instead, it will be called into existence by the very bodies—state legislatures—that breathed life into Philadelphia; the text expresses a similar alternation of official and unconventional authority at the triggering and ratification stages (while speaking delphically on this matter in addressing the final stage of constitutional consolidation).

A deep idea is lurking here. Under the American Constitution, standard institutions are not expected to defend their authority at all cost. They are explicitly invited to work in an uneasy partnership with unconventional institutions that speak in the name of the People. While normal institutions may defer to the plebiscitary claims of revolutionary reformers meeting in anomalous fora, they continue to play a crucial stabilizing role, sustaining deep constitutional continuities even at times of radical institutional disruption. By this means, the text invites us to imagine that Americans may manage to transform moments of grave crisis into democratic triumphs of constitutional creativity. Is this unconventional solution a promising response to crisis?

We shall see. But I first want to return to the Founding and correct what might seem an excessively triumphalist account. While I am unembarrassed in applauding the historic breakthrough achieved by the federal and state conventions, I hardly wish to deny that the Federalists fell far short of the ideal of popular sovereignty, even as it was understood in the eighteenth century. When judged in modern terms, the Founding looks even worse.

Confronting these hard facts is not only essential for a balanced view. It plays an important role in my larger argument. Thus far, I have been using strictly legal tools in my effort to persuade you to abandon a hypertextualist understanding of constitutional change—appealing to the express language of Article Five, the original understanding, the nature of the Founding precedent, and the like. If these haven't completely discredited hypertextualism, perhaps they have at least created some large doubts?

Here is where my moral critique enters. *Perhaps* you might be justified in granting Article Five a monopoly on constitutional change if the Founding had approximated the ideal of popular sovereignty more closely than any later constitutional transformation in American history. But the facts refute such a supposition. While the constitutional practice of the Reconstruction Republicans and New Deal Democrats had their own significant failings, they were, in many respects, far superior to the Federalists'. Given these Founding deficits, it seems morally bizarre, as well as legally inappropriate, to grant the Federalists the constitutional authority to lay down the rules for subsequent efforts to speak in the name of the People. To the contrary, it is only because Reconstruction Republicans and New Deal Democrats managed to correct some of the more obvious Founding failures that we are justified in refusing to throw the Federalist precedent into the historical junk heap. The hypertextualist, in short, is not only historically wrong but morally obtuse to suppose that the Federalists provide us with the last word on constitutional revision. Once we scrutinize their moral failures, it becomes even clearer that the Founding deserves to be treated as at best the beginning, but not the end, of an ongoing American struggle for popular sovereignty.

FOUNDING FAILURES

Three failures stand out. The most obvious is the Founders' politics of exclusion. To win the right to speak for the People, the Federalists did not suppose they needed to appeal to women or slaves or Native Americans. While the Convention's practice was strikingly democratic for its time, it does not stand up to more modern understandings. In contrast, the higher lawmaking practices of Reconstruction and the New Deal—though hardly ideal—embraced far more democratic conceptions of We the People. As we shall see, black Americans first entered constitutional history in a big way with the unconventional ratification of the Fourteenth Amendment. Women voters had won the suffrage by the time Americans responded to the Great Depression by revolutionizing their constitutional traditions. Even today, we remain a long way from the ideal of a citizenry in which each American has a more-or-less equal voice in constitutional politics. But the

Founding project in dualist democracy would have lost all credibility if Americans had not moved far beyond the narrow Founding conception of We the People.

Next to this great matter of exclusion, the other Founding failures may seem like small potatoes. But they are not minor when judged by any other standard. The first problem involves the Federalists' refusal to seek a direct electoral legitimation for the Philadelphia Convention. As critics repeatedly pointed out,[32] the Convention would have greatly enhanced its authority if its members had been elected by the People directly, rather than appointed by state legislatures. Under this scenario, the Philadelphia meeting should have simply issued a call for another convention—this one composed of elected delegates who possessed a clearer mandate for revolutionary reform. Wouldn't such a convention have had a much plainer mandate to speak for the People?

But the Federalists were not conducting a philosophy seminar. They were trying to win. Another round of elections would have given Anti-Federalists a chance to win a lot of seats at the next convention, enabling them to defeat the Federalists' centralizing ambitions. The majority in Philadelphia were utterly unwilling to take this chance. It had taken a lot of hard work to get to Philadelphia, and Madison & Co. were grimly determined to make the most of their opportunity.

In response to their critics, Madison and others salved their consciences by pointing out that the People were perfectly free to reject the Convention's handiwork by selecting Anti-Federalist delegates for the ratifying conventions. Didn't this fact justify the Philadelphia Convention in proceeding despite the delegates' failure to win direct popular election?

Not really. It is true, of course, that the Convention's democratic credentials would have been bogus if it had refused to allow *any* electoral process to test the new Constitution. Nonetheless, the Philadelphians were asserting a very great power in forcing the state conventions to consider its proposal instead of countless others that might have been advanced. After all, lots of the alternatives might have prevailed in an up-or-down vote in the state ratifying conventions. But it was the thirty-eight signatories at Philadelphia who effectively determined which one of these proposals would be given a chance. To make matters worse, these unelected gentlemen asserted the authority to trigger a decisive change in ratification rules, which proved absolutely essential to the success of their Constitution.

Given the immense practical importance of these proposal and triggering functions, the Federalists seriously impaired their legitimacy by taking their shortcut—at least when compared with the more democratic paths pursued by later unconventional actors. Both Reconstruction Republicans and New Deal Democrats had to win many more popular elections than their Federalist counterparts before they earned the constitutional authority to make similar decisions in the name of the People. In this important particular, it is they, not the Federalists, who provide the stronger precedents in popular sovereignty.

Turning next to problems of ratification, it is useful to distinguish between the quality of the Founding debate and the quantity of Federalist support. Qualitatively, the debate was remarkably vigorous and often of high quality—though this was also true of the debates generated during Reconstruction and the New Deal. The Founding looks a lot weaker, however, when we turn to quantitative issues. While the overwhelming majority of white males were eligible to vote for convention delegate,[33] participation rates were unspectacular. In only three states was voter turnout higher than the historical norm; in three, lower; in the rest, about the same.[34] Some elections were held in the dead of winter, not the best time for large turnouts.[35] Participation was further depressed by the fact that balloting was not combined with votes for other positions. This meant that candidates for other offices did not have an incentive to bring their followers to the polls, who then might also cast a ballot for a convention delegate.[36]

Worse yet, we will never know for certain whether the Federalists won a majority of the vote, let alone the decisive kind of majority required by the theory of dualist democracy.[37] We simply do not have much reliable electoral data; and these scraps do not support strong claims.[38] In contrast, the electoral returns provide firmer support to the claims of a popular mandate made by Reconstruction Republicans and, especially, New Deal Democrats at later turning points.

Not that two centuries of development have left us anywhere near an ideal system of higher lawmaking. While the achievements of Reconstruction and New Deal have compensated in part for some

Founding failures, they have also contributed new weaknesses to the evolving structures of dualist democracy. Only one thing is clear: Rather than recoiling at the extent to which Reconstruction Republicans and New Deal Democrats departed from the principles and procedures of Article Five, we should be grateful to these latter-day Americans for pushing the struggle for popular sovereignty far beyond the point where the Federalists left it.

BUT IS IT LAW?

At this stage, hyperformalists tend to retreat to a jurisprudential defense of their position. Article Five, they rightly point out, lies at the conceptual core of the American legal system. Consider, for example, Five's relationship to more famous parts of the Constitution, like the First Amendment—protecting free speech, assembly, and religion. While these guarantees define the substance of American freedom, they owe their status as *law* to Article Five: We could not identify the First Amendment as legally binding if it had not been proposed and ratified in conformity with Article Five. More generally, Five provides a fundamental conceptual tool for distinguishing law from politics. Only with the aid of such "rules of recognition" can lawyers and citizens distinguish between judicial disputes over "the law as it is" from political struggles over "the law as it may become." Of course, the hypertextualist does not expect his rule-oriented version of Article Five magically to dissolve all disputes over the meaning of American law. Even after they recognize the First Amendment as binding law, judges must still interpret the meaning of famously difficult phrases like "the establishment of religion." But these interpretive difficulties should not blind us to the role played by Article Five in focusing legal vision. For instance, I know people who think that, despite the First Amendment, America should create a religious establishment. Even they do not suppose, however, that the Constitution *already* authorizes the establishment of a Church of America comparable to the Church of England. A partisan who made such a claim would only reveal how deeply she had confused her own personal ideals with the principles established by the rule of law. But it is only Article Five that allows us to explain to would-be establishmentarians why they are mistaken in ignoring the First Amendment.

Humanistic Positivism?

In elaborating this point, my hypertextualist interlocutor builds on a jurisprudential school that has been (more or less) dominant throughout the twentieth century: legal positivism. Within his account, my rejection of Article Five's exclusivity threatens to dissolve the very idea of a "*rule* of recognition," and hence the very possibility of the rule of law.

There are two ways to resolve this anxiety. The first is to attack positivism head-on; the second is to reinterpret it. Though trashing positivism has been a popular pastime over the last quarter-century,[39] I cannot join this particular bandwagon without making nonsense of my central claim: that in America, the People rule, and judges and other officials have an *obligation* to follow the People when, after appropriate public debate and decision, a mobilized majority hands down new principles to guide the polity. If this dualistic promise is not sheer puffery, positivists are right to insist on "rules of recognition." How else is a judge to determine when the People have spoken? If I cannot explain how, in principle, a judge (or other law-abiding) citizen is to distinguish higher law from his private moral convictions, dualist democracy is hollow at its core.

I accept this challenge—with the proviso that we not settle for a caricature. If my positivist friends demand a "rule of recognition" that permits machine-like application, I will not be able to oblige. But this should prove disconcerting only to those people—if they still exist—who remain entirely in the grip of machine metaphors. While rules have a place in the law, does anybody really think they exhaust the category of legal judgment? Certainly not H. L. A. Hart, who introduced the notion of a "rule of recognition" in his classic *Concept of Law*.[40] Since humans are not machines, they will not be satisfied with rigid rules in their quest for discriminating judgment. They will also work out criteria that are based on the elaboration of abstract principles and insights into the implications of great historical precedents. These reflections resist algorithmic reduction into cut-and-dried rules, but a humanistic positivism should not purge these elements from an account of the legal system's "basic criteria of recognition." The challenge for lawyers and citizens is to become self-conscious about the use of these humanistic elements of legal judgment that elude rule-like formulation.

A Puzzle

To begin this ongoing process, I focus on a conceptual puzzle that may generate great lawyerly resistance, but it is resistance which dissolves upon further reflection. This threshold objection focuses on my emphasis on the legally problematic aspects of the Founding and subsequent exercises in higher lawmaking: "If unconventional lawmaking involves illegal activities, how can it be a matter for *legal* analysis? Isn't the legal analysis of illegality a contradiction in terms?"

Not at all. Lawyers do it all the time. A good example comes from property law. The doctrine of adverse possession allows a concededly illegal occupant of land to perfect his title despite the efforts of the legal owner to regain possession. To qualify for this extraordinary privilege, the adverse possessor cannot slip onto some land in the dead of night and declare himself the rightful owner on break of morning. Instead, the law imposes a set of rigorous conditions—some of which bear a family resemblance to those elaborated in our study of the Founding precedent.[41] For example, property law requires an adverse possessor to assert his proprietary claims to the general public and induce others to accept these claims in practice. This is also true of unconventional lawmaking: without popular acceptance, a "convention's" claims to constitutional authority cannot be based upon the Founding precedent.

Similarly, the law does not allow the adverse possessor to oust the true owner unless he has successfully maintained his dominion for many years. So too in constitutional law. Popular sovereignty cannot be won in a single moment. As at the Founding, a rising reform movement must engage in a temporally extended process—in which it is obliged to defend its claims to speak for the People time and again in a series of escalating institutional contests for popular support.

Another parallel: most American courts protect only those possessors who have publicly asserted a *legal* right to occupy the property. Of course, this "claim of right," as it is called, can't hold up in court— otherwise the claimant wouldn't need the doctrine of adverse possession to protect his interests. Nonetheless, the courts demand some gesture toward legality, however defective it may turn out to be on inspection.

An analogous pattern emerges from our constitutional case studies. It is not as if the Federalists secretly broke into the Assembly Hall in

Philadelphia in the manner of a common thief. They prepared the way for their possession by gaining legalistic authorizations from their state legislatures, and they continued to buttress their appeals to the People with legalistic support from preexisting institutions. These legalistic supports were plainly inadequate, but they *did* exist, and they gave the Federalist campaign a distinctive quality. Just as an adverse possessor's claim of right distinguishes him from the common thief, the Federalists' unconventional bandwagon distinguished them from outright usurpers disdainful of all preexisting forms of legal authority.

There are disanalogies as well. The most important involves the different forms of community acceptance central to the two cases. Adverse possession is grounded in the common law's glorification of custom as a privileged form of community recognition. It may take twenty years or more of uninterrupted daily practice before the courts will allow the adverse posssessor to perfect his legal claims. But it took the Federalists only four years to win a sometimes-grudging recognition that the People had spoken in support of their new Constitution. Property law requires the claimant to establish that his use has been uncontested by others; but the Founding precedent suggests that an act of popular sovereigny is marked by an escalating series of popular contests, in which legitimacy is established by mobilized acts of consent, not passive acts of acquiescence.

These analogies and disanalogies warrant further exploration. But I have said enough to make my main point. Rather than calling upon lawyers to engage in an absurdly paradoxical analysis of illegality, I am asking them to use the same sophistication that property lawyers have deployed for centuries. Conceptually, this involves the use of multiple time frames in legal analysis. As the doctrine of adverse possession teaches, even if an actor is breaking some established legal norms at Time One, his conduct may look very different when placed within the context of a longer temporal pattern that includes Time Two. If property lawyers can engage in this dynamic form of multi-frame analysis, why not constitutional lawyers?

Perhaps it may prove unnecessary to engage in this more complex legal style during periods of normal politics, when all the major protagonists are willing to play by more or less the same rules. But constitutional law is also made for the great crises of the republic, when the authority and meaning of the old rules becomes deeply problematic—and the American people are called, once again, to give new marching orders to their representatives. At these times, dynamic multi-frame analysis becomes imperative. Without it, we shall never come to grips with the distinctive interactions between established institutions and revolutionary reformers that enabled the American people to confront the burning issues of the nineteenth and twentieth centuries, and then—after much bitter, if democratic, debate—to set their government on a new course.

PART TWO

Reconstruction

CHAPTER FOUR

Formalist Dilemmas

The Unasked Question

FOUNDING AND RECONSTRUCTION: two shaping events, but what is their legal relationship to one another?

This is the great unasked question of constitutional law. Orthodox opinion posits, but does not analyze, a textualist answer. Modern lawyers assume that each Reconstruction amendment was processed in strict compliance with Article Five—they were proposed by two-thirds of Congress and ratified by three-fourths of the state legislatures.

This pat answer might be satisfactory if the facts were straightforward. But, as I shall show, they raise questions of dizzying difficulty—in which case, modern evasiveness itself requires explanation. Why should America's lawyers—noted worldwide for their contentiousness—suddenly fall silent when confronting the very foundations of the greatest constitutional event since the Founding?

If I am successful, this curious silence will come to seem an act of desperation. Suppose it turns out that the Thirteenth and Fourteenth Amendments were not proposed and ratified consistently with the principles of Article Five. If hypertextualists were obliged to confront this truth, they would be forced to a shattering choice: Are they really prepared to say that the Emancipation and Equality Amendments are NOT part of the Constitution? If this is the result of "good textual analysis," there is little wonder that hypertextualists turn a blind eye. Surely blissful ignorance is better than the proclamation of such an awful truth?

But there is always a price for acts of repression. By consigning crucial events to the collective unconscious, the legal community bars itself from deeper truths about America's evolving constitutional identity. This might be acceptable if obscurantism were the only way to sustain the validity of the Reconstruction amendments. We are talking, after all, about the greatest statements of moral principle ever pronounced in the name of the American people. But such a bargain between political morality and legal obscurantism is worth paying only as a last resort. Before the next generation builds its constitutional law on a noble lie, it should satisfy itself that the lie is necessary.

This chapter enumerates a series of legal dilemmas that must be resolved if the current orthodoxy is to be vindicated. But the remaining chapters of Part Two do not try to "solve" these dilemmas. Rather, they seek to dissolve them by fashioning a different relationship between Founding and Reconstruction. The dilemmas arise on the assumption that the Republicans could remain faithful to the Founding only by fulfilling Article Five to perfection. Once we free ourselves from this mistake, we can open up a second path linking the 1860's to the 1780's. Though the Republicans played fast and loose with the Federalists' text, perhaps they remained faithful to the precedent established by the Founding practice? During both periods, spokesmen for the People charted a third way between textual regularity and total revolution—unconventionally adapting older institutions to new purposes until the spokesmen for revolutionary reform had earned the constitutional authority to speak for the People. By following the Republicans step by step down this path of democratic adaptation, we will grasp the deeper constitutional dynamics that generate the formalist dilemmas this chapter introduces.

DECEMBER 1865

I begin the drama *in medias res.* The month is December 1865. Lee has surrendered the preceding spring. Six days later, Lincoln is shot. Before his death, he had begun to reconstruct civil authority in four states.[1] After the Confederacy collapses, Andrew Johnson orders his victorious generals to summon new "conventions" of the People in each of the other Southern states. These conventions meet in the summer to repudiate their states' secession ordinances and to revise their antebellum constitutions to abolish slavery. They are quickly succeeded by newly elected state legislatures. Increasingly, the South takes on the appearance of normal government under the Constitution of the United States.

Then comes December 1865, and two fateful events—one involving the Thirteenth Amendment; the other, the Fourteenth.

Some Questions about the Thirteenth Amendment

On December 18, 1865, Secretary of State William Seward proclaims the Thirteenth Amendment ratified by three-fourths of the states. His proclamation includes eight states of the former Confederacy among the twenty-seven signifying assent.[2] As Seward views the situation, all eight are necessary for ratification under Article Five. His proclamation explicitly asserts that thirty-six states are in the Union; hence, twenty-seven is the absolute minimum required by Article Five's three-fourths rule.

At present, I am interested not in Seward's constitutional calculus but in a threshold question: can the hyperformalist avoid elaborate analysis by resting his case on the Secretary's proclamation? After all, I hear him saying, nobody denies that Seward did have twenty-seven ratifications; nor that three-fourths of thirty-six *is* twenty-seven. So where is the problem? Why doesn't the proclamation supply a pat answer to the validity question?

Turn to the second critical event of December 1865. This one comes two weeks earlier. On December 4, the Thirty-ninth Congress meets for the first time, and it immediately confronts the constitutional status of the Southern governments, whose Senators and Representatives demand admission. In memorable scenes (to be described later), this demand was rejected by the Republican majority—which seated only a single Southern state, Tennessee, during its two year term. Indeed, by the end of its deliberations, the Thirty-ninth Congress had publicly declared that "no legal state governments" existed in the other ten states of the South.[3]

All this raises an obvious problem with Secretary Seward's proclamation. If Seward had followed Congress's December 4 decision, he would have struck the eight Southern states from his tally, leaving only nineteen of the requisite twenty-seven state "legislatures" he thought were required for constitutional validity.[4] What, then, gave him authority to ignore the negative Congressional judgment of December 4? Putting the proclamation to one side, how might a hypertextualist defend the legality of the Thirteenth Amendment?

These questions were of the first importance at the time. Consider, for example, Andrew Johnson's veto of the act of Congress declaring that "no legal state governments" existed in the South:

> The bill also denies the legality of the governments of ten of the states which participated in the ratification of the amendment to the Federal Constitution abolishing slavery forever. . . . If this assumption of the bill be correct, their concurrence cannot be considered as having been legally given, and the important fact is made to appear that the consent of three-fourths of the States—the requisite number—has not been constitutionally obtained to the ratification of that amendment, thus leaving the question of slavery where it stood before the amendment was officially declared to have become a part of the Constitution.[5]

It seems odd to rely on Seward's proclamation when the Secretary's boss is on record as having called it into question.

Some Questions about the Fourteenth Amendment

December 4 also casts a cloud on the Fourteenth Amendment. Textualism's charm lies in its promise of a mechanical solution to the problem of legal validity. By looking up a couple of pages in the *Congressional Globe* of June of 1866, the textualist hopes to establish that the amendment had the support of the requisite two-thirds majorities required by Article Five.

Unfortunately, the purge of December 4 makes this simple solution problematic. Before flipping through the pages of the *Globe,* the textualist must persuade himself that the body of Northerners meeting on Capitol Hill in June of 1866 could properly invoke the Article Five powers of "Congress." Every student of the period recognizes that, were it not for the purge of Southern Senators and Representatives, the "Congress" meeting in June would *never* have mustered the two-thirds majorities required to propose the Fourteenth Amendment.[6] Why, then, does the formalist suppose that the terms of Article Five could be satisfied by taking a head count of those Northerners who managed to survive the heat of Washington in the summer of 1866?

Dilemma Number One

We can now put both of these questions together to define a dilemma: while the hypertextualist may hope to rationalize *either* the ratification of the Thirteenth *or* the proposal of the Fourteenth, it will be very hard to vindicate both. To see why, consider the two most promising responses to the questions we have raised.

Begin with the "ratification" of the Thirteenth Amendment. Here the textualist will predictably argue that, notwithstanding the Congressional decision of December 4, Seward was right to count the Southern states among the "legislatures" empowered by Article Five to ratify amendments. But if this argument is sound, where does it leave the Fourteenth Amendment? If the *state assemblies* ratifying the Thirteenth Amendment are "legislatures" for purposes of Article Five, how can the *federal assembly* excluding these states count as a "Congress" when it proposed the Fourteenth Amendment? As the *New York World,* a leading Democratic paper, put the point on December 7, 1865: "The ratification of a constitutional amendment being the highest act a State can perform in its federal relations, competency to do this implies competency for every other. There could be no greater absurdity than to hold that a State can give a valid ratification, and at the same time deny to it any of the rights or functions of complete statehood."[7]

The reverse problem arises if our formalist friend focuses first on the Fourteenth Amendment and persuades us that the Republican caucus *did* have the constitutional authority to exclude representatives of the South. How, then, could Southern legislatures validly participate in the ratification of the Thirteenth Amendment?

I do not say these puzzles cannot be solved, only that some fancy footwork will be required. The forensic challenge is to elaborate an Argument X that will justify the Republicans' exclusion of the Southern Senators and Congressmen *without impugning the status of the governments from which they came.* If the hypertextualist can execute this maneuver successfully, he might have his cake and eat it too. Thanks to X, Congress would be within its rights to proceed without the Southerners and propose the Fourteenth Amendment. But since X does not discredit the Southern governments, the textualist might successfully explain why they remained constitutionally empowered to ratify the Thirteenth Amendment.

Easier said than done: Are there any X's that will serve?

PARADOX LOST?

Perhaps the answer is to be found in Section Five of Article One:

> Each House shall be the Judge of the Elections, Returns and Qualifications of its own Members, and a Majority of each shall constitute a Quorum to do Business.

This text explicitly contemplates Congress retaining its legitimacy even though it excludes some members. Moreover, the Republicans *did* constitute a majority in each House. So why can't Section Five justify exclusion without disparaging the Southern governments?

The problem comes only when we consider how "Congress" exercised its exclusionary powers. At no point did it inquire into the qualifications of particular Southern Senators or Representatives, excluding those, for example, who were disloyal to the Union during the recent war. Rather than rejecting particular men, Congress excluded *all* representatives, however qualified they may have been, from the Southern states.[8]

At this point, the Qualifications Clause must be limited by other textual considerations. Article One asserts that "each State shall have at least one Representative," and Article Five provides that "no State, without its consent, shall be deprived of its equal suffrage in the Senate." Surely Congress cannot use its power to disqualify particular representatives to defeat a state's claim to all representation. If there is a textual warrant for the proscription of the South, it is not the Qualifications Clause.

PARADOX REGAINED

The Republicans' justification, if there is one, is in Article Four:

> Section 4. The United States shall guarantee to every State in this Union a Republican Form of Government.

Suppose that after seizing power in the state, the King of New York dispatches two Dukes to serve in the United States Senate. Surely Congress would be empowered by the Guaranty Clause to reject the King's delegates to the Senate. While the Constitution does guarantee each *state* representation, it does not allow any and all state *governments,* however un-republican they may be, to intrude their representatives into the halls of Congress.

So much is unarguable. But it is trickier to apply this line of thought to the present problem. Unsurprisingly, both sides vigorously brought the Guaranty Clause into play. Beyond assessing the contending arguments, we should consider whether any of them take the special X-form required to resolve the dilemma.

Saving the Thirteenth?

The Southern constitutions of 1865 looked very similar to the antebellum documents, except for the new provisions outlawing slavery. Under the traditional reading of the Guaranty Clause, this was more than enough to satisfy constitutional requirements. As Madison explained in the *Federalist:*

> the authority extends no further than to a *guaranty* of a republican form of government, which supposes a preexisting government of the form which is to be guaranteed. As long, therefore, as the existing republican forms are continued by the States, they are guaranteed by the federal Constitution. Whenever the states may choose to substitute other republican forms, they have a right to do so, and to claim the federal guaranty for the latter. The only restriction imposed on them is, that they shall not exchange republican for anti-republican Constitutions.[9]

Madison's view was repeated in many leading commentaries,[10] and Congress had consistently rejected abolitionist efforts to invoke the Guaranty Clause as a bar to the admission of new slave states.[11] Given these facts, wasn't it odd to suggest that the South had rendered itself un-republican by freeing the slaves? If the old constitutions qualified as republican, surely the new ones did?

This is a very powerful argument, so long as one accepts its traditional premise. Unfortunately, it does not have the X-form: while it supports Seward's proclamation on the Thirteenth Amendment, it denies the authority of Congress to go forward with the Fourteenth. This so-called Congress was instead a Republican Rump that had no business making higher law for the nation. Throughout the period, traditionalists—led by President Johnson—repeatedly and forcefully raised this objection.

Saving the Fourteenth?

But, of course, there was nothing to stop the Republicans from attempting a revolutionary reinterpretation of the Guaranty Clause—one that went beyond antebellum abolitionism in insisting that "republican" government required not merely that blacks be free but that they be enfranchised.[12] Led by Charles Sumner,[13] some Congressional radicals took this step. While Sumner's great speeches served as a rallying point for radical opinion in the country, most Republicans were troubled by the implication that the federal government would have a permanent role in structuring state governments.[14]

Even Sumner found it imprudent to insist upon one of the most obvious implications of his position—if Republican government required black suffrage, why didn't it require women's suffrage?[15] Throughout the debates, conservatives repeatedly used the women's issue to discredit the radical construction of the Guaranty Clause—reducing the formidable Thaddeus Stevens to evasions as he struggled with the implication.[16]

But women's suffrage was hardly the only obstacle on the path toward a principled construction of the Guaranty Clause. Congressional Republicans even found it hard to elaborate a coherent approach to black suffrage. They were painfully aware that only six Northern states had granted blacks the vote by 1865.[17] During the Exclusion Crisis, seven out of nine Northern states defeated proposals for black suffrage in popular referenda.[18] Against this background, it was hard for most Republicans to agree with Sumner that black suffrage was unconditionally required by the Clause. The best they could do was to distinguish their racist Northern constitutions on quantitative grounds: By depriving a third or a half of their male population of the vote, the Southern governments were transforming themselves from republics into oligarchies; in contrast, the Northern exclusions, while regrettable, eliminated such a small percentage from the suffrage that they could not plausibly be considered oligarchic.[19]

Even this convoluted position could not make sense of Congress's treatment of the suffrage question in the Fourteenth Amendment. Section Two of the amendment did not ban the wholesale exclusion of blacks from the polls—this step was taken only in 1869, with the ratification of the Fifteenth Amendment. Instead, it imposed a special sanction upon the exclusion of large proportions of "male citizens twenty-one years of age" from the ballot box. Any state continuing this practice would suffer a proportionate reduction in its representation in the House of Representatives. While this was a serious penalty, it transparently presupposed the continued constitutional legitimacy of such exclusionary practices. How, then, could Congress justify its refusal to seat the returning Southern governments under the Guaranty Clause when it was not even prepared to ban exclusionary practices in the future?

These doubts and hesitations account for the cautious treatment of the Guaranty Clause by the Republican majority when it sought to justify its behavior in a great state paper issued by the Joint Committee on Reconstruction in June 1866. The document, prepared at a moment of grave crisis (to be described later), sought both to justify Congress's power to exclude Southerners and to propose the Fourteenth Amendment. Although the Republicans were determined to use the Clause as their principal legal basis, they could not accept a purely traditionalist account. At the same time, they crafted an interpretation far removed from the Sumnerian claim that the guarantee of republican government required the South to extend suffrage to blacks. Instead of challenging the substance of the new Southern constitutions, the Committee focused upon the process through which they were brought into force:

[I]t would seem that, before being admitted to the participation in the direction of public affairs, such governments should be regularly organized. Long usage has established, and numerous statutes have pointed out, the mode in which this should be done. A convention to frame a form of government should be assembled under competent authority. Ordinarily, this authority emanates from Congress; but, under the peculiar circumstances, your committee is not disposed to criticize the President's action in assuming the power exercised by him in this regard. The convention, when assembled, should frame a constitution of government, which should be submitted to the people for adoption. If adopted, a legislature should be convened to pass the laws necessary to carry it into effect. When a state thus organized claims representation in Congress, the election of representatives should be provided for by law, in accordance with the laws of Congress regulating representation, and the proof that the action taken has been in conformity to law should be submitted to Congress.

In no case have these essential preliminary steps been taken.[20]

When the Committee speaks of "long usage," it is referring to the process by which Congress regulated the admission of territories into statehood. Once a state had entered the Union, however, Congress had strictly followed Madisonian principles.[21] It did not scrutinize the process by which states undertook further constitutional change— which, in fact, was sometimes quite irregular.[22] The only question was whether the end result remained "republican." Since there had never been a case of a state "exchang[ing] republican for anti-republican Constitutions," Congress had never questioned the validity of a government under the Guaranty Clause.[23]

Nevertheless, as the Committee emphasized, Congress had never encountered a total collapse of governmental order like the one experienced in the South after the Civil War. Under the circumstances, its extension of the Guaranty Clause seems plausible, if not compelling.[24] Those textualists who agree have overcome one large hurdle on the path to the formal validity of the Fourteenth Amendment.

But many more hurdles remain. It is one thing to say that Congress could legitimately exclude the South and still pass ordinary legislation; quite another, that it could legitimately propose a constitutional amendment under Article Five.

After all, whatever the merits of the Congressional exclusion of December, one should pause long and think hard before saying that it had deprived the Northern representatives of the authority to call themselves a "Congress" for the purpose of enacting ordinary statutes under the powers vested in them by Article One of the Constitution.[25] Such a conclusion would mean that *no* federal body existed during the critical Reconstruction years that had *any* legitimate lawmaking authority. And the Constitution is not a suicide pact.

But it is a very big leap to a similar grant of power under Article

Five. So long as "Congress" is conceded the power to pass ordinary legislation, anarchy has been avoided. When it comes to Article Five, the textualist is no longer obliged to play fast and loose with basic principles on plea of necessity. Indeed, the text of Article Five imposes a special caution. It contains a final clause that carves out a permanent exception to the general amendment procedures: "no State, without its consent, shall be deprived of its equal suffrage in the Senate." This clause exists on a conceptually more fundamental level than *any* other part of the Constitution. While every other element—including the Guaranty Clause—may be transformed under Article Five, it is only the Senatorial equality of each state that is a permanent part of our Constitution.

Or is it? Given the foundational character of this text, wasn't it especially wrong for the Republicans to proceed with their proposed amendments until Senators from *all* the States could deliberate together on their constitutional destiny?

As we shall see, President Johnson raised these concerns through out the debate, and they certainly should be taken seriously in a thoughtful reading of the text. Many will conclude that, although both Article One and Article Five speak in terms of "Congress," the text granted the Republican Rump powers of ordinary legislation only under One, without granting them higher lawmaking powers under Five. Others, of course, might disagree and think it more plausible to read the word "Congress" to mean the same thing in both contexts.

Suppose you find yourself in the second group. Not only have you persuaded yourself that Congress acted appropriately in excluding the South on December 4 for purposes of normal legislation; you have also decided that the Southern governments were *so* un-republican that they could be deprived of their rights to participate in the Congressional process of higher lawmaking. With this conclusion, you have successfully vindicated the authority of the Thirty-ninth Congress to propose the Fourteenth Amendment.

But not in a way that saves the Thirteenth Amendment. If, as you have just insisted, the Southern governments were un-republican, what justified Secretary Seward's decision to count these very same governments in proclaiming the ratification of the Thirteenth Amendment?

DILEMMA NUMBER TWO: THE RATIFICATION OF THE FOURTEENTH AMENDMENT

Hypertextualists have not yet reached the end of the maze they have created for themselves. As they move from the proposal of the Fourteenth Amendment to its ratification, a second dilemma awaits—one more perplexing than the last. The facts are these: once the Thirty-ninth "Congress" made its proposal, the Fourteenth Amendment was sent to all existing governments of the South as well as the North. When one Southern government, Tennessee, ratified the amendment, the Republicans immediately admitted its representatives to Congress.[26] But the other ten Southern states rapidly rejected the Congressional initiative—often justifying their decision by asserting that they had been unconstitutionally excluded from deliberating and voting on its proposal.[27] Since there were never more than thirty-seven states in the Union during this period, a blocking veto of ten had been assembled. Worse yet, there were important pockets of opposition in the North as well. The Fourteenth Amendment seemed doomed.

Until Congress intervened with a series of Reconstruction Acts in the spring and summer of 1867. These revolutionary statutes divided the ten Southern states into five military districts and placed the Union Army in control of any further transition to statehood. Commanding generals were authorized to call new constitutional "conventions," but only after they had compiled new voting registers that empowered previously voteless blacks while disenfranchising many disloyal whites. After revolutionizing the South's political class, the acts instructed the Army to supervise the election of delegates to constitutional conventions who would then offer their proposals for approval by the (redefined) People of each state before they were finally submitted to Congress.[28] All this required an enthusiastic embrace of Sumnerian understandings of the Guaranty Clause that has not been seen before or since in the history of the Republic.[29]

As I have noted, Sumner himself blanched at the logical implications of his position. Yet the constitutional problems pale by comparison with those encountered at the next statutory stage. Congress was not content to determine whether the new constitutions were truly "republican" before allowing Southern representatives to take their seats on Capitol Hill. Instead, it left them out in the cold until "said

State, by a vote of its legislature elected under said constitution, shall have adopted the amendment to the Constitution of the United States, proposed by the thirty-ninth Congress, and known as article fourteen." Indeed, even ratification would not suffice. The state would remain unrepresented until "said article shall have become a part of the Constitution of the United States."[30] Only then would the bar be raised and military rule be lifted.

These last two Congressional provisions—enacted over presidential veto[31]—are qualitatively different from all that came before. Up to now, it was possible to drape a legal fig leaf over each Congressional action. But at this point, we are in the presence of naked violations of Article Five. These last two Congressional conditions cannot conceivably be justified by the Guaranty Clause, however expansively interpreted—for the simple reason that Congress had, by this point, already approved the states' constitutions as republican. Nevertheless it was still asserting its power to keep the states out in the cold until they went along with its demand to ratify the Fourteenth Amendment.

This demand made hash of Article Five. While the text gives Congress the right to *propose* amendments, it only allows it to determine whether ratification will proceed through state legislatures or state conventions. There is nothing in the text that contemplates Congress overriding a veto by the states of a proposed amendment.

Yet this is what Congress was doing in its Reconstruction Acts. Rather than allowing the republican governments of the South to accept *or* reject the Fourteenth Amendment, it was telling them, loud and clear, that their decision to reject deprived them of all political power in the councils of the nation. This is flat-out inconsistent with the limited Congressional role described by Article Five. It follows that the process by which Congress procured ratification of the Fourteenth Amendment simply cannot be squared with the text.

Not, mind you, that such a breach is unprecedented. As Part One showed, the Federalist Convention stood in precisely the same relationship to the thirteenth Article of Confederation. But this chapter is trying to analyze the Republican initiative in textual terms without investigating the unconventional alternative. Given this limitation, the "ratification" of the Fourteenth Amendment can be nothing less than a revolutionary act—one that is best dealt with by changing the subject.

And yet it is hard to ignore the tell-tale signs of irregularity that peer out from the fifteenth volume of the *Statutes at Large.* The volume displays a proclamation from Secretary Seward dated July 20, 1868. Congressional Reconstruction had been proceeding apace. Thanks to the Union Army, the black-and-white electorates of six Southern states now possessed Congressionally approved constitutions and were now prepared to reverse their predecessors' rejection of the Fourteenth Amendment. As the Secretary explained, he had received ratifications from "newly constituted and newly established bodies *avowing themselves to be and acting as the legislatures,* respectively, of the states of Arkansas, Florida, North Carolina, Louisiana, South Carolina and Alabama" (emphasis supplied).

As Seward read the relevant statutes, they did not authorize him "to determine and decide doubtful questions as to the authenticity of the organization of State legislatures, or as to the power of any State legislature to recall a previous act or resolution of ratification of any amendment proposed to the Constitution."[32] Worse yet, Seward had another problem. Though he was in possession of twenty-three Northern ratifications, two of these were from Ohio and New Jersey, which had formally retracted their prior assents. What was he to do?

The proclamation concludes conditionally, saying that "if the resolutions of the legislatures of Ohio and New Jersey ratifying the aforesaid Amendment are to be deemed as remaining in full force and effect[33] . . ., then the aforesaid Amendment has been ratified."

Congressional reaction was swift and unequivocal. On July 21, both Houses passed a concurrent resolution listing all twenty-nine states as ratifiers of the amendment, declaring it "to be a part of the Constitution of the United States, and it shall be duly promulgated as such by the Secretary of State." This resolution marks the first time Congress asserted the power to pass judgment on the question of ratification.[34]

However unprecedented, it was also entirely successful. On July 28, the Secretary issued a second proclamation "in conformance"[35] with the Congressional resolution of July 21, certifying the amendment's validity. The ratification story ends as it began: with emphatic markers of its legally anomalous character.

As if the problem of ratification were not enough, it is not our only constitutional dilemma. Our previous paradox was also provoked by a Seward proclamation, this one involving the Thirteenth Amendment. A satisfying solution to the problem raised by Seward's twin proclamations of 1868 should also be consistent with the rationale vindicating his earlier proclamation of 1865. But in this proclamation, Seward validated the Thirteenth Amendment on the basis of the eight assents tendered to him by the *white* governments of the South. As a consequence, the hypertextualist must somehow explain why Seward was right to count these white governments when they said Yes on the Thirteenth Amendment but why Congress could destroy these governments in 1867 when they said No, and keep new governments in the cold until they said Yes.

Is there any way out of the textualist wilderness?

Cutting the Gordian Knot?

I have been assuming that the states of the South did not commit constitutional suicide by rebelling against the Union: While the Southern *governments* had forfeited their claim to legitimacy by rebelling, the *people* of the Southern *states* had not forfeited their right to be counted as constituent parts of the Union—provided, of course, that they reestablished republican governments that *were* loyal to the Union.

But this assumption is open to challenge. Most famously, Charles Sumner argued that Alabama et al. had committed suicide and so should not count as "states" in calculating the three-fourths majority required by Article Five. Thaddeus Stevens and others went even further, arguing that the South was a conquered province at the mercy of the United States.[36] While Stevens's theory differed from Sumner's, they had the same implications so far as Article Five was concerned.[37] If only Northern states in the Union should be counted in applying the three-fourths rule, it is easy to establish formal validity for both the Thirteenth and Fourteenth Amendments.[38] With a single conceptual stroke, the textualist may cut his way free of legal perplexity.

Unfortunately, an embrace of Sumner-Stevens mathematics generates even deeper paradoxes of its own. As President Johnson never tired of pointing out, Congress had explicitly assured the nation that the war's object was "to preserve the Union with all the dignity, equality, and rights of the several states unimpaired. . . . As soon as these objects are accomplished the war ought to cease."[39] This was also the official position of the Lincoln Administration throughout the war.[40] Now, after hundreds of thousands had died for the Union, Sumner and Stevens seemed to be saying the rebels were right: the Constitution had not created an indissoluble Union, and the Southern states could be transformed into conquered provinces or mere territories. For this reason Johnson constantly likened them to Southern secessionists, portraying himself as the spokesman for moderates who hoped to steer clear from dis-Unionists of both the South *and* the North.

To parry this thrust, the Republican majority in Congress never formally endorsed Stevens-Sumner radicalism and its embrace of Northern diktat.[41] While Congress used the Union Army to create new voting rolls and supervise reconstruction, success still depended upon the decisions made by the new black-and-white electorate. No less than the President, Congress sought to create a process in which Southern states *consented* to the constitutional solutions emerging from the Civil War. Although the means of obtaining this consent made a hash of the Article Five framework, Congress refused to attempt an even deeper break with constitutional values by publicly proclaiming this consent to be unnecessary. Its response of July 1868 to Secretary Seward proudly listed the assents from the South as well the North, and on *that* basis it declared the Fourteenth Amendment valid. The Supreme Court took the same approach in its 1870 decision of *Texas v. White*.[42] Chief Justice Salmon P. Chase prudently avoided any clear-cut decision on the constitutional status of the white governments established by President Johnson. But he made it very clear that Southern secession had *not* reduced the region to a conquered province: "the Constitution, in all its provisions, looks to an indestructible Union, composed of indestructible States."[43]

It follows, then, that before he follows Stevens and Sumner, the hypertextualist must repudiate a considered Supreme Court holding[44] that crystallized the constitutional consensus emerging from Reconstruction. In taking this step, he would be asserting a position yet more paradoxical than any we have encountered thus far: Repudiating the considered judgments of Presidents Lincoln and Johnson, Congress and the Court, he triumphantly informs us that we may save the validity of the Reconstruction amendments by accepting secessionist opinions of Southern rebels and Northern radicals that never gained the considered endorsement of the American people.

GRASP OF WAR?

Thoughtful hypertextualists often give up the ghost at this point. If we cannot continue to suppress the problematic origins of the Reconstruction amendments, I hear them say, why don't we just make a virtue out of necessity: Granted that the South had not successfully seceded from the Union; nonetheless, the North was within its rights in holding the South within "the grasp of war"[45] until the South accepted its demands. On this view, the Thirteenth and Fourteenth Amendments are part of our Constitution not by virtue of Article Five, but by virtue of Antietam and Gettysburg and the war power.[46]

Without wishing to appear ungracious, I cannot accept this concession without emphasizing its importance. This book's central target is hypertextualism—the naive, but orthodox, view that Article Five provides a framework within which modern lawyers can explain *all* valid amendments since the Founding. Any constitutionalist who accepts the "grasp of war" argument has broken decisively with this orthodoxy. He agrees with me that Reconstruction did not proceed by the old formula, but that the Republicans put together their new regime in a new way. The question is no longer whether hypertextualism is adequate, but what theory of constitutional change should replace it?

"Grasp of war" strikes me as a bad candidate. Most importantly, it would place the Reconstruction amendments on a radically different, and much less attractive, constitutional foundation than all other parts of our Constitution. The Founding, and other amendments, gain their authority from the constitutional will of the American people; but if we accept "grasp of war," the Civil War amendments emerge from the guns of the Union Army.

Maybe we would have to grit our teeth and accept this harsh truth—if it were the truth. But as I hope to show, "grasp of war" is bad history. When the cannons went silent, the constitutional meaning of the war was unresolved. Many answers were possible, none were inevitable. "Grasp of war" does not emerge from a careful study of the facts, but from a misguided jurisprudence which restricts our choices to a sharp dichotomy—*either* the framework of Article Five governed in all its legalistic splendor *or* the legal framework was destroyed and only force reigned.

But the entire point of this book is to reject this dichotomy between legalistic perfection and lawless force. If I am successful, the Civil War's relationship to the Reconstruction amendments will seem similar to the American Revolution's relationship to the Constitution of 1787. After all, the Revolution was itself a civil war, pitting loyalists against patriots in bloody struggle. And yet we do not suppose that the shape of the Constitution of 1787 was determined by the Battle of Yorktown. We believe—and rightly so—that it was the political struggle provoked by the Philadelphia Convention that determined America's constitutional destiny.

So too with the Civil War and Reconstruction. Only after the killing stopped did Americans begin to struggle in earnest over the meaning of the Union victory: Was it simply a vindication of the old Constitution? Did it authorize the construction of a radically new republic? Or something in between? Despite its pseudo-realistic ring, "grasp of war" goes wrong in ignoring the unconventional but profoundly democratic ways in which the American people—in the South as well as the North—exercised a *genuine choice* amongst the constitutional solutions opening up before them.

There is only one way to recover these unconventional structures of popular sovereignty. As with the Federalists, we must follow the Republicans as they moved, step by step, to gain a mandate from the People for their revolutionary reforms of the old regime.

THE SOUNDS OF SILENCE

Since a long and arduous journey lies ahead, I should respond to a common effort to cut it short: *If* you were right, Bruce, and there is a serious problem about the Reconstruction amendments, why haven't lawyers been talking about it? Lord knows, they manage to talk plenty about less important matters! Silence *must* mean that these legal dilemmas have been decisively resolved so long ago that the answers have been lost in the mists of time.

To the contrary, the legal blockage has more proximate sources. In 1939, the Supreme Court announced that it was going out of the Article Five business. Breaking with a long line of precedents, *Coleman v. Miller*[47] declared that Article Five was off limits, raising "political questions" rather than legal ones. Since then, the Court has been true to its word: it has not decided a single case under Article Five. Within a different scholarly culture, this sudden retreat from legalism might have been the source of great curiosity: Why did the Court decide that Article Five was too hot to handle? If Article Five is the hard law that the hypertextualist supposes, why don't courts enforce it? But the fact is that American legal scholars tend to be court-watchers, and when the Court stops talking about an issue, scholars also put it on the back burner.

Indeed, the only time the problem has surfaced was in the 1950's, when Southern law reviews contained a number of articles that revived the Fourteenth Amendment's problematic pedigree as part of the campaign against *Brown v. Board of Education*.[48] Apart from a weak and belated response in a Northern review,[49] mainstream legal opinion generally ignored this Southern challenge.

But lawyers are merely partners in the preservation of the nation's constitutional memory. And if historians had sustained an interest, the problem would not have dropped so completely from view. Consider James Randall's *The Civil War and Reconstruction,* which served from the 1930's through the 1960's as "as the best one-volume history of the Civil War for general readers, and as a textbook for college classes."[50] Here are some highlights from the chapter dealing with "Postwar Politics and Constitutional Change":

> A notable characteristic of this period of Radical rule was its disregard for the Constitution. Nowhere was this attitude more clearly exhibited than in their disregard for form and procedure in the adoption of the fourteenth amendment. . . .
>
> In reality Congress in 1867–68 was not merely submitting an amendment to the states. It was creating fabricated governments in the South, to which there was given not an untrammeled opportunity of voting *Yes* or *No* on the proposed constitutional article, but only the alternative of voting *Yes* or being denied recognition as states in the Union. As a matter of constitutional law the method of amending the Constitution does not lie within the legislative power of Congress. It is prescribed in Article V of the

Constitution . . . It is for Congress to choose between the convention and legislative ratification, but not to create new factors or conditions as part of the amending process. In this case Congress submitted an amendment which was rejected by more than a fourth of the states; then in effect Congress changed the process, providing that ratification must be effected by a specified type of legislature, elected in a manner provided by Congress, a legislature chosen on the basis of Negro suffrage (though this was prior to the adoption of the fifteenth amendment, designed to force such suffrage) . . .

Maintaining that the Southern states were not in the Union until redeemed by Congress, the Radicals were driven to the absurd conclusion that the states could not qualify as members of the Union until after they had performed a function which only members can perform, i.e. ratify a Federal constitutional amendment. . . .[51]

If constitutional lawyers were regularly exposed to such acerbic commentaries from historians, they would find it difficult to maintain their blithe indifference to the paradoxes we have exposed to view.

But the last generation of historians has also turned a blind eye to these puzzles. Eric Foner's outstanding work of 1988, *Reconstruction: America's Unfinished Revolution,* is symptomatic.[52] It aims for a comprehensive synthesis of contemporary scholarship, but this 600-page book omits a sustained treatment of Randall's sharp doctrinal complaints. What happened?

An intellectual revolution. A vast outpouring of scholarship has rewritten the social and political history of Reconstruction. Working from an expanded set of sources, the last generation has managed a mighty demolition job on the pro-Southern biases that had informed historical scholarship since the late nineteenth century. But in one key respect, this revisionist wave has only reinforced an already existing tendency. Over the course of the twentieth century, professional historians have steadily lost interest in matters of technical constitutional doctrine. While early academics like John Burgess and William Dunning treated constitutional questions with high interest, most historians of the 1920's and 1930's were already dismissing constitutional doctrine as a manipulative smoke screen used to cover up more basic social and economic interests. Despite Randall's stature, his concern with legal doctrine was already quite exceptional at midcentury.[53] This dismissive tendency has, if anything,[54] been reinforced by the last generation's fascination with social history. Rather than focusing on the rarefied heights of Capitol Hill, recent historians have preferred to explore the meaning of Reconstruction history for the ordinary men and women of the South.

No less important has been a subtle change in attitude amongst the small but outstanding band of scholars who have sustained a serious legal interest. Speaking broadly, they have sought to avoid the caustic judgmentalism expressed in Randall's commentary. Rather than responding on the merits to Randall's complaints, the best books and articles have proceeded from a more detached interpretivist stance— seeking to understand, rather than judge, the ways law and politics interacted during the period. Much has been gained by this change, but something has been lost—a sense of the anxiety with which Americans saw the higher lawmaking system unraveling before their eyes, and their grim determination to fill the legitimacy gap that had been revealed.

The sense of crisis came on early. By 1862, Sidney George Fisher's great *Trial of the Constitution* was already explaining to his countrymen that they could not rely on the mechanisms for constitutional change provided by Article Five: "We must understand the Fifth Article, as providing one mode by which amendments may be made, not as excluding others."[55] Buttressing this claim with an extraordinary range of arguments that included—but went far beyond—many developed here, Fisher recalled his countrymen to their ultimate responsibility:

> The Constitution belongs to the people,—to the people of 1862, not to those of 1787. It must and will be modified to suit the wishes of the former, by their representatives in Congress, just as the English Constitution has been modified by Parliament, or it will be destroyed. . . . It may be thought, by some, that it would run greater risks if committed to the caprice of the multitude, or to such a Legislature as the multitude elects. But these perils must be encountered in a republic. If the people cannot preserve the Constitution, it must perish, for it cannot be preserved by the Judiciary.[56]

I cannot do justice to Fisher's brilliant speculations.[57] My concern is with the remarkable way Americans rose to his challenge and managed to reaffirm the possibility of popular sovereignty through unconventional adaptations that even Fisher had not foreseen during the darkest days of the war.

CHAPTER FIVE

Presidential Leadership

From Founding to Reconstruction

THE LAST CHAPTER took aim at the prevailing understanding of our constitutional past. This orthodox approach compares the Founding text to Reconstruction practice and supposes that the latter conforms to the former. As this path trails off into deepening dilemmas, it is time to change course. But in what direction?

Perhaps the only honest response is that Reconstruction amounted to a total repudiation of the higher lawmaking principles established at the Founding? This is a provocative hypothesis, but it can be rejected in the end. We need to reinterpret, not repudiate, the Founding legacy. Orthodoxy goes wrong in cutting down the Founding contribution to a single rule in Article Five that authorized the Republicans to amend the Constitution by specified majorities in Congress and the state legislatures. But the Founders contributed their own precedent to posterity as well as a few rules. Once we take this richer legacy into account, the hypothesis of a radical break between Founding and Reconstruction will begin to seem unnecessary and unwise. We will learn much more about our Constitution by seeing Reconstruction as a rather successful adaptation of the Founders' unconventional precedent to nineteenth-century conditions.

Not that the repudiationist is wrong in emphasizing the remarkable features of Reconstruction. He only underestimates the equally remarkable character of the Founding. As we have seen, the Federalists did not suppose they could win constitutional authority by acting according to established operating procedures. They sought to break the hold of previous arrangements by bringing legally problematic "conventions" to the center of the constitutional stage. At the same time, they did not liberate their conventions entirely from preexisting patterns of constitutional authority. They sought to coordinate legalistic and extralegal elements in a distinctive dynamic that ultimately allowed them to *earn* constitutional authority to speak in the name of We the People. The challenge is to understand the Unionist struggle to gain constitutional authority in analogous terms.

Begin by defining a common problem—which I will call the conflict between medium and message. Both Federalists in the 1780's and Unionists in the 1860's carried a constitutional message that was relatively nation-centered for its time and place. Both confronted a lawmaking medium that was relatively state-centered—giving one (1780's) or a small minority (1860's) of states a constitutional veto over the nationalizers' vision of "a more perfect Union." Hence the conflict: "We are increasingly a People of a *United* States," asserted the messengers. "Get the states to agree," asserted the medium.

But, of course, the Federalists were only relatively nation-centered for their time and place. They knew that the American people were not then prepared to opt decisively for the nation over the states. The Federalist regime expressed this ambiguity by creating an exquisite, and uncertain, balance between state and national elements within the governmental structure.[1] Nowhere was this uncertainty more evident than in Article Five. This text presented the central government and the states as equal partners in the process of constitutional revision. A national consensus, no matter how broad or deep, would not generate higher law unless the states, acting as states, gave their free and overwhelming assent.

It is precisely this Federalist premise that the Unionists challenged with ever-greater seriousness during the 1860's—once again to confront the abiding tension between medium and message. Both the Thirteenth and Fourteenth Amendments were revolutionary reforms, committing the national government to intervene when the states trampled upon newly defined rights that adhered to Americans as Americans. Such strong affirmations of nationhood proved to be unachievable within the medium of an Article Five partnership with the states. How, then, were the Unionists to proceed?

Like the Federalists before them, they were unwilling to allow the state-centered medium to discredit their vision of a "more perfect

Union." At the same time, they were unwilling and unable to impose their evolving vision by military fiat. As at the Founding, Reconstruction would emerge only after it had been vigorously tested through a higher lawmaking system that provided opponents with ample opportunities to mobilize their political forces in the country. The difference between the Founding and Reconstruction lies in the institutions used by the Unionists to generate consent. To put my thesis in a single line: rather than calling a second Philadelphia convention, the Unionists adapted the separation of powers between Congress, President, and Court as a great new engine for refining the constitutional will of the American people.

In retrospect, this development may be seen as an organic response by the constitutional system. Long before the Civil War, the separation of powers had been thoroughly entrenched in normal democratic government, providing all political participants with familiar patterns of engagement. What changed in 1860 is not the separation of powers, but the national political agenda. Before Lincoln's election, government was dominated by leaders who tried to defuse the slavery issue through a series of compromises. Once the Republican victory in 1860 dashed these hopes, is it really so surprising that the American people, already socialized into the separation of powers, would use these patterns to deal with the new problems of national self-definition brought to center stage by Lincoln's victory?

Of course, the Unionists who lived through the 1860's were not blessed with twenty-twenty hindsight. Like the Federalists before them, they confronted a failing system of national authority and tried desperately to pick up the pieces by adapting preexisting constitutional vocabularies to rally the nation behind them. As in the 1780's, this consent-building process involved far more than a momentary triumph in a single institution. If the Republican party was going to establish that Americans were now a People of the *United* States, they would have to defend and elaborate this view repeatedly against determined conservative opponents who sought to mobilize the People to defend the more federalist traditions of the 1787 Constitution. As in the case of the Founding, my aim is to elaborate this dynamic pattern of institutional challenge and unconventional response.

The present chapter introduces one great theme by presenting the Thirteenth Amendment as a case study in Presidential leadership.

Article Five does not envision the President playing any role in constitutional revision; but as we have seen, Article Five does not contain the key to the validity of the Reconstruction amendments. To gain the needed insights, we must confront the unconventional ways in which Lincoln and Johnson induced Congress to propose and the states to enact the Thirteenth Amendment. Without reflecting upon their sustained use of Presidential authority, it will prove impossible to explain how the Amendment was enacted, let alone why it is *legitimately* understood as a valid expression of We the People of the *United States.*

As we turn to the Fourteenth Amendment, the constitutional dynamic remains unconventional but takes a turn for a very simple reason—Andrew Johnson defects from the Republicans and transforms the Presidency into the leading opponent of revolutionary reform. This forces the Republicans back upon their remaining stronghold in Congress, and obliges them to develop a model of Congressional leadership that goes far beyond the framework of Article Five. The Fourteenth Amendment ultimately gains legal validity only because the Republicans manage to adapt the separation of powers in ways that allowed Congress to claim credibly that it, and not the President, had won a mandate from the People to move decisively beyond the Thirteenth Amendment in the ways expressed by the Fourteenth.

This shift of the Presidency in midstream will complicate our case study. In Part One, it was enough to follow the Federalists as they moved through one cycle of constitutional creation, beginning at Annapolis and ending in Rhode Island. But this time we must explore two turns of the unconventional cycle—first as the Republicans vindicate Presidential leadership in the enactment of the Thirteenth Amendment, then as they vindicate Congressional leadership in the enactment of the Fourteenth.

To facilitate comparisons between the 1860's and the 1780's, I will be carrying forward the framework that emerged from our study of the Founding. The present chapter begins with the election of Abraham Lincoln in 1860 and how it operated as a *signal* for an intensive round of unconventional constitutional activity; it then proceeds to Lincoln's Emancipation Proclamation, and its use in the Presidential elections of 1864, to provide a mandate from the People that legitimated the Congressional *proposal* of the Thirteenth Amendment; then to the ways Andrew Johnson used Presidential power to *trigger* an unconventional process of ratification in the Southern states; then to describe how the President managed *to win unconventional ratifications* from the Southern states; and finally to the role played by Seward's proclamation of December 18, 1865, in *consolidating* the new amendment. While this framework may seem overly formulaic, keep in mind the functional logic of each step—the American people could hardly be said to exercise their popular sovereignty without a credible signal that reformers were seriously planning a constitutional transformation, without learning the outlines of the proposal, and so on.[2] Our aim, in short, is to uncover the recurring pragmatic basis for the exercise of popular sovereignty in the United States.

This said, the two Reconstruction cycles share two common themes that set them apart from the Founding. The first is the crucial importance of the rigid electoral schedule established by the Constitution. Despite a very bloody war, nobody took seriously the possibility of suspending elections, which served as a fixed anchor for the rapidly evolving system of unconventional authority. In the interim between elections, President and Congress might launch dramatic and problematic initiatives in the name of the American people. But everybody recognized that these revolutionary initiatives would be repudiated if their opponents won the next election.

By the same token, if the reformers won at the polls, their victory would vastly enhance their constitutional authority. Republicans could claim that their bitterly contested initiatives had now been vindicated by a "mandate from the People," and they would press their mandate aggressively upon the other branches of American government on both the federal and state levels.

These populistic assertions of power would then be transmuted by a second basic reality. Most American officials are elected on a fixed calendar, but not the same calendar. As a consequence, it is very difficult for a rising political movement to gain a quick ascendancy over all the relevant centers of power. As Republicans won particular elections, they would repeatedly encounter holdovers in other centers of power who looked upon their claims to a popular mandate with great skepticism. To the members of these conservative branches, the

Republicans looked more like irresponsible demagogues than inspired prophets of a new higher law.

And yet the remaining conservatives could not casually dismiss the Republicans' talk of a mandate too quickly. Thanks to the electoral calendar, the holdovers knew that they would encounter their day of popular judgment in the not-too-distant future. If the Republican flood tide continued unabated, would they be overwhelmed at the polls unless they ostentatiously cooperated with the spokesmen for the new order? If so, perhaps it was more prudent for the holdovers to cooperate with the Republicans before they lost their jobs. I will call this option "the switch in time," and we will see it recur with considerable frequency.

But nothing forced the conservative branches to switch. They could always opt for continued resistance: if they reacted to the Republican assertion of authority with an inspired defense of the old order, perhaps they might bring the People to their senses?

This choice—between switching and fighting—will arise in a variety of institutional settings. And the decisions made by the conservative branches will have a decisive effect on the ensuing dynamic. When conservatives chose to cooperate with the assertive Republicans, the result was a "bandwagon effect"—as at the Founding, the revolutionary reformers gained greatly enhanced credibility if standpatters recognized their popular mandate. When conservatives resisted, the result was an intensification of constitutional debate. With the separation of powers threatening an impasse between resistant conservatives and assertive reformers, both sides were spurred to greater heights of popular mobilization at the next election. It is only by repeatedly winning this cycle of popular election and institutional confrontation that the Republicans finally gained the constitutional authority needed to hand down the Thirteenth and the Fourteenth Amendments in the name of We the People of the *United* States.

But, of course, this underlying dynamic—and much else besides—was hidden in the mists of time when the Republican Party capped its meteoric rise during the 1850's by nominating Abraham Lincoln for the Presidency. Like the Federalists on the road to the Annapolis Convention, the Republicans on the road to their nominating Convention did not have the slightest idea how it would all turn out. Only one thing *was* clear to Lincoln and his party: existing arrangements were tending toward disaster unless the People would take control of their government and send it in a fundamentally new direction.

STAGE ONE: PRESIDENTIAL SIGNALING

In turning to the election of 1860, I focus first on the Presidency more than on Lincoln, and consider how far it had already departed from the Founding design. One of the Framers' greatest fears was that the Presidency might become the object of excited popular mobilizations on behalf of stirring constitutional principles. Converting the chief magistrate into a popular tribune would enable unscrupulous demagogues to follow Caesar and Cromwell down the path to dictatorship. In response to these fears, the Framers created an Electoral College that aimed to screen out populistic types in favor of men like Washington whose prior public service had established a pattern of resistance to Caesaristic temptation. It was past service to the Republic, not the promise of great constitutional transformation, that was the touchstone of the Founding conception of the Presidency.

But the Electoral College, and the ideal it represented, was the first great casualty of constitutional history, shattered by a potent mixture of personality and organization. The leading personalities were Thomas Jefferson and Andrew Jackson, who began to impress the office with plebiscitarian meanings. The leading organization was the mass political party, for whom the quadrennial struggle for the Presidency became a central event. After Jackson's Presidency, these contests sometimes centered on little more than personality and patronage. Nonetheless, they also functioned as a new conveyor belt of populist legitimacy, allowing the winning Presidential candidate to claim a mandate from the People that would have horrified the Founders. This nineteenth-century transformation was only partial and gradual—especially when judged by twentieth-century standards. Nonetheless, the plebiscitarian Presidency had achieved sufficient historical weight by the 1850's to give Lincoln's election a threatening meaning to the South. Rather than serving as a limited chief magistrate, would the new President use his office to inaugurate a constitutional revolution in the manner of Jefferson or Jackson?[3]

By saying that the election of Lincoln performed a *signaling* function, I mean to analogize it to the Annapolis Convention and the Continental Congress at the Founding. In calling for the Philadelphia Convention, these bodies did something that fell far short of a concrete constitutional proposal. Nonetheless, they did something terribly important—signaling that the new movement had gained sufficient political authority to demand that others take its constitutional intentions seriously. By midcentury, the capture of the Presidency had become a similar symbol of constitutional seriousness.

Without this development, it is hard to understand why the South reacted with such alarm to the election returns. In choosing Lincoln, the Republicans had selected a moderate conciliator over fire-eaters like Seward and Chase.[4] Lincoln's moderating propensities would be reinforced by his failure to win more than 40 percent of the popular vote.[5] What is more, the Republicans remained a Congressional minority,[6] and the Supreme Court remained solidly Southern in its interpretive sympathies. Within this setting, Lincoln's victory would not have been earthshaking if the Founding vision of the Presidency as the office of chief magistrate had retained its vitality.

But Southerners were right to think that this vision had failed to sustain itself, and that the election was a signal that the American people—at least in the North—were no longer willing to allow the old compromises with slavery to go unchallenged. This plebiscitarian meaning catalyzed a burst of higher lawmaking activity by opponents who sought to prevent the emergence of a new Presidential tribune. Between Lincoln's election in November and his inauguration in March, conservatives used traditional Federalist models in three different ways to eliminate the transformative connotations of the Presidential signal.

Higher Lawmaking by Normal Institutions

President Buchanan and the Thirty-sixth Congress, both lame ducks, immediately began the search for a "Compromise of 1860" by framing constitutional amendments that would neutralize the meaning of the election. Early in December, Buchanan suggested an "explanatory" amendment which would, among other things, protect slavery in the states and territories.[7] Since the Republicans had won the White House on a platform explicitly prohibiting the extension of slavery,[8] they moved decisively to protect their "mandate." Here is Republican Senator Ben Wade responding to the Democratic initiative:

> But what have we to compromise? Sir, I am one of those who went forth with zeal to maintain the principles of the great Republican party. In a constitutional way we met, as you met. We nominated our candidates for President and Vice President, and you did the same for yourselves. The issue was made up; and we went to the people on it. Although we have been usually in the minority; although we have been generally beaten, yet, this time, the justice of our principles, and the maladministration of the Government in your hands, convinced the people that a change ought to be wrought; and after you had tried your utmost, and we had tried our utmost, we beat you; and we beat you upon the plainest and most palpable issue that ever was presented to the American people, and one that they understood the best. . . . Sir, I know not what others may do; but I tell you that, with the verdict of the people given in favor of the platform upon which our candidates have been elected, so far as I am concerned, I would suffer anything to come before I would compromise that away.[9]

Conservatives were unimpressed.[10] They denied that Lincoln's minority victory amounted to a mandate for anything and tried to hammer out new constitutional limits on the ascendant Republicans. The most important initiative was Senator John J. Crittenden's package of unamendable amendments.[11] His plan, no less than Buchanan's, challenged the Republicans by authorizing the controlled extension of slavery in the territories. Since this initiative had no chance of ratification by Republican legislatures in the North, Crittenden proposed ratification by state conventions.[12] When the Republicans tried to kill his proposal in committee,[13] Crittenden took to the floor with an unprecedented demand for a national referendum:

> Sir, it may be that we are spell-bound in our party politics, and in opinions which they have generated, and fastened and bound upon us against our will; but I appeal with confidence to that great source from which we derive our power. When the people are in danger, and the people's institutions, I appeal with confidence to them. If we are at fault, if we cannot combine the requisite majority here to propose amendments to the Consti-

tution which may be necessary to the settlement of our present difficulties, the people can. . . .[14]

While Crittenden and William Bigler, the referendum's most vocal supporters, portrayed the vote as more consultative than binding, their proposal aimed to supplant the electoral mandate claimed by the Republicans.[15] But Article Five did not provide for a direct referendum. Though Republicans were bombarded with petitions in favor of the compromise,[16] they refused to endorse Crittenden's end run around Article Five, protecting the integrity of their Presidential mandate from Crittenden's unconventional effort to construct an alternative, and opposing, signal.[17]

The Washington Peace Convention

As Article Five initiatives sputtered, Americans sought to to save the Union by a direct appeal to the precedent established by the Philadelphia Convention. As in the 1780's, the call for a Philadelphia-style convention came from Virginia's General Assembly.[18] The response was overwhelming. Apart from seven Southern states that had already seceded, every state but three sent delegations to Washington—despite the fact that Congress had not authorized the convention under Article Five.[19] Even more remarkably, the Washington Convention quickly hammered out a complex constitutional compromise. By February, it was prepared to submit its proposal to the lame-duck Congress and the nation.[20]

But at this point, the institutional bandwagon came to a screeching halt. At a similar stage of the Founding, the Continental Congress agreed—after bitter debate—to forward the Philadelphia Convention's proposals to the states.[21] The same debate recurred in the Thirty-sixth Congress—with Crittenden, playing the role of James Madison, urging his fellow Senators to defer to the authority of the convention.[22] But the Republicans rejected this initiative just hours before Lincoln's inauguration.[23] In doing so, they prevented a return to eighteenth-century precedents and preserved the nineteenth-century mandate they believed they had earned by electing a President.

Secessionist Conventions

As this was going on, Southerners were successfully organizing "conventions" that enacted secession ordinances in the name of We the People. In hindsight, these turned out to be the first steps in the formation of the Southern Confederacy. But they were also moves within the framework of the Federal Union, inviting a peaceful renegotiation of the basic terms of the Constitution.[24] This was hardly the first time individual states had taken dramatic, and legally problematic, measures to protest federal policy, and the Union had managed to accommodate their protests.[25] The first wave of secession only swept through the seven states of the Deep South, amidst widespread doubts as to this constricted region's economic and political viability. Who was to say, then, whether the Southern "conventions" would provoke yet another effort to redefine the old Union in the name of We the People of the United States—an effort that might be credible despite its illegality under Article Five?

Institutionally speaking, the answer was in the hands of the President of the United States. If an unconventional process of accommodation was possible—and I do *not* say that it was—it would have required a lot more time. And it was precisely this that Lincoln did not allow. While President Buchanan had rejected any military response to secession,[26] Lincoln's decision to reinforce Forts Sumter and Pickens brought the higher lawmaking process to an end.[27] It was not merely a Presidential election that operated as a higher lawmaking signal; it was a Presidential decision that decisively transformed the South's unconventional activity into a challenge requiring a military solution.

STAGE TWO: PROPOSAL

Given the President's decision, the status of the secession ordinances would be determined on the battlefield. But was there anything more at stake?

At first, the answer was No. In the early months of the war, both President and Congress unequivocally affirmed that their aim was "to preserve the Constitution as it is, the Union as it was."[28] During 1862, Congress chipped away at slavery within Union territory,[29] but it was only the President's Emancipation Proclamation that sought to establish that all slaves within the rebel territory "shall be . . . forever free."[30]

The Proclamation and Its Problems

Despite this strong language, the proclamation was a tentative and problematic document. It only "emancipated" blacks where the Union writ did not run, specifically exempting the four loyal slave states and all Southern areas under Union military control.[31] Worse yet, it acted under a claim of "military necessity," allowing Southerners to argue, after the war, that the President's powers as commander-in-chief did not authorize a legal revolution behind the lines.[32] Indeed, the proclamation almost encouraged such questions. Rather than urging blacks to destabilize the Confederate war effort, it "enjoin[ed] . . . the people so declared to be free to abstain from all violence, unless in necessary self-defense; and I recommend to them that in all cases when allowed they labor faithfully for reasonable wages."[33] Jurisdictionally ineffective, constitutionally doubtful, the Emancipation Proclamation even recognized slave owners as holders of legitimate property rights. Lincoln announced that he would "in due time recommend that all citizens of the United States who shall have remained loyal . . . be compensated for all losses . . ., including the loss of slaves."[34]

But none of these caveats should undercut the proclamation's profound constitutional meaning. For most Americans, the proclamation is a symbol comparable to the Constitution itself as a landmark of American liberty. But for most lawyers, it has no similar significance. This gap between popular and legal understanding is due to the hypertextualist view of the amendment process. Within the Article Five structure, the proclamation is no more than a melodramatic prelude to the serious business, which begins two years later with the Thirty-eighth Congress proposing the Thirteenth Amendment on January 31, 1865. But if we use the Founding precedent, and not the text, as our orienting framework, we can see the proclamation for what it was: neither a final decision, nor a meaningless symbol, but an unconventional proposal like the one made earlier at Philadelphia. Just as the Convention of 1787 precipitated an institutional bandwagon that ultimately gave its proposal a powerful mandate from the People, so did President Lincoln.

To the People: The Elections of 1862 and 1864

The President announced a preliminary proclamation on September 22, giving the rebels one hundred days to surrender before they lost their slaves on January 1. This proclamation became one of the central issues in the 1862 elections.[35] Would the people vote the Republicans out of power in Congress, depriving the President of support for his proposal?

When the votes were all in, the question remained open. The Republicans retained control over Congress and defeated legislative efforts to undermine the proclamation, but their House majority had been reduced from from thirty-five to eighteen.[36] Despite these equivocal results, Lincoln pushed forward with his final proclamation of January 1.[37]

The country erupted.[38] Lincoln's act was heralded by the long-suffering abolitionists as "a great historic event, sublime in its magnitude, momentous and beneficient in its far reaching consequences"[39] and condemned by the South and the Democrats as the realization of their fears of 1860.[40]

The President was under no illusions. He knew that Republicans had won election in 1860 on a platform prohibiting the extension of slavery to the territories, not the emancipation of slaves in the states. He recalled the lines of his first inaugural, denying both his power and his inclination to interfere with slavery in the states.[41] Within this context, the "forever free" in the proclamation might last as long as the next Presidential election. If a Democrat returned to the White House after 1864, what was to prevent him from issuing a new proclamation repudiating emancipation?

Lincoln's annual message was not particularly reassuring: "[W]hile I remain in my present position I shall not attempt to retract or modify the emancipation proclamation, nor shall I return to slavery any person who is free by the terms of that proclamation or by any acts of Congress."[42] Nor was Congress willing to place the President's action on a firmer constitutional foundation.[43] The merits of a formal constitutional amendment were debated passionately throughout the first session of the Thirty-eighth Congress.[44] The Senate passed a version in April 1864, but House Democrats—their numbers enhanced by the 1862 elections—voted against, depriving it of the necessary two-thirds majority. Conceding defeat, Representative James Ashley refused to call the amendment to the floor for reconsideration, but with this warning: "The record is made up and we must go to the country on this issue thus presented. When the verdict is rendered next November I trust that Congress will return determined to ingraft that verdict into the national Constitution. I therefore give notice to the House and the country that I will call up this proposition at the earliest possible moment after our meeting in December next."[45]

When Ashley spoke, the future looked grim. With Grant stuck before Richmond and Sherman not yet in Atlanta, widespread uncertainty gripped the North. The Democratic platform flirted with Copperhead notions of immediate peace, and its candidate, Union General George McClellan, was on record against emancipation. The Republicans united behind the President only with difficulty.[46] But once Lincoln reasserted his leadership, he insisted on a platform that called for a constitutional amendment to abolish slavery and support "especially, the Proclamation of Emancipation."[47] With the issue joined, the election gained a special significance. Harold Hyman puts it well: "What was different in 1864 was the intense interest of ordinary voters in issues and principles, men and measures, causes and aspirations."[48]

The Republicans emerged with the decisive victory that had previously eluded them. Lincoln won 55 percent of the popular vote and beat McClellan by a margin of 212 to 12 in the Electoral College.[49] At the same time, Republicans won 145 of the 185 Northern seats in the House and commanded a 42-to-10 super-majority in the Senate.[50] Given the sharp Republican-Democrat division on emancipation in Congress and the campaign, the victorious party "could regard its success at the polls as a popular mandate for [the] amendment."[51]

The Switch in Time

Lincoln moved immediately to transform the excited talk of a popular mandate into the enduring shape of a constitutional amendment. He did "not claim that the election has imposed a duty on members to change their views [on the Thirteenth Amendment]. . . . [But] the voice of the people now for the first time [has been] heard upon the question."[52]

The lame-duck Congress responded positively. With Lincoln himself lobbying key Democrats,[53] enough switched to push the amendment over the two-thirds threshold. Here is Democrat Anson Herrick explaining his changed vote:

> Stripped of all side issues the main question presented [in the 1864 elections] to the people for their decision was whether slavery should be abolished and the seceded States coerced into allegiance to the Constitution, as it is now proposed to amend it, or whether the war should be speedily terminated and the aegis of the Constitution thrown around the social system of the South. The people by a large majority indorsed the policy of the Administration on the slavery issue, and I am now disposed to bow in submission to that popular decree.[54]

On January 31, 1865, the House joined the Senate in proposing the Thirteenth Amendment.[55]

This was an important milestone, and we should be clear about its precise role. Congressional action was not required to place Americans on notice that emancipation had become the central constitutional issue on the nation's agenda: the President's proclamation had done *that* much. Nor did it serve to place the proposed amendment on impeccable legal foundations. Since the war was still raging, "Congress" was the name of an assembly which represented only twenty-five of the thirty-six states of the Union—and Democrats used this fact to deny that a formal proposal was constitutionally appropriate.[56]

The Congressional decision is best seen as part of the Republicans' effort to create an institutional bandwagon similar to the one generated at the Founding—but this time the bandwagon was being constructed out of institutional materials that had only been created in 1787. Within the emerging pattern, the Presidency and the system of national elections had begun to interact together to generate a powerful legitimating dynamic. By the time Congress had acted, the President's unconventional proclamation had catalyzed a broad-ranging national debate that had already shaped the meaning of two general elections. When sustained Presidential leadership finally met with decisive voter response in 1864, the Republicans could claim that there was something more than a normal political victory involved.

To anticipate predictable misunderstandings, I do not wish to present the election of 1864 as a cut-and-dried plebiscite of the kind favored in European constitutional practice. There was something more subtle at work. By providing the party of revolutionary reform with a decisive victory at the polls, the election gave the reformers new momentum in their struggle with conservative institutions—in this case, the House of Representatives. Paradoxically, this made the conservatives the arbiter of the existence of the "mandate." If House Democrats had stood firm in rejecting the Thirteenth Amendment, the President would have been in a terribly weakened position in the great constitutional struggles that lie ahead. But by allowing Congress to make a "switch in time" in response to the election, the Democrats greatly enhanced the Republicans' plebiscitarian claims. With the Democratic switch, Republican talk of a mandate could no longer be dismissed as normal political puffery: *Why else would the conservative institution have switched, if it were not because slavery's traditional friends were coming to recognize, however reluctantly, that the American People had determined to emancipate the blacks?*

This is, of course, the same unconventional logic that we saw at work at the Founding. To schematize the bandwagon effect thus far: The President issued (1) a preliminary proclamation that (2) was followed by ambiguous results in the midterm elections, (3) but the President continued with his constitutional leadership by issuing a final proclamation that (4) Congress refused to reinforce until (5) the sweeping Republican victories of 1864, which led immediately to (6) the formal proposal of the Thirteenth Amendment.

A Formalist Gesture

Since Presidential leadership had served as the engine of this process, there was a deep logic to Lincoln's next step. During the antebellum period, Presidents had never participated formally in the Article Five process. Although the Constitution required the two Houses to present him with "*every* order, resolution, or vote,"[57] this was not the early practice for constitutional amendments. Proposals by Congress had been sent directly to the states for ratification without a Presidential signature. This practice, upheld in an opaque Supreme Court decision of 1798,[58] reflected the original understanding of the President as a chief magistrate insulated from plebiscitarian appeals to the People.

Given Lincoln's central role in generating the popular mandate for emancipation, it is entirely appropriate that he broke these early precedents based on a different model of the Presidency. While Lincoln's decision to sign the proposed amendment provoked a protest from Capitol Hill, it stands to this day as a formal symbol of a deeper transformation in the higher lawmaking system.[59]

PRESIDENTIAL TRIGGERING

Contrast the moment when Lincoln signed the amendment to the day, two years earlier, he signed the proclamation. Thanks to the bandwagon effect, emancipation was no longer the unilateral act of a single branch; it had become the solemn proposal of *all* the political branches of the national government. Congress had reinforced the proclamation substantively as well as institutionally. The amendment proposed to liberate all slaves, including those in the states that had remained loyal to the Union.

But its future was not secure. By expanding the proclamation's proposal to embrace the entire nation, Congress increased the risk that Northern states would reject it—as happened in Delaware on February 8, Kentucky, on February 24, and New Jersey, on March 16.[60] These rejections, in turn, made it easier for the eleven Southern states to hop on the rejectionist bandwagon as they returned to the Union.

The grim prospects were dramatized by Lincoln's first reaction to the news of the amendment's approval by Congress. Both he and Seward were on the ship *River Queen* discussing an end to hostilities with commissioners from the Confederacy. William McFeely provides a good account:

> During the discussion, the Confederates were told that the Thirteenth Amendment . . . had now cleared the House and was being sent to the states for ratification. . . . Lincoln stated his position that he would countenance no reenslavement of people freed under the Emancipation Proclamation, but he listened as the secretary of state suggested that if "the Southern States will return to the Union, . . . with their own strength and

the aid of the connections they will form with other States, this amendment will be defeated." . . .

Lincoln, at this point, had a different suggestion to make to his old Whig friend Stephens: "If I were in Georgia . . . I would go home and get the Governor . . . to call the Legislature together, and get them to recall all the State troops from the war . . . and ratify this Constitutional Amendment prospectively, so as to take effect—say in five years. . . . Slavery is doomed." . . .

Lincoln then reiterated his support of the Emancipation Proclamation and said he would not permit any people freed by it to be re-enslaved. However, when Stephens questioned him he agreed that the Emancipation was a war measure and conceded that those who had not been freed by the time peace was established might still be slaves in the eyes of the law.[61]

These remarks were made in secret and may be discounted as a negotiating ploy. At the very least, they suggest anxiety about ratification prospects. So does Lincoln's very last public address. This was a defense of his reconstruction policy in Louisiana against radical critics. His speech conceded many inadequacies but closed cautiously:

> Again, if we reject Louisiana, we also reject one vote in favor of the proposed amendment to the national constitution. To meet this proposition, it has been argued that no more than three fourths of those States which have not attempted secession are necessary to validly ratify the amendment. I do not commit myself against this, further than to say that such a ratification would be questionable, and sure to be persistently questioned; while a ratification by three fourths of all the States would be unquestioned and unquestionable.[62]

We are reaching the same moment of truth confronted by the Philadelphia Convention when it broke with the preexisting ratification system established by the Articles of Confederation. As we saw, even adventurers like Hamilton blanched at the prospect of a decisive break but went along in the end. Lincoln's ongoing confrontation was then cut off by John Wilkes Booth's bullet. But the problem would not go away: Would the Thirteenth Amendment be ratified on the basis of purely Northern votes? Would national institutions passively allow the eleven states of the South to vote the Thirteenth Amendment up or down as they saw fit? Or would an unconventional solution be found to the triggering problem?

As a stunned nation mourned its loss, one thing became clear: the

Presidency was not dead, and would continue to exercise constitutional leadership. Rather than calling Congress into special session, Andrew Johnson allowed the constitutional calendar to run its course. Seven months would elapse between Lincoln's assassination in April and the first session of the Thirty-ninth Congress in December. During this period, the Presidency would be the only authoritative spokesmen for the United States government, and Johnson used all his powers—and then some—to insure the prompt ratification of the Thirteenth Amendment.

While Lincoln had previously constructed loyal state governments in Arkansas, Louisiana, Tennessee, and Virginia, it was up to Johnson to establish interim policy for the remaining seven Southern states.[63] He responded with a strategic mix of legal and extralegal elements. Certain aspects of his North Carolina Proclamation—which served as a model for the six other states—provided the appearance of legalism if the President's experiment proved successful and the South speedily ratified the Thirteenth Amendment. From this angle, the proclamation's crucial aspect was its decision to treat the states as if they had never legitimately abandoned their antebellum constitutions. In summoning a new constitutional convention, the proclamation specified that the only people who could vote for, or participate as, delegates were citizens qualified to vote "under the Constitution and laws of the State of North Carolina in force immediately before the 20th day of May, A.D. 1861, the date of the so-called ordinance of secession." Substantively, this meant that only whites would be passing on the amendment; formally, it seemed to envision the legalistic restoration of preexisting constitutional authority.

But appearances were deceiving. The proclamations were simultaneously creating concepts and institutions that belied their legalisms. On the textual level, the most significant unconventional element was introduced by the recurrent insistence that only "loyal" citizens of each state could participate in the process of Unionist restoration. To provide a framework for "loyalty," Johnson issued a second proclamation requiring an amnesty oath from all who hoped to qualify for a Presidential pardon. In providing such a system, Johnson followed in Lincoln's footsteps—but with a key difference. So far as slavery was concerned, Lincoln simply required affiants to swear that they would:

faithfully support all acts of congress passed during the existing rebellion with reference to slaves, *so long and so far as not repealed, modified, or held void by congress, or by decision of the supreme court;* that I will, in like manner, abide by and faithfully support all proclamations of the President made during the existing rebellion having reference to slaves, *so long and so far as not modified or declared void by decision of the supreme court.* So help me God.[64]

Johnson's amnesty oath required:

> I, —— ——, do solemnly swear (or affirm), in presence of Almighty God, that I will henceforth support, protect, and defend the Constitution of the United States and the Union of the States thereunder, and that I will *in like manner abide by and faithfully support all laws and proclamations which have been made during the existing rebellion with reference to the emancipation of slaves.* So help me God.[65]

A pardon, according to Johnson, now required unconditional support of the Emancipation Proclamation—identical to the loyalty owed to the Constitution itself!

The remarkable character of this demand was widely noted at the time.[66] To bring the point home, consider a hypothetical case in a more contemporary setting. Suppose that, over the next decade, the women's movement sought to place abortion rights on a deeper foundation by enacting a freedom of choice amendment. After years of political struggle, it was nearing its goal: Congress had proposed an amendment and about half the state legislatures had ratified it. This political success, however, served only to drive opponents to more violent measures. Right-to-Life rallies increasingly degenerated into mass riots requiring federal troops to restore order. With the jailhouses overflowing, the President—who had gained the White House on the Freedom of Choice ticket—ponders his next move. Citing Andrew Johnson's action as a precedent, he offers an amnesty to all Right-to-Lifers, provided they are willing to swear to "abide by and faithfully support *Roe v. Wade* and all other laws with reference to abortion." If they do not sign, the President threatens them with long prison terms. The Right-to-Lifers sign, and proceed from jailhouse to courthouse, demanding a release from the restraints on political participation imposed by their oath. Surely the Supreme Court should vindicate the Right-to-Lifers?

I do not deny that Presidents have broad discretion to grant conditional pardons. But not when they strike at the very core of the First Amendment, especially when the President is trying to silence opposition at a critical time—the moment at which the fate of a higher lawmaking initiative is to be determined in the name of the People. And yet this was precisely the point of Johnson's amnesty oath, when read in conjunction with the North Carolina Proclamation.

The President, in short, was engaged in an unconventional triggering operation. By insisting that North Carolina be organized by "people . . . who are loyal to the United States, and no others," and defining loyalty as requiring support of emancipation, the President had shifted the constitutional baseline from the one established by Article Five. Under Five, state legislatures are free to accept or reject a proposed amendment without endangering their standing in the Union. But this was not the choice presented by the President and his agents: Southern legislators could exercise their Article Five veto and reject the Thirteenth Amendment *only at the risk of tainting themselves and their states as disloyal to the Union.*

But the President was not content with the subtleties of legal implication. He created a powerful provisional governor in each Southern state to represent the national interest—as the President chose to define it. As set out in the North Carolina Proclamation, the governor's role was defined rather narrowly: he was to proceed, "at the earliest practicable period," to supervise the selection of delegates to a convention to "enable such loyal people of the State of North Carolina to restore said State to its constitutional relations to the Federal Government and to present such a republican form of State government as will entitle the State to the guaranty therefore." But as we shall see, the President extended these powers when the ratification effort began to stall. In short, the President had developed a new kind of triggering device—call it *unconventional delegitimation*—that will recur at future crises in American history.

Speaking broadly, white Southerners responded to the President's project by searching for an intermediate solution. They did not elect Confederate firebrands to serve as convention delegates. But they also denied support to a white leadership committed to advanced Republican principles of racial equality. The Southern conventions and legislatures of 1865 were generally dominated by "reluctant Confederates"—who had gone with their states during the war but had been cool or opposed to disunion before secession. These men were unwilling to sacrifice their emerging leadership positions by assenting to a federal *diktat* their constituents considered illegitimate.[67] They thought they had a choice on matters like the Thirteenth Amendment.

But it would not be a choice made within the framework of federal-state partnership envisioned by the Federalists of the eighteenth century.

Unconventional Ratification

To sketch the subtleties of Presidential triggering, I follow the paper trail left by Johnson in two states—one that rejected the Thirteenth Amendment, another that ratified it.

Mississippi

As the first Southern convention began in Mississippi, Johnson sent a telegram to William Sharkey, the provisional governor:

> EXECUTIVE OFFICE
> Washington, D.C.
> August 15, 1865

Governor W. L. Sharkey, Jackson, Mississippi
I am gratified to see that you have organized your convention without difficulty. I hope that without delay your convention will amend your State constitution, abolishing slavery and denying to all future legislatures the power to legislate that there is property in man; also that they will adopt the amendment to the Constitution of the United States abolishing slavery. If you could extend the elective franchise to all persons of color who can read the Constitution of the United States in English and write their names, and to all persons of color who own real estate valued at not less than two hundred and fifty dollars, and pay taxes thereon, you would completely disarm the adversary and set an example the other States will follow. This you can do with perfect safety, and you thus place the southern States, in reference to free persons of color, upon the same basis with

the free States. I hope and trust your convention will do this, and, as a consequence, the radicals, who are wild upon negro franchise, will be completely foiled in their attempt to keep the southern States from renewing their relations to the Union by not accepting their senators and representatives.

Andrew Johnson[68]

Close textual analysis suggests the complexity of the emerging situation. While the telegram quickly became famous throughout the South (and the nation),[69] it is officially directed only to Johnson's appointee: "I am gratified to see that *you* have organized your convention. I hope that without delay *your* convention will . . ." The possessives artfully set up a hierarchical relationship: the convention is identified as the provisional governor's creation; just as the provisional governor is the President's creation.

But the President does not use the imperative voice. He "hopes" that ratification of the Thirteenth Amendment will be secured "without delay"—leaving it to his agent to induce "his" convention to comply. The quasi-imperative character of these "hopes" is clarified by comparison with the President's remarks on black suffrage. Here he is plainly allowing the delegates more leeway, though he is already pointing out the potent threat of unconventional delegitimation by Congress.

The complexity and ambiguity of the President's role increase with the next round of correspondence. Governor Sharkey points out that the President's desire that the convention ratify the Thirteenth Amendment is inconsistent with the fact that Congress had said that state *legislatures* should do this work. The President's answer is worth pondering:

> Your convention can adopt the amendment to the Constitution of the United States, or recommend its adoption by the legislature. You no doubt see the turn that is being given to the attempts in the south to restore State governments by the extreme men of the north; hence the importance of being prompt and circumspect in all that is being done.
>
>   The proceedings in Mississippi will exert a powerful influence on the other States which are to act afterwards.[70]

Note the unconventional assertion of Presidential authority to displace an explicit Congressional triggering judgment. But despite the President's urgency, the "loyal Mississippians" refuse to act with haste.

While the convention repeals the State's secession ordinance and amends its antebellum constitution to abolish slavery, it leaves the fate of the federal amendment to the legislature. As soon as this body assembles, the President renews his demands:

EXECUTIVE OFFICE
Washington, D.C.,
November 1, 1865

Provisional Governor Sharkey, Natchez, Mississippi:

It is all-important that the legislature adopt the amendment to the Constitution of the United States abolishing slavery. The action of the legislature of Mississippi is looked to with great interest at this time, and a failure to adopt the amendment will create the belief that the action of the convention abolishing slavery will hereafter, by the same body, be revoked. The argument is, if the convention abolished slavery in good faith, why should the legislature hesitate to make it a part of the Constitution of the United States?

I trust in God that the legislature will adopt the amendment, and thereby make the way clear for the admission of senators and representatives to their seats in the present Congress.

I congratulate you and your colleague on your election to the Senate.

ANDREW JOHNSON[71]

The Mississippians respond by calling the President's bluff. On December 2, 1865, they solemnly reject the Thirteenth Amendment. In a formal message,[72] the legislature points out that the convention had already amended its state constitution to abolish slavery, and so the Thirteenth Amendment was not legally necessary to free black Mississippians. Moreover, it condemns as positively dangerous the second section of the amendment, empowering Congress "to enforce this article by appropriate legislation":

[We] cannot anticipate what construction future Congresses may put on this section. It may be claimed that it would be "appropriate" for Congress to legislate in respect to freedmen in this state. [We] can hardly conceive of a more dangerous grant of power . . . [We] are apprehensive that if this second section be incorporated in the Constitution, radicals and extremists will further vex and harass the country on the pretext that the freedom of the colored race is not perfect and complete until it is elevated to a social and political equality with the white. The tendency of the section is to absorb in the federal government the reserved rights of the State and people, to unsettle the equilibrium of the States in the Union, and to break down the efficient authority and sovereignty of the State over its internal and domestic affairs.[73]

Mississippi was appealing to the President, and the People, to think again about the meaning of the Civil War: Emancipation was one thing; nationalism quite another; did We the People fight the Civil War to empower the federal government to intrude upon the States' authority to regulate the civil rights of its citizens?

The ball was in the President's court: How would he respond to this effort at a conservative redefinition of constitutional meaning?

We will never know: Mississippi's appeal came too late. On December 5, Secretary Seward was sending a triumphant telegram to Alabama's provisional governor:[74] "The President congratulates you and the country upon the acceptance of the congressional amendment of the Constitution of the United States by the State of Alabama, which vote . . . gives the amendment finishing effect as a part of the organic law of the land."[75] In extending congratulations, the President was also celebrating himself—ratification was due in large part to his aggressive triggering activities.

South Carolina

Given South Carolina's leading role in secession, its decision on emancipation had special significance. And it came at an especially important moment. The four Southern governments organized under Lincoln had ratified the amendment soon after it had been proposed.[76] South Carolina was the first of seven states reconstructed by Johnson to pass upon it. Approval would, in Johnson's words, "set an example which will no doubt be followed by the other States"[77]—as would disapproval. Johnson's anxieties are evident from the documentary record.

Begin with a request by Provisional Governor Benjamin Perry for some clarifying instructions at the time of South Carolina's constitutional convention:

August 28, 1865

I desire to be instructed as to my duty after the State convention shall have framed a constitution abolishing slavery. . . . It is probable that the convention will provide for the election of members of the legislature and the election of governor by the people on the second Monday in October. When these elections have taken place, is it my duty to convene this new legislature, as provisional governor, or are my functions at an end when the new State government is organized? How long shall I continue to act as provisional governor? Do my functions continue until the State is admitted back into the Union? . . . Shall the new governor of the State qualify and call the legislature together? If so, can I act any longer as provisional governor? If I do, what are my duties? . . . And how can the provisional governor and newly elected state governor act together?[78]

These questions probed a weakness in the President's project. On their face, Johnson's proclamations aimed for the *restoration* of republican government by a convention that renounced its secession ordinance and reaffirmed its old constitution (while amending it to abolish slavery). Once this had happened, and South Carolinians had elected a governor and legislature, it was hard to see how a federal governor had any business exercising civil authority.[79] Now that South Carolina was up and running, wasn't Perry's limited mission accomplished?

Yet Johnson and Seward resolutely refused to bite at Perry's constitutional hook:

> DEPARTMENT OF STATE
> Washington
> September 29, 1865

> Sir: I have had the honor to receive, and I have submitted to the President, your letter of August 28, in which you state: . . . [repeating questions reproduced above]. In reply, I have the honor to inform you that the President does not think it now necessary to anticipate events. He will expect you to report proceedings and events as they occur in South Carolina, carefully and freely, for the information of this government. In any case, you will continue to exercise the functions heretofore vested in you by the President until you shall be relieved from that duty by his express orders to that effect.

> Congratulating you upon the favorable aspect of events in your State, I have the honor to be your obedient servant,

> WILLIAM H. SEWARD[80]

So the legislators of South Carolina would not deliberate under normal institutional conditions. They would confront a provisional governor whose very existence expressed the Presidential capacity to challenge South Carolina's statehood if they refused to ratify the Thirteenth Amendment. Indeed, Seward refused to discharge any provisional governors until the day after he issued his December proclamation formally announcing the validity of the amendment.[81]

Seward's telegram is remarkably devoid of any effort to *justify* this decision to maintain unconventional federal authority. Nor does he, at this stage, make ratification of the Thirteenth Amendment an explicit condition for the removal of the provisional governor. Doubtless he and the President would have vastly preferred the legislature to take the hint and ratify without further ado.

But something less subtle would be required. The first rumblings of legislative opposition prompts the President to dash off the only telegram in the series labeled "private":

EXECUTIVE OFFICE
Washington, D.C.
October 31, 1865

B. F. Perry, Provisional Governor, Columbia, S.C.:

There is a deep interest felt as to what course the legislature will take in regard to the adoption of the amendment to the Constitution of the United States abolishing slavery, and the assumption of the debt created to aid in the rebellion against the government of the United States. If the action of the convention was in good faith, why hesitate in making it a part of the Constitution of the United States?

I trust in God that restoration of the Union will not now be defeated, and all that has so far been well done thrown away. I still have faith that all will come out right yet.

This opportunity ought to be understood and appreciated by the people of the southern States.

If I know my own heart and every passion which enters it, my earnest desire is to restore the blessings of the Union, and tie up and heal every bleeding wound which has been caused by this fratricidal war. Let us be guided by love and wisdom from on high, and Union and peace will once more reign throughout the land.

ANDREW JOHNSON[82]

And yet resistance continued. A week later, Seward issues a widely publicized telegram[83] in an effort to head off South Carolina's Article Five veto. The legislature's complaint involves the same issue troubling Mississippi: the second section's grant of an ongoing power to Congress to legislate on behalf of the freedmen. The Secretary responds: "The [legislature's] objection . . . is regarded as querulous and unreasonable. . . . The President considers the acceptance of the amendment by South Carolina is indispensable to a restoration of her relations with the other States of the Union."[84] The President is no longer deflecting the threat of unconventional delegitimation onto Congress. He is speaking in his own voice.

Then more bad news arrives. As Seward delicately puts it, the President "regrets that the state seems to decline the congressional amendment . . . abolishing slavery."[85] But the Secretary refuses to accept this decision as final. He reports that the President is "unchanged" about ratification, and that Perry is to "continue to exercise the duties . . . of provisional governor" until further notice.[86]

Johnson is now mounting a frontal challenge to the federalist premises of the early republic. He is no longer operating within the Article Five framework of equal partnership between state and nation. He is threatening South Carolina with unconventional delegitimation if it rejects Presidential leadership.

And it is at just this point that South Carolina reconsiders.[87] On November 13, it ratifies the Thirteenth Amendment, helping generate a bandwagon joined by three other Johnsonian states—Alabama, Georgia, and North Carolina—before Congress returns to Washington in early December. As a consequence, Secretary Seward could issue his famous telegram on December 5, congratulating Alabama and the nation on the ratification of the Thirteenth Amendment.

In considering South Carolina's "switch in time," we should avoid exaggeration. On the one hand, white South Carolinians had been deprived of the full authority granted to them by Article Five. On the other hand, they had not been reduced to powerlessness. While their choice was unconventional, it was still very real. Suppose, for a moment, that South Carolina had joined Mississippi in leading a Southern bandwagon against ratification.

On this scenario, up to seven Johnsonian governments might have joined Delaware, Kentucky, and New Jersey in rejecting the amendment, depriving it of the necessary twenty-seven of thirty-six ratifications—leaving the American people confronting Lincoln's sober warning that ratification by three-fourths of Northern states "would be questionable, and sure to be persistently questioned."* To be sure, Southern rejection would have heightened the constitutional confrontation. But as the next chapters show, this happened anyway.

Rather than looking upon Southern ratification as either perfectly legal or completely coerced, we should view the mix of legal and translegal elements displayed in South Carolina as a classic case of unconventional adaptation. On the one hand, the legislative assembly of South Carolinians meeting in Columbia were *not*—to use the language of the President's proclamations—a random group of "loyal Americans" speaking their mind about the Thirteenth Amendment. Their capacity to speak for South Carolina had been established through a complex legalistic process based upon electoral competition. On the other hand, the South Carolina assembly would not be giving its consent under the normal conditions specified by preexisting constitutional law. Indeed, there is a deep truth in Johnson's first public telegram that had informed the South that it could ratify the amendment through either constitutional "conventions" or through state "legislatures." If we move beyond labels to concepts, the ratifying assembly that met in South Carolina was more similar to the "convention" that spoke for South Carolina at the Founding than it was to an ordinary legislature. In both 1788 and 1865, South Carolinians were giving their consent under conditions which raised a nationalistic challenge to preexisting constitutional norms.

And yet, while Johnson had inserted the national interest into the ratification process, Southerners continued to have a key role in the decision. As the example of Mississippi indicates, Southern legislators were perfectly capable of saying No to the President—if, after deliberation, they believed that they would destroy their future political careers with their constituents by endorsing the Thirteenth Amendment. Indeed, their consent would have been worthless if they were mere puppets of national authority.

More broadly, there is an almost exquisite correspondence between the nationalistic dynamic of Presidential leadership in the process of ratification and the nationalistic substance of the new Emancipation

---

*Of course, everything might have worked out happily in the end. New Jersey changed its mind in 1866 and sent a symbolic "acceptance" to Secretary Seward after he had issued his proclamation of December 18, 1865. But during the interim, some other government might have tried to change its yea into a nay, leaving the status of the amendment still in doubt.

Amendment. Southern ratification was not a matter for the President, acting alone, *or* the state legislatures, acting alone; it was the distinctive product of a new form of national-state interaction in which the federal government played an enhanced role. And the same is true when we turn to the substance of the amendment itself. As a result of its second paragraph, the national government would now be empowered to intervene into the very core of civil relationships formerly controlled exclusively by the states. Is there any surprise that the states would not concede this control without unconventional federal intervention? But would this great extension of federal power have seemed legitimate without any show of Southern consent?

As a result of Presidential leadership, the constitutional situation emerging in December was very different from the one obtaining on the day in April when Lincoln was shot. No longer could the Thirteenth Amendment be viewed as the exclusive creation of We the People of the North. Representatives of the white South had overwhelmingly, if unconventionally, voted to endorse the amendment.

But it was one thing for the white South to make this gesture under Presidential leadership; quite another, for the rest of the nation to accept it. The problem is analytically similar to the one confronting the First Congress in 1789, when North Carolina and Rhode Island were still out of the new Union. These two holdouts could have clung to the Articles' ratification rules, denouncing the eleven Unionists as illegal secessionists. Similarly, the triggering decisions made by the President could have been repudiated as an illegal mockery of Federalist principles. As Thaddeus Stevens put it in a famous September speech denouncing Johnson and demanding confiscation of land from disloyal Southern whites and its redistribution to loyal blacks:

> The President says to the rebel States "before you can participate in the government you must abolish Slavery and reform your elections laws." *That* is the command of a Conqueror . . . Nor can the constitutional amendment abolishing Slavery ever be ratified by three-fourths of the States, if *they* are States to be counted. Bogus Conventions of these States may vote for it. But no Convention honestly and fairly elected will ever do it.[88]

If you will forgive the jargon, we have moved once more into the consolidation phase. Under both Lincoln and Johnson, the Presidency had won support for its unconventional initiatives on behalf of emancipation time after time from a broad variety of popularly elected representatives of the People. Had this broad and accelerating institutional bandwagon reached the point where, despite the legal anomalies, it deserved the unquestioning acceptance from all sober citizens as the work of We the People? Or was all this sound and fury merely the work of "Bogus Conventions"?

PRESIDENTIAL CONSOLIDATION

In the case of the Founding, this decision was made at the state level, when North Carolina and Rhode Island finally gave their consent and joined the bandwagon. Given the nationalist tilt of Reconstruction, it is predictable that the consolidation decision was made through a complex interaction between the President and Congress.

Point Counterpoint: Sumner's Resolution and the President's Message

As soon as the Senate convened on December 4, Charles Sumner took the floor to offer the first resolution:

> Whereas the Congress, by a vote of two thirds of both Houses, did heretofore propose to the Legislatures of the several States, for ratification, an amendment to the Constitution in the following words, to wit: "Article XIII [reciting text]." And whereas, at the time when such amendment was submitted as well as since, there were sundry States which, by reason of rebellion, were without Legislatures, so that, while the submission was made in due constitutional form, it was not, as it could not be, made to all the States,[89] but to "the Legislatures of the several States," in obedience both to the letter and spirit of the provision of the Constitution authorizing amendments, there being a less number of Legislatures of States than there were States; and whereas, since the Constitution expressly authorizes amendments to be made, any construction thereof which would render the making of amendments at times impossible, must violate both its letter and its spirit; and whereas, to require the ratification to be by States without Legislatures as well as by "the Legislatures of the States," in order to be pronounced valid, would put it in the power of a long-continued rebellion to suspend, not only the peace of the nation, but its Constitution also; and whereas, from the terms of the Constitution, and the nature of the case, it

belongs to the two Houses of Congress to determine when such ratification is complete; and whereas more than three fourths of the Legislatures to which the proposition was made have ratified such amendment: Now, therefore,

Be it resolved by the Senate, (the House of Representatives concurring,) That the amendment abolishing slavery has become, and is, a part of the Constitution of the United States.

Resolved, That notwithstanding the foregoing resolution, and considering the great public interest which attaches to this question, the Legislatures which have not ratified the amendment, be permitted to express their concurrence therein by the usual form of ratification to be returned in the usual manner.

Resolved, That no one of the States, to the Legislature of which such amendment could not be submitted, by reason of its being in rebellion against the United States, and having no Legislature, be permitted to resume its relations, and have its Legislature acknowledged, and its Senators and Representatives admitted, until its Legislature shall have first ratified such amendment in recognition of the accomplished fact."[90]

This is a sweeping effort to deny the constitutional significance of the President's triggering activities on behalf of the Thirteenth Amendment. It also rejects any claim by the President, or his delegate Seward, to judge the contested issues of higher lawmaking process: "it belongs to the two Houses of Congress to determine when such ratification is complete."

The next day was the President's turn. His Annual Message to Congress[91] is a key text. Published on the front page of most newspapers, it was a reference point for public discussion. It emphatically rejects a lengthy period of military rule for the South, which "would have divided the people into the vanquishers and the vanquished, and would have envenomed hatred rather than have restored affection."[92] Such a course was not only counterproductive but unconstitutional: "the true theory is that all pretended acts of secession were from the beginning null and void. . . . The states placed themselves in a condition where their vitality was impaired, but not extinguished; their functions suspended but not destroyed."[93] Rather than setting himself up as a military despot, the President had used his authority to restore constitutional government.

But the message is hardly an out-and-out conservative apologia.

When he turns to the Thirteenth Amendment, President Johnson does not cover up the legally problematic aspects of his enterprise. To the contrary, he takes pride in his unconventional acts of leadership:

As no State can throw a defense over the crime of treason, the power of pardon is exclusively vested in the executive government of the United States. In exercising that power *I have taken every precaution to connect it with the clearest recognition of the binding force of the laws of the United States and an unqualified acknowledgment of the great social change of condition in regard to slavery which has grown out of the war.*

The next step which I have taken to restore the constitutional relations of the States has been an invitation to them to participate in the high office of amending the Constitution. Every patriot must wish for a general amnesty at the earliest epoch consistent with public safety. For this great end there is need of a concurrence of all opinions and the spirit of mutual conciliation. All parties in the late terrible conflict must work together in harmony. It is not too much to ask, *in the name of the whole people,* that on the one side [i.e., citizens of the North] the plan of restoration shall proceed in conformity with a willingness to cast the disorders of the past into oblivion, and that on the other [i.e., the citizens of the South] *the evidence of sincerity in the future maintenance of the Union shall be put beyond any doubt by the ratification of the proposed amendment to the Constitution,* which provides for the abolition of slavery forever within the limits of our country. So long as the adoption of this amendment is delayed, so long will doubt and jealousy and uncertainty prevail. This is the measure which will efface the sad memory of the past; this is the measure which will most certainly call population and capital and security to those parts of the Union that need them most. Indeed, *it is not too much to ask of the States which are now resuming their places in the family of the Union to give this pledge of perpetual loyalty and peace.* Until it is done the past, however much we may desire it, will not be forgotten. The adoption of the amendment reunites us beyond all power of disruption; it heals the wound that is still imperfectly closed; it removes slavery, the element which has so long perplexed and divided the country; it makes of us once more a united people, renewed and strengthened, bound more than ever to mutual affection and support.

The amendment to the Constitution being adopted, it would remain for the States whose powers have been so long in abeyance to resume their places in the two branches of the National Legislature, and thereby complete the work of restoration. Here it is for you, fellow-citizens of the Senate, and for you, fellow-citizens of the House of Representatives, to judge, each of you for yourselves, of the elections, returns, and qualifications of your own members.[94]

Here is a voice unknown to the Founding Fathers: a President demanding that "states . . . give this pledge" to the Thirteenth Amendment in the name of "the whole people," a President who is proudly manipulating his pardoning powers to win "an unqualified acknowledgment of the great social change of condition in regard to slavery."

No less important is Johnson's assertion of authority against Congress. In contrast to Sumner, he does not wait for Congress to determine the legal issues raised by the amendment's ratification. He declares that the amendment *has been* adopted. But would Congress go along?

Seward's Proclamation

Within this context, Secretary Seward's formal proclamation on the amendment was a remarkably provocative act. It does not try to evade the issues separating Sumner from Johnson, but squarely endorses the President on all questionable matters.[95] It forthrightly rejects the view of ratification as an exclusively Northern affair: "the whole number of states in the United States is thirty-six." It rejects any thought that Presidents Lincoln and Johnson had failed to establish republican governments in the South—explicitly naming eight of these governments among the twenty-seven casting dispositive votes. Finally, in accepting the Southern ratifications, the Secretary was finding them untainted by unconstitutional coercion from the federal government (in which he and the President were intimately involved).

As soon as we recognize that the Secretary is trying to render *authoritative* judgment on fundamental questions of higher law, a second remarkable aspect of his proclamation appears to view—its lack of legal support. Certainly Article Five does not explicitly authorize any such role for the Secretary of State. Nor does the applicable statute:

Section 2. *And be it further enacted,* whenever official notice shall have been received, at the Department of State, that any amendment which heretofore has been, or hereafter may be proposed to the constitution has been adopted, according to the constitution of the United States, it shall be the duty of the said Secretary of State forthwith to cause the said amendment to be published in the newspapers authorized to promulgate the laws, with his certificate, specifying the states by which the same may have been adopted, and that the same has become valid, to all intents and purposes, as part of the constitution of the United States.[96]

This section is part of a statute of 1818 "to provide for the publication of the laws of the United States," by authorizing the Secretary to publish all statutes and treaties in newspapers and in bound volumes of collected laws. The context suggests that the Secretary has only been empowered to act as certifier-in-chief, and not as the final authority on fundamental questions of higher law. Any remaining doubts are removed by the opening words of the section, which authorizes him to proceed with newspaper publication only when "official notice shall have been received, at the Department of State, that any amendment . . . has been adopted." While the statute doesn't name the institution that sends this notice, one thing is clear: it can't be the Secretary, otherwise the words would be meaningless. As later events proved, Seward was under no illusion as to his statutory authority. In connection with similar problems surrounding the ratification of the Fourteenth Amendment,[97] he publicly acknowledged that "neither the act [of 1818] nor any other law, expressly or by conclusive implication, authorizes the Secretary of State to determine and decide doubtful questions as to the authenticity of the organization of State legislatures."[98]

Nonetheless, Seward's proclamation on the Thirteenth Amendment proceeds as if none of these legal problems existed. Purporting to act "by virtue and in pursuance of the second section of the act of Congress, approved the twentieth of April, eighteen hundred and eighteen . . . ,"[99] the Secretary blandly fails to identify the "official notice" the statute requires, thereby suppressing his lack of statutory authorization to resolve fundamental constitutional questions. While it is easy to expose the emptiness of Seward's legalistic gesture, I do not mean to suggest its irrelevance. We are once again witnessing the distinctive combination of legal and extralegal elements that serves as the hallmark of unconventional adaptation.

Not that the Secretary's legalistic piece of paper was enough to consolidate the Thirteenth Amendment into higher law. It still remained possible for the Republicans in Congress to rally behind Sumner's banner. When faced with Seward's challenge, would Congress reject executive leadership or jump on the accelerating institutional bandwagon?

Congressional Acquiescence

On the very day of the Secretary's proclamation, Thaddeus Stevens took Sumner's challenge to the floor of the House:

> [It is vitally important] to establish a principle that none of the rebel States shall be counted in any of the amendments of the Constitution. . . . I take no account of the aggregation of white-washed rebels, who without any legal authority have assembled in the capitals of the late rebel states and simulated rebel bodies. Nor do I regard with any respect the cunning by-play into which they deluded the Secretary of State by frequent telegraphic announcements that "South Carolina had adopted the amendment;" "Alabama has adopted the amendment, being the twenty-seventh State;" &c. This was intended to delude the people, and accustom Congress to hear repeated the names of these extinct states as if they were alive.[100]

But the Republican majority was in no mood to take up Stevens's call "to establish a principle."[101] Instead, they quickly jumped on the executive's bandwagon.

This process is nicely revealed by the early Congressional debates over a civil rights bill. The Senate's first pass at the problem was on December 13, five days before Seward's proclamation. Senator Henry Wilson urged immediate action on behalf of blacks without awaiting lengthy deliberation in committee. But despite his emphatic commitment, his draft only protected blacks living in the Confederate states affected by the Emancipation Proclamation, and not in the rest of the country—as he could have done if he believed that the amendment was an unquestionable part of higher law.[102]

Wilson's refusal to rely on the amendment is remarkable for three reasons. First, the Senator publicly subscribed to the Sumner-Stevens view of ratification,[103] under which the ratification by three-fourths of the North sufficed to validate the amendment. On this view, the amendment had become a part of the Constitution six months before

Wilson took the Senate floor on December thirteenth. In steering clear of the amendment, Wilson was deferring to his perception that most Senators did not share his Radical view. Second, by December 13, both Secretary Seward and President Johnson had publicly declared that they had received 27 ratifications from the 36 (Southern and Northern) states of the Union. All that was lacking was an official-looking proclamation by the Secretary. Third, Wilson's hesitation is unrelated to any doubts about the merits. As a leading Senator from Republican Massachusetts, he was a consistent advocate of civil rights. His proposal of December 13 does not reflect faintness of heart, but a realistic recognition that doubts about the validity of the Thirteenth Amendment had not yet been laid to rest either in the Congress or the nation at large.

This point was confirmed by the ensuing debate. Listen to the terms in which leading Republicans rejected Wilson's demand for immediate action:

> MR. SHERMAN: Mr. President, I sympathize heartily with the purpose of the bill. . . . With me, it is a question simply of time and manner. . . . I believe it would be wiser to postpone all action upon this subject until the proclamation of the Secretary of State shall announce that the constitutional amendment is a part of the supreme law of the land. When that is done, there will then be, in my judgment, no doubt of the power of Congress to pass this bill, and to make it definite and general in its terms [including the entire United States and not only the ex-Confederacy]. . . .[104]

Sherman was seconded by Senator Lyman Trumbull, who cautiously suggested that until the Secretary acted "there may be some question (I do not say how the right is) as to the authority of the Congress to pass such a bill as this, but after the adoption of the constitutional amendment there can be none."[105] These remarks by leading moderates dashed any hope of a quick vote.

Once the Secretary acted, Congressional opinion took a different turn. Sumner's invitation to contest the President's authority remained buried in committee, but the Republican leadership promptly moved to confirm the Secretary's proclamation by enacting legislation under its authority. Consider a January colloquy in the debate on Senator Trumbull's bill to expand and extend the Freedmen's Bureau:

MR. SAULSBURY: I say, as one of the representatives of Delaware on this floor, that she had the proud and noble character of being the first to enter the Federal Union under a Constitution formed by equals. She has been the very last to obey a mandate, legislative or executive, for abolishing slavery. She has been the last slaveholding State, thank God, in America, and I am one of the last slaveholders in America.

MR. TRUMBULL: Well, Mr. President, I do not see particularly what the declaration of the Senator from Delaware has to do with the question I am discussing. His State may have been the last to become free, but I presume that the State of Delaware, old as she is, being the first to adopt the Constitution, and noble as she is, will submit to the Constitution of the United States, which declares that there shall be no slavery within its jurisdiction. [Applause in the galleries.]

THE PRESIDING OFFICER: Order! Order!

MR. SAULSBURY: She will.[106]

As "the last slaveholder in America" representing a loyal slaveholding state that had formally rejected the amendment, Willard Saulsbury would be among the last Senators to concede the amendment's validity.[107] Nonetheless, he no longer disputed the Congress's authority once the Secretary had officially proclaimed the amendment's validity. While Republicans would soon regret the existence of Seward's proclamation, even they spoke of the matter as if it represented a *legal precedent* that could not be ignored.[108]

THE CONSERVATIVE SIDE OF UNCONVENTIONALITY

We have taken two steps beyond orthodoxy. The first was to recognize the awkward fit between the rules and principles of Article Five and the process that brought us the Thirteenth Amendment. The second was to see that this break with tradition did not imply the absence of pattern but the elaboration of a new, more nation-centered, configuration marked strongly by Presidential leadership. The emerging institutional grammar of popular sovereignty involves a President (1) taking steps that enable him to claim that a national election amounted to a constitutional mandate from the People and (2) successfully leading other deliberative institutions to give their assent to, or more passive acquiescence in, his claim that *the People have spoken*. Since this pattern challenges orthodox notions of constitutional change, perhaps it will help restore reflective equilibrium if we take a third quick step?

This is to emphasize that unconventionality does not necessarily imply adventurism. Lincoln and Johnson invoked their higher law-making powers to drive the constitutional process in a relatively conservative direction, using their authority to support the smallest departure from the status quo that might be acceptable to the nation as a whole.[109]

Presidential minimalism had fateful consequences. It was Radicals like Stevens and Sumner, and not the men in the White House, who saw the terrible truth that quick reunion would result in Southern betrayal of the new constitutional values trumpeted in the formal text. A President following Radical advice would have used the precious months of 1865 to pave the way for a new class of property-owning and educated black yeoman in the South. He would not have allowed rebel whites to regain their land in exchange for the minimal promises exacted by Johnson's amnesty oath. He would have heeded Stevens's call for a massive land redistribution to loyal freedmen and elaborated Sumner's great vision of a public school system that might compensate for slavery's enforced ignorance.

A Radical President would have rejected the "minimalist" aims expressed in Johnson's North Carolina proclamation. He would have directed his provisional governors to create territorial governments, not state authorities. He would have been prepared to keep the South under federal tutelage during the decade or more required for blacks to gain the educational and economic resources needed to defend their interests at the ballot box. While this Radical program might have failed, wouldn't it have been a better gamble than the one actually taken in the name of the American people?

To be frank, I cannot read the brilliant speeches of Sumner and Stevens without physically experiencing a bitter sense of the moral opportunity lost by America when Andrew Johnson issued his North Carolina proclamation. Nonetheless, something leads me to pause before condemning the conservative use of Presidential power in the evolving higher lawmaking system. The stumbling block is a single, but uncontested,[110] fact: in 1865, a majority of the American people were not prepared to support the Radical program. Given this fact, it is not enough to affirm the moral right of the freedmen to the land and education that they had purchased by centuries of slave labor. One must also affirm the constitutional authority of the President to use his emerging higher lawmaking powers on behalf of a moral position that was *far*[111] in advance of the majority view contemporaneously held by the American people.

The dangers of Presidential vanguardism should be obvious. We are all familiar with the dismal process by which chief executives in countless nations have invoked the imperatives of a higher morality to transform themselves into dictators. It is one thing for us to recognize the fundamental precedent established by Lincoln and Johnson in gaining repeated public acceptance of Presidential leadership in higher lawmaking; quite another to condemn them for rejecting the temptations of vanguardism.[112]

To the contrary, it is a great merit of Presidential leadership in 1865 that it allowed the American people to distinguish clearly between floor and ceiling as they embarked on a lengthy struggle over the design of a reconstructed Union. By December 1865, it was no longer open to serious question whether the great sacrifices of civil war would be frittered away without the American people hammering out some deep sense of constitutional meaning arising from the crisis. Presidential leadership had already helped crystallize a minimum, but fundamental, constitutional understanding that the People had now authorized a national government permanently committed to the emancipation of all human beings. Once this floor had been established, Americans could focus all their energies on the next obvious questions: Was simple emancipation enough? Should the American people demand more of their government, and if so what?

As the next chapters suggest, the constitutional effort to define the grander ideals of the Fourteenth Amendment catapulted the country into a profound constitutional crisis, generating a cycle of bitter disagreement, mass popular mobilization and institutional improvisation. As this struggle threatened to spin out of control, the fact that Americans had already succeeded in hammering out a shared, if minimal, sense of constitutional meaning in enacting the Thirteenth Amendment was more important than it might seem on the surface. If unconventional adaptation might succeed once in gaining consent, why not a second time?

CHAPTER SIX

The Convention/Congress

MEASURING THE MOMENT

THE STRUGGLE over the Fourteenth Amendment marks the greatest constitutional moment in American history. As at the Founding, constitutional law became the preeminent language through which Americans debated and defined their national identity. Reconstruction was also a time when the leading protagonists did not mouth the words scribbled by young assistants. When Sumner or Fessenden, Stevens or Bingham speak on the floor of Congress, you can hear the energy and hesitation of mature thought—just as you can when eavesdropping on Madison or Wilson at the Constitutional Convention.[1]

Only this time, the debate was more wide-ranging and sustained. The Philadelphia Convention, to put it mildly, was not an ecumenical affair. While the Federalists were careful to gain the support of state legislatures for their Convention, they also carefully stacked most delegations in favor of strong nationalizers. The Convention debates became increasingly one-sided as leading Anti-Federalists walked out in protest. Debate during Reconstruction was far more representative. While Congressional Republicans affirmed new ideals of equal citizenship and fundamental rights, they were met by President Johnson's powerful defense of more traditional ideals.

What is more, these debates in Washington were not secret, as in Philadelphia, but served as the focus of a vast national dialogue. Once the Philadelphia Convention went public, its proposals provoked a remarkably vibrant and sophisticated discussion. But despite its dynamism, the Founding dialogue did not penetrate the body politic as deeply as the debate over the Fourteenth Amendment. In part, this was a tribute to the rise of mass political parties. Republicans and Democrats had organized a vast network of party newspapers, party rallies, and party patronage that engaged the interest of ordinary Americans in ways unimaginable in the late eighteenth—or late twentieth—century.[2] In part, the debate's penetration into public life was a function of sheer duration—discussion of the original Constitution took a few months (or less) in most states; it went on for years in the case of the Fourteenth Amendment.

In part, however, the debate's impact was a product of the enormous sacrifices of civil war. The Founding had also followed a civil war between patriots and tories, forcing all to consider questions of political identity that are usually taken for granted. But the collective measure of sacrifice was now on a different scale. The death toll says it all. North and South, 665,000 soldiers gave their lives—14 out of every 100 men between the ages of 15 and 30, 2 percent of the population as a whole.[3] Everybody knew somebody who made the ultimate sacrifice; and most were determined to ensure that these men had not died in vain.

Passionate commitments were so many and so great that they threatened to overwhelm the constitutional tradition. Could the old symbols and institutions channel all this passionate turbulence? Would they offer the contending parties opportunities to reflect upon, as well as react to, the political thrusts of their antagonists? Would they clearly mark off occasions upon which key questions of constitutional identity were ripe for decision? Or identify the winners and losers in ways that most Americans would recognize as legitimate?

Only one thing was clear. The processes specified by the Founding Federalists in Article Five would not suffice. As we have seen, this article invited Americans to direct their constitutional proposals to a federal congress or a federal convention. But it had not explicitly confronted the all-important issue of 1865: how to treat the Senators and Congressmen wending their way to Washington from the eleven states of the former Confederacy?

The answer would have a decisive impact upon the ultimate decision. If "Congress" included both Northern and Southern states, the constitutional meaning of the Civil War would remain where Presidents Lincoln and Johnson had left it—with the words of the Thirteenth Amendment. Once the white South was represented on Capitol Hill, nothing resembling the Fourteenth Amendment would gain the super-majority needed for proposal, much less ratification. If the American people were to move beyond simple emancipation, it would be necessary for "Congress" to remain an assembly of twenty-five, not thirty-six, states. But who was going to decide *this* question? Would it be the Republican majority in "Congress"? Would it be the President?

Or would it be neither? I will argue that it was *the People themselves* who took this decision away from competing political elites in Washington and decided it on their own responsibility. It is this decision of a mobilized People, and not any textual formalism, that lies at the foundation of the Fourteenth Amendment. In speaking of "the People," I am not hunting for some Lockean entity mysteriously emerging out of a "state of nature" to renegotiate the social compact for nineteenth-century America. Instead of lapsing into some prepolitical condition, Americans managed to impress new meanings on old institutions in ways that allowed them to hammer out a democratic solution to their crisis of constitutional identity. Our task is to isolate the distinctive properties of this next great adaptation in the language of popular sovereignty.

Begin by reflecting on a key word, *convention,* that has threaded its way throughout our story. As we have seen, the Federalists borrowed the word from English constitutional law, using the Convention of 1688 as a precedent for their own anomalous assemblies. This precedent from the Glorious Revolution also serves as an illuminating benchmark for Reconstruction.[4] Recall the scene in Westminster Hall after James II fled to France. The "convention" that met in his absence was a constitutionally problematic body—and yet it was this problematic body that managed to frame the Bill of Rights in the name of the English People.

Something similar happened in 1865. Just as the seat occupied by the King was painfully empty in Westminster Hall in 1688, so too the seats occupied by the Southern states remained empty in the Senate and House chambers. To mark this analogy, I shall be describing the Republican-dominated assembly on Capitol Hill as the Convention/Congress. Just as the Convention of 1688 hammered out its great Bill of Rights, the Convention/Congress made its own signal contribution to Anglo-American constitutionalism with the Fourteenth Amendment. But this time, the claims of the Convention/Congress to speak for the People would be subjected to a far more democratic series of tests than anything imagined in 1688 or 1787. I shall be analyzing this democratic dynamic of challenge and response with the five-phase framework deployed in previous case studies.

We begin with the remarkable way the Republicans *signaled* their higher lawmaking intentions by excluding the white South from Capitol Hill. By March, President Johnson had alerted the nation to this unconventional assertion of power in two veto messages rejecting the Republican program. This Presidential assault pushed the Republicans into the daunting task of framing a Fourteenth Amendment that might allow them to triumph over their antagonist in the White House.

With the President and the Convention/Congress reaching an impasse in Washington, the elections of 1866 offered both sides an opportunity to discredit their opponents' claim to speak for the People. Both the Republicans and their opponents made a maximal effort to produce a new Congress that would either repudiate the Congressional decision to exclude the South or reaffirm it. The Fourteenth Amendment, whose fate hung in the balance, was central to the campaign.

The result was a Republican landslide. The next two chapters consider how this victory successfully triggered further unconventional efforts that finally allowed the ratification and consolidation of the Fourteenth Amendment.

THE PRESIDENTIAL BASELINE

Although the meaning of equal protection and due process remains controversial, no sane American supposes that the country would be better off *without* the Fourteenth Amendment. This modern consensus tempts us to suppose that the moral grandeur of the amendment engendered a national chorus of jubilation at the time it was proposed.

Nothing could be further from the truth. Like the Federalists' initiative, the Republicans' proposal sharply divided the country. The problem was straightforward. An overwhelming majority of white Americans—North as well as South—were racists. When Northerners emancipated slaves before the Civil War, it was on legal terms that emphasized their continuing inferiority; indeed, some Western states prohibited "free" blacks from entering their borders. Only in the Northeast could black men vote.[5]

And yet the Republicans were proposing to defy this pervasive prejudice. Not only did their Fourteenth Amendment guarantee all blacks the privileges and immunities of citizens of the United States; it gave them the right to break down borders by claiming citizenship in any state they wished. Not only did it require all states to provide equal protection of the laws; it reduced the Congressional representation of states that denied blacks the vote. To vindicate such revolutionary reforms, Republicans would have to persuade their fellow countrymen to transcend their racist impulses. The real surprise is not that they encountered resistance, but that they managed to win sustained popular support for such a radical challenge to entrenched political, legal, and social practices.*

This basic point has shaped my perspective on President Johnson's role in Reconstruction. When viewing his efforts to restore white authority in the Southern states, twentieth-century historians have tended to cheer or boo, depending on their view of the merits of his program—the cheers predominating in the first half of the century; the boos, in the second. I will be asking a different question: How did the President's spirited defense of conservative constitutionalism contribute to the larger process that ultimately led most Americans to make such a revolutionary commitment to equal freedom for all?

My answer emphasizes a *paradox of resistance.* By struggling so long and hard, the President vastly increased the legitimacy of the decision by the People to embrace revolutionary reform. To begin with the basics, his efforts on behalf of white Southern governments gave the turbulent debate a pragmatic anchor in reality. Rather than losing themselves in heady constitutional abstractions, Americans could pass judgment on the conservative vision of Reconstruction after gaining a concrete sense of what it might, and might not, accomplish. Equally important, Presidential Reconstruction began the complex process through which the South as well as the North participated in the

---

*This is the fundamental weakness in interpretations of the amendment that emphasize the pervasive racism of the time. See, e.g., Raoul Berger, *Government by Judiciary* (1977). The amendment stands as proof of the possibility that Americans *can* transcend their racist instincts in response to the ideal of equal citizenship.

fateful process of defining an enduring constitutional identity. Rather than looking on passively as Northerners debated the nature of the Union, white Southerners played a powerful role in determining the outcome. In particular, if the white electorate had selected leaders who had vigorously followed through on their professed commitments to the Union and emancipation, President Johnson would have gained an immense advantage in defending his conservative vision against Republican critique.

But, in fact, the white South did not match its words with deeds, and the disparity continually eroded the credibility of the President's conservative vision. As the debate over the Fourteenth Amendment proceeded in Washington, the grim character of the "emancipation" promised by the Thirteenth Amendment became clear as one Southern state after another enacted Black Codes that consigned the "freedmen" to serf-like status. Moreover, a steady stream of lurid accounts of violence against black and white Unionists made plain the failure of these "white moderates" to put the full force of public authority behind their governments' formal professions of loyalty. To top it off, the very personalities of the Southern representatives to Congress displayed the dark side of the conservative vision. While some Southerners could take the Unionists' ironclad oath with a good conscience, most could not. Among the eighty Southerners barred from the Thirty-ninth Congress, there were ten Confederate generals, five colonels, nine Congressmen. Indeed, Georgia had sent Confederate Vice President Alexander II. Stephens to represent the state in the United States Senate![6]

With twenty-twenty hindsight, it is easy to suppose that the President's promise of emancipation was certain to be shattered by the facts of life below the Mason-Dixon line. But for most Americans, it was not obvious how the white South would respond to its military defeat. And it was perfectly reasonable for them to withhold their support for more radical measures unless and until the defects of the President's conservative theories were revealed in the real world. In this fundamental sense, the President's constitutional experiment greatly enhanced the deliberative quality of the higher lawmaking process.

It is true, of course, that "the facts" emerging from the South were distorted in countless ways by countless partisans. But it is wrong to judge the President's experiment as if it were conducted in a scientific laboratory or philosophy seminar. Above all else, constitutional politics is a popular politics involving ordinary people caught up in a crisis of constitutional definition. Passionate concern, and bitter conflict, are characteristic of such moments. Rather than hoping for a miraculous suspension of human frailties, a dualist constitution provides mechanisms that encourage ordinary citizens to test their initial reactions against relevant patterns of experience, so that they may finally reach a considered judgment on the matters set before them.[7]

By this standard, Presidential Reconstruction had a very substantial value—albeit different from the one Johnson hoped to achieve. Whatever its weaknesses (and there were many), it guaranteed that the great principles of the Fourteenth Amendment would not be adopted by ordinary Americans at a moment when they hadn't the slightest idea of the large commitments the politicians were proclaiming in their name. As a result of Presidential leadership, Americans were gaining a concrete sense—however partisan and fragmentary—of the way the white South was prepared to interpret its commitments to the Union and to the Thirteenth Amendment. If Americans ultimately moved beyond this conservative vision, it was only after judging it as fundamentally inadequate.

The Signaling Phase

The opening scenes of the Thirty-ninth Congress provided the nation with a dramatic introduction to its constitutional predicament. Enter stage right, Horace Maynard, a newly elected representative from Tennessee. A man of undisputed Unionist loyalties from the President's home state,[8] he perfectly symbolized the larger Presidential enterprise. In demanding his right to a House seat, he was a stand-in for the kind of committed white Unionist Johnson hoped to restore to power. Should not the likes of Maynard/Johnson be trusted to speak for this new loyal South?

This was not the first time Maynard had raised this question. During the Civil War, Congress was happy to seat him as a Representative from a Tennessee district that had remained (more or less) loyal to the Union.[9] If Maynard was good enough then, why not now?

Enter stage left, Edward McPherson, the Clerk of the House and a political appointee of Thaddeus Stevens, Republican majority leader.

Following established practice, McPherson opened the session by calling the roll. But he also followed the instructions of the Republican Caucus and refused to call out the names of the Southerners who had won election. As the roll call proceeded in alphabetical order, Maynard rose in protest as his name was passed over:

MR. MAYNARD. Does the Clerk decline to hear me?

THE CLERK. I decline to have any interruption of the call of the roll . . .

MR. MORRILL. I move that the House do now proceed to the election of a Speaker of the Thirty-Ninth Congress.

MR. MAYNARD. Before that motion is put—

MR. STEVENS. I call the gentlemen to order.

THE CLERK. The Clerk rules, as a matter of order, that he cannot recognize any gentleman whose name is not upon the role.

MR. BROOKS. [Democrat of New York] Mr. Clerk, I hope that motion will not prevail until it is settled who are members of this House— whether the honorable gentleman from Tennessee [Mr. MAYNARD], holding in his hand, I presume, the certificate of the Governor of that State, is entitled to be heard on his credentials or not. I trust that we will not proceed to any revolutionary step like that without at least hearing from the honorable gentleman from Tennessee. For, if Tennessee is not in the Union, and has not been in the Union, and is not a loyal State, and the people of Tennessee are aliens and foreigners to this Union, by what right does the President of the United States usurp his place in the White House and in the capital of the country when an alien, as he must be, a foreigner, and not from a State in the Union?
. . . [I]f a precedent can be established by the Clerk, and he can make a rule to exclude members from the floor of this House by his mere arbitrary will, this then ceases to be a Congress, and the Clerk of the House, but a servant of the House, is omnipotent over its organization. Is not the state of Tennessee in the Union? . . .

THE CLERK. With the consent of the gentlemen I will state that if it be the desire of the House to have my reasons, I will give them. . .

MR. STEVENS. It is not necessary. We know all.[11]

"We know all": Stevens was speaking for the nation in one respect at least. The millions of Americans who were following this scene in the newspapers *did* understand its profound constitutional significance. Henceforward, Stevens would be presiding over a Convention/ Congress.

Perhaps a more formal definition of my neologism is in order. I shall call an institution "convention-like" when its perceived legitimacy resides primarily in its appeal to the ideal of popular sovereignty, rather than its established legality. Like most definitions, this one embraces clear and hard cases. The clear case involves a *blatant* break with established constitutional norms—as occurred, for example, when the Philadelphia Convention broke with the ratification process specified by the Articles of Confederation. As the next chapter describes, the Convention/Congress made a similar break with Article Five after the election of 1866.

But at this early stage, the Convention/Congress was still in a gray zone. While it required a big stretch of traditional understandings, Republicans could use the constitutional responsibility to "guarantee a Republican Form of Government" as a platform for mounting a legalistic defense of their exclusion of the South.[12] Nonetheless, their action was so shocking that they well understood the imperative need to supplement these legalisms with aggressive appeals to popular sovereignty. For example, here is John Bingham, the future draftsman of the Fourteenth Amendment, struggling with an elaborately legalistic speech demanding immediate seating of the South, presented by Democrat Daniel Voorhees on January 9, 1866:

> Now, Mr. Speaker, I am not willing that the gentleman [i.e., Voorhees], after the struggle through which we have all passed, shall assume that he alone, as a Representative of the people, is faithful to the Constitution of his country and to the sacred rights of the people of the whole country. I claim myself to cooperate with a party of men who are as charitable as the gentleman [i.e., Voorhees] can be, even toward these late insurgents, these late conspirators, these men who but the other day struck with their drawn daggers at the white breast of our mother country. I am not willing to concede that these gentlemen [i.e., the Democratic Party] who, by their utterances, but gave aid and comfort to the rebellion during the gigantic struggle, are the only persons to be intrusted with the honor and dignity of this greatest of all trusts ever committed to the care of any people upon this earth, the perpetuity of the Republic. The Republic, sir, is in the hands of its friends, and its only safety is in the hands of its friends. The party of

the Republic proposes only to take security for the future. They do not expect nor hope for indemnity for the past. They propose, however, to take security for the future.[13]

Although Voorhees was voicing the constitutional anxieties of millions, Bingham treats them with dismissive impatience. No exercise in constitutional logic-chopping could obliterate the truth that Voorhees and his party "by their utterances, . . . gave aid and comfort to the rebellion during the gigantic struggle." The supreme fact is that "[t]he Republic, sir, is in the hands of its friends, and its only safety is in the hands of its friends."[14]

Strong stuff, but nothing that would shock the Conventions of 1688 and 1787. Of course, it is one thing to make such claims to popular sovereignty; quite another, to get them accepted as constitutionally legitimate. In 1787, it was the bandwagon of state and federal institutions that gave the Federalists the authority to move beyond the signaling stage and make a serious proposal in the name of the People. A similar need for official confirmation was evident from the opening moments of the Convention/Congress. Recall that it was the Clerk of the House who sought to respond to the Democratic claim that excluding the South meant that "this . . . ceases to be a Congress." But surely somebody more important than the Clerk would have to resolve such a fundamental question.*

Recognizing this, the Republicans made a serious effort to win Presidential confirmation of their decision. Whatever else could be said about Johnson, he was no Copperhead. Nor was Secretary Seward—one of the early leaders of the Republican Party[15] who bore the wounds of Lincoln's assassins. If Johnson and Seward could be induced to accept the need for a temporary exclusion of the South, this would vastly reinforce the Convention/Congress's claims to authority.

More than symbolic politics was involved. Johnson would be a formidable enemy. His power over patronage would allow him to organize party workers in every district against errant Congressmen.

---

*This is not the first time we have come across such an *inversion of authority*. Recall that it was an inferior officer of the executive branch, Seward, who had asserted the power to consolidate the Thirteenth Amendment through a proclamation. But Seward's act came at the end of a long and complex process; MacPherson's, in contrast, came at the very beginning, and it was unreasonable to expect anything like the official acquiescence Seward's proclamation obtained.

He could also use the White House as a platform to elaborate a conservative vision of the Union that would have great appeal to moderate Republicans as well as Democrats. Presidential opposition, quite simply, threatened to destroy the Republican Party—whose ten-year existence hardly guaranteed it a permanent place in American politics.

During the early months of the session, most Republicans in Congress were prepared to concede a great deal to pacify the President.[16] To the disgust of radicals like Sumner and Stevens, moderates refused to insist on black suffrage as part of a deal that would allow Southern representatives to regain their seats.[17] This concession was crucial, since the Johnsonian governments had been organized on an all-white basis. Once Congressional Republicans waived this point, there was no fundamental obstacle to the ultimate recognition of the Johnsonian governments and the return to a normal Congress of thirty-six states.

Central to this accommodationist strategy were two proposed statutes. The Freedmen's Bureau Bill authorized an extension of federal efforts to provide extraordinary relief for newly emancipated blacks. The Civil Rights Act overruled *Dred Scott* by declaring freedmen citizens of the United States and granting them federal rights to the "full and equal benefit of all laws and proceedings for the security of person and property, as is enjoyed by white citizens."[18] If the President accepted these limited, but fundamental, statutory efforts to redeem the promise of the Thirteenth Amendment, Republicans would begin to resolve the exclusion crisis by admitting Johnsonian governments to their seats in Congress. Tennessee provided a good test case: not only was it the President's own state, but its government was dominated by men of undoubted loyalty. By the middle of February, the seating of Tennessee was under serious consideration by the Joint Committee on Reconstruction.[19]

Johnson's response marks a critical moment in the higher lawmaking process. He not only vetoed both Republican statutes, but launched a frontal assault on the legitimacy of the Convention/Congress. Here is the crucial passage from the Freedmen's Bureau veto:

I cannot but add another grave objection to this bill. The Constitution imperatively declares, in connection with taxation, that each State *shall* have at least one Representative, and fixes the rule for the number to which, in future times, each State shall be entitled. It also provides that the Senate of the United States *shall* be composed of two Senators from each State, and adds with peculiar force "that no State, without its consent, shall be deprived of its equal suffrage in the Senate." The original act [establishing the Freedmen's Bureau] was necessarily passed in the absence of the States chiefly to be affected, because their people were then contumaciously engaged in the rebellion. Now the case is changed, and some, at least, of those States are attending Congress by loyal representatives, soliciting the allowance of the constitutional right for representation. At the time, however, of the consideration of and the passing of this bill there was no Senator or Representative in Congress from the eleven States which are to be mainly affected by its provisions. The very fact that reports were and are made against the good disposition of the people of that portion of the country is an additional reason why they need and should have representatives of their own in Congress to explain their condition, reply to accusations, and assist by their own knowledge in the perfecting of measures immediately affecting themselves. . . . I would not interfere with the unquestionable right of Congress to judge, each House for itself, "of the elections, returns, and qualifications of its own members;" but that authority cannot be construed as including the right to shut out in time of peace any state from the representation to which it is entitled by the Constitution. At present all the people of eleven States are excluded—those who were most faithful during the war not less than others. . . .

The President of the United States stands toward the country in a somewhat different attitude from that of any member of Congress. Each member of Congress is chosen from a single district or State; the President is chosen by the people of all the States. As eleven States are not at this time represented in either branch of Congress, it would seem to be his duty on all proper occasions to present their just claims to Congress. . . . Under the political education of the American people the idea is inherent and ineradicable that the consent of the majority of the whole people is necessary to secure a willing acquiescence in legislation.[20]

The President is not only denying that the Rump Congress can represent the "whole people." He is claiming an affirmative role as popular tribune, representing the People in a way the Republican Rump cannot emulate.

The Convention/Congress reeled before these "dark" and "sinister"[21] claims—as do most modern historians, who regularly condemn

Johnson's "obstinacy" in failing to offer an olive branch.[22] I take a different view. I do not deny that Johnson was a stubborn fellow—as were Thaddeus Stevens, Charles Sumner, and countless others. I challenge the premise that "stubbornness" in defense of constitutional principle is always a vice.

From the dualist perspective, Johnson's "stubbornness" played a vital role in structuring the popular ascent to a higher form of lawmaking—in which political leaders sought to mobilize mass followings behind rival visions of constitutional identity. After all, the President was on solid ground in pointing out the profound questions raised by the exclusion crisis. I do not mean to say that he was "right" and his opponents were "wrong" about the "true meaning" of the constitutional guaranty of republican government.[23] My point is more complicated. During moments of grave crisis, our system does not seek to identify a quick and easy "winner" of a constitutional argument. It provides *both* sides with a rich vocabulary to make their case, encouraging them to use the resources of a common language to define critical issues for subsequent debate and, ultimately, democratic resolution by the People.

Perhaps a thought-experiment might clarify. Imagine yourself a dramatist commissioned to write a script conveying the basic constitutional issues raised in the aftermath of the Civil War: "Would Southern whites be allowed to maintain, in altered form, their old political and social supremacy? How much did the North really care about the fate of Southern blacks?" and so forth. Rather than writing a learned disquisition, you are searching for a set of dramatic images that might make these questions meaningful for a mass audience. Could you do any better than to present the scene revealed to the American people in the spring of 1866 by operation of the Constitution of the United States: On one end of Pennsylvania Avenue, a band of popularly elected "friends of the Republic" repulse the pretensions of suspect Southerners who claim admission to the councils of the Union. On the other end, stands a white Southerner who remained faithful to the Union during its time of trial and declares that the white South *has* learned the lessons of the Civil War. Who is right?

As the script worked itself out in the spring of 1866, it continued to dramatize this simple, but basic, question. On February 21, Senate Republicans fell two votes short of an override of the President's veto of the Freedmen's Bureau Act. Even after excluding the South, the Convention/Congress was unable to overcome the veto message's challenge to its constitutional authority. A month later, the Republicans did better, managing to convince a bare two-thirds of the Senate to override the President's veto of the Civil Rights Act—but only after excluding a Democratic Senator from New Jersey on the most doubtful grounds.[24]

By late March, the separation of powers had shifted into high gear as an engine of constitutional articulation. Rival branches were denouncing each other's authority to speak in the name of the People, launching a point-counterpoint that framed the next phase of popular debate, mobilization, and decision. It was this unconventional dynamic, far more than the mechanisms of Article Five, that would organize the upcoming struggle.

The Proposal Phase

Johnson had one great advantage over the Convention/ Congress. He could act unilaterally, without the need to reconcile the conflicting ideas of strong-willed Congressmen. In the agonized words of *The Nation* of March 22:

> We hear a great deal of the President's policy, it is something definite, determined, capable of being set down in black and white and discussed in all its bearings; but we never hear of the policy of Congress, because there is no such thing. The people are ready to keep the South out until it complies with certain conditions, but they want to know what these are. . . . The Reconstruction Committee has produced several valuable measures, each of them meeting some great want of the crisis, but not forming any well-defined plan. . . .
>
> More serious work than we have yet had must now begin. If it does not . . . we greatly fear the coming fall will find the public thoroughly out of patience with Congress and quite ready to let the President and his friends have their own way.[25]

But slowly the threat of impending electoral disaster concentrated the Congressional mind, leading the Republicans to hammer out the Fourteenth Amendment by late June, in time to serve as a platform for the Party in the fall elections.

The Unconventional Defense of the Fourteenth Amendment

But the vote they managed to deliver in favor of the amendment—120 in the House, 33 in the Senate—only emphasized the crucial character of Southern exclusion. With a full complement from the South, a two-thirds majority required 162 votes in the House, 48 in the Senate.[26] It would not be enough for the Republicans to defend the merits of their proposal to the country in the fall. The real question went deeper: What justified the Convention/Congress in making such a revolutionary proposal while excluding the South?

This question lies at the very heart of the great report tendered by the Joint Committee on Reconstruction in support of the Fourteenth Amendment. Prepared by Senator William Pitt Fessenden and approved by leaders of both House and Senate, the report was a principal campaign document. To modern eyes, it contains little of interest, since it barely discusses the meaning of central concepts like "equal protection" and "due process."[27] But the Committee had more urgent things to do than help modern Americans with their doctrinal predicaments. Its crucial task was to explain why Congress had the authority to propose an amendment when it only spoke for twenty-five of the thirty-six states. From the first page onward, the Committee enters into an institutional duel with the President, denying his power to reestablish civil governments in the South. Using the Guaranty Clause as its base, the report presents a mix of legal and translegal arguments characteristic of unconventional claims to authority. On the one hand, it contains an elaborate enumeration of the formal deficiencies in the process by which the Johnsonian governments had constituted themselves in the preceding months—complaining about the lack of legal documentation provided by the new Southern governments, disputing the legal sufficiency of the processes of restoration marked out by the President and so forth.[28] On the other hand, the Committee dismisses the notion that Southern governments might normalize their political status by dotting a few more *i*'s and jumping through a few more legal hoops:

> It should appear affirmatively that they [the Southern states] are prepared and disposed in good faith to accept the results of the war, to abandon their hostility to the government, and to live in peace and amity with the

people of the loyal States, extending to all classes of citizens equal rights and privileges, and conforming to the republican idea of liberty and equality. They should exhibit in their acts something more than an unwilling submission to an unavoidable necessity—a feeling, if not cheerful, certainly not offensive and defiant. And they should evince an entire repudiation of all hostility to the general government, by an acceptance of such just and reasonable conditions as that government should think the public safety demands. Has this been done? Let us look at the facts shown by the evidence taken by the committee.

Hardly is the war closed before the people of these insurrectionary States come forward and haughtily claim, as a right, the privilege of participating at once in that government which they had for four years been fighting to overthrow. Allowed and encouraged by the Executive to organize State governments, they at once place in power leading rebels, unrepentant and unpardoned, excluding with contempt those who had manifested an attachment to the Union, and preferring, in many instances, those who had rendered themselves the most obnoxious. In the face of the law requiring an oath which would necessarily exclude all such men from federal offices, they elect, with very few exceptions, as senators and representatives in Congress, men who had actively participated in the rebellion, insultingly denouncing the law as unconstitutional. . . . Professing no repentance, glorying apparently in the crime they had committed, avowing still . . . an adherence to the pernicious doctrine of secession, and declaring that they yielded only to necessity, they insist, with unanimous voice, upon their rights as States, and proclaim that they will submit to no conditions whatever as preliminary to their resumption of power under that Constitution which they still claim the right to repudiate.[29]

The report is demanding nothing less than a spiritual transformation of the South. Until such time as Southerners repent, Congress will not heed their legalistic demands for admission: "Treason, defeated in the field, has only to take possession of Congress and the cabinet."[30]

We have seen this move before. Just as Fessenden defended the authority of the Convention/Congress, Madison defended the authority of the Philadelphia Convention against the Anti-Federalists' legalistic critique. Here is a comparable text from the *Federalist Papers:*

Let us view the ground on which the Convention stood. . . . They must have reflected that in all great changes of established governments, forms ought to give way to substance; . . . nor could it have been forgotten that no little ill-timed scruples, no zeal for adhering to ordinary forms, were anywhere seen, except in those who wished to indulge, under these masks, their secret enmity to the substance contended for. They must have borne in mind that as the plan to be framed and proposed was to be submitted to *the people themselves,* the disapprobation of this supreme authority would destroy it forever; its approbation blot out antecedent errors and irregularities.[31]

There is danger here. Once Madison likens his formalist opponents to disloyal Tories who use legality as a "mask" to conceal their "secret enmity," once Fessenden treats legalism as a form of "treason," we are reaching the point where convention-like institutions threaten to careen out of democratic control, and the self-proclaimed Party of Virtue breaks free of all constitutional restraints.

But it is here where the key difference between leaders like Madison and Fessenden, and those like Robespierre and Lenin, comes to the fore. While Federalists and Republicans challenge normal procedures, they are unwilling to smash all of the legitimating structures within which they are imbedded. Fessenden does not claim the authority to impose the Fourteenth Amendment on the South by brute force. Like the *Federalist Papers,* his *Report* seeks to adapt preexisting institutions into a new and democratic ratifying pattern.

When addressing the ratification question, the Committee steers a course between two extremes. On the one hand, it nowhere endorses the radical claim that three-fourths of the Northern states will suffice. On the other hand, it explicitly rejects the Johnsonian claim that the new Southern governments should be conceded the *normal* right to reject the amendment for any reason they see fit. Instead, the Committee proposes a remarkable statute that would allow the Southern governments to participate in ratification under anomalous ground rules. This statute seeks to condition the Johnsonian government's future representation in Congress on their approval of the amendment: "Whereas it is expedient that the States lately in insurrection should, at the earliest day consistent with the future peace and safety of the Union, be restored to full participation in all political rights," the statute indicates that if the Johnsonian governments support the Amendment,[32] their representatives could expect to regain their seats in Congress.

This initial effort to design an unconventional triggering mechanism would not, in fact, regulate the ratification struggle. But it does suggest how seriously Congress was already taking the problem.

Presidential Counterpoint

The President had his own ideas. Nine days after Congress proposed the amendment, he responded with an unprecedented message. In its first paragraph, he reported that the Secretary of State had forwarded the proposal to the states for ratification. The concluding two paragraphs should not be paraphrased:

> Even in ordinary times, any question of amending the Constitution must be justly regarded as of paramount importance. This importance is at the present time enhanced by the fact that the joint resolution was not submitted by the two houses for the approval of the President, and that of the thirty-six States which constitute the Union, eleven are excluded from the representation in either House of Congress, although, with the single exception of Texas, they have been entirely restored to all their functions as States, in conformity with the organic law of the land, and have appeared at the national capital by Senators and Representatives who have applied for and have been refused admission to the vacant seats. Nor have the sovereign people of the nation been afforded an opportunity of expressing their views upon the important questions which the amendment involves. Grave doubts, therefore, may naturally and justly arise as to whether the action of Congress is in harmony with the sentiments of the people, and whether State Legislatures, elected without reference to such an issue, should be called upon by Congress to decide respecting the ratification of the proposed amendment.
>
> Waiving the question as to the constitutional validity of the proceedings of Congress upon the joint resolution proposing the amendment, or as to the merits of the article which it submits, through the executive department, to the Legislatures of the states, I deem it proper to observe that the steps taken by the Secretary of State, as detailed in the accompanying report, are to be considered as purely ministerial, and in no sense whatever committing the Executive to an approval or a recommendation of the amendment to the State Legislatures or to the people. On the contrary, a proper appreciation of the letter and spirit of the Constitution, as well as of the interests of national order, harmony, and union, and a due deference for an enlightened public judgment, may at this time well suggest a doubt

whether any amendment to the Constitution ought to be proposed by Congress and pressed upon the Legislatures of the several States for final decision until after the admission of such loyal Senators and Representatives of the now unrepresented States as have been or as may hereafter be chosen in conformity with the Constitution and laws of the United States.[33]

This remarkable protest represents another landmark in the rise of Presidential leadership. Recall that Lincoln had broken with earlier precedents by formally approving the Congressional proposal of the Thirteenth Amendment before sending it to the states.[34] Johnson is now asserting the President's authority to intervene with equal force, but in an opposite direction.

THE TRIGGERING ELECTION

Given the exclusion of the South, the elections for the House of Representatives were charged with extraordinary constitutional meaning. The crucial operational question was whether the Republicans could carry 122 seats. This was the number that gave them a majority of all House seats including those from the South.[35]

If the Republicans fell short, they opened themselves up to a devastating counterattack. The President would then be free to recognize the 122 Johnsonian Representatives from North and South, together with their conservative colleagues in the Senate,[36] as *the* Congress. Such a move would put the more radical Republicans between a rock and a hard place: either they could meekly take their seats in the Johnsonian Congress, or they could try to continue to assert that they were the "true" Congress despite their smaller numbers. In either case, the President would have won a stunning victory: if the Northern Republicans joined the Johnsonian Congress, they would no longer have the votes required to take unconventional measures to induce the white South to ratify the Fourteenth Amendment. If they boycotted the President's Congress, they would reveal themselves for what, in the President's eyes, they already were: radicals willing to dismember the Union in order to achieve their extreme objectives.

A loss of only twenty to thirty House seats exposed the Republicans to this threat;[37] and the danger was a subject of Republican oratory during the campaign.[38] Indeed, when the Republicans later drew up articles of impeachment against the President, his campaign assault became the substance of a "high crime and misdemeanor." Only one impeachment article (Article XI) ever came up for a vote and it began:

> That said Andrew Johnson . . . did . . . on the 18th day of August, 1866, at the city of Washington, in the District of Columbia, by public speech, declare and affirm in substance that the Thirty-ninth Congress of the United States was not a Congress of the United States authorized to exercise legislative power under the same; but, on the contrary, was a Congress of only part of the States, thereby denying and intending to deny that the legislation of said Congress was valid or obligatory upon him, the said Andrew Johnson, except in so far as he saw fit to approve the same, and also thereby denying and intending to deny the power of the said Thirty-ninth Congress to propose amendments to the Constitution of the United States; . . .[39]

Johnson's challenge was also emphatically remembered at the opening arguments at the impeachment trial:

> Does anyone doubt that if the intentions of the respondent [i.e., the President] had been carried out, and his denunciations [during the election of 1866] had weakened the Congress in the affections of the people, so that [his supporters in the North and South had] formed a majority of both or either House of Congress, that the President would have recognized such body as the legitimate Congress, and attempted to carry out its decrees by the aid of the Army and Navy and the Treasury of the United States . . . and thus lighted the torch of civil war?[40]

These remarks come from Congressman Ben Butler—a man not noted for understatement. While talk of civil war may be extreme,[41] Butler's remarks suggest the high constitutional stakes raised by the election in the public mind.

Shortly after the President filed his formal protest against the Fourteenth Amendment, a call came out from Washington inviting partisans who "sustain the Administration in maintaining unbroken the Union of the States under the Constitution" to meet in a National Union Convention to prepare for the elections. The convention's aim was to organize a new moderate-conservative party whose victory would discredit the constitutional proposals of the existing Congressional leadership.

As so often before, the word *convention* dramatized the limits of legal form in establishing political legitimacy. Meeting in Philadelphia (where else?),[42] the convention was the first important assembly since the Civil War to include political leaders from both the North and South.[43] From its first moments, its challenge to Congressional legitimacy was unmistakable: its opening procession was led by the delegations from Massachusetts and South Carolina, who walked arm in arm into the hall together. The message was plain enough: while the Republican "Congress" in Washington only spoke for the North, the "Arm-in-Arm" Convention in Philadelphia *legitimately* represented We the People of the (Re-)United States. To emphasize the breadth of the new movement, Congressman Henry Raymond had been selected to proclaim the convention's declaration of principles. Chairman of the Republican National Committee and publisher of the *New York Times,* Raymond exemplified the Northern moderates whom the National Union sought to enlist in the struggle against the Convention/Congress.[44]

The platform was a paean to Andrew Johnson, "steadfast in his devotion to the Constitution . . . equal to the great crisis upon which his lot is cast."[45] It insisted that "all the States have an equal and indefeasible right to a voice and a vote" in changing higher law.[46] On August 18, the platform was formally presented to the President in Washington, occasioning the speech that was later singled out as a "high crime and misdemeanor."[47]

But Johnson went further. In an unprecedented[48] decision, he went on the campaign trail against Congress. Determined to take his message to the People, Johnson boarded a special campaign train to "swing the circle" of critical Northern states.[49] In response, the Republican Party made the Fourteenth Amendment the ideological centerpiece of its effort to reassert itself as the true spokesman for the Union.[50]

The ensuing struggle forced to the surface competing understandings of American identity. On the conception of the Union championed by Johnson and his partisans, America remained a white man's country. When Johnsonians looked to the South, they saw fellow whites reasserting their rightful place in the Union. While these whites had strayed from the path of righteousness, they had now rejoined the nation by adopting the Emancipation Amendment, which had finally destroyed the slave power that had been the root cause of the Civil War. Having destroyed slavery, weren't these white Southerners indistinguishable from the typical white Northerner, who shared their racist anxieties?

The Republicans divided the world differently.[51] For them, the crucial test of American identity was not racial but political: Were you loyal to the Union or were you a traitor?

As white Southerners had abundantly established, skin color was no guarantee of loyalty. In contrast, blacks had proven their loyalty by dying for the Union by the thousands. And when Republicans looked at the postwar South, blacks were the only large bloc who could be relied upon to stand up for the Union. It was these men and women who were the *true* Americans, not the former Confederates who were rediscovering the glories of states' rights. The Nation must extend its protection to these black men and women, guaranteeing their rights as American citizens before the states could be legitimately allowed to return to the fold.

As the election of 1866 reached its climax, voters were being asked to confront a truly constitutive question. Stripped down to essentials, it was simply this: which was *more* fundamental to the American Union— racial identity or political identity?*

Doubtless, many voters would have preferred to avoid such a probing question; many would have been happy to suppose that Reconstruction could proceed without their having to wrestle with their souls. But the American system did not give them this choice. For good or for ill, they would have to cast a ballot one way or the other. They could vote for the party of a white Southerner who did not disguise his racism but who insisted on its compatibility with loyalty to the Union. Or they could vote for the party of the Fourteenth Amend-

---

*Petroleum V. Nasby, a popular commentator of the time, put the point more cynically: "Rites for a nigger! Why all the difference between a nigger and a Dimocrat is in this matter uv rites. That's the bone uv contention. Give a Georgia nigger the same rites endoored by the whites, and turn loose among them school-masters and skool-marms, and how much inferior are they to the whites uv that state. I'm a bleever in blood, I am, and es nine-tenths uv the niggers in the South hev coursin in their veins the proud patrician blood uv the Rhetts, Davis', Yanceys, Wises, Quitmans, and such wot chance wood I hev who haint got no blood, hevin bin born in Noo Jersey uv paents wich wuz poor but not honest, ef these niggers with sich parentage had their rites, and cood read?" Nasby, *Androo Johnson, His Life, includin' his infancy, his boyhood, and his Dimocrisy and Abolitionism, separate and mixed* 30 (1866) (Beinecke Manuscripts Collection, Yale University).

ment, asserting that "all persons born or naturalized in the United States . . . are citizens of the United States," and that "no State shall abridge the privileges or immunities of citizens of the United States."

When put to this test, Americans gave a remarkably straightforward answer. By the time the votes were counted, the conservatives had suffered a devastating personal, organizational, and electoral defeat. Personally, the "swing around the circle" became a disaster for Johnson. Rather than stating his case with dignity, he provided newspapers with a steady flow of intemperate stump speeches that debased his office in the public mind.[52] Organizationally, Democrats manipulated the National Union label for narrowly partisan ends, making it an unattractive home for moderate Republicans.[53] Electorally, the Union's candidates were overwhelmed in a landslide. Rather than reducing the Republican representation below 122, the President would confront a House containing 144 Northern Republicans, who outnumbered the 49 Northern Democrats by a margin of 3 to 1 (so long as the South continued to be excluded).[54] Republicans also carried every Northern legislature, as well as every contested governorship.[55]

The President's strenuous effort to characterize the Convention/Congress as a body of radical dis-Unionists had backfired. But this did not make it pointless. Were it not for Andrew Johnson, we might never have known that nineteenth-century Americans were prepared to set aside their racist prejudices long enough to support the Republican vision of a Union that made birth-right citizenship, and not skin color, the fundamental bond that sustains our identity as a People.[56]

As we shall see, this great Republican victory was hardly enough to endow the Fourteenth Amendment with higher law status. Nonetheless, it did shift the balance of legitimacy as the Republicans returned to Washington and considered their next steps. Before the election, Presidency and Congress were in equipoise as they forcefully advanced competing diagnoses of the constitutional crisis. But now, the Convention/Congress was in the ascendancy. How would the Republicans interpret their mandate from the People? Would a chastened Andrew Johnson accept their interpretation? If not, would the Republicans be able to repeat their victory when the conservatives challenged them again in 1868?

I take these questions up in the next chapter. But before we push onward, consider some of the broader implications of the unfolding pattern.

TEXTUALISM RECONSIDERED

Consider how much of our story is omitted from the textualist account of the genesis of the Fourteenth Amendment. Article Five fails to mention the Presidency; on its view, the only significant national actor is an assembly like the Thirty-ninth Congress. As a consequence, the textualist misses the key role played by Johnson in forcefully articulating—and personifying—the conservative side in the constitutional debate. Similarly, the article fails to recognize the role national elections can play in testing a proposal's popular support. As a consequence, the textualist fails to notice that the voters of the South, no less than those of the North, played a crucial role in 1866 in determining the fate of the Fourteenth Amendment.

These omissions have a cumulating and distorting impact on textualist understanding, especially when conjoined to the single fact that will predictably gain respectful attention. Since Article Five does emphasize the role of "Congress," the textualist must pause long and hard over the ostentatious way the South was excluded from the Congress that proposed the amendment. When lifted out of context, this single fact will lead to a dark diagnosis of the amendment's authority: Since the Fourteenth Amendment was proposed by a Northern Congress, how can it represent the considered judgment of We the People of the United States? Isn't it more honestly treated as an act of Northern imposition upon a prostrate South?

Within the Article Five framework, the Fourteenth Amendment is a *Civil War* amendment.[57] But for me, this characterization reveals the bankruptcy of the underlying approach. As this chapter shows, representatives of the white South were *very* powerful participants in the higher lawmaking system; it is only an odd preference for eighteenth-century texts over nineteenth-century practices that blinds us to this fact. Once we take practice seriously, we can see that the crucial 1866 elections counted the South, no less than the North, as full participants. As we have seen, the Republicans needed 122 House seats in the Fortieth Congress; yet this calculus placed Southern districts on a par with Northern districts. Indeed, Southern whites were in an especially favored position in this critical test. To see why, simply recall the notorious Three-Fifths Compromise of the original Constitution. Under its terms, the white South gained a bonus in the House of Representives for three-fifths of its black slaves. Since the Thirteenth Amendment did nothing to reduce the whites' electoral bonus, the Southerners retained their advantage in 1866. This meant that the average Northern district contained 160 percent of the potential voters included in the average Southern district!

Once we bring these facts into play, the framing of the Fourteenth Amendment no longer seem an outrageous case of textualist rupture and sectional imposition. Instead, nineteenth-century Americans appear to have brilliantly adapted their constitutional traditions to allow for a remarkably open and even-handed process. Rather than silencing the white South, the Constitution enabled a white Southern President to launch a powerful critique of the Republican proposal. Rather than excluding the South from the critical election of 1866, the Constitution required the Republicans to win 122 House seats to sustain constitutional momentum, *thereby giving Southern white votes a disproportionately heavy weight in the electoral balance.*

Our effort to understand this process is greatly assisted by our previous discussion of the Thirteenth Amendment—which provides a precedent for the two great institutional adaptations isolated in this chapter. The first involves the role of the separation of powers as an engine through which constitutional options are debated and refined. In dealing with emancipation, we saw how the Thirteenth Amendment emerged from a tension-laden dialogue between the President and Congress. Only this time, the two branches played opposite roles—while Lincoln was the partisan of revolutionary reform in the case of Thirteenth Amendment, Johnson was the leader of conservative opposition in the case of the Fourteenth; and vice versa for the Congress. Similarly, it was President Lincoln, not Johnson, who first sought to use a national election as a popular mandate in his struggle to win Congressional confirmation for emancipation—with the difference that the South was ostentatiously absent during the elections of 1864 and very much present in 1866.

It is true, of course, that the Founding Federalists had never contemplated this new dynamic based on the interaction of the separation of powers and national elections. But then again, the Federalists had never anticipated that their Constitution would survive a bloody civil war, and yet provide many of the institutional materials for a renewed popular effort to redefine the Union. Rather than mourning the break with Federalist forms, we will find it more rewarding to follow the Republicans as they sought to give meaning to their decisive electoral victory.

CHAPTER SEVEN

Interpreting the Mandate

A TRIGGERING ELECTION?

THE ASPIRATION of formalism is to provide a specification, in advance, of the meaning of every step in a legal process. This has many benefits, but one big cost. Life is surprising and will evade all efforts to cabin it within preset formulas. The protagonists will then confront exquisite moments of self-conscious indeterminacy. While great events may have disrupted old formulas, they do not carry a clear legal meaning of their own. Debate turns to competing interpretations of the disruptive events, as the protagonists seek to fill the interpretive gap with different meanings. But how to determine which of the contenders will emerge victorious?

The problem, in our case, was posed by the election of 1866. Formally speaking, the Republican victory at the polls simply meant that the Party would be in charge of Congress for the next two years; it had no implications for the ratification of the Fourteenth Amendment, whose structure was preset by Article Five. Under its terms, once Congress had proposed the amendment, it was entirely in the hands of the state legislatures—which were free to accept or reject the amendment as they saw fit.

This formalist view was adopted by President Johnson, who urged the states of the South to use their Article Five power to veto the amendment. In response, the Convention/Congress reconsidered the sources of its authority. Was it an ordinary legal body bound by Federalist principles? Or did the election of 1866 provide it with a popular mandate to move beyond Federalist models of ratification?

The Republicans asserted their mandate from the People in the First and Second Reconstruction Acts. Seemingly sober historians have characterized these acts in wildly different ways. During the first half of the century, they were regularly denounced as revolutionary; more recently, they have been even called conservative.[1] Both sides are right. When judged by Federalist principles, the triggering activities of the Convention/Congress involved a blatant breach of preexisting constitutional law; but when judged by the standards of the nineteenth—or the twentieth—century, they did represent a moderate—even a conservative—solution.

I also hope to clarify the role of triggering elections in the overall process of unconventional adaptation. My treatment of such elections has frequently been misinterpreted. Readers of previous work seem to impose an overly anthropomorphic understanding on my remarks—as if "the People" were the name of a superhuman being who could "speak" at an election in the same way that you or I might speak at a lecture podium. On this view, the election of 1866 served as a magic moment at which THE PEOPLE SPOKE and decisively ratified a Fourteenth Amendment that had previously been the object of elite contestation in Washington.

Since my addiction to metaphor has undoubtedly helped propagate this misunderstanding, permit me to reject it as clearly as I can. For me, "the People" is not the name of a superhuman being, but the name of an extended process of interaction between political elites and ordinary citizens. It is a special process because, during constitutional moments, most ordinary Americans are spending extraordinary amounts of time and energy on the project of citizenship, paying attention to the goings-on in Washington with much greater concern than usual. If the higher lawmaking system operates successfully, it will channel this active citizenship engagement into a structured dialogue between political elites and ordinary Americans—first giving competing elites the chance to elaborate alternative constitutional meanings; then inviting citizens to share in the debate and cast their votes. These votes, in turn, shape the constitutional debate and decisions of political elites during the next period, which are then subjected to citizen debate and decision at the next election; and so forth. If this dynamic is working well, the result will be increasing convergence between the talk that is going on in the country and the talk occurring in the capitol. As a constitutional solution is hammered out, the prevailing elites and the majority of citizens will share common concerns and basic aims to a much higher degree than usual. The process ends as the general citizenry retreats from its extraordinary levels of engagement, leaving political elites to engage in normal electoral competition in a way that is broadly consistent with the terms worked out in dialogue with the People during the preceding period.[2]

The notion of a *triggering election* conveys, I hope, the distinctive role of 1866 in this extended process. These elections marked neither the beginning nor the end of the Fourteenth Amendment story. Instead, they triggered a radical shift in the balance of perceived legitimacies in Washington. Before the ballots were counted, President Johnson and the Convention/Congress were competing with one another on relatively equal terms—each claiming that the People would support their rival constitutional visions. Afterwards, the Convention/Congress was on the offensive. The operational question was no longer whether the majority of Americans supported the President— they didn't, and any fool understood this. The question was what, if anything, the Republicans would make of their popular mandate, and whether the President, and other conservative parts of the government, would go along or insist on making the elections of 1868 into another referendum on the Fourteenth Amendment.

JOHNSONIAN FORMALISM

The first move was the President's. He could read the election returns as well as the next man. If he had responded by abandoning his opposition to the Fourteenth Amendment, he would have been doing nothing unusual. Successful American politicians are not known for ideological rigidity. As we have seen, they had already negotiated a switch in time in the case of the Thirteenth Amendment. Before the elections of 1864, Congressional Democrats had consistently defeated the Republicans' Emancipation Amendment; but opposition collapsed after conservatives saw the election returns, and the amendment passed the two-thirds hurdle on Democratic votes.

Moreover, if Johnson had switched, he had already pioneered a range of unconventional techniques of Presidential leadership in his successful campaign for ratification of the Thirteenth Amendment. As in 1865, so in 1867, the President and his Secretary could have dispatched a steady stream of telegrams containing threats and promises to the white governments of the South. As in 1865, they could have offered the Southerners a deal—ratify the Fourteenth Amendment, and Congress will admit your representatives and thereby call a halt to revolutionary reform. Granted, the President had made similar promises before, only to see Congressional Republicans repudiate them. But this time, the Convention/Congress had already taken steps to enhance Presidential credibility.

Ironically, Congressional reinforcement had come in the case of the President's home state of Tennessee. Johnson had lost political control of the state to political enemies, who used the Fourteenth Amendment as a tool to embarrass him.[3] When Tennessee ratified on July 19, 1866, Republican moderates quickly responded by unconditionally admitting the Tennessee delegation to both Houses of Congress. Much to the disgust of the radicals, a precedent had been established for other Southern states that gave the amendment their endorsement.

But the President rejected the temptations of a "switch in time." In his view, the election returns did not amount to a decisive mandate from the People. They were best understood as a momentary aberration—the product of a cynical Republican effort to manipulate wartime emotions for partisan purposes.[4] The challenge was to remain steadfast in defeat. If he continued to resist the pretensions of the Convention/Congress, the People would come to their senses and support his courageous service to the Constitution at its time of crisis. After all, time was on his side—or so he could readily believe. Under his conservative interpretation, the ten states of the former Confederacy sufficed to form a veto bloc under Article Five.[5] If they remained firm, the Republican amendment would remain in constitutional limbo. Rejectionism, in the language of the time, would lead to a policy of "masterly inactivity."[6] Nothing would be firmly decided before the next round of elections in 1868—at which time the Presidency, as well as Congress, would be up for grabs. Indeed, who was better placed to lead this next great conservative struggle than Johnson himself?[7]

THE CONVENTION/CONGRESS DEFENDS ITS MANDATE

By January 1867, the Convention/Congress understood that it was confronting a constitutional crisis that shook the very foundations of

Article Five. By that point, the President had organized a bloc of Southern states determined to stand firm behind their veto of the Fourteenth Amendment.[8] Once again, the separation of powers was forcing fundamental higher lawmaking questions to the center of political life. If the Convention/Congress did not take steps to trigger the ratification of the Fourteenth Amendment, the President's policy of masterly inactivity would prevail—and the Republicans would be obliged to return to the voters in 1868 in disarray. When faced with this prospect, the Republicans struggled with some basic questions: Did the recent elections give the Convention/Congress an extraordinary mandate from the People? If so, how to translate the heady rhetoric of constitutional politics into the hard lines of constitutional law?

These questions were at the center of a great Congressional debate that began in early January and ended with the enactment of the First Reconstruction Act of March 2, 1867. The importance of this debate has long been recognized by American historians,[9] but legal scholars have failed to follow suit.[10] While they have endlessly scrutinized the earlier debates surrounding the proposal of the Fourteenth Amendment, they have supposed there was nothing left for Congress to decide once it had sent the amendment to the states in June 1866. On this hypertextualist view, the *Congressional Globe* of early 1867 contains a report on an unrelated topic—the "Reconstruction Act of 1867." The debate surrounding this act might be of antiquarian interest, but it is not part of the canon that provides the legislative history of the Fourteenth Amendment.

I reject this hypertextualist view. More importantly, so did the Convention/Congress. Members were perfectly aware that the Fourteenth Amendment would go down to defeat unless they took further decisive action. Indeed, their central aim in passing the Reconstruction Act was to override the veto of the Fourteenth Amendment. This claim might seem surprising to modern readers, who have been taught to look upon Congressional Reconstruction primarily in social and economic terms. But these were not the terms of the Congressional debate. For better and for worse, the language of constitutional law provided the organizing context, with many speakers presenting arguments of extraordinary quality. It is possible to discount all this legalistic rhetoric as a mere mystification of the "real" interests at play. But, as I hope I have made clear, the Convention/Congress was confronting a very real legitimacy problem; and it would require lots of argument—pro and con—before the Republicans would converge on the unconventional solution that promised to override the Southern veto of the Fourteenth Amendment in a way that most Americans might find credible.

Was There a Mandate?

Under the nineteenth century's constitutional calendar, the newly elected Congress would not convene before March 4, 1867. Until then, the old Congress was scheduled to meet in its "lame-duck" session. Nevertheless, the Republicans thought that the democratic authority of their "lame-duck" session had been massively reinforced by the electoral returns. Facing down Democratic pleas against "revolutionary" action,[11] speaker after speaker[12] rose to assert that the People had now given the Convention/Congress a mandate for immediate decisions.

Speeches from conservative Republicans like Henry Raymond were particularly revealing.[13] We last saw him playing a leading role at the National Union Convention of Andrew Johnson's supporters. But when he returned to the public stage as a Congressman from New York, he was singing a different tune:

> [A]s I do not desire to follow the example of the attorney who persisted in arguing his case after the jury had brought in a verdict, I will take occasion to say that in my judgment some aspects of this great question of reconstruction have been virtually settled, so far at least as to remove them from the arena of profitable discussion at this time. By various expressions of public sentiment, through the press, through this body, in legislative assemblies all over the land, and especially through the verdict rendered last fall at the polls, I think I am quite justified in saying that the people have themselves already decided several points of this great controversy. One of the points embraced in that decision I think is this: that they are not willing to accept as a basis of adjustment and restoration what has been put forward as the policy of the President of the United States. In other words, they are not willing that the States lately in insurrection shall resume their former portion of political power as members of this Union, and to give admission to their representatives in the two Houses of Congress without

some provision for the future or without specific authority of law. The President had put this forward as his view of what was just and proper to be done in this case, providing only that the representatives they might send should be loyal men. I concurred in that opinion; and I say frankly that I am still of the opinion that if this had been done at an early stage of the controversy, promptly, cheerfully, generously by the party which ruled the destinies of this country at that time, it would have restored peace and healed to a great extent all the troubles of the body-politic. But because I believed and still believe that to have been the best policy then, I do not feel bound to maintain that it is the best policy now. A physician may prescribe a gargle for a sore throat; and if his prescription is thrown out of the window the sore throat may develop into an inflammation or into a raging and consuming fever; but he would be regarded as wanting in sound judgment and in common sense if for the sake of consistency he should feel bound to prescribe nothing but gargles during the whole progress of the disease. I shall therefore dismiss from consideration as impracticable and out of the question this mode of settling the controversy which divides and distracts the nation. And in the next place, although they have not pronounced decisively upon any specific plan of adjustment, I think the people have decided more nearly than they have decided upon anything else that the constitutional amendment adopted by Congress at its last session and submitted to the several States for ratification affords, on the whole, the wisest and the most satisfactory basis of adjustment of which this question in its present attitude is susceptible. And finally, I think the people have decided that they would rather trust to Congress to devise some mode of settling this question, some mode of restoring those States which were lately in rebellion to the Union, than trust to the executive department of the Government. They regard it as a matter for the legislative power rather than for the President alone.[14]

Although Raymond had loyally struggled for his President, it was now clear to him that the Convention/Congress had *earned* its claim to constitutional leadership. The President's defeat left Johnson in the position of "the attorney who persisted in arguing his case after the jury had brought in a verdict."

But it was one thing for conservative Republicans like Raymond to agree that the People now supported strong measures, quite another to translate the excited rhetoric of constitutional politics into a legally operational solution. How *precisely* was the Convention/Congress to respond to the problem posed by the Southern veto of the Fourteenth Amendment?

Defining the Mandate

Republicans were, as always, divided. Radicals, led by Thaddeus Stevens, had never viewed the Fourteenth Amendment as more than an expedient compromise that might enable the party to survive its battle with Andrew Johnson. They now proposed a more sweeping political and social transformation for the South.

A more numerous group of centrists looked upon the amendment as the final solution to the constitutional crisis. Leaders like John Bingham saw the electoral victory as a massive popular endorsement for their view:

> I stand upon the proposition that the Congress . . . did give out this amendment to the people of the United States as the future basis of reconstruction. . . . Mr. Speaker, the people of the United States so understood and accepted it. There are gentlemen here, not a few I undertake to say, who owe their reelection to the Fortieth Congress to the fact that the [Republican] conventions in the States which they represent upon this floor declared their acceptance of this constitutional amendment, in manner and form as it now stands, as a condition of future restoration.[15]

Speaking for moderate Republicans, Bingham aimed to design a procedure that would credibly override the Southern veto of the Fourteenth Amendment. If this could be accomplished, his interest in excluding the South came to an end. Once the amendment had been cemented into the foundation of higher law, he was prepared to allow the Convention/Congress to convert itself into a normal Congress by admitting Southerners.

Radicals wanted to defer the return of normal politics. As a consequence, it was crucially important for them to reject the centrists' triggering view of the recent elections. Here is Thaddeus Stevens inaugurating the great debate:

> I deny that there is any understanding, expressed or implied, that upon the adoption of the [Fourteenth] amendment by any State, that such State may be admitted. . . . Such a course would soon surrender the Government into the hands of the rebels. Such a course would be senseless, inconsistent, and illogical. Congress denies that any State lately in rebellion has any government or constitution known to the Constitution of the United States, or which can be recognized as a part of the Union. How, then, can such a State adopt the amendment? To allow it would be yielding

the whole question and admitting the unimpaired rights of the seceded states. I know of no Republican who does not ridicule what Mr. Seward thought a cunning movement, in counting Virginia and other outlawed States among those which had adopted the constitutional amendment abolishing slavery.[16]

Stevens conveniently forgot the history surrounding the Thirteenth Amendment—how leading Republicans waited for the Secretary to proclaim the amendment's validity, how most Republicans refused to support radical claims that three-fourths of the North sufficed for ratification under Article Five.[17] Indeed, his all-out effort to deny the triggering interpretation of the past election was controversial amongst his fellow radicals. Even James Ashley—whose plan for Reconstruction was more draconic in some respects than Stevens's—conceded that he would have voted to admit any Johnsonian government that had ratified the Fourteenth Amendment. It was only because "the great body of the men recently in rebellion, under the lead of the Executive, have rejected these mild terms"[18] that Ashley believed himself free to join Stevens in demanding more from the South. Despite these variations on the radical theme, the critical question was clear enough: should the Convention/Congress claim a mandate for a more sweeping transformation of the South or should it seek only to trigger the unconventional ratification of the amendment?

Stevens and Ashley set the initial terms of the January debate in (rival) bills aiming for a sweeping political revolution in the South—enfranchising all blacks while disqualifying whites who could not swear they had opposed the rebellion after March 4, 1864.[19] More important for our purposes, both bills broke the link between Congressional intervention and ratification of the Fourteenth Amendment. Both refused to guarantee Congressional readmission if the new governments ratified the amendment; indeed, they did not explicitly invite Southern participation in the ratification process.[20]

Predictably, Bingham viewed such proposals as a "usurpation of powers which do not belong to the Congress of the United States, [to] induce the people to fling aside the constitutional amendment, and thereby subject the future of this Republic to all those dread calamities which have darkened its recent past."[21] After an intense and protracted debate, he emerged victorious. On January 28, a majority of the House supported Bingham's motion to return the radical bills to the Joint Committee on Reconstruction.[22]

This placed all Republicans at the mercy of the constitutional calendar. On March 4, the lame-duck session would end and the Republicans would have to begin again in the next Congress, losing precious time and momentum. Given the need for quick action, the Joint Committee on Reconstruction tried to avoid another internecine battle. Its new proposal focused on a narrow, but crucial, issue that might win the support of all Republican factions. The Convention/Congress had been bombarded with reports detailing case after case in which loyal Unionists (both black and white) had been killed or oppressed by Southern diehards. Even if the Party could not unite on other matters, surely it could act forcefully to stop the intolerable mistreatment of fellow Unionists?

This was the aim of the "military bill" introduced by Stevens on behalf of the joint committee in early February. The bill contained five short paragraphs, dividing the South into five military districts and authorizing each district commander to "punish all disturbers of the peace" in military tribunals.[23] To insulate martial law from obstruction by federal courts, it suspended *habeas corpus*. It said nothing, however, about the triggering question that had divided Stevens from Bingham. In a bitter speech, Stevens called upon his Republican opponents to defer their combat over this issue and act quickly, lest the Thirty-ninth Congress "go home and leave the President triumphant."[24]

Bingham was unimpressed. On February 13, he opposed Stevens's motion to bring the simple "military bill" to a vote, and once again he emerged victorious.[25] He then proposed an amendment[26] to gain his fundamental aim: to design a triggering mechanism that would override the Southern veto of the Fourteenth Amendment. Bingham's proposal represented a big change in his thinking. When he last addressed the subject in January, he had played with the old radical idea that the amendment might be adopted on the basis of three-fourths of the Northern states. While this notion was strong medicine, it avoided the need for the kind of forceful military intervention supported by Stevens and Ashley. As Bingham then saw the matter, Congress could declare the Fourteenth Amendment valid on the basis of Northern votes and then tell the white South that it held the key to Congressional readmission in its own pocket: each Southern state would be promised its seats in Congress as soon as it ratified the amendment. Bingham thought his offer was irresistible: Since the Fourteenth Amendment would already be on the books, surely Southerners would not fail to go through the meaningless ritual of ratification to regain real political influence on Capitol Hill?

But even in January, Bingham was perfectly aware of the constitutional weaknesses of his scheme:

> But, say some, there are two departments of the Government against this asserted power of the people of the organized States, the executive and judicial. My answer is, neither of these departments has any voice in the matter—no right to challenge the authority of the people. I have no concern or care for any influence which the President may seek to exert. He is powerless with the people. He can in no way reverse their final judgment. But we are told the Supreme Court of the United States will strike down this amendment, if ratified by three-fourths of the organized and represented States and declared duly ratified by authority of an act of this Congress.
>
> I do not share in the fears thus expressed. That supreme tribunal of justice has no power in the premises. It is not a judicial question; it is a political question in the decision of which the Supreme Court can in no wise interfere. . . .

Having dismissed fears of judicial intervention, Bingham went on to indulge them:

> If . . . gentlemen are at all apprehensive of any wrongful intervention of the Supreme Court in this behalf, sweep away at once their appellate jurisdiction in all cases, and leave the tribunal without even color or appearance of authority for their wrongful intervention. . . . If, however, the court usurps power to decide political questions and defy a free people's will it will only remain for a people thus insulted and defied to demonstrate that the servant is not above his lord by procuring a further constitutional amendment and ratifying the same, which will defy judicial usurpation by annihilating the usurpers in the abolition of the tribunal itself.[27]

These apocalyptic visions led Bingham to rethink his triggering strategy. By February, he abandoned radical mathematics and adopted an alternative scheme that envisioned ratification by a super-majority of all the states. To accomplish this, Bingham was now prepared to accept the radical insistence that blacks be allowed to vote, since it was only in this way that Southern Republicans could reasonably hope to create majorities that would reverse the earlier rejections of the Fourteenth Amendment.[28] To enhance the prospect of ratification, Bingham's proposal explicitly tied Southern readmission to Congress upon the amendment's ratification.[29]

Bingham's initiative was soon superseded by others offered by Congressman James G. Blaine, and later by Senator John Sherman. But these were variations on the same theme. Each proposal made an important concession to radical opinion by accepting the need for black suffrage. But each rejected radical hopes for open-ended transformation. Black suffrage was viewed as a means to a well-defined end: the ratification of the Fourteenth Amendment. As soon as the new black-and-white governments joined to ratify the amendment, the centrists explicitly promised the resumption of normal Congressional politics with full Southern representation.

Stevens reacted to all these proposals with unremitting hostility. He repeatedly organized odd coalitions of radical Republicans and conservative Democrats to beat back the centrist initiative.[30] But his brilliant parliamentary maneuvers could not be repeated in the more conservative Senate.[31] After much pulling and hauling, the House finally backed down and accepted the centrist amendment. On March 2, 1867, the Reconstruction Act became law over the President's veto.

The result was a stunning victory for Bingham's triggering interpretation of the 1866 election. This point is easily overlooked, because the act effected an even more dramatic decision. It redefined the very essence of Southern polity by insisting on equal black participation in the process of reconstruction. If the South hoped to gain readmission to Congress, black-and-white electorates would have to begin the process of reconstruction anew, by electing delegates to a constitutional convention. These conventions, in turn, would submit new constitutions to the redefined electorate for self-conscious approval. If the draft gained majority support, it would then be submitted to Congress, which would approve its republican form.

It was at this point that the act's fixation upon the Fourteenth Amendment became evident. Although black-and-white Southerners were now in full possession of a republican constitution, they could not expect their representatives to be seated in Congress until their state legislatures ratified the Fourteenth Amendment. Even then, they would have to wait until the Amendment received the approval of three-fourths of the states and so fulfilled the numerical threshold established by Article Five. Only at *that* point did the act promise readmission, and in exceedingly explicit terms: the new government "*shall* be declared entitled to representation in Congress and senators and representatives *shall* be admitted therefrom."[32] To the radicals' disgust, the extraordinary provisions of Stevens's Military Bill would cease to apply as soon as the Fourteenth Amendment was safely on the books.

Reconstruction as a Re-Founding

For anybody less radical than Stevens, the resulting statute was a revolutionary act of constituent authority. If anything was clear from the structure of Article Five, it was that "Congress" could only propose an amendment and not punish states who refused to accept it. And yet here was the Convention/Congress threatening the Southern states with indefinitely extended military occupation unless they ratified its constitutional initiative! Keep in mind that "the South" placed under unconventional threat was not the lily-white South, but the newly minted governments of black and white voters *after* their constitutions had been certified as complying fully with the requirements of Republican government. What gave the Convention/Congress the authority to make such an extraordinary demand?

The same mix of nationalist ideals and unconventional practice that the Philadelphia Convention had used two generations earlier. To be sure, the Republican nationalism emerging from the crucible of civil war was much more intense than that of the Revolutionary era. This difference was symbolized by the opening words of the Fourteenth Amendment, declaring the primacy of national citizenship and treating state citizenship as derivative. In contrast, the Federalists avoided any effort to define national citizenship, let alone to give it priority. Americans of their generation were profoundly uncertain whether the claims of national identity should trump more local commitments.

Now that the Republicans were seeking to resolve these crucial uncertainties, they confronted them again in the form of Article Five. This article expressed a similar unwillingness to recognize the priority of national over state citizenship. Rather than allowing national organs to enact constitutional amendments, it structured higher lawmaking as a collaborative enterprise between the nation and the states. No matter how emphatically citizens of the nation endorsed an initiative, it could not be enacted unless citizens of the states emphatically assented.

Once Andrew Johnson sought to exploit this point on behalf of "masterly inactivity," the Republicans confronted their moment of truth. Either their Convention/Congress would retreat before the state effort to reject the priority of national citizenship or it would break with the principles of Article Five. The surprise is not that the Republicans made their revolutionary break, but that they tried to save so much of the older tradition. The key here was the election of 1866. If it had not been scheduled, the Republicans would have had to invent some brand-new way to establish that they had the support of a *national* majority in their struggle for national citizenship. Given the constitutional calendar, no such radical break was necessary. Regularly scheduled elections provided a means of testing the Republican mandate from the national citizenry while giving conservatives a fair chance to make their case. Once the Republicans had won the *national* election, they could use it as a means of legitimating a profound shift in the *federalist* system described by Article Five.

There is a deep unity, then, between the nationalizing substance of the Fourteenth Amendment and the nationalizing process through which the Convention/Congress proposed to enact it into law. Both substance and process put national citizenship first. The First Reconstruction Act told Southerners, in no uncertain terms, that they could not act as citizens of their individual states without affirming the priority of national citizenship by ratifying the Fourteenth Amendent. By a remarkable bootstrapping operation, the Convention/Congress was proposing to redefine We the People of the United *States* as We the People of the *United* States.

From this vantage point, the First Reconstruction Act is functionally equivalent to Article Seven of the 1787 Constitution. By substituting nine ratifying conventions for thirteen state legislatures, Seven not only gave the Federalists a realistic chance to win acceptance for their constitutional initiative. It gave institutional substance to their claim that the national government, no less than the states, were creations of

We the People. Like the Reconstruction Act, Article Seven emerged from an elaborate institutional bandwagon that greatly enhanced the reformers' claims to popular sovereignty.

But there are big differences in the way Federalists and Republicans constructed their bandwagons. Most importantly, the Federalists took most of their materials from the state level of government—though even in the 1780's the unconventional contributions of national institutions, notably the Confederation Congress, were very substantial. In contrast, the Republicans were using national institutions created by the Federalists—the separation of powers, national elections—to claim constituent authority in the name of We the People of the *United* States. But this difference in process itself tracks the deeper difference in substance. In advancing Article Seven, the Philadelphia Convention was seeking popular consent to a regime that remained profoundly uncertain about the ultimate relationship between state and national authority.[33] In advancing the Reconstruction Act, the Convention/Congress was proposing to resolve this ambiguity and establish the priority of national citizenship in a reconstructed Union.

The Conservative Side of the Reconstruction Act

At the same time, the Convention/Congress managed to preserve a good deal of the Federalist tradition. Its Reconstruction Act still allowed a bloc of Southern states to reject the amendment—so long as they were willing to remain outside in the cold on Capitol Hill. Of course, if they exercised this remaining right under Article Five, the burden of decision would return to the Convention/Congress and to American voters at the next national elections—who might, or might not, take further steps to put the Fourteenth Amendment on the books without the consent of the South. Taken by itself, the Reconstruction Act had radically transformed, but had not obliterated, the Federalist tradition.

The conservative side of the act also expressed itself in its refusal to provide for active federal intervention in the state-building process. While it dangled the prospect of Congressional readmission if black and white Southerners complied with national demands, it left it entirely up to Southerners to push the process forward. In the words of Senator Sherman, who drafted the crucial statutory terms:

No [administrative] machinery is provided [in the statute]. . . . Here is an invitation to the people. They can call their party conventions, their State conventions, and finally by a movement of the people, without regard to their local legislatures or local tribunals, a constitutional convention can be convened, elected by all the people, and they can form a constitution. . . . If, however, they have gone through all this . . . then we say to them they shall go further, and their Legislature shall adopt the constitutional amendment; [then, and only then, can the South hope for readmission].[34]

In calling for a "movement of the people," Sherman was following the triggering approach taken at Philadelphia. The 1787 Constitution did not try to force conventions of the people to meet on the state level. It was up to the Federalists in each state to convince state legislatures to go along. More generally, both the Federalist Constitution and the First Reconstruction Act supposed that the new initiatives would be legitimated through two *independent* cycles of constitutional politics: the first at the national level, the second at the state level.

It immediately became plain, however, that this Federalist premise was inconsistent with the nationalizing aspirations of the Convention/Congress. Whatever the Republicans might proclaim from their citadel on Capitol Hill, the South was in fact dominated by all-white governments supported by the President. There was no chance that these governments would cooperate, as their Federalist counterparts had done, in their own constitutional reorganization. With white governments hostile, how could new black-and-white voting registries be established, a revolutionary politics of constitutional reconstruction be sustained?

CONGRESS NATIONALIZES THE RATIFICATION PROCESS

Anticipating such problems, the "lame-duck" Congress passed a special statute authorizing its successor to meet immediately after it had expired at noon on March 4. To the Republicans' embarrassment, many Representatives were unprepared to come to Washington eight months before their normal meeting in December. When the clerk of the House called the roll, seven Northern states were entirely unrepresented.[35] The opening scene once again dramatized the unconventional character of Congressional authority. As the Democratic minority emphasized, "seven of the original thirteen states that in 1787 met and created the Constitution" were absent.[36] Despite the minority's "most solemn protest against any and every action tending to the organization of this House until the absent States be more fully represented,"[37] the Republicans organized a House containing Representatives of twenty of the thirty-seven states. By March 23, Republican majorities had enacted a second reconstruction bill into law over the President's veto.

The Second Reconstruction Act gets short shrift in historical accounts. This is a mistake, since it marked a sharp break with Federalist traditions. It served notice that the Convention/Congress would not allow the white governments of the South to sabotage a "movement of the people" in support of the Republican vision of the Union. It transformed the Union Army into a bureaucratic engine expressing the national interest in Reconstruction and the ratification of the Fourteenth Amendment.

The act made it the business of each of the five district commanders to register the black and white voters Congress considered eligible. The Army would then supervise a first round of elections for a constitutional convention, and a second round determining whether a majority supported the new constitution emerging from the convention. At this point, the second act adhered to the triggering proposals of the first—the new state could gain representation in Congress only after it had approved the Fourteenth Amendment and the amendment had gained the support of a three-fourths majority of the states. Nonetheless, the new act had taken a giant step toward the *nationalization of the triggering function.*

This was well understood—and not only by the Democratic opposition. Even the majority leader of the Senate, William Pitt Fessenden, was opposed:

> Instead of leaving it to the people to work the matter out in their own way, as I would be perfectly willing to do, . . . we go further and say, this military government which we send there shall take the initiative, and not only take the initiative, but shall govern all the details and settle the matter in which that is to be done. Now sir, you see the danger of this. I see it, or I think I do. They are not a people satisfied, or likely to be satisfied, with what we do. The large majority of the white population, probably nineteen twentieths of them, are disposed to find fault with everything we do . . .; and I think it becomes us to look well that we give no proper occasion, and not

only no proper occasion, but no plausible occasion, for accusations . . . against us.[38]

Given these concerns, Fessenden offered an amendment that would have authorized the Army to compile a new black-and-white voting registry, but would have required an affirmative decision from the all-white government before proceeding with elections for a new constitutional convention. He recognized that this might greatly delay the entire process. But he thought this a price worth paying:

> I am as anxious as anybody that these States shall be back in full communion with us as soon as possible. . . . [But] by—I use the word again—forcing them, by taking the matter into our own hands . . ., we expose ourselves to . . . disadvantages. . . . They may turn around and say to us that they did not desire to come; that they have been forced back; that they do not thank us for forcing that question [of holding a new constitutional convention] upon their consideration; it should be left to them. . . . This is not for the military. . . .[39]

I report Fessenden's remarks because the Senator was perhaps the single most influential Republican on Capitol Hill.[40] His opposition emphasized the seriousness of the breach with old Federalist values. Nonetheless, the Senate rejected Fessenden's amendment by a vote of 33 to 14.[41] Fresh from their recent victory in the polls over Andrew Johnson, Republicans no longer believed their national mandate could be appropriately blocked by Fessenden's Federalist plea to "leave it to the people [in each state] to work the matter out in their own way." Speaking for the Judiciary Committee, Lyman Trumbull directly confronted Fessenden's critique:

> In some remarks made by the Senator from Maine [Fessenden] yesterday he expressed himself as opposed to forcing upon the people of any of these States a constitution. So am I . . .; and this bill proposes no such thing: it proposes to leave it to the registered voters, excluding certain leading rebels who are not to be registered, to determine through the delegates they shall elect to the convention whether they will form a constitution. . . . Is there any force in this? . . .
>
> The whole object of the bill is to afford the facilities to the people to give expression to their opinions.[42]

While Fessenden protested, in the old Federalist manner, that the national government was forcing the states to take the Republican agenda seriously, Trumbull presents the national government in a new role—as the guarantor of democratic life on the state level. This view is familiar to modern students of the Fourteenth Amendment; but it is fascinating to see it emerge in the very process through which the amendment became higher law. Once again, we can glimpse the unity integrating higher lawmaking process with substance. In nationalizing the triggering function, the Convention/Congress was acting on the very same understanding animating the substance of the amendment—that We the People, speaking through national institutions, may rightfully intervene to safeguard the exercise of equal citizenship in the states.

The Senate adopted two statutory amendments in the service of this emerging constitutional vision. First, in addition to casting a ballot for their favored candidate to the constitutional convention, each voter would be asked whether a convention should be held at all. It was only if a majority said yes that the act authorized the army to notify the victorious delegates to assemble in the name of the People. This amendment, sponsored by Senator Charles Drake, emphasized the national interest in engendering a constitutional politics with genuine popular support.[43] Second, and in a similar vein, the Senate required at least half the registered voters to go to the polls before a convention might be called, or a constitution be approved.[44]

When viewed as a whole, then, the act was a landmark in the adaptation of constitutional forms—the Nation was now telling the People of the Southern states how their constitutional will might validly be expressed, but it was still up to the People in each state to make their own judgment. Reconstruction would still culminate with a writing that *took the appearance* of an Article Five "amendment," though the reality would have horrified the Federalists, who never imagined that nonconsenting states could be barred from the Congress so long as they ignored the expression of the Nation's constitutional will.

Even more fundamentally, the Convention/Congress had not relieved Republicans in each state from the formidable task of repeatedly mobilizing majority support for their effort to represent the People—first, in authorizing a constitutional convention; next, in approving the new Republican constitution; and finally, in gaining legislative consent for the Fourteenth Amendment. However much the First and Second Reconstruction Acts had broken with key Federalist principles, they remained *triggering* decisions—leaving it up to the (nationally defined) People of each state to determine whether they would go along with the nation-centered enterprise of constitutive redefinition initiated by the Fourteenth Amendment.

TRIANGULATING THE PRECEDENTS

We have been seeking, in the manner of the common law, to understand the triggering decisions of the Convention/Congress by setting them against earlier precedents. As our case studies accumulate, comparisons with the Founding can only begin this larger inquiry. In particular, the unconventional activities surrounding the Thirteenth Amendment serve as a more proximate source of light.

When viewed from this angle, a paradox emerges. Despite Andrew Johnson's struggle against the Fourteenth Amendment, he himself had provided the Convention/Congress with key precedents for its own unconventional activities. It was the President, not the Convention/Congress, who had first demanded, "in the name of the whole people," that the Southern states ratify the Thirteenth Amendment as a "pledge of perpetual loyalty."[45] It was the President, not the Convention/Congress, who had first made state ratification a condition for readmission into Congress. It was the President, not the Convention/Congress, who had injected anomalous federal officials into state constitutional processes.

All these path-breaking activities are more noticeable the second time around. But this is in part because the Republicans left their fingerprints on the pages of the *Statutes at Large,* while the President scattered his unconventional activities amongst a variety of sources that are harder to find—proclamations, messages, and telegrams to provisional governors. We should not allow Johnson's emphatic resistance to Congressional Reconstruction to disguise his own role in blazing the nationalizing trail.

The point is particularly important, given our ultimate objective—which is not only to understand Reconstruction in its own terms but to grasp higher lawmaking patterns that have served to organize Americans' response to constitutional crises over the generations. From this perspective, it is very significant that, despite their bitter disagreements, *both* "conservative" President and "reformist" Congress were driven to override the veto powers vouchsafed the states by Article Five. This practical convergence suggests an underlying tendency of the evolving system.

So does a second parallel—in the case of both the Thirteenth and the Fourteenth Amendments, a sweeping victory in a national election gave the reformers the mandate they needed for their unconventional triggering activities. Without the sweeping Republican victory at the polls in 1864, Johnson would never have claimed a mandate from the Nation to induce Southern ratification of the Thirteenth Amendment, any more than Bingham would have made such a claim if the Republicans had not swept to victory in 1866.*

These patterns will regularly recur in American history. Time and again, rival protagonists from competing centers of power in Washington D.C. will struggle to an impasse as they advance conflicting constitutional visions. Time and again, they will appeal to the People at the next national election to resolve the impasse—often failing, but sometimes succeeding, in their effort to gain vindication at the polls. And when they win an electoral mandate, they will follow the path marked out by Johnson and Bingham—taking aggressive steps to induce other, more conservative, parts of the constitutional system to heed the People's will.

I do not suggest that the twentieth century has been a rerun of the nineteenth—any more than the nineteenth was a copy of the eighteenth. But for all the surface differences, may we begin to see different historical episodes as variations on a smaller set of constitutional themes?

---

*Indeed, but for the election returns, it is very unlikely that the Thirty-Eighth Congress would have proposed the Thirteenth Amendment in the first place. See Chapter 5.

CHAPTER EIGHT

The Great Transformation

RATIFICATION AND CONSOLIDATION

As the Convention/Congress ended its special session in early spring, Republicans could look back on a period of creativity rivaling the Founding. From their first post-War meeting, they had signaled their unconventional claim to popular sovereignty by barring Southern Congressmen. When their rightful possession of Capitol Hill was challenged by the President, they used the election of 1866 to demonstrate that the People supported their higher lawmaking pretensions. When the President encouraged the Southern states to veto the Fourteenth Amendment, they triggered another round of ratification activity in their unprecedented Reconstruction Acts.

At each stage of the unfolding process—signaling, proposing, triggering—the Republicans impressed new higher lawmaking meanings upon familiar institutional materials. The emerging pattern was far more nation-centered than in 1787. Article Five supposed that a Philadelphia-like body would dominate national life only at the request of two-thirds of the states. But the Convention/Congress signaled its higher lawmaking authority by excluding almost one-third of the states from their seats. Article Five assumed that Congress or a convention would be the sole important actor on the federal level. But the Fourteenth Amendment was the product of an ongoing struggle between the President and Congress. Article Five limited Congress's function to determining whether state conventions or legislatures should engage in the task of ratification. But the Convention/Congress had gone far beyond this after its claims to speak for the People had been vindicated in a triggering election.

And yet, after all was said and done, the fate of the Fourteenth Amendment remained in doubt. The most obvious source of resistance was the all-white South governments established by Presidents Lincoln and Johnson. According to the Reconstruction Acts, Southern approval of the Fourteenth Amendment would only come at the end of an elaborate state-building process involving the federal registration of a black-and-white electorate, and repeated shows of popular support in the formation of a new constitution and the election of a state legislature. During all this time, all-white power structures continued as "provisional" governments "subject to the paramount authority of the United States at any time to abolish, modify, control or supersede the same."[1] But if the Union Army did not choose to exercise its "paramount authority," the old governments had every incentive to disrupt the elaborate state-building process, as did white vigilante groups. The statutory call for a stately ritual of democratic deliberation, culminating in approval of the Fourteenth Amendment, threatened to back-fire. Would the federal effort only serve to make it unmistakably clear that Southern whites decisively rejected the new Republican Union? Even if white governments did not sabotage the process, could Southern Republicans win a steady stream of electoral victories and thereby create an institutional bandwagon in support of the Fourteenth Amendment?

Only one thing was clear: the Army's sustained support would be crucial in pushing the process despite the resistance of the established governments. This leads us to a second great obstacle: Andrew Johnson, in his capacity as commander-in-chief. Johnson viewed the Republican Congress as an unconstitutional assembly bent upon centralized military despotism. How, then, would the President respond to Congress's call to use the Army to destroy the all-white governments that he and Lincoln had helped create?

Worse yet, the Republicans had yet to hear from the Supreme Court. It was one thing for the President to denounce the Convention/Congress as unconstitutional; quite another for the Court to agree. Would the loyal people of the North continue to support the Republican Rump on Capitol Hill if the Justices declared the Reconstruction Acts unconstitutional?

Though Abraham Lincoln had made five appointments to the Court,[2] they might not stand by the Convention/Congress at its moment of constitutional truth. A judicial counterattack would not only

damage the Republicans' standing before the nation. It would immediately disrupt the institutional balance of power. Armed with a Supreme Court opinion condemning the Reconstruction Acts, President
Johnson would surely order his Southern commanders to shift their
support to the all-white governments that had vetoed the Fourteenth
Amendment. Might he go further and order the Union Army out of
the South, proclaiming that his policies had restored peace?[3] Once the
Army left, would it ever return? Without the Army controlling terror-
ists and supervising state-building, would the Fourteenth Amendment
ever be ratified?

These questions point to a deeper transformation at work. By nationalizing the triggering process in its Reconstruction Acts, the Con-
vention/Congress was bringing forces into play that would nationalize
ratification as well. The fate of the Fourteenth Amendment would no
longer be resolved exclusively by goings-on in each of the states, as
Article Five supposed. It would be determined in large part by the
interacting decisions of Congress, President, and Court. To put my
thesis in a single line: the separation of powers was taking on a key role
in the ratifying process formerly monopolized by the states. I will be
describing this great transformation step by step, as it emerged from
the effort by the Convention/Congress to transcend first one, then
another, challenge to its authority from the President and Court.

This will require us to revisit some of the most dramatic events
of constitutional history—including the effort by the Convention/
Congress to impeach the President and to strip the Supreme Court of
its powers of judicial review. I will be locating these struggles within a
larger pattern of transformation. Two themes will dominate, both with
roots in a single feature of the Constitution. In contrast to the parliamentary system, the institutional protagonists in Washington D.C.
could not call a special election at their convenience, but had to return
to the voters on a fixed schedule. This meant, first, that if the President and Court wished to obstruct Reconstruction, there was only one
way the Convention/Congress could respond before 1868—threaten
the more conservative branches with dire institutional consequences
unless they called off their campaign of resistance.

These *unconventional threats* took different forms in the case of the
Presidency and the Court. In the first case, the Convention/Congress
sought to impeach Andrew Johnson; in the second, it tried to deprive
the Court of the power to rule on the constitutionality of the Recon-

struction Acts. Despite their different form, these two actions performed identical functions. In each case, the Convention/Congress sought to preserve the mandate from the People that the Republicans thought they had won in the 1866 elections and to insist upon the rapid ratification of the Fourteenth Amendment.

The use of unconventional threats was hardly unprecedented as a higher lawmaking technique. We have already seen the Convention/Congress and the President make similar moves against Southern state governments in their efforts to win ratification of the Thirteenth and Fourteenth Amendments. The novelty, insofar as there is one,[4] lies in the Convention/Congress's selection of institutional targets. Previously, the states of the South were the targets of unconventional threats. But now that the ratification process had been nationalized, it was necessary to induce the conservative branches of the national government to cooperate if the Fourteenth Amendment was to become higher law. But how would the President and the Court react to such unconventional threats?

As we elaborate the pattern of conservative resistance and unconventional threat, a second basic implication of the constitutional calendar will appear to view. Call it the race against the clock. When the Convention/Congress passed its Second Reconstruction Act in March of 1867, only eighteen months remained before the elections of 1868. This simple point allows us to detect a cool constitutional logic in events that otherwise might seem—and have often been portrayed— as irrational melodrama. In continuing their struggle against the Republican Rump, neither the President nor the Court were fighting a pointless rear-guard battle. They were engaging in a rational strategic maneuver: if they succeeded in slowing down Reconstruction by only a few months, conservatives could transform the 1868 elections into a final referendum on the Fourteenth Amendment.

On this scenario, the conservative candidate for the Presidency (Johnson imagined himself in this role) could claim that Congress's militaristic efforts had only created endless chaos in the South; each day's news of white resistance to military Reconstruction would emphasize the wisdom of the President's conservative policies. The conservative counteroffensive could well strike a responsive chord with Northerners who were increasingly weary of a generation of constitutional turbulence and profoundly ambiguous about black suffrage. It was unclear, of course, whether Johnson's strategy would succeed. But it was not at all foolish for the President to think that, if he could only hold the fort until 1868, the People *might* come to his rescue.

It is a serious mistake, then, to view the conservative branches as powerless in the face of the Convention/Congress's threats of impeachment and jurisdiction-stripping. Indeed, there are many cases in American history in which conservative branches have defied reformist pressure and have survived unharmed. But at this critical moment, neither President nor Court fought to the bitter end. Both executed brilliant "switches in time," retreating before impeachment and jurisdiction-stripping in ways that saved them from permanent damage.

As a consequence, the Convention/Congress won its race against the clock. With the aid of the Union Army, enough states of the South signed on to the amendment to permit Secretary Seward to proclaim its validity in July of 1868. Rather than marking a further escalation of the higher lawmaking struggle, the election of 1868 served a different constitutional function: consolidation. Though the Fourteenth Amendment was now on the books, everybody was aware of its unconventional pedigree. Indeed, leading Democrats threatened to reverse Reconstruction during the fall elections. It was not too late for the voters to reopen the status of the Fourteenth Amendment by returning the Democrats to power in Washington.

But the election returns of 1868 put an end to all serious questioning. With their hold on national power reconfirmed in the *consolidating election,* Republicans in the White House and Capitol Hill took aggressive steps to pack the Supreme Court with men who would vindicate their new vision of the Union. By 1873, a reconstituted Court unanimously affirmed the validity of the Reconstruction amendments in the *Slaughterhouse* case. With all three branches now solidly behind the amendment, the Republicans' great bootstrapping operation had come, at last, to a triumphant conclusion. To summarize the final stages of the institutional bandwagon:

Challenge by Conservative Branches → Unconventional Threats by
Reformist Branch (Impeachment and Jurisdiction-Stripping) →
Switch in Time by Conservative Branches → Consolidating Election →
Consolidating Opinions by the Supreme Court

Among other things, this schema will serve as a bridge to the next great constitutional turning point. A similar pattern will reemerge during the final phases of the New Deal Revolution—though on this occasion, the Presidency joined Congress as part of the reformist coalition and left the Supreme Court to play the leading conservative role in the "switch in time." But all this is best left to Part Three. Our challenge is to understand the great transformation of the nineteenth century on its own terms.

THE EMERGING CHALLENGE

As soon as the Convention/Congress left Washington after its first special session, other institutions began to fill the void. On April 15, the Supreme Court allowed the Johnsonian government of Georgia to proceed with a motion against Secretary of War Edwin M. Stanton. The petition urged an injunction against the Republicans' effort to destroy the "existing State of Georgia and to cause to be evicted and substituted in its place . . . another distinct and hitherto unknown State, to be called and designated the State of Georgia."[5] Oral argument generated "intense interest":[6] Would the Justices take the lead in the struggle against Reconstruction and the Fourteenth Amendment?

The answer was Not Yet. As the Court ended its term in the middle of May, it dismissed *Georgia v. Stanton* for "want of jurisdiction." This did not imply permanent passivity. Although the Court had refused to hear the plea of an abstract entity called the "State of Georgia," it might hear the complaints of real people suffering real injuries at the hands of Union officers implementing Reconstruction. It would take a few months before such cases would begin arriving. As a consequence, the Court could leave Washington with its future role up in the air.[7]

The next move was up to the President, who was obliged to tell his commanding generals how to interpret the Reconstruction Acts. Like the Supreme Court, he sought to avoid a head-on confrontation, choosing a more subtle way of running out the constitutional clock. At his request, Attorney General Henry Stanbery provided formal opinions that interpreted the Reconstruction Acts in ways that would undermine their practical operation. Stanbery denied that Union generals could discharge uncooperative officials from the all-white governments. He also effectively eliminated their capacity to bar white Southerners of doubtful loyalty from the new black-and-white voting registries.[8] Since the Reconstruction Acts were poorly drafted, these interpretations were not patently absurd—though it would have been easy to provide more expansive readings.[9] In any event, only Secretary of War Stanton[10] dissented when the President consulted his Cabinet on the Stanbery interpretations. With their support, Johnson embarked on a strategy of legalistic obstruction, issuing appropriate orders to his generals on June 20. If these orders were allowed to stand, the Congressional effort to trigger a new round of ratification activity was in deep trouble: with the old governments secure, ex-Confederates flooding the voting registries (and white vigilantes scaring blacks off), the deck would be stacked against the Republicans from the very start.

Given the President's past performance, the Convention/Congress had arranged for an extraordinary summer session if need required. Returning to Washington in a fury, Republicans responded with a Third Reconstruction Act which rejected the Stanbery interpretations—and then dispersed until December.[11]

The first conservative campaign of resistance had wasted a few months but was little more than a sparring match. It was now up to the President and the Court to think again: Had the time come to call off further resistance?

THE ATTACK

From the very beginning, the Convention/Congress was painfully aware of the constitutional clock. The Second Reconstruction Act had explicitly instructed the commanding generals to complete registration of the new black and white voters by September 1.[12] In overruling the Stanbery interpretations in its Third Act, the Republican majority recognized that Presidential obstruction had made this date unrealistic, but only extended the deadline to October 1.[13] Unfortunately for the Republicans, it would be harder to set precise time limits on the further phases of Reconstruction. After the voting rolls were established, the Army commanders had to allow a decent interval—the statute said "not less than thirty days"[14]—for candidates to present themselves to the new electorate. If the voters then approved a constitutional convention, the commanding general had sixty days to "notify the delegates to assemble."[15] The next stage was even less amenable to statutory control; the delegates, if they so chose, could dally forever before proposing a new constitution to the People. Only then did the statute take up the drumbeat, telling the commanding general to submit the constitution to the electorate "after the expiration of thirty days from the date" it was proposed.[16] If everything went right, new multiracial legislatures might be in a position to ratify the Fourteenth Amendment by the late spring or early summer of 1868—just in time for the Republicans to return to the People in the fall.

This would not only allow the Republicans to claim their policy was a success. It would enable them to redefine the very meaning of electoral victory, especially so far as the Presidential election was concerned. If the Southern states remained disorganized, they would not be in a position to cast electoral votes; if, however, they were in the control of a black-and-white coalition of Republicans, the party could look with greater confidence on its prospects for nationwide victory. In short, the Republicans were trying to set up yet another unconventional bandwagon—if their effort to create a new electorate in the South succeeded, then this new electorate could help the Republicans redeem their claim to speak for We the People of the *United* States in 1868.

By the same token, if Johnson hoped to win election in his own right, he would do everything within his power to stop this bandwagon in its tracks. Only one thing was clear: the Republican timetable depended upon the energy and enthusiasm of the five district commanders in the South. It would be child's play for them to shift the state-building machine into low gear, asserting that chaotic conditions required more deliberate speed. As Congress left for the summer, it could be cautiously optimistic, since four of the five district commanders were strong Republicans.[17] At the same time, if Johnson wished to continue legalistic resistance, his next step was obvious: purge the Army chain of command.

This would not be easy, since the Convention/Congress had taken precautionary measures in two statutes, passed over the President's veto, on March 2, 1867.[18] The Command of the Army Act barred Johnson from removing Ulysses Grant as General of the Army without the express consent of the Senate. It also required the President to issue all military orders through General Grant, and threatened any military officer with a minimum prison term of two years if he obeyed a Presidential order without Grant's signature.[19]

Johnson could, of course, defy this unprecedented assault on Presidential power—if he was willing to risk impeachment. But if he chose to follow the law, he would have to convince Grant to join him in the military purge. This was made more difficult by a second statute. The new Tenure of Offices Act protected civilian officials from Presidential removal without Senatorial consent. It would come into play if the Presidential purge included Secretary of War Stanton. Originally appointed by Lincoln, the Secretary was the sole remaining member of Johnson's Cabinet who sympathized with the Congressional cause.[20] Stanton was a more adept political infighter than Grant. So long as he remained in the War Office, it was highly unlikely that Grant would go along with Presidential orders purging Republican district commanders; and if Grant did not go along, Johnson would find it hard to persuade military men to risk a two-year jail term. Hence the Secretary was marked out as Purge Victim Number One.

The Tenure of Offices Act did not give Stanton the explicit protection afforded Grant by the Command of the Army Act. Its first section began by guaranteeing tenure to "every" civil officer whose appointment had been confirmed by the Senate "until a successor shall have been in like manner appointed." But unfortunately for Stanton, the statute immediately continued:

> *Provided,* That the Secretaries of State, of the Treasury, of War, of the Navy, and of the Interior, the Postmaster General and the Attorney General, shall hold their offices respectively for and during the term of the President by whom they may have been appointed and for one month thereafter, subject to removal by and with the advice and consent of the Senate.[21]

This proviso would give Stanton's partisans no end of trouble, since the Secretary had never been formally reappointed by Johnson. Under the terms of the proviso, it would seem that Stanton had been guaranteed tenure only during the term of President Lincoln "and for one month thereafter." As Johnson considered his options in August 1867, the Tenure of Offices Act did not seem to present a serious legal obstacle.

But never underestimate the ingenuity of lawyers. As events proved, Stanton's lawyers would be able to say something on his behalf. Their trick was to adopt a highly conceptual understanding of Lincoln's "term" in office. On this view, Lincoln's second term did not end with

John Wilkes Booth's bullet in April of 1865; it continued until the moment on March 4, 1869, that Lincoln would have retained the legal right to remain in office. As a consequence, Republican lawyers would claim that Andrew Johnson was merely filling out Lincoln's "term." On this reasoning, any Cabinet officer appointed by Lincoln during his second term was protected from Johnson's displeasure. Even this strained interpretation did not help Stanton much, since he had been appointed by Lincoln during his first term in office and had not received a formal reappointment. It was therefore necessary for the lawyers to twist again and assert that the statute compelled second-term Presidents to stick with the choices they made during their previous term unless they could convince the Senate to accept a replacement. Although the legislative history explicitly rejected this view (which was intrinsically implausible in any event), this did not stop some Republican partisans.[22]

These convoluted legalisms should not obscure the main institutional point. However farfetched Stanton's statutory interpretations, the Supreme Court would not return to Washington until December; nor would Congress get a chance to amend the statute until it returned in late November. In the interim, it would be up to the President and his Secretary to resolve the matter on their own. On August 5, 1867, only days after Congress had left town, Johnson wrote to Stanton:

> Sir: Public considerations of a high character constrain me to say, that your resignation as Secretary of War will be accepted.[23]

To which Stanton replied:

> . . . I have the honor to say that public considerations of a high character, which alone have induced me to continue at the head of this Department, constrain me not to resign the office of Secretary of War before the next meeting of Congress.[24]

Not for the first time, a key actor was defending a threatened constitutional position by taking the distinctive posture of an adverse possessor. Though his legal case was gossamer, Stanton was asserting his authority to hold office in the name of the Convention/Congress.

The President's next move reveals the cool deliberation with which he played his cards. From a strictly legal point of view, he held a winning hand.[25] But Johnson was not interested in self-indulgent invocations of Presidential authority if it got in the way of his immediate objective: to purge the Army command and thereby slow down Reconstruction and the Fourteenth Amendment. Instead of challenging Stanton's interpretation of the Act, he invoked a statutory escape hatch. Section Two allowed the President, during a Senate recess, to suspend a tenured official if he had been "shown, by evidence satisfactory to the President, to be guilty of misconduct in office, or crime, or for any reason shall become incapable or legally disqualified." Under this procedure, the President had to justify his decision to the Senate within twenty days of its next meeting; if the Senate refused to concur, the statute provided that the suspended officer "shall forthwith resume the functions of his office."[26] By proceeding under this provision, Johnson was creating a future problem for himself. But for the moment, his legal tactics gave him a priceless strategic advantage. By triggering Section Two, the President deprived Stanton of the last shred of legal argument justifying disobedience.

No less important, by ostentatiously proceeding within the letter of the law, he obtained the cooperation of Ulysses S. Grant, even convincing the General to serve as Stanton's replacement as Secretary of War *ad interim*. Tactically, this was a masterstroke. When Grant presented Stanton with the suspension order on August 12, the Secretary had no real choice but to give way to the nation's most popular war hero. So long as Grant remained in Johnson's Cabinet, he could not honorably invoke the Command of the Army Act and refuse to countersign the President's commands. With a single stroke, the President had cut through the Republicans' efforts to tie his hands as commander-in-chief.

Five days later, Johnson began his purge. His initial target was General Philip Sheridan, the most aggressively Republican district commander. By the end of the month, the President also removed Republican General Daniel Sickles from the sensitive Second District (containing North and South Carolina). Despite verbal protests, Grant neither resigned his *ad interim* appointment nor refused to execute the President's orders. To cap off his summer offensive, Johnson issued a proclamation of amnesty for all but a handful of Confederates, once again reminding the country of the Resolution of 1861, which put Congress on record in declaring that "this war is not waged upon our part for the . . . purpose of overthrowing or interfering with the rights or established institutions of those States [in rebellion] . . ., but to defend and maintain the supremacy of the Constitution and to preserve the Union, with all the dignity, equality, and rights of the several States unimpaired."[27]

SOME PULSE-TAKING: THE ELECTIONS OF 1867

So matters stood as the nation paused for the elections of 1867. These contests could not directly affect matters in Washington, but the voters were poised for some symbolically significant decisions. The eyes of the country turned to Ohio. Elections would determine whether Senator Ben Wade, the radical who would succeed Johnson in case of a successful impeachment, would win another term. Ohioans were also voting on a constitutional amendment granting suffrage to blacks. The campaign, marked by virulent racist appeals, led to the defeat of black suffrage and Ben Wade.[28] Black suffrage was also rejected by the voters in Kansas and Minnesota. Republicans suffered clear-cut defeats in the legislatures of Pennsylvania, New York, New Jersey, and Maryland, and their majorities were significantly reduced throughout the North.[29]

So far as Johnson was concerned, these returns had only one meaning: "I am gratified, but not surprised at the result of the recent elections," he explained to serenaders at the White House, "I have always had undoubting confidence in the people. They may be misled . . . but never perverted, in the end they are always right. In the gloomiest hours through which I have passed—and many of them God knows have been dark enough—when our Constitution was in the utmost peril . . . I had still an abiding confidence in the people and felt assured that they in their might would come to the rescue. They have come and, thank God! they have come."[30] If he only stayed his course, and continued to sustain the white Southern governments, would not next year's federal elections provide final vindication?[31]

In the meantime, his August takeover of the War Department was showing results. Johnson's replacement for Sheridan was the deeply conservative Winfield S. Hancock—who immediately began to reinstate Johnsonian officials discharged by his predecessor,[32] declaring in his first order: "The General commanding is gratified to learn that peace and quiet reign in this department. It will be his purpose to maintain this condition of things. As a means to this great end, he regards the maintenance of the civil authorities [i.e., Johnson's white governments] as the most efficient, under existing circumstances."[33]

Encouraged on both the administrative and electoral fronts, Johnson proceeded with his purge. On December 28, he obtained Grant's consent to the removal of John Pope and Edward Ord, the last two Republican district commanders. As the New Year approached, he had every reason to celebrate the coming of 1868, and the national elections it would bring.

THE CONGRESSIONAL CHALLENGE

The Congressional leadership appreciated the gravity of their situation.[34] Unless they took decisive action, the upcoming elections would be held with white governments in the South, and the Fourteenth Amendment in constitutional limbo.[35] How to avoid this fate?

The Republicans could pass more statutes, but the President had shown an uncanny ability to evade command. If words would not bind, there was only one alternative: impeachment. The man next in line for the White House was the radical Senator, Ben Wade, who required no convincing about the imperative need for speedy Reconstruction.

But it would not be easy to impeach the President. The great stumbling block was the legalistic character of his resistance. Johnson had taken great pains to avoid any outright breach of the rules laid down by Congress.[36] How, then, could he be found guilty of "high crimes and misdemeanors"?

Radicals like Thaddeus Stevens were willing to dismiss legalistic quibbles, but the Republican majority had not lost its sense of restraint. On December 7, the House rejected impeachment by 57 to 108, with 68 Republicans voting with the Democratic minority.[37] Even as late as February 14, the majority rejected Stevens's effort to return impeachment to the floor of the House.[38]

And yet, the President still had a long way to go before he could achieve his objectives. His purge of the high command had not prevented the army from completing the first stages of the Reconstruction process. Except for Texas, the military registrars had generally met their October 1 deadline. During the final months of 1867, the military had supervised the first set of elections required by the Second Reconstruction Act, at which the voters were asked to authorize, and select delegates to, a new constitutional convention. The results of this first round went overwhelmingly to the Republicans. In all nine states holding elections, conservatives failed to convince the black-and-white Southern electorate to reject the call for a constitutional convention.

The early months of 1868 would be crucial. Throughout the South, conventions would be meeting to propose constitutions; if voters approved, the days of the old governments would be short. If the President hoped to stop the transition, his commanders would have to use their discretionary authority to encourage local conservatives to delay and disrupt the conventions, and to organize actively to defeat the new constitutions at the next round of elections. But before the President could act decisively in the South, he must somehow solve a legal problem he had created for himself in Washington.

To clear the way for his purge of the high command, Johnson had taken the path of least resistance against Secretary Stanton. Rather than firing Stanton outright, he had suspended him under the Tenure of Offices Act. When Congress convened in late November, the President bought more time by submitting the notice of Stanton's suspension within the twenty-day period specified by the statute.[39] As the new year opened, Johnson could no longer evade, by artful legalism, the statutory challenge to his authority. On January 13, the Senate refused to concur in Stanton's removal. By the terms of the act, the time had come for Stanton "forthwith [to] resume the functions of his office."

Johnson responded with great tactical skill. On Saturday, January 11, he had a private talk with his Secretary *ad interim*, Ulysses S. Grant, about the future of the War Office. He now explained that he had always considered the Tenure of Offices Act unconstitutional and proposed to test his power to remove Stanton in the courts. Offering to pay any fine levied on Grant for violating the act, the President implored him to remain in office. Grant refused, finally aware of the damage he was doing to his own Presidential prospects. What happened next was the subject of bitter dispute. The President asserted, and the General denied, that Grant promised to return control of the War Office to Johnson rather than allow Stanton to regain possession.

This would permit the President to appoint a new interim Secretary willing to reject Stanton's claims under the Tenure of Offices Act. Under this scenario, the President would keep the upper hand in his battle with the Convention/Congress. All through the next round of interbranch struggle, it would be the President's man who would be wielding power from the War Office, while Stanton stood helpless in the wings. If Stanton went to the courts, he might only succeed in gaining judicial confirmation of his defeat—after all, his legal case was very weak.

As the President awaited the Senate vote ordering Stanton's reinstatement, Johnson had reason to look to the future with grim confidence. All the more bitter was his disappointment. For the first (and only) time in constitutional history, it would not be the President or the Congress or the Court who made the decisive constitutional move. It would be a military man: Grant returned the War Office to Secretary Stanton and denied that he had made any contrary promise to the President.

The balance of unconventional authority had begun to swing against the President. No longer could he expect unquestioned obedience as commander-in-chief, since Stanton would predictably challenge Presidential commands and encourage Grant to withhold the signature required by the Command of the Army Act. Whatever the weaknesses in Stanton's legal claims, his simple ability to sustain possession of the War Office undermined Johnson's capacity to get his orders followed by his field commanders. If Johnson wished to continue his campaign, he would have to find a way to remove Stanton physically from the War Office and replace him with a Secretary *ad interim* committed to Presidential authority.

As the President pondered his next move, news from the South emphasized the high stakes. On February 4, Alabama became the first Southern state to vote on the work-product of a constitutional convention. To the Republicans' despair, a majority of registered Alabamans failed to show up at the polls and so the new constitution failed to satisfy the test for validity established by the Second Reconstruction Act.[40]

Other Southern states were lagging behind Alabama. Conventions had begun meeting during January and February 1868. Early news was not encouraging. When moderates in Florida walked out of a convention dominated by radicals, Johnson's new commander, General George Meade, allowed them to form their own separate convention. When the radicals adjourned, Meade forced enough of them to join the moderates so as to give their convention a quorum.[41] The fate of Reconstruction, and the Fourteenth Amendment, was hanging in the balance.

Johnson's next decisions deepened the sense of crisis. On February 12, he created a new Military Division of the Atlantic, with headquarters in Washington, D.C. This gave the President a military force independent of General Grant. At the same time, he proposed to promote William Sherman to the full generalship only Grant possessed, and to bring this popular but conservative war hero to Washington as commander of the new military district. Since Sherman was well disposed to Johnson, the President hoped to use him as his tool to oust Stanton from the War Office and play Grant's old role as interim Secretary. When Sherman resolutely refused to mix himself up in constitutional politics,[42] Johnson turned to the bumbling Adjutant General, Lorenzo Thomas. On February 21, Thomas crossed Pennsylvania Avenue to the War Office to announce: "By virtue of the power and authority vested in me as President by the Constitution and laws of the United States you are hereby removed from the office as Secretary for the Department of War, and your functions as such will terminate upon the receipt of this communication."[43] As the President explained this step, it was a continuation of his strategy of legalistic resistance: its aim was to precipitate a legal test before the courts.[44]

The next move was up to the Convention/Congress. It could accept the President's invitation to view their dispute as just another issue of normal politics, appropriately resolved by the Supreme Court. Or it could assert its unconventional authority as a tribune of the People and use its power of impeachment to protect Reconstruction against the President's assault.

It took the latter course, which was played out in dramatic scenes that seared themselves into the consciousness of nineteenth century Americans. Stanton refused to obey Thomas's order and barricaded himself into his office with a phalanx of Republican Senators. In the meantime, the House preempted the President's effort to present the dispute to the Supreme Court. After a brief debate, it impeached

Johnson by a vote of 126 to 47, with Democrats alone in the minority. The Speaker then appointed a special committee to address the legalities.[45] It responded with an elaborate bill of impeachment containing nine articles charging specific violations of the Tenure of Offices Act or the Command of the Army Act—only to find their efforts challenged by the Representatives selected to manage the impeachment before the Senate. Distressed by the legalistic tenor of the bill, these Managers convinced the House to add two more articles that altered the nature of the proceeding. The first of these—article ten—omitted any mention of illegality, impeaching Johnson for "set[ting] aside the rightful authority of Congress," by asserting that "in fact it is a Congress of only part of the States." The House then added an eleventh article that impeached the President both for illegal acts involved in removing Stanton and for publicly denying the legitimacy of a "Congress" that excluded Southerners.[46] This last article—uniquely combining legal and unconventional charges—became the focus of the Senate's decisive vote on Presidential removal.

These additional articles required the Senate to answer some very basic questions: To what extent should it operate as a court, impartially determining whether the President had engaged in willful violations of statutory law? To what extent was it a tribune of the People seeking to vindicate its authority against a President who denied Congress's right to exclude the South?

The Senate trial was scheduled to begin on March 30. In the meantime, another institutional dynamic helped shape the outcome.

EX PARTE MCCARDLE

As the Convention/Congress squared off against the President, the Supreme Court emerged from the shadows. In the spring, it had refused to intervene at the behest of the Johnsonian government of Georgia. When it returned to Washington in December, it confronted a new lawsuit, masterminded by the President's confidant, the formidable Jeremiah S. Black.[47] This petition sought to vindicate the concrete rights of a real person, William McCardle, whose editorial attacks on Reconstruction in Mississippi had led to his military arrest under the Reconstruction Act.[48] In bringing McCardle's predicament to the Court, Black and his co-counsel launched a sweeping attack on Congress's authority to displace the Johnsonian governments[49]—often repeating the same arguments Black had developed when working with the President on veto messages.[50] While McCardle's concrete predicament gained the Court's attention, the suit was part of the larger Presidential strategy.

Responding to this emerging threat, Republican Senator Lyman Trumbull sought to persuade the Court that it lacked jurisdiction over McCardle's case. As chairman of the Senate's Judiciary Committee, Trumbull was entitled to serious consideration—after all, his committee had passed the relevant jurisdictional statute only a year before. Nonetheless, the Court unanimously rejected his arguments on February 17.

No less important, it gave the case expedited treatment. The normal waiting period was then two years,[51] but the Court reserved the entire week of March 2 for this single case—awarding each side six full hours for oral argument. (This was three times the norm.) During this same week, the House was formally submitting its bill of impeachment to the Senate. The interbranch struggle was reaching its climax.

Consider the delicate balance. The President had a strong legal case if he made a second effort to remove Stanton. As we have seen, the Tenure of Offices Act offered scant protection to a cabinet officer in Stanton's position; moreover, the act itself was of doubtful constitutionality.[52] But viewing the matter unconventionally, Congress held the upper hand. Whatever the strict legalities, Stanton was in possession of the War Office, flouting Presidential authority behind the barricades in the name of the Convention/Congress. Johnson could not change this without attempting a micro-military invasion. With the Senate poised for an impeachment trial, Johnson would be playing with fire if military thugs broke through the barricades to evict Stanton.[53]

But judicial intervention might shift the balance once again. Armed with a Court opinion, Johnson could renew his demand for Stanton's removal. He could also order his conservative district commanders to cease enforcing acts that the Court had declared null and void. And he could present himself to the Senate as a heroic defender of legality, not the perpetrator of "high crimes and misdemeanors." If a Senate of

Northerners voted to convict, would he comply with such a blatantly unconstitutional decision?*

Only the most drastic measures would suffice to head off such a devastating counterattack. On March 12, the Republicans passed a statute removing the McCardle case from the Court's jurisdiction even though the Justices had already heard argument. Such an action would normally serve as a devastating confession by Congress of the unconstitutionality of Reconstruction. But, as these chapters have shown, the unconventional character of Congress's authority was hardly a secret to the American people by March of 1868. The Republican assault on the Court dramatized the obvious: "Congress" was not relying on the Founding document for its legitimacy, but on its contemporaneous mandate from We the People of the *United* States to insist upon Reconstruction and the Fourteenth Amendment.

But would the Court retreat before this unconventional assertion of authority? The Constitution gave the President ten business days to consider a veto; and it would take Congress a day or two to override it. This gave the Court two weeks to beat Congress to the punch by announcing its final decision.[54] According to Chief Justice Chase, if "the merits of the McCardle Case [had] been decided the Court would doubtless have held that his imprisonment for trial before a military commission was illegal."[55] How many Justices were prepared to go beyond the question of military trials, and declare the entire Reconstruction effort unconstitutional, is less certain. At least four of the eight sitting Justices seemed willing; whether a fifth vote could be

---

*Most ominous was the President's warning in his latest Annual Message: "How far the duty of the President 'to preserve, protect and defend the Constitution' requires him to go in opposing an unconstitutional act of Congress is a very serious and important question, on which I have deliberated much, and felt extremely anxious to reach a proper conclusion. Where an act has been passed according to the forms of the Constitution . . . executive resistance to it . . . would be likely to produce violent collision between the respective adherents of the two branches of the Government. This would be civil war; and civil war must be resorted to only as the last remedy for the worst evils. . . . The so-called reconstruction acts, though plainly unconstitutional as any that can be imagined, were not believed to be within the class last mentioned." See James Richardson, ed., 6 *Messages and Papers of the Presidents* 568–569 (1898).

But would a conviction by the Senate on a bill of impeachment fall into "the class last mentioned"?

found is less clear.[56] Even if only four justices had signed a broad opinion, while others voted to discharge McCardle on the "narrow ground," the result would have been devastating.

The decisive problem for the Justices was not the merits but the question of institutional self-preservation: Was continued resistance worth the risk that the Republicans would retaliate by inflicting even more serious damage upon the Court's institutional independence?

By a vote of 6 to 2, the Justices retreated. Given the procedural posture of the case, the majority negotiated its "switch in time" by doing nothing and allowing the jurisdiction-stripping statute to come into effect. But Justices Robert Grier and Stephen Field made the stakes clear enough in their dissent, which the court reporter somehow failed to publish in his official Reports.[57]

> Protest of Mr. Justice Grier:
>
> This case was fully argued in the beginning of this month. It is a case that involves the liberty and rights not only of the appellant, but of millions of our fellow-citizens. The country and the parties had a right to expect that it would receive the immediate and solemn attention of this court. By the postponement of the case we shall subject ourselves, whether justly or unjustly, to the imputation that we have evaded the performance of a duty imposed on us by the Constitution, and waited for legislation to interpose to supersede our action and relieve us from our responsibility. I am not willing to be a partaker of the eulogy or opprobrium that may follow; and can only say:
>
> Pudet haec opprobrium nobis
> Et dici potuisse;
> et non potuisse
> repelli
>
> [*Trans.:* I am ashamed that such opprobrium should be cast upon the court, and that it cannot be refuted. Ovid, *Metamorphosis,* Book 1, lines 758–759]
>
> R. C. Grier

> I am of the same opinion with my brother Grier, and unite in his protest.
> Field, J.

But most Justices were more impressed by Congress's unconventional threats than their colleagues' charge of cowardice. As soon as the jurisdiction-stripping statute became law over the President's veto on

March 27, McCardle's lawyers urged the Justices to give expedited treatment to their constitutional challenge to this unprecedented statute. But the Court refused,[58] deferring the matter to its December term.[59] By that point, the election returns would cast a different light over the dispute.

THE IMPEACHMENT TRIAL

The Court's retreat left the President in an exposed position. Only three months earlier, he was on the verge of triumph, with Grant in the War Office and the field command purged of Republican activists. But after the Convention/Congress's counteroffensive, the President confronted a hostile Stanton in the War Office, an alienated Grant as Commanding General, and a Senate poised to consider the question of "high crimes and misdemeanors" without the instruction of the Supreme Court on the status of Reconstruction.

As the impeachment trial began on March 30, Johnson was left with some unattractive options. He could still try to disrupt Reconstruction by asserting his power, as commander in chief, to issue orders over the heads of Stanton and Grant. But would his commanders obey?

Continued Presidential provocations would have a disastrous impact on the Senate. Granted, the President still had a very strong legal case against the Tenure of Offices Act. But as Representative Ben Butler, one of the Managers of the impeachment, put the point in his opening argument on March 30: "[Y]ou are bound by no law, either statute or common, which may limit your constitutional prerogative. You consult no precedents save those of the law and custom of parliamentary bodies. You are a law unto yourselves, bound only by the natural principles of equity and justice, and that *salus populi suprema est lex.*"[60] On his view, it was enough to remove the President for "high crimes and misdemeanors" if Senators concluded that Johnson's Southern strategy was *"subversive of some fundamental or essential principle of government or highly prejudicial to the public interest."*[61] The President's counsel took the opposite view—the Senate was a court, and it could remove the President only if he had committed a criminal act.[62]

As the Senate teetered uncertainly between rival characterizations,[63] the constitutional clock kept on ticking. Even if Johnson behaved himself, it was anybody's guess whether the Republicans would return to the voters in the fall with the Fourteenth Amendment on the books and black-and-white governments established on the ground. But if the commander-in-chief made yet another effort to disrupt Reconstruction, the resulting chaos in the War Office and the Southern command could easily doom the Republican race against the clock.[64]

This meant that the President would largely determine whether the Senate would view the impeachment process as a political inquest or a legalistic trial. If he initiated another round of open resistance, Republicans in the Senate would undoubtedly rally around Butler's vision and replace Johnson with the radical Benjamin Wade. If Johnson allowed Reconstruction to proceed to the triumphant ratification of the Fourteenth Amendment, he stood half a chance of sustaining the legalistic characterization of impeachment—and serve out his term in the White House. Which would it be: fight or switch?

The President retreated. Not only did he cease all serious acts of resistance,[65] he made more affirmative gestures as the Senate's climactic vote of May 16 came closer. On April 24, Johnson agreed to nominate John Schofield as Secretary of War, who accepted the appointment only on the understanding that the President would make no further efforts to interfere with Reconstruction.[66] By early May, he confronted a new test on receiving the first new constitutions approved by the voters of two states, Arkansas and South Carolina, which had complied with Congress's commands. Against the advice of Cabinet diehards, Johnson showed his good will by forwarding the new constitutions to the Congress on May 5. In private meetings, Johnson assured moderates that he would do nothing to violate the law or the Constitution if acquitted.[67] The overall impact of the President's switch in time is best described by Michael Benedict:

> Perhaps even more important than the President's assurances to conservative Republicans was the actual cessation of his interference while impeachment progressed. In explaining "What Has Happened During the Impeachment Trial," the Chicago Tribune wrote simply, "Andrew Johnson has been a changed man. The country has been at peace. The great obstruction to the law has been virtually suspended; the President . . . has been on his good behavior." The President's new docility enabled Republicans to recoup some of their losses in the South. In six of the unrecon-

structed States [the number needed for ratification of the Fourteenth Amendment], Republicans were able to win ratification of the Reconstruction laws, although by narrow margins. . . . By the time senators voted on impeachment, it was clear that only Virginia, Mississippi, and Texas would remain unrestored and liable to presidential interference. It is remarkable how quickly the sense of crisis that gripped the capital a few months earlier eased.

To a large extent, therefore, impeachment had succeeded in its primary goal: to safeguard Reconstruction from Presidential obstruction.[68]

The President's switch also had its predictable effect on the Senate's evolving understanding of the impeachment process. It weakened the intense pressure on Republican moderates to abandon their legalistic interpretation of impeachment as a quasi-criminal trial. The importance of this point is suggested by the fascinating series of opinions filed by individual Senators after the President's acquittal. The very idea of filing quasi-judicial opinions was eloquently denounced by radicals like Charles Sumner.[69] But for Republican moderates,[70] the opinions provided them with a crucial opportunity to deflect partisan criticism. In the words of Lyman Trumbull:

> The question to be decided is not whether Andrew Johnson is a proper person to fill the presidential office, nor whether it is fit that he should remain in it, nor, indeed, whether he has violated the Constitution and laws in other respects than those alleged against him [in the bill of impeachment]. . .
>
> Unfit for President as the people may regard Andrew Johnson, and much as they may desire his removal, in a legal and constitutional way, all save the unprincipled and depraved would brand with infamy and contempt the name of any Senator who should violate his sworn convictions of duty to accomplish such a result.[71]

Senator Trumbull had not always responded to the crisis with such emphatic legalisms. As recently as March, he had taken a leading role in stripping the Supreme Court of jurisdiction over McCardle's case. But the Court was then threatening the very existence of the Republicans' constitutional project; now that the President had retreated, Trumbull was more than willing to legalize an unconventional situation. Since Johnson was acquitted by a single vote in the Senate, it is plain that Johnson's switch in time saved the Presidency from a very damaging precedent.

Not that the Presidency immediately rose out of the flames of impeachment in Phoenix-like splendor. The emerging Republican regime of normal politics would, in Woodrow Wilson's phrase, be one of Congressional government. Not until the 1930's would the Presidency rival Congress in the American scheme. Yet, even at their low points, Presidents never had to struggle with the specter of a convicted Andrew Johnson obliged (by a show of force?) to leave the White House for the "crime" of opposing Congress.

THE RATIFICATION STRUGGLE CONTINUES

With the Court and the President in retreat, the Union Army proceeded to supervise a wave of elections in the South.[72] During the spring, the Republicans emerged victorious at the polls in six Southern states, losing only in Mississippi.[73]

Alabama posed a more complicated problem.[74] Its reconstituted citizenry was the first to cast ballots on an interracial constitution—voting 72,000 to 1,000 in favor. But this margin did not satisfy the demands of the Second Reconstruction Act, which required the participation of at least half of all registered voters. Alabama had fallen short of this threshold by 10,000 votes.[75] This news had generated such anxiety in March that the Republicans passed a Fourth Reconstruction Act that repealed this requirement.[76] Under the new ground rules, it would no longer matter that most Southerners were boycotting the polls—so long as the Republicans got a majority of the voters who braved the boycott, the Fourth Act professed itself satisfied with the new constitution's legitimacy. While the Republicans managed to get their bill enacted in time to govern all subsequent elections, the Fourth Act did not try to change the rules retroactively. Instead, the draftsmen supposed that the boycott of white Alabamans had successfully defeated Reconstruction.

By June, this supposition assumed strategic importance. Despite the six recent victories in the South, events in the North threatened to unravel the ratification effort. The Republican defeats in the elections of 1867 were coming home to roost as Northern legislatures convened in 1868. Already New Jersey and Ohio had withdrawn their earlier ratifications of the Fourteenth Amendment. Recent elections in Oregon threatened another legislative defection. In response, the

Congressional leadership moved aggressively to recognize the constitutional legitimacy of all seven Southern governments, including Alabama, and thereby put the Fourteenth Amendment over the top.

One of these states—Arkansas—had already ratified the amendment, and her representatives were immediately admitted to Congress on June 22.[77] As to the others, Congress took a more unconventional course. Its act of June 25 proclaimed that all six (including Alabama) had "framed constitutions of state government which are republican" and "shall be entitled and admitted to representation in Congress . . . when the legislature of such state shall have duly ratified the amendment to the Constitution . . . known as article 14."[78] Speaking for the Joint Committee on Reconstruction, Congressman Bingham explained why he opposed all efforts to amend the statute to eliminate Alabama or other states whose constitutions seemed defective to some of his colleagues.[79] Citing the recent Republican defeat in Oregon, Bingham called for action "above all—and it is to this I call the attention of the House and of this country— because upon the admission of these six states, upon the express condition named in the bill, may depend the final ratification and incorporation into the Constitution of the Republic of the fourteenth article of amendment."[80]

This candid confession emphasizes the blatant refusal by the Convention/Congress to respect the structure of the Federalist's Article Five. Since the act of June 25 explicitly proclaimed the six Southern states to be fully republican governments, there was no longer *any* textual foundation for barring their representatives from the House and Senate. And yet this is *precisely* what the Convention/Congress was doing by conditioning admission on the further act of ratifying the Fourteenth Amendment. As President Johnson put the point in his veto:

> . . . [T]his bill supersedes the plain and simple mode prescribed by the Constitution for the admission to seats in the respective Houses of Senators and Representatives from the several states. It assumes authority over six States of the Union which has never been delegated to Congress, or is even warranted by previous unconstitutional legislation upon the subject of restoration. . . . In the case of Alabama it violates the plighted faith of Congress by forcing upon that State a constitution which was rejected by the people, according to the express terms of an act of Congress requiring

that a majority of the registered electors should vote upon the question of ratification.[81]

Let us grant, with Bingham, that the fate of the Fourteenth Amendment hung in the balance. But so long as the operative norms governing constitutional amendment were rooted in the Federalist text, this hardly justifies the Congressional override of the President's veto.

From the textualist perspective, the whole point of a written constitution is to provide an anchor in times of crisis. If Article Five means anything, it gives each state the right to vote no as well as yes to any proposal coming out of Washington D.C. If the Congress, in its desperate effort to impose the Fourteenth Amendment, blatantly contravened this fundamental principle, so much the worse for the Fourteenth Amendment!

This exclamation returns us to my central thesis: the anxiety provoked by the Congressional override is based on a fundamental mistake in legal method. Modern lawyers are wrong to suppose that the validity of the Fourteenth Amendment is to be determined by a principled application of the text laid down by the Federalists. They should follow instead the methods of the common law and look upon both Founding and Reconstruction as co-equal precedents in an ongoing tradition of higher lawmaking.

From this point of view, there are striking analogies between the decision by the Convention/Congress to override President Johnson and decisions made during the Founding. In particular, President Johnson's veto message resembles the public protest of Governor Collins of Rhode Island when the Philadelphia Convention ran roughshod over a principled reading of the Articles of Confederation. Bingham's candid warnings are analogous to those issued by James Wilson and James Madison against a misplaced textualism that threatened to destroy the Federalist venture in constitutional politics.[82] Rather than papering over such assertions of unconventional authority, I have tried to locate them within an unfolding dynamic of institutional adaptation that allowed both Federalists and Republicans—each in their own time and place—to earn credibility for their claim to speak for We the People of an increasingly *United* States.

Having come this far, we can now turn to yet another episode that challenges hypertextualist understandings.

Seward's Last Stand

A month later, the six Southern states had complied with the Congressional demand for ratification, and it was up to the Secretary of State to make legal sense of the consequences. In his proclamation of July 20, Seward reacted with consternation to the notices he had received from "newly constituted and newly established bodies *avowing themselves to be and acting as* the legislatures, respectively, of the states of Arkansas, Florida, North Carolina, Louisiana, South Carolina, and Alabama."[83] After publicly demeaning these new Congressional creations, his proclamation followed up with a remarkable disparagement of the amendment's validity. Seward did not take the provocative step of explicitly proclaiming that the six Southern assents were null and void. He pointed to a defect that Republicans found more embarrassing: the decisions by the newly elected legislatures of New Jersey and Ohio to revoke their previous ratifications. Wringing his hands with mock anxiety, the Secretary awarded the amendment only a conditional validity "if the resolutions of Ohio and New Jersey . . . remain[] of full force and effect."[84] All in all, an artful performance: the Southern ratifications were publicly impugned, but it was the Northern ones that Seward identified as impairing the amendment's claim to higher law status.

But the Convention/Congress was not in the mood for forensic subtleties. On the day after Seward's proclamation, both Houses enacted a concurrent resolution "declaring the ratification of the fourteenth amendment" on the basis of the assent of all the states—both North and South—that had ever ratified it. Like so much else in this history, the effort by the Convention/Congress to resolve the question of validity was entirely unprecedented. Previously, such decisions had always been left to the Secretary of State to resolve by issuing an appropriate proclamation.

This meant that the institutional dynamic would return to the executive: Would Secretary Seward respond to Congress's aggressive resolution with a counterattack denouncing the validity of the Fourteenth Amendment? Or would he execute a strategic retreat?

The answer, once again, was a switch in time. Seward's proclamation of July 28 no longer asserted his independent authority to examine the merits of the ratification process. After reciting the Congressional resolution in full, he treated it as precluding any further doubt: "in execution . . . of the aforesaid concurrent resolution of the 21st of July, 1868, and in conformance thereto, . . . I do hereby declare that the said proposed amendment has been adopted."[85]

Though this tale of two proclamations can only embarrass the hypertextualist, we can now see it in a different light. It is not an awkward anomaly, but a surface reflection, in the official documents, of the structural transformation that had occurred. Time after time, Reconstruction Republicans had been obliged to challenge the monopoly over the ratification process that the Federalists had granted to the states. Time after time, they had won their struggle by adapting the federal separation of powers to new higher lawmaking purposes. Is it not appropriate, then, that the last act of ratification involved decisions made at the federal, and not the state, level?

CONSOLIDATION: THE ELECTION OF 1868

But as the Secretary gave ground, it was by no means clear whether his retreat was permanent or merely strategic. July was also the month when the Democratic National Convention was charting its electoral course. Its platform set the tone, offering Andrew Johnson "our thanks for his patriotic efforts" in "resisting the aggressions of Congress upon the Constitutional rights of the States and the people."[86] Even more threatening were the pronouncements of the Democrats' Vice-Presidential candidate, Frank Blair. In a public letter, Blair confessed that his party would be unable to dislodge the Republican majority in the Senate even if it won the Presidency and the House of Representatives. Since Democrats could not hope to repeal the Reconstruction Acts by normal methods, Blair proposed an unconventional solution:

> There is but one way to restore the Government and the Constitution, and that is for *the President-elect to declare these acts null and void, compel the army to undo its usurpations at the South, disperse the carpetbag State governments, allow the white people to reorganize their own governments and elect Senators and Representatives.* The House of Representatives will contain a majority of Democrats from the North, and they will admit the Representatives elected by the white people of the South, and with the

cooperation of the President, it will not be difficult to compel the Senate to submit once more to the obligations of the Constitution.[87]

Blair, in short, was offering a rerun of the election of 1866—where a conservative victory in the House would have enabled Johnson to force the Republican Rump on Capitol Hill to end its campaign for the Fourteenth Amendment.

Blair's letter caused an uproar—with Republicans denouncing it as "revolutionary" and Democrats backing away as they saw its potential for electoral disaster. Nonetheless, Blair remained on the ticket. Together with the Democratic platform's repeated constitutional denunciations of Reconstruction, a Democratic electoral victory would have reopened the questions raised by Secretary Seward's abrupt about-face on the Fourteenth Amendment. Here is the way the *New York Times* framed the issue in an editorial on "The Question Before the People":

> The all-important question presented to the people, North and South, is not whether a Republican or Democratic Administration shall rule the country. The political conflict which agitates every section of this continent is not simply partisan, as in ordinary cases . . .
>
> The military success which closed the war for the Union only furnished a basis for the restoration of peace. . . . The laws, which during the war had been silent, must now speak again and ratify and secure the results gained on the battle field. But ordinary legislation might be repealed; hence the necessity of incorporating in a constitutional amendment the legal conditions of a more perfect union . . .
>
> In a great measure this result has been achieved, through the fourteenth amendment. But the people cannot shut their eyes to the fact that this has been accomplished in the very teeth of the former Secessionists, and that the means through which it has been accomplished are pronounced unconstitutional and invalid by the Democratic Party. The feeling of insecurity, therefore, as to this most vital element in the restoration of peace, still remains. It has still to be decided by the popular vote whether the war had any real significance, whether it accomplished anything of permanent value for the nation.[88]

Such editorials emphasize the decisive importance of the race against the constitutional clock in the American scheme of government. As we have seen, the Fourteenth Amendment barely reached the finish line at the end of July—and then only as a result of switches in time by the President and Court. If the Convention/Congress had lost this race because the President or Court had remained intransigent, the editorials would have contained a very different message. Republican papers like the *Times* would have been unable to point to the Fourteenth Amendment as evidence that the great constitutional aim of the war had been largely "achieved," and that the only task which remained was to remove a residual "feeling of insecurity." Instead of holding up the Blair letter as evidence of the Democrats' "revolutionary" campaign to destroy the emerging status quo, the Republicans would have been still in the midst of their own revolutionary effort to ratify the Fourteenth Amendment. With chaos continuing in the South, would Northern voters have continued to support the Republicans?

We will never know, but the importance of the switches in time are suggested by the election returns. The Republicans won big in Congress—gaining a 2-to-1 majority in the House, 5-to-1 in the Senate[89]— but the Presidential returns told a different story. Grant's substantial Electoral College majority was belied by his thin margin of 300,000 popular votes. Since more than a half-million black Americans voted under the terms of the Reconstruction Acts, this meant that most whites voted for Democrats Horatio Seymour and Frank Blair![90]

The exclamation point marks a high point in the Republicans' boot-strapping operation. Recall that, under the leadership of Bingham and other moderates, the Convention/Congress had imposed black suffrage on the South for the express purpose of implementing the popular mandate for the Fourteenth Amendment that the Republicans had earned from the elections of 1866. Having redefined the Southern polities in the name of the nation to include blacks, the Convention/Congress now invited these very same black people to play a decisive role in consolidating the amendment in the elections of 1868. The result was a conceptually complex, but politically exhilarating, triumph of constitutional redefinition. We the People of the United States had somehow managed to reconstruct itself—whereas before, We the People consisted of a union of states that defined their own citizenship criteria, it now consisted of a union in which the People of the Nation imposed fundamental criteria of citizenship on the people of each state. While such a revolutionary redefinition of nationhood has often required a radical break with preexisting institutions, the Americans had somehow managed the process through a

chain reaction of unconventional adaptations culminating in 1868—
when the black citizens of the South used the unconventional voting
rights granted them by the Reconstruction Acts to consolidate the
very amendment that guaranteed them equal citizenship in the first
place. By continuing to adapt national elections for purposes never
contemplated by the Federalists, We the People of the *United* States
had now fully dedicated itself to the proposition that "[a]ll persons
born or naturalized" in America were entitled to "the privileges [and]
immunities of citizens of the United States" that were beyond the
power of any state or locality to abridge.

Viewed from a nuts-and-bolts perspective, Grant's election also
solidified the constitutional baseline established provisionally by the
second proclamation issued by Secretary Seward on the Fourteenth
Amendent. Given the Secretary's July retreat before the Conven-
tion/Congress, only a Democratic electoral victory could have prevented the consolidation of the Fourteenth Amendment into higher
law. Only then would it have been possible for a President to carry out
Blair's threat by ordering the new Secretary of State to issue a third
proclamation on the Fourteenth Amendment, reasserting the doubts
expressed in Seward's first—and generating yet another cycle of unconventional struggle in Washington and the South.

By cutting this cycle short, the Republican victory resolved—in the
words of the *New York Times*—"the feeling of insecurity" that still
surrounded the amendment. In my lingo, it was a *consolidating* event,
comparable to similar episodes in the aftermath of the Founding.
Recall that, despite the Federalists' success in gaining the formal ratification of the original Constitution, the First Congress opened with
two states—Rhode Island and North Carolina—defiantly in dissent.
So long as they remained outside the Union, the illegalities involved in
the Founding remained on the very surface of public life, and could
not be dismissed as historical curiosities. With the two dissenters
insisting on their rights under the Articles of Confederation, it was
perfectly possible for the Constitution to unravel. If one or more states
had defected from the new Union and rejoined Rhode Island and
North Carolina under the Articles, the problematic legality of the
Founding would have remained a burning issue. Only when the two
dissenters abandoned the Articles did the legal problems surrounding
the Founding lose their political sting.

The election of 1868 marked a similar watershed. With Grant in the White House, and Republican majorities solidly in control of Congress, Reconstruction had reached a point of no return. With the Republicans in firm command of national institutions, the remaining states of the South had little choice but to ratify the Reconstruction amendments as the price for readmission to Congress.

For all their other differences, the Presidencies of Grant and Washington were discharging similar constitutional functions. By the end of their first term in office, these relatively apolitical generals were presiding over an institutional order that—on the surface at least—belied the fierce struggles of the day before yesterday. No longer were leading American institutions regularly denouncing each others' constitutional legitimacy; nor were they issuing unconventional threats to one anothers' very existence. As in 1792, so in 1872, the new regime had emerged as the only game in town.

I do not mean to deny the obvious. Both in the 1790's and the 1870's, there were lots of people around who were grimly determined to undermine the unconventional victories that Federalists and Republicans had proudly proclaimed in the name of the People. At least in hindsight, both moments of constitutional consolidation are laden with bittersweet ironies. Looking back across the centuries, it is clear—to us at least—that the political pendulum was already beginning to swing away from the revolutionary nationalisms of the Federalists/Republicans just as they were proclaiming their triumph in the name of the People.

But not before they managed to anchor their legal contribution into the very bedrock of our constitutional order. We turn, then, to the final act of consolidation—the moment at which the Supreme Court made it plain that, despite their problematic pedigree, the Reconstruction amendments would serve as a source of enduring constitutional meaning for the indefinite future.

CONSOLIDATION AND THE COURT

When we last noticed the Court, it was in helter-skelter retreat—deferring to December any further consideration of the Convention/Congress's assault on its jurisdiction in McCardle's case. But once December arrived, the Court's next step was by no means foreordained: Would it follow the election returns or launch another legalistic attack on Reconstruction that would disrupt the consolidating tendencies of the Grant Administration?

The Justices first moved in the direction of disruption—before pulling back onto the consolidating course.

Court-Packing and Its Aftermath

As soon as Grant took office, the Republicans moved quickly to extend their control over the Court. This involved undoing some of the extraordinary steps they had taken in the recent past. In July of 1866, at the height of its struggle with the President, the Convention/Congress had responded to Johnson's nomination of his Attorney General, Henry Stanbery, as a Justice by enacting a remarkable "court-shrinking" statute. Under its terms, the retirement of a sitting Justice would not create a vacancy until the number of Justices was reduced to seven—thereby making it impossible for Johnson to appoint Stanbery, or anybody else, over the near term. With Grant in the White House, the Forty-first Congress quickly passed a statute expanding the Court back to nine, effective at the December term in 1869.[91] After some delay occasioned by the death of one nominee and the unpopularity of another, Grant managed to gain Senate confirmation of Justice William Strong in February and Justice Joseph P. Bradley in March of 1870.

The results were dramatic. A week before Strong arrived, the Justices had voted 4 to 3 to invalidate one of the great acts of the Convention/Congress making paper money into legal tender of the United States.[92] While fiat money may seem uncontroversial to modern Americans, it profoundly shocked nineteenth-century lawyers—who had great trouble seeing how, given the Federalists' notorious hostility to paper money, their Constitution could be read to authorize Congressional creation of greenbacks. It is merely anachronistic for moderns to look with bemused condescension upon the decision of Chief Justice Chase invalidating the Legal Tender Act. To the contrary, the seriousness of Chase's legal concerns is heightened by the fact that he was the Secretary of the Treasury at the time the greenbacks were issued. Chase's willingness to repudiate his own decisions at the Treasury cannot be explained without supposing that the Chief Justice was acting upon his good-faith understanding of Federalist constitutional principles.[93]

But as soon as the two new Justices came on the bench, they immediately moved to reverse this judicial assault on Republican economic policy.[94] The new five-man majority did not even wait to publish an opinion before announcing their decision upholding greenbacks in May of 1871.[95] The opinions, when they were finally published the next January, were bombshells. Speaking for the Court, Justice Strong disdained the textual path that might seem obvious to moderns. After all, the Constitution explicitly says that Congress can "coin Money [and] regulate the Value thereof," and nowhere does it limit this power to the issuance of currency backed by gold and silver. It does not seem much of a stretch to read this language as authorizing greenbacks whenever Congress deems it necessary and proper.

But Strong insisted on making life difficult for himself. His opinion refused to rely on the Constitution's textual grant of power over money, implicitly conceding that the dissenters were right in insisting that the Founders would have been horrified by fiat money. Casting about for other sources of national power, Strong led the Court to repudiate other elements of constitutional orthodoxy. It is a mistake, he declared for the Court, to suppose that the Federalist Constitution established a national government of limited powers. To the contrary, "important powers were understood by the people who adopted the Constitution to have been created by it, powers not enumerated, and not included incidentally in any of those enumerated. . . ."[96] The other new appointee, Justice Bradley, joined the nationalistic chorus in a concurring opinion:

> The United States is not only a government, but it is a National Government, and the only government in this country that has the character of nationality. . . .
>
> Such being the character of the General Government, it seems to be a self-evident proposition that it is invested with all those inherent and implied powers which, at the time of adopting the Constitution, were generally considered to belong to every government as such. . . .[97]

Though Bradley and Strong both indulged ritual gestures toward the Founding, no Federalist would have made such extravagant claims. But in the new Republican vision of the Union, the national government could assert "inherent" authority based on its standing as "the only government in this country that has the character of nationality."

Consolidating Reconstruction

Given its emphatic switch on legal tender, I have no doubt that a reconstituted Court would have responded with the same assertive nationalism if it had been obliged to face a constitutional challenge to Reconstruction and the Fourteenth Amendment. Just as Strong and Bradley rejected the restraints imposed by Federalist text and principle when it came to Republican economic policy, they would have done the same when it came to Republican constitutional policy—treating the Federalist principles of Article Five with no greater respect than the Federalist principles of sound money. During the Grant Administration, the Court came very close to this moment of truth—only to swerve and take a less melodramatic approach.

As with legal tender, the story begins with a legalistic opinion by Chief Justice Chase. On April 12, 1869—almost two years after it dropped McCardle—a unanimous Court defended its decision. Its retreat, Chase explained, had nothing to do with prudence, everything to do with principle. After all, the jurisdictional statute under which McCardle came to the Court had only been enacted in the previous year. If Congress could grant the Court new jurisdiction in 1867, why could it not take it away in 1868?

Given this strong affirmation of Congressional power, Chase readily acquitted the Court of any hint of impropriety suggested by its helter-skelter retreat: "Jurisdiction is power to declare law, and when it ceases to exist, the only function remaining to the court is that of announcing the fact and dismissing the cause. And this is not less clear upon authority than upon principle."[98] But there were hidden dangers in this resounding transformation of prudence into principle: Wasn't Chase proclaiming the death knell of judicial review? Whenever a future Court threatened to declare a statute unconstitutional, couldn't the dominant faction in Congress strip it of jurisdiction?

Chase responded in one of the most brilliant concluding paragraphs in Supreme Court history:

> Counsel seem to have supposed, if effect be given to the repealing act in question, that the whole appellate power of the court, in cases of *habeas*

corpus is denied. But this is an error. The act of 1868 does not except from that jurisdiction any cases but appeals from Circuit Courts under the act of 1867 [like the one made by McCardle]. It does not affect the jurisdiction which was previously exercised.[99]

Having dressed up the Court in a mantle of principle, Chase had majestically redefined the principle. Though everybody had thought that *McCardle* was a "great case" involving the plenary power of Congress to destroy the Court's jurisdiction, Chase blandly informed the world that it was mistaken. *McCardle* merely decided that Congress could deprive litigants of one path to the Supreme Court *so long as another had been left open.* Later generations returning to *McCardle* in search of a clear answer to a basic question will be rewarded only by Chase's enigmatic smile. On the one hand, the fact remains that the Court *did* acquiesce to Congress at a critical moment of constitutional transformation; on the other, the Court's opinion did *not* recognize Congress's unconditional and plenary power to strip it of jurisdiction.

While Chase's brilliant maneuver had reduced *McCardle*'s long-run institutional damage, it had a different short-run consequence. Lawyers for other aggrieved Southerners would predictably seek to exploit the opinion to blaze other jurisdictional trails to the Court, and propel the Justices into a belated confrontation with Grant and the Republican Congress over Reconstruction—which in 1869 was still proceeding in Georgia, Mississippi, Texas, and Virginia.[100] It fell to Edward Yerger to serve as legal trailblazer. Yerger had been accused of killing a Union officer assigned as mayor of Jackson, Mississippi. As in *McCardle,* the commanding general denied Yerger's request for a jury trial, ordering him to stand before a military commission under Section 3 of the Reconstruction Act.

After hearing the case, the commission sentenced Yerger to death. However violent his crime, Yerger's case raised most of the same issues as McCardle's.[101] Could Congress deny a Southern civilian a jury trial when the civilian courts were open?[102] Did it have the power to use the Union Army to destroy a Johnsonian government in an effort to gain ratification of the Fourteenth Amendment?

With Chase's opinion in *McCardle* now before him, Yerger's lawyer invoked the Supreme Court's jurisdiction through traditional habeas corpus procedures that antedated the statute Congress had repealed in McCardle's case. This gambit was successful. On October 25,

1869, the Chief Justice accepted Supreme Court jurisdiction over Yerger's case. *Ex parte Yerger* was now at the same point at which Congress had been provoked into its jurisdiction-stripping measures in *McCardle*. Since Strong and Bradley had not yet ascended to the bench, there was every reason to fear a negative outcome. As Charles Fairman puts it, "on a candid estimate, a decision on Yerger would probably go against the Government; indeed, in a substantial sense the Government could not possibly win."[103]

Republicans once again moved on the offensive. As Congress reconvened in December 1869, Senator Charles Sumner filed a bill[104] depriving the Court of *all* appellate jurisdiction over habeas corpus.[105] The judiciary committee transformed Sumner's bill into a vehicle for a different, but no less extreme, response. Striking everything except the title, it substituted the very same proposal that its chairman, Lyman Trumbull, had made two years previously. This would have explicitly forbidden any court from questioning the constitutional validity of Reconstruction.[106] If either Sumner or Trumbull had succeeded, the Chief Justice could no longer deny, by artful statutory construction, that the Convention/Congress was deadly serious about subordinating the Court to the Republican vision of the Union.

Once again, the Court seemed to be propelling itself into a war it could not win. If it moved quickly to vindicate Yerger, it either confronted another round of jurisdiction-stripping or a variation of the Legal Tender scenario, in which Justices Strong and Bradley came to the rescue with a ringing defense of the intrinsic power of the Convention/Congress to insist on Reconstruction in the name of the Nation.

But at this point, President Grant intervened to cut short the cycle of constitutional confrontation.[107] Even before Congress convened in December, the new Republican Attorney General had taken steps to assure that the Court would never hear Yerger's case. The day after Chase handed down his opinion asserting jurisdiction, the following note appeared in the minutes:

> Mr. Phillips stated to the Court that on account of an arrangement in progress between the Attorney General and the counsel of petitioner, no motion will be made this morning for further proceedings; but if there be no objection on the part of the Court, counsel will postpone moving until a subsequent day of the term.
>
> The Chief Justice said, It is undoubtedly matter of discretion with the counsel for the petitioner to move for the writ of Habeas Corpus. The

point of jurisdiction having been determined, the Court will hear a motion for the writ whenever counsel shall see fit to make it.[108]

Phillips then waited until February 23, 1870, when the reconstructed state of Mississippi was finally recognized in the halls of Congress. On the very same day, he reported an agreement to transfer Yerger to the new state authorities to allow them to prosecute him for murder.[109] A similar settlement was reached in a companion case from Texas.[110]

And then there were none. Once Georgia was readmitted in July of 1870, there were no longer any more whites who could bring concrete cases challenging Army administration of Reconstruction. There is, then, a humdrum procedural reason why the Legal Tender Acts generated a highly visible vindication of national sovereignty while no similar episode marks the consolidation of the Fourteenth Amendment into higher law. Since greenbacks were circulating into the indefinite future, an endless stream of litigants would badger the Court about their constitutional status. With Reconstruction winding down under Grant, the Justices could avoid any further struggles among themselves—not to mention the President, Congress, and the People—by playing a waiting game.

Until a very different kind of lawsuit came along. After 1870, Southern whites found themselves in a paradoxical position. They suddenly became leading advocates of the very amendment they had so bitterly opposed. The new Republican governments of the South were now dominated by interracial coalitions that left many whites out in the cold. So long as these coalitions remained in power, conservative whites would respond to legislative defeat in the good old American way—by going to the courts, and using all available legal tools to reverse their legislative defeats. And what could be a better weapon than the shiny new Fourteenth Amendment's promise of citizenship, liberty, and equality?

So matters stood in 1873, when the Court finally handed down its first considered decision on the Fourteenth Amendment. The *Slaughterhouse Cases* were brought at the behest of *white* butchers of New Orleans against their new state government, which had created a slaughterhouse monopoly that threatened to freeze them out of business. On the butchers' view, the Reconstruction amendments gave whites, as well as blacks, fundamental rights as American citizens—

including the right to compete in a free market without unjustified legislative restriction. In a famous 5-to-4 decision, the Supreme Court rejected this claim.

But it is not this aspect of the case—already discussed in the first book of this series[111]—that need concern us. Our focus here is not substance but process, not with *Slaughterhouse* as the first great case interpreting the meaning of the Reconstruction amendments, but as the last great step in their consolidation. Given this interest, the Court's prologue commands special attention. After stating the facts of the case, Mr. Justice Samuel Miller locates his problem in the flux of time. He begins by viewing the Federalist Constitution, and its early amendments, from a very great distance. These fundamental texts, Miller explains, "have become . . . historical and of another age." The next sentence juxtaposes this historical past with the living present: "But within the last eight years three other articles of amendment of vast importance have been added by the voice of the people."[112]

Miller's declaration may seem bland, but it represents a crucial turning point. The Court's hostility to Reconstruction had been a continuing source of grave anxiety to Congress and the President; but this single sentence places the country on notice that its period of anxiety is at an end. The Justices speak with a unanimous voice. While they later divide sharply over the *meaning* of the amendments, all nine unconditionally accept their *validity*.

Reflect upon the precise words through which the Court expresses this epochal act of recognition: ". . . have been added *by the voice of the people*."[113] Justice Miller speaks the unmediated language of popular sovereignty without trying to establish the amendments' legal pedigree under Article Five. His entire rhetorical framework is hostile to such formalisms. Rather than creating the fiction of a smooth transition from the 1780's to the 1860's, he has presented a radical disjunction between the Founding texts of "another age" and the living "voice" of contemporary Americans. As the Court describes the genesis of each amendment, its unconcern with the formalities becomes apparent. Consider Miller's treatment of the Fourteenth Amendment. In his stylized account, the "statesmen who had conducted the Federal government in safety through the crisis" recognized that "something more" than the Thirteenth Amendment was necessary to protect "the unfortunate race who had suffered so much. They accordingly passed through Congress the proposition for the fourteenth amendment, *and they declined to treat as restored to their full participation in the government of the Union the States which had been in insurrection, until they ratified that article by a formal vote of their legislative bodies.*"[114]

These are my italics, not Miller's. While the italics cry out for a modicum of legalistic hand-wringing over Article Five, this is the last thing the Court has in mind. Rather than explaining why an amendment obtained under such conditions merits recognition as legally valid, Justice Miller passes on to other things, as if nobody had ever thought to raise constitutional questions about the decision by Republican "statesmen" to override the Southern veto of the Fourteenth Amendment.

Not that the Justices supposed they were fooling anybody. As Miller explains, his "recapitulation of events, almost too recent to be called history,"[115] involved episodes that are "fresh within the memory of us all."[116] The ease with which he evades the problematics of validity cannot be attributed to a sudden attack of amnesia—either amongst the nine Justices or the population at large. It is a tribute to the influence of common law methods on constitutional adjudication. Unlike constitutional courts in Europe, the Supreme Court gives no advisory opinions. Like a common law court, it waits for real-life litigants to bring unresolved constitutional questions to its attention. But neither side of the *Slaughterhouse* controversy was interested in raising the question of validity—certainly not the white butchers, who were trying to use the new amendments to attack the new monopoly imposed by the ascendant black-and-white authorities in Louisiana; certainly not the defenders of the slaughterhouse monopoly, who could denounce Reconstruction only at the cost of renouncing their own special privileges. Since both sides were happy to finesse the question of validity, the Court acted consistently with common law norms in ignoring the deep questions that everybody knew lurked just below the surface.[117]

Nonetheless—and here again common law methods are at work—*Slaughterhouse* effectively ended all serious legal debate on the validity of the Fourteenth Amendment. For common lawyers, the key is not what a court says, but what it does. Although the Justices had not explained the basis of their action, their unanimous decision on validity operated as a decisive precedent. Henceforth, a lawyer would be laughed out of court if he tried to persuade a judge to scrutinize the doubtful pedigree of the Reconstruction amendments. With every passing year, the courts would generate a mountain of case law burying the amendments' problematic pedigree under layers upon layers of learned discussion that simply took for granted the binding force of the Reconstruction amendments. With *Slaughterhouse,* the bandwagon had come to rest at its final destination.

THE RETURN OF NORMAL POLITICS

Just in the nick of time. As consolidation was proceeding in the courts, the Ku Klux Klan was embarking on a guerrilla campaign of terror that aimed for nothing less than the obliteration of the Republican experiment in interracial politics. Grant responded with an erratic use of the Union Army to sustain law and order, but he was simply not up to the strategic and moral demands of leadership.[118] Under a reign of death, blacks retreated from the polls, allowing whites to vote one Republican government out of office after another. By the end of Grant's Administration, only three Republican governments remained (barely) standing with the aid of Union troops.

National politics was also turning against the Republicans. The devastating Panic of 1873 generated a Democratic landslide in the 1874 elections. For the first time since 1860, Democrats would control the House, and they had cut into the Republican majority in the Senate.[119]

Within this changing political context, the electoral crisis of 1876 operated as an acid test of the consolidation process. The Democratic candidate, Samuel J. Tilden, was the clear popular winner, beating the Republican Rutherford B. Hayes by 250,000 votes.[120] But Tilden was deprived of the White House by an extraconstitutional Electoral Commission convened to resolve disputed returns from the three Republican states remaining in the South.[121] These states had reported two rival sets of election returns—one awarding the electoral vote to Tilden, the other to Hayes—and it was up to the Commission to decide which ones to recognize. The body, consisting of five Senators, five Representatives, and five Justices, upheld all the Republican electors on a party-line vote of 8 to 7—with Mr. Justice Bradley, who owed his seat to the Republicans' court-packing statute of 1870, casting the decisive ballot in each case. This decision made Hayes President by a one-vote majority in the Electoral College, despite his clear defeat in the popular vote.[122] To the disgust of millions of his Democratic partisans, Tilden accepted this outcome in a remarkable show of statesmanship that deserves a place of great honor in the annals of the Republic. Hayes, in turn, stopped giving military support to the remaining Republican governments of the South, leading to their rapid collapse.

From the distance of 125 years, we can now recognize that the stage was being set for a new national politics. The burning issues of race and Union began to be displaced by the crises of industrial capitalism. New movements would emerge from the farms and the cities to challenge the emerging status quo. As the 1870's moved into the 1880's, the air filled with denunciations of big business and its corruption of American government. Like their fathers and grandfathers and great-grandfathers, a new generation would express their populist impulses by founding a new political party, the Populists, as a vehicle for a frontal assault on the status quo. But as always, these variations on old themes generated a surprising outcome. The rising Populists would never celebrate the victory of a Jefferson or a Jackson or a Lincoln. They would see their candidate William Jennings Bryan decisively defeated in the Presidential elections of 1896 and 1900. If you will forgive my lingo, the new century would open with a *failed constitutional moment*—with fateful consequences that still reverberate today.

But in the America of 1876, all this was for the trackless future. The operational question was how to treat the immediate past—the period of Reconstruction that was so evidently coming to a close. In particular, Americans were then very conscious of a choice that we have long forgotten: Should the next generation accept the Fourteenth Amendment as a valid act of higher law, or should it use the amendment's problematic pedigree to discredit it?

From this vantage point, the answer given by the Democrat Tilden is especially important. Here is his open letter published at the height of the fall campaign:

The questions settled by the war are never to be reopened. The adoption of the thirteenth, fourteenth, and fifteenth amendments to the Federal

Constitution closed one great era in our politics. . . . They close the chapter; they are and must be final; all parties hereafter must accept and stand upon them, and henceforth our politics are to turn upon questions of the present and the future, and not upon those of the settled and final past.[123]

Even if Tilden had gained the White House, there is no reason to believe he would have sought to erase the Reconstruction amendments from the books (how they would have fared on the ground is another matter). Suppose the contrary, however, and imagine President Tilden repudiating his campaign rhetoric once in office. Even then, he would have confronted a Court that had *unanimously* received the Reconstruction amendments into higher law three years before in *Slaughterhouse*. It was no longer within the power of a single President to reverse this judgment, even if he could convince the Senate to confirm Supreme Court nominees devoted to the Johnsonian interpretation of the ratification crisis. Given the 9-to-0 vote, reversing *Slaughterhouse* would require decades of Democratic ascendancy in the White House and the Senate, as well as remarkable ideological consistency in the selection of nominees to the Supreme Court. President after President would have had to fend off potential nominees who did not toe the Johnsonian line but were politically attractive for other reasons. In short, a formal repudiation of the constitutional legacy of Reconstruction was now operationally impossible.

Contrast this with the situation prevailing when Secretary Seward had reluctantly proclaimed the amendment's validity in July of 1868. Imagine, for example, that the electoral crisis of 1876 had occurred in 1868. Instead of beating Seymour by 250,000 votes, Grant went down by 250,000 (which was the margin of the Republican popular vote deficit in the Tilden-Hayes contest). Suppose next that the Republicans had attempted to defy the will of the majority by constructing an Electoral College victory for Grant with the assistance of Republican electors from the newly reconstructed Southern states. Suppose next that Seymour had responded with the same remarkable statesmanship that Tilden displayed, and allowed Grant to move into the White House without further agitation. Suppose, finally, that Grant responded in the manner of Hayes—with an appropriate gesture of reconciliation to the majority of Americans who had voted against him at the polls. Within the context of 1868, what would this gesture have looked like? In particular, *would the Fourteenth Amendment have been sacrificed as part of the accommodation?*

After all, we are speaking of a time when Seward's July proclamation casting doubt on the amendment was still fresh in the public mind, when Blair's denunciations of Reconstruction provided a defining issue of the election campaign, when the Supreme Court had not yet been re-expanded from seven to nine, when . . .

To put it mildly, it is easy to tell a story that ends unhappily for the Fourteenth Amendment. At the very best, the pages of the *United States Reports* would have told a much more turbulent tale—full of ringing opinions denouncing and defending the effort by the Convention/Congress to override the Southern veto of the Fourteenth Amendment. Perhaps the *Reports* might have contained many such confrontations, as judicial majorities shifted to and fro, in the manner of the *Legal Tender Cases,* before settling down one way or another sometime in the 1880's.

This thought-experiment puts in bold relief the importance of the Grant years to the legitimation of the Fourteenth Amendment. It also suggests why dualist theory places a high value on successful consolidation. This emphasis is alien to constitutional theorists who suppose Americans should continue the burdens of constitutional politics indefinitely. These strong democrats[124] cannot conceal their disappointment as they see the American people retreat in 1877 from the heavy sacrifices they had been enduring in the name of citizenship. For them, the fact that a few constitutional amendments were now securely on the books is small consolation for America's retreat from racial justice in the South.

Things look different to the dualist, who neither seeks nor expects the indefinite extension of constitutional politics. So far as he is concerned, Americans have a fundamental right to say ENOUGH IS ENOUGH to the mobilized engagements demanded by a politics of popular sovereignty, and to declare that the time has come to turn to other things—either the pursuit of more private interests or the slow elaboration of a new constitutional agenda for fundamental change (or both).[125] Within this framework, the Constitution makes a key contribution when it brings an era of successful mobilization to a decisive end, as in the *Slaughterhouse Cases,* rather than allow the collective sense of accomplishment to be frittered away by a series of inconclusive elite manipulations envisioned by my alternative thought-experiment.

Similarly, as the dualist observes Hayes allowing the fall of the last Republican governments of the South, he does not suppose that this moment could have been long delayed if only the Republicans had sustained the burning faith of 1866. He takes it for granted that popular disengagement from yesterday's constitutional agenda is bound to occur, and asks a different question: How well did American institutions—and in particular, the Supreme Court—manage to preserve the spirit of 1866 during the long period of normal politics inaugurated by the Hayes Administration? What does this judicial experience teach us about the strengths and limits of dualist constitutionalism?[126]

I will return to these questions in volume three.

BEYOND TOCQUEVILLE

For now, let us return one last time to the hypothetical Grant-Seymour "Compromise of 1868." Suppose that Grant did not simply abandon the Fourteenth Amendment as part of a deal with Seymour to gain the White House. Instead, he stands by Seward's second proclamation and instructs his Attorney General vigorously to prosecute cases like *Yerger* that call upon the Supreme Court to resolve the constitutional status of Reconstruction and the Fourteenth Amendment. Suppose further that the Court flip-flops for a decade until, after several more Presidential elections, it finally comes down unanimously in favor of the Fourteenth Amendment. Suppose, finally, that you agree with me that this outcome would have been much worse for the country than what actually happened in *Slaughterhouse*.

Then, you will reach a final paradox. Though the hypothetical outcome would have been much worse for Americans of the nineteenth century, it would have advantaged one small group who live much later on. This is the group composed by the readers of this book—which would never have been written, since the problematic pedigree of the Fourteenth Amendment would have been a standard topic in every course on constitutional law that attempted a comprehensive overview of the "great cases" rendered by the Supreme Court.

The very existence of this book is, then, a testimony to the remarkably narrow fixation of modern scholarship on the Supreme Court. *Pace* Tocqueville, it is *not* the case that every important constitutional question ends up in the courts for full-dress resolution. Sometimes, as in *Slaughterhouse,* courts simply acknowledge the constitutional conclusions reached by others after long and bitter years of argument.

The challenge is to take these non-Tocquevillean truths seriously. The great precedents established by Presidents and Congresses, in dialogue with their fellow citizens, command respect even if their significance is given scant acknowledgment in judicial opinions. It is about time for lawyers to move beyond their myopic focus on the work of the courts. It is not too late for them to redeem the promise made by the first words of the constitutional text, and to treat We the People as the principal architect of America's constitutional destiny.

PART THREE

Modernity

CHAPTER NINE

From Reconstruction to New Deal

ON METHOD

AS WE MOVE from the nineteenth century to the twentieth, our perspective on the past suffers different distortions, requiring compensating changes in interpretive method. In dealing with Reconstruction, we confronted collective amnesia. The last American who personally participated in the struggle over the Fourteenth Amendment was buried a half-century ago. Even grandchildren who dimly recall childhood stories of Thad Stevens and Andy Johnson are dying out. As a consequence, we had to spend lots of time and energy rediscovering institutional interrelationships that once were intuitively obvious. If the higher lawmaking legacy of the nineteenth century is to survive, each generation must make a similar effort to rediscover the remarkable way Americans organized their debate over the constitutional meaning of the Civil War.

By contrast, the great constitutional struggles of the New Deal are closer to us. Ronald Reagan voted for Franklin Roosevelt in 1936. When he recalled the Democratic landslide of that year, he could effortlessly place it in a sequence that began with Roosevelt's first victory in 1932 and continued through the Court-packing crisis of 1937 to the consolidation of the welfare state by the early 1940's. Memories of these scenes returned men like Reagan to their youth, when they began to share in the political struggles of their parents. The lessons they learned served as benchmarks for many later exercises in political judgment.

As in politics, so in law. When the New Deal generation won positions of authority in the courts and the law schools, they took full advantage of their opportunity to warn their successors against repeating the Old Court's mistakes. These doctrinal teachings were greatly enhanced by the penetration of New Deal premises into American government. The millions of Social Security checks mailed each month attest to the government's ongoing concern with fair income distribution. The thousands of pages published annually in the *Federal Register* (founded in 1936) contain countless reminders by a host of alphabet agencies—SEC, NLRB, EPA, OSHA, . . .—that unregulated capitalism endangers a series of fundamental values, ranging from environmental purity to worker dignity. Each day's headlines report on the ongoing effort by the national government to sustain general prosperity through the flexible tools of macroeconomic policy made possible by the New Deal's repudiation of the Gold Standard. Until the Reagan Presidency, no victorious political movement had questioned the propriety of this complex governmental effort to improve upon the invisible hand. To one or another extent, each Administration had built upon the efforts of its predecessors in the three basic areas of activist concern marked out in the Roosevelt years: the pursuit of distributive justice, the correction of market failure, and the assurance of general prosperity.

Little wonder that modern lawyers have little trouble recalling the broad outlines of the great constitutional crisis of the 1930's. It is only their recollection of the Supreme Court's retreat before the New Deal that provides the vast statutory superstructure of the activist state with a firm constitutional foundation. It was different before 1932. Each new activist initiative then provoked anxious foreboding: How to evade the entrenched constitutional principles that cast intervention into the "free market" under a dark cloud? The answer, in particular cases, depended upon the complexities of constitutional doctrine and the vagaries of judicial personnel. But there was no mistaking the constitutionally problematic character of the activist enterprise. So far as the judges were concerned, We the People had *not* authorized state regulation of the marketplace whenever political majorities concluded that this would serve the nation's general welfare; the Constitution emerging after the Civil War contained fundamental limitations on such dubious enterprises.

These boundaries disintegrated during the New Deal revolution. A complex web of doctrine, woven by two generations of judges in the long period between 1873 and 1932, was swept away in the space of a decade. If the partisans of laissez-faire lost their battle in the legislature, they could no longer hope that the courts might reverse their opponents' victory. After the New Deal revolution, it became clear to judges that We the People had stripped free market solutions to social problems of their previously privileged position.

Lochner v. New York serves as the paradigm. In 1905, the Court struck down the effort by New York to limit the work week to sixty hours as a violation of freedom of contract.[1] By the end of the Roosevelt era, *Lochner* became the symbol of a repudiated era of laissez-faire jurisprudence. Henceforward, courts would uphold the authority of American government to act against all forms of social or economic exploitation that were condemned by a democratically elected majority.

This turnaround was all the more wrenching in connection with the national government. The Supreme Court had never denied the states a broad (though not unlimited) power to police the economy, but it had taken a different view of Congressional authority. *Hammer v. Dagenhart* can serve as paradigm. In 1916, Congress had acted against child labor by excluding its products from interstate commerce. But the Court struck down this effort: "[t]he Commerce Clause was not intended to give to Congress a general authority to equalize . . . conditions."[2] If Congress could not take steps to express the nation's condemnation of a shocking abuse like child labor, its powers were limited indeed. If the New Deal was to prevail, this vision of limited government could not survive.

And it did not. By the early 1940's, the New Deal Court was ringing the death knell in unanimous decisions that would have astounded lawyers a decade before. But the bar proved very adaptable. Under the Court's emphatic tutelage, lawyers learned to look upon the case law of the preceding Republican regime with the peculiar mix of ignorance and contempt reserved for abandoned precedent. Whatever their personal political convictions, they quickly mastered the New Deal language for courtroom use. A half-century later, the New Deal Constitution—far less respectful of the rights of property and contract, far more respectful of national power—had been woven into the very fabric of the modern polity, shaping the expectations of ordinary citizens as well as the daily interactions of the President, Congress, and the Supreme Court.

All this is changing. The meaning of the New Deal revolution is no longer a matter of lived experience. The political stage is dominated by generations for whom other events served as the formative context for political awareness: the war against Hitler, the crusade against Communists, the struggle for civil rights, the agony of Vietnam, the resurgence of the right under Reagan. With the Republican takeover of Congress in 1994, New Deal premises are an object of sharp legislative critique. As usual, these tendencies take hold much more slowly in the courts—though even here, the first expressions of doubt are noticeable.[3]

It is too soon to say what will come of this rite of generational passage. Perhaps it heralds the ultimate unraveling of New Deal doctrine, bringing an end to the third great constitutional regime in American history. Perhaps it will provoke Americans to reinvigorate and deepen their New Deal commitments to social justice and the general welfare. Or maybe it will lead to something else entirely. Whatever lies in our constitutional future, the New Deal revolution is now becoming "historical and of another age."[4]

Which does not mean that it will be unimportant. So long as America remains a dualist democracy, the death of a generation does not consign its constitutional achievements to the junk heap. But if they survive, they can no longer depend on the emphatic certainties of those who were present at the creation. They can flourish only through the engaged efforts by citizens, judges, and scholars to reflect on the meaning of the historical traces left behind.

I approach the New Deal, then, with a different ambition from the preceding case studies. Previously, my challenge was to bridge vast historical distances and see the Federalists and Republicans as they saw themselves—as revolutionary reformers struggling against formidable odds to redeem the will of We the People. Now my problem is different. I will be reflecting on the yawning gap—the unbridgeable distance of mortality—that has begun to separate the Roosevelt revolution from the lived experience of the American people. There is little value in repeating the stories told to us by the New Dealers after they took power in the nation's courts and classrooms; rather, the challenge is to hold them at a critical distance.

My target will be the standard account of the birth agony of the modern republic. Political scientists regularly refer to the New Deal creation of a "Second American Republic,"[5] but lawyers tell a different tale. They do not compare New Deal Democrats to the great regime-makers of previous centuries. They attribute the great constitutional crisis of the 1930's to a few reactionaries on the Supreme Court who perversely distorted the Constitution's true meaning. In opposing the New Deal, the Old Court of the early 1930's had departed from the main line of the constitutional tradition established by John Marshall and the other great nationalizers of the early republic. If only the Justices had not strayed from Marshall's path, all this unpleasantness could have been avoided!

On this traditional line, there was nothing new about the New Deal—except that it was cursed with some peculiarly reactionary Justices. The founders of the welfare state in America were not Roosevelt and his Democrats but Marshall and other Federalists who built the constitutional foundations of national power. In rediscovering the relevance of the Marshallian tradition after 1937, the New Deal Court was simply reestablishing itself in the main stream of American constitutional law.

Or so we have been taught. In calling this a "myth of rediscovery," I do not dismiss it as worthless. There *is* an important truth in the last generation's teaching. In placing activist government on a secure constitutional foundation, the New Dealers did not destroy all their legal and institutional connections to the past in the manner, say, of the Bolsheviks. As a consequence, the reigning professional narrative is right in pointing to the historical precedents for the New Deal revolution. But it deeply misleads by focusing on only half of the truth. Granted, the New Dealers maintained some important links with the past; they *also* gained popular consent for a sweeping redefinition of the aims and methods of American government.

I am calling for the same kind of balanced treatment that lawyers automatically accord to the 1780's or 1860's. Like the New Dealers, both Federalists and Republicans maintained many traditional elements in their constitutional theory and practice; but this does not prevent lawyers from recognizing the transformative thrust of the original Constitution or the Reconstruction amendments. Why not take a similar stance when dealing with the New Deal? Why pretend that it was Marshall and his friends who did *all* the really important constitutional work?

The answer returns us, once again, to the hypertextualist view of Article Five. Within this framework, the New Dealers could only lead Americans to a revised political identity by formally amending the Constitution. Since Roosevelt & Co. did not follow this path, hypertextualists are obliged to deny the constitutional creativity of the New Deal without deigning to investigate the facts. If there are no formal amendments, there can be no legitimate change, and that is that.

But, alas, it can't be so simple—at least for those hypertextualists who are fated to live out their lives as lawyers and judges. In their daily work, they confront an endless array of legal doctrines and structures that presuppose the legitimacy of the New Deal revolution. And as sober professionals, they are not disposed to go on a constitutional rampage against the work of the last half-century. When faced with the yawning gap between hypertextualist theory and real-world practice, many lawyers have embraced the myth of rediscovery as a convenient legal fiction. Perhaps, they may concede, Marshall or Madison look a bit awkward when portrayed as proto–New Dealers; but this is an acceptable price to pay for a myth that allows modern lawyers to vindicate the constitutionality of modern American government. So let's stop picking nits and get on with the business of constitutional adjudication in today's America, dominated by the activist regulatory state. Next case.

For obvious reasons, such sentiments don't appear in print too often. But I have heard them many times in private conversation. My aim is to confront the hypertextualist prejudices that make a descent to legal fiction seem necessary. While Roosevelt and Congress did not accept the preexisting system of higher lawmaking, neither did Madison and the Convention or Bingham and the Convention/Congress. Perhaps, after reviewing the facts, you will be unpersuaded by my claim that the New Deal is fundamentally similar to these earlier great acts of popular sovereignty. But surely the hypertextualist is a bit rash to dismiss my thesis on *a priori* grounds without deigning to consider the facts?

Now is the time to play a trump card and turn to the place where the hypertextualist might naturally look for support: the Supreme Court. After all, judges are apt to be more formalistic than most folk.

Surely the last two hundred years have given them ample opportunity to endorse a hypertextualist reading of Article Five and thereby establish that these oracles of the law are squarely opposed to my thesis?

This is not what we find in the *United States Reports*. In its leading case on the subject, the Supreme Court does not focus narrowly on the text, but employs the precedent-based reasoning to which this book has been dedicated. More remarkable still, the Court emphasizes the unconventional character of the leading precedents. In short, hypertextualism is built on absolutely nothing of legal substance: neither the philosophy of the Founding, nor the history of the country, nor the law on the books. It is based on our failure to trouble ourselves with the facts and consider the remarkably self-conscious way the New Dealers grappled with, and ultimately transcended, the limits on popular sovereignty established by Article Five.

THE FORMAL REJECTION OF FORMALISM

Coleman v. Miller[6] came to the Court at an especially illuminating moment. When it was decided in 1939, Roosevelt had already appointed four committed New Dealers to the Court—Hugo Black, Stanley Reed, Felix Frankfurter, and William O. Douglas. This left only two conservatives—Pierce Butler and James McReynolds—to recall the constitutional principles of the laissez-faire era. The three remaining old-timers—Charles Evans Hughes, Harlan Stone, and Owen Roberts—provided the deciding votes in the case. Each group contributed an opinion: Butler's dissent was joined by McReynolds; Black's concurrence gained the assent of his fellow New Dealers Frankfurter and Douglas, as well as Roberts; Chief Justice Hughes provided an "opinion of the Court."[7]

The case concerned the validity of a constitutional amendment proposed by Congress in 1924 after the Old Court had repeatedly denied Congress the power to act against the exploitation of child labor. In seeking to override cases like *Hammer v. Dagenhart,* the proposed amendment did not repudiate the fundamental principle of limited national government. It merely granted Congress the "power to limit, regulate, and prohibit the labor of persons under eighteen years of age."[8]

Even this modest proposal was too radical for Americans of the

1920's. By mid-1927, twenty-six states had rejected the amendment, and only five had ratified.[9] The amendment's fate was sealed—until the electoral tidal wave of the 1930's. Fourteen legislatures ratified the amendment in 1933 alone, and eight more said yes by 1937.[10] When Kansas voted to jump on the bandwagon in January, Republican legislators protested. Kansas was one of the states that had rejected the amendment in the 1920's, and as the Republicans construed Article Five, this meant the state could not change its mind. They asked the Court to declare that the 1924 proposal had lapsed and that Congress was required to propose it again if it hoped to gain the consent of the People to a ban on child labor.

When the Kansans began their lawsuit in January of 1937, there was nothing odd about their demands. The Court had given no indication that it was abandoning the basic principles elaborated in *Hammer*. But shortly afterwards, the Court embarked on a massive retreat before the partisans of activist national government. During the spring of 1937, a majority of the Justices upheld the National Labor Relations Act and the Social Security Act in a series of sharply contested opinions. (Chapters 10–12 discuss this switch at much greater length.) Given this "switch in time," *Coleman* took on a more ominous meaning. If the Court agreed with the Kansans, it would be casting doubt on its recent conversion to the welfare state. The challenge became more pointed when the New Deal Congress tried once again to abolish child labor by statute in its Fair Labor Standards Act of 1938. Congress had acted as if it were confident that the Court would no longer defend cases like *Hammer* and would allow statutory action without the need for further constitutional amendment. But if the Court had upheld the Kansans' complaint, it would be placing this assumption, and hence the Fair Labor Standards Act, under a cloud.

So far as Butler and McReynolds were concerned, this was no reason for dismissing the Kansans' arguments. Since these two judicial conservatives never recognized the legitimacy of the "switch in time," the lawsuit raised a live issue: the Republican-era decisions invalidating activist national interventions on such "local matters" as child labor remained good law until Congress and the states managed to enact a valid Article Five amendment. Moreover, the conservatives had little trouble finding that the proposed child labor amendment had lapsed after its massive repudiation in the late 1920's, and that Article Five required its reapproval by two-thirds of Congress before it could be considered by the states for ratification.

More surprisingly, the seven Justices who endorsed the "switch in time" did not disagree with the conservatives' contention that the New Dealers were playing fast and loose with Article Five in reviving a proposal that had been so roundly rejected a decade earlier. At the same time, they were completely unwilling to insist that Congress had to restart the Article Five process if it ever hoped to gain regulatory authority over child labor. Since 1937, the Court had been working hard to reassure the nation that the Justices would no longer defend the Republican vision of limited government expressed in cases like *Hammer v. Dagenhart.*

But after only two years, the Court remained on probation. It was not yet clear whether the switch of 1937 was a strategic maneuver or a serious effort to consolidate the constitutional foundations of activist national government. Doubts would have flared into active political opposition if the Justices began, once again, to join Butler and McReynolds in opinions that cast a constitutional shadow upon the New Deal revolution.

How, then, to avoid both Scylla and Charybdis? Could the majority write an opinion that refrained from a renewed assault on the New Deal *without* offending its legal conscience by breathing new life into an amendment that had been so roundly repudiated by the states in the 1920's?

Much to the Court's credit, this question provoked the deepest judicial inquiry into the law of higher lawmaking in American history. Rather than offending their legal integrity or undermining their "switch in time," the seven Justices advanced a new approach to Article Five. Speaking for the Court, Chief Justice Hughes declared that the central issues in the Kansans' case raised "political questions" most appropriately resolved by the political branches, not by judges.

This holding was unprecedented. During the first hundred fifty years of the Republic, the Court had treated Article Five as a standard legal text. Justices differed about its meaning, but nobody doubted that his task was to interpret the text's commands. In calling Article Five "political," the Court was not mindlessly repeating some traditional formula. It was declaring that the time had come for lawyers to confront the fact that our higher lawmaking tradition could not be cabined within a neat legalistic understanding of Article Five.

To drive this point home, Hughes dealt with the Kansans' legalistic complaint by confronting the unconventional pedigree of the Fourteenth Amendment. For the first (and only) time in Supreme Court history, Hughes sketched some of the problems canvassed in Part Two. He pointed out that the white Southern states rejected the Fourteenth Amendment when it was first proposed; that Congress responded by erecting new governments that tendered their assent; that Secretary Seward responded with a proclamation that expressed doubts about these Southern assents; that Congress replied with a joint resolution purporting to overrule the Secretary's doubts; and that Seward acquiesced in the second proclamation.[11]

Hughes's next move was even more significant. He refused to affirm that the Reconstruction Republicans conformed to Article Five in overriding the Southern veto of the Fourteenth Amendment. *All* the Court is willing to say was this:

> This decision by the political departments of the Government as to the validity of the adoption of the Fourteenth Amendment has been accepted.
>
> We think that in accordance with this historic precedent the question of the efficacy of ratifications by state legislatures, in the light of previous rejection or attempted withdrawal, should be regarded as a political question pertaining to the political departments, with the ultimate authority in the Congress in the exercise of its control over the promulgation of the adoption of the amendment. . . .[12]

Guided by its rediscovery of the unconventional aspect of the Republican past, the Court made short work of its New Deal present. As in the 1860's, so in the 1930's, the Court refused to channel the revolutionary shift in opinion expressed by Kansas and its sister states through a legalistic interpretation of the rules of Article Five. Hughes left it to the "political departments" to decide whether the People of Kansas in 1937 could properly change its mind about the child labor amendment.

In writing his opinion, the Chief Justice restricted himself to the narrow questions[13] raised by the Kansans' case. This lawyerly caution only served to provoke New Dealers Black, Frankfurter, and Douglas, as well as Roberts (who had played a key role in the 1937 switch). Writing a special concurrence, Black declared that the entire amendment process was "'political' in its entirety . . . and is not subject to judicial guidance, control or interference at any point."[14]

For fifty years, *Coleman* has been the "leading case" on Article Five, the first place a well-trained lawyer should look in his search for enlightenment. Yet both Hughes and Black repudiate a reading of Article Five that is uninformed by the "historic precedents." As they dealt with the New Deal struggle over higher law, both emphasize the distinctive processes by which the "political branches" gained public acceptance for new constitutional principles.

I will be building on their insights here. Like Hughes, I will be looking for specific guidance in the precedents from the 1860's. But like Black, I will not limit my concern to the particular problems that generated the Kansans' complaints. I will show that the entire New Deal revolution takes on a deeper meaning when set against the "historic precedent" of the 1860's. With the aid of this precedent, I attempt a systematic challenge to the myth of rediscovery—beginning with the way the New Dealers signaled their constitutional intentions in 1932 and ending with the consolidation of the new regime in the early 1940's. This comparative exercise will suggest that, time after time, the New Dealers elaborated legitimating techniques that bear an uncanny resemblance to those worked out by Reconstruction Republicans.

But history never repeats itself exactly. When we trace the differences between Reconstruction and the New Deal, we will find that many of them are the product of a single accident of history—John Wilkes Booth's murder of Abraham Lincoln in Ford's Theater. Thanks to Booth's bullet, the Presidency passed from a Republican stalwart to an increasingly conservative critic, forcing the party of revolutionary reform to fall back upon a model of Congressional leadership. Since the New Deal Democrats never had to cope with the consequences of an assassin's bullet, Roosevelt could use the Presidency in ways that Lincoln contemplated but never executed.

In emphasizing the significance of Presidential leadership, I move beyond the *Coleman* Court in a second way. While Hughes rightly emphasized the role of the Reconstruction Congress in overcoming Seward's legal doubts about the Fourteenth Amendment, he ignored the role of Presidential leadership in the proposal and ratification of the Thirteenth Amendment. This fixation on Congress is attributable to Hughes's narrow focus on the particular issues raised by *Coleman*. The Kansans' effort to change their mind on the child labor amendment naturally recalled similar state turnarounds on the Fourteenth Amendment. But nothing about the Kansans' case invited Hughes to recall the unconventional uses of Presidential authority in the struggle for the Emancipation Amendment. Once we reflect more broadly upon the institutional parallels between the 1860's and the 1930's, the importance of the Presidency will become unmistakable.

Learning from Reconstruction?

Begin with signaling: at what point did Reconstruction Republicans and New Deal Democrats place their constitutional agendas at the very center of the political stage?

In both cases, it was with Presidential victories—Lincoln's in 1860 and Roosevelt's in 1932. In neither case did these initial triumphs represent a massive endorsement of the ultimate constitutional solutions consolidated a decade later. To the contrary, these signaling elections did not even focus on the proposals that would ultimately win the day. The Republican platform of 1860 disclaimed any intention to assault slavery in the states where it was established. The Democrats did not put the voters on notice of Roosevelt's intentions for his first Hundred Days. In both 1860 and 1932, the Presidential victories served more to put new constitutional options on the agenda, rather than to legitimate new solutions.

In this sense, they are analogous to the provision in Article Five authorizing two-thirds of the states to call for a new Philadelphia-like convention. Just as such a call would signal the need for fundamental reconsideration, so did the initial elections of Lincoln and Roosevelt. Of course, such signals may lead nowhere—sometimes they do not generate a serious constitutional proposal, let alone the successful consolidation of a new solution.

But after 1860 and 1932, Republicans and Democrats pushed the process into the proposal phase in very similar ways. Both Lincoln and Roosevelt devoted their first term to a remarkable set of constitutional innovations, but neither spent much time on Article Five. The emerging Republican and Democratic visions of a "more perfect Union" were elaborated through a dynamic interaction between President and Congress. Like Lincoln and the wartime Congresses, Roosevelt and the New Deal Congresses sought to mobilize the People behind a wide range of activist initiatives that raised a profound challenge to the constitutional status quo.

As before, this challenge provoked a sharp response from conservatives in other key institutions. In the 1930's, this did not come from Southerners prepared to fight for their state-centered understanding of the Union; it came from the conservative judiciary prepared to defend the property-centered constitution inherited from the prior era. Fortunately, conservative opposition did not touch off a second civil war—this one between social classes rather than geographic regions. But as in the 1860's, institutional resistance did dramatize the extent of the New Deal's departure from prior constitutional norms and tested the seriousness of public commitment to revolutionary reform. When the Supreme Court began to strike down a host of New Deal innovations, the President and Congress could have retreated from their vision of activist national government—just as the Republicans could have retreated from their commitment to emancipation and "equal protection" in the light of Southern resistance during and after the Civil War. Instead, the New Dealers took a course that would have proved politically suicidal in more normal times. They responded by enacting a second round of revolutionary reforms during the Second Hundred Days, escalating the institutional tension between reformist and conservative branches.

Here is where the institutional paths followed by Reconstruction Republicans and New Deal Democrats diverge. After Lincoln is shot, the Republicans lose control of the Presidency as Andrew Johnson becomes the leading exponent of a conservative vision of the Constitution. For analytic purposes, let me bracket this big difference to identify the common threads that continue to connect the unfolding stories.

Begin with the role of triggering elections. Just as Congressional Republicans used their electoral triumph in 1866 to claim a mandate from the People, so did Franklin Roosevelt in 1936. Upon returning to Washington, both Republicans and Democrats faced the same problem. Conservative branches of government, operating on a different constitutional calendar, still blocked revolutionary reform. Given their loss of the Presidency, the Reconstruction Republicans were in a worse position than the New Deal Democrats—since they had not only to confront an unsympathetic Court but an aggressively hostile Andrew Johnson.

Taking this change into account, we can see that both parties dealt with the problem in the same way—by threatening the leading conservative branch with personnel change. The Republicans' threat of impeachment was functionally equivalent to the Democrats' threat of court-packing. In each case, it was an effort to shift the constitutional balance without waiting for more elections. More remarkably still, these unconventional threats engendered an identical response. The conservative branches suddenly shifted gear with a "switch in time" that allowed the constitutional revolution to proceed.

The parallels continue into the consolidation phase. Once the conservative branches switched, they escaped permanent institutional damage—both impeachment and court-packing narrowly failed in the Senate. The party of constitutional reform, in turn, continued winning elections. Thus, the Republicans regained control of the Presidency in 1868, and their grip on Congress did not begin to slip until 1874. The Democrats, of course, did even better. This meant that both parties could consolidate their grip on the Supreme Court—though the New Deal Democrats managed to avoid the blatant court-packing of the Grant era. As the last judicial holdover from the old regime retired from the Court in 1941, the stage was set for the final act of juridical consolidation. Just as the *Slaughterhouse Cases* of 1873 decisively ended all serious legal questions about the validity of the Republican transformation, so did the New Deal Court's unanimous decisions upholding activist national government in the early 1940's.

By this point, it would take much more than a few electoral victories by the conservative party to undermine the newly ascendant constitutional regime. It would take a mobilized effort by the American people equal in force, but opposite in direction, to the movement that established the Republican/Democratic regime in the first place.

THE VIEW FROM ARTICLE FIVE

We can now begin to triangulate our problem by considering the New Deal's relationship to the Founding. Speaking broadly, the higher lawmaking efforts of the 1930's broke with the premises of Article Five in two ways.

The first involved a break from the Founding system of authorizing institutions. Article Five rests upon a federalist premise: in order to speak in the name of the People, a movement must gain the assent of *both* national and state institutions. The New Dealers took a more nation-centered course—using a series of national electoral victories as mandates that ultimately induced all three branches of the national government to recognize that the People had endorsed activist national government. So long, then, as modern lawyers suppose that all successful popular movements must take a federalist path to higher lawmaking authority, they will never surmount this first hurdle to a mature recognition of the New Deal's constitutional creativity.

But it shouldn't be too hard to jump over this hurdle. As we have seen, it was the Reconstruction Republicans, not the New Deal Democrats, who first established that We the People could speak through national institutions and demand that the states accept the primacy of American citizenship. If Reconstruction Republicans could use national institutions to legitimate their claims, why not New Deal Democrats—especially when they had gained the sustained consent of majorities in *all* regions of the country, while the Republicans had a lot more support in the North than in the South?

Which brings us to a second aspect of the New Deal break with Article Five. While the Reconstruction Republicans repudiated the federalist premises of the Founding, they memorialized their revolutionary reforms by placing them in legal packages that resemble Article Five amendments—bearing the numbers XIII and XIV and placing themselves in sober sequence with other amendments of less uncertain pedigree.[15] In contrast, when modern lawyers seek to recall the New Deal's contribution, they do not turn to writings that pose as Article Five amendments but to *transformative judicial opinions* written in the aftermath of the Court-packing crisis. These great cases mark the decisive institutional moment at which the Supreme Court joined the other branches in rejecting the Republican vision of limited government, symbolized by *Hammer v. Dagenhart* and *Lochner v. New York*. Indeed, modern judges are more disturbed by the charge of *Lochnering* than the charge of ignoring the intentions of the Federalists and Republicans who wrote the formal text. To mark this point, I shall say that the transformative opinions handed down by the New

Deal Court function as *amendment-analogues* that anchor constitutional meanings in the same symbolically potent way achieved by Article Five amendments.

Undoubtedly, this New Deal use of amendment-analogues requires thoughtful reappraisal of some pious platitudes—including the sense in which Americans live under a *written* constitution. Two centuries after the Founding, this platitude remains valid only on an expanded understanding of the constitutional canon. The corpus of authoritative texts includes not only those formal amendments generated by the procedures of Article Five but also: (a) the *amendment-simulacra* generated by the Republicans under the nationalistic procedures developed during Reconstruction and (b) the transformative opinions that serve as *amendment-analogues* under the nationalistic procedures developed by the Democrats during the Great Depression. So long as lawyers continue to accept the text-simulacra generated by the Reconstruction Republicans, they should not lightly reject the amendment-analogues generated by the New Deal Democrats.

Especially when this use of transformative opinions is hardly unprecedented in American constitutional history. As we already saw, the Republican Court's opinions in the *Legal Tender* and *Slaughterhouse Cases* discharged analogous constitutional functions toward the end of Reconstruction; and even before the Civil War, the opinions of the Taney Court had served to codify the constitutional meaning of Jacksonian Democracy.[16]

Looking beyond the confines of constitutional law, there are countless other cases in which judicial opinions substitute for formal legislative texts. Consider the problem that arises when judges are obliged to coordinate statutory commands and the common law tradition. In this familiar situation, common law courts regularly appeal to common law cases whenever they find a hole in a statutory scheme.[17] Indeed, this use of judicial precedents in the absence of statutes is the single most important feature distinguishing Anglo-American legal systems from those dominant in Europe. From this vantage, the New Deal innovation is best seen as another case in which American lawyers, at moments of great crisis, creatively adapt traditional ideas (here, the common law use of cases in the absence of statutes) for new constitutional purposes (here, the use of cases in the absence of formal amendments). While this unconventional adaptation does challenge constitutional theory, this is the kind of challenge that has allowed the American people to sustain a continuous constitutional identity for the past two centuries.

INSTITUTIONAL FOUNDATIONS FOR AMENDMENT-ANALOGUES

The New Deal revolution, then, broke with Article Five in two different ways: (1) it substituted a model of Presidential leadership of national institutions for a model of assembly leadership based on a dialogue between the nation and the states; (2) it used transformative opinions as amendment-analogues. The next question is whether (1) and (2) are related. My answer is yes: (2) is a surface manifestation of (1). Rather than appearing as an inexplicable formal breach of Article Five, the New Deal Court's development of transformative opinions was an organic response to the rise of Presidential leadership in higher lawmaking.

A grim thought-experiment makes the point. Suppose that, early in 1935, Roosevelt had met Lincoln's fate in Ford's Theatre. While dedicating a WPA project, he is gunned down by a hard-line Republican, convinced that Roosevelt was leading the nation toward Fascism. A stunned America witnesses John Nance Garner take the oath of office as the next President. The ritual is redolent with recollections of Reconstruction. Garner would have been the first Southern politician since Andrew Johnson to gain the White House; and he would have gained it the same way. Like Johnson before him, he owed his vice-presidential nomination to his Party's desire to "balance" a ticket headed by a progressive Northerner with a more traditional Southerner.[18]

After a brief period of mourning, Garner's conservatism becomes manifest. When the Supreme Court declares the National Industrial Recovery Act unconstitutional in the spring of 1935, Garner does not support the New Deal Congress in its second great Hundred Days of creativity—which produced such modern landmarks as the National Labor Relations Act and the Social Security Act. Instead, he seeks to organize an anti–New Deal coalition composed of Republicans and conservative Democrats. Denouncing Social Security and the NLRA as unconstitutional, Garner sends a steady stream of vetoes that rely heavily on Supreme Court precedents. How would the New Dealers in Congress have responded?

In the same way Republicans reacted to President Johnson's vetoes of the Civil Rights Act and Freedmen's Bureau Bill. Given the President's assault, the Republicans had no choice but to propose the Fourteenth Amendment to serve as the platform for an electoral appeal to the People. Like their embattled predecessors, liberal Democrats would not have allowed an "accidental" President to turn the language of constitutional law against their movement. As President Garner, with the aid of the traditionalist Supreme Court, called upon the American people to defend the principles of the traditional constitution, the reform Democrats would have answered with a New Deal amendment to serve as their platform for the decisive electoral struggle that loomed in 1936. And if they had won this struggle, they would have been sorely tempted to take extraordinary actions to assure the assent of three-fourths of the states.[19]

As we shall see, the New Deal Congress seriously considered coming forward with formal amendments during the constitutional crisis. I will defer a study of these Article Five exercises to a later point, since the Garner/Johnson scenario is enough to suggest the link between the rise of the Presidency and the substitution of transformative opinions for formal amendments.

Roosevelt's success in keeping control over the Presidency shifted higher lawmaking incentives in two related ways. First, since the New Deal Congress was not in a life-and-death struggle with a conservative President, it lacked an overriding incentive to propose a formal amendment as part of its defense against a Presidential onslaught. It could afford to take its cues from its party leader in the White House. Second, with both President and Congress working together, the appointment of new Justices would be firmly under reformist control. This meant that the New Dealers had a choice unavailable to the Reconstruction Republicans. Instead of pushing forward under Article Five, they could appoint a steady flow of New Dealers to the bench who could uphold revolutionary reforms through a series of landmark judicial opinions. For the moment, the particular choice made by the New Dealers is not important. The crucial point is the underlying institutional change that gave New Deal Democracy a new degree of higher lawmaking freedom.

The "court-packing" issue looked very different to the Republicans after the Civil War. Once Johnson defected from the reform coalition in 1866, he was intent on filling vacancies with solid conservatives who would invalidate the Reconstruction Acts and sabotage the ratification of the Fourteenth Amendment. When the death of Justice John Catron gave Johnson his first chance, the Republicans responded with a remarkable "court-shrinking" statute. Under its terms, Catron's vacancy simply disappeared, and the size of the court would continue to shrink with every death or resignation until it was reduced to seven seats. The statute not only prevented Johnson from filling the vacancies, but allowed the Republicans to reexpand the size of the Court to nine when Grant won back the White House in 1869. This made it easier for the Court to consolidate the Fourteenth Amendment in the *Slaughterhouse Cases.*[20]

This remarkable story helps round out our two models of unconventional change. Under the Reconstruction model of Congressional leadership, the reformers try *to shrink* the Court to prevent new Presidential appointments from reinforcing conservative constitutionalism. But under the model of Presidential leadership, it is court-packing, not court-shrinking, that becomes a functional tool for translating constitutional politics into constitutional law. Sometimes the ascendant movement actually engages in court-packing—as the Republicans did under Grant. Sometimes it only threatens to expand the bench, and retreats when the Court carries out its own switch in time—as happened during the New Deal. But in both cases, the opinions of the Supreme Court can serve as the functional equivalents of formal amendments—dramatically and authoritatively shifting the terms of doctrinal development for generations to come.

The New Deal's substitution of transformative opinions for formal amendments was not the result of some inexplicable failure to attend to the terms of Article Five. It was a creative elaboration of higher lawmaking changes initiated much earlier in American history. The struggle over Reconstruction, not the Great Depression, first led Americans to break with the federalist premises of Article Five. The struggle over Reconstruction, not the Great Depression, first led the President, Congress, and Court to develop new higher lawmaking procedures more in keeping with the constitutive will of We the People of the *United* States. The basic New Deal innovation followed from the Democrats' greater success in sustaining their control over the Presidency throughout the period of constitutional creativity.

TURNING THE TABLES ON RECONSTRUCTION

I have been following Chief Justice Hughes in treating Reconstruction as an "historic precedent" for the higher lawmaking activities of the 1930's. Having come this far, we can reverse field and use our analysis of the 1930's to enrich our understanding of the 1860's. If the practice of Presidential leadership is such a central part of twentieth-century constitutional history, why wasn't this also true in the nineteenth century? In particular, why did Congress, and not the President, emerge as the leading spokesman for constitutional change during the critical years after the war?

Surely it would be a mistake to ignore the role of John Wilkes Booth in this affair. Before the assassination, the constitutional dynamic of the Lincoln Administration was evolving along the Presidentialist lines later developed by Roosevelt. Not only did Lincoln's victory in 1860 operate as a constitutional signal much like Roosevelt's in 1932. But Lincoln's effort to initiate a new era of freedom for blacks was institutionally elaborated in ways similar to Roosevelt's effort to initiate a new era for working people. Recall that the Thirteenth Amendment was only proposed by the "lame-duck" session of the Thirty-eighth Congress *after* Lincoln had led the Republican Party to a decisive victory in the elections of 1864. During the heart of Lincoln's first term, the Republicans proceeded in a very New Dealish way— anxiously aware of the threat to their program raised by the conservatives on the Supreme Court. When Roger Taney's death in 1863 gave Lincoln a chance to name a Republican as Chief Justice, we can glimpse the beginnings of a strategy more fully developed in the 1930's. Lincoln nominated Salmon P. Chase chiefly because ". . . we wish for a Chief Justice who will sustain what has been done in regard to emancipation and the legal tenders."[21]

It is hard to say whether Lincoln could have sustained Presidential leadership over Congress during his second term. If so, he would have found himself at the same constitutional crossroads Roosevelt confronted later. On the one hand, he could have pursued the path marked out by Article Five and encouraged the Convention/Congress to propose a "Fourteenth Amendment." On the other hand, he could have tried to secure the legal substance of the "Fourteenth Amendment" by leading the Senate to appoint a series of strong Republicans to the Court.[22] Under this scenario, the Reconstruction Congress would not have enacted the "court-shrinking" statute that its historical counterpart used as an unconventional weapon against Andrew Johnson. It would have kept the Court at its existing size—which, thanks to a statute of 1864, was not nine but ten—and supported Lincoln's nomination of a series of radical Republicans to the bench.[23] Indeed, there was nothing to stop it from expanding the Court yet further—from 10 to 15, say. Certainly, such a step was not as unconventional as many others taken by the Republicans in their struggle for the Fourteenth Amendment.*

Suppose that Lincoln and the Republicans in Congress had taken the second option, and consider how Reconstruction might have worked itself out. Rather than Congress proposing the first sentence of the Fourteenth Amendment guaranteeing Americans national and state citizenship, a reconstituted Lincoln Court might have achieved the same result by a ringing reversal of *Dred Scott* and a powerful judicial elaboration of the nature of American citizenship in the Republican Union. Rather than a formal amendment's guarantee of "equal protection" and "due process," the Lincoln Court might have proclaimed such protections to be essential "privileges and immunities of citizens of the United States." In short, Reconstruction would have looked a lot like the New Deal, where transformative opinions, not formal amendments, serve as the principal memorials of constitutional meaning.

If Lincoln had taken this course—and his remarks about the Chase appointment suggest that the thought would have crossed his mind—we come to a fascinating question: Would this have been good for the development of American law?

Maybe yes, maybe no. Today's lawyers would have had to live without the formal text of the Fourteenth Amendment, and the modern Supreme Court could not have pointed to canonical formulae like

---

*In fact, such a proposal was made by Senator Charles Drake as part of the debate that ultimately led to the reexpansion of the Court in 1869 (40th Cong., 3d Sess., *Congressional Globe*, at 1484). Although his proposal was rejected (id. at 1487), nobody seemed scandalized.

"equal protection" in cases like *Brown v. Board of Education.* But we would have legal resources available that are now painfully lacking. When lawyers look back to the late 1860's, they do not find a sustained effort by the Chase Court to elaborate the Republican ideals that had engendered so much sacrifice from the American people. If my hypothetical Lincoln Court had discharged this transformative function with the eloquence of other great opinions, perhaps its ringing affirmation of equal national citizenship might have served as a *better* memorial of Reconstruction than the cryptic formulae left behind by the Fourteenth Amendment?

We will never know. All we do know is that John Wilkes Booth deprived Lincoln of his chance to steer Reconstruction to a conclusion, leaving Johnson to generate a fact-pattern that occurs with sufficient frequency to merit a special name: *the Vice-Presidential exception.* The pattern arises because the Vice Presidency is regularly used as a consolation prize to candidates, regions, and ideologies that fail to capture the Presidential nomination. In his moment of triumph at the party's convention, the successful Presidential candidate is not in the mood to contemplate his death; but he is mindful of the need to maximize his electoral chances by "balancing the ticket" with a Vice-Presidential nominee who appeals to a different constituency. This means that the death of the President does not bring a devoted supporter of the deceased President to the White House; instead, it typically yields the succession of somebody very different. The Lincoln-Johnson episode provides the most tragic example, but others have proved consequential: McKinley-Roosevelt, Kennedy-Johnson, for example.[24] The Vice-Presidential successor may be more reformist or more conservative. But in either event, the system suffers a shock—and the participants have to struggle to reach a new political equilibrium. From this vantage, the Congressional decision to propose the Fourteenth Amendment seems more like a brilliant, but rather desperate, effort to adapt unconventionally to an exceptional situation: *Given* the assassin's bullet, and *given* Johnson's conservatism, there was a grave danger that the institutional system would spin out of the control of the mobilized majority of Americans. If *anybody* in Washington was going to stand up for the Republican vision in 1866, it was going to be the Convention/Congress; if the higher lawmaking system was going to register *any* fundamental constitutional change before the next round of elections, it would take the form of an Article Five simulacrum. To mark this point, I shall say that the Fourteenth Amendment experience, culminating in an amendment-simulacrum, is best viewed as our most dramatic example of the constitutional consequences of the Vice-Presidential exception.

If this is right, the hypertextualist's worship of Article Five appears in a most peculiar light, as it gives decisive weight to the tragic accidents of American history. After all, Roosevelt was also the object of assassination, only narrowly missing the fatal bullet.[25] If his attacker had been a better marksman, and Lincoln's a worse one, modern hypertextualism would have had a very different spin. It would have urged modern interpreters to focus intently on the text of the New Deal amendments, while casting a skeptical glance at the Chase Court's invocations of equal protection.

But surely American lawyers owe more to their fellow citizens than such a heavy-handed formalism. Rather than indulge in hypertextualist certainties, we should patiently explore the facts surrounding the New Deal revolution before confidently pronouncing upon any claims about its constitutional creativity. This seems especially important when Roosevelt's model of Presidential leadership may serve as a more reliable guide to future exercises in constitutional politics. Hopefully, assassins will not regularly strike at the Presidency just as the People are preparing for fateful constitutional decisions. If we are lucky, the model of Congressional leadership, as exemplified by the Fourteenth Amendment, will be a rare event, while our Presidentialist case study of the 1930's may well serve as *the* "historic precedent" for future constitutional revolutions.

This provisional conclusion is reinforced by more recent episodes in American history. When Ronald Reagan led his fellow Americans to re-think fundamental elements of their constitutional legacy, he did not put great emphasis on Article Five, but relied far more heavily on precedents inherited from the Roosevelt revolution. To be sure, Reagan invoked the Rooseveltian model to invite a reconsideration of the very New Deal principles that Roosevelt had successfully constitutionalized. Yet this irony only suggests how deeply the "historic precedents" of the New Deal have entrenched themselves into constitutional culture.

So does the fate of the "Republican Revolution" of 1994. The

Republicans came into power in Congress with all the familiar flags flying: the Speaker of the House proclaimed himself a "revolutionary," waving a new social contract with America and demanding that it be fulfilled. If a President had come into power under similar auspices, he would have been a very formidable figure. Yet the ease with which Speaker Gingrich was defeated by a skillful, but not very popular, President Clinton suggests once again how difficult it is for a revolutionary movement to succeed without controlling the Presidency.

I haven't the slightest idea how the present struggles over the future of America will play themselves out in the decades ahead. But the recent patterns of our politics do provide additional reasons for a serious confrontation with New Deal precedents—not only to define their enduring significance but also to expose the evolving model of Presidential leadership to critical inquiry: What are its dangers? Can it be reformed?

CHAPTER TEN

Rethinking the New Deal

THE RISE OF PRESIDENTIAL LEADERSHIP

THE LAST CHAPTER challenged the myth of rediscovery that clouds our vision of the 1930's. While the Philadelphia Convention and John Marshall provided some of the constitutional foundations for contemporary government, the crucial decisions were made by Americans of the twentieth century. If any single person is the founder of the modern activist state, it is Franklin Roosevelt, not James Madison; if any assembly, it is the New Deal Congress, not the Philadelphia Convention; if any Justice, it is Hughes, not Marshall.

I do not deny that the Founding precedent can usefully put the New Deal into historical perspective. But the salient similarities are noticeable only on a wider canvas. As in the 1780's, so in the 1930's, a relatively nationalistic group of revolutionary reformers refused to play by the old higher lawmaking rules—without, however, utterly obliterating the institutional matrix that had previously organized political life. As in the 1780's, so in the 1930's, the reformers created new legitimating patterns out of older institutional materials—finally earning the credibility needed to make new higher law in the name of We the People. As in the 1780's, so in the 1930's, their accelerating institutional bandwagon proceeded from a signaling phase through a series of appeals to the People at the polls to a period of consolidation. In all these senses—and more—the New Deal revolution carried forward the Founders' unconventional experiment in popular sovereignty into the twentieth century.

But it is a mistake to ignore the nineteenth-century contribution. Not only are Lincoln and Bingham closer in time than Washington and Madison, but they were obliged to struggle with a key problem that haunted the New Dealers and challenges us still: How to adapt the Founding institutions to express the powerful sense of American nationhood that emerged after the Civil War? The Republican answer involved pioneering uses of the Presidency, the separation of powers, and national elections to win popular mandates for fundamental change. These innovations not only serve as the true constitutional foundation for the Thirteenth and Fourteenth Amendments, but are decisive historic precedents for the New Deal revolution.

This crucial point, once conceded, prepares the way for a more complex critique and reconstruction of received opinion. The prevailing myth portrays the Supreme Court of the *Lochner* era as dominated by a bunch of fools or knaves (or both). I argue, to the contrary, that the *Lochner* Court was doing what most judges do most of the time: interpreting the Constitution, as handed down to them by the Republicans of Reconstruction. *Lochner* is no longer good law because the American people repudiated Republican constitutional values in the 1930's, not because the Republican Court was wildly out of line with them before the Great Depression. Since I develop this argument elsewhere,[1] I will proceed at once to a second key question: Should the Roosevelt revolution be viewed as a constitutive act of popular sovereignty that *legitimately* changed the preceding Republican Constitution?

As with Reconstruction, a full answer requires a study of two distinct rounds of unconventional development. Just as the ratification of the Thirteenth Amendment involved different dynamics from that of the Fourteenth, the Roosevelt revolution went through two cycles. During the 1930's, the nation struggled with the constitutional implications of the Great Depression; during the 1940's, with those of the Second World War. In both cases, the basic thrust was the same—away from laissez-faire and toward activist government first at home and then abroad. Since a serious treatment of both cycles would make this book too bulky, I have taken up the transformation of the foreign relations power in a separate essay.[2] I will focus here on the conflict between the Old Court and the New Deal during the 1930's.

The myth of rediscovery treats this struggle as a grievous misfortune, a tragic waste of time. I emphasize, in contrast, its positive contribution to the democratic quality of debate and decision. As in

Reconstruction, the conflict between the branches presented critical choices to the American people with extraordinary drama and clarity. The ultimate outcome was a redefinition of Americans' relationship to government that was more reflective and more democratic than it would have been otherwise.

I begin by inquiring into the popular mandate Roosevelt brought with him to Washington in 1933. This was more equivocal than supposed by the prevailing myth. Once the ambiguities are recognized, it will be easier to appreciate the positive role played by the Old Court. While judicial resistance angered New Deal loyalists during the President's first term, it emphasized to the larger public that the Democrats' initiative raised questions far beyond the ordinary competence of elites in Washington to resolve; and that it was up to the People to decide whether the traditional values elaborated by the conservative Justices were worth preserving.

THE SIGNALING ELECTION

Beware the perils of reading history backwards. Modern lawyers find it easy to suppose that the Democrats of 1932 were already proclaiming their activist vision throughout the land. The reality was more complex. By casting their ballots for Roosevelt, most Americans were certainly voting *against* Hoover and all he stood for; but what they were voting *for* was a lot less clear.[3]

Presidential Signaling

What, then, did Herbert Hoover represent?

In 1928, he was anything but a stand-patter. His election marked a shift to the Progressive wing of the Republican Party that had been shunted to the sidelines by Harding and Coolidge. Hoover was a social engineer who believed in the affirmative uses of government power. His response to the Great Crash of 1929 was quite activist. His Reconstruction Finance Corporation, for example, represented an ambitious effort to shore up the credit structure and support business recovery. At the same time, Hoover was clear that the Constitution did not give the federal government plenary powers to manage the national economy. By 1932, his energetic, but limited, recovery effort had the paradoxical effect of demonstrating the obsolescence of the constitutional tradition. With unemployment in 1932 soaring to a quarter of the workforce, and national income less than half of 1929 levels,[4] Americans were not going to tolerate Hoover's principled assertions that the relief of poverty was a local concern and that national options were limited by Republican constitutional principles.

While public opinion had decisively repudiated Hooverism by 1932, it was not obvious that the Democratic Party would inherit the whirlwind. The party remained deeply shaped by its Jeffersonian origins, which emphasized states rights, limited government, and market freedom. This Jeffersonian message had been muffled a bit by the addition of Populist and Wilsonian themes,[5] but it is anachronistic to view the party as committed to the aggressive use of national power—especially given the pivotal role of Southern Democracy. Though Southerners might welcome economic aid for their impoverished region, they valued white supremacy even more. Memories of Reconstruction, and the assertive liberalism of some Northern Democrats, enhanced their fear that active national government might ultimately undermine Jim Crow.

Historically speaking, it was the Republicans, not the Democrats, whose heroes included proponents of national power like Lincoln and (Theodore) Roosevelt. Nor had Democrats been particularly activistic during previous economic crises. When the Democratic President Grover Cleveland confronted the wrenching Panic of 1893, his response was far more conservative than Hoover's—and, in response, an angry electorate swept the Democrats from power in the elections of 1894 and 1896.

Moving closer to the present, the Presidential election of 1928 had done little to reverse the Democrats' association with laissez-faire. While their nomination of Al Smith in 1928 had mobilized and deepened their urban and ethnic constituencies in the North, it did not signal the rise of a new philosophy of activist government. Smith was more interested in getting Washington out of the business of moral regulation by repealing Prohibition. If any candidate was interested in poverty, it was Hoover—whose claim to fame was his success in organizing the relief effort in war-torn Belgium.[6] By 1932 Hooverism had failed in the court of public opinion, but it was not clear that the Democrats had anything new on offer.

Against this background, progressives like Paul Douglas, later a liberal Democratic Senator from Illinois, urged the organization of a new party in 1932:

> It is a sobering thought that twenty years ago many Progressives were pinning similar hopes on Woodrow Wilson, who, with all respect to Governor Roosevelt, was a far keener thinker and a more determined fighter. . . . Yet, after eight years, Wilson retired with the Democratic party as cancerous as ever in its composition and as conservative in its policies. If such was the fate of Wilson, how can we hope for better things from Franklin Roosevelt?[7]

Roosevelt's answer during the campaign was equivocal. Breaking hallowed precedent, he did not wait modestly at home for news of his nomination, but flew to the Chicago convention to announce his New Deal:

> My program, of which I can only touch on [a few] points, is based upon this simple moral principle: the welfare and the soundness of a Nation depend first upon what the great mass of the people wish and need; and second, whether or not they are getting it. . . .
> Our Republican leaders tell us economic laws—sacred, inviolable, unchangeable—cause panics which no one could prevent. But while they prate of economic laws, men and women are starving. We must lay hold of the fact that economic laws are not made by nature. They are made by human beings.

This activist philosophy was elaborated throughout the campaign.[8] But it coexisted with many more traditional themes. The first three planks of the Democratic platform "solemnly promise[d]":

> An immediate and drastic reduction of governmental expenditures . . . of not less than 25 percent.
> Maintenance of the national credit by a Federal budget annually balanced . . .
> A sound currency to be preserved at all hazards . . .

And candidate Roosevelt committed himself to these principles as well.[9] True, he made a number of fragmentary activist proposals, but none remotely foreshadowed the breathtaking initiatives of his First Hundred Days.[10] It would be a mistake, then, to suppose that Americans knew what they were bargaining for when they swept the Democrats into the White House and Congress in 1932.

But it is also a mistake to dismiss the 1932 campaign as lacking in serious communicative content. Despite its discordant and fragmentary character, the general direction of Roosevelt's campaign was clear enough—away from limited government and toward the activist regulatory state. As he put the point repeatedly, "[w]e need to correct, by drastic means if necessary, the faults in our economic system. . . . The country needs and, unless I mistake its temper, the country demands bold persistent experimentation. . . . Above all, try something."[11]

This is what made 1932 into a signaling election. Just as the Federalists of 1787 managed to persuade state legislatures to send delegates to Philadelphia to experiment with constitutional principles, Roosevelt was going to Washington with a mandate to experiment with traditional understandings.

The closest analogy is Lincoln's victory of 1860. Just as the 1932 Democrats promised to cut federal expenditure and preserve a sound currency, the 1860 Republicans repeatedly reassured the South of the sanctity of slavery within the existing states. Despite these emphatic conservative gestures, Lincoln's election had put a new constitutional agenda onto the forefront of national debate.

To forestall predictable misunderstanding, I do not want to claim too much for either Presidential signal. Lincoln's 1860 victory only began a protracted period of institutional conflict, punctuated by a series of elections in 1862, 1864, 1866, and 1868. The same is true of Roosevelt's victory. Without the Democratic success in gaining popular consent to their developing vision of activist national government in 1934, 1936, and beyond, the New Dealers would never have pushed the higher lawmaking process beyond the signaling stage.

Party and Presidency in Constitutional Transformations

Having located New Deal Democrats and Reconstruction Republicans within a common matrix, I want to point to a key difference.[12] The Republicans were a new party in 1860 and so their electoral victory promoted men whose entire career had been shaped by the anti-slavery struggle. Even "moderates" like Bingham took matters of constitutional principle with high seriousness and were eager to use Congress as a vanguard in the struggle for revolutionary reform.

In contrast, many in the Democratic leadership in Congress had built their careers in a Jeffersonian world far removed from Rooseveltian activism. As good politicians, they would defer to their new and powerful Party leader, as well as the noisy New Dealers swept into Congress on his coattails. But they would predictably drag their heels whenever Presidential leadership disrupted their traditional web of political understandings and arrangements.

Speaking broadly, then, the new party–old party difference generated a very substantial shift in Congressional-Presidential relations during the periods of Republican and Democratic ascendancy. Despite Lincoln's many unconventional acts of leadership, he was consistently a moderating brake upon the transformative energy coming out of Congress. During the New Deal, Roosevelt would be the engine and Congress the brake.

All this could have turned out differently. After all, Lincoln was reluctant to abandon the Whig Party. If the Whigs had managed to survive the crisis of the 1850's, Lincoln would have been happy to use the Presidency to renovate traditional party ideologies and structures. By the same token, there was nothing inevitable about Franklin Roosevelt's fourth-ballot victory over Al Smith at the Democratic convention of 1932. Since Smith had become very conservative on economic questions,[13] his victory could have led to a rerun of the Democrats' disaster under Grover Cleveland. Under this scenario, the Democrats might have gone the way of the Whigs. After a period of chaos, perhaps a new party (or two) would have come to the fore led by a man like Douglas of Illinois (or somebody much less attractive).[14] In such a case, we would have seen the Congress of the late 1930's flooded with New Party ideologues resembling those who were abundant on Capitol Hill in the 1860's.

My thought-experiment emphasizes a distinctive problem confronting the higher lawmaking system during the New Deal. Call it the problem of *constitutional clarity*. While the President was signaling the rise of a new agenda, Congress would *not* be putting pressure on him to sharpen his constitutional vision. *If* any institution would induce the Presidency to give sharper form to the emerging constitutional vision, it would be the Supreme Court.

Whatever its disadvantages, old age gave the Democratic Party one big plus. No newcomer could have gained such broad support from the American people in so short a time.

Both the Federalists and the Republicans provide useful benchmarks. When the Federalist Convention and the Republican Convention/Congress began to debate the shape of their revolutionary reforms, they were painfully aware of their uncertain claim to majority status in the nation. As a consequence, they relied very heavily on the later phases of their institutional bandwagons to provide the democratic momentum ultimately required for higher lawmaking legitimacy.

In contrast, the New Deal Democrats could begin from a very broad electoral base. The 1932 landslide swept an unprecedented 310 Democrats into the House, leaving only 117 Republicans; the Senate, on a six-year cycle, saw the number of Republicans shrink to 35 from 56 four years earlier.[15] The New Dealers' problem was not the breadth, but the depth, of their popular support.[16] Once they enacted a concrete action program into law, Americans might not like what they saw. It was all very well for the President to plead for experimentation; but experiments have the nasty habit of blowing up in your face before the next election.

As always, the constitutional calendar exerted its sobering logic. Given the need to return to the voters in two short years, would the Democrats turn cautious and content themselves with a few halting steps beyond Hoover? Or would they seek to revolutionize the relationship between the national government and ordinary Americans?

The First Wave

Roosevelt's answer was the National Industrial Recovery Act (NIRA), signed into law less than four months after the inauguration. The Act did not try to cure a particular abuse of the free market system—as the Interstate Commerce Act had focused on railroad monopolies or the Pure Food and Drug Act on health risks. It proposed to *abolish* market capitalism and replace it with a corporatist structure under Presidential leadership. Henceforward each industry would legislate its own code of economic life—in which the interests of organized labor, no less than organized capital, would be represented. Once a code was approved by the President, NIRA sought to make this new corporatist order, not the "free market," the measure of economic justice. To be sure, Roosevelt did not propose that NIRA should immediately become a permanent structure of American society. The experiment, given a two-year trial run, was scheduled to expire unless the next Congress passed new legislation.

Nonetheless, the break with constitutional tradition was plain enough. A snippet from the House debate provides the tone:

> Mr. BECK. [I]t does seem to me important to make a record, if it is possible, of what is a very critical hour in the history of the Republic, so that future generations, if they turn back to the Congressional Record, may know that there were some Members of the House, who at least protested against a transformation of that form of government, under which we had grown surpassingly rich and powerful, into a new form of government, which those who framed the Constitution, if they could "revisit the glimpses of the moon," would today be unable to recognize.
>
> As the shadows of evening are lengthening with us now, the shadows of a lasting night are falling upon the old constitutional edifice, which the genius of Washington, Franklin, Madison, Hamilton, and Jefferson built with such surpassing wisdom. . . .
>
> Mr. KELLY of Pennsylvania. My colleague, Mr. BECK, is a great student of history . . . I am only a humble student . . ., but I believe that the George Washington who built a new order in the wilderness of his own times would not hesitate to build a new order now in the wilderness of economic conditions which surround us.
>
> I believe that the Thomas Jefferson, who stretched the Constitution until it cracked in order to make the Louisiana Purchase for national expansion, would be the first to urge any needful action to save this nation from industrial and economic collapse.
>
> I believe that the Abraham Lincoln, who . . .[17]

And so forth.

The speed of NIRA's enactment recalled the four-month frame of the Philadelphia Convention. But this time, the process of decision heralded the rise of Presidential leadership. Roosevelt had initially called a special session of Congress to pass emergency legislation, intending to defer a comprehensive recovery package to the first regular session. But when Senator Hugo Black's proposal for a maximum thirty-hour work week took on momentum, an alarmed Roosevelt tried to head off this simplistic Congressional assault on the complexities of modern life. In patterns that heralded the emerging regime, anxious Brain Trusters huddled together in crisis sessions to hammer out alternative paths to recovery. After Roosevelt locked two competing teams into a single room, the NIRA emerged as the Administration position.[18]

The next stage was no less remarkable. The new Congress did not respond to this Presidential initiative with angry protests against executive usurpation; nor did it use NIRA's problematic constitutionality as an excuse for delay or revision. After only minor modifications, Congress reinforced the President by passing NIRA with heavy majorities. As at Philadelphia, Washington was now the scene of a revolutionary effort to reform America's constitutional tradition before it disintegrated under the weight of the impending crisis.*

Though NIRA was the most important initiative of the first New Deal Congress, others paled only by comparison. Its authorization of Roosevelt's decision to go off the gold standard and devalue the dollar went far beyond anything Lincoln and Congress had attempted when they floated "greenbacks" during the Civil War. Yet this earlier experiment with fiat money had been struck down by the Supreme Court— until a successful court-packing effort by President Grant induced the Court to reverse itself by 5 to 4.[19] As if this were not enough, Congressional approval of the Tennessee Valley Authority inaugurated a national experiment with outright socialism.[20] At the same time, Congress was revolutionizing policy in fields like agriculture, energy, and pensions—making nonsense of the notion that the Constitution delegated it a list of strictly limited powers. Given these breakthroughs, even the epochal decision to impose sweeping and continuing regulation on Wall Street seemed almost humdrum—though the establishment of the Securities and Exchange Commission also raised some serious constitutional questions.

But it was one thing for the President repeatedly to assert, and

---

*The question was dramatized by the simultaneous rise of Adolf Hitler to power as Reich's Chancellor in January of 1933.

Congress repeatedly to support, the claim that the American people demanded revolutionary reform; quite another to win general acceptance for such an unlikely assertion. How much more would the Constitution require before the New Dealers' heady rhetoric of popular sovereignty would be transformed into the hard lines of higher law?

Returning to the People

An initial test came with the fall elections of 1934. The revolutionary character of the New Deal reforms was now obvious to any thinking American—as was the best way to stop the experiment dead in its tracks. Historically speaking, the President's party has never fared well during mid-term elections. Without a victorious President at the head of the ticket, his partisans in Congress lose seats. This drop-off "is more than a mere *tendency*. Midterm loss is an almost invariable historical *regularity*."[21] Given the preceding Democratic sweep, a loss seemed even more likely. The 117 Republicans left standing in the House were from hard-core conservative districts. Though the Senate seats had last been contested in the halcyon days of 1928, the historical record was no less clear. Even a modest recovery in Congress would allow Republicans to question whether the country supported the endless series of revolutionary reforms cascading out of Washington; and a substantial victory might allow them to form a solid coalition with conservative Democrats disturbed by Roosevelt's repudiation of Jeffersonian principles.

When read against this background, the Democrats' smashing victory in 1934 carried a clear meaning. Only 103 Republicans remained standing after the New Deal tidal wave that swept 322 Democrats into the chamber. Not only did the number of Senate Republicans drop from 35 to 25, but the party's composition changed. Eight leading conservatives lost their seats, while the bloc of Republican progressives remained unchanged at ten.[22] This dwindling minority now confronted 69 Democrats, the largest majority in history.[23] In the words of *New York Times* columnist Arthur Krock, the Democrats had won "the most overwhelming victory in the history of American politics."[24] Perhaps the New Dealers were no flash in the pan? Perhaps they were to be taken seriously as spokesmen for the People?

Roosevelt had no doubts. Armed with his mandate, he moved to consolidate the NIRA. Declaring his experiment a success, he proposed a further two-year extension. He invited perfecting amendments but insisted that "[t]he fundamental purposes and principles of the Act are sound. To abandon them is unthinkable. It would spell the return of industrial and labor chaos."[25]

But *was* corporativism sound? Surely the time had come for the New Dealers to confront the implications of their revolutionary break with constitutional tradition?

REFINING THE PROPOSAL

Here is where the Supreme Court got into the act. Before moving to particulars, I want to challenge the way the reigning professional narrative sets the stage for the epic struggle between the Old Court and the New Deal.

Resetting the Stage

The Court crisis is too often treated as an unhappy accident of the mortality tables. Unlike every previous President in history, Roosevelt went through his first term without making a single nomination to the Supreme Court. The New Deal came before a bench dominated by Republican appointees, with only a couple of holdovers from the Wilson Administration. Little wonder that Roosevelt had such a hard time. The Court he had inherited consisted of three blocs—four conservatives, three liberals, and a two-man center of Charles Evans Hughes and Owen Roberts. Given this setup, the reigning narrative naturally focuses on the flips and flops of the centrists as they struggled with constitutional perplexities.

Only at this point does scholarly disagreement begin. For legal realists, the political character of the centrists' "switch in time" in 1937 is painfully apparent. For shocked legalists, the switch provides the supreme test of faith. As they unfold the subtleties of judicial doctrine, it becomes clear (to them) that the centrists' flips and flops were more apparent than real. The decision by Hughes and Roberts to endorse the New Deal in 1937 was the (more or less) predictable outcome of deeper doctrinal shifts that had already occurred before the high-visibility battle had begun. The so-called switch in time was not the product of politics, but the result of the law working itself pure.[26]

As my argument proceeds, I will be incorporating the insights of both sides without going to either extreme. The legalists are right in insisting that the New Deal Court did not reconstruct constitutional law out of thin air; the realists are right in emphasizing that the doctrinal revolution would not have happened without sustained Presidential leadership. But at this stage, it is more important to challenge the basic premises of the traditional debate. Both realists and legalists assume that the conflict between the Old Court and the New Deal was a waste of time. They only disagree as to its cause—the realists invoking insufficient political awareness, the legalists invoking a regrettable failure by Hughes and Roberts (especially the latter) to grasp the implications of doctrinal innovations they had previously endorsed. Both sides assume that America would have been a better place if the Old Court had not resisted the First New Deal. One can almost hear them sigh in chorus: If only Roosevelt had been given a chance to appoint a couple of politically savvy/legally acute Justices in his first term, the Court could have evaded this stain on its historical record![27]

In my view, the conflict was not an aberration. Parliamentary systems allow a victorious party to seize immediate control of leading institutions, but America's dualist system *purposely* makes it difficult for a rising movement to seize total control at once. As a convincing literature in political science has established,[28] the Supreme Court will characteristically serve as the conservative branch, leading a principled challenge to a rising movement of revolutionary reform.

This is as it should be. Within the dualist tradition, no movement for revolutionary reform can rightfully expect an easy victory for its transformative vision. It must earn its claim to speak for the People by repeatedly winning electoral support in the face of sustained constitutional critique. In putting the New Deal to this test, the Old Court was redeeming—not betraying—America's constitutional tradition.

Indeed, it is too quick to suppose that Roosevelt could have evaded his period of constitutional struggle if fate had given him the chance to make an early appointment or two. After all, Hoover had not done such a terrible job filling the three seats opening up between 1930 and 1932. As a moderately progressive Republican, his appointments tilted to the center-left of the traditional continuum. When the conservatives Taft and Sanborn left the Court in 1930, they were replaced by the progressives Hughes and Roberts. And when Oliver Wendell Holmes left in 1932, Hoover replaced him with the yet more progressive Benjamin Cardozo.

Would Roosevelt have done as well? Supreme Court nominations are not merely tokens in an ideological struggle; they also provide the President with political patronage through which he can cement weak links in his coalition. As a consequence, each opening requires the President to balance the demands of constitutional politics against the normal demands of politicians for a place in the sun.[29] In Roosevelt's case, this demand was particularly exigent, since it was made by his Senate majority leader, Joseph Robinson, whose life's ambition was a Supreme Court seat. As Senator from Arkansas, Robinson symbolized the distinctive problems Roosevelt confronted in transforming the Democratic Party into a vehicle for revolutionary reform.[30] While Robinson was a loyal supporter of his President, he had been raised in the Jeffersonian traditions of the Southern Democratic Party. This was, of course, the very tradition that Roosevelt was seeking to revolutionize. And yet it was widely understood that he had promised Robinson the first available appointment as a reward for his service in pushing the New Deal through the Senate—a promise that Roosevelt could break only by paying a very heavy price with Robinson and the rest of the Congressional leadership.[31] Imagine, then, that Mr. Justice Holmes had not retired at the age of ninety but had hung on until he reached his ninety-second year in 1934. Instead of Hoover's Cardozo joining Brandeis and Stone on the Court's left wing, Roosevelt's Robinson would have been sorely tempted to join the conservative Four Horsemen in their heroic defense of the Jeffersonian vision of limited government!

The Old Court's resistance, then, should not be casually attributed to the accidents of judicial turnover; nor do the Four Horsemen of legal legend deserve the diabolic role so often attributed to them. On some very crucial matters, the Old Court did not divide 5 to 4, or 6 to 3, but 9 to 0.

The Court Draws a Line

As the lawyers began to debate the constitutionality of the NIRA, something very peculiar happened. On the one hand, leading government lawyers did not disguise the initiative's problematic constitutionality. Attorney General Homer Cummings was so convinced of its defects that he refused to defend the NIRA before the Supreme Court; Donald Richberg, the Recovery Administration's general counsel, tried to avoid judicial review by dismissing cases that raised the constitutional question.[32] As Milton Handler explained in a balanced, but sympathetic, essay of August 1933, "[c]andor demands . . . the admission that for the statute . . . to be sustained . . . requires a change of attitude on the part of the Supreme Court no less revolutionary than the law itself."[33] Even leading legal realists like Thurman Arnold could stretch the cases only to justify the NIRA as an emergency measure.[34] Government lawyers tended to do the same when the question hit the courts.[35]

Under ordinary conditions, the government's expression of such anxieties would encourage a blistering attack from its opponents in the private bar. Nothing could be further from the truth. Ronen Shamir summarizes a comprehensive review of the sources:

> [I]n spite of the mounting evidence that the NIRA threatened established legal principles and practices, the opposition of lawyers . . . on grounds of its administrative and constitutional shortcomings had not been played wholeheartedly [for three reasons]: . . . the wide support it enjoyed among leading commercial and industrial groups, the uncertainty concerning the way the Supreme Court would eventually treat this constitutionally doubtful law, and the administration's justification of the act in the name of national emergency.[36]

This role reversal is striking, but not unprecedented. As we have seen, Federalists and Anti-Federalists displayed a similar pattern at the Founding. Rather than relying heavily on legalistic rationales, the Federalists conceded the revolutionary character of their reforms and appealed to their opponents to accept the need for unconventional action in the name of a national emergency; rather than indulging in legalistic defenses, Anti-Federalists waived their constitutional objections to Philadelphia's call for state ratifying conventions and mobilized for the ongoing electoral struggle.

A similar pattern emerges during Reconstruction. This second time around, the Supreme Court began to bulk larger in the reformers' unconventional calculations. Recall that, after winning their triggering election in 1866, the Republicans confronted the threat to Reconstruction posed by the Court in *ex parte McCardle.* Rather than allowing the Justices to strike down Reconstruction, the Convention/Congress stripped the Court of jurisdiction.

While the New Deal Democrats had launched an initiative in the economic realm as sweeping as Reconstruction, such unconventional measures did not yet seem appropriate for two reasons. First, the Democrats' situation could not yet be fairly compared to that of the Republicans at the time of *McCardle.* After all, the Republicans' challenge to the Court came after they had managed to sustain popular support through four electoral cycles—1860, 1862, 1864, 1866. While the Great Depression had led most ordinary citizens to focus on questions of economic organization with comparable seriousness, the Democrats had only put together a string of two electoral victories.

Second, the Hughes Court's reaction to the NIRA was a good deal less predictable than the Chase Court's obvious hostility to the Reconstruction Acts. A year earlier, Hughes himself had written a 5-to-4 opinion that showed the way for the revolutionary shifts suggested by Arnold and Handler. Confronting an extraordinary debtor relief statute passed by Minnesota, the Chief Justice did not deny that the Founders would have judged such measures patently unconstitutional. But he upheld the statute, explicitly rejecting the claim "that the great clauses of the Constitution must be confined to the interpretation which the framers, with the conditions and outlook of their time, would have placed upon them."[37]

Even more recently, Hughes had led a 5-to-4 majority to support the sweeping New Deal decision to go off the gold standard and make fiat money the permanent coin of the realm. If Hughes had failed to carry the Court in the *Gold Clause Cases,* there is every indication that Roosevelt would have responded with a *McCardle*-like effort to invalidate the Justices' decision.[38] But if Hughes could lead the majority to support the New Deal's revolutionary monetary policies, perhaps he might also win majority support for its revolutionary industrial policies?

It was, in short, entirely premature for Roosevelt to intervene. There was no need to consider unconventional actions when the Court's future conduct was so unpredictable.

But it is at this point that the Justices took their stand, and with remarkable aggressiveness. The second most prestigious court in the nation—the Second Circuit Court of Appeals—had handed down its judgment, largely approving NIRA, on April 1, 1935, only months before the statute's two-year term expired. The Justices could have rendered the lawsuit moot by setting the case down under the normal schedule for appeal and briefing. Instead, they granted the government's request for expedited treatment and scheduled argument for early May. On May 27, they announced their opinion in *Schechter Poultry Corporation v. United States*. With blinding speed, the Justices not only rejected the NIRA; they did so unanimously. The Chief Justice set himself firmly against the talk of economic emergency he had floated the year before:

> We are told that the provision of the statute authorizing the adoption of codes must be viewed in the light of the grave national crisis with which Congress was confronted. . . . Extraordinary conditions may call for extraordinary remedies. But the argument necessarily stops short of an attempt to justify action which lies outside the sphere of constitutional authority. . . . Such assertions of extra-constitutional authority were anticipated and precluded by the explicit terms of the Tenth Amendment,— "The powers not delegated to the United States by the Constitution, nor prohibited by it to the States, are reserved to the States respectively, or to the people."[39]

The words were double-edged. They allowed the Court to assess the NIRA under traditional constitutional principles; but they also challenged the President to run against the Court in the next election and seek to gain a mandate from the People in support of his corporatist initiative.

The Court then proceeded, with great clarity, to lay down two traditional principles that would require popular re-vision if the President took to the higher lawmaking path. The first involved the structure of the national government. In establishing NIRA, Congress had delegated vast regulatory powers to business and labor groups that met together to write up codes of fair competition. Once these codes were prepared, the President was granted broad discretionary authority to approve them. The Court struck this system down, finding that Congress had abdicated the central lawmaking role established at the Founding and reaffirmed at Reconstruction. On its view, the Democrats assembling on Capitol Hill in 1933 had not earned the popular authority to displace the tradition of Congressionally centered government with a corporatist regime based on Presidential leadership.[40]

The Court also built a bulwark around the states. According to the Justices, the Schechter Poultry Corporation, distributor of kosher chickens in Brooklyn, New York, was an archetypal local operation. If any government could control its labor and distribution practices, it was New York, not the New Deal monolith. The Court granted that "almost all" of Schechter's chickens were coming from other states,[41] and that the code had been drawn up for an interstate market region consisting of New York, Connecticut, and New Jersey.[42] But if this were enough to justify national control, "there would be virtually no limit" to "completely centralized government."[43] Schechter only had an "indirect" impact upon interstate commerce. Once the company picked up the chickens from its wholesaler, "[t]he interstate transactions in relation to that poultry ended."[44] What Schechter did with them was no concern of Congress under the commerce power: "The distinction between direct and indirect effects . . . must be recognized as a fundamental one, essential to the maintenance of our constitutional system."[45]

The President Responds

The ball was in the President's court. He had three basic options:

1. To retreat and enact a new and more modest legislative program that accepted the Court's constitutional critique.
2. To take up the gauntlet and reenact (something like) the NIRA; then appeal to the People in 1936 for a mandate to insist on his initiatives despite the Court.
3. Neither to retreat nor to reenact, but to rethink the New Deal. Was the centralizing style of Presidential corporatism really the

best way to control the abuses and injustices of a free market economy?

The President took the third path in a remarkable press conference that was immediately recognized, in the words of the *Washington Post,* as "of the most far-reaching political significance. . . . His observations, informally presented but carefully weighed in advance, must be regarded as being of even greater moment in the future of the Nation than the court decision which aroused them."[46] Speaking without interruption for an hour and a half, the President declared *Schechter* to be more important "than any decision of my lifetime . . . more important than any decision probably since the Dred Scott case."[47]

The most striking feature of Roosevelt's presentation was its high constitutional seriousness. True, he began the press conference by reading a selection of telegrams from constituents outraged by the Court's decision, but he then moved to a different plane—reading out passages of Hughes's opinion and subjecting them to thoughtful and sustained commentary. After disputing the Court's dismissive treatment of the emergency rationale, Roosevelt distinguished cleanly between two prongs of its constitutional critique. "[T]he delegation of power [from Congress to the President] is not so very important" because the Court indicated that it could be cured by more specific statutory guidelines. But its decision on the Commerce Clause was a different matter: "[T]he Supreme Court will no longer take into consideration anything that indirectly may affect interstate commerce; . . . the only thing in interstate commerce . . . is goods in transit plus, perhaps, a very small number of transactions which would directly affect goods in transit."[48] If the Justices held to this view, vast areas of national life would remain beyond the reach of the New Deal. After elaborating this point at length, Roosevelt defined the key question:

> It is infinitely deeper than any partisan issue, it is a national issue; yes, and the issue is this . . .: Is the United States going to decide, are the people of this country going to decide that their Federal Government shall in the future have no right under any implied power or any court-approved power to enter a national economic problem, but that that economic problem must be decided only by the states?
>
> The other part of it is this: Shall we view our social problems—and in that I bring employment of all kinds—shall we view that from the same

point of view or not, that the Federal Government has no right under this
or following opinions to take any part in trying to better national social
conditions? Now that is flat and that is simple![49]

As the mangled syntax suggests, Roosevelt is not reading a carefully
crafted statement prepared by underlings. This press conference provides a glimpse of a President actually engaged in genuine constitutional thought. Rather than accepting or rejecting or ignoring
Schechter, Roosevelt is using the opinion to sharpen his constitutional
priorities, distinguishing the important from the fundamental.

Many have suggested that the Court did Roosevelt a favor by
jettisoning the increasingly unpopular NIRA.[50] But this is not how
the President saw the situation. He had come out strongly for renewal, and his smashing victory in the 1934 elections gave him no
reason to abandon his major project.[51] It was Supreme Court resistance that forced him to sober second thought: Would the People
really support him if he made the 1936 election into a mandate for the
NIRA?

Whatever his own personal attraction to corporatism, Roosevelt did
not have much trouble answering this question in the negative. The
press conference shows him immediately searching for more solid
constitutional ground in the impending struggle for public opinion.
Not corporatism, but nationalism, would serve as his watchword—
"the right to legislate and administer laws that have a bearing on and
general control over national economic problems and national social
problems."[52] Roosevelt was under no illusion about a quick victory:
"[I]t is the biggest question that has come before this country outside
of time of war and it has got to be decided, and, as I say, it may take
five years or ten years."[53]

Even at this early stage, Roosevelt was dropping sophisticated hints
about the variety of possible constitutional outcomes. Early in his
discussion of Hughes's opinion, he described *Schechter*'s restrictive
definition of interstate commerce as "dictum" and asked his audience
to "remember that the dictum is not always followed in the future."[54]
Further along, he described the challenge for the future as "whether in
some way we are going to turn over or restore to—*whichever way you
choose to put it*—turn over or restore to the Federal Government the
powers which vest in the national governments of every other nation
in the world."[55] Such remarks already introduced the possibility that a

judicial switch in time might serve as an alternative to a formal constitutional amendment—perhaps planting a thought that provoked the following exchange at the very end of the press conference:

> Q. You referred to the Dred Scott decision. That was followed by the Civil War and by at least two amendments to the Constitution.
>
> THE PRESIDENT. Well, the reason for that, of course, was the fact that the generation of 1856 did not take any action during the next four years.
>
> Q. You made a reference to the necessity of the people deciding within the next five or ten years. Is there any way of deciding that question without voting on a constitutional amendment or the passing of one?
>
> THE PRESIDENT: No; we haven't got to that yet.
>
> Q. Or a war? (Laughter)
>
> THE PRESIDENT: Just qualifying the issue, that is all.

With the constitutional options opening before them, the press corps went off to report the President's remarks under front-page headlines: ROOSEVELT ADVOCATES CONSTITUTION CHANGES, announced the *Los Angeles Times,* ROOSEVELT OUT FOR UNLIMITED POWER, shouted the *Chicago Tribune.* Whatever the eye-catching assessment, the meat of the story was a lengthy, and generally accurate, summary of the President's constitutional analysis—as well as an appreciation of the wide-ranging set of Presidential options. According to the *Los Angeles Times,* "a dozen trial balloons have risen from administration sources, including the White House itself, to sound out public sentiment toward a change . . . One scheme is to increase the number of Supreme Court justices so as to create a pro–New Deal majority therein. Another is so to alter the Constitution as to destroy the Court's present power to negative acts of Congress. Still another would re-define Federal and State rights as now constitutionally enunciated."[56] The *Washington Post* concluded:

> Taken as a whole, the President's remarks were interpreted as meaning that if he does not press for an amendment of the Constitution to give the Federal Government more explicit control over commerce, he is hopeful that the country would so forcefully express its hostility to the States Rights doctrine enunciated by the court that the latter would abandon or modify it in subsequent rulings.[57]

The *New York Times* followed up the next day with a first-page lead: WASHINGTON STUDIES PLAN FOR A QUICK AMENDMENT OF FEDERAL CONSTITUTION.[58] The story elaborated the potential application of the method that had been recently used to expedite repeal of the Prohibition Amendment. Rather than submitting repeal to the state legislatures, Congress had triggered the method of ratification by state conventions—with voters going to the polls to cast ballots for slates of convention delegates pledged in advance to support or oppose the proposal. This converted the ratification process into a series of quasi-referenda and allowed the proponents of repeal to win the support of three-fourths of the states within a year.

The *Times* gave banner headline treatment to the potential use of this precedent: "Administration officials today were reported to be considering a specific plan for a 'quick' method of amending the Constitution by what would be the equivalent of a popular referendum, so that the people might, within sixty days, declare their will on the problems posed by the Supreme Court decision in the Schechter case."[59] Under this plan, the Administration would change the procedure used to repeal Prohibition. Rather than allowing each state to call its own ratifying convention, Congress would itself "name the time, the method, and the place of constitutional conventions in the States as well as how the conventions shall be composed. Under such procedure there would be the closest possible approximation to a popular referendum that could be arranged for under this Constitution."[60] Leading columnists were no less adventurous, Arthur Krock suggesting that the President might "go to the point of advocating a [federal] constitutional convention to modernize the document in other particulars."[61]

As can be imagined, such suggestions generated a great deal of editorial opposition. But it was difficult to tell whether the largely Republican press spoke for ordinary men and women. Sympathetic commentators, like Arthur Krock, were relatively optimistic: "This much is certain at the end of a historic week: Whatever the legal destiny of the New Deal, the country rallied with a rush to its objectives after they were imperiled, and President Roosevelt, after a staggering rebuke and defeat, emerged as the leader of a newer New Deal to be outlined hereafter."[62] More conservative columnists prophesied "a titanic struggle with large consequences for the future,"[63] without commenting on the outcome. At this point, however, the President disappointed apocalyptic expectations. Rather than continuing his campaign, he lapsed into virtual silence throughout the remainder of his first term, even as the Court continued to strike down crucial aspects of the First New Deal.

Some have attributed this switch to the President's surprise at the ferocity of the opposition.[64] But this strikes me as implausible—both because an experienced politician would have expected an initial round of critique, and because there were signs of popular support as well as opposition.[65] A better explanation is to be found on the level of constitutional strategy, not tactics.

To see my point, return to the three basic options confronting Roosevelt. If he had chosen to reaffirm his faith in NIRA, he would have had little choice but to prosecute his campaign against the Court. After all, the Court had made its opposition absolutely clear, and the only way to move forward was to appeal to the People to remove the constitutional obstacles to success.

But if the President was planning to respond to *Schechter* by rethinking the New Deal, his forward-and-backward movement made a lot of sense. His sharp reaction to *Schechter* put the Court and the country on notice of his intention to press fundamental constitutional questions. But once he had removed the NIRA from the agenda, an immediate push for a constitutional amendment—or an unconventional alternative—was distinctly premature. It was far more important for the President to come up with a well defined alternative to the NIRA. Only if he won a popular mandate on behalf of this "second New Deal" would the higher lawmaking questions ventilated by the press conference deserve a central place on the political stage.

Reshaping the Proposal

It was only right and proper, then, for the President to turn his attention to Congress, and not the Court, in charting his next response to *Schechter*. William Leuchtenburg describes the scene:

> The Schechter verdict climaxed a disastrous five months for Roosevelt. Although the President had apparently won a smashing victory in the November, 1934, elections, the new Congress had passed only a single piece of legislation—the work relief bill . . . By March, government was at a standstill. "Once more," wrote Walter Lippman, "we have come to a

period of discouragement after a few months of buoyant hope . . ."
Roosevelt seemed uncertain where he was headed, barely able to manage
his unruly Congress, and downright contrary in his refusal to indicate his
main line of direction.[66]

Schechter's principled challenge served "as the final goad"[67] to a new
collective effort by the President and Congress to give a clearer shape
to the New Deal. Although Congress was preparing to adjourn,
Roosevelt insisted that it remain over the summer to enact a sweeping
new legislative program. The result was a Second Hundred Days of
creative activity, yielding such landmarks as the Wagner Labor Act,
the Social Security Act, and the Public Utility Holding Company
Act.[68]

This Second New Deal marked an important change in constitutional course. Rather than seeking to displace the competitive market
with the NIRA, Roosevelt and Congress now accepted the market as a
legitimate part of the emerging economic order—so long as regulatory
structures could be introduced to correct abuses and injustices
defined through the democratic process. Thus, the Wagner Act gave
disorganized workers new tools to bargain effectively with their
bosses; the Holding Company Act eliminated abusive concentrations
of big capital; the Social Security Act guaranteed all workers the
prospect of a decent old age after their usefulness to the market was
over.

In launching this series of focused structural initiatives, the New
Dealers did not break completely with their earlier legislative experiments. The Securities Acts of 1933 and 1934 had already taken a
similar approach. Until *Schechter,* however, this strategy competed
with the all-embracing corporativism of the NIRA. Now it emerged,
with increasing clarity, as the New Deal's central thrust.[69] As the
Democrats prepared for the 1936 elections, they would return to the
voters as advocates of a regulated capitalism, proposing a series of
focused structural initiatives by which the People might control, but
not obliterate, the competitive market.

Refining the Proposal: The Court's Critique

I have been focusing on the supreme importance of the *Schechter*
decision in refining the emerging New Deal vision of activist govern-

ment. But the Old Court resisted the emerging ideal of government on a broad front during 1935 and 1936. Although the reigning myth discredits these decisions, consider how they contributed to the democratic character of the ultimate outcome. Most importantly, the Court put Americans on notice that the New Deal was shaking the foundations—and that it was not too late to withdraw their mandate. The emerging pattern of decision also invited the public to take a more discriminating view of New Deal projects. Some innovations, like the new SEC, passed the Court's constitutional test on the first go-round.[70] Many went down but with strong dissenting opinions. The revolutionary effort by Congress to force a federal pension program on the railroads, for example, lost by 5 to 4;[71] its precedent-breaking attempts to regulate vast sectors of the economy—most notably agriculture and coal mining—lost by 6 to 3.[72] These sharp divisions suggested—accurately—that the revised New Deal program of structural reform was less of a break with the past than the NIRA.

At the same time, the Old Court helped broaden the field of debate. While Roosevelt focused on the need to gain popular consent for a dramatic expansion of the powers of the national government, the Court's decisions correctly emphasized that there was much more at stake. Since the Civil War, the Justices had worked out principles of liberty that constrained the operation of government at all levels— state no less than federal. Speaking broadly, these principles of restraint presented private property and freedom of contract as the central constitutional bulwarks of individual freedom against majority tyranny. But such laissez-faire understandings would systematically frustrate the ongoing structural reforms that New Deal Democracy was coming to represent in the minds of Americans.

The Court made this clear in *Louisville Bank v. Radford*[73] on the same "Black Monday" it invalidated the NIRA. The Court's constitutional challenge in *Radford* was no less fundamental than in *Schechter*. It dealt with the Frazier-Lemke Act of 1934, a paradigmatic New Deal response to the economic crisis that was sweeping hundreds of thousands of farmers from their lands in a wave of foreclosure sales. Instead of allowing this massive dislocation to proceed, Congress gave mortgage debtors extraordinary relief—guaranteeing them five years of undisturbed possession if they paid their creditors a "reasonable rental fixed by the court," and allowing them to discharge their debt by paying the assessed value of their property.[74]

Within a modern constitutional framework, there is nothing very anxiety-provoking about Frazier-Lemke. Granted, Congress forced creditors to accept rent payments in lieu of their common law right to immediate possession. But so long as courts scrutinized rent levels for "reasonable[ness]," weren't creditors getting their money's worth? It is also hard to detect a grave constitutional grievance in the provision allowing debtors to buy their properties at assessed value: Could any bank reasonably insist on more-than-market compensation?

Given the banks' minor complaints, Congress seemed on firm ground in determining that its innovative regulatory scheme would generate very substantial benefits. Rather than allowing the banks to keep uprooting hordes of farmers and homeowners, Frazier-Lemke promised these people a way to sustain themselves with dignity within their traditional communities. In a time of massive economic disruption, surely this was an especially great value?

At the very least, this is the kind of cost-benefit judgment that Congress is perfectly entitled to make—or so the modern constitutional lawyer has been trained to conclude. *Radford,* then, serves as an apt symbol of the deep divide that separates the present era from the one coming to an end in 1935. Not only did the Court strike down this innocuous exercise in social engineering; it did so unanimously. No less remarkably, the opinion was written by Louis Brandeis, the patron saint of the "liberal" bloc. So far as he was concerned, the Congressional plan deprived creditors of the very "essence of a mortgage."[75] Disdaining as irrelevant the "[e]xtensive economic data" tendered by the defenders of the statute,[76] Brandeis held that the taking of the creditor's possessory interest was a violation of the Fifth Amendment.

The opinion, in short, was an altogether remarkable performance from the man who had made the "Brandeis Brief" a watchword for the innovative legal use of social science. Yet there was a deeper wisdom in Brandeis's decision to write an opinion of the Court that could easily pass for a *Lochnerian* masterpiece penned by Justice Sutherland or Butler. In joining hands with his more conservative brethren, Brandeis and his fellow "liberals" were making it clear that the New Deal was proposing to do more than nibble around the edges of the laissez-faire constitutional tradition. It was out to repudiate the constitutional baseline previous generations had constructed out of core principles of property and contract. Once Americans glimpsed the depth of the New Deal critique of the common law, did they really wish to endorse it?

Having raised this question, the liberals were happy in other cases to dissent from the conservatives' more robust commitments to laissez-faire constitutionalism. In his famous 1932 dissent in *New State Ice Company v. Leibmann,*[77] for example, Brandeis protested against the Court's vindication of a small entrepreneur's right "to engage in a lawful business enterprise" despite the state's refusal to grant a certificate of convenience and necessity. In this context, Brandeis was untroubled by the fact that a "certificate [of convenience and necessity] was unknown to the common law," and he defended the authority of the democratic state to respond to the necessities of "the machine age" by reshaping property rights "to promote the public interest."[78] Indeed, on particular issues, the liberals sometimes attracted a majority for their more instrumental view of private property.[79]

At no point, however, was there a suggestion that the Court was prepared to overthrow the entire traditional framework.[80] Consider its parting gesture before the 1936 elections. On June 1, the Court struck down a New York statute prescribing minimum wages for women. Rather than reopen the question for fresh debate, the majority thought it sufficient to invoke the authority of Mr. Justice Sutherland's landmark opinion of 1923, *Adkins v. Children's Hospital.*[81] This time Hughes joined the three liberals in dissent, though in a very cautious opinion. While Justice Stone wrote a stronger dissent, calling for the repudiation of *Adkins,* it is a mistake to overinterpret the text. As we have seen, neither Stone nor anybody else was prepared to call for the repudiation of the entire framework of laissez-faire constitutionalism.

The larger pattern of decisions, then, made a very useful contribution. A unanimous Court stood firm on core principles of contract and property in *Radford,* just as it had on traditional principles of federalism and Presidential power in *Schechter.*[82] At the same time, the Court conducted a vibrant debate on the extent this basic framework should be adapted to accommodate New Deal activism—with the liberals giving more scope to government power and the conservatives insisting on more protection to the principles of federalism and the free market. Like many family disputes, this one sometimes degenerated into bitter name-calling. But it should not divert us from the role played by the Court in the larger debate.

Here the disagreements between liberal and conservative Justices paled besides the conflict between the Court and the President. In his response to *Schechter,* Roosevelt put the country on notice that the New Deal was seeking to dismantle the very framework of traditional constitutionalism; and he was now convincing Congress to endorse a second, and more refined, statutory program that sought a revolutionary redefinition of the citizen's relationship to the nation-state. An irresistible force was on a collision course with an immoveable object. The outcome would depend on the 1936 election.

THE TRIGGERING ELECTION

As Herbert Hoover put it at the Republican convention:

> The American people should thank Almighty God for the Constitution and the Supreme Court. They should be grateful to a courageous press.
>
> You might contemplate what would have happened if Mr. Roosevelt could have appointed enough Supreme Court justices in the first year of his Administration. Suppose those New Deal Acts had remained upon the statute books. We would have been a regimented people. Have you any assurance that he will not have the appointments if he is reelected?[83]

By the end of this speech—a slash-and-burn assault on the New Deal and all its works—Hoover had stirred the Republican faithful into a frenzy. For a moment, the cheering throng seemed on the verge of bolting toward political destruction by awarding Hoover a third run at the Presidency.[84]

But the moment passed and political sanity returned. The convention turned to Alf Landon, the only Republican governor to win reelection in 1934. Landon was not merely a fresh face. He was by no means an all-out critic of the New Deal, accepting the legitimacy of a number of structural initiatives—including federal aid to agriculture, public assistance, and (even more remarkably) old age pensions. On these matters, his protest took the modern Republican form, directing itself at means, not ends—the waste, bureaucracy, and centralization which have become the watchwords of campaign critiques ever since.[85] While Landon's voice became shriller during the campaign, and was sometimes overwhelmed by diehards in the Republican chorus, his nomination represents a first and very tentative recognition by the leading party of the old regime that the People were indeed in the process of rethinking the very foundations of American government.

At the same time, Landon was still calling upon the People to stop short of a constitutional revolution. He emphasized this point in his closing speech at Madison Square Garden in New York City. With only days remaining before the election, Landon restated his critiques of particular New Deal programs—AAA, NRA, Social Security, and the like. After each assault, he challenged his audience to consider how the President's policies would evolve if he were reelected: "The answer is: No one can be sure."

I will let Landon speak for himself as he reached his rhetorical climax:

> I come finally to the underlying and fundamental issue of this campaign. This is the question of whether our American form of government is to be preserved.
>
> Let us return once more to the record.
>
> The President has been responsible for nine acts declared unconstitutional by the Supreme Court.
>
> He has publicly urged Congress to pass a law, even though it had reasonable doubts as to its constitutionality.
>
> He has publicly belittled the Supreme Court of the United States.
>
> He has publicly suggested that the Constitution is an outworn document. . . .
>
> Every one of these actions—and the list is by no means complete—strikes at the heart of the American form of government.
>
> Our Constitution is not a lifeless piece of paper. It is the underlying law of the land and the charter of liberties of our people. The people, and they alone, have the right to amend or destroy it. Until the people in their combined wisdom decide to make the change, it is the plain duty of the people's servants to keep within the Constitution. It is the plain meaning of the oath of office that they shall keep within the Constitution.
>
> Our Federal system allows great leeway. But if changes in our civilization make amendment to the Constitution desirable it should be amended. It has been amended in the past. It can be in the future.
>
> I have already made my position clear on this question. I am on record that, if proper working conditions cannot be regulated by the States, I shall favor a constitutional amendment giving the States the necessary powers.
>
> And what are the intentions of the President with respect to the Consti-

tution? Does he believe changes are required? If so, will an amendment be submitted to the people, or will he attempt to get around the Constitution by tampering with the Supreme Court?

The answer is: No one can be sure.[86]

Landon was quite right. Roosevelt had opened up these questions in his *Schechter* response, and the Democratic platform, written on the President's express instructions, did not resolve them. True, it pledged to meet "pressing national problems . . . through legislation within the Constitution." If this failed, it promised to seek a "clarifying amendment . . . to regulate commerce, protect public health and safety and safeguard economic security."[87] But these formulations left the status of court expansion unclear: past Congresses had often "tamper[ed]" with the size of the Court. Landon was on firm ground in charging that Roosevelt might have similar plans in mind.

Despite the urgings of some of his advisors, the President refused to respond explicitly to Landon's charges. While he was concerned with basic values, he refused to allow Landon's questions of higher law-making technique deflect attention from the central constitutional choice he wished to put before the People. As he explained in his acceptance speech at the Democratic convention in Philadelphia:

> Philadelphia is a good city in which to write American history. This is fitting ground on which to reaffirm the faith of our fathers; to pledge ourselves to restore to the people a wider freedom; to give to 1936 as the founders gave to 1776—an American way of life.
>
> That very word freedom, in itself and of necessity, suggests freedom from some restraining power. In 1776 we sought freedom from the tyranny of a political autocracy—from the eighteenth century royalists who held special privileges from the crown. . . .
>
> Since that struggle, however, man's inventive genius released new forces in our land which reordered the lives of our people. The age of machinery, of railroads; of steel and electricity; the telegraph and the radio; mass production, mass distribution—all of these combined to bring forward a new civilization and with it a new problem for those who sought to remain free.
>
> For out of this modern civilization economic royalists carved new dynasties. . . .
>
> It was natural and perhaps human that the privileged princes of these new economic dynasties, thirsting for power, reached out for control over

Government itself. . . . And as a result the average man once more confronts the problem that faced the Minute Man. . . .

Liberty requires opportunity to make a living—a living decent according to the standard of the time, a living which gives man not only enough to live by, but something to live for.

For too many of us the political equality we once had won was meaningless in the face of economic inequality. . . . For too many of us life was no longer free; liberty no longer real; men could no longer follow the pursuit of happiness.

Against economic tyranny such as this, the American citizen could appeal only to the organized power of Government. The collapse of 1929 showed up the despotism for what it was. The election of 1932 was the people's mandate to end it. Under that mandate it is being ended. . . .

Today we stand committed to the proposition that freedom is no half-and-half affair. If the average citizen is guaranteed equal opportunity in the polling place, he must have equal opportunity in the market place.

These economic royalists complain that we seek to overthrow the institutions of America. What they really complain of is that we seek to take away their power. In vain they seek to hide behind the Flag and the Constitution. In their blindness they forget what the Flag and the Constitution stand for. Now, as always, they stand for democracy, not tyranny; for freedom, not subjection; and against a dictatorship by mob rule and the overprivileged alike.[88]

Forget, for the moment, whether you think that Roosevelt or Landon has the better of this argument. *Both* were raising basic issues. It is no small thing for a political system to focus on fundamentals in this incisive way. Most of the credit goes to the American people—who rejected the demagogues around them eager to drag them toward the moral abyss.

But the Constitution also deserves its share—for the way it structured the evolving struggle so as to allow the antagonists to join issue, rather than talk past one another. Despite Roosevelt's assertion to the contrary, the election of 1932 had little relationship to "the people's mandate" as he was now defining it. At that time, Americans had simply repudiated Hoover's style of progressive Republicanism as utterly inadequate; Roosevelt's mandate, as he well understood, was to experiment with more activist approaches—without any certainty that

Americans would approve. Only with the 1934 elections could the President begin to claim genuine popular support for his more affirmative program. Even then his vision was very different from the one he was presenting to the Philadelphia convention. The NIRA was no assault on "economic royalism." If anything, it consolidated the hold of the business elite on their industrial fiefdoms—suspending the antitrust laws and giving dominant firms a central role in the emerging industrial order. This was, of course, why men like Brandeis enthusiastically joined in striking it down.

Only in response to the Supreme Court did Roosevelt and his New Dealers rethink their course—leading to the statutory initiatives of the Second New Deal and the Philadelphia effort to frame the meaning of their initiatives in self-consciously constitutional terms. Roosevelt's watchword was now the rebirth of freedom, not the imperative of central planning. But it was a new freedom, defined in the light of modern realities that would otherwise defeat the claims of equal opportunity. It was a freedom that could not be achieved in opposition to the state, but only through democratic control of the marketplace: "If the average citizen is guaranteed equal opportunity in the polling place, he must have equal opportunity in the market place."

This is the point where the Republicans jumped off the train. While Landon was willing to endorse a more activist version of progressive Republicanism, he was unwilling to revise the old constitutional definition of freedom—tightly linked to principles of limited national government, freedom of contract, and private property. At most, he could endorse a constitutional amendment that authorized state (not federal) regulation of hours and wages. But he was entirely unwilling to accept the New Deal claim that modern freedom could only be achieved through the state and not against it; or endorse Roosevelt's assertion that the old constitutional regime had degenerated into a legalistic smokescreen for a world in which "life was no longer free; liberty no longer real; men could no longer follow the pursuit of happiness." To the contrary, the New Deal promise of freedom raised alarming prospects: "[Will] he attempt to get around the Constitution by tampering with the Supreme Court?"

With such questions ringing in their ears, Americans went to the polls—and gave Roosevelt and the New Deal Congress the greatest victory in American history. Landon gained the electoral votes of only

Maine and New Hampshire; he managed to win only 36.5 percent of the popular vote, his share rising as high as 45 percent in no more than four states. The Republicans were left with eighty-nine seats in the House; sixteen in the Senate.[89] No less important, the election of 1936 cemented the hold of the Democratic Party on American life for the next generation. Indeed, we have yet to see another example of such a massive and enduring political realignment.[90]

The same is true if we look backwards. Despite breakthroughs in the theory of popular sovereignty, the majoritarian achievements of the Federalists and the Republicans were actually quite modest. On both occasions, the revolutionary reformers won the consent of paper-thin majorities for their unconventional movements toward a "more perfect Union." In contrast, New Deal Democracy achieved in practice what Federalists and Republicans had sought in theory—the escalating support of a decisive majority of Americans throughout the nation in the face of an eloquent effort by conservatives to draw the line short of revolutionary reform.

Of course, all Americans had not been magically transformed into enthusiastic New Dealers. Alf Landon did attract 17 million voters into the Republican column in 1936, and the Supreme Court's resistance played an especially important role in reconciling these dissenters to the larger transformation. However bitterly the remaining Republicans might condemn "that man in the White House," there was something that none of them could reasonably deny. In gaining reelection, Roosevelt had been obliged to seek popular support in the face of a withering constitutional critique led by the Court. But when Landon energetically called the People to rise up in defense of their traditional Constitution, Americans were more impressed with the urgent need for revolutionary reform. While Republicans might conscientiously believe that their fellow citizens had made a tragic mistake, they could hardly deny that the People had given decisive support to the Democrats with their eyes open. By raising the question of constitutional principle so eloquently during Roosevelt's first term of experimentation, the Supreme Court had played a key role in establishing, *even to New Deal opponents,* that the People were indeed supporting a change in their governing philosophy.

How, then, did Roosevelt and the Congress propose to interpret their mandate?

CHAPTER ELEVEN

The Missing Amendments

HYPERFORMALISM?

IN THE LAST CHAPTER I challenged the reigning view of the struggle between the Old Court and the New Deal. Received opinion discredits the Court and suggests that the Nine Old Men should have given the First New Deal their constitutional seal of approval. I emphasized how judicial resistance contributed to the democratic character of the outcome. First, it forced Americans to recognize that the emerging New Deal did challenge their constitutional commitments to free markets and limited national government. Second, it invited Americans to discriminate between the full-blown corporatism of the NIRA and an activist liberalism that sought to regulate the market, not abolish it. Third, it deepened the political dialogue: What did the American people really think about *the principles* behind the minimum wage laws,[1] or old age pensions,[2] or agricultural subsidies?[3] Finally, it emphasized—as nothing else could—that the political elite in Washington, D.C., had not yet authoritatively decided the questions of constitutional identity raised by the New Deal; and that it was up to the American people to make this decision, against a background that emphasized the principled aspect of the struggle.

All this might have been lost if, as the reigning myth suggests, the Court had approved the first wave of New Deal initiatives. On this scenario, the 1936 election would have occurred under foggier conditions. President and Congress might have been teetering uncertainly between full-blown corporativism and liberal welfarism. Roosevelt might have run a campaign that focused entirely on personal charisma and presidential pork. Such factors always play an important role in

American politics, but the Court's opposition made it impossible to evade the questions of principle. In fact, Roosevelt's campaign of 1936 elaborated the basic premises of the emerging New Deal far more incisively than anything Roosevelt had said in 1932.

At the same time, Landon and his partisans emphasized the danger of court-packing in their last-ditch efforts to mobilize the American people. In the words of H. L. Mencken:

> During his second term, if he has one, [Roosevelt] will have the choosing of at least three judges, and perhaps of all nine, for the youngest of the sitting ones is beyond sixty. . . . That he will appoint men who actually believe in the Constitution is hardly likely. It is immensely more probable that they'll be advocates of the kind of revision that will greatly enlarge his own powers.
>
> Thus his reelection will set off the most violent attack upon the Constitution ever made, at least since the Hon. Abraham Lincoln adjourned it during the Civil War. He will waste no time (and run no risk) trying to change it by the orderly process of amendment. Instead, he will set his juridic stooges upon it, asking them only to make a thorough job.[4]

Mencken was stating the obvious—the traditional Constitution was reaching the point of no return.

To put my thesis in terms of a single (if much abused) word, the reigning myth is insufficiently dialectical. It focuses on each No handed down by the Supreme Court without trying to understand how these rejections helped shape the subsequent Yeses by the New Dealers in Washington and the American people at large. The Court's No in *Schechter* forced the New Deal to make up its mind on corporatism and say Yes to systematic structural reform; the Court's No to particular liberal reforms gave concrete meaning to the New Deal's assault on traditional principles. In response to the Court's emphatic warning that there *was* something new about the New Deal, would the American people reign in the Democrats in the election of 1936?

The results were overwhelming. Democrats returned to Congress and the White House with a show of popular support that has not been seen before or since. But brute numbers never interpret themselves. It was up to the President, the 331 Democrats in the House, and the 76 Democrats in the Senate to elaborate the meaning of their mandate—all the time aware that they would be obliged, once again, to defend their interpretation at the polls in two short years.

This chapter focuses on the way the constitutional issues were defined during the period before the Court began its famous switch in the spring of 1937. Until then, neither the President nor the Congress nor the country had any inkling that the Justices might help resolve the constitutional crisis. Instead, they had to rely on themselves to define the crucial constitutional issues raised by the triggering election.

Roosevelt made the first big move with his plan for judicial reorganization—which would have allowed him to make six new appointments to the Supreme Court. This provoked a remarkably sophisticated constitutional debate.[5] The President's leading opponents did not present themselves as staunch defenders of the traditional jurisprudence. No less then Roosevelt, they recognized that the People were demanding a fundamental change in constitutional direction.

They denied, however, that the President had hit upon the right way to implement the shift. On their view, there was only one way the President and his party could credibly speak for the People in a higher lawmaking voice—and that was by using the forms provided by Article Five of the original Constitution. To establish their good faith, opponents came forward with constitutional amendments and pleaded with the Administration to put its weight behind one or another proposal. In response, the President was obliged to explain why Article Five was inadequate, presenting an increasingly self-conscious defense of Presidential leadership in higher lawmaking.

The President's initiative, in short, catapulted the country into a great debate of central importance to my main thesis: Was the President right in claiming that the Democrats' electoral victories had given the New Dealers a mandate from the People to take unconventional action to constitutionalize their revolutionary reforms? Or were his opponents right in insisting on a monopolistic interpretation of Article Five?

Just then, the Court chose to make its switch in time. While particular decisions became landmarks, the Justices' new-found consistency was even more important. Never again would the Court find a New Deal reform beyond the power of government. As a consequence, the political protagonists relaxed their own creative efforts to work out the terms of a new constitutional solution and allowed the Court to codify the terms of the New Deal revolution.

This point allows us to put the "switch in time" into a new perspective. We have all been taught that the Court waited far too long before it decided to retreat. Modern constitutional law looks with undisguised relief as the Court responds to court-packing by vindicating the New Deal on the basis of some Ancient Truths handed down by John Marshall and the Federalists. If, however, the President, Congress, and the country were doing quite well confronting the crisis without the Court's assistance, we must ask a different question: Did the Court retreat too soon?

I shall take up this question later, but one point needs emphasizing here. The Court's strategic role in aborting the higher lawmaking debate further undermines the case for hypertextualism. On numberless occasions, I have encountered thoughtful lawyers who respond to my arguments by raising the same question: If the New Dealers won a mandate from the People on behalf of a new constitutional solution, why didn't they use Article Five to codify the terms of their mandate?

This chapter shows that Americans were asking themselves this very question *until the Supreme Court killed the debate by making its switch in time.* Of course, we will never know what would have happened if the Court had remained intransigent. Perhaps Roosevelt would have convinced Congress that its mandate from the People extended to unconventional steps like court-packing. Perhaps his opponents would have forced him to yield to their demands that he put forward a package of Article Five amendments. We will explore both possibilities. But these alternative scenarios should not divert attention from my central thesis: in the American system, *the Supreme Court largely determines whether a constitutional revolution will be codified in Article Five terms.* Only if the Justices refuse to recognize the legitimacy of a transformation do the President and Congress have an incentive to take the Article Five path.

If this is right, it places a new burden upon the hyperformalist demand for New Deal amendments. It was one thing for the New Dealers to have failed to enact amendments in the face of a continuing challenge from the Court; quite another for them to keep pushing down the Article Five track after the Justices' emphatic 1937 signal that they could be trusted to codify the New Deal revolution without the further need for formal instruction.

Given this judicial signal, and its predictable impact on the evolving debate, a special kind of hyperformalism is required before lawyers and judges of today might suppose themselves justified in ignoring the constitutional achievements of the 1930's. On this line of argument, the New Dealers were constitutionally derelict when they decided to wind down their debate about the need for Article Five amendments in response to the emphatic signals from the Court. So far as the hyperformalist is concerned, Roosevelt and the Congress should have ignored the Court's offer of cooperation and insisted on laboring in the vineyards of Article Five. The fact that the Democrats were lulled by the Court's switch into a sense of security should not provide an excuse for their failure to continue pushing down the formal track. As a consequence, tomorrow's lawyers may legitimately ignore the New Deal Court's efforts to heed the People's will and put American government on a new foundation.

But isn't this *very* implausible?

THE PRESIDENT'S INITIATIVE

The New Deal–Old Court confrontation had already generated a wave of proposals for constitutional amendment before the 1936 election. Thirty-nine distinct amendments directed at the crisis were submitted during the preceding Congressional term. They ranged widely, but most focused on the issues of federal power and free market freedom raised by the President in his front-page assault on *Schechter.* As the Seventy-fifth Congress began its work after the election, both the Senate majority leader, Joseph Robinson, and the Speaker of the House, William Bankhead, gave the question a high priority: "Admittedly such an amendment would provoke much debate and require time," Robinson stated on January 2, but it "may prove the best method." This announcement made the front page of the *New York Times,* which concluded that "Senator Robinson's support of the amendment idea served to make the question one of the main issues awaiting the new Congress."[6] On January 8, the *Times* ran another front-page headline, "Basic Law Change Gains in Congress":

> Declaring himself in complete sympathy with President Roosevelt's objectives, Speaker Bankhead said: "I hope a way can be found to reach these objectives without resort to a constitutional amendment, but, unless the personnel of the Supreme Court changes we will run head-on into the same situation we faced before. I still do not see how we can escape a constitutional amendment."[7]

The Congressional leadership, naturally enough, focused on the possibility of formal amendment, since this would give them the greatest control in formulating the terms of the New Deal revolution.

But the next move was Roosevelt's. Since Article Five does not explicitly involve the Presidency in the process, he could afford to speculate more broadly about his options. In the aftermath of the electoral landslide, we hear him telling close associates: "Since the election he had received a great many suggestions that he move for a constitutional convention for the United States and observed that there was no way of keeping such an affair from getting out of hand what with Coughlin and other crackpots about. But there is more than one way of killing a cat."[8]

Roosevelt's remark is arresting. At a time when Stalin was running Show Trials and Hitler was proclaiming Nuremberg Laws, could Americans show the world that a mobilized citizenry might radically reconstruct their government "through reason and choice"?[9]

What is more, the modern republic has paid a heavy price for the President's failure to seize the moment. In many ways the 1787 text is unequal to the realities of Presidential leadership and bureaucratic government. America might have a better constitution today if Americans of the 1930's had tried to rewrite the text to confront these emergent realities.

Then again, Roosevelt might well have been right to shy away. Perhaps his fears of a demagogic field day expressed more than his personal anxieties about losing control over the agenda. Even if a convention had come up with a serious response to the problems and promises of activist government, perhaps its solutions would not have withstood the test of time?

We will never know. Our task is to understand the Constitution we have, not the one that might have been. And the real Constitution owes much to Roosevelt's decision to "kill his cat" without calling a convention—and without ceding his leading role to Congress.

Presidential Leadership

On February 5, the President unveiled his famous court-packing plan. He proposed a statute that would give him the power to nominate a new Supreme Court Justice whenever any sitting member reached the age of 70. Incumbents would not be required to resign; but if they held on, the Court would be expanded in size to admit the younger Justice as an equal. The size of the Court would be in the control of the elder Justices; if they tightened their grip on power, the panel could expand to the new statutory limit of fifteen; but if they took the hint, the Court would remain at nine: it is a "subject of delicacy," the President gently put it, but the old folks were not generally up to the physical and intellectual challenges of modern litigation. So why shouldn't the Justices do the right thing, accept a guaranteed pension tendered by the statute in the name of a grateful nation, and give way to younger jurists more in tune with the times?

In his opening presentation, Roosevelt avoided a direct critique of the Court's constitutional doctrine. He presented his initiative as part of a broader reform that applied to judges at all levels. His rejuvenation effort was, in turn, presented as only one part of a larger reorganization of the entire judicial system.

Rather than attacking the conservatives on the court, the President playfully pointed out that the very conservative Justice McReynolds had made a similar proposal when he was Wilson's Attorney General—except that McReynolds had restricted himself to the lower courts. Roosevelt blandly assured his audience that he was simply extending McReynolds's clever idea to all courts. In the same spirit, Attorney General Homer Cummings supplied a technocratic appendix suggesting that old-timers on all levels needed help keeping up with their dockets. Overall, the President presented himself as if he were a pragmatic problem solver more than a constitutional revolutionary.[10]

In the eyes of opponents, this pose merely added deceit to the President's other sins. But from a technical point of view, the President's initial indirection improved his legal position. There is nothing in the constitutional text that specifies the size of the Court—which, as we have seen, was changed especially frequently during the Civil War and Reconstruction. No serious constitutionalist has ever denied that Congress and the President have the power to reorganize the judiciary to enhance its efficiency. By explicitly placing his actions on this ground, the President vastly increased the likelihood that the Old Court would accept the constitutionality of court-packing, should it be adopted.[11]

Moving beyond such (important) questions of strategy, the President's proposal was grounded in a more general approach to constitutional change. As William Leuchtenburg has shown (in the single best article on the subject),[12] Roosevelt's initiative was not—as is sometimes thought[13]—patched together in a few hurried post-election sessions with his Attorney General. It came after years of reflection. Roosevelt's mind repeatedly recurred to the way English Prime Ministers had reduced the veto power of the House of Lords over legislation through a process one might call "Lords-packing." When confronting a resistant upper house, prime ministers had threatened to ask the King to name a sufficient number of peers to guarantee passage by the Lords of the bill approved by the Commons. Such threats were effective in gaining the Lords' assent to the great reform bill of 1832 that began to democratize the House of Commons; two generations later, the strategy was employed in response to the Lords' veto of Lloyd George's budget, which made a first effort to correct the prevailing maldistribution of wealth. On neither occasion was the prime minister obliged to carry out his threat; the very prospect of "Lords-packing" induced the upper house to back down.[14]

Roosevelt repeatedly referred to these precedents as he mulled over his constitutional options during his first term.[15] Since the President understood his New Deal as a continuation of this trans-Atlantic tradition of liberal reform,[16] he was understandably impressed by the British technique. If the threat of "Lords-packing" had been effective in overriding the veto by unelected aristocrats in England, why not use the same technique against the legal aristocracy on the Supreme Court?

This is hardly the first time American revolutionaries had lifted English precedents for their constitutional purposes. As you will recall from Chapter 3, the Federalists had drawn from the well of English precedent in calling for a "constitutional convention" to reorganize the frame of government. Just as Madison looked back to the Glorious Revolution, Roosevelt looked back to the glory days of the 1832 reform bill and the Lloyd George budget.

The difference in historical reference should not blind us to a common understanding of the constitutional project. So far as both Madison and Roosevelt were concerned, they were participating in a larger trans-Atlantic enterprise that had been attempting for centuries to secure and broaden the foundations of constitutional democracy in the English-speaking world.

Congressional Response

When Roosevelt went public with judicial reorganization, he had every reason to expect success. With 331 Democrats in the House and 76 in the Senate, he could afford lots of defections and win the bare majorities needed to pass the statute. Loud protest from the tiny band of Republicans in Congress would only play into his hands—as would the predictable outcry of the overwhelmingly Republican press. He had defeated these "economic royalists" in November and he could defeat them again. The more assertively the Republicans took the lead, the more Roosevelt could portray their protest as a refusal to accept the electoral verdict of 1936.

Recognizing this, the Republicans in Congress did something quite remarkable for politicians. They shut up and tried to recruit Democrats to play the leading oppositionist role.[17] Some conservative Democrats were happy to oblige, but the crucial question was whether any Democrats with liberal credentials would join.

Senator Burton Wheeler's quick and affirmative decision was crucial. A long-time Roosevelt supporter, Wheeler was a strong New Dealer. His bitter break with the Administration cost him a lot back home in Montana, a state exceptionally dependent upon federal largesse. Nonetheless, he took on the leadership of the bipartisan Senate opposition.[18] His place in the national spotlight dramatized to the folks back home that even good New Dealers might find that the President had overstepped the limits of his mandate.

It also deprived Roosevelt of a priceless organizational advantage. Without somebody like Wheeler leading the resistance, the President could have quickly lined up a solid majority through a combination of personal charm, political patronage, and an appeal to the bandwagon effect—get on board now, before I get enough of your fellow Democrats to join and your vote isn't necessary any more! Once Wheeler and a few others put themselves out on a limb, it made sense for other Democrats to play a waiting game—would the tide of public opinion turn for or against the President?

Despite Wheeler's centrality, his constitutional views have not been given adequate attention. Operationally, they represented the terms for a potential compromise. By calling Wheeler into the Oval Office and accepting his terms, Roosevelt would have cut the heart out of the opposition. Nor can there be any doubt that Wheeler—a man who harbored serious Presidential ambitions[19]—would have been happy to return to the fold on his own terms.

Wheeler's views were well-developed. First, he did not try to defend the Old Court's case law. No less than Roosevelt, he recognized that the People were demanding a fundamental change in constitutional direction. Second, and more surprisingly, Wheeler was a strong critic of Article Five. This became clear on February 17, when he introduced (along with Senator Homer Bone) a resolution "that the following article [be] proposed as an amendment to the Constitution":

Section 1. In case the Supreme Court renders any judgment holding any Act of Congress or any provision of any such Act unconstitutional, the question with respect to the constitutionality of such Act or provision shall be promptly submitted to the Congress for its action at the earliest practicable date that the Congress is in session . . .; but no action shall be taken by the Congress upon such question until an election shall have been held at which Members of the House of Representatives are regularly by law to be chosen. If such Act or provision is re-enacted by two-thirds of each House of the Congress to which such Members are elected at such election, such Act or provision shall be deemed to be constitutional and effective from the date of such reenactment.[20]

This proposal is not different in ultimate aim from the President's. If Wheeler's amendment had been enacted, the Supreme Court would have wielded a "suspensive veto," conditional on an override by elected politicians.

But this was precisely the force of Roosevelt's analogy to "Lords-packing." After the crisis provoked by Lloyd George's budget, the Lords had not been reduced to a constitutional nullity. The King's threat to pack the Lords had induced them to trade their traditional veto on legislation for a more conditional one. Henceforward, the Lord's veto could be overridden by the Commons after a pause for reconsideration. Similarly, if Roosevelt had prevailed, most Presidents would have accepted most decisions of the Court without great protest. But if the Justices came down with a line of precedents that generated great public uproar, Presidents would have undoubtedly cited Roosevelt's court-packing precedent and threatened the Court with further packing unless it reconsidered.

In short, *both Wheeler and Roosevelt were devising mechanisms that sought to supplement the existing provisions of Article Five by limiting the Supreme Court to a suspensive veto rather than the absolute veto it had traditionally exercised over democratic legislation.* Indeed, there was a sense in which Wheeler's proposal was more radical. As Harvard's Thomas Reed Powell pointed out in a lead article in the magazine section of the *New York Times:*

> There is a curious paradox about the [President's] proposal. . . . It involves the least interference with existing judicial power of any suggestion that has been made. The court may still act as it has acted before, by ordinary majority and free from overriding of its judicial veto by any legislative reenactment or from recall by any popular vote. All that happens is that the present holders of judicial office are given some helpmates to add fresh viewpoints to their counsel.[21]

Powell is a bit disingenuous, since the precedent-setting character of the President's initiative would have undoubtedly cast a shadow into the future. Nonetheless, isn't he right to suggest that, by providing a formalized mechanism that enabled two-thirds of Congress to override the Court, Wheeler was establishing a mechanism that could be used far more regularly than Presidential threats of court-packing?

The remarkable convergence between the President and his leading critic is suggested further if we return to the path Roosevelt followed in framing his own proposal. As early as December 1935, the President was already consulting his Cabinet about alternatives. Here is how Secretary of the Interior Harold Ickes summarized his views at that time:

> The President pointed out that there were three ways of meeting such a situation: (1) by packing the Supreme Court, which was a distasteful idea; (2) by trying to put through a number of amendments to the Constitution to meet the various situations; and (3) by a method that he asked us to consider very carefully.
>
> The third method is, in substance, this: an amendment to the Constitution conferring explicit power on the Supreme Court to declare acts of Congress unconstitutional, a power which is not given anywhere in the

Constitution as it stands. The amendment would also give the Supreme Court original jurisdiction on constitutional questions affecting statutes. If the Supreme Court should declare an act of Congress to be unconstitutional, then—a congressional election having intervened—if Congress should repass the law so declared to be unconstitutional, the taint of unconstitutionality would be removed and the law would be a valid one. By this method there would be in effect a referendum to the country, although an indirect one. At the intervening congressional election the question of the constitutionality or unconstitutionality of the law would undoubtedly be an issue.[22]

In short, Roosevelt and Wheeler were on the same wavelength.

This convergence is no surprise. Both Wheeler and Roosevelt were expressing opinions that had gained broad currency after decades of political initiatives against the courts by the Progressive and labor movements.[23] Indeed, the roots of Wheeler's proposal reach back to his days as Robert La Follette's running mate on the Presidential ticket of the Progressive Party in 1924. The slate had pledged itself to a similar constitutional amendment as part of a campaign to reinvigorate popular sovereignty: "over and above constitutions and statutes and greater than all, is the supreme sovereignty of the people, and with them should rest the final decision of all great questions of national policy."[24] While Roosevelt remained a regular Democrat during this period, he was in constant contact with Progressive and labor circles.[25]

The President continued to consider Wheeler-style amendments seriously up to the very last moment. Even as he was working with Attorney General Cummings on a court-packing proposal, he was encouraging two leading staffers, Ben Cohen and Tom Corcoran, to work up their own favored option: a formal Article Five amendment. By the time the President went public on February fifth, Cohen and Corcoran had developed an elaborate memo in support of an Article Five amendment similar to Senator Wheeler's.[26] I have also uncovered a memorandum from Cohen to the President, written in the midst of the crisis, that continues to assess the Wheeler-Bone amendment as one of the President's principal alternatives: "If it is possible for any one within the present session to draw an amendment that will command the support of the Senate, I know no one better equipped to do the job than . . . the Senator from Montana [Wheeler]."[27]

I will return to the larger implications of this point later. For now, it is enough to suggest that Wheeler's leadership helped focus the ensuing debate on a narrow, but fundamental, issue—not the need for a substantive revolution in constitutional doctrine, nor even the need for a supplement to the classical amendment procedure of Article Five, but the meta-question: How should the appropriate supplement to Article Five be enacted into higher law?

Wheeler thought that Article Five should be used to amend Article Five; Roosevelt thought that past precedents authorized him to act through court-packing.

THE PUBLIC DEBATE

The President's Court proposal hit the country like a bombshell. "For five months, the mass media, Congress, and the president focused on little else . . . the Court has not since then surfaced so long and so prominently on the public agenda, even during the salad days of the Warren Court"—in the words of Greg Caldeira, whose quantitative study of public opinion should be required reading.[28] The public debate raged on in rallies, assemblies of countless groups and associations, newspaper stories—and also, a sign of the times, the radio. The networks handed out prime time for speechmaking with great generosity.

Another sign of modernity was the Gallup Poll. George Gallup had emerged as the principal beneficiary of the notorious poll conducted by the *Literary Digest* predicting a Landon victory in 1936. The *Digest* had used a telephone survey at a time when few had the device; Gallup deployed more scientific sampling methods and detected the impending landslide. He now followed up by providing weekly probes on the Court issue. Given the primitive state of polling, I do not want to put much weight on the results. But the data do suggest that the broader public was actively engaged. By the seventeenth of February—twelve days after Roosevelt's announcement—only 10 percent of Gallup's sample failed to express an opinion, and this number did not fluctuate much until the "switch in time" began.[29] Gallup's polling also suggested that public opinion was in flux. In its regular broadcasts of Gallup's results, NBC reported that a strong majority favored some basic change in the Court, but the country was sharply divided on Roosevelt's particular proposal—with New England and the Midwest opposed, the mid-Atlantic states in a dead heat, and the South and West in favor of the President. NBC regularly reported national opinion as narrowly against court-packing during February; but, as we shall see, it evolved significantly as the debate proceeded.[30]

Tapes of network radio broadcasts confirm Wheeler's central role. Not only did he give a hard-hitting speech on February 19 but other progressives—ranging from Senator Gerald Nye[31] to former Brain Truster Raymond Moley[32]—presented prime-time speeches in support of the Wheeler-Bone approach. Even Herbert Hoover began his radio address by saying that he would "gladly follow" the leadership of "eminent Senators belonging to the President's own party"[33] and endorsed their insistence on Article Five as the proper path for constitutional revision.[34]

At the same time, the Administration fielded a powerful set of speakers for the radio audience. Attorney General Cummings took the lead on February 14, recounting the long history of efforts to encourage the retirement of elderly judges and denying that any constitutional violation was involved in reinvigorating the judiciary with younger men.[35] He was followed by Senator Sherman Minton, who treated his listeners to a long historical account of Presidential struggles against the Court—placing special emphasis on Reconstruction precedents involving Court contraction and expansion.[36] The political case was developed further in a powerful speech by the governor of Wisconsin, young Phil La Follette, who specifically argued against the amendment proposal of Burton Wheeler, his father's 1924 running mate.[37]

The debate culminated with two addresses by the President in early March. His first speech targeted the Court and asked how the Administration could fulfill its campaign commitments to farmers, workers, and other groups given judicial resistance to "a progressive solution of our problems."[38] Democracy had failed throughout the world because people had "become so fed up with futile [d]ebate and party bickerings." The "three horse team of the American system of government" could not function "if one horse lies down in the traces or plunges off in another direction."[39] He then invoked his popular mandate: "In three elections during the past five years great majorities have approved what we are trying to do. To me, and I am sure to you, those majorities mean that the people themselves realize the increasing urgency that we meet their needs now. Every delay creates risks of intervening events which make more and more difficult an intelligent, speedy, and democratic solution of our difficulties."[40]

This message contrasts sharply with Roosevelt's initial presentation in February. He no longer treats court-packing as a bland matter of enhancing efficiency. He now advances the proposal as a spokesman for "the people themselves," who insist on a Court that expresses the will of the "great majorities" the Democratic Party has gained "[i]n three elections during the past five years."

Roosevelt's second speech came the night before the Senate Judiciary Committee began its hearings. In his "fireside chat," Roosevelt directly confronted the demand for a formal amendment:

> There are many types of amendment proposed. Each one is radically different from the other. There is no substantial group within the Congress or outside it who are agreed on any single amendment.
>
> It would take months or years to get substantial agreement upon the type and language of an amendment. It would take months and years thereafter to get a two-thirds majority in favor of that amendment in *both* Houses of the Congress.
>
> Then would come the long course of ratification by three-fourths of all the States. No amendment which any powerful economic interests or the leaders of any powerful political party have had reason to oppose has ever been ratified within anything like a reasonable time. And thirteen States which contain only five percent of the voting population can block ratification even though the thirty-five States with ninety-five percent of the population are in favor of it. . . .
>
> Two groups oppose my plan on the ground that they favor a constitutional amendment. The first includes those who fundamentally object to social and economic legislation along modern lines. This is the same group who during the campaign last Fall tried to block the mandate of the people.
>
> Now they are making a last stand. And the strategy of that last stand is to suggest the time-consuming process of amendment in order to kill off by delay the legislation demanded by the mandate.
>
> To them I say: I do not think you will be able long to fool the American people as to your purposes.
>
> The other group is composed of those who honestly believe the amend-

ment process is the best and who would be willing to support a reasonable amendment if they could agree on one.

To them I say: we cannot rely on an amendment as the immediate or only answer to our present difficulties. When the time comes for action, you will find that many of those who pretend to support you will sabotage any constructive amendment which is proposed. Look at these strange bed-fellows of yours. When before have you found them really at your side in your fights for progress?

And remember one thing more. Even if an amendment were passed, and even if in the years to come it were to be ratified, its meaning would depend upon the kind of Justices who would be sitting on the Supreme Court bench. An amendment, like the rest of the Constitution, is what the Justices say it is rather than what its framers or you might hope it is.[41]

This radio broadcast marks the first higher lawmaking success of 1937. A crucial test for a dualistic constitution, especially at moments of crisis, is to induce protagonists to join issue on central problems. This is tougher than it sounds, given the strategic temptations to evade arguments rather than answer them. And yet, in this fireside chat, the most powerful politician of the twentieth century was obliged to accept dialogic discipline even in the aftermath of his greatest electoral triumph.

This turnaround is, pretty transparently, a product of the separation of powers. But we should avoid an unduly mechanistic account of the dynamic: it took courage for Senator Wheeler to accept the big political risks involved in leading the opposition in February. Wheeler's decision, in turn, altered the Presidential calculus. Since court-packing would now pass through a *serious* process of Senatorial deliberation, Roosevelt would have been foolish to let his critics monopolize the field of constitutional principle. It was in Roosevelt's interest not only to speak in a higher lawmaking voice, but also to mobilize public support for his side of the argument.

The impact of Wheeler's leadership went further. The President would have vastly preferred treating his opponents' praise of Article Five as a smokescreen for a cynical conservative effort "to block the mandate of the people." With New Dealers like Wheeler at the forefront of opposition, Roosevelt was now obliged to recognize the good faith of "those who honestly believe the amendment process is best."

Part of Roosevelt's response was fundamental but familiar: Article Five gives a small minority of states too large a role in the higher lawmaking system. Like the Reconstruction Republicans before him, Roosevelt believed his Party had won a "mandate" from the People by winning a series of decisive victories on the national level. So far as he was concerned, Five was defective in allowing a small minority to frustrate this national mandate: "thirteen States which contain only five percent of the voting population can block ratification even though the thirty-five States with ninety-five percent of the population are in favor of it." And like Madison and Bingham before him, he refused to allow this to occur.

Only this time, he could appeal to the People of the *United* States with far greater confidence than his predecessors. He was speaking at a unique moment in American history—unlike eighteenth-century Federalists or nineteenth-century Republicans, twentieth-century Democrats had swept all regions of the country by wide margins. Given this fact, the President was on strong ground in arguing that Article Five was unnecessary to protect a powerful regional interest from a national override. He could plausibly portray formal amendment as a mechanism enabling special interests to concentrate their financial resources on a few unrepresentative states and frustrate the broad and deep judgments of the Nation. So far as federalism was concerned, the case for unconventional action was stronger in 1937 than it was in 1866 or 1787.

There is a second and more novel aspect to Roosevelt's fireside chat. It explicitly questions the capacity of Article Five formalisms to channel constitutional law into new directions: "An amendment . . . is what the Justices say it is rather than what its framers or you might hope it is." Neither Federalist Founders nor Republican Reconstructers held such deep doubts about the power of legal formulae to shape the future.[42] This jurisprudential strand of Roosevelt's argument was powerfully reinforced at the Senate hearings.

THE SENATE HEARINGS

The opening days of the hearings mirrored the evolution of the Administration's position over the past weeks. Attorney General Cummings presented the line of early February: old judges couldn't keep up the pace, and the fact they were on the Supreme Court did not make the problem go away. He was followed by Robert Jackson, the Assistant Attorney General, who elaborated more recent Presidential themes.

Jackson's Brief

Like Roosevelt's fireside chat, Jackson's testimony defended court-packing as a *legitimate* "method of bringing the elective and nonelective branches of the Government back into a proper coordination. Its frequent use has avoided amendments which would make the Constitution a document of patches and details."[43]

As in the radio debates, Jackson emphasized that the size of the Court had changed six times in American history, making particularly powerful use of Reconstruction-era precedents.[44] He also pointed to the limited success of previous efforts to overrule the Court by amendment. The efforts of the Reconstruction Congress to overrule *Dred Scott* with three formal amendments had not transformed the Court into a reliable guardian of minority rights. The Court had not fully respected constitutional amendments that had overruled its decisions on the income tax and sovereign immunity from suit in federal court. Yet these problems were easy in comparison with the ones faced by the New Dealers: "To offset the effect of the judicial attitude reflected in recent decisions it would be necessary to amend not only the commerce clause and the due-process clause, but the equal protection clause, the privilege and immunities clause, the tenth amendment, the bankruptcy power, and the taxing and spending power."[45] Jackson challenged his listeners to grapple with the formalist idea, at the core of Article Five, that constitutional law may be transformed through a few cogent formulae: "It may be possible by more words to clarify words, but it is not possible by words to change a state of mind."[46] If "you cannot amend a state of mind," isn't court-packing the best way to push constitutional law in a new direction?

Wheeler's Testimony

Eager for a quick vote, the Administration called a halt to its testimony after two weeks, leaving it to Wheeler to open the argument for the opposition. He began by brandishing a surprise weapon: a letter from Chief Justice Hughes confronting the efficiency arguments presented by Roosevelt in early February. Far from slacking at their job, Hughes assured the Senate that the Justices were up on their work. Indeed, an expansion from nine to fifteen only threatened to bollix up the works. Hughes's letter was a public relations bombshell—marking the express entry of the Court into constitutional politics.[47]

But Wheeler was much more than the Court's publicity agent. As a result of his efforts, both Roosevelt and Jackson had moved the case for court-packing far beyond the efficiency questions with which Hughes's letter was concerned. And Wheeler was determined to use his platform to reassert the constitutional principle that separated him from the President. As before, he denied that he spoke for a bunch of Senatorial stand-patters who rejected the need for constitutional revision: "if the President will abandon the scheme to pack the Supreme Court, [we will] vote to submit to the people of this country any reasonable amendment to carry out his objective that he will submit to this Congress."[48] To establish his good faith, Wheeler restated the case for his amendment:

> SENATOR WHEELER. . . . The necessities of the time have made it necessary for us to pass many laws where there may be doubt as to whether they are constitutional and when we do we say that after all the Supreme Court will pass upon it, and if it is not constitutional then they will so decide. If the Supreme Court held that some of these laws were unconstitutional, there would be very few of their decisions, in my judgment, which would be overruled, and they would not be overruled unless there was an overwhelming sentiment in this country against those decisions; and if there was such sentiment, then I think that it should be declared the law, notwithstanding, because I am one of those who believe in democracy with a small "d." . . .

> SENATOR PITTMAN. But is it not a fact that waiting until after another election would make it a political question?

> SENATOR WHEELER. No; not at all. The object is to give time for deliberate consideration to the Senate of the United States and to the House. . . . [I]f you allowed that cooling time, then the House and the Senate would say, after they had looked at that decision, "After all, the Supreme Court has said this is unconstitutional. I voted for it then, but I never gave it much consideration as to its constitutionality; or I

thought it was constitutional, but I have got before me the decision of the Supreme Court saying it is unconstitutional."

SENATOR PITTMAN. . . . [I]t seems evident that, as you place it after a congressional election, you desire that the people should have the right to elect a Congress to act upon that matter.

SENATOR WHEELER. . . . I think the question would undoubtedly be made an issue in the next campaign. The question would be whether or not the people of this country favor this law, and if the overwhelming majority of two-thirds is elected which favor that law, and the people demand it, I think if we are going to preserve democracy in this country it is entirely proper, the people having spoken, that we should pass that law, notwithstanding the decision of the Supreme Court.[49]

These remarks share a common aspiration with Roosevelt's. The Senator, no less than the President, is searching for a new higher lawmaking mechanism that will cut the states out of the process.

They differ only in selecting the national institution that should take the lead in speaking for the nation. Wheeler built his model on Congressional leadership—designing a procedure through which two-thirds of the House and Senate could plausibly claim a mandate from the People for taking action after a general election. According to Roosevelt, the Democrats had already won such a mandate: "In three elections during the past five years great majorities have approved what we are trying to do. To me, and I am sure to you, those majorities mean that the people themselves realize the increasing urgency that we meet their needs now."[50]

The competition between models of Presidential and Congressional leadership also structured the protagonists' proposed remedies. Under Wheeler's scheme, the Presidency did not have any role in overriding the Supreme Court. A Congressional super-majority, after an intervening electoral debate and decision, was enough to do the trick. Under Roosevelt's approach, a constitutional revolution could occur if the President obtained the consent of a majority of the Senate to a series of transformative judicial appointments. Congress qua Congress was cut out of the system.

The same competition informed the debate about Article Five. Since Wheeler was unprepared to accept the model of Presidential leadership, he believed that an *appropriate* popular mandate had not yet been elaborated, and that a formal amendment was needed to make it clear, once and for all, that We the People could legitimately speak through national institutions. In contrast, Roosevelt held that the Democrats had already won the requisite mandate.

But Wheeler did more than testify. He was busily at work generating Senatorial support for his proposal. On March 2, Republican Senator Arthur Vandenberg took to the radio, and in the words of the *New York Times:* "Abandoning the earlier Republican strategy of letting the Democrats fight out the issue of Supreme Court reorganization among themselves, Senator Vandenberg tonight denounced the President's proposal and expressed favor for the Wheeler-Bone amendment." The Senator added an important caveat: "Measures violating the human rights guaranteed in the first ten amendments . . . would be excepted, perhaps, in this amendment."[51] Wheeler was quick to agree to Vandenberg's suggestion[52]—though the bipartisan coalition never seemed to worked out explicit language on this point. Two weeks later, the first page of the *New York Herald Tribune* was reporting that the "leaders of the Senate opposition . . . had agreed to consolidate on a constitutional amendment as a 'constructive alternative'":

> The choice today appeared to be narrowing to two proposals. One is the Wheeler-Bone amendment permitting Congress after an intervening election to override by a two-thirds vote a judicial invalidation . . .
>
> The other is the O'Mahoney amendment requiring at least two-thirds of the Supreme Court to agree on the unconstitutionality of an act of Federal or State Legislatures before such a law should be invalidated.
>
> Within two weeks a meeting is expected to be held at which a definite choice will be determined by the opposition spokesmen.[53]

Wheeler's dramatic testimony at the hearings gave a further boost to his alternative. But as the opposition considered its next step, a new reality began to emerge. On Monday, March 29—the precise day named by the *Tribune* for the unveiling of the opposition's "constructive alternative"—the Supreme Court went public with its first great decision announcing a doctrinal "switch in time."

Before assessing the significance of this move, reflect on the remarkable evolution of debate in the two months since Roosevelt's initiative of February 5. At that point, the President dressed up his constitutional revolution in the language of normal politics and confronted his Democratic supporters in Congress with a fait accompli. If Roosevelt had possessed the powers of a British prime minister, he could have whipped his Party in line despite the shouts of a few backbenchers.

But the constitutional separation of powers had enabled Wheeler to pick apart the constitutional issues that the President had hoped to jumble together. Wheeler spoke for New Dealers who were fully prepared to accept Roosevelt's demand for substantive constitutional change but insisted that it be channelled through Article Five. There was more than drama here: Wheeler's proposed amendment showed a genuine effort to struggle with many of the very themes that motivated Roosevelt's end run around Article Five.

It was now in the President's strategic interest to confront his constitutional critics and explain why the federalist forms of Article Five could not be relied upon to codify the nation-wide mandate the Democrats had obtained through repeated landslide victories. The Administration pursued its critique before a variety of audiences and at different levels of sophistication: in fireside chats by the President, in legal presentations by Assistant Attorney General Jackson. In response, the opposition was hard at work formulating its own constructive alternatives.

By any reckoning, this give-and-take must be reckoned as one of the great triumphs of America's dualist constitution. Until the Court intervened, the protagonists were leading the nation into a profoundly serious debate about the future of higher lawmaking in the next era of American public life.

The Switch—and Its Alternatives

But the Court did intervene, by switching sides, and thereby took the steam out of this great debate. Gallup polls, analyzed by political scientist Greg Caldeira, show that early public reaction to court-packing was unfavorable, with negatives outpolling positives by seven or eight percentage points during the first four weeks. But once the President changed his rhetorical strategy and took to the airwaves in early March, the polls tell a different story. On the eve of the Court's "switch," Gallup was reporting a close division of opinion.[54]

Then came two sharp, and statistically significant, breaks in Presidential support. The Court's 5-to-4 decision upholding the Wagner Act in April was immediately followed by a drop of almost five percentage points. When conservative Justice Van Devanter announced his resignation in May, support for the President dropped by five more points—for good reason, since it suggested that the "switch" was not temporary, but that the liberals would gain further judicial reinforcement without the need to expand the court. Only at this point had the balance of public opinion swung decisively against the President. All in all, these data suggest that large sections of the public were following the debate very closely and quite rationally withdrew their support from Roosevelt after the Court gave a visible assurance that it would no longer endanger the emerging constitutional order. In Caldeira's words, "regardless of the intentions of the participants, the Supreme Court's behavior made a difference [on public opinion]. . . . Through a series of shrewd moves, the Court put President Roosevelt in the position of arguing for a radical reform on the slimmest of justifications."[55]

It is easy to find similar assessments in the commentary of the period. In its banner headline story on the Supreme Court's surprising decision to uphold the Labor Act, the *New York Times* reported that "Senator Wheeler, generalissimo of the fight in Congress against the President's court plan, seemed particularly elated. . . . 'The decisions were great,' he said, 'I feel now that there cannot be any excuse left for wanting to add six new members to the Supreme Court.'"[56] Joseph Alsop and Turner Catledge, two leading newspapermen, interviewed the leading participants in the crisis, except for Roosevelt himself, and published an insightful book, *The 168 Days.* Here is their assessment: "Two great tactical advantages . . . helped the President—the Democratic party tie, and the need for a solution to the court problem—and it was pretty clear that unless the second advantage could somehow be taken from him he would win in the end."[57] By the time the Justices were coming down with their final big decision of the term, upholding the Social Security Act, *Time Magazine* was reporting that "to many an ardent New Dealer there would have been a very silvery lining in a decision finding this New Deal law unconstitutional. That would have given them fresh proof that more Justices were needed to liberalize the Court."[58]

But the switch not only undercut popular support for the President.

It also took the sails out of the movement for Article Five amendments. It was increasingly unclear which amendments, if any, were still
necessary. Perhaps the Court's switch would make all further work
unnecessary? By May, Congressional leaders were already putting Article Five back on the shelf until they got a chance to see what the
Court would do next.[59]

And then there was the challenge of obtaining the support of three-
fourths of the states. It was one thing to leap over this barrier if the
Court kept provoking public opinion by striking down New Deal
measures on behalf of workers, farmers, and the elderly. But why
spend time and energy on an exhausting campaign for formal amendment when the Court was legitimating activist government through its
transformative opinions?

All this returns us to an issue posed at the outset: Did the switch
come too soon? A speculative question, but a useful one if we hope for
a deeper understanding of the New Deal revolution. So let us consider
the range of likely outcomes that an intransigent Court might have
provoked.

The Court-Packing Scenario

Most obviously, the President could have won the battle for court-
packing.[60] Just as the Court's switch prompted a marked decline in
Roosevelt's public support, continued judicial resistance would have
played into his hands, allowing him to present court-packing as the
only practical solution to the crisis. Would Wheeler and the rest have
been able to withstand the resulting Presidential juggernaut?

The fragility of the opposition is suggested in an outstanding study
by William Leuchtenburg. Despite the President's loss of public support by May, his court-packing initiative underwent a remarkable
renaissance in June. Roosevelt then reluctantly accepted his Congressional leaders' proposal of a "compromise" under which he would
have to wait until a Justice turned 75, rather than 70, to nominate a
replacement, and would be limited to one such nomination in a single
year. Since there were four members (in addition to Van Devanter)
over 75, this would have guaranteed the President five appointments
by 1940. When viewed in political terms, this represented a significant concession by the President—since the original plan allowed

him to make six appointments all at once. But from the long-term view of constitutional principle, it was no compromise at all.

And yet, as Leuchtenburg shows, the Congressional leadership used the "compromise" to engineer a remarkable recovery in the President's political fortunes. By the time the amended bill reached the Senate floor in July, Majority Leader Robinson was confidently claiming majority support. Leuchtenburg argues that he wasn't only puffing: "[t]hough the press was overwhelmingly antagonistic to the proposal, Capitol Hill correspondents credited Robinson with fifty or more commitments."[61] It is true, Leuchtenberg concedes, that "the opposition, with its estimated forty-four votes, might well mount a filibuster, but many doubted that a filibuster would succeed."[62]

We will never know, thanks to one of the great accidents of constitutional history. After the first days of impassioned debate, Senator Robinson died of a heart attack, and with his death expired all the political debts he had cashed to create the Administration's majority. Roosevelt found his support melting in the heat of a particularly hellish Washington summer. Worse yet, a fierce struggle broke out amongst the Senate Democrats for Robinson's position. Roosevelt responded by concentrating his energies on putting a committed New Dealer into this crucial position. He succeeded, but only at the cost of jettisoning the court plan.

I do not claim that only Robinson's death stopped court-packing; to me, the speedy collapse of support suggests the opposite.[63] But Leuchtenburg's study suggests how formidable the President would have been if his support had been soaring instead of sagging as an intransigent Court continued to provoke public opinion. If the Congressional leadership got so far despite the loss of popular support, how hard would it have been to win assent from 49 of 76 Democrats in the Senate and 218 of 331 Democrats in the House when the public was up in arms?

Not that Congressional passage of a court-packing bill would have ended matters. The Republicans could have responded by making court-packing the centerpiece of the upcoming elections—filibustering against the nominations of new Justices, denouncing the crime of 1937, and so forth. At this point, 1938 might have been marked down with 1866 as an "off-year" election of epic significance. With Roosevelt and the Democrats campaigning forcefully in favor of court-packing, and the Republicans declaiming against, the results would have been redolent with constitutional meaning. Given the lopsided Democratic majorities of the time, it is hard to imagine an all-out Republican victory.[64] But would a sufficient increase in Republican support have precipitated a movement to repeal court-packing?

Of course, if the Democrats had won in 1938, the result would have had a powerful "bandwagon effect"—once the President had gotten both the Congress and the voters behind court-packing, could there be any serious doubt that he had won the People's support for his unconventional initiative?

The Article Five Scenario

Suppose, in contrast, that Wheeler and his coalition had managed to sustain a filibuster even as the Administration organized blocs of workers, farmers, and old folks enraged by the Court's continued war on the liberal welfare state. After seeing his court-packing initiative bogged down in endless guerrilla war in the Senate, suppose the President called the Senator into the Oval Office to recall Wheeler's promise at the hearings:

> Do not misunderstand me. I have no pride of authorship. I am willing to submerge my views. I am more than willing, and every other man I have talked to who has introduced an amendment is willing to submerge his views, and we are willing to accept, if the President will abandon the scheme to pack the Supreme Court, to vote to submit to the people of this country any reasonable amendment to carry out his objective that he will submit to this Congress.[65]

Taking up this offer, Roosevelt would have had little trouble persuading his fellow Democrats in Congress to extricate themselves from their internecine battle by giving their overwhelming support to the Wheeler-Roosevelt amendments.

What would these missing amendments have said?

An Aborted Conversation

The crisis had provoked the submission of sixty-six distinct proposals for amendment during the Seventy-fifth Congress, but all were not created equal. Only a few were taken seriously by the press and the Congress, and they displayed recurring patterns.

The first group consisted of federal power enhancers. These took the Old Court at its word when it insisted that the 1787 Constitution had created a federal government of limited powers, and sought to add more to the list. Speaker Bankhead and Senate leader Robinson had already moved in this direction before the President sprung his February surprise. Their proposals were relatively modest, granting the federal government authority over hours, wages, and working conditions. The amendment sponsored by the powerful Chairman of the Senate Judiciary Committee, Henry Ashurst, was broader, enabling Congress "to regulate agriculture, commerce, industry, and labor."[66] I suspect that Roosevelt would have insisted on more encompassing language along the lines proposed by "Senator Costigan of Colorado [who] urged the president to seek an amendment empowering Congress to legislate for the general welfare where states could not effectively do so . . . FDR thought enough of the proposal to want to discuss it further with Costigan in a White House meeting."[67] Since the President would have taken an embarrassing step by withdrawing his court-packing proposal and seeking a compromise with Wheeler, the Congressional leadership would have given him broad leeway in formulating the Article Five alternative.

Congressional debate on a second front was less advanced. There was a pervasive recognition of the Court's yeoman's service in protecting individual rights, but Congress found it hard to frame amendments that would preserve this function without causing other difficulties. The most obvious problem was posed by the "due process" clauses of the Fifth and Fourteenth Amendments. The Old Court had used these provisions primarily to protect private property and freedom of contract, but it had also safeguarded other rights—most notably, freedom of expression and religion. How were the New Dealers to separate the wheat from the chaff?

Proposed solutions lacked the incisiveness displayed by the power-granting amendments. A proposal by Senator Edward Costigan, for example,[68] began by granting the federal government "power to regulate hours and conditions of labor and to establish minimum wages in any employment and to regulate production, industry, business, trade, and commerce to prevent unfair methods and practices." It went on:

Sec. 2. The due process of law clauses of the fifth and fourteenth amendments shall be construed to impose no limitations upon legislation by the Congress or by the several states with respect to any of the subjects referred to in section 1, except as to the methods or the procedure for the enforcement of such legislation.

This "linking strategy" expressed the New Deal determination to bar the Court from obstructing the use of government's new powers over the economy. But it did so in a blunderbuss fashion. Suppose, for example, that a state denied unemployment compensation to Jews and Seventh-Day Adventists who refused to work on Saturday. Section two would have barred a court from scrutinizing this practice. But wasn't this going too far?[69]

Some amendments tried to be more discriminating. Senator Hamilton Lewis restricted the Fourteenth Amendment "only to natural persons and not to corporate or other artificial persons created by law."[70] But this was too timid, allowing a conservative Court to strike down maximum-hours legislation as a violation of *workers'* contractual rights.

Some proposals were more ingenious. Senator William Borah's amendment, like Costigan's, insisted that the "due process clause" should be restricted "only to the procedure [used in connection with] the execution and enforcement of the law." It then went on to enumerate particular rights, traditionally protected by "substantive due process," that should be preserved in the emerging regime:

No State shall make or enforce any law respecting an establishment of religion or prohibiting the free exercise thereof; or abridging the freedom of speech, or of the press; or the right of the people peaceably to assemble; and to petition the State or the Government for a redress of grievances.[71]

Borah is filling the conceptual vacuum left by the disintegration of *Lochnerian* notions of private property and freedom of contract by lifting some hallowed formulae from the First Amendment. This approach would have a bright future in the modern republic. Over time, the Court would go beyond Borah's limited "incorporation" of First Amendment formulas and impose on the states all provisions of the Bill of Rights it considered fundamental to American liberty. Indeed, the Court would move beyond "incorporation" of traditional texts to redefine basic rights in terms that spoke in the twentieth-century language of New Deal liberalism.[72]

It is hard to say whether a similar conversation would have taken place in the New Deal Congress if it had been forced by an intransigent Court to take its higher lawmaking responsibilities seriously. This particular debate had not gotten very far at the time of the Court's switch. An approach to rights-definition might well have emerged that was very different from Costigan's or Lewis's or Borah's.

Turning finally to a third strand in the Congressional conversation, a host of proposals sought to redefine institutional relationships. Some were simple spin-offs of the court-packing controversy. For example, diehard opponents of the President proposed amendments that explicitly limited the number of Justices to nine, while others in the middle sought to constitutionalize aspects of the President's plan—requiring the Justices to retire at 70 or 75.[73] Of the relatively modest proposals, Senator Joseph O'Mahoney's was taken most seriously. This would have required a two-thirds vote by the Justices before the Court could strike down a statute as unconstitutional.[74] This would have made a short-term difference to particular pieces of New Deal legislation, but its long-term impact would have depended on how the Justices administered the rule.[75]

In contrast to Senator O'Mahoney, Senator Wheeler had much larger ambitions—aiming for nothing less than a broad-ranging redefinition of the relationships between Court, Congress, and the People. Moreover, the President was himself strongly attracted to Wheeler's plan—which shared his own ambition of creating a system whereby the People of the *United* States could make their constitutional will known independently of state political processes. It seems a good bet, then, that a Wheeler-style amendment would have had a prominent place in the New Deal proposal, joined by a suitable federal power enhancer and an individual rights guarantee.

This is, to be sure, a formidable package. But after all, the New Deal Democrats who were preparing these proposals had actually won the kind of broad and sustained mandate from the People that the Founding Federalists and Reconstruction Republicans had only dreamed about. Surely they were no less entitled to make higher law than their predecessors?

The Ratification Scenario

Of course, the question remains whether the New Dealers could have carried three-fourths of the states in the campaign for ratification. We have already heard Roosevelt attack this federalist feature of Article Five, and there can be no doubt that he genuinely feared the power of "economic royalists" to buy their way to victory in thirteen states. At the same time, defeat was by no means foreordained. Here is the way Wheeler put the point in his radio address of February 19:

> We have just taken part in an election in which the President of the United States carried 46 out of the 48 states. In 38 states Democratic governors were elected and in three other states liberal governors were elected. In view of this recent election, if the President of the United States would put his influence back of an amendment such as [I propose], it would be ratified in a very short time. Apparently there are those among the President's advisors who suggest that such a measure could not be enacted, but I say to them that if the recent election was not a mandate for social reform, as I believe it was, then it is time for all of us to find out who won the election. . . .
>
> I am for a liberal Constitution. I recognize that the instrument is the fundamental expression of the People's will. . . . I am ready for the amendment to the Constitution, and I believe that the people of this country are ready for such an amendment, but I want it to be amended by the People in the way they have provided and not by packing the Court to make it subservient to anyone's desires. . . .
>
> We must do the right thing in the right way. This is no strategy of delay. It is the strategy of the right, of permanence, of real and abiding relief.[76]

While Wheeler emphasizes the results of the gubernatorial races, the 1936 elections had also swept Democrats into power in the state legislatures throughout the land, putting them in charge of both houses in thirty-three states. Of the remainder, two states were non-partisan, seven were divided between Democrats and Republicans, and only six were solidly Republican.[77]

Wheeler's audience was also well aware that Prohibition repeal had gained approval after Congress specified that the amendment be ratified through special conventions elected for the purpose in each state. The result was a quick series of special elections that resembled referenda—with slates of delegates pledged to opposite sides of the Prohibition question. As Wheeler noted, these special elections generated the necessary three-fourths majority within the short space of ten months.[78] There was nothing to prevent Congress from taking a similar step if Roosevelt were seriously troubled by the prospect of special interests sabotaging the New Deal initiatives in the state legislatures.[79]

After a detailed study of the underlying data, Rafael Gely and Pablo Spiller have recently concluded that "the 1936 election results . . . provided for the first time a realistic threat of a constitutional amendment being enacted at the state level."[80] If this is true, perhaps we have been too quick to applaud as Chief Justice Hughes and Mr. Justice Roberts finally saw the light and led the Court to embrace the New Deal revolution?

HYPERTEXTUALISM REVISITED

The next chapter takes this question up in earnest. But let me conclude this one by returning to the problem with which it began—my encounters with lawyers and judges who suppose that the absence of Article Five amendments preclude them from self-consciously recognizing the constitutional creativity of the New Deal.

Of course, this entire book tries to establish that a monopolistic reading of Article Five does not make sense of either the Founding or Reconstruction, let alone the New Deal. But I think that this chapter's microhistory provides independent support for a pluralistic reading of our great higher lawmaking precedents. It not only reveals that the Court killed off a great debate that could well have led the People to express themselves in the way the formalist demands. It also suggests that the Court was a prime target of this debate—with Article Five's leading defender, Burton Wheeler, proposing to use the formalist system to destroy the Court's traditional veto power over ordinary legislation. Even if Wheeler had forced Roosevelt to take the Article Five path, the Court was the likely loser. In short, the Justices were confronting a fundamental decision in March of 1937: on the one hand, they could stick to their guns in defense of the *Lochnerian* Constitution and run the clear and present danger that the People would formally repudiate the Court's traditional role in the separation

of powers; on the other hand, they could eliminate the risk of hostile
Article Five amendment by unequivocally recognizing the constitutional legitimacy of the New Deal vision of activist government. Given
this reality, it would be especially wrong for today's judges to dismiss
the significance of the New Deal revolution on the ground that it had
not given birth to formal amendments—when it was only by avoiding
such amendments that the Supreme Court eliminated the risk of permanent institutional damage.

I want to distinguish this point from the old and tired debate about
the subjective motivations of the two Justices—Hughes and
Roberts—who engineered the switch by forming a solid bloc with the
three so-called liberals, Brandeis, Cardozo, and Stone. Unsurprisingly,
the evidence on this matter is equivocal.[81] But even if Roberts and
Hughes had been apolitical legalists of legendary proportion, I could
not care less. I am not interested in the hidden wellsprings of their
private motives, but in the constitutional meaning of their public
actions. Whatever they intended, their actions had a predictable
meaning in the Court's ongoing conversation with the President, the
Congress, and the People of the United States. Instead of asserting the
continued relevance of the old Constitution, the switch allowed the
Court to put a new question into play in its dealings with the outside
world: "Now that we have switched, is it really necessary to consider
seriously a fundamental change in the structure of the Supreme
Court? Or should you trust us to consolidate the New Deal by handing down a series of landmark opinions legitimating the new vision of
activist national government?" In response to *this* question, the
spokesmen for the People in both Congress and the White House
quite reasonably gave the Court a second chance to redeem its continued democratic legitimacy without imposing harsher measures in the
form of court-packing or an Article Five amendment.

This judgment commands our respect. I have no doubt that the
lives of today's lawyers would be easier if the New Dealers had played
by the Article Five rules. Formalism does allow people who have
forgotten (or never learned) their history to identify the constitution-
building intentions of their predecessors. If the New Dealers had sent
us some neat time capsules of meaning in the classic Article five mode,
lawyers could have set down to work at once, without confronting the

ponderous tome you are now reading—and that would have been an advantage. But there are more important things than the cognitive convenience of lawyers and judges.

I mean to raise a question of legitimacy.[82] I write as a member of a generation that, over the last twenty years, has conspicuously failed to gain broad and deep popular support for any major constitutional initiative. During such times as these, our principal task is to keep alive the American tradition of popular sovereignty by preserving, as best we can, the memory of previous achievements. Rather than throwing the New Deal out of the court of constitutional opinion on a formalism, the higher calling is to understand its profound contribution to the sense that Americans still live under government *by the People.*

Granted, this sense of a common project is in jeopardy today; granted, the recollection of past achievements does not guarantee future success. But we do not improve our future prospects by cutting ourselves off from past successes.

CHAPTER TWELVE

Rediscovery or Creation?

DEFENDING THE SWITCH IN TIME

WHO killed Article Five?
Not the President, not the Congress, but the Supreme Court.

How did the Justices do it?

By negotiating their "switch in time," thereby taking the wind out of a debate over formal amendments that threatened to weaken the Court permanently.

Or so the last chapter argued, as it urged lawyers and judges to look beyond the four corners of Article Five to recognize that the New Dealers accomplished their revolution through other institutional means, and with different legal texts. For purposes of this argument, I accepted the formalist supposition that it would have been better if the American people had been led by Wheeler and Roosevelt to express their constitutional will through the classical Article Five system.

But it is time to expose this premise to critical scrutiny.

Alternative Scenarios

While there was a real chance of success through Article Five, it was only a chance. Other scenarios loomed. Suppose, for example, that the Court had refused to switch, that Roosevelt and Congress had responded with a package of New Deal amendments, but that the Democrats didn't find it so easy to win the rapid support of thirty-six states. As the country prepared for the 1938 Congressional elections, well-financed opponents in a scattering of small states began to defeat the amendments, leaving the Old Court in command. Does anybody suppose that Roosevelt and the Democrats would have taken defeat lightly?

To the contrary, Roosevelt would have returned to the People to renew his mandate in the elections of 1938: "In the Spring of 1937, I deferred to my critics, and tried to gain the consent of the states to constitutional amendments. But, as I warned you, this has only allowed 'economic royalists' to sabotage the national will by manipulating the vote of a few small states. We can no longer afford to let the workers, the farmers, the old folks wait for a few of the Nine Old Men to leave the Court."

Given the overwhelming New Deal majorities of the time, it is inconceivable that Republicans could have retaken either House in 1938 by urging the People to protect a Court that had recently struck down the Labor and Social Security Acts.[1] Having returned to Congress after a campaign that had demonized the Justices as the enemies of popular sovereignty, the Democrats could have claimed an express mandate for the President's court-packing measure. At the very least, such a claim would have led to a further deepening of the constitutional crisis.

It is pointless to spin out prophecies further, but do not ignore one point—a world war was already looming on the horizon in 1938. By pushing its constitutional challenge beyond 1937, the Court ran the risk that the country would remain in the throes of a constitutional crisis at the time of Pearl Harbor.[2] In contrast, its switch permitted Americans to confront their next great challenge with a sense that they had sucessfully weathered the storms of the previous decade.

Constitutional moments must come to an end. The People must be allowed to move on to other things with a sense that all of their passionate political argument and activity hasn't been in vain: *that government has heard their voice in a way that will not be long forgotten.* Granted, the Court's switch meant that lawyers and judges would have to memorialize the New Deal revolution in a different way: through judicial opinions rather than through formal amendments. But was this too large a price to pay for bringing the matter to a successful conclusion?

I do not think so—especially when the New Dealers had serious doubts about the power of Article Five to express the distinctive character of their revolution.

Jurisprudence: The Pragmatic Revolt

New Deal doubts about Article Five reflected the larger pragmatic revolt against formalism that had swept through much of American culture during the early twentieth century.[3] They also expressed the distinctive ideological orientation of the New Deal itself—occupying a political space somewhere between Locke and Marx, exploring the possibility of a "third way" between capitalism and socialism. The New Deal spirit was ostentatiously pragmatic: experimenting, building on what seemed to work, applauding creative adaptation, and so forth. It went against the grain to enshrine some definitive-seeming formula into the Constitution that might freeze further pragmatic adaptations. Let the Europeans kill each other off with their final ideological solutions; Americans would confront the challenges of the twentieth century in a different spirit. As Robert Jackson explained in *The Struggle for Judicial Supremacy:*

> What we demanded for our generation was the right consciously to influence the evolutionary process of constitutional law, as other generations had done. And my generation has won its fight to make its own impression on the Court's constitutional doctrine. It has done it by marshalling the force of public opinion against the old Court through the court fight, by trying to influence the choice of forward-looking personnel, and, most of all, by persuasion of the Court itself. It must not be forgotten that many of the most important changes in legal theory were announced before there was any change in Justices.[4]

Hear the note of satisfaction in Jackson's discovery that the Old Court turned out to be pragmatic in the end.

Perhaps a half-century of constitutional experience with New Deal pragmatism can teach us something about the costs, as well as benefits, of its approach to constitutional change. Perhaps we should rethink Jackson's praise of informal adaptation and inject new formal structures into the modern higher lawmaking process. This is, at any rate, my conclusion in the final chapter.

But it is one thing to urge (partial) reformalization; quite another, to impose this preference retroactively on the 1930's and refuse to appreciate the constitutional achievements of the New Deal. So far as the New Dealers were concerned, formalism was the problem, not the solution. America's constitutional crisis could not be solved by adding a few more formulae, but required the Justices to undertake their interpretive task with a different cast of mind.

The Court's "switch" served as an apt symbol of the pragmatic spirit that Americans were endorsing in giving their sustained support to the New Deal revolution.

The Critique of Federalism

It also provided an elegant solution to an aching problem threatening the adaptive capacities of the system as a whole: the veto power given to the states by Article Five. So far as the Founding Federalists were concerned, Article Five was a technique for *weakening* the veto that the states were wielding under the Articles of Confederation. But by Reconstruction, this weakened federalism was still too strong: America was now a nation, and it was wrong to allow a minority of states to veto new constitutional solutions that had gained the sustained and considered support of mobilized national majorities. We have already heard Roosevelt making this same point in his defense of court-packing. Rather than contesting it further, wasn't the Court wise to recognize its saliency by adapting constitutional law to the national will without insisting upon Article Five?

The Court's switch did not, of course, deprive Americans of the classical Article Five system based on dual federalism. It simply provided the People with another, more nation-centered, alternative in which the Court responds pragmatically to the sustained demands for constitutional change voiced by the President and Congress on the basis of an escalating series of electoral mandates from the citizenry. Wasn't such an adaptation appropriately expressive of the nationalist spirit of the New Deal's popular mandate?

Consider the Alternative

No less important, the New Deal system has probably worked a lot better than the formal amendments Americans were likely to enact in the 1930's. As we have seen, leading partisans of Article Five like Senator Wheeler had no intention of defending federalism to the death. They merely wished to provide it a different burial. If they had had their way, two-thirds of Congress could have overridden Supreme

Court vetoes by reenacting statutes after a single general election, without any referral to the states. We have also seen that the President might well have endorsed such Progressive ideas if he had been politically required to join Wheeler in traveling down the path of Article Five.

Consider how such a scheme might have worked in practice. The Court declares that the Constitution requires X; Congress overrides and declares that not-X but Y is the more appropriate ideal in one-or-another area of life. Henceforward, the Court's X governs in one area, and Congress's Y in another. Or worse yet, the overriding statute might contain a host of details without very much in the way of organizing vision. Henceforward, the Court's X is eclipsed by a mass of statutory detail. As time marches on, repeated Congressional overrides would have generated a crazy-quilt Constitution that increasingly mocked the very idea that the People might give a series of coherent directions to their governmental agents.

The Court's switch allowed Americans to avoid this fate. By undertaking to rework the fabric of existing law so as to express the New Deal vision of activist government, the Court retained institutional responsibility for giving overall coherence to the shape of constitutional doctrine. My next volume, *Interpretations,* will follow the Court as it struggled to reconcile older constitutional traditions of liberty and equality with newer affirmations of activist government for the general welfare.

For now, it is enough to contrast the dialogic character of the Court's effort with the mechanical solution that would have prevailed if a Wheeler-Roosevelt amendment had been enacted under Article Five. Under this alternative, the Court might have continued to uphold the *Lochnerian* tradition in its opinions while Congress episodically asserted New Deal activism in a proliferating set of overriding statutes—without *any* organ of American government attempting to synthesize the old with the new. Whatever difficulties the modern Court has experienced in its synthetic enterprise, would America have been better off with a mechanical alternative?

I doubt it. By holding up a vision of a constitutional order that sought to synthesize New Deal activism with older traditions of liberty and equality, the Court has not only challenged the modern bureaucratic state to live up to its claims to constitutional legitimacy. It has encouraged others to make the same demand—yielding a far more serious public dialogue over constitutional principle than would have obtained under Wheeler's mechanical alternative.

In Praise of the Unconventional

I refuse, then, to join a formalist lament at the failure of an earlier generation of Americans to announce their constitutional intentions through Article Five amendments. My attitude is closer to celebration than disdain. After sixty years, many New Deal doctrines have been found wanting, and more are in need of rejuvenation. But the ongoing need for doctrinal reconstruction should not divert us from the central achievement of New Deal constitutionalism. Rather than forcing Americans into federalist formalisms, its unconventional adaptations enabled the citizenry to express sustained support for a more nationalistic, activist, pragmatic, and dialogic understanding of its commitments as a People. Will Americans of the twenty-first century respond to future crises with similar creativity?

FROM RATIFICATION TO CONSOLIDATION

Imagine yourself an ordinary citizen observing the Washington scene from afar in the summer of 1937. No longer did you confront an ongoing struggle between the New Deal and the Old Court that challenged the People to decide between different visions of American government. Nor were you immersed in a bitter debate between President and Congress on whether a formal amendment was needed in order to compel the Court to heed the People's will. With the switch in time, all three branches were now operating on the premise that *the New Deal spoke for the People in enacting revolutionary reforms like the Wagner Act and Social Security Act.*

As a result, ordinary citizens could begin to relax: if the big boys in Washington played their cards right, normal folk might move on to other matters—either public or private—that had been pushed aside as the great constitutional debate occupied center stage. Since the ordinary citizen's perspective is crucial to the project of dualist constitutionalism, I shall say that the "switch" marked the beginning of the process of ratification—the point at which citizens might plausibly assume that their representatives in Washington had begun to heed their demand for fundamental change.

But it was only the beginning, and it could have broken down.

Transformative Appointments

If Hughes and Roberts had voted so differently in 1936 and in 1937, couldn't they switch back again in 1938?

The depth of this anxiety was revealed by the big impact on public opinion of Justice Van Devanter's announcement of retirement in May of 1937. His departure promised to make another switch less likely, and so increased the probability of a steady flow of opinions elaborating the activist vision. The Court's course was still uncertain, depending on the character of appointments, their willingness to revolutionize reigning doctrine. But wasn't it sensible to wait and see?

This is the tack taken by a 10-to-8 majority of the Senate Judiciary Committee in its June report on the President's court-packing proposal. Writing after Van Devanter's announcement, as well as the Court's decisions upholding the Labor and Social Security Acts,[5] the majority opposed the President's court-packing proposal:

> Even if every charge brought against the so-called "reactionary" members of this Court be true, it is far better that we await orderly but inevitable change of personnel than that we impatiently overwhelm them with new members. Exhibiting this restraint, thus demonstrating our faith in the American system, we shall set an example that will protect the independent American judiciary from attack as long as this Government stands.[6]

As in the general debate, the majority report did not attempt a full-scale defense of the Old Court's effort to preserve the Constitution of the middle republic. Its protest was focused on the manner in which the transition to the new regime was to be accomplished—rejecting the President's desire to "impatiently overwhelm" the Supreme Court in favor of a more "orderly" process of change in response to the "inevitable."

But what would this "orderly" process look like? Would the President take advantage of openings to appoint committed New Dealers prepared to endorse a revolutionary transformation of constitutional doctrine? If so, would the Senate confirm them?

Neither answer should be taken for granted. It is rare for Presidents to use Supreme Court nominations for transformative purposes. Normally, they lack the will to do so. Even when they are dissatisfied with existing doctrine, other factors often bulk larger: paying off political debts, appealing to a politically important region or interest, or simply appointing a long-cherished friend. Indeed, Roosevelt had already expressed this normal political logic by promising Senator Joseph Robinson a Supreme Court seat. While Robinson had been a loyal majority leader, his elevation to the Supreme Court did not augur well for the New Deal. Rooted in the Jeffersonian traditions of Southern Democracy, Robinson would have been deeply attracted to the states'-rights conservatism of Justices like McReynolds (who, it should be noted, had been appointed by Woodrow Wilson).[7] It is simply impossible to say whether this ideological affinity would have triumphed over his partisan loyalties to Roosevelt.

Robinson's sudden death not only killed the court-packing initiative, but liberated the President to explore a different logic of judicial appointment—characteristic of rare moments of constitutional politics. Only then are Supreme Court nominations something more than juicy political plums—which may, or may not, be used by the President to gratify his taste in constitutional philosophy. They become crucial counters in the ongoing struggle over the looming transformation. At such times, constitutional ideology regularly becomes more salient in Presidential nominations—though even then, it has not been the only factor.

This was true in the days of Jefferson, and Jackson, and Lincoln and Grant. And it became true once again as Roosevelt successfully reasserted Presidential leadership in times of constitutional politics. Between 1937 and his death in 1945, Roosevelt made eight nominations to the Court. Only once—in the case of James Byrnes in 1941—did he indulge the normal nomination logic. Byrnes was a disappointed Vice-Presidential candidate and a long-time friend whose constitutional philosophy—if he had one—was traditional Southern Jeffersonian. But Roosevelt indulged himself on this appointment only after his others had consolidated the New Deal revolution, and in any event, Byrnes didn't like the job and resigned after a year in office.[8]

Otherwise, the President restricted his nominations to public adherents of the New Deal philosophy of activist government. And it is here where he broke new ground—creating a founding precedent of the modern republic. For good or for ill, the image of the President redeeming the voice of the People by a series of transformative appointments has profoundly shaped the modern understanding of legitimate constitutional transformation.

I shall be taking up the latter-day consequences of this precedent in the next chapter. For now, I concentrate on how Roosevelt managed to turn the trick the first time around. It was one thing for him to make transformative appointments a central Presidential priority; quite another, for the Senate to agree; and yet another, for the new Justices to redeem the President's intentions by revolutionizing constitutional doctrine. Consider each of these steps in turn.

SENATORIAL CONFIRMATIONS AND RATIFYING ELECTIONS

Why didn't conservatives in the Senate prevent the President from implementing a strategy of transformative appointment? Liberals had not shown equal restraint when Herbert Hoover was in the White House. They waged a successful ideological campaign against Hoover's nomination of John Parker; and even Charles Evans Hughes— one of the most distinguished statesmen of the age—was bitterly opposed as a big business candidate and won confirmation by 52 to 26 in 1930.[9] Why, then, didn't the Congressional conservatives prove equally rambunctious during the late 1930's?

Undoubtedly, Roosevelt had such questions in mind when nominating Hugo Black to replace Van Devanter in the wake of the court-packing crisis. While Black was an emphatic New Dealer, he was also a Senator—and therefore could count on Senatorial courtesy to win support. Despite this advantage, Black's nomination did not float through, but prompted bitter debate and partisan division, with 16 Republicans voting against 63 Democrats at a time when passions were still very raw.[10]

With the nomination of Stanley Reed, conservatives began to confront their moment of truth. As Solicitor General, Reed had been making the New Deal's case before the Court and could be expected to uphold liberal arguments consistently as a Justice. Roosevelt's transformative intentions could not be more obvious.

The President sent Reed's name to the Senate in January of 1938, at a time when the Republicans were looking forward with anticipation to November. Not only had they begun to score against Roosevelt in the court-packing controversy, but the economy had recently taken a nose dive, calling into question the New Deal's capacity to lead the nation out of the Depression.[11] Would conservatives continue their political initiative by launching a campaign against the President's nomination? Even if they lost the battle against Reed, wouldn't it serve as an ideal campaign issue, as Republican candidates solemnly promised to filibuster against further liberal nominations?

On the Role of Ratifying Elections

The question becomes sharper when we place it against the background of analogous developments during Reconstruction. The "switch in time" of 1937 was hardly the first occasion on which leading defenders of the traditional Constitution have retreated before the aggressive assertion of a mandate from the People. As in March of 1937, so in March of 1868, the conservative branches were on trial before public opinion—with President Johnson facing the prospect of conviction at his impeachment trial and the Court weighing the prospect of the loss of its jurisdiction in *McCardle*.

As in 1937, these unconventional threats were followed by rapid conservative retreat. By the next regular election, both President and Court had acquiesced in the authority of the Convention/Congress to impose Reconstruction and the Fourteenth Amendment in the name of the American people. But was the conservative switch merely a tactical retreat, or did it represent an enduring recognition that the People had spoken?

It was here that the election of 1868 played a crucial role in *consolidating the switch* by giving the conservatives a final realistic chance to challenge the emerging institutional consensus. The Democrats took advantage of this opportunity—with their candidate for Vice President, Frank Blair, threatening an all-out repudiation of the Republicans' constitutional solution. While Blair's threat backfired, helping Grant to win the election, it was still taken very seriously. Only after beating back this threat in 1868 could the Republicans proceed in earnest to use their control over all three branches to consolidate the new constitutional order.

So too here. The switch of 1937 had given institutional momentum to the New Deal revolution, but the Republicans were still free to make a Blair-like effort to reverse the bandwagon. Would the elections of 1938 and 1940 display a similar pattern of conservative challenge?

The Dog That Didn't Bark—and the One That Did

The answer is no and yes. While Republicans in the Senate failed to make the President's transformative strategy a campaign issue in 1938, their nominee for the Presidency showed no similar reluctance two years later.

Begin with the dog that didn't bark. After the successful nomination of Black, Senatorial resistance to Roosevelt's strategy simply collapsed. Reed was confirmed without opposition.[12]

No less remarkable was the Republican response to their electoral victory in November. For the first time in the 1930's, the party experienced an upswing in support. Granted, the shift only increased the number of Republican Senators from 16 to 23.[13] But wasn't this enough to encourage them to join with conservative Southern Democrats to hold back the New Deal revolution in the courts?

While this conservative coalition was very powerful in other areas,[14] it did not seriously challenge the nomination of three emphatic liberals to the Court in the next two years.* Frankfurter and Frank Mur-

---

*A vignette beautifully expresses the spirit of the President's strategy: "On New Year's Day of 1939, President Roosevelt met with Robert H. Jackson, Homer Cummings, and Harry Hopkins to discuss candidates who might be suitable to fill a vacancy on the Supreme Court created by the death of Benjamin N. Cardozo. There was some support for candidates from the west, but Jackson, who supported Felix Frankfurter, opposed them. He maintained that too much was at stake—no less than the course and direction of constitutional interpretation—to approach the appointment in terms of geography. The crucial consideration, he thought, was the prospective appointee's ability to interpret the Constitution 'with scholarship and with sufficient assurance to face Chief Justice Hughes in conference and hold his own in the discussion.' 'Any man you would be likely to appoint from the west,' he told the President, 'would be possessed of an inferiority complex in the presence of the Chief Justice, who looks like God and talks like God. He would be completely unable to help give direction to the action of the Court.' Whereupon FDR said, 'I think Felix is the only man who could do that job, Bob.' Four days later Frankfurter was named to the Court." David Danelski and Joseph Tulchin, *The Autobiographical Notes of Charles Evans Hughes* xxviii (1973).

phy won unanimous confirmation from the Senate; and the only thing that inspired four Senators to oppose William O. Douglas was a fear that he was too cozy with big business while serving as chairman of the SEC![15]

As the Presidential election approached, matters were reaching a point of no return. Here is Wendell Willkie describing the situation in the nationally circulated *Saturday Evening Post* of March 9, 1940:

> Mr. Roosevelt has now won. The court is now his.
>
> In order to understand what this means, it is necessary to be clear concerning the nature of law itself. The full import of the law is not to be found in written enactments or constitutional provisions and amendments. These are parts of the skeleton, but the body of law is progressively built—with occasional interruptions and diversions—by deciding each case upon precedents furnished by prior decisions. . . .
>
> [W]hen a series of reinterpretations overturning well-argued precedents are made in a brief time by a newly appointed group of judges, all tending to indicate the same basic disagreement with the established conception of government, the thoughtful observer can only conclude that something revolutionary is going on. And that is what has happened here. . . .
>
> Now the people of the United States may approve of what is happening, and if they do, that is their affair, but legal decisions are couched in language difficult for the layman to understand. Consequently, the average citizen may well be unaware of the revolutionary nature of the court decisions. . . .

After an intelligent review of the Court's recent decisions dealing with interstate commerce, taxation, and social welfare legislation, Willkie presented his readers with some striking conclusions:

> These decisions have made the United States a national and no longer a Federal Government. . . .
>
> The American public . . . has not yet tested all the whims, vagaries and caprices of a securely enthroned central government reaching into the daily lives of all the people. And the social philosopher may well speculate what that public's reaction will be when the tests have been made. If the present public is anything like its ancestors, I wager that when it does understand, it will mightily rebel.[16]

But, of course, Willkie was not just any ordinary "social philosopher." Articles like this one were propelling him into the center of Republican politics. His meteoric rise was itself remarkable, since Willkie was a big businessman who had never run for public office and had only recently changed his registration from the Democratic Party. Nevertheless, the Republican convention chose him as its Presidential standard-bearer on the sixth ballot over such party stalwarts as Robert Taft.[17]

The Republicans got what they paid for. In his acceptance speech, Willkie declared himself "a liberal Democrat who changed his party affiliation because he found democracy in the Republican party rather than the New Deal party."[18] And he was quite unwilling to make his jurisprudential essay in the *Post* the basis of a campaign onslaught against the New Deal Court. It was far more important for him to reach across party lines by repeatedly emphasizing his support for the National Labor Relations Act, the Social Security Act, and the Fair Labor Standards Act.[19] Given his fealty to these New Deal landmarks, it was quite impossible for him to pine too visibly for the good old days when the conservative Four Horsemen were triumphant on the Court.[20]

Instead, Willkie trained his sights on a much more inviting constitutional target: Roosevelt's decision to break hallowed precedents of self-limitation stretching back to Washington and run for a third term. Roosevelt had invoked the outbreak of war in Europe to justify this breach with Washington's principle;[21] but for Willkie, this was just a facile cover for Roosevelt's slide toward dictatorship.[22] Willkie's constitutional critique of a third term resonated powerfully; but it was not enough to defeat Roosevelt, who beat his "liberal Democratic" rival by a 55 to 45 margin.[23]

Nonetheless, it is enlightening to imagine the implications of a Willkie victory. On this scenario, once the Republican's "liberal Democratic" nominee was safely in the White House, he might have taken the themes of his *Post* essay more seriously. As Hughes and McReynolds retired from the Court during his term, President Willkie might have urged Americans to reassess the doctrinal revolution that had "made the United States a national and no longer a Federal Government." Pointing to Roosevelt's series of liberal appointments, he might have begun a campaign for "balance" on the Court. With the Court tilting so heavily in the direction of activist nationalism, wasn't it time to nominate strong conservatives to continue McReynolds's impassioned defense of the traditions of an earlier day?

Perhaps Willkie's answer might have been yes. Perhaps he might have convinced the Senate to go along. But after Roosevelt won his unprecedented third term, the time for such questions was past. Both Roosevelt and the country had other matters to worry about—notably the raging world war and its implications for America. So far as the New Deal revolution of the 1930's was concerned, Roosevelt had absolutely no reason to change the strategy he had developed to assure its further consolidation. As Hughes and McReynolds retired from the bench, he nominated replacements who would predictably support the New Deal vision of activist national government. Though the number of Republican senators continued to move upward from 23 to 28 after the elections of 1940, all of the President's transformative appointments were confirmed without a single vote of opposition— the liberal Stone replacing Chief Justice Hughes, the liberal Jackson replacing Stone, the liberal Wiley Rutledge replacing the misplaced Byrnes replacing the conservative McReynolds.

The Bandwagon Effect, Revisited

I draw three lessons from this story. First, the constitutional significance of the Supreme Court's transformation was no secret to ordinary Americans. Second, if the Republicans wanted to make it into a big issue, they would have selected a candidate like Robert A. Taft, rather than Willkie, to raise the banner of old-style conservatism. Third, they did not take this step because they knew that the country had no inclination to refight the constitutional battles of the 1930's. The Republican convention of 1940 correctly understood that the country was *proud* of the way in which it had weathered the storms that had destroyed so many democracies in Europe; and that it would have no patience with a party that promised to fight to the bitter end for lost constitutional causes.

These conclusions may seem so obvious that they hardly needed a couple of elections to establish them. But this is a mistake. I am not interested in what a political scientist or a newspaper pundit might say about the evolution of public opinion in the late 1930's. I am interested in the way Americans themselves conducted a political dialogue that finally led to the considered conclusion that *the People had spoken*. From this vantage point, the elections of 1938 and 1940 forced the conservative opposition to a moment of truth: Now that they had beaten back the President's frontal assault on the Court's formal independence, did they continue to contest his claim that the People had given him a mandate to constitutionalize the principles of New Deal Democracy?

The Republicans' answer may have been reluctant, but their performance in the Senate, and in the campaigns, was loud and clear: It was time to jump on the institutional bandwagon, concede that the People had indeed endorsed activist national government, and define a new opposition strategy that might garner majority support within the new constitutional consensus.

Transformative Opinions

We can now look back upon an evolving pattern of events and search for their larger constitutional meaning:

Triggering Election of 1936 → Unconventional Threat by President →
Switch in Time → Transformative Appointments →
Consolidating Election of 1938 → Transformative Appointments →
Consolidating Election of 1940 → Transformative Appointments →
Final Acts of Judicial Consolidation

We have been considering this pattern from the vantage point of ordinary American citizens, people who have not suffered through the ordeals of a professional legal education. From their perspective, the bandwagon effect had generated a plain meaning by the consolidating election of 1940. At that point, it was clear to ordinary Americans that the folks in Washington had finally gotten the message: We the People had endorsed the New Deal vision of activist government.

I now change perspective and consider how the legal community integrated this message into the emerging constitutional order. Having killed off Article Five amendments, the Court filled the gap it created with a series of landmark opinions. Since these texts have decisively shaped the law of the modern republic, their formulation deserves careful attention.

From Common Law to Constitutional Solution

To manage its doctrinal revolution, the Court took full advantage of the disjointed character of common law reasoning. Common lawyers traditionally pride themselves in their skeptical treatment of judicial opinions. Whatever the Court says, they are more impressed by what it does. Over the centuries, they have cultivated the art of distinguishing an opinion's sweeping "dicta" from its "holding"—the latter consisting of those legal propositions strictly necessary to decide the particular case before the Court. While later judges are free to abandon "dicta" they find unpersuasive, the principle of *stare decisis* requires them to take prior "holdings" more seriously.

Under normal circumstances, the distinction between dicta and holding operates as a brake on judicial innovation. While one court may make revolutionary proclamations in its opinions, the next court may dismiss them as dicta and whittle its predecessor's judgments down to size. But in the context of a constitutional revolution, this disjunction operates quite differently. During the early stages of the revolution, the Court's dicta may give the naive reader an impression of substantial doctrinal continuity. The only trouble is that a yawning gap has opened between these quasi-traditional dicta and the course of concrete decisions—making it clear to a common lawyer that some new propositions of law, unexpressed in the opinions, are doing much of the real work.

This disequilibrium between revolutionary holdings and traditional dicta creates cultural pressure for a second stage of opinion-writing—in which a transformed Court elaborates new canonical doctrines that make sense of its earlier revolutionary holdings.

This two-stage process enabled the Justices to satisfy two different audiences as the Court worked itself out of the constitutional crisis. Most obviously, the Court had to reassure the President, Congress, and the general public that it had called off its assault on the New Deal. But throughout 1937, the Justices had to satisfy a second crucial audience as well, consisting of two people: Hughes and Roberts, who had to be persuaded to continue joining Brandeis, Cardozo, and Stone in support of New Deal constitutionalism.

These two audiences had different interests. The general public was primarily interested in the bottom line—was the Court going to up-

hold the Labor Act, the Social Security Act, and other activist legislation? To put this point into legalese, the general public was most
interested in the Court's *holdings*.

The swing Justices were particularly interested in the *dicta*. They
were concerned with the principled character of their own performance. Since they understood the Constitution in relatively traditional
terms, they would find it easier to endorse the switch if opinions
created the appearance of doctrinal continuity. Hence the path of least
resistance: traditionalist dicta, revolutionary holdings.

It was a path, moreover, that fit beautifully into the larger dynamics
of constitutional legitimation I have described. As we have seen, it was
still open to the Republican Party to contest the constitutional legitimacy of the New Deal in the elections of 1938 and 1940. Only after
Roosevelt defeated Willkie did it become obvious that further serious
appeals to the People to reverse the judicial revolution were utterly
fruitless.

And it was precisely then that the New Deal Court reached a
second and final phase in the process of constitutional consolidation.
In landmark opinions during Roosevelt's third term, a transformed
Court was no longer content to conjoin revolutionary holdings with
traditional constitutional dicta in the manner of 1937. It settled for
nothing less than a root-and-branch repudiation of the old constitutional learning, and a new equilibrium between theory and practice,
dicta and holding. The Court's transformative opinions of the early
1940's have served as the functional equivalents of Article Five
amendments, establishing fixed points for legal reasoning during the
next era.

Suppose, however, that Willkie had won the election of 1940. Then
the Justices of the 1940's might have resolved the tension generated
by the mix of traditionalist dicta and revolutionary holdings in a
different way. Rather than announcing newly authoritative principles
to legitimate the revolutionary holdings, they might have reasserted
traditional dicta and repudiated some of the revolutionary holdings of
1937. There was nothing inevitable about the New Deal Court's
movement from phase one to phase two. The dynamic should be
viewed as part of the larger story of constitutional creation brought
about by continuing acts of Presidential leadership in gaining Senate
assent to a stream of transformative appointments.

This two-phase view contrasts with the standard account presented by scholars in thrall to the myth of rediscovery. For them, the Old Court's resistance was a waste of time, a painful comedy of errors. To minimize the pain, many of them minimize the extent of the judiciary's blunders. Adopting an apologetic framework, they portray the Old Court's struggle as a passing aberration, concentrated principally in the bad years of 1935 and 1936.[24] Apologists concede that the Justices blundered badly for a while, but they can barely conceal their impatience with the Court's bungling. As soon as they can decently end their tale of woe, they bring the Court out of the wilderness into the promised land of 1937. Once the Justices rediscover "the truth" in 1937, their story comes to an end. Roosevelt's additional appointments don't accomplish anything important. In David Currie's words, they only put the "icing on the cake; the essential change had occurred before any new appointments were made."[25]

But is Currie right?[26]

Phase One

Writing for the *New Republic* on January 13, 1937, Harvard's Thomas Reed Powell considered "it almost certain that the Wagner Labor Act will be denied application to manufacturing concerns by six votes and possibly by nine." Probably the leading court-watcher of his time, Powell was especially noted for his political realism, and yet he supposed that the Court had bound its hands in its recent decisions: the National Labor Relations Act was doomed. Three months later, Chief Justice Hughes managed to uphold the Act for a five-man majority, but did he overrule the decisions that Powell considered such insuperable obstacles?

No. He repeatedly and ostentatiously emphasized his fidelity to *Schechter*'s "distinction between what is national and what is local" and proclaimed it "vital to the maintenance of our federal system."[27] His opinion in *NLRB v. Jones & Laughlin Steel* called for the empirically sensitive application of traditional ideas. After all, wasn't it silly to treat a giant steel company as if it were like Schechter's chicken business? Given the giant firm's "far-flung activities," Hughes refused to "shut our eyes" to the "obvious" and potentially "catastrophic" impact of a strike on interstate commerce. Given these facts, the

Court's prior cases "are not controlling here."[28] What could be more sensible?

Since Hughes had voted in favor of earlier decisions distinguishing the "direct" from the "indirect," his commitment to limited federal intervention seemed entirely credible. Indeed, his opinion explicitly refused to give the Labor Act an unconditional bill of health, vindicating it only as it applied to vast companies like Jones & Laughlin. On the surface, his opinion seemed utterly unrevolutionary.

Until you turn to a companion case in the same volume, involving the Friedman–Harry Marks Clothing Co.[29] This company looks much more like Schechter, selling only $800,000 worth of clothes in 1932, and $2 million in 1933. Yet Hughes does not even deign to mention this obvious point, blandly upholding the act "for the reasons stated in our opinion in NLRB v. Jones & Laughlin Steel Corp."[30] End of opinion! Who is Hughes trying to fool?

Certainly not Mr. Justice McReynolds, who spoke for four dissenters: "The Clothing Company is a typical small manufacturing concern which produces less than one-half of one per cent of the men's clothing produced in the United States and employs 800 of the 150,000 workmen engaged therein. If closed today, the ultimate effect on commerce in clothing obviously would be negligible."[31] When placed against this dissent, Hughes's silence about Schechter is deafening. The 5-to-4 decision in Friedman–Harry Marks reveals a classic phase-one disequilibrium between dicta and holding. The Court speaks the language of continuity while the holding bespeaks the fact of rupture. A similar disjunction is visible in another crucial decision upholding the Social Security Act.[32]

A third great case involved the states, not the federal government: West Coast Hotel v. Parrish[33] upheld state laws establishing minimum wages and maximum hours for women and minors. Standard accounts get carried away by the melodrama of the moment. Parrish was the first great decision to be announced in the spring. Coming down a couple of months after Roosevelt's court-packing plan, it revealed that Justice Roberts had changed his mind on the issue. Only last term, he had joined four conservatives to strike down a very similar law on the authority of Justice Sutherland's 1923 opinion in Adkins v. Children's Hospital. Now Roberts joined Hughes and the three liberals to uphold the statute without writing an opinion explaining his sudden change.

As a consequence, his motivations have been subjected to endless controversy—with realists making his switch into a symbol of the potency of the President's unconventional threat, and legalists defending Roberts against the taint of political jurisprudence.

But this entire debate proceeds on an exaggerated view of the case's importance. Insofar as Roberts was crucial, it is not because of his single vote in *Parrish,* but because of the remarkably consistent support he now gave to activist statutes that offended his previously proclaimed principles. If he had switched back to the conservative side in subsequent cases, the decision in *Parrish* would have been insufficient to defuse the crisis.[34] Moreover, the opinion in the case is a typical phase-one product, which could have easily been reversed in future years but for the success of the President's subsequent strategy of transformative appointments.

After all, even the *Lochner* court had upheld a maximum-hours statute for women three years after it struck down one for men, finding that "woman's physical structure and the performance of maternal functions place her at a disadvantage in the struggle for subsistence."[35] This 1908 decision was overruled in 1923 by a 5-to-3 vote in *Adkins.* Now that *Parrish* overruled *Adkins* with Roberts's help, this hardly meant that he had signed up for a legal revolution.

To the contrary, Hughes's opinion cited *Lochner* with approval,[36] accepted the idea that the Due Process Clause contains a principle of freedom of contract, and patiently reviewed the cases limiting this basic *Lochnerian* principle. After engaging in an extended lawyerly analysis, he concluded that the Court's judgment in 1908 was sounder than in 1923: the health interests of the weaker sex justified a special measure of protection against "unscrupulous and overreaching employers."

Up to this point, Hughes's opinion seems similar to one written by Justice Roberts in 1934 for a six-man majority in *Nebbia v. New York.* In that case, Roberts had upheld New York's minimum price for milk after an examination of the economics had convinced him that it had "a reasonable relation to a proper legislative purpose, and [was] neither arbitrary nor discriminatory."[37] In saying this, Roberts had recast the balance of preexisting doctrine, but he had not overturned the entire structure. Indeed, when he and Hughes revisited the same New York milk marketing scheme in 1936, they struck down another provision as an "arbitrary" infringement of economic liberty protected by the Fourteenth Amendment.[38]

If a catchword is useful, *Parrish* largely reads as one of the countless *mid-course corrections* that a healthy system is making all the time in the elaboration of fundamental constitutional principles. Rather than calling these principles into question, an ongoing process of judicial recalibration attests to their vitality. But then Hughes concluded *Parrish* on a discordant note:

> There is an additional and compelling consideration which recent economic experience has brought into a strong light. The exploitation of a class of workers who are in an unequal position with respect to bargaining power and are thus relatively defenceless against the denial of a living wage is not only detrimental to their health and well being but casts a direct burden for their support upon the community. What these workers lose in wages the taxpayers are called upon to pay. The bare cost of living must be met. We may take judicial notice of the unparalleled demands for relief which arose during the recent depression and still continue to an alarming extent. . . . The community is not bound to provide what is in effect a subsidy for unconscionable employers. The community may direct its law-making power to correct the abuse which springs from their selfish disregard of the public interest.[39]

These words open up new constitutional vistas. Justice Rufus Peckham, the author of *Lochner,* would have been shocked by the claim that the community provides "a subsidy" to employers when it allows them to pay market wages to their workers. Granting that wages might be very low, he would have denied that the employer was "unconscionable" in using the market price as his reference point. For Peckham, the boss didn't owe his workers a decent living; nor did the community. It was up to each individual to fend for himself, and for charity to care for those who couldn't.

Within this *Lochnerian* vision, the market operated as a prepolitical baseline establishing basic entitlements. It was *only* the state that could provide unconstitutional "subsidies" when it enacted "class legislation" that picked the pockets of one group merely to enhance the welfare of another. It is precisely this wanton redistributionism that *Lochner* set itself against.[40]

Hughes's welfarist vision sets the minimum-wage problem against a different background. The political community owes each citizen a minimum entitlement: "[t]he bare cost of living must be met." If it is not met by the employer, the taxpayers must take on the burden. Given this framework, the market system loses its constitutionally privileged status as a baseline. If the market fails to discharge the community's obligation to provide a "living wage," the community may constitutionally find that it is the employer, not his worker, who is failing to live up to his social obligations.

This is indeed a revolutionary reversal of constitutional baselines, and one which has profoundly shaped the course of post–New Deal jurisprudence.[41] But *Parrish* introduces this reform cautiously—it serves as "an additional and compelling consideration" that supplements, but does not displace, the classical *Lochnerian* analysis with which Hughes's opinion is largely concerned. If the Court of 1938 had been so minded, it would have been entirely within its common law rights to declare that Hughes's welfarist notions weren't nearly as "compelling" as he imagined, and that it was far sounder to return to the grand *Lochnerian* tradition of the (contextually sensitive) vindication of market freedom.

Nevertheless, given Hughes's remarkable conclusion, it would be wrong to treat *Parrish* as if it were merely a garden-variety example of a mid-course correction; better call it an uncertain herald of revolutionary reform.

A Turning Point?

This brief tour of the leading cases of 1937 has revealed a rich variety of mid-course corrections, uncertain trumpets, and arbitrary fiats—in other words, nothing very unusual. Any lawyer will tell you that the Supreme Court fills the *United States Reports* with an abundant supply of similar specimens *every* year. Have we been wrong, then, in marking 1937 as a fabled anno mirabilis in the life of the Constitution?

No. But we will have to reconceive the basis of 1937's distinctiveness. Its special character emerges only by juxtaposing it to the judicial production of 1936 and 1938. Normally, each year generates a rich and varied judicial harvest, but there isn't a dramatic difference in succeeding vintages. What is more, it is usually folly to examine a year's production in search of a master theme. Different cases propel different areas of law in different directions. Perhaps patterns will emerge that reconcile antagonistic impulses. But it takes a lot of time to figure them out. Year one's mid-course correction may provoke another in Year five and yet another in Year ten—a generation later, an entire area of law may be unrecognizable. Many uncertain trumpets go unheard, and others resound only after a decade or two. Most *ipse dixits* sink without a trace; but others provoke serious efforts to elaborate legal principles that redeem the intuitions expressed by the anomalies. And so forth.

For all these reasons, a single year is usually much too short to mark something as pretentious as a "judicial revolution." Indeed, the whole idea of revolution generally serves as an extravagant conceit concealing a more evolutionary reality. In any single doctrinal area, significant change typically occurs after a decade or two of probing and testing; the entire constitutional terrain shifts even more slowly as judges modify one thing, then another, then another, and these changes interact to suggest new argumentative strategies, distinctive legal principles. The very effort to transform the entire framework of constitutional thought may strike legal cognoscenti as hopelessly naive. think of the countless unintended consequences that inevitably follow such hubristic acts of self-confidence!

This exclamation, I am happy to concede, captures the normal mentality of common law development—and thereby provides a measuring rod for assessing the truly distinctive character of the late 1930's. In contrast to the common law norm, a year like 1936 or 1937 does *not* display the dispersive tendencies of case-by-case decisions. Cases in different areas *do* march to the beat of the same drummer. Despite the variety of facts and doctrines, the Justices are transparently struggling with the same question: will they continue to defend the federalist and free market Constitution? Despite the common law disdain for such grand abstractions, the Justices—and every other lawyer—are perfectly aware that the very framework of constitutional thought is on the line. Moreover, the Court's answer to this Big Question changed with blinding speed: in 1936, the answer was Yes to the traditional Constitution; in 1937, it was No.

To be sure, the 1937 Court had expressed its No in a common-lawish way. Whereas Roberts and Hughes often voted with the conservatives in 1936, they suddenly and systematically voted with the liberals *all the time* in 1937—not only in "leading" cases, but in all cases where federal power was challenged. Given the common law's sensitivity to a systematic pattern of holdings, lawyers had no trouble detecting the deeper theme: Despite the Court's quasi-traditionalist dicta, the partisans of the traditional Constitution were now *always* on the losing side.

Since lawyers are interested in winning cases, they do not take this point lightly. As the Justices opened their next term of Court, their messages would be of especial legal interest. Would the new judicial majority begin to expound principles of New Deal constitutionalism that would make more sense of its emphatically changed behavior?

Phase Two

By the end of the Court's 1938 term, President Roosevelt had gained Senate confirmation of his first two transformative appointments— Black and Reed replacing Van Devanter and Sutherland. As a consequence, Hughes and Roberts no longer played the same strategic role: Black, Reed, Brandeis, Cardozo, and Stone could make a majority without them. Of course, neither Hughes nor Roberts was particularly inclined to reconsider his epochal decision of the year before. And the new Justices understood that the constitutional authority of the emerging activist vision would be greatly enhanced if moderates like Hughes and Roberts remained on board the constitutional bandwagon. Nonetheless, the new math created a new atmosphere, encouraging the emerging majority to move beyond quasi-traditional formulations in support of genuinely transformative opinions—texts that gave affirmative doctrinal meaning to the constitutional revolution under way.

Two decisions from the 1938 term are indicative. In contrast to the leading cases of the prior term, *United States v. Carolene Products*[42] did not involve a statute of great political importance. While the larger public was deeply concerned with the validity of the Labor and Social Security Acts, it would little note nor long remember the fate of the Federal Filled Milk Act. *Carolene* is important for what it said, not for what it did.

In challenging the act, the company offered to prove that its filled milk was entirely safe, and that the federal ban was an arbitrary abridgment of the economic freedom the Court had traditionally protected under the Due Process Clause. On the merits, this was not a frivolous claim.[43] But speaking for the Court, Justice Stone announced a fundamental change in the rules of the game. He flat-out denied that the Justices were regularly required to conduct a contextualized inquiry into the arbitrariness of "regulatory legislation affecting ordinary commercial transactions." Not only did he "presume" that activist legislators knew what they were doing, but he made this presumption virtually irrebuttable. Critics were given the impossible burden of producing facts that would "preclude the assumption that [the statute] rests upon some rational basis within the knowledge and experience of the legislators."[44] Since these words were written, the Court has never again struck down a regulatory statute as arbitrary. *Carolene*'s "rational basis" test has become a fixed star in the modern constitutional universe—no less important than formulae like "equal protection" that derive directly from the constitutional text.[45]

Fixed operational formulae play a crucial role in the life of the law. Tests like "rational basis" operate to place vast areas of policy beyond legal question, and thereby allow courts to define a manageable constitutional agenda. But to take the next step in developing an operational approach, courts require something more than fixed formulae; they need a jurisprudence that sets out the broad orienting lines for further legal development. Given the demise of traditional principles of limited government and economic freedom, what alternative principles could discharge this role?

Here too *Carolene* pointed the way. Its famous Footnote 4 began to fill the gap left by the disintegration of traditional principles. Instead of states' rights, property, and contract, *Carolene* offered up a theory of New Deal democracy as an organizing framework. While judges should defer to the legislature in ordinary economic disputes, "a more exacting judicial scrutiny" might be required when the democratic process malfunctioned—either when the majority denied opponents crucial political rights or when legislation was motivated by prejudice against "discrete and insular minorities." At this stage, such suggestions were little more than trial balloons, suitable for discussion in footnotes. It would take years for the emerging majority to wrestle with their affirmative implications in full-blown opinions of the Court.[46]

In contrast, 1938 was not too soon for a self-conscious assault on the jurisprudential foundations of the old order. Without giving any notice to the parties, the new majority transformed *Erie Railroad v. Tompkins* into a vehicle for a root-and-branch repudiation of the premises of *Lochnerian* thought. On its surface, the case was utterly humdrum: "Tompkins, a citizen of Pennsylvania, was injured on a dark night by a passing freight train of the Erie Railroad Company while walking along its right of way,"[47] and he sued to collect damages for negligence under the common law. But its everydayness invited Justice Brandeis to plunge into the philosophical depths. For a century since Justice Joseph Story's decision in *Swift v. Tyson,* the Court had resolved such disputes on the basis of the common law of torts, contracts, and property. Of course, the Justices sometimes found that their understanding of the common law diverged from the views of state courts, but they did not find this fact terribly disturbing. For them, the common law was something bigger than any single court. It was the collective wisdom of the Anglo-American judiciary working itself out over time; ongoing dispute between courts was part of a common search for the best answers. Within this traditional framework, the common law of property, contract, and tort was not the outcome of political will, but the product of judicial reason—and it was the self-evident obligation of the highest court in the land to make an independent contribution to this more general effort.

Whatever the jurisprudential merits of this idea, one thing was clear: it could not survive the triumph of the activist regulatory state. For twentieth-century critics of laissez-faire, the common law was the problem, not the solution: its vision of property, contract, and tort had created a false vision of economic freedom—ignoring the questions of distributive injustice, monopoly power, and other market failures that condemned millions to poverty and exploitation. Rather than genuflecting before this common law vision, the New Dealers sought to create a new foundation for economic freedom through democratic politics and legislative reform. From this perspective, the great sin of the *Lochnerian* era was the Court's effort to constitutionalize the categories of the common law—striking down legislative reforms in the name of their own judge-made definitions of property, contract, and torts.

Now that the New Deal Court had seen the light, it moved decisively to destroy the foundations of *Lochnerian* jurisprudence by demystifying the common law. In applying its understanding of the common law to humdrum railroad accidents, a long line of previous Courts had supposed they were engaged in the judicial search for right reason; but now Brandeis exposed the "common law" as another name for the exercise of sheer political will. With this jurisprudential turn, *Tompkins* raised a new question: What gave Nine Old Men in Washington the right to impose their will on this railroad accident and dismiss the contrary law worked out by the legislature and courts of Pennsylvania?

Brandeis's answer was loud and clear: Nothing at all. Unless and until Congress legislated on the problem of railroad accidents, the Court had no business meddling in state decisionmaking in the name of "common law":

> The fallacy [of the existing doctrine] . . . is made clear by Mr. Justice Holmes. The doctrine rests upon the assumption that there is a "transcendental body of law outside of any particular State but obligatory with it unless and until changed by statute," that federal courts have the power to use their judgment as to what the rules of common law are; and that in the federal courts "the parties are entitled to an independent judgment on matters of general law":
>
> But law in the sense in which courts speak of it today does not exist without some definite authority behind it. The common law . . . is not the common law generally but the law of that State existing by the authority of that State without regard to what it may have been in England or anywhere else. . . .
>
> Thus the doctrine of Swift v. Tyson is, as Mr. Justice Holmes said, "an unconstitutional assumption of powers by courts of the United States which no lapse of time or respectable array of opinion should make us hesitate to correct."[48]

These remarks are sometimes read as if they were a professorial lecture expressing an emerging jurisprudential consensus about the nature of law.[49] But the nature of the common law is an essentially contestable matter; both in 1938 and today, one may find profound spokesmen on both the rationalist and voluntarist sides of the debate.[50] Brandeis's opinion is important not because it adds new philosophical arguments, but because it authoritatively put the Court on a different side of the jurisprudential barricades. Henceforward, it was *unconstitutional* for the Court to indulge rationalist phantasies about the common law of property, contract, and tort; these common law frameworks were merely judicial expedients that could be revised at will by democratic legislatures. This holding made the inquiry suggested by *Carolene*'s Footnote 4 even more pressing. If it was unconstitutional for the Court to follow *Lochnerian* presuppositions about the common law, what *were* legitimate grounds for judicial review in the New Deal era?

Erie was silent on this crucial question: it was intent on destroying the old jurisprudential world, rather than defining the new one. But if one digs a bit deeper, there are two elements of Brandeis's opinion that were more constructive. First is its remarkable resuscitation of federalism: just at the moment that the New Deal Court was destroying the old notion that Congress had limited powers over the economy, Brandeis was creating a new—if more modest—constitutional role for states' rights in the courts. Unless Congress intervened with a statute, federal judges were to give a new deference to the common law judgments reached by state courts.[51] Over time, this Brandeisian vision would spawn an elaborate body of constitutional lore of great professional interest—though of secondary importance to the larger public.[52]

Erie also supplied methodological tools for the construction of new constitutional foundations. It inaugurated a remarkable act of transvaluation. Normally, lawyers and judges are trained to follow majority opinions and look skeptically on arguments found only in dissents. But with *Erie*, the Court began to promote a very different orientation: Holmes's dissents were canonized, while the solemn decisions of the pre-1937 majority were demonized as jurisprudential monstrosities.

This remarkable transvaluation would play a central role in the final stages of consolidation. But in 1938, it was still too soon for confident predictions about the future. For one thing, Brandeis's opinion gained the express endorsement of only five members of the Court, with even a New Dealer like Reed denying the need to reach such high constitutional ground; for another, *Erie* was only a single case, though an important one, and it might have proved a mutant in legal evolution. While the New Deal Court had taken a quantum leap forward during the 1938 term, judicial consolidation could have been reversed by the outcome of the 1940 elections.

But the majority of Americans were not inclined to rethink the New Deal. They were not even willing to elect a self-declared "liberal Democrat" like Wendell Willkie—despite his powerful invocation of the constitutional taboo against a third-term Presidency. As a consequence, Roosevelt could continue his strategy of transformative appointment, enabling the Court to carry the process to its final stage.

A landmark was reached on February 3, 1941, when the Court handed down *United States v. Darby.* The case involved the Fair Labor Standards Act of 1938, which made it a crime to ship any goods in interstate commerce that were manufactured either by children or by workers making less than the national minimum wage.

Darby upheld the statute, but by 1941, this was utterly predictable. The remarkable thing was the Court's opinion. It was unanimous. Three days earlier, the last of the *Lochnerian* jurists, James Clark McReynolds, had retired from the Court;[53] as a consequence, when a lawyer consulted *Darby,* he found *no* indication that the *Lochnerian* principles elaborated over two full judicial generations were still to be taken seriously.

The significance of unanimity cannot be underestimated. Even when one or two Justices are willing to elaborate a doctrinal tradition, the older principles remain a vital part of the living constitution. Not only does a constant stream of dissenting opinions testify to the continuing relevance of the tradition, but practicing lawyers will continue to study them with painstaking care—if only because dissenters vote and may make a difference when splits in the majority ranks appear. Over the long haul, the dissenters may have a larger impact. Their ongoing critique may subtly influence the opinions expressed by the dominant majority. No less important, they will serve as a priceless resource should a new President come into office responsive to the constitutional values the dissenting tradition emphasizes. If he convinces the Senate to support his nominations to the Supreme Court, the new appointments can reinforce a living tradition of constitutional discourse, already containing a familiar and elaborate critique of the prevailing doctrine. Through a gradual process of evolutionary reinterpretation, the dissenting doctrine will begin increasingly to shape the path of the law.

But once McReynolds abandoned the field, practical men and women of affairs no longer had any reason to learn or remember the intricate doctrine fashioned by the Justices of the middle republic—

especially when they looked at the Court's unanimous opinion. Justice Stone's text reinforced the tendencies already visible in 1938. On the level of doctrinal statement, *Darby* was even more categorical than *Carolene* in its sweeping affirmation of national regulatory authority. So far as the powers reserved to the states were concerned, Justice Stone announced that the Tenth Amendment "states but a truism that all is retained which has not been surrendered. There is nothing in the history of its adoption to suggest that it was more than declaratory . . ."* Stone wasted only a single paragraph dismissing the notion that the Due Process Clause might restrict the government's power to regulate "free market" bargains between workers and their bosses. *Lochner*'s contrary holding was not even cited, much less discussed.[54]

But Stone could not so easily evade a second great case from the middle republic: *Hammer v. Dagenhart*. In this decision from 1918, a divided Court had declared unconstitutional an earlier effort by Congress to ban the products of child labor from interstate commerce. Since *Hammer*'s reasoning condemned the more ambitious New Deal statute, Stone had little choice but to confront it, if only to inter it. In discharging this task, he recurred to the technique Brandeis used in *Erie,* overruling *Hammer* on the basis of "the powerful and now classic dissent of Mr. Justice Holmes setting forth the fundamental issues involved."[55]

This opinion vastly reinforced the remarkable transvaluation of majority and dissent that is a defining feature of modern constitutionalism. Over time, the great Holmes would be joined by Brandeis and other dissenters of the middle republic to join in a privileged canon of jurisprudential truth, while the majority opinions of the Old Court

---

*United States v. Darby, 312 U.S. 100, 124 (1941). This message was reinforced by Wickard v. Filburn, 317 U.S. 111 (1942), rejecting a farmer's protest against a federal effort to limit the amount of wheat he could grow for use on his own farm. Since this wheat would never leave the farm, how could it be involved in interstate commerce?

A decade earlier, this question would have admitted only one answer. Even more than the kosher butcher in *Schechter,* the family farm in *Wickard* was a paradigm case of local production activity previously immune from the centralizing grasp of the federal government.

But no longer: "Even if we assume that it is never marketed, it supplies a need of the man who grew it which would otherwise be reflected by purchase on the open market." Id. at 128. The Court's unanimity emphasized the decisive character of this revolutionary transformation.

were sweepingly consigned to the junk heap of "discarded" precedent.[56] Justices on the modern Court predictably disagreed about the best way to avoid the bad mistakes of *Lochner,* but *everybody* agreed that the best way to discredit an argument was to taint it with the sin of "Lochnering."

Reconstruction Reconsidered

The only real parallel for this root-and-branch repudiation is Reconstruction. Just as the Supreme Court would never again cite *Dred Scott* with approval after the *Slaughterhouse Cases* of 1873, it would never again cite *Lochner* with approval after *Darby* in 1941. In both transformations, the previously dominant view of the Constitution had not been reshaped and reevaluated by the slow and subtle processes of common law critique and adaptation. Within the short space of a decade, the old structure had been leveled to the ground and replaced with a new foundation: from slavery to freedom; from laissez-faire to the activist welfare state.

I need hardly remind you that these two consolidations occurred through different legal means: the Republicans won their juridical revolution with the assistance of formal amendments that had pretensions to an Article Five pedigree, while the Democrats dispensed with these amendment-simulacra and built their new foundation directly out of transformative judicial opinions. This difference in legal materials prompts an obvious question: did the fact that the Republicans used amendment-simulacra contribute to the greater endurance of their achievements than those of the New Deal?

On formalist accounts, there is nothing like an Article Five text to secure the long-run impact of a generation's constitutional contribution; a constitutional revolution marked only by judicial opinions is somehow less secure. But this simple theory does not square with the facts. Today's Justices of the Supreme Court are *far* more ready to ignore some of the greatest texts left by Reconstruction than they are to ignore the New Deal charge of *Lochnerism.* For example, all legal historians recognize that the Reconstruction Republicans—both in and out of Congress—placed their highest hopes on the Fourteenth Amendment's solemn guarantee that no state shall "abridge the privileges or immunities of citizens of the United States." And yet the courts have never seriously redeemed the promise of this text. While judges are constantly on the lookout for the least signs of the *Lochnerian* heresy, most go to their graves without giving an hour's thought to the provision of the Fourteenth Amendment that the Republicans supposed would serve as the central memorial of their achievement.[57]

Darby's staying power also challenges conventional wisdom on the role of *stare decisis* in constitutional law. According to the usual banalities, modern law is characterized by its casual treatment of precedent, its disrespect for the principles of *stare decisis*. How, then, to account for the enduring character of the New Deal landmarks?

By refining our idea of precedent. Most judicial opinions are merely markers in an ongoing professional conversation; as they are exposed to new factual circumstances, and ongoing professional critique, many will be found wanting. Their rise and fall is simply the product of the gradual and inevitable change in professional opinion. Rather than a cause for mourning, this flux is a sign of vitality—a recognition that lawyers must forever be adapting their craft to new insights and realities.

But there is another kind of precedent. These decisions do not mark the provisional conclusions of a narrowly professional discourse. They memorialize the rare determinations of a massive and sustained conversation by the American people. These transformative precedents have, and should have, a special status in the legal conversation. Since lawyers did not make them, lawyers cannot unmake them. *Darby* is one of these great precedents.[58]

Not that all Americans of the early 1940's had been magically converted to the New Deal vision of the Constitution, any more than a previous generation had all been converted to the Republican vision of the Union. There were millions of traditionalist Republicans in the 1930's who still believed in *Hammer*, just as there had been millions of traditionalist Democrats in the 1860's who still believed in *Dred Scott*. But by 1941, it was clear to the dissenters that most Americans had soberly repudiated the old views. Perhaps a time would come when a new Lincoln or Roosevelt would seek to challenge the New Deal consensus; perhaps the American people would respond affirmatively to this challenge, and, after a long struggle, perhaps the new President and his rising party would earn authority from the People to repudiate

Darby and replace it with the laissez-faire vision expressed by *Lochner* and *Hammer?*

But this would not come about without another generation taking on the burden of constitutional politics. For the present, the People had spoken decisively on behalf of activist national government, and the Court was now determined to elaborate the doctrinal implications of this new constitutional commitment.

Conclusion: Creation or Rediscovery?

Americans of the 1930's knew what they were doing—and were not shy about saying that they were rebuilding, and not merely rediscovering, the foundations of popular sovereignty in America. While I have been scattering bits and pieces of their conversation into these chapters, I have saved the best for last. Shortly after the Senate rejected court-packing, it fell to the President to celebrate the 150th anniversary of the Philadelphia Convention. This is what he said:[59]

> One hundred fifty years ago tonight, thirty-eight weary delegates to a Convention in Philadelphia signed the Constitution. . . .
>
> A third of the original delegates had given up and gone home. The moral force of Washington and Franklin had kept the rest together. Those remained who cared the most; and caring most, dared most. . . .
>
> The Constitution of the United States was a layman's document, not a lawyer's contract. *That* cannot be stressed too often. Madison, most responsible for it, was not a lawyer; nor was Washington or Franklin, whose sense of the give-and-take of life had kept the Convention together.
>
> This great layman's document was a charter of general principles, completely different from the "whereases" and the "parties of the first part" and the fine print which lawyers put into leases and insurance policies and installment agreements. . . .
>
> But for one hundred and fifty years we have had an unending struggle between those who would preserve this original broad understanding of the Constitution as a layman's instrument of government and those who would shrivel the Constitution into a lawyer's contract.
>
> Those of us who really believe in the enduring wisdom of the Constitution hold no rancor against those who professionally or politically talk and think in purely legalistic phrases. We cannot seriously be alarmed when they cry "unconstitutional" at every effort to better the condition of our people.

Such cries have always been with us; and, ultimately, they have always been overruled.

Lawyers distinguished in 1787 insisted that the Constitution itself was unconstitutional under the Articles of Confederation. But the ratifying conventions overruled them. . . .

Lawyers distinguished in their day persuaded a divided Supreme Court that the Congress had no power to govern slavery in the territories, that the long-standing Missouri compromise was unconstitutional. But a War Between the States overruled them.

Lawyers distinguished in their day persuaded the Odd Man on the Supreme Court that the methods of financing the Civil War were unconstitutional. But a new Odd Man overruled them.

Less than two years ago fifty-eight of the highest priced lawyers in the land gave the Nation (without cost to the Nation) a solemn and formal opinion that the Wagner Labor Relations Act was unconstitutional. And in a few months, first a national election and later the Supreme Court overruled them.

For twenty years the Odd Man on the Supreme Court refused to admit that State minimum wage laws for women were constitutional. A few months ago, after my message to the Congress on the rejuvenation of the Judiciary, the Odd Man admitted that the Court had been wrong—for all those twenty years—and overruled himself.

In this constant struggle the lawyers of no political party, mine or any other, have had a consistent or unblemished record. But the lay rank and file of political parties *has* had a consistent record.

Unlike some lawyers, they have respected as sacred *all* branches of their government. They have seen nothing *more* sacred about one branch than about either of the others. They have considered as *most* sacred the concrete welfare of the generation of the day. . . .

[The] lay rank and file can take cheer from the historic fact that every effort to construe the Constitution as a lawyer's contract rather than a layman's charter has ultimately failed. Whenever legalistic interpretation has clashed with contemporary sense on great questions of broad national policy, ultimately the people and the Congress have had their way.

But that word "ultimately" covers a terrible cost.

It cost a Civil War to gain recognition of the constitutional power of the Congress to legislate for the territories.

It cost twenty years of taxation on those *least* able to pay to recognize the constitutional power of the Congress to levy taxes on those *most* able to pay.

It cost twenty years of exploitation of women's labor to recognize the constitutional power of the States to pass minimum wage laws for their protection. . . .

We know it takes time to adjust government to the needs of society. But modern history proves that reforms too long delayed or denied have jeopardized peace, undermined democracy and swept away civil and religious liberties. . . .

We will no longer be permitted to sacrifice each generation in turn while the law catches up with life.

We can no longer afford the luxury of twenty-year lags.

You will find no justification in any of the language of the Constitution for delay in the reforms which the mass of the American people now demand.

Yet nearly every attempt to meet those demands for social and economic betterment has been jeopardized or actually forbidden by those who have sought to *read* into the Constitution language which the framers refused to *write* into the Constitution.[60]

My aim has been to provide materials that will allow a serious confrontation with this Presidential text. Along with Roosevelt, we have located the struggle between the New Deal and the Old Court as part of a recurring dialectic between populism and legalism in American history. We too have glimpsed the institutional patterns generated by proponents of fundamental change who refuse to be "seriously alarmed" when their opponents "cry 'unconstitutional' at every effort to better the condition of our people." We too have used the Founding and Reconstruction as the best precedents for understanding the New Deal.

At the same time the President recalls America's unconventional history of popular sovereignty, there is a disturbing blindness—indeed arrogance—to his address. Not once does he mention that his proud claims to speak for the People had only recently been rejected by the Senate in the court-packing controversy. He cannot conceal his impatience with the "twenty-year lags" that the separation of powers requires before it allows "the law [to] catch up with life." So far as he is concerned, "we can no longer afford the luxury" of such lengthy periods of institutional testing. It is as if Roosevelt had emerged from the court-packing struggle with a total victory.

There is a sense in which the modern view of the New Deal tracks the blind side of the President's speech. Like the President, modern constitutionalists hold that the period of conflict between 1932 and 1937 was a ghastly mistake; that it would have been better if the Old Court had upheld the New Deal in 1933 and 1934; that the Court's precipitous retreat in 1937 was a constitutional debacle of the first magnitude.

Perhaps, then, I can best conclude my critique by reflecting on the inadequacies of the President's speech. Begin with his claim that the American people cannot "afford the luxury of twenty-year lags" which "sacrifice each generation in turn while the law catches up with life." The question the President begs is that many different visions of "life" compete with one another in the United States, and that the effort of the law to "catch up" with "life" in one direction often demands a departure from much in "life" that other Americans value.

Moreover, the particular vision of social life elaborated by the New Deal had not dominated American public opinion during the long period of Republican ascendancy between the Civil War and the Great Depression. Thus, before the President could credibly claim a popular endorsement for a new vision of American government, he and his fellow Democrats had their work cut out for them. They had to move beyond the ambiguities of their 1932 Party platform and give the American people a clearer sense of direction; only then could they return to the people and convince them that their experiment in activist government was worth endorsing; having gained sweeping electoral victories, they would have to convince millions of doubters that this triumph was not some momentary flash in the pan, but was best interpreted as a considered judgment by a majority of Americans that activist government deserved a fundamental place in our political system; and as popular consent was at last secured, they would have to define more clearly the legal principles that would shape the new regime.

In all of this, legalistic resistance was not a pointless "luxury." The Old Court's early show of opposition encouraged the President and Congress to make some hard choices between the full-blown corporatism of the NIRA and the more focused strategy of structural reform that sought to control, but not abolish, the free market system. As a consequence of the Court's constitutional critique, even the 17 million Americans who voted against Roosevelt in 1936 would find it hard to deny that the People had embraced the ideal of regulated capitalism *with their eyes open.* In short, the Old Court's early effort to say No to the New Deal made the People's Yes in 1936 more credible, especially to those who remained unconvinced on the merits. When the Old Court finally began to respond with its switch in time, surely it was time for the conservatives in the country to begin to reconcile themselves, however bitterly, to the thought that the People had spoken?

This dialectical process of legitimation is entirely missed by the President in his Constitution Day Address. Rather than contenting himself with an important role, Roosevelt wants to be all-important—as if a President invariably speaks with the voice of the People whenever he demands that Congress and the courts "catch up with life." But this, to put it gently, is an exaggeration.[61] My model of modern constitutional change recognizes the rise of the Presidency to a plebliscitarian role, but roots this development in a larger process mediated by Congress, the Supreme Court, and ordinary Americans at the polls. Within this framework, the initial election of a President can at best serve as a signal for serious debate on the nation's constitutional future, a signal that can ripen into a serious constitutional proposal only if the Congress gives the President its sustained support despite the Court's sustained constitutional critique; only if the Presidential/Congressional initiative is then emphatically endorsed by the voters at the next Presidential election should the Old Court begin to consider whether a switch in time is in order.

If, after sober second thought, the Court concedes that a mobilized majority of Americans is demanding fundamental change, it may begin to retreat from judicially entrenched constitutional principles, giving the President and Congress an opportunity to consolidate their reformed constitutional vision by replacing retiring justices with transformative appointments. Only if the Presidentially led movement maintains electoral support for the period required to transform the bench will the time come when the Supreme Court consolidates the new regime by unanimous opinions that repudiate the old order in the name of new principles.

This reading of the New Deal precedent forces modern constitutionalists beyond the myth of rediscovery. At the same time, it urges them to focus on the perils of ignoring the very real role the modern Presidency plays in the process by which We the People debate and decide our constitutional future. Such blindness has its source in the formalistic belief that the rules of Article Five are the beginning *and* the end of our historical engagement with the complexities of higher lawmaking. As the President's Constitution Day Address suggests, this blindness was not shared by the New Dealers themselves, who were perfectly aware, and very proud, of their relationship to the tradition of unconventional transformation symbolized by the Philadelphia Convention and the Reconstruction Congress. If modern lawyers allow formalist presuppositions to ignore the constitutionally creative aspect of the New Deal, they are not doing justice to the protagonists' own understanding of the period. Worse yet, they are depriving themselves of essential insights for understanding today's Constitution, which owes more than formalists suppose to the constitutional achievements (and failures) of the New Deal generation.

It is past time for us to turn to this crucial aspect of the matter.

CHAPTER THIRTEEN

Reclaiming the Constitution

RULES, PRACTICES, PRINCIPLES

THE AMERICANS: a restless and unruly people—yet remarkably restrained when it comes to playing by the rules of government. The French Revolution provoked two centuries of upheaval in Europe, but the American Revolution had the opposite effect. Two hundred years later, and only twenty-six amendments[1] to the original Constitution—what a consensus!

Or so I have been told by many admiring foreigners and, less forgivably, by many Americans. No matter how often repeated, this story is false. America's modern Constitution was created during the Roosevelt Administration through processes unknown to Article Five. It displaced an earlier arrangement established after the Civil War— the biggest bloodbath fought in the West between 1815 and 1914. Since the Federalist Founders had hoped to avoid this war at all costs, it isn't surprising their system of constitutional revision proved inadequate in its aftermath. During both Reconstruction and the New Deal, the protagonists were all too aware of the revolutionary game they were playing. If we are to forget their unconventional achievements, we should have the grace to recognize that it is *we* who are doing the forgetting.

It is better to remember—if only to recapture deeper truths concealed by banalities about the "rules of the game." I do not deny that American constitutional experience has been exceptional, or even that it has been exceptionally continuous. But these continuities cannot be understood through the model of rules.[2] If Americans have not been faithful to the rules, in what sense have they been faithful at all?

I have been developing two answers—one pointing to enduring

principles, the other to institutional practices. My first volume elaborated key dualist ideas that continue to inform the Constitution: most notably, the belief that the People should not be confused with their government, but that they can speak in an authoritative accent through sustained and mobilized political debate and decision. This book has focused on institutional practice—the distinctive patterns through which claims to popular sovereignty have been tested, and sometimes confirmed. The key notion has been unconventional adaptation: at periods of peak mobilization, victorious movements use their control over standing institutions to take actions that go well beyond normal legal authority. Unconventional adaptation bends accepted legalisms to the breaking point, generating deep anxieties in the minds of all and plausible charges of outright illegality from outraged opponents. The constitutional fabric threatens to disintegrate.

But this is not (quite) what happens. As the citizenry peers over the precipice, the sense of crisis concentrates the collective mind. Slowly, painfully, the People affirm the need to build a new legal order out of materials inherited from the past. Presidency, Congress, Court—the names remain the same, but fundamental relationships are reshaped through unconventional activity. The same is true of the relationship between central government, the states, and private rights. As we explore these recurring processes of reconstruction, we glimpse a paradox: Americans owe their extraordinary constitutional continuity to the same anarchic spirit visible elsewhere in national life; it is only by unconventional responses to mobilized movements that our dualistic system has endured. How have we managed to succeed in such a perilous enterprise?

DEEPER STRUCTURES

As the organizing power of ordinary legality declines, Americans discover that the Constitution contains deeper imperatives that continue to shape their struggle for power and legitimacy.

Two in particular. The first is the electoral calendar, which has proceeded remorselessly for two hundred years. Even when protagonists challenge existing rules and principles, they are well aware that the voters' judgment will not be long delayed. And they know that their opponents will forcefully bring their legal irregularities to public attention.

Here is where the second basic structure comes into play: the separation of powers between House, Senate, President, and Court. Given the electoral cycle, it is very difficult for revolutionary reformers to win control over all four branches simultaneously. This not only means that unconventional movements must be prepared for a long and difficult struggle. They must also take their opponents' arguments seriously, at least during the interim period when traditionalists still control some of the key institutions.

This can result in a very creative period of constitutional dialogue—in which reformers are invited to rethink their critique of traditional constitutional arrangements, and redefine their transformative ideals in response to sustained resistance. During both Reconstruction and the New Deal, this give-and-take led to a certain degree of moderation. In both cases, the most extreme projects for transformation—Thaddeus Stevens's radical reconstruction, Roosevelt's NIRA—lost out. But the reforms that survived still seemed quite revolutionary to millions of traditional Americans. Rather than crediting the claim of Republicans or Democrats to speak for the People, these traditionalists looked upon the reformers as cynical demagogues, exploiting a moment of crisis to transform the Constitution in profoundly harmful ways. Given their convictions, traditionalists were tempted to respond with political boycotts and vigilante violence, generating an accelerating cycle of incivility.

There was a lot of this during Reconstruction—and a good deal during the lockouts and sit-down strikes of the New Deal. Nonetheless, the relatively long interim period of divided power helped contain this fearsome dynamic. The separation of powers invited traditionalists to take part in an extended constitutional drama—in which their champions played leading roles for a very long time. Rather than turning away from the scene in Washington with disgust, conservatives remained emotionally involved in the struggles of President Johnson or the conservative Supreme Court against the demagogic Republicans or Democrats—hoping against hope that they would continue to resist until "the People came to their senses." This continuing psychological engagement made it easier for conservatives to live with the results. If even President Johnson or the Supreme Court finally gave way before the repeated electoral mandates won by the Republicans or the Democrats, perhaps it was time for conservatives in the country to reconcile themselves to the new regime?

The separation of powers, in short, restrained both sides even at their most unconventional moments. It encouraged reformers to use bits and pieces of traditional constitutional language in efforts to persuade resistant branches to give way. Traditionalists, in turn, were encouraged to continue playing the game by unconventional rules in the hope that the voters might deal them better cards at the next election. Since they only gradually came to see that the People had dealt them a losing hand, it was harder for them to cash in their chips and refuse to play the new game as it displaced the older one. After all, even the new game allowed the traditionalists to protect some of their basic interests—albeit under terms less advantageous than those they enjoyed under the previous regime. Rather than giving their opponents free reign, didn't it make more sense for traditionalists to master the new system—and turn it to their own advantage?

As the traditionalists—or at least many of them—continued to play the game, new issues started dominating the political agenda, leading to new alliances that crossed old divisions. It became increasingly pointless to raise the old legal questions that generated such passionate division during the prior period of unconventional activity. Sober conservatives accepted the new status quo and left the legalistic quibbling to diehards and historians.*

CONSTITUTIONAL IDENTITY

Over two centuries, a form of constitutional continuity has emerged that resembles a type recently discussed in philosophical circles. These discussions have typically involved questions of personal identity, but they cast a useful light on our present problem. To test our understanding of personhood, philosophers have proposed a series of

---

*There is an obvious danger here. Over time, conservatives may use their power in the new system to subvert the revolutionary reforms made previously in the People's name. This is essentially what happened in the aftermath of Reconstruction—though it took place more gradually, and less inevitably, than is often supposed. See Chapter 8, n. 126. The next volume considers this crucial problem of erosion—and what can be done to solve it—at greater length.

thought-experiments that disrupt normal expectations: Imagine that half of Bruce's brain is transplanted into Owen's body. The rest of Bruce's brain dies in Bruce's body, but Browen wakes up with Bruce's memories, does a good imitation of Bruce's characteristic actions, and insists that you call him Bruce. Are you willing to treat him as if he were Bruce?

Maybe.

Suppose next that Bruce as well as Browen survive the brain transplant operation, and both have Bruce's memories and both claim to be Bruce!

Here, it would seem, Browen's claim should be rejected—since the half-brained Bruce is a "closer continuer" than Browen of the single Bruce who existed before the operation.[3]

This notion of "closer continuity" helps explain the sense in which the American Constitution remains continuous despite periods of unconventional activity. During these periods, the normal rules governing relationships between different institutional components suffer severe disruption. By the end of the unconventional transition, the appearance of American government may differ as radically as Browen from Bruce. Yet, *so long as the old government has died,* the new one is the "closest continuer" despite its unconventional pedigree.

Imagine, for example, two governments claiming authority in North America in 1870. One of them, USA, had managed to maintain the Constitution of 1860 perfectly intact. Since the second one had gone through all the unconventional processes of Reconstruction, I call it RUSA. On this scenario, USA would have had a better right than RUSA to assert continuity with the Founding Fathers—just as the half-brained Bruce would have been a "closer continuer" than Browen.

But, of course, USA was not in existence in 1870. There was only RUSA, a creature like Browen—one that maintained many institutional memories of the first republic, one that acted in ways reminiscent of USA. Granted, the shift from USA to RUSA didn't occur according to preexisting legal rules and principles; but at every moment during the transition, there were people in Washington claiming authority as President, Congress, and Court, and they were regularly redeeming these claims by electoral appeals to the People.

RUSA, in short, had deep institutional connections with USA and was the "closest continuer" remaining in existence. Moreover, its genesis was consistent with many of the fundamental principles of dualist democracy that gave the earlier republic its constitutional identity. Shouldn't we recognize it as continuous with the earlier republic despite its unconventional creation?

Especially when the Republican break with Federalist principles revealed deep weaknesses in the foundational premises that had originally given meaning to Article Five. As we have seen, the Founding system presupposed answers to two questions that went to the very heart of American constitutional identity: Who are "We the People" anyway? What institutions best express our considered judgments?

On the first question, the Federalists supposed that Americans could express themselves as a People only if they managed to speak in the accents of both nation and state: the new national center was the only place that could propose a re-vision, but the states were the only ones that could ratify the proposed amendments.

On the second question, the Founders had simply adopted the English answer: The People expressed themselves in deliberative assemblies—like the House of Commons or the great Convention-Parliament that codified the meaning of the Glorious Revolution. While Presidents and Justices might play important roles in normal politics, Article Five banished them from the scene when the People were to deliberate on constitutional fundamentals.

These answers made sense in the aftermath of the Revolution, but they did not endure the destruction of the early republic in civil war. Reconstruction Republicans denied the authority of the white Southern states to reject the mandate for the Fourteenth Amendment earned through national elections. Two generations later, Franklin Roosevelt advanced a similar critique of Article Five. Only this time it was big business, rather than Southern whites, who threatened to use their power over state legislatures to veto the People's will as expressed in a series of national elections.

The Founders' exclusive focus upon deliberative assemblies was also challenged during Reconstruction and shattered during the New Deal. Roosevelt's plebiscitarian use of the Presidency marks a decisive breakthrough, but it built on generations of constitutional politics, including the remarkable efforts by Presidents Lincoln and Johnson on behalf of the Thirteenth Amendment.[4] Unlike their eighteenth-century predecessors, modern Americans treat Presidential elections as a principal forum through which they can engage in mobilized debate and decision on our future as a nation.

Without this kind of unconventional creativity, it is hard to see how Americans could have democratically transformed themselves from a decentralized Union of white men to a Nation of all races and creeds whose government—on both federal and state levels—is actively engaged in assuring a better life for all citizens.

Nor is there reason to suppose that Americans have reached the end of history. Future crises await. As established legitimacies disintegrate, we will once again glimpse the ultimate question: Shall we let the entire enterprise go under, or will we creatively adapt ongoing structures to sustain and renew the collective sense that the People *do* govern in America?

But I refuse to look too intently into the crystal ball—not because it is blank, but because it is too easy to conjure up crisis scenarios. Different scenarios expose existing institutional patterns to different strains and stresses. Rather than play the prophet, it makes more sense to cast a critical eye on the existing regime. Sixty years have passed since the New Dealers transformed the basic structure of American government. What has become of these great Rooseveltian precedents?

FROM ROOSEVELT TO REAGAN—AND BEYOND

Founding precedents run deep. The New Deal experience was seared into the consciousness of an entire generation. When citizens of the modern republic made their own efforts to gain higher lawmaking authority, it offered them an established language and process within which to proceed. What can happen once, can happen twice. If Roosevelt could inaugurate a new era of constitutional law through Presidential leadership, why not his successors?

Efforts to reenact the Roosevelt scenario propelled the founding precedent forward in time. It also precipitated further precedents that refined, and transformed, earlier meanings. The 1980's provide a paradoxical example.[5] While President Reagan challenged New Deal liberalism, he used Rooseveltian precedents to make the effort. In particular, the Reaganites failed to make a serious Article Five effort to repudiate the activist welfare state through formal amendments. Instead, the 1980's proved to be a variation on the transformative themes set out in the 1930's.

Presidential Signaling

By electing Ronald Reagan in 1980, the American people used the Presidency much as they did in 1932: as a constitutional signal, authorizing our representatives to place a new subject on the agenda of fundamental political debate. Ironically, this subject was nothing other than the continuing validity of New Deal liberalism, as it had been elaborated during the preceding half-century.

In choosing Ronald Reagan over Jimmy Carter, the American people had not authoritatively repudiated New Deal Democracy. But as in 1932, Americans *were* willing to elect a President with enormous charm who was transparently eager to challenge fundamental aspects of the constitutional legacy. The question was whether Reagan would use the Presidency in the Rooseveltian manner to lead the citizenry to redefine their fundamental relationship to national government.

The parallels between Roosevelt and Reagan continued into their first years in office. Reagan won early Congressional support for epochal tax legislation that threatened to deprive the activist regulatory state of the resources required to remain credible. By radically reducing tax rates on the rich, the reform also opened up a debate on the legitimacy of the redistributive activities of the activist state.

Reagan's early triumphs were especially impressive given the political composition of the Congress. While Republicans won control of the Senate for the first time in a quarter-century, the Democrats remained dominant in the House. Despite this, Reagan managed to convince enough of them to jump on the bandwagon. Could the Republicans sustain their momentum in the next election by wresting control of the House from their opponents?

Anatomy of Failure

Here is where the Presidentialist scenarios diverge. Reagan failed to break out of the normal "off-year" election pattern—the Republicans moved up from 53 to 54 seats in the Senate, but fell from 189 to 167 in the Democrat-dominated House.[6] This failure undermined Reagan's short-term capacity to push more transformative initiatives through Congress. It also forced a basic question to the center of the stage: As the American people began to consider the "Reagan Revolution" more soberly, perhaps they would not find its leading principles worthy of their support?

To put the point in Article Five terms, suppose a second constitutional convention had met in Philadelphia upon the request of two-thirds of the states, but the assembled delegates failed to agree on amendments and dissolved in disarray. We might call such a case a *failed constitutional proposal*. Reagan's failure to repeat Roosevelt's "off-year" triumph raised a similar possibility within the evolving model of Presidential leadership.

The President's smashing electoral victory of 1984 did nothing to resolve this question. Reagan's personal triumph was of Rooseveltian proportions, but Republicans failed to win a breakthrough in Congress—the House remained safely in Democratic hands, and the number of Republican Senators dropped from 54 to 53. In contrast, the New Deal landslide of 1936 left only 16 Republicans remaining in the Senate and 89 in the House.

Numbers tell only part of the story. More important is what the New Dealers did with their majorities. Neither President Roosevelt nor the New Deal Congress remained content with their early triumphs of the First Hundred Days. When the Court struck down key initiatives, the New Dealers took up the constitutional challenge in landmark legislation like the Labor Act and the Social Security Act. In contrast, the Republicans' failure to sweep Congress meant that their transformative promises went unredeemed. Reagan's tax reform simply generated massive budget deficits, as Congress refused to scale down government aspirations to match the tax cuts. As the years proceeded, the kind of escalating confrontation between the "political branches" and "preservationist Court" simply did not occur—at least when measured against the benchmark of the Roosevelt years.

The contrast became starker after the elections of 1986, when the Administration lost its majority in the Senate. By this stage, the New Dealers were already sealing their constitutional triumph through a series of transformative appointments to the Supreme Court. But despite the vastly different fate of his political effort, Reagan was trying to follow the Roosevelt example—nominating first Antonin Scalia and then Robert Bork to the Court. If allowed to continue, this pattern of nomination would have predictably culminated in a new series of *Darby*-like opinions—with the New Republican Court of the 1990's condemning the "era of *Roe v. Wade*" with the same ferocity as the New Deal Court condemned *Lochner v. New York*.

But it was not to be.

Appointments, Normal and Transformative

Before moving into the details, consider the challenge confronting any Administration that seeks to reenact the Rooseveltian precedent.

Normal Change

The Court is a conservative institution. The Justices are surrounded by a thick web of case law that defines a world of constitutional meaning.

The world turns as time moves on. New problems force new understandings of established principles to the fore; the arrival of new Justices slowly changes the balance of opinion. Clusters of new decisions provide perspectives that challenge older principles and decisions. And so forth.

For present purposes, only two aspects of this normal evolutionary process are important. The first is the time frame: large changes typically occur only over the course of twenty or thirty years, or more. Second is the extent to which the overwhelming majority of lawyers and judges—especially the most successful ones—are committed to the ethos of interstitial change. This commitment is ingrained in decades of habitual practice, in which clients and courts reward lawyers who make tightly contextualized judgments, and punish those who deal in sloppy abstractions and broad-brush analogies.

Presidential Preconditions

If, then, a President is intent upon reenacting the Roosevelt precedent, he must be very careful in his appointment practices. It will not suffice to nominate *distinguished professionals* who have vaguely supported the President and his party in the past—such Justices will find it far too easy to relapse into their ingrained habits of interstitial adaptation.

He must use his opportunities to advance a different kind of Justice to the bench. As Roosevelt's practice suggests, *constitutional visionaries* can come from three different backgrounds. They may be politicians, like Hugo Black, who have not spent most of their careers parsing cases for clients and courts. They may be leading lawyers in the executive branch, like Stanley Reed or Robert Jackson, who have been spearheading the President's legal campaign in the courts. Or they may be legal academics, like Felix Frankfurter or William Douglas, who have devoted much of their lives to a spirited jurisprudential critique of the old order. (Or they may be shaped by two or three of these molds.)

For a transformative strategy to succeed, it is not enough that the Presidency be allied with the same set of ideological forces for a significant period of time (determined by the mortality rate of sitting Justices). Presidents must be so interested in constitutional transformation that they are willing to sacrifice other, shorter-term, objectives. First, they must resist the temptation to use the Court as a source of high-level political patronage. Lots of the Presidents' political allies dream of crowning their careers with a Justiceship—or they may, more altruistically, wish to win a seat on the Court for one of their own clients. But the faithful servant with the most powerful patronage claim may not be deeply committed to the Presidency's transformative project. If appointed to the Court, he or she will only delay the day of constitutional triumph.

A second, and yet more compelling, countermotive is the President's interest in his own reelection. Supreme Court nominations provide symbolic rewards for crucial electoral groups. In the nineteenth century, this meant a lot of appointments from swing regions of the country. Nowadays, the appeal is to women and to ethnic, racial, and religious groups.

This motive is clearest in the case of Presidents who have no compelling transformative objectives. Consider Eisenhower's appointment of William J. Brennan. As the President considered the replacement of Sherman Minton in the summer of 1956, his November reelection campaign wasn't very far from his mind. Nominating a Catholic Democratic state judge from New Jersey was simply good campaign strategy—maximizing the chances of carrying Brennan's closely contested home state, and appealing to Democratic Catholics throughout the North. Next to these straightforward calculations of normal politics, Brennan's legal views were distinctly secondary.[7]

A similar calculus is visible even in more transformative Presidencies. Take the case of Sandra Day O'Connor, President Reagan's first appointment to the Court. While she would have been disqualified if she had declared the liberal Brennan as her role model, ideological purity was hardly the President's first concern. By nominating the first female Justice in the Court's history, Reagan was appealing to a crucial electoral constituency that tended to favor the opposing party disproportionately.

From Scalia to Kennedy

The contrast with Reagan's second term couldn't be plainer. Neither Antonin Scalia nor Robert Bork owed their nominations to the juicy mix of tribal and regional calculation that looms so large in normal politics. Reagan wanted to place them on the Court for the same reasons Roosevelt chose Felix Frankfurter and William Douglas. Like these New Dealers, Scalia and Bork were legal academics who were able and willing to write transformative opinions that might consolidate a newly ascendant constitutional order.

But there was a crucial difference. When Roosevelt nominated Frankfurter and Douglas, there were 69 Democrats in the Senate.[8] If there had been 69 Republican Senators when Robert Bork was nominated, does anybody doubt he would be on the bench today?

This is too narrow a way of putting the point. If the Reagan Revolution had swept the country in the way required to win such sweeping majorities in Congress, the nominations of Scalia and Bork would have been crowning notes in a triumphalist chorus coming out of Washington. Along with a new breed of legal intellectuals on the bench, the Reaganites in Congress would be enacting new framework statutes elaborating upon their earlier assaults on the activist welfare state.

Instead of functioning as part of a larger constitutional process, the nominations of Scalia and Bork looked more like clever stratagems by an ideological Presidency to transform the Constitution without gaining the kind of broad and deep support required by dualist principles. In the case of Justice Scalia, the gambit succeeded since the Republicans still controlled the Senate; but when President Reagan nominated Bork after the Senate went Democratic in 1986, it is hardly surprising that his transformative nomination went down to defeat.

The next move was the President's and it was crucial. Reagan could have responded by nominating a second constitutional visionary who, like Bork, had made his career as an eloquent critic of the modern Court's jurisprudence. If the Senate had rejected this nominee as well, the stage would have been set for a serious struggle during the election of 1988. The Republican candidate for President could have made the Senate's obstructionism a central part of his electoral appeal; his Democratic opponent might have praised the Senate's defense against extremism. In the course of this debate, the definition of "mainline" constitutionalism would have been revised—in ways difficult to foresee.

But Reagan chose to evade this public confrontation. Like others before him, the President recognized that interbranch struggle might only reveal the shallowness of his support. Rather than provoke a sustained constitutional debate with another Bork-like nomination, he chose the path of normal political accommodation.

The nomination of Anthony Kennedy was more important for what it wasn't. Kennedy was vaguely conservative, but there was nothing about him that suggested a Bork-like determination to destroy the foundations of existing jurisprudence. The President was offering up a nominee who would engage in the normal judicial adaptations that, over the decades, generate difficult-to-predict constitutional modifications, rather than quick and sharp breaks. The evident relief with which the Senate and the country seized this olive branch helped push the system back into normal mode.

From Souter to Breyer

Subsequent events have broadly confirmed that politics has returned to normal. The selection of George Bush as the Republican candidate for the Presidency in 1988 was itself a sign of lost transformative energy. It was difficult to imagine a candidate with feet more firmly planted in the status quo—unless it was the Democratic challenger, Michael Dukakis. Vaguely to the left of an ill-defined center, the Democrat was more of a smart technocrat than a revolutionary reformer.

Against this background, President Bush's nomination of David Souter was constitutionally appropriate. In sharp contrast to Robert Bork speaking of change at his confirmation hearings, Souter assured the Judiciary Committee that his judicial hero was John Marshall Harlan, the great interstitialist. Sharp and wide-ranging breaks with the past were the last thing he had in mind.

Souter's selection was not only significant in itself; it reinforced the constitutional meaning of Kennedy's previous selection. It had been possible to read the Kennedy maneuver as a tactical retreat—buying time for an aggressive return to the transformative strategy with the next judicial opening. But Bush's decision to follow up with Souter suggested that there was more than tactics involved. His actions revealed a recognition that the Republican Presidency was failing to win a Roosevelt-style mandate to transform higher law.

To some extent, this was also the message of the Clarence Thomas affair. Bush's nomination continued a great tradition of normal politics—just as Dwight Eisenhower used Brennan, and Ronald Reagan used O'Connor, President Bush used Thomas to appeal to a constituency, black Americans in this case, that was largely in the opposing party's camp.

But there was also a clever transformative edge to this move. For the first time since Bork went down, the President had chosen a nominee linked to the New Right's constitutional agenda. Thomas had taken a host of controversial stands as chairman of the Equal Employment Opportunity Commission during the Reagan years. By nominating a black conservative, the Administration was hoping to defend against the liberal Democratic onslaught that had defeated Bork. Did liberals have enough constitutional conviction to transcend the normal politics of race to vote against a black man whose views they abhorred?

During the first round of hearings before the Judiciary Committee, it became clear that the answer was No. The President's clever politics seemed to be paying off, when his opponents made a tricky move of their own—transferring their attack from the substance of Thomas's views to his personal morality.

A second round of televised hearings, featuring Anita Hill's charges of sexual harassment and Thomas's impassioned counterattack, revealed new weaknesses in the evolving process of Senate confirmation. Millions of television viewers were treated to a carnival reminiscent of the McCarthy Hearings of the 1950's. Existing Senate procedures were incapable of determining the truth of the charges. Neither accuser nor defender were given the tools—cross-examination, compulsory process—that might have allowed a fair trial of issues of fact. Rather than deferring the matter for the period needed to make dispassionate findings, the Senate rushed to a vote, and Thomas squeaked through without a fair chance to redeem his tattered reputation (as only a scrupulously fair inquiry could have accomplished). Whatever else may be said about the process, it reemphasized the cycles of incivility let loose by Presidential attempts to make transformative appointments without the requisite political support in the Senate and the country.

The election of President Clinton made it even clearer that the Reagan-Bush years would not culminate in a Roosevelt-style transformation. Clinton was not content to stop the Republican revolution in its tracks; although he had won only 43 percent of the popular vote, he aggressively launched a large campaign of his own for universal health care. But this only served to reveal the weakness of public support for large transformative enterprises at present—as did the subsequent failure of the Republican Congress to sustain support for its Contract with America.

Clinton's Supreme Court nominations, in turn, fit perfectly into this larger political context. His selection of Ruth Ginsburg falls broadly within the category of normal judicial politics. As a pathbreaking lawyer for the woman's movement, Ginsburg had marked herself out by the moderation of her argument and her success in making interstitial constitutional gains in the courts. While more sympathetic to the liberal landmarks of the Warren-Burger era, she was no left-wing Scalia, intent on bulldozing large blocks of established doctrine. The President's nomination of Stephen Breyer also suggested moderation. With the opposition party now in control of the Senate, Clinton avoided a rerun of the Bork-Thomas scenarios by appointing a distinguished professional acceptable to key Republican Senators. With every appointment, the transformative thrust of the Reagan years was muffled further.

The Meaning of Casey

As the Presidency and Senate were moving erratically back into normal mode, the Court was also measuring the moment. A crucial arena for appraisal centered on *Roe v. Wade.* The Republican Party, and its Presidential candidates, had run against the Court on this issue time and again. As Presidents Reagan and Bush won popular support against pro-choice Democrats in three consecutive elections, their Solicitors General had repeatedly invited the Court to reconsider *Roe.* An increasingly mobilized right-to-life movement gave substance to the claim that, in opposing *Roe,* the Presidents were not engaged in normal political posturing, but expressed the deep convictions of a large number of American citizens.

This pattern of Presidential leadership should, by now, be familiar. But as we have seen, it is not enough for the Presidency to serve as a signaling mechanism; the cause of constitutional reform must repeatedly carry the party to victory in Congress as well as the Presidency before it can claim a mandate from the People of Rooseveltian proportion; only then may the time be ripe for a judicial switch of the 1937 type.

This broader pattern was absent during the Reagan-Bush years. As a consequence, the Republican effort to overrule *Roe* fell far short of its objective. In the Court's 1989 decision in *Webster v. Reproductive Health Services,*[9] a narrow majority weakened the particular rules *Roe* had laid down to protect the pregnant woman's right to choose. But the two normal appointments of the Reagan years—O'Connor and Kennedy—refused to join Justice Scalia's call for a root-and-branch repudiation of *Roe* and the Warren Court jurisprudence it presupposed. By 1992, the Reagan-Bush failure to go to the mat for Bork-like appointments had decisive effect. If Republican Administrations had responded to the Bork defeat by successfully mobilizing nationwide support for further transformative nominations, the 1992 Court would have contained, in addition to Justice Scalia, three more voices urging the decisive repudiation of *Roe.* This recent wave would have swept along at least two Justices who owed their original appointments to a more distant past—William Rehnquist and Byron White. Just as the third term of the Roosevelt Administration saw the Court demonizing *Lochner,* the third term of the Reagan-Bush period would have seen a transformed Court demonizing *Roe* as the great anti-precedent of a new constitutional age.[10]

Instead, the Reagan-Bush retreat meant that their Administrations' higher lawmaking pretensions would be assessed by a Court containing three of their own normal appointments, O'Connor, Kennedy, and Souter. In emphasizing the non-transformative character of these appointments, I do not suggest that their decision on *Roe* was inevitable. The Reagan-Bush retreat had a subtler significance: Rather than leaving *Roe*'s fate to the gentle mercies of constitutional visionaries, the Court would be dominated by Justices who thought of themselves as distinguished professionals exercising autonomous legal judgment.

What is more surprising, in this bureaucratic age, was the eloquence with which the three Justices undertook their legalistic mission in their famous separate opinion. They insist that it is possible to develop professional criteria for determining whether a "switch in time" is legitimate. What is more, they spoke for a majority of the Court on this central matter.

The opinion[11] searched in the right places for legally operational criteria. On its view, only two precedents "from the last century" served as appropriate benchmarks: the New Deal Court's repudiation of *Lochner* in 1937, and the *Brown* Court's rejection of *Plessy* in 1954. The test it proposed was straightforward: if *Roe*'s opponents could establish a compelling analogy to the situation obtaining in 1937 or 1954, the three Republican legalists were prepared to join the Scalia group in another "switch in time"; if not, not. This is, of course, precisely the approach this book means to encourage.*

The timing of *Casey* was no less significant than its content. It only took the vote of a single one of the Reagan-Bush professionals to create a majority for overruling *Roe*. And if this had occurred, the election of President Clinton would have generated another bitter round of appointment politics. Since both the President and the Democratic Party were committed to freedom of choice, Clinton's judicial nominations would have catalyzed a mighty struggle in the Senate. If pro-*Roe* nominees made it to the Court (on the first or the *n*th try), the result would have been a decade of jurisprudential crisis as a new 5-to-4 majority overruled *Casey*'s 5-to-4 overruling of *Roe*—leading perhaps to an effort by the next President to reverse the reversal . . . The Court's opinion called a halt to this degeneration into

---

*Since I discussed *Brown,* and its relationship to *Plessy,* in my first volume, *We the People: Foundations* (1991), ch. 6, I restrict myself here to *Casey*'s characterization of the situation in 1937.

normal Presidential politics, and gained constitutional weight precisely because it came from Reagan-Bush appointees. Rather than a dying gasp of the old order, it was the distinguished professionals of the present who were declaring that, unlike 1937, the time was not (yet) ripe for a fundamental break with the past.

This declaration will not end the political strife surrounding the abortion question—nor should it. But it put the participants on notice that *Roe* will be overruled only if the conservative movement mobilizes more successfully in the 1990's than it did in the 1980's. In the fullness of time, the American republic will undoubtedly go through another successful effort at radical redefinition and renewal. But it will occur only on the basis of broader and deeper support amongst the People than the Republicans have thus far managed to generate.

Quibbling with the Justices

Constitutional law lives on many levels—as a generator of political meaning for the general public, as a positive set of commands for politicians and bureaucrats, as an ongoing professional discourse for the legal community.

I have been deferring *Casey*'s contribution on the last front because it is inevitably more provisional, opening lines of argument for further professional critique and development.

In this spirit, I have problems with parts of the Court's analysis. Here is the meat of its discussion of the "switch in time":

> The Lochner decisions were exemplified by Adkins v. Children's Hospital, in which this Court held it to be an infringement of constitutionally protected liberty of contract to require the employers of adult women to satisfy minimum wage standards. Fourteen years later, West Coast Hotel Co. v. Parrish signaled the demise of Lochner by overruling Adkins. In the meantime, the Depression had come and, with it, the lesson that seemed unmistakable to most people by 1937, that the interpretation of contractual freedom in Adkins rested on fundamentally false factual assumptions about the capacity of a relatively unregulated market to satisfy minimal levels of human welfare. As Justice Jackson wrote of the constitutional crisis of 1937 shortly before he came on the bench, "The older world of laissez faire was recognized everywhere outside the Court to be dead." . . . Of course, it was true that the Court lost something by its misperception,

or its lack of prescience, and the Court-packing crisis only magnified the loss; but the clear demonstration that the facts of economic life were different from those previously assumed warranted the repudiation of the old law.[12]

This discussion trivializes the dominant concerns of early-twentieth-century jurisprudence. The *Lochner* era was not based on a simple misapprehension of "the facts." First and foremost, it was concerned with the preservation of values—especially the very value of liberty that Casey also reaffirms.[13] When the New Deal Court repudiated *Lochner* after 1937, it was repudiating market freedom as an ultimate constitutional value, and declaring that, henceforth, economic regulation would be treated as a utilitarian question of social engineering.

Such a paradigm shift represents a constitutional change of the most fundamental kind. In Robert Jackson's words, it signifies the disintegration of "[t]he older *world* of laissez-faire."[14] For the constitutional lawyer, this world was constituted by interlocking assertions of fact and value that supported a complex pattern of legal doctrines. When Jackson proclaimed the "death" of such a world, he was doing far more than quibbling with a few facts, however fundamental. He was doing the same sort of thing that Mr. Justice Scalia would dearly love to accomplish today: sweeping away an entire world of argument that had been dominant in the preceding era.

Once we move beyond the Court's superficial characterization of the 1930's, its similarities to the 1990's become unmistakable. Both in the 1930's and the 1990's, the Court was called upon to assess the durability of a constitutional world built up by a generation and more of juridical effort—each world dedicated to the protection of a (different) conception of liberty (as well as other values). During both decades, the Justices confronted powerful political voices denouncing the legitimacy of the established world—urging the Justices to allow the political branches a much freer hand in "balancing" the competing interests at stake. During both decades, they were obliged to confront the question whether the old world was dead, or worthy of continued preservation.

The majority points to a deeper difference, however, when it quotes Jackson's remark that the death of laissez-faire was "recognized everywhere outside the Court." Here the emphasis is on the Old Court's intellectual isolation, not its erroneous factual findings. Even more interesting, when the Justices restate Jackson's point, they correct its exaggerated triumphalism: rather than repeating Jackson's assertion that the bankruptcy of laissez-faire was "recognized everywhere," they are more circumspect: "the Depression had come and, with it, the lesson that seemed unmistakeable *to most people* by 1937, that the [Old Court's] interpretation of contractual freedom . . . rested on fundamentally false factual assumptions."[15]

This more cautious formulation is entirely justified. Alf Landon won seventeen million votes in 1936, many of them from firm believers in the moral economy of laissez-faire. Nor was the "death" of laissez-faire recognized in all philosophical or economic circles. Like most such obituaries, Jackson's was vastly premature. Rather than waking up one day to discover that the old order had "died," the Supreme Court of the 1930's was called upon to confront a contestable question of judgment: Was the bankruptcy of *Lochner*'s jurisprudence "unmistakeable to most people"?

This was also the ultimate question in 1992, when the status of *Roe,* and the constitutional world that made it legally plausible, was called before the bar. Rather than trivializing its problem, it would have been better for the Justices to confront it squarely: Had the Reagan-Bush Presidency, like its New Deal predecessor, established the illegitimacy of *Roe* as "unmistakeable to most people" by engaging in a lengthy contest with the Old Court, carrying the country and Congress in support of a legislative framework to protect the human fetus, and making a triumphant series of transformative judicial appointments who ushered in a new age of constitutional understanding?

To ask this question is to answer it—the Justices were on sound ground distinguishing the Reagan-Bush years from Roosevelt's. The weaknesses of their analysis should not blind us to the soundness of their judgment. Thanks to *Casey,* the institutional order at the end of the Bush Administration differed radically from the pattern arising in the wake of Roosevelt's precedent-shattering third term. Rather than all three branches proclaiming the dawn of a new era, the Reagan-Bush Administrations retire from the scene with the Supreme Court reaffirming the need for continuity with the recent constitutional past.

We have returned to normal politics. This does not mean that the President and Congress have nothing important to do with their time. Though no political party or movement has mobilized the energetic and sustained support of the People for its cause, a lot remains on the agenda: balancing the budget, comprehensive health care, social security, and so forth. Similarly, the Court will be constantly called upon to revisit the past as it seeks to preserve the People's constitutional commitments—how to integrate the principles of the Founding, Reconstruction, and the New Deal into a compelling whole that makes sense of our present predicaments? Reasonable judges will come up with different answers—and we should expect the dominant answers to evolve as they are exposed to ongoing professional critique and the lessons of practical experience. But the watchword here should be evolution, not revolution. It is wrong to suppose that the judges can play a vanguard role when the People themselves are silent. It is more than enough for them to try to preserve the achievements of the past in ways that do them justice.

My next volume, *Interpretations,* will try to clarify the judicial challenges that lie ahead. But I want to end this book with some reflections on the higher lawmaking lessons we may draw from our recent experience. The retreat from the Reagan years should not lull anybody into complacency about the Presidency. While I can't predict the date or the cause, I am certain that some future President will once again claim a mandate from the People for radical constitutional change; and that the citizenry, Congress, and the Court will be obliged to take the measure of these claims. We have not heard the last of Franklin Roosevelt's Constitution Day Address.

When that day comes, the Reagan-Bush years should set off a warning signal, alerting us to the dangers lurking in the Rooseveltian legacy of transformative judicial appointments. Indeed, it should suggest the need for serious higher lawmaking reform before the next plebiscitarian Presidency overtakes us.

After enumerating the disadvantages of the Rooseveltian system, I sketch an agenda for reform. Granted, it will take time to alert the larger public to the dangers of the status quo, but it is never too soon to start the ball rolling.

What's Wrong with Transformative Appointments?

I want to revive a conversation begun in 1937. Recall that Roosevelt's leading critics responded to Presidential court-packing by urging a formal revision of Article Five. Only the "switch in time" allowed the President and Congress to terminate the discussion inconclusively. Once the Court began to uphold the framework statutes of the New Deal, it was easier for the politicians to relax and let Roosevelt replace the Old Court gradually through a series of transformative appointments. But as we have accumulated experience with the use and abuse of the Roosevelt precedent, it increasingly looks like his critics had the better idea. The evolving practice has grave deficiencies as a method of democratic change.

Legal Focus

Under the classical system of Article Five amendment, a formal proposal comes early in the process. While a textual statement of principle hardly eliminates ambiguity and confusion, it does provide a focus for democratic discussion.

Contrast the studied ambiguity of modern practice. Whenever the President makes a nomination to the Court nowadays, he does so under the shadow of the precedents of the Roosevelt and Reagan years: Is he embarked on a systematic effort to jolt constitutional law into a new direction? It will often pay for the President to deny this intention even if he harbors it—since it is usually much harder to gain Senate consent for a constitutional visionary than a distinguished professional.

Presidential denials will predictably fail to convince. Skeptical critics will search frantically through the candidate's record, looking for tell-tale signs of the candidate's revolutionary intentions. In response, Presidents may come up with "stealth" nominations, who may harbor transformative ambitions but are so undistinguished that they have never voiced these sentiments in public.

Even if the President resists the "stealth" temptation, and nominates a committed constitutional visionary, the resulting confirmation struggle can generate a great deal of smoke. The nominee may bob and weave, while critics rip his comments out of context. In the end, the nominee's true views may be lost in clouds of rhetoric. They will be deflected further by his personal style, charisma, and frailties. A graceful television presence may conceal an unattractive constitutional vision. Or opponents may stoop to character assassination. The substantive issues at stake will soon be lost amidst the mud-slinging—only to reemerge if the candidate makes it to the Court.

Institutional Weight

Under the classical system, an amendment must surmount a formidable set of institutional barriers on both the national and state levels. Compared to this obstacle course, the modern practice of Presidential leadership is relatively insubstantial.

In coming to this judgment, I do not underestimate the rigors of the modern system. A single transformative appointment is not the functional equivalent of a constitutional amendment. As we have seen, it took Roosevelt many appointments, and many elections, before the Court consolidated the New Deal revolution. During periods of normal politics, no single party may dominate the Presidency and Senate long enough to reenact Roosevelt's precedent. Moreover, even potentially transformative Presidents often have political incentives to appoint Justices who lack a compelling constitutional vision.

Nonetheless, the New Deal precedent may be abused by future Presidents with far more equivocal mandates than Roosevelt's. After all, each President's power to influence the Court depends on the vagaries of death and resignation. A significant number of vacancies may open up during the term(s) of an ideological President who lacks broad and deep support. Given the ease with which Senatorial confirmation battles can obscure the underlying issues, it is just too easy for randomly selected Presidents to revolutionize constitutional law without the kind of popular support required in dualist theory.

Popular Responsiveness

Changing the Constitution by changing the Court is also less democratic, especially since the process of gaining Senatorial consent does not invite the mass participation properly required for a new constitutional beginning. Think again about Article Five's stipulation that our representatives in Washington may only propose amendments, and that a broader debate is required in the states before an amendment can be ratified. While Americans may no longer believe that the states should always have a veto over national political change, this hardly implies that Senate hearings provide an adequate alternative. If the Senate is controlled by the same party as the President, the hearings may serve as a very superficial probe indeed.

Even if a different party is in control, hearings are inadequate. Since concerned participants have little prior notice of the vacancy and the nominee, they cannot mobilize a sustained constitutional debate in the country on the underlying issues. At the very most, they can catalyze a momentary spasm of high interest by seeking to demonize the candidate, focusing as much as possible on personal deficiencies. Once the mud-slinging begins, Senators will be eager to end the candidate's misery with an up-or-down vote within a few months of initial nomination.

Surely we can do better than this to organize public participation in a process of debate and decision that may, over time, yield decisive changes in constitutional doctrine.

Problem-Solving Potential

Finally, the Supreme Court is simply not well suited to confront many of the constitutional problems of modern life. While the Justices may transform—for good or for ill—the substance of constitutional rights, they are poorly situated to resolve questions of institutional structure. If some future generation of Americans wants to reorganize the bureaucracy or public finance or reconstruct the foundations of federalism, these tasks cannot be readily accomplished by a series of transformative opinions. There is a need for a broader-ranging set of institutional tools.

REFORM?

Legal focus; institutional weight; popular responsiveness; problem-solving capacity. Looking backward, it is easy to see why these problems did not surface during the 1930's. Quite simply, the majorities won by the New Deal were unprecedented in American history, crossing all the traditional lines of region, race, and even class. Given the New Deal's broad support in the country, the President could openly nominate a series of committed visionaries to the Court without generating the pathologies of the Reagan-Bush years.[16] We will run into trouble only when Presidents with weaker mandates use Rooseveltian precedents as a springboard for constitutional transformation.

I begin with a modest proposal. At present, a bare majority in the Senate suffices to confirm a Presidential selection. This is too low a barrier. A super-majority of two-thirds would take much of the sting out of the Rooseveltian precedent. No longer could an ideological President with a weak mandate use a slim Senatorial majority to ram through a constitutional revolution. Since the opposition party almost invariably possesses a third of the seats, Presidents could no longer expect to succeed by appointing constitutional visionaries. They would be obliged to consult with the political opposition and select distinguished professionals who would adopt an evolutionary approach to constitutional interpretation. Super-majority requirements have proved their value in modern European systems; we should take these lessons seriously as we reflect on our recent experience.[17]

But we can and should do more. Indeed, a super-majority requirement might be counterproductive if adopted without more sweeping reforms. Taken by itself, my "modest" proposal would deprive the President, and the nation, of the only method that has yet evolved to permit the expression of the nationalistic aspect of modern constitutional identity. By putting an end to the practice of transformative appointment, it would leave the nation with the state-centered tools provided by Article Five—tools that have repeatedly proved inadequate at the great turning points of the past.

Whatever the weaknesses of present practice, it would be even worse to turn back the clock to the first Republic and ignore the fact that, as a result of the searing experiences of the Civil War and the Great Depression, Americans see themselves as citizens of a nation that is more than a federation of states.* The unconventional responses to these crises establish that the rules of Article Five cannot

---

*The nationalistic self-understanding emerging from the Great Depression gained further constitutional depth in the aftermath of the Second World War and during the civil rights revolution. To be sure, America's experience of total war was very different from its later struggle over civil rights. But the mobilization of civic commitment during both periods ultimately led to the same result—a great enhancement of the typical citizen's appreciation of the Constitution as an expression of a distinctively *national* community that binds him to all Americans, independently of the states in which they happen to live. For more on these issues, see my book with David Golove, *Is NAFTA Constitutional?* (1995).

monopolize our higher lawmaking system. If we hope to move beyond the present practice, we must come up with an alternative that also expresses the modern American understanding that We the People of the *United* States can express its constitutional will in a process in which the President plays an important role. Rather than ignoring Reconstruction or the New Deal, the challenge is to channel nationalistic, and Presidentially centered, understandings into a better lawmaking structure.

Begin by reflecting on the unsatisfactory character of the Rooseveltian precedent, even when it works without the pathologies revealed during the last decade. Imagine, for example, that some future President and Party once again gains the overwhelming and considered support of the country for some fundamental change in constitutional course; suppose, once again, that the President successfully gains the Senate's consent to a series of transformative appointments. After a decade of sustained Presidential leadership, supported by overwhelming electoral victories in Congress, a transformed Supreme Court is happily churning out landmark opinions that, like *Darby* and unlike *Casey,* unanimously commit it to the new constitutional order adumbrated by the previous activities of President and Congress. Isn't there something wrong with this pretty picture?

I don't want to sound querulous: America could do a lot worse when confronting its next great crisis. Nevertheless, the Rooseveltian scenario assigns too active a role to the Supreme Court and too passive a role to the President, Congress, and the voters. Just as politicians in the White House and Capitol Hill are finally earning the authority to speak for the People, they suddenly stop in mid-stream—and hand the job of constitutional articulation over to the Supreme Court. Wouldn't it be better if President, Congress, and the voters hammered out principles on their own authority, before the Court began to get into the act?

This is, after all, the path taken by Article Five. Under its federalistic procedures, the leading politicians on the national and state levels hammer out a constitutional amendment in the name of the People *before* the Court steps in. I believe that We the People of the *United* States should be afforded a similar opportunity—this time using actors and processes that operate exclusively on the national level. Only after providing such a nation-centered alternative can we responsibly close off the existing system of transformative appointment by adding a super-majority requirement.

Before sketching my affirmative proposal, it will help to recall the general outlines of the process we are seeking to regulate.

The Challenge

During normal politics, the center of American politics is occupied by politicians and parties content with interstitial modifications of the existing regime. Speaking broadly, the mass of American citizens look on with detachment, satisfying themselves with minimal forms of civic involvement. While there are many groups devoted to fundamental reform, each wants to transform the system in very different ways, and none can plausibly claim to set the agenda for the mainstream of American opinion.

This is what changes during a constitutional moment. As a result of many electoral victories on many different levels, a broad movement of transformative opinion has now earned the authority to set major aspects of the political agenda.

But a constitutional moment need not ripen into a new constitutional solution. A movement's success in organizing a broad base of Americans for fundamental change may only lead to a backlash—in which most Americans, after considering the transformative proposal, reject it.

And yet success is always possible. The mark of such periods of constitutional solution is a rare convergence in the language and concerns of leaders in the capital and ordinary citizens in the streets. Ordinary Americans are no longer looking upon their leaders with their usual skepticism. The constitutional rhetoric in Washington resonates in billions of conversations on the job, around the breakfast table, and countless social settings.

Not, mind you, that everybody is happy with the emerging outcome. But there is a broad sense, shared (bitterly) by many opponents, *that the People have spoken.*

The challenge[18] is to design a higher lawmaking system that expresses these distinctive rhythms of popular sovereignty, one that builds on the experiences of nationhood articulated during Reconstruction and the New Deal and consolidated thereafter.

The Proposal

Let us add two institutions into the higher lawmaking matrix. The first is the Presidency: Upon successful reelection, the President should be authorized to signal a constitutional moment and propose amendments in the name of the American people.

When approved by Congress, such proposals would not be sent to the states for ratification. They should be placed on the ballot at the next two Presidential elections, and they should be added to the Constitution if they gain popular approval.

In contrast to the system prevailing under Article Five, each voter will be treated as an equal citizen of the nation. His judgment on the referendum question will not count more if he happens to live in Wyoming than in California. The aim is to register the considered judgments of We the People of the *United* States.

This proposal is open to many interesting variations. Perhaps we should insist on a super-majority at one or both elections? Perhaps we should disqualify the referendum results if too few voters go to the polls to express a judgment? Perhaps we should change the number and timing of electoral tests?

But for the present, I limit myself to the two basic innovations— Presidency and referendum—and how combining them into a larger system reduces the risks associated with each device.

The Problem with Referenda

The constitutional politics of the Progressive era led to the adoption of initiatives and referenda in many states. Experience teaches that these mechanisms have many weaknesses as well as strengths.[19]

Most important, it is usually too easy to get initiatives on the ballot. Voters are regularly confronted with long lists of unfamiliar proposals and cast their ballots on the basis of hurried reactions to a media blitz. Such charades, remorselessly repeated over the decades, generate well-founded skepticism about cheap appeals to popular sovereignty. Whatever their deficiencies, elected representatives are often more knowledgeable than normal voters about the selfish motives that lurk behind attractive slogans; and they have many political incentives to safeguard the public against excessive factional depredation—incentives that are lacking when the general electorate is invited to make a single up-or-down vote on a complex issue.

Nonetheless, the referendum retains its democratic appeal under the special conditions of constitutional politics—when millions of citizens have indeed been mobilized and confront the political agenda with a rare seriousness. The trick is to design a mechanism for triggering the device at the right time—during the period in which a movement has precipitated a constitutional moment, but has not yet won the authority to enact a constitutional solution. Within this crucial period, a referendum provides both opponents and proponents with a chance to make their case to the country in a fair and focused fashion.

How, then, to design a mechanism that will trigger a referendum at constitutional moments and not at other times?

Here is where the Presidency enters. All Presidents should not be granted the referendum power, since many come into office without anything resembling a mandate. But our constitutional experience suggests that a second Presidential victory is sometimes—not invariably—accompanied by plausible claims that the People are up to something.[20]

The Problem with the Presidency

We should not allow the President to design referenda without restraint. An unchecked President could use his proposals for personal or partisan advantage, rather than for expressing considered judgments that might ultimately win the sustained support of the community.

The first check is obvious: Congress should approve the terms of the proposal, probably by a two-thirds vote. But a second check is also important. Call it the test of time. When the President and Congress act, it may be hard for them to identify the likely candidate in the next Presidential race—let alone those in the one afterward. By proposing a constitutional amendment, they will be shaping the agenda of the next two Presidential campaigns in unforeseeable ways. Partisan proposals may prove to be political albatrosses five or six years later, embarrassing the party that originally endorsed them.

The test of time places the protagonists in a position resembling the "veil of ignorance" described by John Rawls.[21] Given the difficulty of calculating their partisan advantage, won't the President and Congress use their new higher lawmaking power to formulate principles that may reasonably gain the considered judgment of their fellow citizens?

THE CASE FOR REFORM

Maybe not. No set of rules can guarantee against all abuse. But if I succeed in provoking debate, further analysis will yield improvements in my proposals.[22] Even my reform package, as it stands, promises big gains over present practice.

Transformative Appointments, Compared

Recall the four weaknesses of the existing system of Presidential leadership through transformative judicial appointments.

Legal focus: If we required a super-majority vote in the Senate for Supreme Court nominees, Presidents no longer would have big incentives to hide their transformative intentions by cleverly selecting judicial candidates. But if they win reelection, they will be able to express their constitutional objectives openly, and in ways that invite focused support and dissent.

Institutional weight: Rather than slipping a number of "stealth" candidates through the Senate, the President would have his transformative ambitions checked by the entire Congress and the citizenry at large.

Popular responsiveness: The President's opponents would not need to mobilize their supporters in a series of *ad hoc* and *ad hominem* campaigns against particular Supreme Court nominees. They would be placed on notice to organize a long hard struggle for the hearts and minds of the American people, punctuated by two scheduled referenda. Their steady and pointed attacks on the President's proposals, moreover, would require a mobilized defense from the ascendant political movement—leading to the kind of considered judgment that the American constitution should aim to articulate and support.

Problem-solving potential: Constitutional amendments are tools that may be deployed to confront institutional and structural issues that have escaped serious control by the Supreme Court during the modern period.

The Classical System, Compared

My proposal bears a strong family resemblance to the classical system described by Article Five. Like the existing procedure, the new one invites a reform movement to frame proposals in the lapidary style of a constitutional amendment; it allows the normal institutions of national government to propose, but not to ratify, the initiative; and it requires national institutions to evidence an extraordinary degree of seriousness before they can place a proposal before the people.

Precisely because of these similarities, my proposal highlights the basic problem with the status quo: the mismatch between modern constitutional identity and the classical forms of constitutional amendment. Modern Americans put their national identity at the center and expect the Presidency to take a leading role in the process of articulating the nation's future. The classical system puts federalism at the center and assumes assembly leadership over the process. It is no accident, then, that most Americans look upon Article Five as a cumbersome and antique device, rather than as a powerful instrument of constitutional redefinition. If we had a new system that allowed for the expression of the nationalistic side of modern identity, the very existence of the system would renew a practical sense of the efficacy of popular sovereignty.

Consider, for example, how the old federalist system processed the Equal Rights Amendment. On the one hand, Article Five deserves high marks for the way it generated a serious political conversation between the women's movement and its critics as the proposal was considered in state after state. On the other hand, it has taught us once again the dangers of allowing a veto by a minority of the states to stifle higher lawmaking in this country. While the campaign for the ERA did generate a far deeper and more considered judgment in this country, the outcome was a strong national majority consistently in its favor. Rather than leading to a renewed sense by Americans that the People *can* govern itself, the outcome was a frustrated sense that the federalist forms had somehow stifled the considered judgment of the national majority. Such frustrations, in turn, feed fixation on the Supreme Court as an alternative forum for constitutional change—rather than trying again to run down a higher lawmaking system that is out of synch with national self-understandings, isn't it much more important to make sure that solid feminists get on the Supreme Court?

I use the ERA as an example because it is the only recent case in which a popular movement has leaped over the initial hurdle to propose a constitutional amendment. But it should be plain that my reform allows conservative as well as liberal movements to take their case to the nation. While many on both sides will fail to win the crucial referenda, the very exercise will reinvigorate popular sovereignty in America.

We the People can reclaim our power to rewrite the Constitution in ways that express our modern constitutional identities. We can become masters of our own house—if, like the Federalists themselves, we have the strength to revise the higher lawmaking rules to express the evolving rhythms of constitutional politics.

The Popular Sovereignty Initiative

Will the political agenda turn this way any time soon? Certainly, there are signs of dissatisfaction with normal politics, and an increasing tendency to search for structural change—recurring efforts to reform campaign finance, the recent movement for term limits on Congressional incumbents. And certainly there have been widespread expressions of discontent with the process of Supreme Court nomination and appointment. But most leading politicians have not yet traced the problem back to its roots in our obsolescent higher lawmaking system.[23]

Perhaps this is all to the good, since lawyers are only beginning to confront the problem. After another few years, constitutionalists may have a clearer sense of the plausible range of reform alternatives. At the same time, popular discontent with existing structures may ripen into a broader recognition of their source in our obsolescent higher lawmaking system. As the year 2000 approaches, politicians may be prepared to ask probing questions and legal professionals might be prepared to provide serious answers. Admittedly, this is an optimistic scenario, but stranger things have happened in the life of the Republic.

It is not too early, then, to open up the conversation on a second level. For this purpose, assume a broadening appreciation of the need for reform. Serious political groups come forward with serious proposals to revise the existing system of Presidential leadership: How should they proceed to enact their reforms into higher law?

One might, of course, proceed along the path marked by Article Five. Other things being equal, this is the better way—since it will appeal to the rule-bound part of the legal community and the general public. But, as you may have noticed, our higher lawmaking system is no longer governed by the rule of rules—if it ever has been. It is a law of principles, practices, and precedents. And these sources of law suggest that it is appropriate to look beyond the rules in the present case.

The problem is familiar: federalism—the very problem which led Americans during both Reconstruction and the New Deal to move beyond Article Five. A Popular Sovereignty Amendment would ask three-fourths of the states to cede their formal monopoly over constitutional change. This is something state politicians may well refuse—but not because they are blind to the fact that most Americans are Americans first, and Nevadans or Rhode Islanders second. State politicians are interested parties.

The applicable precedents do not require reformers to play a lawmaking game so dramatically tilted against them. Rather than aiming for an Article Five amendment, the vehicle for constitutional change should be a special statute that I will call the Popular Sovereignty Initiative. Proposed by (a second-term) President, this Initiative should be submitted to Congress for two-thirds approval, and should then be submitted to the voters at the next two Presidential elections. If it passes these tests, it should be accorded constitutional status by the Supreme Court.

The Court's opinion should track the argument presented in this book. Citing *Coleman v. Miller*, it should explain that Article Five has failed to accommodate the nationalistic aspect of our constitutional identity ever since the Civil War—leading to the proliferation of amendment-analogues during Reconstruction and amendment-simulacra after the New Deal. While the Court facilitated this process in *Ex parte McCardle* and *Coleman v. Miller*, as well as its landmark opinions in the 1940's, this ongoing exercise at creative adaptation has had its costs—most notably the hyperpoliticization of Supreme Court nominations in the modern republic. Rather than resisting the supplementation of Article Five by the Popular Sovereignty Initiative, the Court should greet it with great relief: After more than a century of struggle, We the People of the *United* States have managed to give a formal structure to our higher lawmaking capacities—and one that parallels the structures used by Article Five to express the constitutional will of We the People of the United *States*.

JURISPRUDENTIAL DOUBTS

Isn't there something curious about this proposal? This book has devoted chapter after chapter to exposing the inadequacy of legal rules in regulating the great movements of constitutional law. Having come all this way, isn't it odd to end with a plea for more rules?

Why Formalism?

But there is no paradox here. It is one thing to say that rules have not been all-important; another thing to say they are unimportant. Taken by themselves, rules are lifeless things—marks on paper that neither control nor restrain. Once placed within a setting of principles, institutions, and precedents, they can play a useful supporting role.

As in our particular case. Without a dose of rulishness, the dynamic of Presidential leadership threatens basic principles of popular sovereignty. By setting the Presidency into a better structure, we will not only minimize the dangers but gain some advantages generally associated with legal forms. First, and most obviously, there is the question of notice. With the Popular Sovereignty Initiative on the books, future generations will have a clearer sense of the steps they can take to speak for the People through a nation-centered process. No less important, opponents will understand what they can do to defeat the pretensions of the reformers. Prior notice will tend to legitimate the proceedings in the eyes of all concerned.

Especially, and this is the second point, since the Initiative system was not designed by any of the present protagonists. While the rules may well turn out to have deficiencies, at least they were not caused by a partisan effort to manipulate them to present-day advantage.

Third, the rules will make it easier for lawyers, after the event, to identify *when* a successful constitutional solution occurs and *what* it means. While the present system of transformative opinions has operated rather well over the last half-century to discharge these functions, the crisp markers provided by a new formalism might help from time to time.

None of this suggests that the Popular Sovereignty Initiative provides a final solution to the problem of constitutional adaptation. Along with the benefits of formalism come its costs. At some fateful time, a movement may arise that will find the forms provided by the Popular Sovereignty Initiative as uncongenial as those provided by Article Five—*and yet the People will be heard.* The challenge, once again, will be to act unconventionally in ways that allow a serious and ongoing test of the new movement's pretensions, and that devise credible means for recording its constitutional solutions if they meet with sustained and considered support.

But the fact that rules cannot answer this ultimate challenge does not mean that they cannot answer the particular challenge we presently confront. One of the reasons I end on this formalist note is to emphasize the importance of using *all* the resources of legal understanding if constitutionalists are to sustain dualist democracy.

Beyond Realism

But still, it may be insisted, I have not really confronted the truth about rules—one that has been seared into our constitutional consciousness by none other than Franklin Roosevelt:

> And remember one thing more. Even if an amendment were passed, and even if in the years to come it were to be ratified, its meaning would depend upon the kind of Justices who would be sitting on the Supreme Court bench. An amendment, like the rest of the Constitution, is what the Justices say it is rather than what its framers or you might hope it is.[24]

This fireside chat, in the midst of the court-packing crisis, told the realist truth to the American People. So long as we hold to this Truth, my Popular Sovereignty Initiative seems hopelessly naive. Why take the trouble to modernize the formal lawmaking system, when the judges can do anything they want with any amendment anyway?

But the Initiative not only includes a new lawmaking system; it also contains a proposal requiring a super-majority in the Senate for the confirmation of new Justices.

This, according to the realist, is even worse—especially if it succeeds in encouraging the appointment of solid professional types to the Court, who might take the task of constitutional interpretation seriously. For the strong realist, these poor souls are the victims of false consciousness. There is no such thing as legal interpretation distinct from political preference: "Everything is politics." Judges who deny this dictum are blind. At least those who celebrate the essentially political character of adjudication do not suppress the only impulses that could possibly serve as their guide.[25]

In short: Even if my reforms fulfilled their objectives, they would only yield more lost souls on the bench and new empty formalisms in the text. This is progress?

———

Yes, but only if we have the strength to question the realist banalities of contemporary legal thought. When Roosevelt used realist rhetoric, he enlisted it as part of a larger battle fought in the name of the People against laissez-faire constitutionalism.

But over the past half-century, realism has transformed itself into an apologia for the constitutional status quo. Rather than allowing us to consider alternatives to the system of transformative appointment, it scoffs at the very notion that judges have an obligation to make sense of authoritative texts. Once this realist premise is conceded, the very notion that the People might give marching orders to their government is excluded a priori: Since the judges will play politics with any text, the *only* way to change the constitution is to change the judges. The alternative path, described by my Initiative, is simply an illusion.

There is a self-fulfilling prophecy at work: the more lawyers and judges believe in realism, the more they vindicate its predictions by playing politics, and the more it will seem that rule by the People is a hopeless anachronism.

On the other hand, there is the other hand: the more seriously the legal community takes interpretation, the more it will encourage Americans to take the arduous journey down the formal path of higher lawmaking—in the hope that the judges will sustain their textual commitments long after the reformers have left the scene of political struggle.

How then will lawyers and judges respond? With more realism or a renewed commitment to interpretation?

While interpretivists have launched a jurisprudential counteroffensive over the last decade,[26] I have been on a different mission here. Though the concept of interpretation certainly can use abstract elaboration and philosophical defense, lawyers and judges do not live in the abstract, but in the all-too-concrete conflicts of the present. In the final analysis, the only way interpretivists will be persuasive is by providing concrete interpretations of the constitutional past—and urging others to join in the effort to make sense of authoritative texts and precedents of our past.

We will not always like what we see. As this project took shape during the 1980's, it seemed likely that *We the People* would be published at the same moment that judges like Scalia, Bork, and others would be proclaiming the dawn of a new constitutional order. As a liberal committed to social justice, I was not amused at the prospect of playing into the hands of the Reagan Revolution.

But I was determined to publish nonetheless. The Constitution is not the exclusive possession of those who share my politics. It reaches out to all Americans, conservative as well as liberal, in an effort to find a common language and practice for voicing, and sometimes resolving, disagreements. In elaborating this language and practice, constitutional lawyers are not doing something either better or worse than politics—just different.

Of course, it would be terrible if everybody spent their time worrying about the meaning of the constitutional past at the expense of creating a better future. But there isn't much danger of this. Americans have never been excessively backward-looking; and this will not change in the computer age. If the Republic is to maintain a constitutional memory, it will continue to rely heavily on its lawyers and judges.

During the 1980's, this meant that I would not join my fellow liberals on the field of constitutional polemics—castigating the Rehnquist Court and all its works, and insisting that the Warren Court had gotten the Constitution right once and for all. Instead of treating the Reagan Revolution in a presentist fashion, I owed it to my fellow citizens to test the Reagan years against the relevant constitutional benchmarks—in particular, the Roosevelt years. And if the Reaganites

had managed to measure up to the Roosevelt precedents, I was determined to tell the truth to my fellow citizens—however painful that
truth might be to me.

As it turns out, history has not forced me to this test of civic
friendship. Like it or not, the last constitutional moment has failed.
We have returned to normal politics. Perhaps in a decade or two, a
new generation of conservatives will return and succeed in convincing
the American people to make good on the promise of the Reagan
Revolution; perhaps it will be the liberals who regain the advantage
and make a decisive advance toward social justice; perhaps some
radically new movement will establish its higher lawmaking voice by
displacing the established left-right axis of current political opinion.

Whatever happens, it will be the task of constitutional lawyers to
judge the new movement by the benchmarks of the past—and tell the
truth, as best they can, to their fellow citizens. The enactment of a
Popular Sovereignty Initiative would ease this burden. By disciplining
the pattern of Presidential leadership, it would make it easier for
lawyers to judge the moment at which the excited rhetoric of constitutional politics should be allowed to harden into the contours of new
constitutional law.

But if, as is likely, the Popular Sovereignty Initiative doesn't get off
the ground, we still owe it to our fellow citizens to confront the
lawmaking precedents of the past. These precedents are unconventional, but they provide a key to the American success in sustaining
self-government for two centuries. American lawyers have it in their
power, over the next generation, to throw away this key—in the name
of a false realism that denies the central importance of the past in the
formation of the legal mind.

But we also have it in our power to recall the past with a renewed
sense of the revolutionary truths it contains—and challenge our fellow
citizens to continue the project of popular renewal and redefinition in
the crises that lie ahead.

FREQUENTLY CITED WORKS

NOTES

INDEX

Frequently Cited Works

B   Edmund C. Burnett, ed., *Letters of Members of the Continental Congress* (1936)

CG   *Congressional Globe* [citation format: Congress, Session CG (year), at page]

CR   *Congressional Record* [citation format: CR (year), at page]

D   Merrill Jensen, ed., *The Documentary History of the Ratification of the Constitution* (1976)

E   Jonathan Elliot, ed., *The Debates in the Several State Conventions on the Adoption of the Federal Constitution* (2d ed., 1854)

F   Bruce Ackerman, *We the People: Foundations* (1991)

FDR   Samuel Rosenman, ed., *The Public Papers and Addresses of Franklin D. Roosevelt* (1938–1950) [citation format: year in parentheses indicates the volume in the series]

I   Charles C. Tansill, ed., *Documents Illustrative of the Formation of the Union of American States* (1927)

MPP   James Richardson, ed., *Messages and Papers of the Presidents* (1898)

R   Max Farrand, ed., *The Records of the Federal Convention of 1787* (rev. ed., 1937)

S   Arthur Schlesinger, ed., *History of American Presidential Elections* (1971)

T   Francis Thorpe, *The Federal and State Constitutions, Colonial Charters, and Other Organic Laws* (1911)

Notes

1. Higher Lawmaking

1. See Sacvan Bercovitch, *The American Jeremiad* (1978); Robert Ferguson, *The American Enlightenment* (1996); Perry Miller, *Errand into the Wilderness* (1956).
2. See Albert Hirschman, *Shifting Involvements* (1982); Arthur Schlesinger, *The Cycles of American History* (1986).
3. See Ronald Dworkin, *Law's Empire* (1986), for a useful elaboration of this concept.
4. In the twentieth century, this view is most powerfully developed by Carl Schmitt, *Verfassungslehre,* sec. 8 (1928), who unsurprisingly became the Nazis' principal legal apologist.
5. See E. H. Carr, *The Bolshevik Revolution, 1917–1923,* 109–120 (1950).
6. Id. at 115.
7. See, e.g., Laurence Tribe, "Taking Text and Structure Seriously," 108 *Harv. L. Rev.* 1221, 1293–4 (1995).
8. For further elaboration of this theme, see *F,* esp. chs. 7–10.
9. For further discussion, see *F,* ch. 9.
10. See Ronald Dworkin, *Taking Rights Seriously,* chs. 2–3 (1978); Karl Llewellyn, *The Common Law Tradition: Deciding Appeals* (1960).

2. Reframing the Founding

1. Charles Beard, *An Economic Interpretation of the Constitution of the United States* (1913). This chapter is derived from Bruce Ackerman & Neal Katyal, "Our Unconventional Founding," 62 *U. Chi. L. Rev.* 475 (1995), which contains more documentation for many of its claims, as well as other themes that do not play a central role in this book's argument.
2. Thurgood Marshall, "Commentary: Reflections on the Bicentennial of the United States Constitution," 100 *Harv. L. Rev.* 1 (1987).
3. Among the most perceptive are Robert Burt, *The Constitution in Conflict* (1992); Alexander Bickel, *The Least Dangerous Branch* (1962).
4. See Merrill Jensen, *The Articles of Confederation* 57, 103, 126–139, 183, 238 (1970); Jack P. Greene, *Peripheries and Center* 154 (1986).

5. After July 11, New York never voted in the Convention. Compare Journal for July 10, in 1 R 565, with Journal for July 11, in 1 R 577. See 2 R 641 for the final vote on the Constitution.

6. See 1 D 203. Delaware's problem was broadly recognized at Philadelphia. See 1 R 4, 6, 37.

7. See I 45–46 (emphasis supplied).

8. See 1 D 209 (New York's resolution). Massachusetts' first resolution, passed on February 22 and before the state legislature knew about Congress's resolution the day before, did not contain this limit, but the state later substituted a new one with Congress's "sole and express" limitation. Id. at 205–207. Connecticut was the only other state with the "sole and express" limitation. Id. at 215–216.

9. Id. at 196, 201, 203, 204, 222, 224.

10. *Acts Passed at a General Assembly of the Commonwealth of Virginia, 16 Oct. 1786–11 Jan. 1787*, at 11 (Richmond, 1787) (emphasis added). Such wording appeared in virtually every resolution. See 1 D 199–200, 203, 204, 213, 222, 225. The second Massachusetts resolution provided for Congressional and state approval (id. at 207), as did other states (id. at 214, 216). North Carolina only mentioned approval by the state (id. at 201). The only real exception was New Jersey, whose one-sentence resolution omitted any discussion of anything besides "Taking into consideration" and "devising . . . provisions" (id. at 196).

11. 1 D 187.

12. Ruth Bogin, *Abraham Clark* 134 (1982). Abraham Clark turned down an appointment for similar reasons. Id.

13. Gordon Wood, *The Creation of the American Republic* 226–227, 231–232 (1969).

14. 3 T 1890 (N.H.); 4 T 2454 (Mass.); 5 T 3091 (Pa.).

15. Willi Adams, *The First American Constitutions* 137–144 (1980).

16. In four states, legislatures proposed and implemented the constitution without any advance authority or subsequent ratification: Virginia (1776), New Jersey (1776), Rhode Island and Connecticut (reenacting their colonial charters). In three states, constitutions were adopted by legislatures authorized by popular vote to approve changes but were not submitted to the people: Delaware (1776), Georgia (1777), and New York (1777). In four instances, legislatures with advance authority from the voters distributed pre-enactment drafts to give the people a chance to suggest changes: Maryland (1776), Pennsylvania (1776), North Carolina (Dec. 1776), and South Carolina (1778). See Roger Hoar, *Constitutional Conventions* 4 (1917).

17. John Quincy Adams to William Cranch, 14 D 223–224.

18. Bogin, supra n. 12, at 82–83.

19. Linda De Pauw, *The Eleventh Pillar* 33 (1966).

20. In response to pressure by the Continental Congress and the neighboring states of Connecticut and New Jersey, New York reconsidered its position on the impost in February 1787, and rejected it by a 2-to-1 vote. Ernest Spaulding, *His Excellency George Clinton* 170–171 (1938). This was not necessarily New

York's last word, since pressure from its neighbors remained intense. We will never know the outcome, since attention shifted to the campaign for the new Federalist Constitution.

21. See John Fitzpatrick, ed., 31 *Journals of the Continental Congress* 494–498 (1934).

22. See, for example, *Votes and Proceedings of the House of Delegates of the State of Maryland,* 1st Sess., March 12, 1785: "[T]he proposed meeting, though originating from the best intention, may tend to delay the adoption of the [1783 impost], and the vesting that assembly with proper powers to regulate trade, by the states who have hitherto delayed to accede to these measures, and also that unforeseen consequences may result from such meeting, this legislature has declined to appoint commissioners for this purpose" (available at the Maryland Hall of Records).

23. Here is Rufus King opposing the Convention (in which he later served) on the floor of the Massachusetts House as late as October 1786: "If all the States could be brought into the Continental Impost, the resource indeed might be anticipated, and the national credit strengthened in that way, but there remained two States which had not acceded to it, Pennsylvania and New York. The situation of the former was known, and should that State be brought over, New York would not dare longer to oppose the Union." Speech of October 12, in *Worcester Magazine,* 3rd week of Oct. 1786, at 353.

24. Even in 1788, many members of the state ratifying conventions still wanted the impost instead of a new constitution. See 2 *E* 80; 3 *E* 278; 4 *E* 70.

25. Richard Morris, "The Mount Vernon Conference: First Step Toward Philadelphia," 6 *This Const.* 38, 40 (1985); Nancy McManus, "The Bicentennial of the Mount Vernon Conference," 8 *This Const.* 43 (1985).

26. Broadus Mitchell, *Alexander Hamilton* 356 (1957).

27. Richard Bernstein, *Are We to Be a Nation?* 99 (1987).

28. *Original Laws of Maryland, 1785* (in Maryland Hall of Records); *Votes and Proceedings of the House of Delegates of the State of Maryland,* 1st Sess., Nov. 21, 1785, at 19; "An Act authorizing the states of Maryland and Virginia to lay out and improve a road within the limits of this state, between the waters of the River Patowmack and of the river Ohio," *Maryland Journal* (Baltimore), Feb. 21, 1786, at 3.

29. Max Farrand, *The Framing of the Constitution* 8 (1913).

30. 1 *D* 180.

31. To James Monroe, May 13, 1786, in Gaillard Hunt, ed., 2 *Writings of James Madison* 242–243 (1901).

32. To James Monroe, March 19, 1786, in id., at 233–234.

33. "Since states were forbidden by the Articles of Confederation [Art. VI] to enter into treaties or alliances with each other without Congressional consent, any action by the Annapolis Convention would be clearly illegal. But Madison, if not yet desperate, was determined to do something." William Peters, *A More Perfect Union* 9–10 (1987).

34. Mervin Whealy, "The Revolution Is Not Over," 81 *Md. Hist. Mag.* 231 (1986).
35. Madison explained in 1786 that "Connecticut declined not from a dislike to the object, but to the idea of a Convention, which it seems has been rendered obnoxious by some internal Conventions, which embarrassed the Legislative Authority." 2 *Writings of Madison,* supra n. 31, at 262.
36. *Votes and Proceedings of the Senate of the State of Maryland,* 1st Sess., March 8, 1785, at 84–85.
37. Id.
38. New Hampshire, Massachusetts, Rhode Island, and North Carolina had elected delegates, but they had not arrived. On September 8, Madison wrote in despair: "I came to this place a day or two ago, where I found two [commissioners] only. A few more have since come in, but the prospect of a sufficient [number] to make the meeting respectable is not flattering." To Ambrose Madison, Sept. 8, 1786, in 2 *Writings of Madison,* supra n. 31, at 269.
39. 1 D 182–185.
40. Unfortunately, I have been no more successful than others in uncovering evidence that would reveal the course of the Commissioners' discussions. My analysis is based simply on the text of Hamilton's report.
41. See Walter Mead, *The United States Constitution* 18 (1987); Mitchell, supra n. 26, at 366.
42. Compare Robert Feer, "Shays's Rebellion and the Constitution," 42 *New Eng. Q.,* at 393–394, who minimizes the role of the Rebellion, with David Szatmary, who gives it more emphasis in his *Shays' Rebellion* 127 (1980).
43. An Other Citizen, "On Conventions," in *Worcester Mag.,* 1st week of Sept. 1786, at 273. For similar attacks, see An Old Republican, "Strictures upon County Conventions," *Worcester Mag.,* 3d week of Sept. 1786, at 291.
44. Address of Selectmen of Boston, *Worcester Mag.,* 3d week of Sept. 1786, at 301–02.
45. The dilemma confronting New England legalists was appreciated throughout the country. As late as the state ratifying convention in Virginia, William Grayson remarked: "When this state proposed that the general government should be improved, Massachusetts was just recovered from a rebellion which had brought the republic to the brink of destruction. . . . Massachusetts was satisfied that these internal commotions were so happily settled, and was unwilling to risk any similar distresses by theoretic experiments. Were the Eastern States willing to enter into this measure. Were they willing to accede to the proposal of Virginia? In what manner was it received? Connecticut revolted at the idea. The Eastern States, sir, were unwilling to recommend a meeting of a convention. They were well aware of the dangers of revolutions and changes. Why was every effort used, and such uncommon pains taken, to bring it about? This would have been unnecessary, had it been approved of by the people. . . . There was no complaint, that ever I heard of, from any other part of the Union, except Virginia." 3 E 274–275.
46. Rufus King, "Proceedings of Government," *Worcester Mag.,* 3d week of Oct.

1786, at 353. A month later, Nathan Dane restated King's concerns in another speech to the House, reprinted in the *Newport Mercury,* Nov. 27, 1786, at 1.

47. Only Massachusetts approved Philadelphia before Congress acted. The others responded to Congress's February decision: New York (Mar. 6), Connecticut (May 17), New Hampshire (June 27), and Rhode Island not at all.

48. These included New Jersey (Nov. 23), Virginia (Dec. 4), Pennsylvania (Dec. 30), North Carolina (Jan. 6), Delaware (Feb. 3), Georgia (Feb. 10), South Carolina (Mar. 8), and Maryland (May 26).

49. Lee to Tucker, Oct. 20, 1786, 8 *B* 489–490. Madison says that "[t]he objections which seemed to prevail against the recommendation of the convention by Congress, were with some: (1) that it tended to weaken the federal authority by lending its sanction to an extra-constitutional mode of proceeding—with others (2) that the interposition of Congress would be considered by the jealous as betraying an ambitious wish to get power into their hands." Madison, Feb. 21, 1787, in 1 *D* 188. Madison also notes that New Englanders were less enthusiastic, attributing this in part to "the effect of their late confusions" (i.e., Shays' Rebellion). Id. at 189.

50. 1 *D* 187 (emphasis supplied).

51. Letter of Feb. 11, 1787, in Charles King, ed., *The Life and Correspondence of Rufus King* 201–202 (1894).

52. On February 4, General Lincoln's army took the Shaysites by surprise in Petersham. On the same day, the Massachusetts General Court declared a state of rebellion, which gave Governor Bowdoin virtually unlimited powers. He used them to raise 2,600 troops. Twelve days later, Massachusetts passed an act disqualifying Shaysites from voting, serving as jurors, or holding public office. This ended the threat of major Shaysite assaults. Szatmary, supra n. 42, at 102–107.

53. To General Knox, February 8, 1787, in Thomas Higginson, *The Life and Times of Stephen Higginson* 113 (1907).

54. Letter of Sept. 15, 1787, in William Staples, *Rhode Island in the Continental Congress* 575–576 (1870).

55. See Jay's revealing letter to Washington, in King, supra n. 51, at 208–209.

56. Letter of Sept. 15, 1787, in Staples, supra n. 54, at 576.

57. The problem of illegality burst onto center stage with the first of Virginia's fifteen points, which contended that "a union of the states merely federal will not accomplish the objects proposed by the articles of confederation." Both Pinckney of South Carolina and Gerry of Massachusetts warned that such proposals went beyond their commissions (1 *R* 39, 42–43). These men were crucial for the Virginians, and they quickly deferred further discussion—only to encounter more legalistic resistance to their second resolve, demanding a radical break with the Confederation's "one state–one vote" system in Congress. In response to the predictable objections from Delaware—which Gouverneur Morris joined—the nationalizers rapidly retreated (1 *R* 37). At the time of these debates in late May, representatives from only eight states had appeared in

Philadelphia. A legalistic walkout by Delaware could have pushed the Convention down the road to Annapolis.

58. 1 R 178.

59. Even Hamilton admitted that the plans of the nationalizers "are very remote from the idea of the people. Perhaps the Jersey plan is nearest their expectation. But the people are gradually ripening" (1 R 301). Many intelligent commentators seem blind to the problem of legal authority: "The defenders of the New Jersey plan could not come up with a positive argument for their plan, their best defense of it was that it was less radical and therefore more in touch with what the people wanted" (Fred Barbash, *The Founding* 87 [1987])—as if legality were not a "positive argument."

60. 1 R 250 (Paterson).

61. Id.

62. Id. at 336 (Lansing); id. at 531 (Bedford); id. at 469 (Ellsworth).

63. Madison floated a trial balloon in a speech suggesting that the nationalists' plan could legally count as an appropriate "revision" of the Articles within the terms of Congress's Resolution. After all, the Resolution did suggest that delegates were to "render the federal constitution adequate to the exigencies of government and the preservation of the Union." He also disputed Paterson's claim that the Articles could not be legally dissolved without the unanimous consent of all thirteen states. On his view, there might be occasions where the breach of the Articles by some states allowed others to declare them void. 1 R 314–315.

These remarks had little influence on the debate. Others did pick up a bit on Madison's broad interpretation of the Congressional call, but even strong nationalists like Hamilton conceded he was "not yet prepared to admit the doctrine that the Confederacy, could be dissolved by partial infractions of it." Id. at 324. Ellsworth denounced "the doctrine that a breach of [any of] the federal articles could dissolve the whole. It would be highly dangerous not to consider the Confederation as still subsisting." Id. at 335.

Given this cold reception, it is not surprising that Madison abandoned his legalisms when defending the Convention's triggering decision in public. See generally, Ackerman & Katyal, supra n. 1, at 508–510, 539–558.

64. 1 R at 255. See the similar sentiments of Hamilton, id. at 283; and Mason, id. at 338.

65. Id. at 266 (reported by King). Madison's report of the same remarks does not contain an explicit reference to "revolution principles": "With regard to the power of the Convention, he conceived himself authorized to conclude nothing, but to be at liberty to propose any thing." Id. at 253.

66. 1 E 480.

67. 2 R 475.

68. Id. at 475. The 1776 Maryland Constitution declared that no changes could occur "unless a bill so to alter, change or abolish the same should pass the General Assembly, and be published at least three months before a new election." John Jameson, *American Constitutional Law* §224 (1869).

69. 2 R 476.
70. Id. Luther Martin "repeated the peculiarity in the Maryland Constitution." Id.
71. 2 R 476–477. Actually, it was 1795. Madison might have misheard or King might have misspoken.
72. Id.
73. Id. at 476.
74. Id. at 478.
75. Id. at 560.
76. Id. at 561.
77. Id. at 562.
78. Id. at 563. After Lansing and Yates left the Convention, Hamilton was no longer allowed to cast New York's vote since he did not represent the majority of the state's delegation. The single vote cast in favor of Hamilton's motion was that of Connecticut.
79. 1 D 317.
80. Id. at 336 (quoting Melancton Smith's notes for Sept. 27, 1787).
81. The return seems to have been prompted by his fears of Congressional sabotage. See letter from Carrington to Madison, New York, Sept. 23, 1787, in 1 D 326.
82. Madison did not deny "the right of Congress" to propose amendments, but argued that it would be "inexpedien[t]." Madison to Washington, Sept. 30, 1787, in 8 B 27.
83. Id. Madison parried Lee and Dane's claim that "as the new Constitution was more than an alteration of the articles of Confederation . . . and even subverted those Articles altogether there was a constitutional impropriety in their taking any positive agency in the work" by arguing that "if beyond those powers, the same necessity which justified the Convention would justify Congress."
84. 1 D 329–330.
85. Id. at 332.
86. John Kaminski and Gaspare Saladino, eds., 8 *The Documentary History of the Ratification of the Constitution* 301 (1976).
87. Even the existence of the debate in Congress was suppressed from public view. The Continental Congress deleted all references to it in its official journals. See id. at 301. We owe our knowledge to Julius Goebel, Jr., who found the crucial manuscript in the archives of Melancton Smith, "Melancton Smith's Minutes of Debates on the New Constitution," 64 *Colum. L. Rev.* 26 (1964). A comprehensive collection of the relevant sources is in 1 D at 323–342.
88. Matthew Herrington, "Popular Sovereignty in Pennsylvania 1776–1791," 67 *Temple L. Rev.* 575, 602–603 (1994).
89. Pennsylvania Constitution of 1776, sec. 47, 5 T 3092.
90. The Address of the Seceding Assemblymen, 2 D 112, 113–114. The "seceding assemblymen" consoled themselves that they had forced the majority to expand the campaign period from nine days to six weeks. Id. at 114.
91. See id. at 128.

92. For the only time in its history, all thirteen states attended sessions. Congress met on 132 days in 1788—more than in some other years—and conducted business on a wide variety of matters. See Ackerman & Katyal, supra n. 1, at 519-525.

93. The Federalists' unconventional strategy was quite deliberate. See, e.g., Nicholas Gilman to the President of New Hampshire, Oct. 31, 1787, in 8 B at 670 ("[I]t was not my intention to have taken a seat in Congress this year but as it was conceived important to have a full House on the Subject of the new plan of Government I was induced to take a seat"); Hawkins to the Governor of North Carolina, Aug. 14, 1787, in id. at 639 ("It is of the first importance that our State be represented when the Convention make their report to Congress"); Otis to Warren, Nov. 27, 1787, in id. at 683-684 (same); Blount to the Governor of North Carolina, July 10, 1787, in id. at 618 (referring to Thompson's letter stating that "a Congress was absolutely necessary for the great purposes of the Union").

94. Roscoe Hill, ed., 34 *Journals of the Continental Congress, 1774-1789*, at 304 (July 8, 1788) (1937).

95. For examples of nonratifying states voting on matters pertaining to the organization of the new government, see 34 id. 317-318 (July 14, 1788)(New York and North Carolina); id. at 359 (July 28, 1788) (North Carolina); id. at 367 (July 30, 1788) (North Carolina); id. at 383 (Aug. 4, 1788) (North Carolina and Rhode Island); id. at 394 (Aug. 5, 1788) (same); id. at 395-402 (Aug. 6, 1788) (same); id. at 399 (Aug. 6, 1788) (same); id. at 400 (Aug. 6, 1788) (same); id. at 400-402 (Aug. 6, 1788) (same). Even Hamilton went out of his way to reassure leading Rhode Islanders: "A doubt might perhaps be raised about your right to a vote under the present circumstances. There is not a member of Congress but one who has even *pretended* to call your right in question." Hamilton to Olney, Aug. 12, 1788, in Harold Syrett and Jacob Cooke, eds., 5 *The Papers of Alexander Hamilton* 199-200 (1962).

96. For example, at the North Carolina convention, Mr. Spaight argued: "The gentleman says, we exceeded our powers. I deny the charge. . . . The proposing a new system, to be established by the assent and ratification of nine states, arose from the necessity of the case. It was thought extremely hard that one state, or even three or four states, should be able to prevent necessary alterations. . . . It was, therefore, thought by the Convention, that if so great a majority as nine states should adopt it, it would be right to establish it. It was recommended by Congress to the state legislatures to refer it to the people of their different states. Our Assembly *has confirmed what they have done,* by proposing it to the consideration of the people. It was there, and not here, that the objection should have been made." 4 E 206-207 (emphasis supplied). See also id. at 16 (similar remarks of Mr. Davie at the North Carolina convention).

97. Delaware, New Jersey, Georgia, and Connecticut ratified the Constitution within the first seventeen weeks. The convention vote in all these cases, with the

exception of Connecticut, was unanimous; in Connecticut's case, it was three-to-one.

98. See Charles Roll, "We, Some of the People, Apportionment in the Thirteen State Conventions Ratifying the Constitution," 56 *J. Am. Hist.* 29–30 (1969).

99. "Thomas Person . . . tried unsuccessfully to prevent the call of a convention." Hugh Lefler and Albert Newsome, *The History of a Southern State: North Carolina* 267 (1963). Senate journals confirm that on 5 December, "Mr. Person having spoken as often as the rules of the House would permit," was unable to block the final vote. Walter Clark, ed., 20 *State Records of North Carolina* 369–370 (1902).

100. Robert Dinkin, *Voting in Revolutionary America* 127 (1982).

101. *New York Daily Advertiser,* Feb. 12, 1788.

102. Id., Feb. 8, 1788.

103. John Kaminski, "New York: The Reluctant Pillar," in Stephen Schechter, ed., *The Reluctant Pillar* 79 (1985).

104. John Bartlett, ed., 10 *Records of the State of Rhode Island* 271–272 (1865); *Providence Gazette,* March 1 and 8, 1788.

105. Bartlett, supra n. 104, at 291.

106. Compare 2 *E* 117 with 2 *E* 157–158 (Mass.); 3 *E* 636–637(Virginia).

107. See Samuel Harding, *The Contest Over the Ratification of the Federal Constitution in Massachusetts* 67 (1896) ("Had a vote been taken on the adoption of the Constitution as soon as the convention assembled, there can be no question but that it would have been overwhelmingly against the proposed plan"); Beard, supra n. 1, at 226–228; Forrest McDonald, *We the People: The Economic Origins of the Constitution* 183 (1958).

108. Id. at 185.

109. Id.

110. Three of Massachusetts' ten proposals became part of the bill of rights. See 2 *E* 177 (reprinting Massachusetts' nine proposed amendments).

111. 1 *E* 386–388.

112. The key to the gerrymander was Federalist Charleston—which had 46 percent of all convention delegates but contained 11.3 percent of the non-slave population. See Roll, supra n. 98, at 21, 30–31 and n. 15.

113. At the convention, the Anti-Federalists managed to convert ten delegates from Kentucky, three Federalists, and one undecided member. See McDonald, supra n. 107, at 258–259.

114. 3 *E* 6.

115. Id. at 21, 23; see also id. at 277 (remarks of Mr. Grayson at Virginia Convention).

116. Id. at 28.

117. See, e.g., id. at 187, 200, 454, 594, 603, 642.

118. Id. at 277.

119. Id. at 61. See also id. at 315.

120. For the intricate development of Randolph's views, see John Reardon, *Edmund Randolph* 82–84, 98–105, 115–119, 142–147 (1974).

121. 3 *E* 652.

122. 3 *E* 654.

123. New York's strategic dilemma has been noted by modern social choice theorists. See Russell Hardin, "Why a Constitution?," in Bernard Grofman and Donald Wittman, eds., *The Federalist Papers and the New Institutionalism* 100, 109 (1989); Robert McGuire and Robert Ohsfeldt, "Public Choice Analysis and the Ratification of the Constitution," in id. at 175, 185.

124. See Kaminski, supra n. 103, at 101–102.

125. Federalists supported the clause-by-clause motion (proposed by Livingston) because the delay permitted them to hear the news from New Hampshire. Anti-Federalists, wanting to appear fair, agreed to the motion; moreover, they had just received word from Patrick Henry and other Virginians asking New Yorkers to send copies of their proposed amendments, which a clause-by-clause debate facilitated. Id. at 101–102.

126. 2 *E* 322.

127. See Kaminski, supra n. 103, at 106.

128. 9 *Writings of Madison,* supra n. 31, at 179–180, 183.

129. Id. at 185; see also Kaminski, supra n. 103, at 115.

130. 2 *E* 413–414.

131. Surely the movement, in New York and other states, for a second constitutional convention would have been greatly advanced. See Linda De Pauw, "The Anticlimax of AntiFederalism: The Abortive Second Convention Movement, 1788–89," *Prologue* 98 (1970).

132. See, e.g., 4 *E* 212–213 (Mr. Lancaster); 4 *E* 24 (Joseph Taylor); 4 *E* 25 (Jas. Galloway); 4 *E* 201 (Mr. Lenoir); 4 *E* 203–204 (Mr. Lenoir: "The Confederation was binding on all the states. It could not be destroyed but with the consent of all the states. There was an express article to that purpose. The men who were deputed to the Convention, instead of amending the old, as they were solely empowered and directed to do, proposed a new system. If the best characters departed so far from their authority, what may not be apprehended from others, who may be agents in the new government. . . . The states are all bound together by the Confederation, and the rest cannot break from us without violating the most solemn compact. If they break that, they will do this").

133. 4 *E* 243–252.

134. *Providence Gazette,* January 23, 1790.

135. Robert Cotner, ed., *Theodore Foster's Minutes of the Convention Held at South Kingstown, Rhode Island, in March 1790, Which Failed to Adopt the Constitution of the United States* (1929); *Providence Gazette,* Mar. 6 & 13, 1790.

136. Joseph Gales, ed., 2 *Annals of Congress* 1638 (1834).

137. Kenneth Bowling & Helen Veit, eds., 9 *Documentary History of the First Federal Congress* 260–268 (1988).

138. Id. at 458.

139. Staples, supra n. 54, at 666 (1870).
140. 2 *Annals of Congress,* supra n. 136, at 1685.

3. *The Founding Precedent*

1. Sanford Levinson provides an expanded list in his *Responding to Imperfection: The Theory and Practice of Constitutional Amendment* 5–6 (1995).
2. See, for example, David Dow, "The Plain Meaning of Article V," in id. at 117–144.
3. But see id. at 127; Laurence Tribe, "Taking Text and Structure Seriously: Reflections on Free-Form Method in Constitutional Interpretation," 108 *Harv. L. Rev.* 1232–1233, 1240–1249, 1286–1303 (1995). Other commentators who tend strongly in the formalist direction nevertheless are cagey about the possibility of legitimate change outside of Article Five. See Michael Paulsen, "A General Theory of Article V," 103 *Yale L. J.* 677, 687 n. 27 (1993).
4. 2 *R* 561.
5. 2 *R* 557.
6. 2 *R* 559.
7. 2 *R* 629–630.
8. 2 *R* 630.
9. See Akhil Amar, "The Consent of the Governed," 94 *Colum. L. Rev.* 457, 475–481 (1994) (reviewing revolutionary constitutions of the states).
10. James Wilson, "Remarks at the Pennsylvania Convention (November 24, 1789)," (version by Thomas Lloyd), in 2 *D* 350, 362.
11. 2 *D* 376.
12. Jack Rakove provides a fine summary of this campaign in *Original Meanings* 113–128 (1996). As he explains, the Federalists first sought to deflect their opponents by asserting that the state conventions' mandates were limited to a simple yes or no vote on the Constitution, and that it was beyond their power to take any more creative actions to trigger another round of deliberative activity. But the conventions dismissed this legalistic fetter on their higher lawmaking powers, and the Federalists retreated. In key states like Massachusetts, New York, and Virginia, the state ratifying conventions operated on the premise that the restrictions handed down by the Philadelphia Convention in Article Seven did not bind their own exercise of popular sovereignty. While this rejection of an exclusivistic interpretation of Article Seven is analytically distinguishable from the question whether Article Five should be read monopolistically, I think that the two issues looked very similar to eighteenth-century Americans, and that Rakove's discussion supports the pluralistic interpretation of Five presented here.
13. 3 *E* 37. Professor Henry Monaghan slights these remarks by Pendleton and Wilson, and ignores those of Smilie, in "We the People(s), Original Understanding, and Constitutional Amendment," 96 *Colum. L. Rev.* 121, 151–156 (1996). He emphasizes other discussions in which Federalists generally praised

Article Five, and Anti-Federalists worried about it, without self-consciously considering whether it provided the exclusive means for future constitutional revision. Monaghan interprets this silence to support the exclusivist position. I don't see why. Surely people were entitled to mention Article Five without expressly directing their attention to the issue.

14. Robert McCloskey, 1 *The Works of James Wilson* 79 (1967).

15. I thank Akhil Amar for bringing this episode to my attention. See supra n. 9, at 491–492.

16. See Bernard Schwartz, 2 *The Bill of Rights: A Documentary History* 1026 (1971).

17. Id. at 1077. See also James Jackson ("the words, as they now stand, speak as much as it is possible to speak; it is a practical recognition of the right of the people to ordain and establish Governments, and is more expressive than any other mere paper declaration"), id. at 1072; and John Vining ("the constitution enforced the principle in the strongest manner by the practical declaration prefaced to that instrument; he alluded to the words, 'We the people do ordain and establish'"), id. at 1041.

18. John Jameson, *Constitutional Conventions* 209, n. 1 (1887), counts 25 such conventions, but his list should be pruned to eliminate three from Georgia that met in defiance of explicit constitutional texts (see 2 *T* at 785, 789 (semble), 801) and one from New Hampshire that seems to have met in conformity with its charter (4 *T* 2470). I also treat specially the two states that retained their old colonial charters: Rhode Island (whose legislature held four conventions before a new constitution was established) and Connecticut (which held one). Since the King had not contemplated popular revision, it was plainly appropriate to read his charters' silence in a nonexclusive way. Making the appropriate subtractions, 16 conventions remain on Jameson's list.

19. Id. at 527.

20. See Roger Hoar, *Constitutional Conventions* 25–29, 214–219 (1917); Walter Dodd, *The Revision and Amendment of State Constitutions* 101–103 (1910); Akhil Amar, "Philadelphia Revisited: Amending the Constitution Outside of Article V," 55 *U. Chi. L. Rev.* 1043–1044 (1988); and Amar, supra n. 9, at 458–494. Professor Monaghan ignores the implications of this pattern of antebellum state practice in his recent essay, supra n. 13, at 162–165, only discussing the single example of Dorr's Rebellion in Rhode Island.

21. 1 *MPP* 213, 220.

22. Early commentaries cast an uncertain light. Joseph Story describes and praises Article Five in a discussion that tends in the exclusivist direction but does not squarely confront the question. See 3 *Commentaries on the Constitution of the United States* 685–690 (1833). William Rawle explicitly rejects exclusivism in *A View of the Constitution of the United States* 12 (1825).

23. Quoted by Lois Schworer, *The Declaration of Rights, 1689* 126 (1981). Chapter 6 contains a fine analysis.

24. See John Miller, "The Glorious Revolution: 'Contract' and 'Abdication'" Recon-

sidered," 25 *Hist. J.* 541 (1982); Thomas Slaughter, "'Abdicate' and 'Contract' in the Glorious Revolution," 24 *Hist. J.* 323 (1981).

25. Among leading Federalists, James Wilson contributed the most penetrating analysis of the Convention of 1688, defending its precedential value against conservatives like William Blackstone who wrongly sought to "den[y] it to be a ground on which any constitutional principle can be established." See his *Lectures on Law,* in McCloskey supra n. 14, at 78–80.

26. The Parliament of 1690 rushed to promulgate "an act for recognizing King William and Queen Mary, and for avoiding all questions touching the acts made in the parliament assembled at Westminster, the thirteenth day of February, one thousand six hundred eighty eight," which declares "[t]hat all and singular the acts made and enacted in said parliament were and are laws and statutes of this kingdom, and such as ought to be reputed, taken and obeyed by all the people of this kingdom." E. Neville Williams, *The Eighteenth-Century Constitution, 1688–1815: Documents and Commentary* 46–47 (1960). J. P. Kenyon treats the entire affair with great subtlety in his *Revolution Principles: The Politics of Parties, 1689–1720* 37–41 (1977).

27. Gordon Wood, *Creation of the American Republic* 340–343 (1972); Hoar, supra n. 20, at 6–7.

28. See Jameson, supra n. 18, at §§ 132, 157–158; Wood, supra n. 27, at 340–343.

29. Interestingly, early Swiss referendum practice also avoided the sharp yes-no alternatives of modern plebiscites. See Benjamin Barber, *The Death of Communal Liberty* 189–194 (1974).

30. See Daniel Rodgers, *Contested Truths* 87 (1987), whose chapter on constitutional conventions is outstanding.

31. Gordon Wood, *The Radicalism of the American Revolution* (1992); James Pope, "Republican Moments: The Role of Direct Popular Power in the American Constitutional Order," 139 *U. Pa. L. Rev.* 287 (1990).

32. See Chapter 2.

33. Only in Connecticut and Rhode Island did a combination of property and oath requirements limit eligibility to 60 percent of white males. For a state-by-state rundown, see Bruce Ackerman & Neal Katyal, "Our Unconventional Founding," 62 *U. Chi. L. Rev.* 563–564, n. 255.

34. New York, Georgia, and Connecticut probably had higher turnouts for their ratifying elections. In New York more than 24,500 persons went to vote, 43 percent of the electorate, while in the accompanying election for the New York Assembly, 32 percent voted in the five counties where data are available. This contrasts with much lower percentages in prior elections for state offices. Robert Dinkin, *Voting in Revolutionary America: A Study of Elections in the Original Thirteen States, 1776–1789* 122 (1982).

Though little statewide data exist for Georgia, we have some numbers from Chatham County: 59.8 percent of adult white males (401 people) voted for delegates, in contrast to 36.3 percent (246 people) in 1784. Id. at 129. Connecticut was plagued by low turnout in the governors' races through the 1780's (about 15 percent of adult men and about 25 percent of qualified voters), and participation may have been higher for the ratifying election, though data are sparse. Id. at 119–20.

In most other states, turnout remained constant. In South Carolina, about 20 percent of the free adult males voted in state and local elections. Id. at 128. The only returns available for the ratifying election are for St. Philip's and St. Michael's Parish (Charleston), where about 22 percent voted (and overwhelmingly for Federalists). Id.; Forrest McDonald, *We the People: The Economic Origins of the Constitution* 203 (1962).

In North Carolina, turnout fluctuated between 30 and 40 percent in state elections. Dinkin, supra, 127. The only figure for the ratifying elections is from Dobbs County, and it shows a 40 percent turnout before the Federalists ran off with the ballot box. Id. In Rhode Island, turnout at the 1788 vote to decide ratification was about 25 percent—a sizeable percentage given the Federalist boycott, and comparable to the one-third figure in the preceding 1786 election. Id. at 111–12. In Massachusetts, participation was about 27 percent, in line with other elections. Id. at 117–118.

Maryland enjoyed one of the highest turnout rates in post-Revolutionary America. Id. at 115. The data for the ratifying convention are mixed, one report suggesting a 25 percent turnout, another reporting 43 percent in Baltimore and 49 percent in Montgomery County. Id. at 116.

In Virginia, data from seven counties show that the turnout was lower at the ratifying election (27 percent of white adult males) than for the 1788 and 1789 state elections. Id. at 125. In Pennsylvania, where more data are available, about 25 percent voted in the annual elections from 1783 to 1788, but only 17 percent voted in the rushed elections for delegates. Id. at 114–115; John McMaster and Frederick Stone, eds., *Pennsylvania and the Federal Constitution, 1787–1788* 72 (1888). Turnout in New Hampshire may have decreased as well—though data are scant. Dinkin, supra, at 108–110.

There is insufficient information from Delaware and New Jersey to form any conclusion. Id. at 122–124.

35. Bad weather seems to have especially affected the turnout in Virginia and New Hampshire. Robert E. Brown, *Charles Beard and the Constitution: A Critical Analysis of "An Economic Interpretation of the Constitution"* 167 (1956).

36. Georgia, New York, and New Hampshire were exceptions to this rule. Dinkin, supra n. 34, at 129; McDonald, supra n. 34, at 237.

37. See F, chap. 10.

38. Hard data are very scarce. We know that the Federalists were overwhelmingly defeated in New York by a vote of about 16,000 to 7,000. McDonald, supra n. 34, at 286. And we know that in Rhode Island the vote against the Constitution was 2,708 to 237. Id. at 322. We must then descend to tea-leaf reading. In Pennsylvania, the Federalists won a large majority in the counties of Philadelphia, Northampton, and Northumberland. Id. at 165. In Maryland, the vote in favor of ratification seems to have been about two to one. Id. at 149. And the

Federalists seem to have won by a landslide in New Jersey. Dinkin, supra n. 34, at 18. They also seem to have prevailed in Virginia. See 3 D at 652–654.

Delaware's convention voted unanimously for the Constitution, but there are charges of voter fraud. Dinkin, supra n. 34, at 17. There are no hard returns in either Georgia or Connecticut, but there is no reason to doubt that the Federalists won in both. See McDonald, supra n. 34, at 130, 136–138.

The Anti-Federalists entered the state conventions with strong majorities in North Carolina, New Hampshire, New York, and Massachusetts, but (apart from New York) we do not know how this correlates with the popular vote. There does seem strong reason to suspect that malapportionment in South Carolina deprived the Anti-Federalists of the fruits of a statewide electoral victory. See Charles Roll, "We, Some of the People: Apportionment in the Thirteen State Conventions Ratifying the Constitution." 56 J. Am. Hist. 30–32 (1969).

Overall, it is impossible to say how all this adds up in a mathematical way. This point is obscured by scholarly "vote counts" that assume that the proportion of delegates at each convention track the percentage of the popular vote. See, e.g., Evelyn Fink and William Riker, "The Strategy of Ratification," in Bernard Grofman and Donald Wittman, eds., The Federalist Papers and the New Institutionalism 220, 230 (1989).

39. The idea of law described in the text is rooted in the dominant positivistic tradition of Anglo-American jurisprudence whose classic statement remains H. L. A. Hart's Concept of Law (1961). Leading defenders in the present generation include Jules Coleman, Joseph Raz, and Fred Schauer. Ronald Dworkin took the lead in critique, but the list is now endless.

40. See Neil MacCormick, H.L.A. Hart, chs. 2, 9 (1981).

41. The traditional formula requires that possession be (1) actual, (2) open and notorious, (3) exclusive, (4) continuous, and (5) hostile under a claim of right. R. H. Helmholz, "Adverse Possession and Subjective Intent," 61 Wash. U. L. Q. 331, 334 (1983). Helmholz argues that modern courts have implicitly added another requirement of subjective good faith, insisting that the claimant be innocent of knowledge of the superior title. If this is so, it represents a departure from traditional understandings, which serve as the basis for the discussion in the text.

4. Formalist Dilemmas

1. Union-controlled portions of Arkansas, Louisiana, and Tennessee had been reconstructed under Lincoln's "Ten Percent" plan during the war. Eric McKitrick, Andrew Johnson and Reconstruction 122 (1960). Lincoln had also recognized the puppet government of Governor Pierpoint in Alexandria, Virginia, but primarily to allow for the creation of West Virginia. See James Randall, Constitutional Problems under Lincoln, ch. 18 (1951).

2. See 13 Stat. 774–775 (1865). The eight states are Virginia, Feb. 9, 1865;

Louisiana, Feb. 17, 1865; Tennessee, Apr. 7, 1865; Arkansas, Apr. 14, 1865; South Carolina, Nov. 13, 1865—leaving Alabama, North Carolina, and Georgia to push the amendment over the "three-fourths" barrier between December 2 and 6, 1865. The assent of West Virginia was also counted—which generates another set of problems that deserves a separate essay. See Randall, supra n. 1. After Seward proclaimed the Thirteenth Amendment ratified, seven additional states eventually ratified: California, Dec. 19, 1865; Florida, Dec. 28, 1965; Iowa, Jan. 15, 1866; New Jersey, Jan. 23, 1866; Texas, Feb. 18, 1870; Delaware, Feb. 12, 1901, and Kentucky, Mar. 18, 1976. His proclamation only counted states that had ratified by December 6.

3. Reconstruction Act, ch. 153, 14 *Stat.* 428–429 (1867).

4. Seward only counted the 19 Northern states that had ratified the amendment by December 6, when he drew up his proclamation. By the time the proclamation was published on December 18, Oregon had ratified, and California assented the next day. This means that 21 Northern states had ratified at the time of publication.

5. Veto of First Reconstruction Act, 6 *MPP* 508. See a similar analysis in his veto of the Third Reconstruction Act, id. at 540.

6. "It was obvious at the time, as is evident in retrospect, that no civil rights amendment could have received the requisite two-thirds vote of both Houses of Congress with the South fully represented." LaWanda Cox and John Cox, *Politics, Principle, and Prejudice, 1865–1866* 203 (1963).

7. The editorial is entitled "Congress versus the President."

8. This position was explicitly stated and defended in the Majority Report of the Joint Committee on Reconstruction. Edward McPherson, ed., *History of the Reconstruction of the United States* 86–88 (3d ed., 1880).

9. *Federalist* No. 43 at 275. (C. Rossiter ed. 1961).

10. See, e.g., Joseph Story, 3 *Commentaries on the Constitution* 679–685 (1833); George Curtis, 2 *History of the Origin, Formation, and Adoption of the Constitution of the United States* 82 (1858); William Duer, *A Course of Lectures on the Constitutional Jurisprudence of the United States* 340–342 (2d ed., 1856); William Rawle, *A View of the Constitution of the United States of America* 296 (2d ed., 1829).

11. Charles Lerche, "The Guarantee of a Republican Form of Government and the Admission of New States," 11 *J. Pol.* 579–589 (1949); William Weicek, *The Guarantee Clause of the U.S. Constitution* 140–165 (1972).

12. There were a few antebellum abolitionists who went so far as to insist on black suffrage. Weicek, supra n. 11, at 159. But this was conceived as a fringe position even in a radical crowd. James McPherson, *Ordeal by Fire: The Civil War and Reconstruction* 403–404 (1982).

13. Sumner did not insist on black suffrage before the war but only came to this view in 1864. David Donald, *Charles Sumner and the Rights of Man* 199–200 (1970). Weicek, supra n. 11, at 187–88.

14. Michael Benedict, "Preserving the Constitution: The Conservative Basis of Radical Reconstruction" 61 *J. Am. Hist.* 75–76 (1974).

15. "Charles Sumner said, years afterward, that he wrote over nineteen pages of foolscap to get rid of the word 'male' and yet keep 'negro suffrage' as a party measure intact; but it could not be done." Ellen DuBois, *Feminism and Suffrage: The Emergence of an Independent Women's Movement in America, 1848–1869* 60 (1978). Quoting from Elizabeth Cady Stanton et al., 2 *History of Women's Suffrage* 97 (1881–1922). When presenting a petition for female suffrage to the Senate, Sumner took "the liberty of saying that I do not think this a proper time for the consideration of that question." 39, 1 *CG* (1866), at 829.

16. Listen to an interchange between Stevens and the Democrat James Brooks on a predecessor to the Fourteenth Amendment:

> BROOKS: I will only say that at the proper time I will move to amend . . . this proposed amendment by inserting the words "or sex" after the word "color," so that it will read: "*Provided,* That whenever the elective franchise shall be denied or abridged in any State on account of race or color or sex, all persons of such race or color or sex shall be excluded from the basis of representation."
>
> STEVENS: Is the gentleman from New York [Mr. Brooks] in favor of that amendment?
>
> BROOKS: I am if negroes are permitted to vote.
>
> STEVENS: That does not answer my question. Is the gentleman in favor of the amendment he has indicated?
>
> BROOKS: I suggested that I would move it at a convenient time.
>
> STEVENS: Is the gentleman in favor of his own amendment?
>
> BROOKS: I am in favor of my own color in preference to any other color, and I prefer the white woman of my country to the negro. [Applause on the floor and in the galleries promptly checked by the speaker.] (39, 1 *CG* [1866], at 379–380)

Perhaps the best effort to distinguish blacks from women was attempted later on in 1867. Congressman Broomall defined republican government as "that form of government in which the rules are chosen by the suffrages of the people, and in which every citizen may either exercise the right of suffrage himself or have it exercised for him by someone who may be fairly considered as representing his interests by reason of legal, social, or family relations." 39, 2 *CG* [8 Jan 1867], at 350–351

In this way, one might have argued that women were "fairly" represented by their husbands (but what of the unmarried!) while blacks had no similar proxies. This line of thought was not powerfully developed in the *Congressional Globe.* Indeed, during the debates on the Thirteenth Amendment, not even the most radical Republicans had suggested that the mere emancipation of blacks would, without more, require their enfranchisement as well. G. Sidney Buchanan, "The Quest for Freedom: A Legal History of the Thirteenth Amendment," 12 *Houston L. Rev.* 1, 12 (1974).

17. By 1860, blacks had equal suffrage rights in five states—Massachusetts, Maine, Rhode Island, New Hampshire, and Vermont. In New York, blacks could vote

only if they met age and residency requirements, and if they met a property qualification of $250. Leon Litwack, *North of Slavery* 83, 91 (1961).

18. These numbers count Minnesota twice, because it held two votes on black suffrage. In 1865, black suffrage was voted down in Wisconsin, Connecticut, and Minnesota. Kansas, Ohio, New York, and Nebraska Territory followed suit subsequently. But in 1868, both Iowa and Minnesota passed referenda to enfranchise blacks. Eric Foner, *Reconstruction: America's Unfinished Revolution* 222–223 (1988).

19. Weicek, supra n. 11, at 200.

20. MacPherson, supra n. 8, at 89.

21. Weicek, supra n. 11, at 63–67.

22. See Chapter 3, p. 143, and n. 18.

23. In the federal government's major antebellum confrontation with the clause, it was the President, not Congress, who made the critical decisions. This problem was presented by Rhode Island's continuing difficulty in adapting itself to the American constitutional system. The state legislature had responded to the Revolution, and later to the Constitution, by making minor amendments to the Royal Charter of 1663. By the late 1830's, the property qualifications imposed on voters by the Charter had become increasingly anomalous in an age of universal manhood suffrage; the lower House of the General Assembly had also become extremely malapportioned, awarding effective control to a small rural minority at the expense of the rising manufacturing center in the northeast corner of the state. Nonetheless, the governing authorities were unwilling to make any reforms that would adapt government to nineteenth-century realities.

Finally a group of insurgents, led by Thomas Dorr, called an illegal convention of their own, which proposed a new constitution that endorsed universal male suffrage. They then conducted an unauthorized poll at which 14,000 Rhode Islanders approved the new constitution while only 52 voted against it. Given the boycott of this poll by defenders of the Charter government, it is impossible to say whether the Dorrites were in the majority. See Weicek, supra n. 11, 86–110 (which contains the best modern discussion of the factual background). In any event, the Dorrites proceeded to form a rival government and claim legitimate authority.

The Charter government responded with force, and also appealed to President Tyler for support under the Guaranty Clause. Acting under a Congressional statute of 1795, the President declared himself ready to intervene militarily on behalf of the Charter government should this prove necessary. This threat seems to have put an end to armed opposition. See Luther v. Borden, 7 How. 1, 44 (1849). In the meantime, the Charter government moved to reconstitute political authority on a lasting basis, calling a "convention" of its own although the Charter had never contemplated such an action. It was this legally anomalous convention that finally proved to be the mechanism for the restoration of legitimate authority—it wrote a new constitution, which gained electoral approval, that permitted the installation of a new government in 1843.

With peace restored, the old partisans continued the joys of combat in the courts. *Luther v. Borden* began as an action in federal court by a partisan of the Dorr government against a Charter partisan, complaining of trespass during the micro-civil war. If it had upheld this action, the Supreme Court would have undercut the legitimacy of the new Rhode Island government, which traced its authority to the Charter government's convention, not the Dorr convention.

This point was of great concern to Chief Justice Roger Taney when the case finally came before the Court in 1849—six years after the new Rhode Island constitution had come into practical effect. On his view, the courts had no business second-guessing the decision of the President to give military support, if necessary, to the Charter government:

It may be said that this power in the President is dangerous to liberty, and may be abused. All power may be abused if placed in unworthy hands. But it would be difficult, we think, to point out any other hands in which this power would be more safe, and at the same time equally effectual. When citizens of the same State are in arms against each other, and the constituted authorities unable to execute the laws, the interposition of the United States must be prompt, or it is of little value. The ordinary course of proceedings in courts of justice would be utterly unfit for the crisis. And the elevated office of the President, chosen as he is by the people of the United States, and the high responsibility he could not fail to feel when acting in a case of so much moment, appear to furnish as strong safeguards against a willful abuse of power as human prudence and foresight could well provide. At all events, it is conferred upon him by the Constitution and laws of the United States. (Id. at 44).

This is the holding of *Luther v. Borden*—a point often ignored in favor of some famous dicta that Taney offered up on behalf of Congress: "[A]s the United States guarantee to each State a republican government, Congress must necessarily decide what government is established in the State before it can determine whether it is republican or not. And when the senators and representatives of a State are admitted into the councils of the Union, the authority of the government under which they are appointed, as well as its republican character, is recognized by the proper constitutional authority. And its decision is binding on every other department of the government, and could not be questioned in a judicial tribunal." Id. at 42.

But such dicta came by way of a consolation prize to the Dorrites. The fact is that Congress never acted on behalf of the Dorr faction, and we will never know how the Taney court would have responded to a Rhode Island case resembling the evolving situation in 1865. In this imaginary scenario, the Charter government, aided by President Tyler, succeeded in establishing civil order in Rhode Island only to have their success undercut by a Congressional decision to expel the Charter senators and representatives in favor of the defeated Dorrites. Would Taney have supported a Congressional decision to reopen a civil war that had been concluded by the successful intervention of the President on behalf of a Charter government that, despite its restrictive suffrage, nevertheless fell within the traditional definition of republican government?

Even if the answer were yes, a final step would be required before Taney's dicta could be invoked on behalf of the Reconstruction Congress's decision to exclude the South. The Thirty-ninth Congress did not merely disagree with the President over which state government was truly republican; it rejected the *only* governments that could even plausibly be called republican, and thereby deprived the Southern states of all representation of any kind. Thus, a court would be required to weigh not only the President's judgment that the United States had satisfied its guarantee of republican government, but also the explicit constitutional command that all states receive at least one Representative and two Senators in Congress. Since this latter factor was entirely absent from Taney's contemplation in *Luther,* it would be rash to apply Taney's dicta in a mechanical way to the Exclusion Crisis.

Indeed, when considered as a general matter, I doubt that any thoughtful constitutionalist would defend the existence of a plenary power in Congress to depart from traditional conceptions of republican government in determining whether a state is to be admitted into the councils of the Union. (As Weicek, supra n. 11, makes clear, it is only during the Reconstruction era itself that such strong claims were made on behalf of Congressional power under the clause. See also W. Dunning, *Essays on the Civil War and Reconstruction* 131–132 [1898].) Imagine, for example, that the Republicans won a majority in both Houses in the next election and wished to emulate their illustrious predecessors of the Thirty-ninth Congress—the Congress that brought us the Fourteenth Amendment—by gaining two-thirds majorities through a purge of the Democratic opposition. Discovering that their opponents disproportionately represent states that had legalized the sale of marijuana, the Republican caucus acts decisively against this evil: no government can be republican, it declares, if it tolerates the possibility of a drugged electorate on Election Day. Unless and until the errant states satisfy the Congress of the renewed sobriety of their citizens, no further representatives will be admitted to the House or Senate. And so, with a flick of the Guaranty Clause, the Republicans gain two-thirds majorities in "Congress." Does anyone really believe that a Congressional majority has this power? Rather than viewing a President who protested as a usurper, would we not hope that Presidential opposition encouraged the Supreme Court—and the population generally—to resist the prospect of impending tyranny?

24. The Majority Report also made weaker arguments in its defense, suggesting that the election of so many Confederate sympathizers to office in the new Southern governments had somehow disqualified the governments as republican under the Guaranty Clause. See McPherson, supra n. 8, at 90–93. But the clause only guarantees the republican *form* of government. It makes a mockery of the principle of republican self-government for Congress to make recognition contingent upon the politics of those elected by the people of each state. While

each House has the undoubted power to refuse to seat treasonous individuals, Congress cannot disqualify an entire state merely because it sends a number of unqualified people to serve as representatives.

25. Though whether such legislation, especially when passed over a Presidential veto, should be accorded the ordinary presumption of constitutionality by the courts is quite another matter. Where this leaves formalists as to the status of fundamental legislation, like the Civil Rights Act of 1866, I leave for them to decide.

26. See Joseph James, *The Ratification of the Fourteenth Amendment* 20–24 (1984), on the serious irregularities attending Tennessee's ratification of the amendment.

27. See id. at 59, 98, 117.

28. See Chapters 7 and 8.

29. Weicek, supra n. 11, at 200–207.

30. First Reconstruction Act, 14 *Stat.* 428, 429 (1867).

31. 6 *MPP* 499.

32. See 15 *Stat.* 707 (1868).

33. This last paragraph does not explicitly repeat Seward's doubts about the Southern ratifications.

34. Walter Dellinger, "The Legitimacy of Constitutional Change: Rethinking the Amendment Process," 97 *Harv. L. Rev.* 386 (1983).

35. 15 *Stat.* 708, 712 (1868). During the week between the two Seward proclamations, a seventh Southern state, Georgia, had tendered its ratification to the Secretary; as a consequence, it was added to the list of ratifying states, making thirty in all.

36. This is the "forfeited rights theory" described in the works of generations of historians. See, e.g., Dunning, supra n. 23, at 109–112; Eric McKitrick, *Andrew Johnson and Reconstruction* 113–19 (1960).

37. For good explanations of the two theories, see Dunning, supra n. 23, at 105–109; McKitrick, supra n. 36, at 110–113, 113–119.

38. On this line of reasoning, there were 25, not 36, states in the Union in December of 1865, requiring 19 yeses to ratify the Thirteenth Amendment. Seward already had 21 assents by the end of December. See n. 4. On the Fourteenth Amendment, see n. 41.

39. 37, 1 *CG* (1861), at 223. Johnson remembered these words well, since he had introduced the Crittenden Resolution in the Senate.

40. See Herman Belz, *Reconstructing the Union* 7 (1969). Belz' last chapter contains a good summary of the President's evolving positions throughout the war.

41. See, e.g., Carl Schurz, 3 *The Reminiscences of Carl Schurz* 223 (1907–8) ("the theory of State-suicide advanced by Mr. Stevens and a comparatively small school of extremists"). This point has been repeatedly recognized by historians from very different schools. Compare Dunning, supra n. 23, at 109, with Benedict, supra n. 14, at 65, and Michael Perman, *Reunion without Compromise* 3–12 (1973). Thus, when Secretary Seward responded to a Congressional

request by listing the twenty Northern states that had ratified the Fourteenth Amendment by July 1867, Congress did not go forward to proclaim the amendment valid on the basis of radical mathematics, but let the matter rest in limbo until Reconstruction generated more assents from the South. See 40, 1 *CG* (1867), at 740.

As we shall see, centrists like John Bingham did flirt with radical mathematics at times but later led Congress to adopt a very different course. See Chapter 7. As mainstream Republican James G. Blaine explained in his revealing *Twenty Years of Congress* (1886):

> The great majority of the Republican leaders, however, did not at all agree with the theory of Mr. Stevens and the mass of the party were steadily against him. The one signal proof of their dissent from the extreme doctrine was their absolute unwillingness to attempt an amendment to the Constitution by the ratification of three-fourths of the Loyal States only, and their insisting that it must be three-fourths of all the States, North and South. Mr. Stevens deemed this a fatal step for the party, and his extreme opinion had the indorsement of Mr. Sumner; but against both these radical leaders the party was governed by its own conservative instincts. They believed with Mr. Lincoln that the Stevens plan of amendment would always be questioned, and that in so grave a matter as a change in the organic law of the Nation, the process should be unquestionable—one that could stand every test and resist every assault. (2 id. at 140).

The last line is especially fascinating—for, of course, the Republicans did achieve their aim, despite their patent violation of Article Five. The challenge is to understand how the Republicans achieved this remarkable outcome, and why it was appropriate for them to do so in the name of the People.

42. 74 U.S. (7 Wall.) 700, 717 (1868).

43. Id. at 725. Moreover, the Court specifically cited Seward's proclamation declaring the validity of the Thirteenth Amendment "by the requisite three-fourths of the States." Id. at 728, n. 13.

44. This *was* a holding, not mere dictum. At the time of its decision, the representatives of Texas remained excluded by Congress. Mr. Justice Robert Grier made much of this point in his dissent (id. at 738–739).

45. In a famous speech, Richard Henry Dana made the point thusly: "We have a right to hold the rebels in the grasp of war until we have obtained whatever the public safety and the public faith require." Richard Dana, ed., *Richard Henry Dana Jr.: Speeches in Stirring Times* 234, 247 (1910). For a more elaborate statement, see 13 *Opinions of Attorney General* 59 (1869) (opinion on Congressional Reconstruction).

46. Professor Laurence Tribe flirts with this view in "Taking Text and Structure Seriously," 108 *Harv. L. Rev.,* 1221, 1294 (1995).

47. 307 U.S. 433 (1939).

48. See, e.g., Joseph Call, "The Fourteenth Amendment and Its Skeptical Background," 13 *Baylor L. Rev.* 1 (1961); Pinckney McElwee, "The Fourteenth Amendment to the Constitution of the United States and the Threat that It

Poses to Our Democratic Government," 11 *S.C.L.Q.* 484 (1959); Walter Suthon, "The Dubious Origins of the Fourteenth Amendment," 28 *Tul. L. Rev.* 22 (1953).

The unconventional history of these amendments is also recalled in sundry court cases. See, e.g., Lindsay v. Alabama, 139 So. 2d 353 (1961); Dyett v. Turner, 439 P.2d 266 (1968).

49. See Ferdinand Fernandez, "The Constitutionality of the Fourteenth Amendment," 39 *S. Cal. L. Rev.* 378 (1966), whose response ignores or evades the questions raised in this chapter.

50. This is David Donald's assessment in his introduction to the second edition, explaining why he had decided to update the book. See p. v (2d ed., 1961).

51. Id. at 633–635. The discussion is essentially unchanged from Randall's first edition of 1937. There is also a footnote that suggests another of the paradoxes we have developed: "There was, of course, the further point, as noted above, that states of the former Confederacy, though unreconstructed, had been counted in the ratification of the thirteenth amendment and had been included in estimating the total number of states." Id. at 635–636, n. 6. The problem surrounding the ratification of the Thirteenth Amendment is spelled out at greater length by Randall in supra n. 1, at 396–401.

52. See also McPherson's fine general history, supra n. 12, which notes that Johnson's efforts on behalf of the Thirteenth Amendment were "unconstitutional" (id. at 501) but fails to take seriously the implications of this remark.

53. For a sensitive essay dealing with this turn, see Harold Hyman, *The Radical Republicans and Reconstruction,* esp. xl–xlii (1967).

54. "Still, the fact remains that reconstruction as a problem in theory has been out of vogue for some time and no longer has the vitality that it once had. . . . Most of the writing done on this period over the past generation has assumed not only that Johnson's position was the 'constitutional' one but also that the other arguments were in themselves meaningless—that they were really blinds for programs essentially political (or even economic) in nature. . . . Still, there is something arbitrary and self-denying in the assumption, now more or less tacit and orthodox, that the constitutional side of reconstruction may safely be passed over with no more than perfunctory notice." McKitrick, supra n. 36, at 94.

55. Sidney George Fisher, *Trial of the Constitution* 142 (1862).

56. Id. at 96–97.

57. For some appreciations of Fisher's book, see Harold Hyman, *A More Perfect Union* 110–115 (1973), and Daniel Lazare, *The Frozen Republic* 136–139 (1996).

5. Presidential Leadership

1. For a classic statement, see *Federalist* No. 39 (C. Rossiter ed., 1961).

2. See Chapter 2.

3. See James Ceasar, *Presidential Selection,* ch. 1 (1979); Ralph Ketcham, *Presi-*

dents above Party 89–140 (1989). I discuss the themes raised in the last two paragraphs at greater length in a forthcoming book, *The Roots of Presidentialism.*

4. Ludwell Johnson, *Division and Reunion: America 1848–1877* 63 (1978); Don Fehrenbacher, *Prelude to Greatness* 155 (1962); William Zornow, *Lincoln and the Party Divided* 24 (1954).

5. Lincoln's 39.9 percent of the popular vote was the lowest in the history of presidential elections. David Potter, *Lincoln and His Party in the Secession Crisis* 112 (1942).

6. According to a Southern estimate, Republicans would have only 29 of 66 Senate seats, and 108 of 228 seats in the House. Dwight Dumond, *The Secession Movement, 1860–1861* 130, n. 24 (1931). Others have awarded Republicans 31 Senate seats, but this is still a minority. See 2 *S* 1124 (1971).

7. 5 *MPP* 638.

8. See Harold Hyman, "The Narrow Escape from a 'Compromise of 1860': Secession and the Constitution," in Harold Hyman & Leonard Levy eds., *Freedom and Reform: Essays in Honor of Henry Steele Commager* 152–156 (1967).

9. 36, 2 *CG* (1860), at 99–104, quoted in Albert Hart, ed., 4 *American History Told by Contemporaries, 1845–1900* 199–201 (1901).

10. See, e.g., 36, 2 *CG* (1861), at 272 (Representative Cobb). See also 5 *MPP* 628 for President Buchanan's characterization of Lincoln's victory as "effected by a mere plurality, and not a majority of the people, and has resulted from transient and temporary causes, which may probably never again occur."

11. Potter, supra n. 5, at 105–110.

12. 36, 2 *CG* (1860), at 114.

13. See Potter, supra n. 5, at 170–176. See also Stephen Keogh, "Formal and Informal Constitutional Lawmaking in the United States in the Winter of 1860–1861," 8 *J. Legal H.* 280–283, 286–288 (1987).

14. 36, 2 *CG* (1861), at 237.

15. See Potter, supra n. 5, at 237, 351–352, who suggests that Crittenden's proposal would have probably won a referendum in both North and South. Id. at 189–200.

16. Id. at ch. 5.

17. Crittenden's failure left one proposal on the table: the Corwin Amendment, which would have constitutionally entrenched, for all time, the states' rights to slavery within their borders. In 1861, Lincoln believed that this much was constitutionally guaranteed, and the amendment passed both houses by the requisite two-thirds on March 2. Ratification in the states was interrupted by the shots at Fort Sumter, April 12, 1861. Edward McPherson, *The Political History of the United States of America during the Great Rebellion* 59–60 (1864).

18. Robert Gunderson, *Old Gentlemen's Convention: The Washington Peace Conference of 1861* 24–25 (1961).

19. Arkansas was too busy considering the secession question to send a delegation.

Minnesota and Michigan, both staunchly Republican, considered the convention an illegal attempt to force concessions on the North and refused to play a part. Id. at 33–41.

20. Its proposals were a variation on the Crittenden plan with a more elaborate scheme for determining the legal status of slavery in the territories. John J. Crittenden, *A Report of the Debates and Proceedings in the Secret Sessions of the Conference Convention for Proposing Amendments to the Constitution of the United States* 471–473 (1864); see also Keogh, supra n. 13, at 288–292.

21. See Chapter 2.

22. According to Senator Crittenden, "These amendments have been submitted to us, and the question is: whether we will submit them to the States or not? That I take to be the specific and solitary question. This imposes no obligation on us to sanction these constitutional amendments by proposing them to the people. . . . Now, the question here is, whether the resolutions have come to us with a sufficient sanction to constitute in our minds a reason for referring to the States the amendments which the States themselves have asked. That is all." 36, 2 *CG* (1861), at 1309. His opponents argued, in the manner of Richard Henry Lee at the Continental Congress (see Chapter 2), that Congress should not surrender its role in higher lawmaking to an irregular body. 36, 2 *CG* (1861), at 1311.

23. The proposal lost in the Senate by a vote of 7 to 28. Id. at 1405. Its partisans in the House failed to win the two-thirds majority required to suspend the rules necessary for consideration on the floor. Id. at 1333.

24. Jefferson Davis proclaimed upon his arrival in Montgomery on February 16, 1861: "No compromise; no reconstruction can be now entertained." Dunbar Rowland, ed., 5 *Jefferson Davis, Constitutionalist: His Letters, Papers and Speeches* 48 (1923). But others recognized that all bridges had not yet been burned. For a revealing statement by the Confederacy's Vice President at the end of the war, see Alexander Stephens, 1 *A Constitutional View of the Late War Between the States* 532 (1868).

25. A short list includes the Kentucky and Virginia resolutions of the late 1790's, the Hartford Convention of 1814–15, and South Carolina's effort to "nullify" the federal tariff in the 1830's.

26. See Buchanan's Fourth Annual Message in 5 *MPP* 628–653.

27. The link between Sumter and peaceful compromise is exemplified by Lincoln's offer, on February 27, to several Southern delegates to the Washington Peace Convention. The President-elect offered to evacuate the fort if the Virginia convention then sitting in Richmond would dissolve and the state remained in the Union. Potter, supra n. 5, at 353–354.

28. In his inaugural address, Lincoln endorsed a constitutional amendment "that the Federal Government shall never interfere with the domestic institutions of the States, including that of persons held to service." 36, 2 *CG* (1961), at 1433; 6 *MPP* 5–12. Four months later, he reaffirmed these views. 37, 1 *CG* (1861), at app. 3; 6 *MPP* 30–31 (though close readers will detect new ambiguities creep-

ing into the text). At the same session, both House and Senate endorsed the Crittenden-Johnson resolution: "That this war is not waged on their part in any spirit of oppression, nor for any purpose of conquest or subjugation, nor purpose of overthrowing or interfering with the rights or established institutions of those States [in revolt], but to defend and maintain the supremacy of the Constitution, and to preserve the Union with all the dignity, equality, and rights of the several States unimpaired; and that as soon as these objects are accomplished the war ought to cease." H.R. Mis. Doc. No. 17, 37th Cong., 1st Sess. (1861), at 1; S. Misc. Doc. No. 7, 37th Cong., 1st Sess. (1861), at 1. See generally, Herman Belz, *Reconstructing the Union* 14 *et passim* (1969).

29. During the spring of 1862, Congress passed four statutes. On March 13, it prohibited the army from returning fugitive slaves. 12 *Stat.* 354 (1862). On April 10, it provided compensation to any state attempting emancipation. 12 *Stat.* 617 (1862). On April 16, it abolished slavery in the District of Columbia, compensating loyal owners. 12 *Stat.* 376 (1862). On June 19, it abolished slavery in the territories. 12 *Stat.* 432 (1862). See James McPherson, *The Struggle for Equality* 97–98 (1964).

30. 6 *MPP* 157, 158. Before the President acted, Congress had passed two Confiscation Acts. Both were important, but neither was a direct assault on Southern slavery. The Act of 1861 confiscated rebel property and slaves used in the insurrection but did not expressly free the slaves. It provided escaped slaves with a defense in court, if they had been "employed in hostile service against the Government of the United States." 12 *Stat.* 319 (1861). Senator Lyman Trumbull later lamented that "not a single slave ha[d] been set at liberty under [the act]." 38, 1 *CG* (1864), at 1313. The Act of 1862 was broader, but continued to make the disloyalty of the slave owner a necessary condition for emancipation. 12 *Stat.* 589 (1862). Worse yet, it failed to specify the court procedure through which disloyalty could be adjudicated. See Patricia Lucie, *Freedom and Federalism,* ch. 2 (1986); McPherson, supra n. 29, at 72, 111–112, 247; James Randall, *Constitutional Problems under Lincoln* 357–363 (1963). Once again, it is not clear whether a single slave gained freedom under this statute.

31. Proclamation No. 17, 12 *Stat.* 1268 (1863); 6 *MPP* 158. The four slave states were Missouri, Kentucky, Maryland, and Delaware.

32. For a sketch of the arguments, pro and con, see James Welling, "The Emancipation Proclamation," 130 *N. Am. Rev.* 163 (1880); Richard Dana, "Nullity of the Emancipation Edict," 131 *N. Am. Rev.* 128 (1880); Aaron Ferris, "The Validity of the Emancipation Edict," 131 *N. Am. Rev.* 551 (1880). For a good selection of documents, see Hans Trefousse, *Lincoln's Decision for Emancipation* (1975).

33. Lincoln followed his plea for the orderly and peaceful conduct of "emancipated" slaves by stating "that such persons, of suitable condition, will be received into the armed service of the United States to garrison forts, positions, stations, and other places, and to man vessels of all sorts in service." Proclama-

tion No. 17, 12 *Stat.* 1269 (1863); 6 *MPP* 157–159. In fact, tens of thousands of slaves crossed Union lines to serve as soldiers and assist the war effort. This permitted a plausible, if hardly compelling, claim of military necessity in the future legal defense of the proclamation.

34. The quotation is from the preliminary proclamation of September 22, 1862. 6 *MPP* 96, 98.

35. See McPherson, supra n. 29, at 119; James McPherson, *Ordeal by Fire* 293–298 (1982); Phillip Paludan, *A People's Contest,* ch. 4 (1988).

36. Harold Hyman, "The Election of 1864," in 2 *S* 1163 (1971); McPherson, supra n. 35, at 296.

37. As Lincoln put it in his third annual message to Congress: "With other signs, the popular elections [of 1862] . . . indicated uneasiness among ourselves, . . ." 6 *MPP* 188.

38. McPherson, supra n. 29, at 121.

39. Id. at 121, quoting abolitionist William Lloyd Garrison.

40. On December 11, 1862, Unionist Representative George Yeaman of Kentucky introduced a bill declaring the edict unconstitutional. The bill was tabled that same day. 37, 1 *CG* (1862), at 76, quoted in McPherson, supra n. 17, at 229. Similarly, Democratic Representative Joseph Edgerton of Indiana offered a resolution on December 17, 1863, which read in part: "[I]n the judgment of a large number of faithful citizens, [these executive measures] have a tendency to give to the rebellion 'the advantage of a changed issue,' and 'to reinvigorate the otherwise declining insurrection in the South,' and to prolong the war." The resolution was tabled 90 to 66. 38, 1 *CG* (1863), at 45, quoted in id. at 230.

41. 6 *MPP* 6.

42. 6 *MPP* 190 (emphasis supplied). See McPherson, supra n. 29, at 125–126, for the similar concerns of abolitionists; 38, 1 *CG* (1864), at 1313–14, for Representative Trumbull's arguments on the need for substantive reinforcement.

43. Although Republicans repeatedly called for statutory approval of the President's decision, they could not deliver the votes. On January 12, 1863, Representative James Wilson of Iowa introduced a joint resolution "to approve, ratify, and confirm" the Emancipation Proclamation as a war measure. It languished in the Judiciary Committee. 37, 3 *CG* (1863), at 281, quoted in McPherson, supra n. 17, at 230. Representative Isaac Arnold of Illinois introduced a bill, on December 14, 1863, declaring the Emancipation Proclamation constitutional under the President's war power. It suffered an identical fate. 38, 1 *CG* (1863), at 20, quoted in id. at 229–230. Senator Daniel Clark of New Hampshire offered a similar bill on February 10, 1864. It was referred to the Committee on Slavery and Freedmen. 38, 1 *CG* (1864), at 553, quoted in id. at 229. Senator Sumner of Massachusetts attempted to provide statutory support a fourth time on July 1, 1864. His bill was defeated outright, 11 to 21. 38, 1 *CG* (1864), at 3460, quoted in id. at 318.

44. For a summary of the debates, see H. D. Hamilton, *The Legislative History of*

the Thirteenth Amendment, ch. 1 (1970); Henry Wilson, *History of the Anti-slavery Measures of the Thirty-seventh and Thirty-eighth United States Congresses* 249–272 (1864).

45. 38, 1 *CG* (1864), at 3357.

46. Both Chase and John Fremont sought to replace Lincoln as the Republican nominee. McPherson, supra n. 29, at 281–282; Paludan, supra n. 35, at 249–252. As late as August 23, 1864, Lincoln was writing: "This morning, as for some days past, it seems exceedingly probable that this administration will not be reelected." Roy Basler, ed., 10 *Complete Works of Lincoln* 203 (1953).

47. 2 *S* 1180, 1181.

48. 2 *S* 1174.

49. Id. at 1175; McPherson, supra n. 35, at 456–458.

50. Id. at 456.

51. Zornow, supra n. 4, at 166.

52. 6 *MPP* 252.

53. Edward Gambill, *Conservative Ordeal* 21 (1981).

54. 38, 2 *CG* (1865), at 525. For similar assessments by Republicans, see comments of Orth, 38, 2 *CG* (1865), at 142; Higby, id. at 155; Scofield and Broomall, id. at 144, 220; and Davis, id. at 155.

   Of course, there were Democratic naysayers. See, e.g., Cravens, id. at 220.

   I do not suggest that the elections were the only factor at work. The President used patronage to advantage as well. See Trefousse, supra n. 32, at 56. But he had done so previously, without decisive effect.

55. Full support from the Republicans, seventeen crossover votes by Democrats and Unionists, and eight Democratic abstentions gave the measure a 119-to-56 majority. Lucie, supra n. 30, at 117.

56. See, e.g., 38, 1 *CG* (1864), at 2981 (Congressman Mallory). Republicans argued that the Southern states could not complain of Congressional action taken in their *voluntary* absence. Id. at 2955 (Congressmen Kellogg).

57. The only textual exception authorizes Congressional decisions to adjourn. See art. 1, sec. 7.

58. The Court's one-paragraph opinion in Hollingsworth v. Virginia, 3 U.S. (3 Dall.) 378 (1798), rejected an attack by a private litigant on the Eleventh Amendment because the President's signature was lacking. How the Court would have responded to an effort by a *President* to demand presentment is anyone's guess.

59. On February 7, Senator Trumbull denounced the President's decision and tendered a resolution asserting the presentment of the proposed amendment to the President was a mistake. 38, 2 *CG* (1865), at 629. After Senator Reverdy Johnson defended the President's participation on textual grounds, the Senate approved Trumbull's resolution without a recorded vote. I have not found a similar debate in the House. Nor did Lincoln attempt any defense during the short time he survived. All we have is a copy of his signature to the joint resolution, reproduced at 8 *Complete Works of Lincoln,* supra n. 46, at 253.

60. New Jersey reversed its decision and ratified the Thirteenth Amendment on January 23, 1866. Much later, Delaware, February 12, 1901, and Kentucky, March 18, 1976, also reversed themselves. *U.S. Code Annotated,* Const. amend. XIV.

61. William McFeely, *Grant* 205–06 (1981).

62. Last Public Address, 8 *Collected Works of Lincoln,* supra n. 46, at 399, 404.

63. See Chapter 4, n. 1.

64. 6 *MPP* 213–214 (1863) (emphasis supplied).

65. 6 *MPP* 310–311 (1865) (emphasis supplies).

66. See *New York World,* May 30, 1865; *Hartford Daily Times,* May 31, 1865; *Chicago Times,* May 31, 1865.

67. See Michael Perman, *Reunion Without Compromise: The South and Reconstruction, 1865–1868* (1973). For a thoughtful survey of the election returns, see Dan Carter, *When the War Was Over,* ch. 3 (1985).

68. These and subsequent telegrams are to be found in a Presidential Message to the Senate of March 6, 1866, Exec. Doc. 26, 39th Cong., 1st Sess.(1866). The Mississippi telegram is at p. 229.

69. Eric McKitrick, *Andrew Johnson and Reconstruction* 200–201 (1960).

70. Presidential Message, supra n. 68, at 230.

71. Id. at 233.

72. Id. at 79–80.

73. Id.

74. Id. at 109–10.

75. Id. at 110.

76. Virginia (Feb. 9, 1865), Louisiana (Feb. 17, 1865), Tennessee (Apr. 7, 1865), and Arkansas (Apr. 14, 1865). *U.S.C.A., Amendments 13 and 14* 5 (1972).

77. Presidential Message, supra n. 68, at 253.

78. Id. at 116–117.

79. Of course, the military side of the matter would remain unchanged.

80. Id. at 118.

81. See Georges Clemenceau, *American Reconstruction* 60–63 (1928), for a perceptive discussion. Alabama's governor was discharged on December 18. South Carolina's turn came on December 21. Id.

82. Presidential Message, supra n. 68, at 120.

83. This telegram was continually discussed during Congressional debates of the following months.

84. Presidential Message, supra n. 68, at 197–198.

85. Id. at 198–199.

86. Id.

87. Id. at 199.

88. Speech of Hon. Thaddeus Stevens, Delivered in the City of Lancaster 6 (September 7, 1865) (available at Library of Congress).

89. Sumner seems to be wrong in saying that the amendment was not sent to the Southern states. See 39, 2 *CG* (1867), at 598 (Rep. Cooper). At least this is

what Secretary of State Seward says in response to an inquiry from the provisional governor of South Carolina on November 6, 1865: "I . . . find that the constitutional amendment was posted, immediately after its passage, to the governors of all the States, without exception. The accidents of war, no doubt, prevented it from reaching the acting governor of South Carolina, which was in rebellion." Presidential Message, supra n. 68, at 198.

90. 39, 1 *CG* (1865), at 2.

91. The message was dated December 4. It was submitted to Congress on December 5, the day Seward congratulated Alabama for ratifying the Thirteenth Amendment. See p. 144 supra.

92. 6 *MPP* 356.

93. Id. at 357.

94. Id. at 358, emphasis supplied.

95. See Chapter 4, p. 101.

96. Fifteenth Congress, Sess. 1, chap. 80, 3 *Stat.* 439 (1818).

97. See Chapter 8, p. 233.

98. Proclamation No. 11, 15 *Stat.* 706, 707 (1868).

99. Proclamation No. 52, 13 *Stat.* 774, 775 (1865).

100. 39, 1 *CG* (1865), at 2.

101. Sumner's resolution was quickly buried in committee. 39, 1 *CG* (1865), at 38. Floor debate was postponed indefinitely on June 20, 1866. 39, 1 *CG* (1866), at 3276–77.

102. 39, 1 *CG* (1865), at 39.

103. 39, 1 *CG* (1865), at 41.

104. 39, 1 *CG* (1865), at 41.

105. 39, 1 *CG* (1865), at 43.

106. 39, 1 *CG* (1866), at 321.

107. Indeed, before the Secretary had issued his proclamation, Saulsbury had developed the formalist paradox elaborated in Chapter 4, denouncing the inconsistencies involved in counting Southern ratifications of the amendment while excluding Southern representatives from Congress. See 39, 1 *CG* (1865), at 43.

108. See the revealing speech by the radical Glenni Scofield to the House at the time ten Southern legislatures had rejected the Fourtenth Amendment. 39, 2 *CG* (1866), at 597–598.

109. Indeed, the Thirteenth Amendment left open the question whether slave owners would gain compensation. Only the Fourteenth resolved this question in the negative.

110. At least, this is a fact that has never been contested by any historian, or any serious history book, I have ever encountered.

111. I insert this weasel word to allow leeway for good-faith judgment. But, as the next chapter will suggest, it is painfully obvious that a majority of Americans were not radicals in 1865, or at any other time.

112. For an implicit endorsement of Presidential vanguardism, see McPherson, supra n. 35, at 501.

6. The Convention/Congress

1. President Johnson is an exception to this rule, though even he sometimes did his own work. See John Cox and LaWanda Cox, "Andrew Johnson and His Ghost Writers," 48 *Miss. Val. Hist. Rev.* 460 (1961).

2. See generally Joel Silbey, *The American Political Nation, 1838–1893* (1991).

3. For the mortality figures, see Richard Current, 1 *Encyclopedia of the Confederacy* 338 (1993). Total non-mortal casualties added up to 1,166,000. Id. The total population of the United States in 1860 was about 31 million; the number of men between the ages of 15 and 30 was 4.56 million. See U.S. Department of the Census, *Historical Statistics of the United States, Part 1, Chaps. A–M* 15 (1989). These grim numbers dwarf the 405,000 deaths of World War II—America's second-bloodiest war. Allan Millett and Peter Maslowski, *For the Common Defense* 653 (1994). While data are weak for the Revolution, it appears that about 25,000 died, and 8,500 (?) were wounded. Id. In relative terms, this death toll represents 1 percent of the total population—Richard Balkin, *Revolutionary America* 123 (1995)—about one-half the Civil War ratio.

4. I expand here on John Pocock's *Three British Revolutions* (1980), by suggesting that the British roots of American constitutional experience continue through the nineteeth and twentieth centuries.

5. Blacks could vote on the same basis as whites in New England (with the exception of Connecticut). In New York, they could vote if they satisfied special property requirements. Edward Gambill, *Conservative Ordeal* 23 (1981). About 90 percent of free Northern blacks lived in states that excluded them from the ballot. Leon Litwack, *North of Slavery* 75 (1961).

6. See Dan Carter, *When the War Was Over* 229–230 (1984).

7. For more on the concept of considered judgment, see F, ch. 10.

8. See Oliver Temple, *Notable Men of Tennessee* 138–141 (1912).

9. Though Stevens was, even then, protesting this decision. See 37, 2 *CG* (1861), at 2.

10. Brooks himself was subsequently expelled from the House on a Republican challenge to his credentials. He was recalled, however, by his fellow Democrats at the time of the vote on the Fourteenth Amendment:

> MR. ELDRIDGE. I desire to state that if Messrs. Brooks and Voorhees had not been expelled, they would have voted against this proposition. [Great laughter]
>
> MR. SCHENCK. And I desire to say that if Jeff. Davis were here, he would probably also have voted the same way [Renewed laughter]. (39, 1 *CG* [1866], at 3149)

11. 38, 2 *CG* (1865), at 3–4.

12. See Chapter 4.

13. 39, 1 *CG* (1866), at 157.

14. Samuel Shellabarger speaks with a similar voice in an influential speech of January 8:

> There were, during the first years of the war, twenty-three rebel Senators . . . That was more than one third of the Senate. These twenty-three in the Senate are enough to deprive the Senate of all power ever to make a treaty, or to expel a member from the Senate, or to remove from office by impeachment . . . an imbecile President who thought secession unconstitutional, and its prevention equally unconstitutional, like Buchanan. How long, sir, could your government survive with such a Senate, one-third rebel? . . . Not a week, sir.
>
> But, Mr. Chairman, this is precisely what . . . may occur today if the States be indeed disloyal yet at heart . . .
>
> If you reply, I will reject these twenty-three rebel Senators, not because their States can elect none, but because they are "rebels," in the case you put; the reply is vain. When Mason, Slidell, Davis, and Breckenridge last took their seats in your Senate, who knew, or could have proved, that they came here to embarrass and destroy your government? Could either have been excluded from any known or ascertainable personal disqualification?
>
> No, Mr. Chairman, there is no escape. (39, 1 *CG* [1866], at 145.)

Shellabarger's complex interweaving of legalistic and unconventional elements is worthy of extended study.

15. Indeed, Seward was the *Radical* candidate for the Republican nomination for the Presidency in 1860, losing to the moderate Lincoln in a close contest.
16. See, e.g., Carl Schurz, 3 *Reminiscences* 225–229 (1908).
17. Michael Benedict, *A Compromise of Principle* 216–222 (1974).
18. Sec. 1, 14 *Stat.* 27 (1866)
19. See Eric McKitrick, *Andrew Johnson and Reconstruction* 286 (1960).
20. 6 *MPP* 403–405 (veto message of Andrew Johnson, Feb. 19, 1866); see also the less elaborate discussion in id. at 405, 406 (veto of civil rights bill, March 27, 1866). There is reason to believe that the quoted section was written by Johnson himself. See Cox and Cox, supra n. 1, at 470–472.
21. These characterizations come from Schurz, supra n. 16, at 226, 229.
22. McKitrick, supra n. 19, at 292–293; Hans Trefousse, *Andrew Johnson* 252 (1989).
23. See Chapter 4 for the arguments pro and con.
24. A relatively balanced account of Senator John Stockton's shocking exclusion is presented by Schurz, supra n. 16, at 233.
25. *The Nation,* March 22, 1866, quoted in McKitrick, supra n. 19, at 344.
26. 39, 1 *CG* (1866), at 3149 (House: yea, 120; nay, 32; not voting, 32) (June 13, 1866); id. at 3042 (Senate: yea, 33; nay, 11; absent, 5) (June 8, 1866). In the House, the eleven excluded states would have been entitled to 61 votes: Alabama 6, Arkansas 3, Florida 1, Georgia 7, Louisiana 5, Mississippi 5, North Carolina 7, South Carolina 4, Tennessee 8, Texas 4, Virginia 11, raising the

voting base from 184 to 243. (These figures come from Joel Treese et al., *Biographical Directory of the American Congress 1774–1996,* 37 (1996).) In the Senate, the eleven excluded states would have had 22 seats.

27. The only cursory discussions appear at *Report of the Joint Committee on Reconstruction,* in Edward McPherson, *Political History of Reconstruction* 88, 91, 93 (1880).

28. I have considered this aspect of the *Report* in Chapter 4.

29. *Report,* supra n. 27, at 90.

30. Id. at 87.

31. *Federalist* No. 40 (C. Rossiter ed., 1961) at 252–253. I discuss this passage at greater length in *F* at 173–175.

32. To be more precise, the statute did not allow a Southern state to expect readmission to Congress until "the above-recited amendment shall have become part of the Constitution of the United States, and any State lately in insurrection shall have ratified the same, and shall have modified its constitution and laws in conformity therewith." *Report,* supra n. 27, at v. Thus, even if an individual Southern state approved the amendment, it would remain in limbo so long as the exercise of an Article Five veto by other states remained possible. This suggestion—and its blatant breach with Article Five—would be taken up in earnest later on. See Chapter 7.

33. 39, 1 *CG* (1866), at 3349.

34. See Chapter 5.

35. Benedict, supra n. 17, at 207.

36. Seventeen Northern seats in the Senate, 13 held by Republicans and 4 by Democrats, were also up for election. The President could have gained an absolute majority only if he had continued to hold the 4 Democratic seats and captured 9 of the 13 Republican seats available. Such a landslide seemed most unlikely. Cf. Joseph James, *The Ratification of the Fourteenth Amendment* 87 (1984). Even so, a substantial success might have enabled Johnson to coax conservative Republicans to join a "Presidentially recognized" Senate, or—more likely—to place overwhelming pressure on their colleagues to end the crisis by admitting the South.

37. Benedict, supra n. 17, at 207.

38. See, e.g., *The Nation,* Sept. 20, 1866, at 230 ("secure the all-important point, *the election of at least 122 Republicans to the next House of Representatives,* the only way . . . by which the country can be saved from an outbreak of violence"), quoted in Benedict, supra n. 17, at 207.

39. See Chapter 8. Article X is entirely devoted to the President's conduct during the election campaign of 1866, but it played a small role at the trial.

40. *Proceedings in the Trial of Andrew Johnson, President of the United States, on Articles of Impeachment Exhibited by the House of Representatives* 77 (1868).

41. Echoes of Butler's fears can be found in the writings of many more sober men: "I almost fear he [Johnson] contemplates civil war." Letter from J. Sherman to W. T. Sherman (July 8, 1866), reprinted in *The Sherman Letters, Correspon-*

dence between General and Senator Sherman from 1837 to 1891 276 (1894), quoted in LaWanda Cox and John Cox, *Politics, Principle, and Prejudice, 1865–1866, 222–223* (1963).

42. The parallel to the 1787 Convention was milked for all it was worth. Professor Thomas Wagstaff, for example, describes the message advanced by Senator James Doolittle as he accepted the chairmanship: "The National Union Convention would carry forward and perfect the work begun by the Fathers in 1787." Thomas Wagstaff, "The Arm-In-Arm Convention," 14 *Civ. War. Hist.* 101, 113 (1968).

43. The call to convention went out to all thirty-six states, nine territories, and the District of Columbia. Joseph James, *The Ratification of the Fourteenth Amendment* 31 (1984). Each state was entitled to a number of delegates equal to twice the number of its normal full Congressional representation. Wagstaff, supra n. 42, at 101, 104. In the North, each state was to send four delegates from each Congressional district, two Unionists and two Democrats. Benedict, supra n. 17, at 193. This equal division was not required of Southern delegates. Gambill, supra n. 5, at 65. While the selection of Northern delegates was controlled by state party organizations (id.), Southern selection was less centrally organized. Carter, supra. n. 6, at 247.

The original intent of the convention organizers was to prevent the selection of delegates who had been "very prominent or active either for or against secession" (id. at 246), to keep out extreme Copperheads (McKitrick, supra n. 19, at 405), and to attract conservative and moderate Republicans as well as like-minded Democrats. Ideally, the delegates would "subscribe to the principles of no secession, no slavery, and no right to keep states unrepresented." James, supra, at 31.

44. After this act of apostasy, Raymond was removed from the chairmanship by vote of an illegal meeting of the Union Republican National Committee at Philadelphia on September 3. McKitrick, supra n. 19, at 420.

45. Wagstaff, supra n. 42, at 101, 117. This paean was contained in the last of the ten declarations that composed the National Union platform. See Edward McPherson, *The Political History of the United States of America during the Period of Reconstruction* 241 (1875).

46. The sixth principle of the National Union Platform declared: ". . . amendments to the Constitution of the United States may be made by the people thereof as they may deem expedient, but only in the mode pointed out by its provisions; and in proposing such amendments, whether by Congress or by a convention, and in ratifying the same, all the States of the Union have an equal and an indefeasible right to a voice and a vote thereon." Id. at 241.

47. For the text of the speech, see "Reply to Committee from Philadelphia National Union Convention," in Paul Bergeron, ed., 11 *Papers of Andrew Johnson* 92–96 (1994).

48. See McKitrick, supra n. 19, at 429. (Johnson's personal speaking tour involved "the first modern campaign train.")

49. Id. at 428.

50. James, supra n. 43, at 29.

51. For an especially perceptive discussion, see Kenneth Stampp, *The Era of Reconstruction* 87–108 (1970).

52. For examples of these often heated extemporaneous exchanges, see James, supra n. 43, at 430–437.

53. See Gambill, supra n. 5, at 65.

54. Of the 17 Senate seats up for election, Republicans won 15, losing only one of the 12 they controlled previously and capturing 3 of the 4 Democratic seats. Indeed, the Senate refused to seat the one Democrat who had ousted a Republican. See Jean Baker, *The Politics of Continuity: Maryland Political Parties from 1858 to 1870* 173 (1973). This left the Republicans in control of the Senate by 44 to 9.

55. McKitrick, supra n. 19, at 447.

56. For a perceptive discussion of the leading themes of Republican constitutionalism in 1866, see Robert Kaczorowski, "Revolutionary Constitutionalism in the Era of the Civil War and Reconstruction," 61 *N.Y.U.* 863, 871–900 (1986).

57. So long as we embrace this framework, it is unsurprising that pro-Southern historians like James Randall can derisively dismiss the constitutionality of the Fourteenth Amendment, while pro-Northerners squirm anxiously and seek to change the subject or embrace "grasp of war" theories of the kind discussed in Chapter 4.

7. *Interpreting the Mandate*

1. Compare Howard Beale, *The Critical Year* (1930), and Claude Bowers, *The Tragic Era* (1929), with Michael Benedict, *A Compromise of Principle* (1974), and Eric McKitrick, *Andrew Johnson and Reconstruction* (1960).

2. For more, see *F,* chs. 9–10.

3. As Governor William Brownlow gently put it in a famous telegram to the clerk of the Senate: "We have ratified the Constitutional Amendment . . . Give my respects to the dead dog of the White House." Quoted by Hans Trefousse, *Andrew Johnson* 253 (1989).

4. As Johnson explained in an interview with the *London Times* (Jan. 10, 1867): "The President said that the light in which he regarded public affairs at the present moment was that a minority in the country was seeking to impose its views on the majority. . . . In the elections last Autumn false issues were dexterously introduced, and upon them the people pronounced a judgment. . . . But, continued the President, it is impossible that the question should rest here." Paul Bergeron, ed., 11 *Papers of Andrew Johnson* 596 (1994).

5. See McKitrick, supra n. 1, 454–455; Michael Benedict, *The Impeachment and Trial of Andrew Johnson* 16 (1973).

6. McKitrick, supra n. 1, at 467–473.

7. See Trefousse, supra n. 3, 336–339.

8. By the end of January, nine of the former Confederate states, together with Kentucky, had rejected the amendment. If taken at face value, this tally deprived the amendment of the needed three-fourths approval. By the end of March, these ten rejections increased to thirteen when the states of Louisiana, Delaware, and Maryland added their nays. Charles Fairman, *History of the Supreme Court: Reconstruction and Reunion, 1864–88,* Part One, 255 (1971). It is misleading to focus too much attention on precise dates. As soon as observers learned the results of the November elections in these states, the grim prospects were clear. Joseph James, *Ratification of the Fourteenth Amendment* 128 (1984).

9. Benedict, supra n. 1, chs. 10–11 (1974).

10. The exception is Charles Fairman, who recognizes that the debate on the Reconstruction Act "may be viewed together" with those on the Fourteenth Amendment "as a continuing pursuit of one persistent problem: On what basis should the Union be restored—and what should be done when the South rejected the proffered basis?" Fairman, supra n. 8, at 332. I am indebted to Fairman for this insightful formulation.

11. See, e.g., speeches by Eldridge, 39, 2 CG (1867), at 561–564; Kerr, id. at 622–625; Ross, id. at 778–781; LeBlond, id. at 1077–79; LeBlond, id. at 1323–24; Eldridge, id. at 1324–25.

12. See, e.g., speeches by Pike, 39, 2 CG (1867), at 254; Holmes, id. at 265; Spalding, id. at 288–290; Bingham, id. at 502; Warner, id. at 566; Plants, id. at 598; Koontz, id. at 595; Miller, id. at 600; Higby, id. at 625; Cullom, id. at 815; Thayer, id. at 1098; Garfield, id. at 1104; Kelley, id. at 1177; Allison, id. at 1180; Garfield, id. at 1183; Raymond, id. at 1182–83; Van Horn, id. at 1201–02; Garfield, id. at 1320; Thayer, id. at 1321; Delano, id at 1325; Woodbridge, id. at 1323; Banks, id. at 1328; Miller, id. at 1332; Darling, id. at 1337; Stewart, id. at 1361; Fessenden, id. at 1556.

13. See also speech by Spalding, 39, 2 CG (1867), at 289–290.

14. Id. at 715. Raymond parted company with most Republicans in expressing a willingness to water down Section 3 of the amendment, which disqualified leading Confederates from high political office. This plea fell on deaf ears.

15. Id. at 500.

16. Id. at 252.

17. See Chapter 5.

18. 39, 2 CG (1867), at 783–784.

19. Id. at 250 and 253.

20. Stevens's January proposal left it to future Congresses to determine whether to readmit representatives and Senators from the new governments. Id. at 250. In arguing against moderate amendments to his new statutory initiative in February, Stevens exclaimed, "[W]hy tie us up by this pledge in advance to the constitutional amendment?" Id. at 1214.

21. Id. at 501.

22. The vote was 88 to 65. Just before, Stevens had denounced Bingham on the

floor of the House: "In all this contest about reconstruction I do not propose either to take his [Bingham's] counsel, recognize his authority, or believe a word he says." Id. at 816.

23. Although George Williams, the author of the Military Bill, had not intended it to be a radical measure, it was Stevens who presented it to the House, and he gave it a radical cast. The preamble and the first section referred to the "so-called states" of the South, and Stevens repeatedly emphasized that they had been "conquered" and should be treated like any other "conquered" "foreign government[s]" under "the law of nations." Id. at 1076. This interpretation made the statutory language unacceptable to moderates and conservatives, and Bingham tried to amend it. Id. at 1081. While Bingham's motion was not successful, Stevens consented to change the reference to the Southern states in Section One from "the so-called states" to "the late so-called confederate states," which helped to appease moderate concerns. Id. at 1206. Subsequent attempts in the House to change the bill were unsuccessful, but in the Senate, references to the Southern states' status was removed, and the preamble was changed to declare only that the South had "[n]o legal state governments," and so self-consciously avoided any endorsement of the "state suicide" theory. Id. at 1459.

24. Id. at 1104.

25. The vote was 79 to 54. Id. at 1210.

26. At no point did Bingham deny the need for martial law in the South. See id. at 1081. He simply barred the enactment of any legislation that failed to explain to the South that it could regain admission to Congress by ratifying the Fourteenth Amendment.

27. Id. at 501–502. The entire speech is from p. 500 to p. 505.

28. Before the proposal of the Military Bill and its amendments, Bingham had supported impartial rather than universal suffrage— allowing literacy and property qualifications to deny the vote to most if not all blacks, especially in the South. Benedict, supra n. 1, at 223. But on February 13th, he demanded that all males be allowed to vote, since it would put "the loyal men . . . in the majority" and set the stage for ratification. 39, 2 CG (1867), at 1211.

29. Although some suggested that ratification was a convenient means to signal an end to military rule (see, e.g., Stewart's comments, id. at 1366), Bingham's goal was to trigger ratification. He not only required each former Confederate state to ratify the Fourteenth Amendment, but before any of them could gain representation in Congress, he demanded "that . . . the . . . amendment shall have become part of the Constitution of the United States." Id. at 1211. This theme was taken up by Senator John Sherman, who drafted the triggering provision that was finally enacted.

30. The clearest analysis of the parliamentary maneuvering is to be found in David Donald, *The Politics of Reconstruction,* ch. 3 (1965).

31. When the Military Bill arrived in the Senate, its fate was quickly tied up with the Louisiana Bill, which had passed the House shortly before. That bill left re-

sumption of representation in Congress unsettled and did not try to trigger ratification of the Fourteenth Amendment. 39, 2 *CG* (1867), at 1397. Radicals, like Sumner, supported passage of both bills: the Military Bill for the protection of Southern loyalists, and the Louisiana Bill, which they wanted to generalize to all Southern states, to initiate actual Reconstruction. Id. at 1303. Moderates and conservatives successfully resisted these proposals. Fearing a pocket veto by the president, the Republicans quickly created a special committee under Senator Sherman to negotiate a compromise. After less than a day of discussion, Sherman emerged with a new version of the Military Bill that adopted a moderate triggering provision very similar to the one Stevens had defeated in the House. Sherman's proposal guaranteed the Southern states readmission to Congress after three conditions were satisfied: first, that new state constitutions guaranteed universal suffrage; second, that new legislatures ratified the Fourteenth Amendment; and third, that "said article . . . shall . . . become a part of the Constitution of the United States." Id. at 1459. Sherman called this triggering requirement the most important aspect of the measure. Id. at 1462. The bill passed the Senate easily, 29 to 10, the same evening. Id. at 1469.

But in the House, Stevens led an odd coalition of conservative Democrats and radical Republicans that refused to concur with the Senate amendments. The House requested a conference committee to settle the chambers' differences. Recognizing the fragility of Stevens's coalition, Sherman urged the Senate to refuse a conference and to insist that the House either agree to the Senate amendments or modify them in a manner acceptable to both houses. His tactic worked. The House concurred with only two minor changes, neither relating to the triggering requirement. The Senate quickly agreed, and the Military Bill, as amended, was sent to the President.

32. 14 *Stat.* 428, 429 (March 2, 1867). Emphasis added.

33. *Federalist* No. 39 remains the classic statement of this deep uncertainty concerning the locus of popular sovereignty amongst Americans of the Revolutionary era.

34. 39, 2 *CG* (1867), at 1564. Sherman was the draftsman of the triggering language that finally was enacted, but he was not alone. Others in both Houses believed that the South should be allowed to reconstruct itself. See, e.g., Baker, id. at 137; Bingham, id. at 501; Bingham, id. at 1212; McRuer, id. at 1331; Trimble, id. at 64.

35. States with absent Representatives included California, Connecticut, Kentucky, Nebraska, New Hampshire, Rhode Island, and Tennessee. In most of them, no elections had yet been held, and only Nebraska and New Hampshire would be represented before Congress adjourned in April. Three more would have Representatives in the House when the Congress met in July, but the seats for California and Tennessee would remain empty until November 21, when Congress met for the third and final time that year. 40, 1 *CG* (1867), at 6, 185, 468, and 768.

36. Id at 3. The seven unrepresented states that were founding members of the

Union were New Hampshire, Rhode Island, Connecticut, Virginia, North Carolina, South Carolina, and Georgia.

37. Id. at 2–3.
38. Id. at 161.
39. Id. at 110.
40. See, e.g., McKitrick, supra n. 1, at 269–273.
41. 40, 1 *CG* (1867), at 118.
42. Id. at 110.
43. Id. at 155.
44. As we shall see, later events forced the Republicans to weaken this second requirement in the Fourth Reconstruction Act. See Chapter 8.
45. 6 *MPP* 358.

8. The Great Transformation

1. Sec. 6, 14 *Stat.* 428–429 (1867).
2. Lincoln's appointees were Justices Stephen Field, David Davis, Samuel Miller, Noah Swayne, and Chief Justice Salmon P. Chase.
3. Johnson had already proclaimed that "peace, order, tranquillity and civil authority now exist in and throughout the whole of the United States of America." Proclamation of 20 August 1866, 6 *MPP* 434, 438. See also 6 *MPP* 445.
4. In fact, both Jefferson and Jackson had experimented with this technique—at least so far as the Supreme Court was concerned—much earlier. See *F* at 70–80, and my forthcoming book, *The Roots of Presidentialism.*
5. At the same time, the Court refused to hear a suit from the Johnsonian government of Mississippi that would have sought directly to enjoin the President, as opposed to his inferior officers, from enforcing the Reconstruction Acts. Charles Fairman, *History of the Supreme Court: Reconstruction and Reunion, 1864–88,* Part One, 385 (1971).
6. *National Intelligencer,* quoted in id. at 386.
7. The Justices did not file an opinion in *Georgia v. Stanton* until the following February—so tea-leaf reading was impossible.
8. It took Stanbery two opinions to cut the Reconstruction Acts down to size. In the first, dated May 24, 1867, Stanbery minimized the impact of the disqualification provision of the Second Act. 15 *Stat.* 2 (1867). He found that militia, municipal, and county officers were not "officers of the state" and so were not disqualified unless they had explicitly sworn previously to uphold the Constitution. United States Department of Justice, 12 *Opinions of the Attorney General* 151–163 (1867). Even more significantly, Stanbery denied the federal voting registrars the power to make an independent investigation of an applicant's qualifications. If a would-be voter swore that he satisfied Congressional loyalty tests, the registrar was required to add his name to the voting rolls: "The oath itself is the sole and only test of the qualification of the applicant." Id. at

168. Even Jefferson Davis could demand registration, subject only to a later trial "on an indictment for perjury." Id.

Stanbery's second opinion, dated June 12, was equally obstructionist. It denied that military commanders were superior to the Johnsonian governments. While Congress had asserted its power "to abolish, modify, control, or supersede," Stanbery denied that it had delegated this power to military officers, who could neither remove or appoint officials of these governments. The military's sole role was to maintain the peace and effect the registration and elections specified by the acts. Id. at 182, 183–184.

9. Indeed, Johnson's earlier veto messages had interpreted the acts in a very different spirit: "The power . . . given to the commanding officer over all the people of each district is that of an absolute monarch. His mere will is to take the place of all law." Veto Message, 6 *MPP* 500 (1867). As Senator Roscoe Conkling exclaimed, "[The veto messages] proceed largely upon the idea that the acts they denounce contain the very ingredients, that they are odious and vicious because they contain the very ingredients, which are now found wanting by the Attorney General." 40, 1 *CG* (1867), at 529.

10. The proceedings of the June 18 Cabinet meeting are summarized in 6 *MPP* 528–531.

11. 15 *Stat.* 14 (1867). Southern commanders were expressly authorized to remove uncooperative officials in existing governments (sec. 2), and registration authorities were told that the oath of a would-be voter "shall not be conclusive . . . and no person shall be registered unless such board [of registration] shall decide that he is entitled thereto." Sec. 5, 15 *Stat.* 15 (1867).

12. Sec. 1, 15 *Stat.* 2 (1867).

13. Sec. 6, 15 *Stat.* 14, 15 (1867).

14. Second Reconstruction Act, Sec. 2, 15 *Stat.* 2, 3 (1867).

15. Sec. 4, 15 *Stat.* 3 (1867).

16. Id.

17. Only General John Schofield, whose district included the single State of Virginia, was a conservative. In fact, Reconstruction in Virginia did proceed slowly, leading to readmission of Senators and Representatives only in 1870. See Fairman, supra n. 5, at 598–601.

18. The very same day it had overridden the President's veto of the First Reconstruction Act.

19. Sec. 2, 14 *Stat.* 485, 486–487 (1867).

20. When other Republicans resigned from the cabinet in 1866, the Republican leadership called upon Stanton to remain as a bulwark for Congressional interests. See Benjamin Thomas and Harold Hyman, *Stanton: The Life and Times of Lincoln's Secretary of War* 471–494 (1962). Nominally, however, he was a Democrat.

21. Sec. 1, 14 *Stat.* 430 (1867).

22. See Michael Benedict, *A Compromise of Principle* 297–298 (1974).

23. Hans Trefousse, *Andrew Johnson* 81 and 206, n. 66 (1989).

24. Id. at 295.
25. Looking backward from the safety of the twentieth century, Chief Justice William Howard Taft had no trouble pronouncing the statute unconstitutional—see Meyers v. U.S., 272 U.S. 52, 176 (1925)—though, as a former President, he might not have been the most impartial judge imaginable.
26. Sec. 2, 14 *Stat.* 430 (1867).
27. See Proclamation of Sept. 7, 1867, 6 *MPP* 547.
28. See Trefousse, supra n. 23, at 91.
29. Id. at 91.
30. *N.Y. Times,* November 14, 1867, at 1.
31. Despite all his subsequent setbacks, Johnson attempted to win the Democratic nomination for the Presidency in 1868. See Edward Gambill, *Conservative Ordeal* 138, 140 (1981).
32. See Michael Benedict, *The Impeachment and Trial of Andrew Johnson* 89 (1973).
33. Quoted in Trefousse, supra n. 23, at 115.
34. "The fact is that Reconstruction is now on a pivot . . . [t]he action of Congress for the next 10 or 15 days will decide whether the whole South will be Republican or Democratic." Circular letter of December 30, 1867, by Congressman Foster Blodget. Quoted in Benedict, supra n. 32, at 91.
35. See Trefousse, supra n. 23, at 115–122.
36. The best evidence of the President's obedience to the letter, if not the spirit, of the law is the inability of his radical opponents to make out a case for impeachment that would convince their more moderate Republican colleagues. See the minority report of the moderate Republican chairman of the committee, James Wilson, who dissented from the majority recommendation in favor of impeachment. Impeachment of the President, *House Reports,* 40th Cong., No. 7, at 1–11. With Wilson leading the opposition, impeachment was defeated on the floor of the House on December 7 by a vote of 57 to 108. See Trefousse, supra n. 23, at 106. The technically legal character of Johnson's obstruction is conceded even by those historians, most notably Michael Benedict, who wish to portray Congress' decision to impeach as a reasonable response to Presidential provocation. See, e.g., Benedict, supra n. 32, ch. 5.
37. Trefousse, supra n. 23, at 129–130, 112.
38. Eric McKitrick, *Andrew Johnson and Reconstruction* 503–504 (1960).
39. Trefousse, supra n. 23, at 117.
40. Of the 165,813 registered voters in Alabama, only 71,817 showed up at the polls, short of the majority by more than 10,000. Even though 70,812 voted for the new constitution, it failed under the Second Reconstruction Act. Walter Fleming, *Reconstruction in Alabama* 541 (1905).
41. See Charlton Tebeau and Ruby Carson, 1 *Florida From Indian Trail to Space Age: A History* 222–223 (1965).
42. Johnson's courtship of Sherman is elaborated by Trefousse, supra n. 23, at 124–128.

43. Reprinted in id. at 133.

44. Id. at 136.

45. Its resolution simply asserted, without any further support, "That Andrew Johnson, President of the United States, be impeached of high crimes and misdemeanors in office." 40, 2 *CG* (1868), at 1400.

46. 40, 2 *CG* (1868), at 1638–42.

47. Black's coordinating role in the litigation is chronicled by Fairman, supra n. 5, at 371, 386, 433–440, 449–459, 467–476, 478, 492. His role in writing the President's veto messages is described by John Cox and LaWanda Cox, "Andrew Johnson and His Ghost Writers," 48 *Miss. Valley Hist. Rev.* 468 (1961).

48. Section 3 of the First Reconstruction Act made it the duty of the District Commander "to punish . . . all disturbers of the public peace and criminals." McCardle faced four separate charges alleging disturbance of the peace through the publication of libelous attacks on Reconstruction.

49. Although McCardle was arrested solely for his fierce newspaper attacks on Reconstruction, the briefs mention the First Amendment only in passing. Black and his associates could have argued that the Reconstruction Act did not, in fact, authorize the military action taken against McCardle. But, as Fairman notes, the brief "eagerly conceded" the point on page two. Fairman, supra n. 5, at 457. Counsel did do better in dealing with the fact that Congress had given jurisdiction over McCardle to a military commission in time of peace, depriving him of a jury trial in federal court, or even habeas corpus. Since the Court had, during its previous Term, eloquently protected jury trials in *ex parte Milligan,* Black did argue that *Milligan* should be extended to cases, like McCardle's, that arose in rebellious states like Mississippi. Even this argument was secondary to the broad-based attack described in the text.

50. Both Johnson's veto messages and the legal briefs in *McCardle* (1) begin with an attack upon the validity of the preamble to the First Reconstruction Act; (2) assert that the republican form of government clause prohibits federal efforts to reconstruct the South; (3) list the Bill of Rights guarantees as secondary evidence of Congressional illegality, with the rights to grand jury presentment and trial by jury emphasized more than others, e.g., freedom of speech and press; and (4) argue that *ex parte Milligan* invalidates the military trials exemplified by McCardle's case.

51. Fairman, supra n. 5, at 450–451.

52. See n. 25, supra.

53. Indeed, the Senate had already condemned the President's defiance of the Tenure of Offices Act as illegal. U.S. Senate, 16 *Executive Journal* 171 (Feb. 21, 1868).

54. See, e.g., 40, 2 *CG* (1868), at 2062 (statement of Cong. Wilson).

55. Reported in Fairman, supra n. 5, at 494; Stanley Kutler, *Judicial Power and Reconstruction Politics* 112.

56. Stanley Kutler asserts that the death of Justice James Wayne, in the summer of

1867, left the Justices deadlocked 4 to 4. See Kutler, supra n. 55, at 99–100. Charles Fairman is less certain. See Fairman, supra n. 5, at 584, as well as 494.

57. The protest is reprinted in Fairman, supra n. 5, at 473–474.

58. Id. at 474–476.

59. See id. at 478.

60. 40, 2 CG (1868), at 30.

61. Id. at 29.

62. Indeed, one of the President's lawyers asserted that Johnson could be removed only for high crimes or misdemeanors *as they were defined when the Constitution was proposed in 1787,* thereby insulating his client from any complaints involving the Tenure of Offices Act. See generally Benedict, supra n. 32, at 145–146.

63. The Senate began its struggle over self-definition in considering rules proposed by a special committee to govern the impeachment proceeding. These explicitly asserted that the Senate would "resolve itself into a high court of impeachment" that would adjourn formally whenever the Senators transacted legislative business. After two days of confused but passionate debate, the Senate eliminated the term "high court of impeachment" whenever it appeared in its rules. Id. at 115–116.

This vote did not conclude the matter. Almost immediately the Senate confronted it afresh in defining the role of Chief Justice Chase who, according to the Constitution, was to "preside." In voting to delete all references to a distinct "high court of impeachment," the Republican majority was seeking to deprive Chase of a vote that would come with membership in such a "court." It also rejected its committee's proposal to authorize the Chief Justice to make a preliminary ruling on all questions of law and evidence, his opinion to stand as the judgment of the "court" unless overruled by a majority vote. Senator Charles Drake moved to strike this rule, explaining that "It is not proper that the judgment of the Senate upon questions of law . . . should be warped, in any degree affected by the previous announcement of an opinion upon that question by so high a judicial officer as the Chief Justice."

In response, Senator Jacob Howard proposed an ambiguous substitute that merely asserted that the Chief Justice "may in the first instance submit to the Senate, without a division, all questions of evidence and incidental questions." Id. at 116. Drake accepted this substitute, which was adopted by a majority in its final rules: the Chief Justice was well on his way to becoming a ceremonial figurehead without power to shape questions of procedure and evidence, let alone the final outcome.

This is not the view that Chase took when he arrived in the Senate to begin the conduct of the trial. Chase immediately announced that since the rules only said that he "may" submit preliminary questions to the Senate, it did not require him to do so. When Senator Drake appealed his decision, Chase ruled him out of order. Once again insisting on the judicial analogy, Chase declared that only the

House Managers (for the prosecution) or the President's lawyers (for the defense) could object to his rulings; a mere Senator like Drake could not do so. When the House Managers objected to this effort at judicialization, the problematics of legality took yet another turn. Senator Wilson moved that the Senate retire for consultation on the critical matter raised by the Managers' objection. When the Senate divided 25 to 25 on the motion, Chase immediately announced that he would break the tie by voting in the affirmative: a move that supposed that, despite the Senate's earlier rejection of all mention of itself as a "high court of impeachment," he was presiding over a Court in which he was a full member.

In the ensuing senatorial consultation, Charles Sumner moved the Senate to declare that "the Chief Justice is not a member of the Senate, and has no authority, under the Constitution, to vote on any question during the trial, and he can pronounce decision only as the organ of the Senate, with its assent." Id. at 121. But the Senate rejected this motion 22 to 26 and accepted a resolution declaring the Presiding Officer's decision the judgment of the Senate unless a Senator asked for a formal vote. The next day the Senate refused to declare that Chase had acted beyond his authority in casting his tie-breaking vote. Of course, these votes fell short of an *explicit* senatorial endorsement of the view, advanced earlier by the draftsmen of its proposed rules, that it had become a distinct "high court of impeachment" whose authority was exclusively of a court-like kind. While the Senate had, for the moment, acquiesced in the Chief Justice's court-like definition of the situation, it was impossible to say whether Chase's limited position of procedural leadership would continue to have Senate support. After all, Sumner's motion had lost by only four votes; and recent history had amply demonstrated Congress's capacity to change its mind. The trial opened under conditions that dramatized the problematic mix of legalistic and unconventional elements in the Senate's assertion of constitutional authority. See id. at 115–123.

64. Between mid-March and early May, six Southern states held the crucial second round of elections. See Martin Mantell, *The Election of 1868* 144 (Columbia University diss., 1969). Only Alabama had voted before this point. Three states—Mississippi, Texas, and Virginia—lagged in the rear.

65. The Library of Congress archive contains an order from Johnson to Grant, directing him to send all War Department communications to Thomas rather than Stanton. The order was dated March 10 but was never sent. See Mantell, supra n. 64, at 136.

66. James McDonough and William Alderson, "Republican Politics and the Impeachment of Andrew Johnson," 26 *Tenn. His. Q.* 177 (1967).

67. Sullivan Cox, *Union—Disunion—Reunion: Three Decades of Federal Legislation, 1855 to 1885* 592–594 (1886). By May 14, John Henderson assured Republican representatives that Johnson intended to enforce the Reconstruction laws and even change his Cabinet to give Republicans control. *House Report* No. 75, 40th Cong, 2nd Sess, at 18.

68. Benedict, supra n. 32, at 138–139.

69. Opinion of Charles Sumner, see F. J. Rives & George Bailey, eds., *Proceedings of the Trial of Andrew Johnson* 958–967 (1868).

70. Of the seven Republican Senators who voted to acquit, five filed Opinions: Fessenden (id. at 936), Grimes (p. 870), Henderson (p. 1065), Trumbull (p. 863), and Van Winkle (p. 893). Unsurprisingly, the moderates contributed a greater proportion of Opinions (5 out of 7) than did other Senators—less than half of whom took the time and effort to write Opinions (22 out of a possible 47, to be precise).

71. Id. at 863.

72. While Johnson did nothing to undercut this process on the ground, he continued to deny its legality in more symbolic ways. For example, in vetoing the Electoral College Act, he called the new Southern governments "illegitimate and of no validity whatever," and in connection with Southern ratifications of the Fourteenth Amendment, he referred to resolutions "purporting" to be legislative acts, and certifying signatures of a man "who therein writes himself governor." 7 *MPP* 653, 656–670.

73. See Fairman, supra n. 5, at 106–107 (table).

74. Virginia and Texas had not yet voted on new constitutions. See id. (table)

75. See p. 221, infra.

76. Sec. 1, 15 *Stat.* 41 (1868).

77. 15 *Stat.* 72 (1868).

78. In addition, the states were forbidden to amend their constitutions' grant of suffrage to blacks. Special conditions were also imposed on Georgia. 15 *Stat.* 73 (1868).

79. Florida's constitution was thought to be particularly defective. Bingham's candid confession came in connection with the debate on Florida, after the debate on Alabama had been concluded. Georgia was also a problem—indeed, its representatives were later ejected from Congress when black legislators in Georgia were evicted by their white colleagues.

80. 40, 2 *CG* (1868), at 3094. When Bingham's confession brought gleeful protests from the opposition, the Congressman held his ground: "I said that upon the admission of the sixth State might depend the ratification of that amendment. . . ." Id. at 3095.

81. Veto Message of June 25, 1868, 6 *MPP* 650, 651.

82. See Chapter 2.

83. Proclamation No. 11, 15 *Stat.* 706, 707 (1868) (emphasis supplied).

84. Id. at 707.

85. 15 *Stat.* 710 (1868). See also Chapter 4, n. 35

86. Democratic Platform, 2 *S* 1267, 1269.

87. Matthew Carey, Jr., *The Democratic Speaker's Handbook: containing everything necessary for the defense of the national democracy in the coming presidential campaign* 355 (1868).

88. *N.Y. Times,* August 18, 1868, at 4.

89. Fairman, supra n. 5, at 487.

90. See John Franklin, "The Election of 1868," in 2 *S* 1247, 1265–66.

91. Act of April 10, 16 *Stat.* 44 (1869). The statute generated very little debate, in part because a predecessor had been discussed at greater length during the closing days of the previous Congress. Though the political motivation passed unmentioned by most Congressman, Senator Charles Buckalew let the cat out of the bag: "We know very well that formerly the judges of that [supreme] court were ten in number. . . . It has been reduced. The reduction was made under peculiar circumstances, and with some reference to political considerations two or three years since. Now that those have passed away, I see no objection to increasing the number of the judges of that court by one or two." 40, 3 *CG* (1869), at 1487.

92. Hepburn v. Griswold, 75 U.S. (8 Wall.) 603 (1870). At the insistence of Justice Field (see Fairman, supra n. 5, at 713), Chase's opinion invalidated the act only as it applied to debts contracted prior to its passage, leaving the question of post-enactment debts to another day. When the problem returned the second time around, Field endorsed complete invalidation. Legal Tender Cases, 79 U.S. (12 Wall.) 457, 634 (1871).

93. Perhaps Chase's public-regarding motivation would not have been so clear if the decision had come down earlier, when he was seeking the Democrats' nomination for the Presidency in 1868. But by this point, Chase was suffering a serious illness, which precluded a future run for the Presidency. (He died in 1873.)

94. Fairman presents the bitter internal squabble in supra n. 5, at 738–757, though he strains to minimize the legally remarkable elements of the affair.

95. Id. at 759.

96. See 79 U.S. (12 Wall.) 457, 534 (1871).

97. Knox v. Lee, 79 U.S. (12 Wall.) 457, 556 (1871).

98. Ex parte McCardle, 74 U.S. (7 Wall.) 506, 514 (1869).

99. Id. at 515.

100. See the useful time line provided by Fairman, supra n. 5, at 106–107.

101. Obviously, he could not raise McCardle's First Amendment claim. But this was not the centerpiece of McCardle's argument. See n. 49, supra.

102. Ex parte Milligan, 71 U.S. (4 Wall.) 2 (1866).

103. Fairman, supra n. 5, at 584. I fully agree with the analysis presented by Fairman to support his position.

104. S. 280, 41st Cong., 2d Sess. (1869).

105. Senator Drake proposed an even more extreme measure, S. 274, that would have deprived the courts of *all* power of judicial review. See Fairman, supra n. 5, at 586–588.

106. See S. 363, 40th Cong., 2d Sess. (1868).

107. While Trumbull's bill reached the Senate floor, it never came up for a vote. Fairman, supra n. 5, at 588, explicitly attributes this to the Attorney General's activities.

108. This item appears in the Court's Minutes for Tuesday, October 26, 1869. It is reprinted in id. at 585.
109. See id. at 589.
110. Ex parte Brown is discussed in id. at 590.
111. See *F* at 94–96.
112. Slaughterhouse Cases, 83 U.S. 36, 67 (1873).
113. Emphasis supplied.
114. Id. at 70–71.
115. Id. at 71.
116. Id. at 68.
117. I do not suggest that the Court was legally incapable of raising the question of validity on its own—only that professional norms allowed it to evade the question.
118. The best account is provided by William Gillette, *Retreat from Reconstruction* (1979).
119. For further analysis, see n. 126.
120. 2 *S* 1487.
121. And one vote from the North (Oregon).
122. See Charles Fairman, *Five Justices and the Electoral Commission of 1877* (1988), for a recent if overly apologetic—account.
123. Letter to Hewitt, *N.Y. Times*, October 25, 1876, at 2.
124. See Benjamin Barber, *Strong Democracy* (1984), for the best recent statement by a political theorist. In the legal academy, John Hart Ely's *Democracy and Distrust* (1980) provides the most influential theory that indulges in strong democratic presuppositions (though often covertly and in an unexamined way).
125. See *F*, ch. 11.
126. Michael McConnell has provided a different view of the end of Reconstruction in "The Forgotten Constitutional Moment," 11 *Con. Comm.* 115 (1994). He claims that a consistent application of my theory requires that 1874 be recognized as inaugurating a new and successful constitutional moment in which the People authorized the construction of a racist "Jim Crow Republic."

McConnell does not offer this interpretation to commend my theory, but to bury it. If my general approach legitimates Jim Crow, he suggests, shouldn't good-hearted lawyers avoid it like the plague?

Whatever its motivation, I commend McConnell's inquiry. A close analysis of proposed counterexamples permits the clarification of criteria that distinguish the many failed constitutional moments in American history from the few successes. Is McConnell right, then, in suggesting that Jim Crow was established through a mobilized and self-conscious decision by the American people?

I do not think so. His demonstration runs out of steam at the first step—establishing that Americans were signaling a serious desire to rethink the Reconstruction amendments. McConnell is quite right to point out that, after the Panic of 1873, the Republicans suffered a big defeat in the elections of 1874.

For the first time since the Civil War, the Democrats would control the House, and by the lopsided margin of 169–109. But despite their defeat, the Republicans were still in control of the Senate by 45–29; and they continued, of course, to control the Presidency. Nevertheless, McConnell wishes to endow the Democrats' electoral victory with profound constitutional significance. On his account, the election should be treated as a signal of a rising movement bent on questioning the constitutional solutions hammered out by the People in the 1860's.

I disagree. Off-year elections almost always result in victories for the party that is out of the White House. (The New Deal landslide of 1934, for example, is the only exception in the twentieth century.) Allowing a single off-year victory to function as a signal threatens to destroy the entire dualist project—which is to force normal politicos to achieve truly distinctive institutional and electoral victories before they are to gain the constitutional authority to speak in the name of the People.

McConnell's claim loses further credibility in its particular historical context. Despite their increased numbers, the Democrats failed to enact *any* legislation that raised a sweeping challenge to the statutory legacy of civil rights that the Republicans had continuously enhanced throughout the first half of the 1870's. Professor McConnell ignores this crucial institutional fact, emphasizing instead some statements on the Congressional floor by Democrats questioning the Fourteenth Amendment and proclaiming white supremacy. His collection is remarkably unimpressive, consisting of a few remarks by well-known racists. Even if McConnnell had dug up a more substantial set of quotations, there is a deeper methodological difficulty. Normal politics is full of talk—from extremists on all sides and moderates of different persuasions. Constitutional moments are signaled only when Congress and the President begin to translate this talk into deeds by passing statutes and taking other extraordinary actions that bespeak wide-ranging popular support for a new constitutional agenda. Nothing happened between 1874 and 1876 that remotely qualifies.

But perhaps the Hayes-Tilden affair indicates that the system was shifting into higher lawmaking gear? If Tilden had campaigned on a Blair-like platform questioning the amendments, I would accept the parallel to the signaling election of Lincoln in 1860—though the Democrats would have had to do a lot more work before moving through the next four phases of unconventional legitimation. Given Tilden's *explicit* embrace of the Reconstruction amendments in his campaign, McConnell's view of Tilden as the Lincoln of Jim Crow does a grave injustice to this very impressive statesman.

But what of Hayes's decision, in the Compromise of 1877, to remove military support from the remaining three Republican governments in the South? Did not this decision signal a self-conscious assault on the Reconstruction amendments? To the contrary, it was the ongoing use of troops to intervene politically in fully admitted states of the Union that was irregular. Taken by itself, Hayes's decision to rely on more ordinary methods of enforcing the amendments simply represents a return to normal politics.

But Professor McConnell suggests that this decision had a much larger impact. After 1877, he explains, "civil rights became a political liability . . . [t]hereafter, neither of the great political parties of the Nation retained a commitment to fulfillment of the ideals of the Fourteenth Amendment." Id. at 130.

McConnell is simply wrong on the facts. A major test came in 1879. The Democrats had finally gained majorities in both Houses of the Forty-fifth Congress and mounted a major assault on the civil rights statutes left behind by the Republicans. In particular, they tried to repeal the provisions of the Force Act, which authorized federal marshals to monitor the polls during federal elections and to call in federal troops to keep the peace. If Hayes had signed these repealers, or Congress had passed them over his veto, McConnell's signaling claim might have begun to seem plausible; and if the Democrats had followed through on this initial victory by winning the Presidency in 1880, the stage might well have been set for a very serious effort to repudiate the Reconstruction settlement in the name of the People.

But this is not what happened. Time and again, Hayes vetoed the Democratic Congress's assault on the Republicans' statutory legacy in messages that emphasized the constitutional issues. See 10 MPP 4475, 4484, 4489, 4493, 4497 (1879). In general outline, the ensuing conflict was very similar to the recent struggle between the Republican 104th Congress and President Clinton. Both in 1879 and 1995, an insurgent Congress used the very same technique to demonstrate high seriousness in assaulting the status quo—like the Republican 104th, the Democratic 45th tacked its repealers to key appropriations bills, and threatened to close down the government if Hayes did not accept the elimination of effective federal oversight of the electoral process in the states.

As in 1995, the move backfired. Hayes's vetoes revitalized the Republican Party and gained broad popularity, and the Democrats were obliged to accept defeat and pass appropriations without the riders. See Frank Vazzano, "President Hayes, Congress and the Appropriations Riders Vetoes," 20 *Cong. and Pres.* 25 (1993); Ari Hoogenboom, *Rutherford B. Hayes,* ch. 22 (1995).

Instead of backing away from the Republican commitment to the Reconstruction amendments, the Hayes Administration ended with their ringing reaffirmation. Indeed, Hayes's most recent biographer regrets Hayes's refusal to run for a second term: "Four more years would have allowed Hayes to widen the executive application of civil-service reform principles, and if he had secured a Republican Congress, he could have enforced the election laws and protected black voters in the South." Hoogenboom, supra, at 538.

Despite Hayes's withdrawal from the Presidential race, the Republicans won with Garfield, whose inaugural address suggested, once again, that McConnell's obituary notice on civil rights was premature. It contained a ringing and extended defense of the "elevation of the negro race from slavery to the full rights of citizenship . . . No thoughtful man can fail to appreciate its beneficent effect upon our institutions and people." 10 *MPP* 4598 (1881).

At that point, America suffered through another successful assassination. As in the case of Andrew Johnson, a Vice President from a very different branch of the party came into control of the White House. Garfield's successor, Chester Arthur, was from the New York wing of the party that was much more interested in the distribution of patronage than any matter of principle. Professor McConnell would be hard-pressed to portray Arthur as the leader of a mobilized movement seeking to inaugurate the Jim Crow Republic.

Indeed, the next time the Republicans won control of the White House and Congress in 1888, they came within a hair of enacting new civil rights legislation. Their proposed Force Act of 1890 successfully passed the House, had the support of a committed majority in the Senate, and barely failed to defeat an extended filibuster. Moreover, Senator George Hoar, the bill's primary sponsor, saw it as a prelude to further national legislation that would "secure for every child on American soil the education which shall fit him for citizenship." See Richard Welch, Jr., "The Federal Elections Bill of 1890," 52 *J. Am. Hist.* 511, 518 (1965).

Professor McConnell's interpretation is, in a word, anachronistic. There was no moment in the late nineteenth century in which a mobilized national majority repudiated the Reconstruction amendments. Indeed, the erosion of these amendments in the South took place in a far more complex fashion than McConnell supposes. See C. Vann Woodward, *The Strange Career of Jim Crow* (3d ed., 1974).

In rejecting Professor McConnell's claims, I do not deny the obvious. American institutions increasingly failed to preserve the commitments previously made by the People to black Americans. I simply deny that this failure occurred because the proponents of Jim Crow mobilized the majority of Americans to repudiate the Reconstruction amendments in the manner contemplated by higher lawmaking. If we hope to understand the tragic failure to live up to the amendments, we shall have to ask different questions: Did the Supreme Court betray its task of preserving constitutional commitments during normal politics? Or was there something inherently defective in the approach to racial justice taken by the amendments—defects which doomed them to failure even if judges had done their best to redeem the People's commitments?

I return to these questions in the next volume.

9. *From Reconstruction to New Deal*

1. 198 U.S. 45 (1905).
2. 247 U.S. 251, 273 (1918). This decision was reached by a sharply divided court, but it was confirmed in the Child Labor Tax Case, 259 U.S. 20 (1922)—

in which another divided Court struck down Congress's effort to use the taxing power to abolish child labor.

3. See United States v. Lopez, 115 S.Ct. 1624 (1995), the first case since 1937 to strike down a federal statute as exceeding the Commerce Clause, which is generating a new round of scholarly discussion. See, e.g., "Symposium," 94 *Mich. L. Rev.* 554 (1995).

4. I am using the words of Mr. Justice Miller in the *Slaughterhouse Cases.* See Chapter 8. For some further reflections on this theme, see Bruce Ackerman, "A Generation of Betrayal?" 65 *Fordham L. Rev.* 1519 (1997).

5. See, e.g., Theodore Lowi, *The Personal President* xi, chs. 2–5 (1985).

6. Coleman v. Miller, 307 U.S. 433 (1939).

7. Justice Frankfurter also contributed an opinion which sought to avoid any encounter with the merits, but this failed to gain the support of a majority. As a consequence, all the Justices signed one of the three opinions discussed in the text.

8. Id. at 435.

9. Id. at 436.

10. Id. at 451.

11. Id. at 448–449.

12. Id. at 449–450.

13. In particular, the Chief Justice focused on two questions: (1) how long a proposed amendment may remain open for ratification before it lapses, and (2) whether a state like Kansas can change its mind and ratify an amendment it had previously rejected.

14. Id. at 459.

15. There are problems with the Fifteenth Amendment as well, but an elaborate discussion will not advance my general argument. For the standard, but inadequate, treatment, see William Gillette, *The Right to Vote* (1969).

16. See *F* at 76–78.

17. Indeed, all common lawyers are familiar with episodes in which English and American courts have, over the course of centuries, absorbed ancient statutes into the fabric of the common law itself—to the point where decisive judicial opinions have utterly displaced the statutory text in operational legal authority.

18. See Arthur Schlesinger, *The Crisis of the Old Order* 308–309 (1957).

19. Unlike the Republicans of Reconstruction, the Democratic Congress of 1937 had an excellent chance of gaining the voluntary assent of three-fourths of the states. See chaps. 11–12, infra. If they had failed to win the requisite super-majority, they would have faced the same decision that the Republicans confronted at Reconstruction: should they use unconventional measures to induce the dissenting states to change their vote on their hypothetical New Deal amendments?

In making this decision, the New Deal Congress would have had a wide range of options open to them. For example, instead of intervening with the Union Army as in Reconstruction, Congress might have threatened the dissenting states with a cutoff of all federal funds unless and until they agreed to the New Deal amendment. Such a technique would have violated the fundamental principles of Article Five, if not quite as blatantly as the events of the 1860's.

20. See chap. 8.

21. Letter to Boutwell, quoted by Warren, 2 *History of the United States Supreme Court* 400–01 (1928). New Dealers were very aware of this precedent. See, e.g., Robert Jackson, *The Struggle for Judicial Supremacy* 32 (1941).

22. In addition to the fundamental principles of section one, four, and five, the Fourteenth Amendment contained, in sections two and three, restrictions on the political power of Southern whites once the region regained its representation in Congress. Even Andrew Johnson recognized that it made sense to propose an Article Five amendment to resolve these latter issues, and Lincoln would have undoubtedly taken this path as well.

23. Congress expanded the Court to allow for the appointment of Justice Field from California. Charles Fairman, *Reconstruction and Reunion, 1864–88, Part One* 4 (1971).

24. For remarks on the understudied implications of the Garfield assassination, see Chapter 8, n. 126.

25. See Schlesinger, supra n. 18, at 464–466.

10. Rethinking the New Deal

1. See *F,* chs. 3 and 4. My argument gains support from recent historical scholarship, see, e.g., Howard Gilman, *The Constitution Besieged* (1993); Michael Benedict, "Laissez-Faire and Liberty," 3 *Law and Hist. Rev.* 293 (1985); William E. Forbath, "The Ambiguities of Free Labor," 1985 *Wis. L. Rev.* 767 (1985); Harry Scheiber, "American Federalism and the Diffusion of Power," 9 *U. Tol. L. Rev.* 619 (1978); and I will develop it further in the next volume.

2. *Is NAFTA Constitutional?* (with David Golove) (1995).

3. For an insightful interpretation of the Presidency, which has influenced my account throughout, see Stephen Skowronek, *The Politics Presidents Make* (1993).

4. Arthur Schlesinger, *The Crisis of the Old Order* 248 (1957).

5. See David Burner, *The Politics of Provincialism* (1986).

6. See George Nash, 2 *The Life of Herbert Hoover* (1983); Allan Lichtman, *Prejudice and the Old Politics,* ch. 1 (1979).

7. Paul Douglas, *The Coming of a New Party* 168–170 (1932).

8. "I Pledge You—I Pledge Myself to a New Deal for the American People," July 2, 1932, in *FDR* 647 (1932). See, for example, his speech to the Commonwealth Club of San Francisco, Sept. 23, 1932, id. at 742; and Campaign Address at Detroit, Michigan, Oct. 2, 1932, "The Philosophy of Social Justice through Social Action," id. at 771.

9. See, e.g., "The Candidate Discusses the National Platform," radio address, Albany, N.Y., July 30, 1932, *FDR* 659 (1932).

10. Most notably, the pathbreaking NIRA was not fairly suggested by the campaign rhetoric.

11. See his thoughtful Address at Oglethorpe University, May 22, 1932, *FDR* 639, 646 (1932). See Schlesinger, supra n. 4, at 277, 289–291, 313 (1957); William Leuchtenburg, *Franklin D. Roosevelt and the New Deal* 11–12 (1963). My treatment parallels Michael Nelson's, "The President and the Court: Reinterpreting the Court-packing Episode of 1937," 103 *Pol. Sci. Q.* 267 (1988), to which I am indebted.

12. My thinking about party development has been deeply influenced by the school of V. O. Key and Walter Dean Burnham. For a good summary, see James Sundquist, *Dynamics of the Party System* (1983).

13. In fact, Smith quickly broke with the New Deal and became one of its most aggressive and visible critics.

14. For a good survey of the possible residual legatees, see Arthur Schlesinger, *The Politics of Upheaval* 15–211 (1960).

15. See Donald Bacon et al., eds., 3 *Encyclopedia of the United States Congress* 1557, Table 1 (1995).

16. For more on depth and breadth, see *F* at 272–275.

17. 77, pt. 4 *CR* (1933) at 4212 (Beck); id. at 4217 (Kelly).

18. See generally Donald Brand, *Corporatism and the Rule of Law* (1988); Ellis Hawley, *The New Deal and the Problem of Monopoly* (1966); Robert Himmelberg, *Origins of the National Recovery Administration* (1976). For the anecdote about the Presidential lock-in, see Arthur Schlesinger, *The Coming of the New Deal* 96–98 (1959).

19. See Chapter 8, pp. 239–241.

20. This was, at least, the opinion of Hoover and many other conservatives. See Herbert Hoover, 2 *Memoirs* 232 (1952).

21. Erikson, "The Puzzle of Midterm Loss," 50 *J. Pol.* 1011 (1988).

22. Clyde Weed, *The Nemesis of Reform* 44–45 (1994).

23. See Leuchtenburg, supra n. 11, at 116.

24. Arthur Krock, "Tide Sweeps Nation," *N.Y. Times,* Nov. 7, 1934, p. 1.

25. See Presidential Message of Feb. 20, 1935, *FDR* 80, 82 (1935).

26. Michael Parrish provides a thoughtful summary of the debate in "The Hughes Court, the Great Depression, and the Historians," 40 *The Historian* 286 (1978). More recently, the legalist side of the argument has been aggressively developed in Barry Cushman, "Doctrinal Synergies and Liberal Dilemmas," 1992 *Sup. Ct. Rev.* 235 (1992) and "A Stream of Legal Consciousness," 61 *Ford. L. Rev.* 105 (1992); Richard Friedman, "Switching Time and Other Thought Experiments," 142 *U. Penn. L. Rev.* 1891 (1994); Lawrence Lessig, "Understanding Changed Readings: Fidelity and Theory," 47 *Stan. L. Rev.* 395, 443–471 (1995). Even more recently, Stephen Gardbaum has made the legalists' life more difficult by elaborating on a host of other fundamental doctrines that were revolutionized after 1937. In order to make out their case, the legalists would be obliged to explain why these radical changes also occurred

for adequate doctrinal reasons. See Stephen Gardbaum, "New Deal Constitutionalism and the Unshackling of the States," 64 *U. Chi. L. Rev.* 483 (1997).

Historians and political scientists continue to take a more realistic view of the matter. See, e.g., Laura Kalman, *The Strange Career of Liberal Legalism* 349–351 (1996); William Leuchtenburg, *The Supreme Court Reborn* (1995); John Gates, *The Supreme Court and Partisan Realignment* (1992).

27. This is also true of another legalistic strand that emphasizes the role of bad statutory drafting in accounting for the Court's hostile reception of the First New Deal. See, e.g., Barry Cushman, "Rethinking the New Deal Court," 80 *Va. L. Rev.* 201, 249–255 (1994); Peter Irons, *The New Deal Lawyers* (1982).

28. For a good summary, see Gates, supra n. 26, at 10–25.

29. I elaborate on this point at Chapter 13, pp. 392–394.

30. For an excellent analysis of Roosevelt's revolutionary ambitions as a party leader, see Sidney Milkis, *The President and the Parties,* pt. 1 (1993).

31. This caused the President a great deal of embarrassment when Willis Van Devanter resigned at the height of the court-packing crisis, and Robinson called in his chips. Joseph Alsop and Turner Catledge, *The 168 Days* 208–216 (1938).

32. This discussion is indebted to a recent book by Ronen Shamir, *Managing Legal Uncertainty: Elite Lawyers in the New Deal,* ch. 2 (1995), which confirms and deepens the research I had done independently on this subject.

33. Milton Handler, "The National Industrial Recovery Act," 19 *Am. Bar Assoc. J.* 440, 483 (1933).

34. Thurman Arnold, "The New Deal Is Constitutional," *New Republic* 989 (Nov. 15, 1933). The most thoughtful defense of the constitutionality of the NIRA is by Edward S. Corwin, *The Twilight of the Supreme Court,* ch. 1 (1934), though it is made with such scholarly indirection that its thrust can be missed.

35. As Peter Irons notes, supra n. 27, at 38, 53–54, the lower courts proved unsympathetic to government appeals to the economic emergency.

36. Shamir, supra n. 32, at 20–21.

37. Home Building & Loan Association v. Blaisdell, 290 U.S. 398, 442 (1934).

38. As William Leuchtenburg has shown, Roosevelt had prepared a defiant radio address refusing to "permit the decision of the Supreme Court to be carried through to its logical inescapable conclusion." Quoting Lincoln's first inaugural, the speech insisted that "if the policy of the government, upon vital questions affecting the whole people, is to be irrevocably fixed by decisions of the Supreme Court, . . . the people will have ceased to be their own rulers." As the President and his Cabinet met in special session to await the news of the Court's decision, there was no doubt that a major constitutional crisis loomed. See Leuchtenburg, supra n. 26, 86–88.

39. Schechter Poultry Corp. v. United States, 295 U.S. 495, 528 (1935).

40. This theme was also elaborated in Panama Refining Co. v. Ryan, 293 U.S. 240 (1935), and Humphrey's Executor v. United States, 295 U.S. 602 (1935).

41. *Schechter,* supra n. 39, at 495, 542.

42. Id. at 523.

43. Id. at 548.
44. Id. at 543
45. Id. at 548.
46. *Wash. Post,* June 1, 1935, at 8.
47. Roosevelt, 5 *Complete Presidential Press Conferences* 309, 315 (Press Conference No. 209, May 31, 1935).
48. Id. at 322–323.
49. Id. at 328–329.
50. See, e.g., Ellis Hawley, *The New Deal and the Problem of Monopoly,* ch. 7 (1966).
51. As late as 1941, Roosevelt was saying that the NIRA had been "point[ing] the way to a new economic order which I am sure will be fully realized in years to come." See Alan Brinkley, *The End of Reform* 40, 290 (1995). See also, Leuchtenburg, supra n. 26, at 146; and Otis Graham, Jr., "Franklin Roosevelt and the Intended New Deal," in Thomas Cronin and Michael Beschloss, eds., *Essays in Honor of James MacGregor Burns* 83–84 (1989).
52. Roosevelt, supra n. 47, at 333.
53. Id.
54. Id. at 319.
55. Id. at 333 (emphasis supplied).
56. Editorial, *L.A. Times,* June 2, 1935, at 14.
57. *Wash. Post,* June 1, 1935, at 4 (continuation of lead story on page 1).
58. *N.Y. Times,* June 2, 1935, at 1.
59. Id.
60. Id.
61. *N.Y. Times,* June 2, 1935, sec. 4 (News of the Week in Review), at 3.
62. Id.
63. Raymond Clapper, "Between You and Me," *Wash. Post,* June 1, 1935, at 2.
64. See Leuchtenburg, "The Origins of Franklin D. Roosevelt's Court-packing Plan," in supra n. 26, at 82.
65. For example, the *N.Y. Times* of June 2 (sec. 1, at 28) reported:

> SENATORS VEERING TO ROOSEVELT VIEW
> A marked change of front was perceptible today on the part of leading Senators of both major parties with regard to President Roosevelt's appeal to the nation on the Supreme Court's NRA decision.
>
> Few would permit direct quotation, but in most quarters there was apparent a tendency, the result in many cases of telegrams and letters from home, to view with greater equanimity the possibility of a constitutional redefinition of interstate commerce. . . .
>
> One dominant Democratic leader suggested today that the President might even try to get the present session of Congress to propose a constitutional amendment to the States, without further delay, provided the reaction for Federal control was sufficiently strong.

Speaking broadly, editorial reaction ran the gamut from strong hostility, e.g., "Freedom or Despotism," *Chicago Tribune* at 12 (June 5, 1935); "A Losing Game," *L.A. Times,* pt. 2, at 4 (June 4, 1935); to anxious handwringing of a mildly negative sort, "Amending the Court," *N.Y. Times,* sec. 4, at 8 (June 2, 1935); to positive comments on the need to take constitutional reform seriously, e.g., "On Changing the Constitution," *St. Louis Post-Dispatch* at 20 (June 3, 1935); "The Constitution and Planned Economy," *Des Moines Register* at 14 (June 2, 1935).

66. Leuchtenburg, supra n. 11, at 146.

67. The phrase is Leuchtenburg's. See id. at 150. We can never know, of course, whether Roosevelt and Congress would have regained the initiative without the assistance of the judicial dialectic. The President had, for example, already decided to support the Wagner Act a week before *Schechter;* and Social Security was long in the works. For a persuasive argument that emphasizes *Schechter*'s role, see Skowronek, supra n. 3, at 311–313.

68. The full range of initiatives is usefully described by Schlesinger, supra n. 18, chs. 17–20.

69. See Schlesinger, supra n. 14, ch. 21. Alan Brinkley sensitively discusses this shift in *The End of Reform,* chs. 2 and 3 (1995).

70. Though with sharp warnings on the subconstitutional level, see Jones v. Securities Commission, 298 U.S. 28 (1936).

71. Retirement Board v. Alton Railroad Co., 295 U.S. 330 (1935).

72. See United States v. Butler, 297 U.S. 1 (1936); Carter v. Carter Coal Co., 298 U.S. 238 (1936). For a wooden, but useful, defense of the majority opinions in these cases as grounded in the dominant lines of precedent, see Richard Maidment, *The Judicial Response to the New Deal,* ch. 6 (1991).

73. Louisville Bank v. Radford, 295 U.S. 555 (1935).

74. Id. at 593.

75. Id. at 580.

76. Id. at 599.

77. New State Ice Company v. Leibmann, 285 U.S. 62, 280 (1932).

78. Id. at 282.

79. See, e.g., Nebbia v. New York, 291 U.S. 502 (1934). This case is sometimes treated as a revolutionary decision destroying the foundations of established doctrine. I reject this view at Chapter 12, pp. 359–377 and nn.37, 38.

80. This basic point is missed by Friedman, supra n. 26, at 1891. While Friedman has many insights into particular cases, he proceeds within the traditional metanarrative that disparages the period of Old Court resistance. Even within this framework, Friedman gives too much emphasis to split decisions and too little to unanimous ones like *Radford.*

81. Morehead v. New York ex. rel. Tipaldo, 298 U.S. 587, 604 (1936).

82. On presidential power, see also Humphrey's Executor v. United States, 295 U.S. 602 (1935).

83. Hoover, *Platforms and Speeches at the Republican and Democratic Conventions* (1936; typescript available at Library of Congress).

84. See, e.g, Richard Smith, *An Uncommon Man: the Triumph of Herbert Hoover* 224–228 (1984).
85. Landon convinced the convention to write some of these accommodationist themes into the party platform. 3 *S* 2865–64. For a selection of Landon's essays and speeches, see his *America at the Crossroads* (1936).
86. Address by Governor Landon, October 29, 1936, 3 *S* 2894, 2898.
87. 3 *S* 2851, 2854–55.
88. *FDR* 230, 231–234 (1936).
89. Leuchtenburg, "The Election of 1936," 3 *S* 2842–43.
90. See, Byron Shafer, ed., *The End of Realignment?* (1991).

11. The Missing Amendments

1. Morehead v. New York ex. rel. Tipaldo, 298 U.S. 587 (1936).
2. Railroad Retirement Board v. Alton Railroad, 295 U.S. 330 (1935).
3. United States v. Butler, 297 U.S. 1 (1936).
4. H. L. Mencken, "Burying the Dead Horse," August 17, 1936, reprinted in *Carnival of Buncombe* 314–315 (1956).
5. Most of the studies on this campaign stress the political wheeling and dealing at the expense of the constitutional debate. Leonard Baker, *Back to Back* (1967), provides the most comprehensive treatment; Joseph Alsop and Turner Catledge, *The 168 Days* (1938), is an indispensable contemporary source.
6. "Amendment Rises as a Session Issue," *N.Y. Times,* January 3, 1937, at 1.
7. "Basic Law Change Gains in Congress," *N.Y. Times,* January 8, 1937, at 1. (The quotation comes from the runover section of the story)
8. Quoted in Barry Karl, *Executive Reorganization and Reform in the New Deal* 27 (1963), from the manuscript edition of Louis Brownlow, *A Passion for Anonymity* 378–382 (1958). Much of the quoted passage is omitted from the published version of the book.
9. *Federalist* No. 1, at 3 (C. Rossiter ed. 1961). For a widely reviewed book advocating such a proposal, see William Elliott, *The Need for Constitutional Reform,* esp. ch. 9 (1935). Even more impressive is *Whose Constitution?*, by Secretary of Agriculture Henry Wallace (1936). It contains a brilliant exposition of the unconventional "forms of statecraft" practiced by Madison and Hamilton during the Founding period, and of their implications for the political practice of the 1930's. See esp. pt. 1, ch. 6 (entitled "1936, Shake Hands with 1787!") and all of pt. 3 ("We the People").
10. See, generally, *FDR* 51–66 (1937).
11. Ever since Fletcher v. Peck, 10 U.S. 87 (1810), courts have been reluctant to probe too deeply into the real motivations of political actors, contenting themselves with rationalizations tendered in official documents.
12. "The Origins of Franklin D. Roosevelt's 'Court-packing' Plan," reprinted in expanded form in William Leuchtenburg, *The Supreme Court Reborn,* ch. 4 (1995).
13. See, e.g., Alsop and Catledge, supra n. 5, ch. 1.

14. A good account of the British practice, centering on the struggle precipitated by Lloyd George's budget, is provided by Roy Jenkins, *Mr. Balfour's Poodle* (1954).

15. See, e.g., Roosevelt's elaborate (if historically inaccurate) discussion of the British practice at his Cabinet meeting of December 27, 1935, reported in *The Secret Diary of Harold Ickes* 493–495 (1953). Leuchtenburg provides other examples in supra n. 12, at 94–95, 277.

16. See the fine book by Robert Kelley, *Transatlantic Persuasion* (1969).

17. The remarkable character of the "Republican 'strategy of silence,' which has been a more or less spectacular feature of the Supreme Court struggle," was widely noted. *N.Y. Times,* April 4, 1937, at sec. 4, p. 6. See also, Arthur Krock, "First Kickback of New Republican Policy," *N.Y. Times,* April 9, 1937, at 20; Alsop and Catledge, supra n. 5, at 97–100.

18. Alsop and Catledge, supra n. 5, at 100–105.

19. Wheeler was on the list of serious Democratic prospects in 1940, but his opposition to court-packing and other Rooseveltian measures had hurt his chances. Herbert Parmet and Marie Hecht, *Never Again* 11–12 (1968).

20. 75th Cong., 1st Sess., S.J. Res. 80 (February 15 [calendar day February 17], 1937).

21. Thomas Reed Powell, "For 'Ills' of the Court: Shall We Operate?," *N. Y. Times Magazine* 3, 26 (April 18, 1937).

22. Ickes, 1 *The Secret Diary* 495 (1953).

23. See generally William Ross, *A Muted Fury* (1994).

24. See La Follette's platform of 1924, planks 5 and 11, in Kirk Porter and Bruce Johnson, *National Party Platforms* 252, 254–255 (1970). See Ross, supra n. 23, ch. 11, and esp. 196–200.

25. During the 1924 elections, Roosevelt had tried to broker the divide between regular Democrats and La Follette Progressives. See Frank Freidel, *Franklin D. Roosevelt: The Ordeal* 173–175 (1954).

26. More precisely, Cohen-Corcoran would have permitted "Congress to override by a two-thirds majority any Supreme Court decision on federal legislation immediately after such decision was rendered, or do so by simple majority after an intervening election." It also "enable[d] Congress to validate state legislation that the Court had rejected." Kenneth Davis, *FDR: Into the Storm, 1937–1940* 52 (1993). This proposal differed from Wheeler's in allowing a super-majority in Congress to overrule the Court even before the voters had a chance to consider the question at an intervening election.

27. Library of Congress, Benjamin V. Cohen Papers: Subject File 1918–83, Container 14: Supreme Court—Draft Folder. Cohen's memo also singles out another proposed amendment, by Senator William Borah, as a specially serious candidate for enactment. I discuss this proposal at p. 339 infra.

The 24-page memo does not bear a date, but it is obviously written in the midst of the crisis. It is far more critical of the Wheeler-Bone approach than the previous Cohen-Corcoran memo. The difference may be attributable to its different strategic purpose. While it is formally addressed to the President, it is written so that the President can readily pass it along to Wheeler in an effort to persuade the Senator to withdraw his proposal and return to the President's camp.

28. See Greg Caldeira, "Public Opinion and the U.S. Supreme Court: FDR's Court-Packing Plan," 81 *Am. Pol. Sci. Rev.* 1139, 1140, 1144 (1987).

29. The high was 15 percent on March 24. See id. at 1147 (fig. 3). This number seems to include respondents whose judgment was in equipoise and therefore may overestimate the group with no opinion.

30. NBC/Gallup regularly put their estimates in precise quantitative terms, reporting, for example, that 59 percent favored one or another proposal that would significantly change the Court's role, but that only 47 percent favored the President's plan (with 53 percent opposed). Obviously, such precision should not be taken too seriously. See NBC Museum of Broadcasting t37-21, disks 4946-49. (All referenced disks are available at the Library of Congress and the Yale Law Library.)

31. Radio Address, Gerald P. Nye, Feb. 21, 1937, 9 P.M., NBC t37-17, disk 4389-90.

32. Radio address, February 12, 7:45 P.M., NBC t37-5, disc 3485.

33. Speech of Herbert Hoover to the Union League Club of Chicago, February 20, 1937, 10 P.M., NBC t37-11, disk numbers 3668-9.

34. Republican Senators were conspicuously absent from NBC in February, leaving it to academics (like former Harvard President Abbott Lowell), Southern Democrats (like Josiah Bailey), and Progressives (like the men mentioned in the text) to take to the airwaves. The only exception was Styles Bridges, then a very junior Republican Senator from New Hampshire. See NBC t37-10, disc 3640; t37-12, disk 3689-90.

35. Radio Address, February 14, 1937, 7 P.M., NBC t37-7, disk 3518-19.

36. Senator Minton addressed the NBC National Radio Forum on February 15, 1937, at 9 P.M. NBC t37-10, disk 3655. See Chapter 8 for a discussion of the Legal Tender controversy.

37. Radio Address, February 17, 1937, 8:30 P.M., NBC t37-12, disk 3691-2. Robert La Follette himself joined the radio lists in favor of the President on March 7. NBC t37-17, disk 4393-4.

38. *FDR* 120 (1937).

39. *FDR* 116 (1937).

40. *FDR* 120 (1937).

41. *FDR* 132 (1937).

42. Though Madison had his skeptical moments—see *Federalist* No. 37, at 229-30 (C. Rossiter ed. 1961).

43. 75th Cong., 1st Sess., *Reorganization of the Federal Judiciary: Hearings on S. 1392 before the Committee on the Judiciary,* 40 (1937).

44. See id. at 40-41. Jackson also pointed to political motivations involved in decisions on the size of the Court made during the Administrations of Adams, Jefferson, and Jackson. Id.

45. Id. at 43.

46. Id.

47. I use the word *politics* advisedly, because Hughes's intervention breached basic norms of judicial propriety. The Chief Justice had not circulated his letter to all his fellow Justices, probably because he would have failed to get unanimous support for a statement that amounted to an advisory opinion. Rather than run this gauntlet, he merely obtained the signatures of his two senior colleagues, Brandeis and Van Devanter, and failed to correct the widespread impression that he was speaking for a unanimous court.

    This performance places a heavy burden of persuasion on latter-day legalists who portray Hughes's conduct in 1937 as motivated by purely doctrinal considerations. See, e.g., Richard Friedman, "Switching Time," 142 *U. Penn. L. Rev.* 1891, 1965 (1994). Hughes's 1937 decisions undoubtedly have some doctrinal roots, but they are also blatantly inconsistent with other decisions. See Chapter 12, n. 34. All in all, Hughes's performance in 1937 is best seen as the product of constitutional statesmanship of the first order, by a man whose career—as governor of New York, secretary of state, and candidate for the presidency—enabled him to recognize the need for unconventional activity at a moment of grave crisis.

48. See *Hearings,* supra n. 43, at 504–505.

49. Id. at 502–504.

50. See supra, pp. 325–326.

51. "Vandenberg Joins Court Plan Fight," *N.Y. Times,* March 3, 1937, at 10.

52. See Wheeler's testimony, *Hearings,* supra n. 43, at 502.

53. "Court Change Foes Unite on Amendment," *N.Y. Herald Tribune,* March 15, 1937, at 1.

54. Caldeira, supra n. 28, at 1147 (Figure 3).

55. Id at 1149–1150.

56. "Supreme Court Upholds Wagner Labor Law," *N.Y. Times,* April 13, 1937, at 1, col. 4. The *Times* editorial page declared "that the advocates of the President's plan . . . must feel that most of their thunder has been stolen." Id. at 24. See also "Four 5–4; One 9–0," *Time Magazine,* April 19, 1937, at 15 (arguing that decision had "reduced the great debate over the President's Supreme Court enlargement plan to an all but academic position, for the immediate reason which drove many liberals to support it was their wish for Labor legislation").

57. Alsop and Catledge, supra n. 5, at 105.

58. "Security Secure," *Time Magazine* 16 (May 31, 1937).

59. "Court Bill Defenders Want Roosevelt Aid," *N.Y. Times,* May 9, 1937, sec. 4, at 10, col 2.

60. Barry Cushman denies this possibility in "Rethinking the New Deal Court," 80 *Va. L. Rev.* 208–228 (1994), on the basis of a review of the secondary literature. Unfortunately, Cushman does not cite, let alone confront, Leuchtenburg's essay, originally published in 1985, or Caldeira's study of public opinion, supra n. 28, published in 1987, or Rafael Gely and Pablo Spiller's study of the electoral returns, "The Political Economy of Supreme Court Constitutional Decisions:

The Case of Roosevelt's Court Packing Plan," 12 *Intl. Rev. Law & Econ.* 45 (1992). These essays, together with my own study of the original sources, suggest that Cushman's confidence is misplaced. Nonetheless, he usefully reviews the substantial obstacles Roosevelt would have had to overcome in pursuing his court-packing plan.

61. Leuchtenburg, "FDR's Court-packing Plan," in supra n. 11, at 132, 148–149.

62. See William Leuchtenburg, "FDR's Court-Packing Plan: A Second Life, A Second Death," 1985 *Duke L.J.* 673 (1985), for a considered assessment of the latter-day struggle over the amended plan. The quotation comes from p. 681.

63. Moreover, the Administration still had to confront the bitter opposition of Hatton Sumners, chairman of the House Judiciary Committee, though it probably could have overcome this obstacle when push came to shove.

64. In fact, the Republicans scored a major victory in the 1938 elections as voters treated the economic downturn of 1937 as evidence of New Deal failure. But if the Court had continued its constitutional assault, Roosevelt could have blamed the economic downturn on the Court's refusal to provide the tools needed to stabilize the economy. Of course, it is impossible to know how well this appeal would have worked.

Once the Court had switched, the basic framework of electoral competition had changed. The voters could punish the New Dealers without supposing that they were endangering the constitutional revolution that was already in progress. As we shall see, the Republicans recognized this by their actions in the new Congress. Though they remained a distinct minority in the new Congress, with 164 Representatives and 23 Senators, they could now join conservative Democrats to block many (but not all) efforts to expand the range of New Deal statutory initiatives. However, they did not even try to roll back the constitutional revolution by vetoing the appointment to the Supreme Court of a steady stream of committed New Dealers. See Chapter 12, pp. 355–356, infra. For a thoughtful account of the 1938 election, and its constitutional implications, see Sidney Milkis, *The President and the Parties,* ch. 4 (1993).

65. *Hearings,* supra n. 43, at 504–505.

66. S.J. Res. 285, 74th Cong., 2d Sess. (1936). This proposal was reintroduced by Representative Faddis as H.R.J. Res. 64, 75th Cong., 1st Sess. (1937).

67. David Kyvig, *Explicit and Authentic Acts* 297 (University Press of Kansas: 1996). This incident occurred in 1935, not 1937, but nothing suggests that the President would settle for less than Senator Costigan's sweeping initiative. Dean Garrison of Wisconsin Law School made a similar proposal that was frequently noted in the 1937 debate: "Congress shall have power to promote the economic welfare of the United States by such laws as in its judgment are appropriate, and to delegate such a power in whole or in part to the states. Existing state powers are not affected by this article, except as Congress may occupy a particular field." See Charles Haines, "Judicial Review of Acts of Congress and the Need for Constitutional Reform," 45 *Yale L.J.* 816, 847 (1936). For other broad formulations, see the proposal submitted by Senator Marvel Logan and Repre-

sentative Kent Keller, granting Congress the power to legislate "for the general welfare," H.R.J. Res. 316, 74th Cong., 1st Sess. (1935) (Keller), S.J. Res. 8, 75th Cong., 1st Sess. (1937) (Logan).

68. S.J. Res. 3, 74th Cong., 1st Sess., Jan. 4, 1935. For other examples of this approach, see H.R.J. Res. 17, 75th Cong., 1st Sess. (1937); H.R.J. Res. 258, 75th Cong., 1st Sess. (1937).

69. Sherbert v. Verner, 374 U.S. 398 (1963).

70. S.J. Res. 208, 74th Cong., 2d Sess. (1936).

71. S.J. Res. 92, sec. 3, 75th Cong., 1st Sess. (1937).

72. See F at 119–129.

73. See, e.g., S.J. Res. 86, 75th Cong., 1st Sess. (1937) (Burke).

74. S.J. Res. 98, 75th Cong., 1st Sess. (1937).

75. For example, the Court might have developed a convention under which Justices who found themselves "on the fence" deferred to their brethren whenever they accumulated five votes.

76. Speech of February 19, 1937, 10 P.M., NBC Museum of Broadcasting, box t37-23, disks 4995–6.

77. Gely and Spiller, supra n. 60, at 45, 63 (Table 5).

78. The amendment was proposed by Congress on February 21, 1933, and was ratified by 36 states on December 5. Donald Bacon et al., eds., 4 *Encyclopedia of the U.S. Congress* 1996 (1995).

79. The Administration had considered such measures as early as 1935. See Chapter 10.

80. See Gely and Spiller, supra n. 60, at 47.

81. Though, as I have already suggested, a narrowly legalistic account of Hughes's motivation strikes me as naive (see n. 47, supra). As to Roberts, the reasons he gave for reversing himself in *Parrish* simply don't hold up on legalistic grounds, as even a legalist like Friedman concedes, supra n. 47, at 1950. But I refuse to be drawn too deeply into this morass, since my larger argument does not depend on the ineffabilities of private motivation.

82. I elaborate on this legitimacy question in "A Generation of Betrayal?" 65 *Fordham L. Rev.* 1519 (1997).

12. Rediscovery or Creation?

1. In fact, the Republicans did score a substantial victory in 1938, but they still did not get close to a majority in either House. For further analysis of the significance of this victory, see Chapter 11, n. 64.

2. Accidents of mortality would not have sufficed to end the crisis before the war: Butler died on November 11, 1939; McReynolds, on August 24, 1946; Sutherland, on July 18, 1942; Van Devanter, on February 2, 1941.

3. Legal Realists, then gaining prominence in American jurisprudence, expressed similar doubts, but it is a mistake to exaggerate their direct role in this affair. The academics with the greatest influence on Roosevelt—men like Frankfurter

or Edward Corwin—were not Realists in any narrow sense, but they *were* pragmatists, and this was quite enough to generate a good deal of skepticism. For a fine study of the intellectual background, see Morton White, *Social Thought in America: The Revolt against Formalism* (1949).

4. Robert Jackson, *The Struggle for Judicial Supremacy* xiv (1941). The book was published as the author ascended to the Court.

5. Actually, the crucial vote of the Judiciary Committee took place in the middle of May, after the President refused to take the compromise course he later accepted.

6. 75th Cong., 1st Sess., Sen. Comm. on Jud., *Reorganization of the Judiciary,* Report No. 711, at 14 (1937).

7. McReynolds was appointed by the "liberal" Wilson largely because the President found his Attorney General obnoxious and wanted to "kick him upstairs." Henry Abraham, *Justices and Presidents* 177–178 (1992).

8. See id. at 232.

9. See Laurence Tribe, *God Save This Honorable Court* 148 (1985).

10. Id.

11. See James Patterson, *Congressional Conservatism and the New Deal,* chs. 6–8 (1967).

12. 83 *CR* (1938), at 1069.

13. See Donald Bacon et al., eds., 3 *Encyclopedia of the U.S. Congress* 1556–58 (table 1) (1995). There were 76 Democrats after the 1936 elections, 69 after 1938, and 66 after 1940.

14. Among its other efforts, the conservative coalition made a big push to enact an administrative procedures act that promised to curtail drastically the powers of the rising bureaucracy. See George Shepard, "Fierce Compromise," 90 *Nw. L. Rev.* 1557, 1586–1632 (1996). While conservatives failed to win enactment before war suspended further efforts, their new statutory focus reflected a recognition that they could no longer rely upon the Court as a constitutional bulwark against bureaucratic government.

15. See 84 *CR* (1939), at 3706–13, 3773–88. (See especially remarks of Senator Frazier.) Frankfurter and Murphy were confirmed unanimously, see Tribe, supra n. 9, at 148.

16. Wendell Willkie, "The Court Is Now His," *Saturday Evening Post,* March 9, 1940, at 29, 71, 74, and 79.

17. For a good account of the politics, see Herbert Parmet and Marie Hecht, *Never Again* (1968).

18. See *N.Y. Times,* August 18, 1940, at sec. 1, p. 13.

19. See, e.g., Seattle Address, Sept. 23, 1940, reprinted in 4 *S* 2974, 2975–76.

20. Willkie's speech accepting the Republican nomination did not criticize the Supreme Court's decisions in the manner of his pre-nomination article in the *Saturday Evening Post.* To the contrary, he endorsed many of the New Deal's fundamental principles. See *N.Y. Times,* supra. n. 18. For a useful summary of Willkie's themes, see Robert Burke, "The Election of 1940," in 4 *S* 2917.

21. See Parmet and Hecht, supra. n. 17, at 176.
22. See, e.g., Willkie's wind-up speech at Madison Square Garden on November 2, 1940, reprinted in 4 S 2999.
23. A total of 50 million votes were cast. The Electoral College vote was 449 to 82. See 4 S 3006.
24. Richard D. Friedman, "Switching Time," 142 *U. Penn. L. Rev.* 1891 (1994), provides an outstanding recent example of this emphasis.
25. David Currie, *The Constitution in the Supreme Court: The Second Century* 206 (1990).
26. This is an important point of contact with Barry Cushman's interpretation of similar events in "A Stream of Legal Consciousness," 61 *Ford. L. Rev.* 105, 156–160 (1992), which shares my skepticism and also emphasizes the role of transformative appointments by President Roosevelt in bringing about the paradigm shift in the opinions of the early 1940's.
27. NLRB v. Jones & Laughlin Steel Corp., 301 U.S. 1, 30 (1937).
28. Id. at 40.
29. NLRB v. Friedman-Harry Marks Clothing Co., 301 U.S. 58 (1937).
30. Id. at 75.
31. Id. at 87.
32. See, for example, Cardozo's effort to distinguish, rather than overrule, the majority's decision in United States v. Butler handed down a year before, in Steward Machine Co. v. Davis, 301 U.S. 548, 591–593 (1937), and his favorable citation, id. at 598, of another case destined for the junk heap, Carter v. Carter Coal Co.
33. West Coast Hotel v. Parrish, 300 U.S. 379 (1937).
34. If any single case is crucial, it was *Jones & Laughlin,* not *Parrish.* If Justice Roberts had joined the four conservatives in striking down the act, the Justices would have deprived the New Deal of its only creative solution to the proliferating sit-down strikes that were precipitating all-out class war in America's industrial heartland. See U.S. Bureau of Labor Statistics, "Industrial Disputes," 44 *Monthly Labor Rev.* 1211 (1937) (documenting dramatic increase in strike activity from 1936 to 1937, noting that there were "more strikes in March 1937 than in any single month in the last 20 years"). Little wonder, then, that the majority's decision in *Parrish* had no measurable impact on the Gallup Polls, but that its subsequent opinion in *Jones & Laughlin* provoked an immediate and substantial decline in popular support for the President's court-packing initiative. Greg Caldeira, "Public Opinion and the U.S. Supreme Court: FDR's Court-Packing Plan," 81 *Am. Pol. Sci. Rev.* 1147–48 (1987). Whatever the motivation for Roberts's vote in *Parrish,* nobody can deny that both Hughes and Roberts decided to uphold the Wagner Act in *Jones & Laughlin* with full knowledge of Roosevelt's threat and despite their votes' blatant inconsistency with their prior opinions in Carter v. Carter Coal Co., 298 U.S. 278, 316 (1936). See Peter Irons, *The New Deal Lawyers* 283 (1982) (oral argument in

Supreme Court on Wagner Act began four days after Roosevelt's court-packing announcement).

35. Muller v. Oregon, 208 U.S. 412, 421 (1908).

36. *Parrish,* 300 U.S. 379, at 392 at n. 1.

37. Nebbia v. New York, 291 U.S. 502, 537 (1934). Recent legalist writers tend to present *Nebbia* as a revolutionary decision in their effort to diminish the significance of the later doctrinal transformation in the aftermath of 1937. See, e.g., Friedman, supra n. 24, at 1919–22; Cushman, supra n. 26, at 127–131.

38. See Mayflower Farms Inc. v. Ten Eyck, 297 U.S. 266 (1936), in which Roberts wrote an opinion of the Court that is transparently inconsistent with the principles proclaimed two years later in *Carolene Products.* See infra, at pp. 368–369. In joining the *Mayflower* majority, Roberts and Hughes made it abundantly clear that they continued to endorse the Court's historic mission of aggressively protecting free market liberties under the Fourteenth Amendment.

I do not suggest that *Mayflower* was flatly inconsistent with *Nebbia.* The later case protected the right to enter a business, while *Nebbia*'s retreat concerned price regulation. As a consequence, it remained open for the Court to rationalize both cases or use either one as a lever for the subsequent reconsideration of the other. Only after the switch of 1937 did it become clear that *Nebbia,* rather than *Mayflower,* would prosper in the years ahead.

This means that legalist scholars, see n. 37, are begging a big question when they use *Nebbia* to disparage the importance of 1937. On their view, *Nebbia* had already undercut substantive due process in 1934, and so it is melodramatic to focus on 1937 as a crucial moment in the demise of laissez-faire constitutionlism. But this interpretation of *Nebbia* itself presupposes the importance of 1937. Without the switch in time, *Nebbia,* and not *Mayflower,* might have been the case with the brief half-life! In short, the legalists are themselves presupposing the decisive importance of 1937 even as they use *Nebbia* to disparage it.

39. *Parrish,* 300 U.S. 379, at 399–400.

40. See Howard Gilman, *The Constitution Beseiged,* chs. 2–4 (1993).

41. See Cass Sunstein, "Lochner's Legacy," 87 *Colum. L. Rev.* 873 (1987); Sunstein, *The Partial Constitution* (1993).

42. United States v. Carolene Products, 304 U.S. 144 (1938).

43. Geoffrey Miller, "The True Story of Carolene Products," 1987 *Sup. Ct. Rev.* 397 (1987).

44. *Carolene,* 304 U.S. 144, at 152.

45. Justice Stone's standard was initially written in an opinion approved by only four of the seven justices participating in the decision. See 304 U.S. 144, at 155. Neither the ill Cardozo nor the newly appointed Reed participated. The two remaining conservatives predictably disassociated themselves from Stone's opinion—McReynolds dissenting, and Butler concurring on independent grounds. The real surprise was Black, who refused—without any giving any

reasons—to join the crucial section of Stone's opinion. While Stone's opinion technically qualifies as an "opinion of the Court," since it speaks for a majority of the quorum, it is important today only because Roosevelt's ongoing strategy of transformative appointment ultimately made it the cornerstone of subsequent doctrinal development.

46. See *F*, ch. 6, and my "Liberating Abstraction," 59 *U. Chi. L. Rev.* 317 (1992).

47. Erie Railroad v. Tompkins, 304 U.S. 64, 69 (1938).

48. Id. at 79.

49. See, e.g., Lawrence Lessig, "Understanding Changed Readings," 47 *Stan. L. Rev.* 395, 426–432 (1995).

50. Contrast Ernest Weinrib, *The Idea of Private Law* (1995), with Roberto Unger, *What Should Legal Analysis Become?* (1996).

51. See Henry Friendly, "In Praise of Erie—and of the New Federal Common Law," 39 *N.Y.U. L. Rev.* 383 (1964), suggesting how *Erie*'s positivism liberated federal, as well as state, courts to create a new "common law."

52. See Paul Bator et al., *Hart & Wechsler's The Federal Courts and the Federal System* (3d ed. 1988).

53. Retirement of Mr. Justice McReynolds, 312 U.S. v (1941).

54. United States v. Darby, 312 U.S. 100, 125 (1941).

55. Id. at 115.

56. Ferguson v. Skrupa, 372 U.S. 726, 730 (1963).

57. I have discussed some of the reasons for the trivialization of this central guarantee in *F*, at 94–99, and will return to this question in the next volume.

58. What are the others? I shall consider this problem of canonization at greater length in the next volume.

59. Joseph Lash reports that Felix Frankfurter was one of the ghost-writers of this speech. Lash, *Dealers and Dreamers* 315 (1988).

60. FDR 359–366 (1937) (emphasis in original).

61. See Robert Dahl, "The Myth of the Presidential Mandate," 105 *Pol. Sci. Q.* 355 (1990), for a skeptical treatment and a call for a "fundamental alteration" in the constitutional framework to respond to the problem. I am sure that Dahl has something more fundamental in mind than the proposals I present in the next chapter, see his *Democracy and Its Critics* (1989), but perhaps my modest proposals may help spark the larger conversation he has in mind.

13. Reclaiming the Constitution

1. Some people have the impression that a twenty-seventh amendment was enacted in 1992. That year marked the end of an effort to breathe new life into an amendment, proposed two hundred years earlier by the First Congress, which restricted the power of Congressmen to raise their own salaries. The proposal failed to gain the approval of the states during the early years of the Republic and had long lapsed into the collective unconscious. But then its partisans

revived it in the late twentieth century and ran a low-visibility campaign amongst the state legislatures for its ratification, which ultimately resulted in approval by three-fourths. Since the amendment purportedly restricts the power of Congress to raise its own salaries, the present incumbents found it too embarrassing to protest at this antiquarian revival and accepted its validity.

Despite this, it is silly to suppose that a constitutional proposal can be revived despite its lapse into desuetude for two centuries. As Justice Van Devanter explained, speaking for the Court in Dillon v. Gloss, 256 U.S. 368, 374–375 (1921), the theory of popular sovereignty underlying Article Five requires representatives of *both* the nation and the states to think a proposed amendment is a good idea—and this is not satisfied if the assent of the nation is obtained in the eighteenth century and the assent of the states in the twentieth century. Instead, We the People must speak on both national and state levels within a reasonable amount of time of one another. See also Justice Butler's discussion in Coleman v. Miller, 307 U.S. 433, 470 (1939). Whatever the implications of *Coleman*'s "political question" doctrine for a judicial challenge, the so-called twenty-seventh amendment should be treated as a bad joke by sensible citizens.

For a different view, see Michael Paulsen, "A General Theory of Article Five: The Constitutional Lessons of the Twenty-Seventh Amendment, 103 *Yale L.J.* 677 (1993).

2. I am using the word *rule* in the sense elaborated by Ronald Dworkin in *Taking Rights Seriously*, chs. 2 and 3 (1977).

3. See Robert Nozick, *Philosophical Explanations* 29–37(1981); Derek Parfit, *Reasons and Persons*, pt. 3 (1984).

4. I discuss the New Deal revolution's relationship to other Presidentialist precedents in my forthcoming book, *The Roots of Presidentialism.*

5. I concentrate on the Reagan-Bush years because they provide a cautionary tale that sets the stage for serious proposals for reform of the higher lawmaking process. But I do not wish to ignore the significance of other decades, see, e.g., Bruce Ackerman and David Golove, *Is NAFTA Constitutional?* (1995), including the Civil Rights revolution. My discussion of the 1960's is particularly inadequate at present, see *F,* at pp. 108–111.

6. Donald Bacon., ed. 3 *Encyclopedia of the U.S. Congress* 1558 (1995).

7. See Henry Abraham, *Justices and Presidents* 265–266 (3d ed. 1992).

8. Bacon, supra n. 6, at 1557.

9. Webster v. Reproductive Health Services, 492 U.S. 490 (1989).

10. Even on this scenario, the parallel to the New Deal would have remained incomplete. By the early 1940's, the Court was unanimously behind its decisive doctrinal break with the past; the Court of the early 1990's, in contrast, would have contained two or three dissenters who insisted on the continued significance of the old jurisprudence.

This is, as Chapter 12 suggested, a big difference. It is only when the Court is of one mind that the legal profession may be expected to remit a previously dominant view to the ashcan of history. Nonetheless, an opinion for the Court written by Justice Scalia, on behalf of six or seven Justices, would have sustained the momentum of the Reagan Revolution in constitutional law. The destruction of *Roe,* moreover, would have shaken the ground beneath all of the great landmarks built up by the Justices in the half-century between Roosevelt and Reagan—leaving it to the Court of the 1990's (gradually changed through further transformative appointments?) to determine their fate.

11. Planned Parenthood v. Casey, 505 U.S. 833, 861–864 (1992).

12. *Casey,* at 861–862, citations omitted.

13. For preliminary statements, see *F,* chs. 4–6, and my "Liberating Abstraction," 59 *U. Chi. L. Rev.* 317 (1992).

14. Emphasis supplied.

15. Emphasis supplied.

16. Moreover, the New Dealers did not believe that constitutional law provided an appropriate response to the problems of bureaucracy, public finance, and decentralization of power raised by activist government. Consequently, they were unimpressed by the narrow focus of judicially guided transformative practice.

17. See Bruce Ackerman, *The Future of Liberal Revolution* 105–106 (1992).

18. For more, see *F,* chs. 9–10.

19. For a recent review by a leading scholar, see David Magleby, "Governing by Initiative," 66 *U. Col. L. Rev.* 13 (1995).

20. Second-termers like Eisenhower and Clinton, for example, are a different breed from Roosevelt and Reagan. See the insightful typology in Stephen Skowronek, *The Politics Presidents Make* 36 (1993).

21. See John Rawls, *A Theory of Justice,* sec. 31 (1971).

22. See Philip Weiser, "Ackerman's Proposal for Popular Constitutional Lawmaking: Can It Realize His Aspirations for Dualist Democracy?," 68 *N.Y.U. L. Rev.* 907 (1993). This thoughtful essay suggests that it would be too risky to accept my proposals without taking further steps both to deepen the educational foundations for citizenship and to control the power of money in politics.

I am very sympathetic to this critique, see, e.g., my "Crediting the Voters: A New Beginning for Campaign Finance," *American Prospect* 71–80 (1993), and my discussion of liberal education in *Social Justice in the Liberal State,* ch. 5 (1980). But there are obvious political dangers involved in burdening my particular initiative with further reforms. Even though these other initiatives may be desirable in their own right, it will be hard enough to gain broad political support for my not-so-modest package.

Weiser's caution might be appropriate if the existing higher lawmaking system were operating satisfactorily. But it isn't. If we fail to channel the Presidentialist model into a more elaborate system of popular referenda, future Presidents will predictably place increasing pressure on the present practice of transformative appointments. If you agree that this is a dangerous course, it may seem wisest to focus on an attainable improvement rather than to aim too high.

I do not deny that my proposal carries some of the risks that Weiser identifies; but these seem less serious than the clear and present dangers posed by the existing Presidentialist system.

23. But see Jack Kemp, *American Renaissance* 187–189 (1979).
24. *FDR* 132 (1937).
25. See Thurman Arnold, *Symbols of Government* (1935), and Jerome Frank, *Law and the Modern Mind* (1930).
26. See, most notably, Ronald Dworkin, *Law's Empire* (1986).

Index

Library of Congress Cataloging in Publication Data

Ackerman, Bruce A.
We the people / Bruce Ackerman.
p. cm.
Includes bibliographical references and index.
Partial Contents:
I. Foundations. ISBN 0-674-94840-8 (cloth)
ISBN 0-674-94841-6 (pbk.)
II. Transformations. ISBN 0-674-94847-5 (cloth)
ISBN 0-674-00397-7 (pbk.)
1. United States—Constitutional history. 2. United States—
Constitutional law. I. Title.
KF4541.A8 1991
342.73'029—dc20
[347.30229]

91-10725

DATE DUE

Harvard University Press is a member of Green Press Initiative
(greenpressinitiative.org), a nonprofit organization working to
help publishers and printers increase their use of recycled paper
and decrease their use of fiber derived from endangered forests.
This book was printed on 100% recycled paper containing
50% post-consumer waste and processed chlorine free.